space.time.narrative

*for those
who unite the curiosity of the inventor
with the adventure in design*

acknowledgements

This book is the sediment of a still ongoing research project, called *narrative environments*, which started in the fall of 2005 with the organization of a series of seminars on the art of exhibiting. As head of the *scenographical design* course at the Zurich Academy of Art and Design in Switzerland, I was in the position to initiate this seminal event, whose realization wouldn't have been possible without the unlimited help of my colleagues at the time, Christoph Lang and Stefan Kreysler, not to mention the entire class of graduate students who took care of the staging and technical support of the four successive and now memorable Wednesday-evenings in the lobby of the Museum Bellerive. That lobby had been put at our disposal by its director Eva Afuhs, who generously welcomed the happening within the venue of her museum. All of this, however, would have remained an illusion without the financial help and intellectual support of Sigrid Schade, head of the Institute for Cultural Studies in Zurich, which adopted all of the hotel and travel expenses of our international guests and provided a budget for me to visit these *scenographers* at their home bases and record the marathon-interviews, which the reader may find in the middle section of the present book. This stage of the interviews proved to be crucial as it allowed me to extensively test my hypotheses in deep conversation with the succesive experts of exhibition-making. I am in great debt of Herman Kossmann, Mark de Jong, Dinah Casson, Roger Mann, François Confino, Ruedi Baur, Barbara Holzer, Tristan Kobler and Uwe Brückner for their time and their shared insights. This book couldn't have been written as it is, without their open-minded attitude. However, the research project would never have turned into a book without a confident publisher and I owe a great deal of gratitude to Dinah Casson, who kindly introduced me to Nigel

space.time.narrative

Farrow of Ashgate Publishing Ltd, who made me feel at home right from our first conversation. Nevertheless, *Space Time Narrative* was damned to remain a ghost image without the financial coverage of all translations by the Zurich University of the Arts, for which I am particularly grateful to its president Hans Peter Schwarz at that time. It marked a phase of reflection and writing from which I could personally and professionally benefit a great deal. I enjoyed working with the two excellent translators, Alex Skinner and Pieter Kiewiet de Jonge, who respectively turned the German and Dutch original texts into the eloquent Englisch versions, which shape the body of the book. Not after Abigail Grater thoroughly copy-edited all bits and pieces of text and took care of the consistency of the whole, for which I would like to express my deep appreciation. At the same time overall visual consistency was achieved with the basic layout of the book by Pieter Kiewiet de Jonge, who was so much more to me than a translator and really appeared to be a great companian in the successive stages of this expedition. Together we developed the concept of the cover, of which the clarity expresses more than words. Another great companian was Valerie Rose, my editor at Ashgate, whose optimism and unbreakable mood gave serious business a touch of great joy. She, and her assistants Sarah Horsley and Emma Gallon who excellently guided the book towards its stage of final production, safeguarded the project from the pitfalls of any complex production, which is driven beyond mainstream by the utopian ambition of its author. I am eternally thankful for that, not to mention the fact that in the end, all material landed on the desktop of Kirsten Weissenberg, who dedicatedly turned the manuscript into a real book. And here again, I have to express my gratitude to Sigrid Schade of the Institute of Cultural Studies, as well as Ruedi Baur and Clemens Bellut of the Institute Design2Context, both in Zurich, who financially supported the two picture-essays, which seemed indispensable compositional components to me. Finally, I shall always be grateful to my companian in life, Lenneke Büller, who generously set me free from all sorts of duties in order to safeguard the mere process of writing.

Frank den Oudsten
November 2010

foreword

Routes to a new scenography

'People only go to the museum because they've been told that's what a civilised person has to do, not out of interest. People aren't interested in art. At any rate, ninety-nine per cent of humanity has absolutely no interest in art.'[1] While it is rather unlikely that Thomas Bernhard would ever have been a friend of scenography, in his acerbic comedy *Alte Meister* the Austrian writer nonetheless takes aim at the Achilles' heel of the traditional culture industry of the 1960s. He accuses it of lacking a public with the self-understanding, formed in the nineteenth century and of educated middle-class provenance, that still dominated the official institutions of cultural mediation in the mid-twentieth century. However unintentionally, Bernhard provides us here with an excellent explanation of why scenography is necessary as intermediary between past and present, between the understanding of experts and the general public, between everyday experience and the production of visionary ideas.

In January 2010, Peter Greenaway gave a lecture entitled '*Neue Möglichkeiten: Film, Architektur, Szenographie*' ('New possibilities: film, architecture, scenography') at the Zürcher Hochschule der Künste (Zurich University of the Arts – ZHdK).[2] He was asked, given his transdisciplinary inclinations, which of the disciplines mentioned in the title of his lecture was his first love. Instead of a response – or in response – he presented the latest version of the interface for his mammoth project *The Tulse Luper Suitcases*.

With the help of 92 suitcases, this multimedia installation presents the adventurous biography of his (fictional) colleague Tulse Henry Purcell Luper. What makes this installation, which extends into cyberspace, so special, is

space.time.narrative

that it not only presents a biography but makes the action into a sensory experience in both real and virtual media spaces.

In fact, for me the Tulse Luper project is a paradigm of what the new potential of scenography might actually mean: the hybrid narrative environment, which truly comes into its own only through a crossover between virtual and real space, an environment that extends the boundaries of the staged space into new realms, that imbues the idealised 'white cube' of the exhibition designer with the potential for real experiences and shifts the chronological filmic space into the analogue here and now.

It is of course rather more than a coincidence that I begin my foreword to Frank den Oudsten's in-depth investigation of the scenographic space by summoning as witness and protagonist none other than Peter Greenaway, who started out as a painter, architect and graphic artist, achieved worldwide fame as a filmmaker and, since presenting his project '100 Objects to Represent the World' at the close of the twentieth century, has provided the scenography of the twenty-first century with entirely new perspectives. As an individual, and in his truly transdisciplinary oeuvre, Greenaway unites all the key qualities I believe characterise the development of scenography – a term used for some time now to refer to the overarching disciplinary home of endeavours such as stage design and exhibition design, set design and urban design. These qualities are: an interest in and capacity to engage in transdisciplinary projects; the unique collision of time-based and space-oriented media; and the rediscovery of the narrative potential of the architectural space.

At the beginning of the last century – perhaps as a necessary response to the fictionality of the architectural concepts of space typical of historicist academicism, which were felt to be aesthetically and morally dishonest – various avant-garde figures of modernity emptied space entirely of its narrative capacities, at least in their theoretical polemics. Towards the end of the twentieth century, postmodern discourse – whose interest, if one looked beneath the surface, clearly went beyond the merely visual potential of the facade – certainly reinvested conceptions of space with a genuine expressive power: 'fiction not function' was the rather simplistic motto. Yet there was always something static about a notion of fictionality – rarely expressed with much precision in postmodern theories – that was meant to capture the tension between the haptic and visual reception of the architectural space, as Andrea Gleiniger shows in her study of the relationship between fiction and narration:

foreword

> Postmodernity 'developed' concepts of fictionalisation in which, each in its own way, history and narrative, as contextualising points of reference, were given architectural form and quite consciously staged. In contrast to the rather static concept of fiction, that of narration opens up a perspective on the processual dimension of narrative, a narrative that becomes manifest not so much through images as architecturally.[3]

In order to avoid rashly imposing the streaming dimension of narrative (as opposed to fiction) and the concept of the narrative space (which was developed out of a narratology heavily focused on the discipline of literary studies) on the operation of the architectural space, Gleiniger introduces the concept of the code, which points beyond the traditional boundaries of pictorial and verbal languages:

> So when people refer today to 'storytelling with code', they mean a new quality of architectural narration, which no longer consists solely of a semantic, metaphorical understanding of code, but of a physical, operational field of sheer scenographic possibility as well.[4]

What Gleiniger claims for the architectural space of the twenty-first-century present, in other words a kind of operative narration, was already foreshadowed by the twentieth-century *Raum der Gegenwart* or *Room of Today* planned by the Hungarian Bauhaus virtuoso László Moholy-Nagy in 1930 as an alternative to El Lissitzky's *Proun Rooms* of the preceding decade, though the tools available to him were primitive in comparison with contemporary media technologies. Both concepts aimed at a more complex understanding and awareness of the space–time phenomenon, but their difference lies primarily in the materials and media applied. With *Proun*, Lissitzky still entirely relied on wood and paint as the components of his construction; while Moholy-Nagy went considerably further in his his *Raum der Gegenwart* by using film projections, photographs, kinetic walls and the now famous light–space modulator. This not only brings out the highly ambivalent, often covert relationship of the early-twentieth-century avant-garde to the narrative capacity of the architectural space, but also lays bare, at least conceptually, the major role played by the then new media in the modern notion of time-based space. In his works of film theory, Gilles Deleuze goes so far as to state that the century of space has been superseded by the century of time.[5] Over the course of the last century, through the

space.time.narrative

collision with film and television, and later above all with virtual spaces, the breakdown of the rock-steady relationship between space and time took on quite new dimensions as a result of the lightning succession of perceptual shifts caused by media technology, from expanded cinema through cyberspace to the omnipresent World Wide Web.

As fine artists, architects, filmmakers and practice-oriented media theorists worked together across disciplines, they developed concepts for a new space–time continuum that began to place a new question mark over Deleuze's dictum that the age of space was giving way to the era of time – people such as John Cage and Robert Rauschenberg, Coop Himmelb(l)au and Archigram, Stan Vanderbeek and Peter Greenaway, referred to above, and of course Marshall McLuhan were the key exponents of these concepts in the early days, a period marked by the dictum of crossover, while latterly the media artists and architects of the 1990s pioneered and cultivated interactive space as a streaming phenomenon.[6] Tellingly, this entailed the revival of the panorama – an aesthetic conception of space that had dominated the notion of the narrative space before the triumph of film as an early mass medium. Hence, leaving new media technologies aside for the moment, it was always the oscillating relationship between space and time that determined the eloquence of the *skene*, of the site of dramatic action, whether in the theatre, film or the exhibition.

However, within these different spheres of the artistic appropriation of space, the need to refocus on the narrative capacities of space was emphasised to very different degrees. As early as the mid-twentieth century, the exhibition space in particular, which began to suffer under the dictum of the 'white cube', developed a need to be more than a mere casing for the auratic artefact.[7] In the context of world fairs, thematic exhibitions saw the first attempts to intoxicate space by the use of a mix of time-based media. The Pepsi-Cola pavilion at Expo '70 in Osaka, developed by engineer Billy Klüver in collaboration with E.A.T., or the IBM pavilion in New York in 1964 by Charles and Ray Eames were milestones in an experimental period that was ultimately central to the – highly ambivalent – notion of the (exhibition) space as 'event'.[8]

Making exhibitions no longer consisted merely of assembling, researching and presenting historically striking, aesthetically accepted and hopefully interesting artefacts, while generally leaving the hermeneutic process entirely to the artefact's auratic emanations – especially in exhibitions of contemporary art – or relegating it to the interpretive diatribes of ever-more-comprehensive information panels and exhibition catalogues.[9]

foreword

In the field of the fine arts, it was the exhibition maker Harald Szeemann, with his obsessive exhibition scenarios, who became the leading hero for us young exhibition designers or museum curators. And with a critical take on one of the quintessential visions of artistic modernity, he provided a template for the new notion of a unity of time and space, or to be more precise of analogue spatio-temporal experience, namely the *Gesamtkunstwerk*.[10] In his great Zurich exhibition of 1983 – '*Der Hang zum Gesamtkunstwerk*' or 'The proclivity for the total work of art' – he brought out both its potential for aesthetic fascination as well as the risk of its being deployed to socially deleterious ends.

Perspectives on the *Gesamtkunstwerk* were of course different in the second half of the twentieth century than in the first half of the nineteenth century, when the term was introduced to artistic discourse by Karl Friedrich Eusebius Trahndorff in the second volume of his *Ästhetik oder Lehre von der Weltanschauung und Kunst* from 1827, popularised by Richard Wagner in his *Zürcher Schriften zum Kunstwerk der Zukunft* from 1849 and to some extent internationalised shortly afterwards by Charles Baudelaire.

Now, in the 1970s and 1980s, it was of importance to the re-evaluation of the *Gesamtkunstwerk* that it does not represent an object, however complex, but a process whose complexity varies according to its degree of transdisciplinarity. Rather than its formal aesthetic aspects, the idea here was to investigate the production of aesthetics and interrogate the total artwork's aesthetic reception in light of its impact on participants, as both producers and recipients.

In the context of this commentary and in keeping with the new relationship between space and time elaborated above, the relationship between unity and fragment inherent in the *Gesamtkunstwerk* must be described more as a constant oscillation than as a finely tuned balancing act. And as Anke Finger highlights in her study *Das Gesamtkunstwerk der Moderne* from 2006, the new pleasure taken in and the quest for the *Gesamtkunstwerk* is anchored in the very fact that

> [it is] actually the degree of cooperation and dedication to the artwork under construction that, even today, fascinates and captures our attention. It is the quality and intensity with which the arts have fused together and separated out again over the centuries, in parallel to the diversification and development of the disciplines, regardless of the marking of

space.time.narrative

But another paradigm is also being expressed here, one that accommodated the new interest in the *Gesamtkunstwerk*: transdisciplinarity.

When Fluxus artist Dick Higgins published his *Statement on Intermedia* in 1966, the ecstatic reunion of the arts under the influence of happenings, pop, performance and action art was at its peak.[12] Open-air concerts, spectacular quadrophonic environments and mass happenings were the settings for this exhilarating multimedia frenzy, which, despite internal resistance, also impacted on the established institutions of theatre, concert and exhibition.

But critics, trained to remember Guy Debord's warnings about the 'society of the spectacle', were soon to emerge from within, reminding us of the dangers of unthinking attempts to realise dreams of synaesthetic fusion.[13] As Peter Weibel, for a time the head of Ars Electronica, the outstanding festival of media art, asserts:

> An emphatic, ecstatic fusion of the arts, pounding simultaneously on every sensory organ, is [...] an illusory and false act of reconciliation. In fact, art's true task should be to develop subversive strategies of difference, absence, unsealing and dissolution, in order to recognise the things of which society is unconscious,to see through the masks of the social text and media dramatisation.[14]

I know from my own experience – including through supervising the scenography for the *'Wissen–Information–Kommunikation'* (knowledge, information, communication) pavilion at EXPO 2000 in Hanover, realised by a group of artists around German 'machine performer' Olaf Arndt – the addictive qualities of the spectacle, in which the visionary organisation of a major event can all too easily become bogged down. Yet, at least since they have expressed their cultural ambitions through so-called theme parks, the expos have been extremely important in sounding out the possibilities of a new scenography.

However, in the face of justifiable suspicions about the idea that intermedia or interdisciplinary media linkage is always the best way to proceed, a process was soon set in motion that was intended to expand on an intermediality or interdisciplinarity of merely aesthetic significance to produce a socially effective transdisciplinarity. In the 1960s and 1970s, with their faith in planning and enthusiasm for participation, there came the first interdisciplinary attempts, beyond the arts, to relate disciplinary fields more strongly to one another. This was especially true of those fields intended

foreword

to reconstitute public life: urban and regional planning, social policy and technological innovation and, following the first oil crisis, resource planning. Later, as a product of the risk society of the 1980s and 1990s, the fields of ecology, technology assessment and sustainability were most vigorous. Now it's globalisation. It was the emotionally charged slogans of natural scientific and, with some reluctance, humanities research networks, that took on the great questions of the day with transdisciplinary élan – with no lack of visible successes. The arts – with the above-mentioned intermedia exceptions, which had in turn run out of steam towards the end of the 1970s – remained strangely uninvolved, stuck in escapist and later postmodern marginality.

Yet what used to be merely the fine arts can potentially make an enormous contribution to the highly complex challenges thrown up by a globalised communication-based society. The challenges of globalisation affect the very heart of the aesthetic experience. These challenges arise from intercultural structures of perception, they reconstitute the problem of gender, and their aim is the sensory appropriation of the world – deploying all the senses – in both a negative and positive sense. Global communication technologies entail both the opportunity to extend our sensory powers so that we can engage in communicative action, and the risk of reducing sensory experience to passive consumption, the standard mode of behaviour in Guy Debord's 'society of the spectacle'. And in this crisis situation we once again need to cross the dividing lines between the artistic disciplines and between the arts, sciences and economy: in the transdisciplinary atelier of today.

Attempts to imagine a new space–time continuum through innovations in media technology, the rediscovery of intermedia crossover in the more respectable guise of transdisciplinarity and, not least, the dangers of a 'society of the spectacle' as attested by the Situationists, constitute the system of coordinates underlying the notion of a new scenography, which has been tried out for real in various exhibition and museum projects, though at the time in experimental form.[15]

The key characteristic of the practical museum setting in which I had the opportunity to carry out scenographic innovations in collaboration with Frank den Oudsten and other partners – the Deutsches Architekturmuseum in Frankfurt am Main in the 1980s and the Medienmuseum in the Karlsruhe Zentrum für Kunst und Medientechnologie in the 1990s – was the need to begin by virtually reinventing, or at least mediatising, the various fields of interest; in other words, tailoring them to the museum space. I happened to be in a position to make the most of this opportunity as curator of the

space.time.narrative

former and founding director of the latter, by way of numerous temporary and permanent exhibitions. And from the furnace of these endeavours, whose dynamics certainly resulted in part from the kind of productive failure that has always accompanied pioneering efforts, there emerged the basic elements of a course of study originally conceived as 'Museum Studies' by Frank den Oudsten. Adapted to the university setting as 'Scenographical Design', this was then introduced to the curricula of the Hochschule für Gestaltung und Kunst (School of Art and Design) in Zurich early in the first decade of the new millennium. On the basis of a very similar, quasi-scenographic framework, I was later able to merge the local departments of design, art, music, film, dance and theatre to create a genuine 'university' of the arts in 2007: the Zürcher Hochschule der Künste.

In the Deutsches Architekturmuseum (DAM), which owed its existence to the massive museum building boom that gripped West Germany in particular in the 1980s, the agenda was dominated by so-called 'multivisions'. This tallied with the technological capacities of a period in which computers had certainly learnt to produce images, but of a generally poor quality, and film/video and slides were the key visually compelling exhibition media. As audiovisual projects enriched by sound and language – awkward media for exhibitions which achieve their impact primarily through visual means – these multimedia installations, which later grew into genuine total art works in the early-1990s exhibition '*In der Tradition der Moderne*', not only produced an impressive reconstruction of historical realities.[16] They also offered a wide range of routes to intellectual and sensory engagement with the exhibited artefacts and introduced the kind of authentic experience that brought museums and exhibitions in the 1980s visitor numbers that had been considered impossible in an age dominated by the mass medium of television. The visit to the exhibition became the exhibition experience, and the exhibitions produced by DAM, staged in such places as the Centre Pompidou in Paris and national museums of architecture from Barcelona to Tokyo, served as models for the presentation of architecture in museums, actually the medium most resistant to exhibition.

While the scenography of architectural exhibitions was generally a matter of temporary displays, an entirely new conception of space was – and indeed had to be – created for the permanent exhibition of the Karlsruhe Medienmuseum, as the interactive, digital media art installations presented there would have been out of place in the classical 'white cube' (or its inversion, the 'black box') of the twentieth-century museum. Like the Zentrum für Kunst und Medientechnologie (ZKM) as a whole, its 'showcase', the first museum for interactive media art, was not reacting to the twentieth century but anticipating the twenty-first. And as we have said, the intention was for it to do so not only in its artworks, but also in its scenography.

In the early 1990s, designing an entirely new type of museum meant first coming to terms with the discourse on the alleged 'museumisation' of (post)modern society. During the 1980s, this discourse was carried on beyond museological circles and their associated theorists. In 1978, Jean Baudrillard had already pithily remarked that 'the museum now exists everywhere as a dimension of life'.[17] At the same time he laid bare, on a theoretical level at least, the dangers of dissolving the boundary lines traditionally drawn around the museum vis-à-vis the society of the spectacle, though his concept of the museum was very broadly conceived. And there was good reason for his concern. Theodor W. Adorno began a 1953 essay entitled 'Valéry Proust Museum' with the observation that the expression '*museal*' in German had an 'unpleasant hue'. Here he was alluding to the generally negatively charged relationship between avant-garde and museum evinced in numerous impressive polemics from Herder through Romanticism to the *Museumsstürmer* of Modernism.[18]

When Henri-Pierre Jeudy published his study *Die Welt als Museum* in 1987, this relationship had changed markedly.[19] Large swathes of the public had reacted to the intimidating complexity of the risk society, which Ulrich Beck sees beginning with a second modernity in the late 1970s,[20] by developing a consciousness of history, albeit a rather imprecise one. The great stagings and fictionalisations of historical and art-historical events attracted hundreds of thousands of visitors, and contemporary art celebrated its Olympiad at the Documenta exhibitions in Kassel. 'History on its own was contemporary (again)', and the revival of historicism kicked off a frenzy of nostalgia at the aesthetically sensitive and dominant architectural projects, as well as in urban planning and the mass media.[21] The number of people in Germany visiting museums matched the entire population of the old West Germany; in other words, statistically, every West German visited one exhibition a year. It is in this social milieu, which was not limited to Germany but was particularly well developed there, that Jeudy begins his diagnosis. Much like Baudrillard's thesis of the duplication of the world through simulation, he asserts that history is being duplicated through museophilia: 'Beyond the system of remembering, another reading of what has happened to modern societies is emerging – a second reading of a collective and public character.'[22]

It was above all two key motifs from Jeudy's at times rather cryptic

space.time.narrative

critique of museumisation that influenced the concept of the Karlsruhe Medienmuseum. Firstly, his deconstruction of the staging of historical or artistic realities so popular in the museum of the 1980s. He points out how these construct a fictitious context that culturalises history as the 'theatre of remembering', destroying it – or 'fossilising' it, as he puts it – as a productive legacy for the individual. The second key influence is Jeudy's compelling examination of how the new apparatus of media and communication technology increasingly risks the 'disinheritance' of the museum, most notably through the comprehensive museumisation of its history, present and future.

So the aim of a truly novel conception of the museum, in both curatorial and scenographic terms, had to be to provide a field of experimentation for a public that is critical (of media), a field of experimentation that enables the visitor, as interactive participant, to take part in that process of collective remembering that re-establishes history as a living legacy and opens up the arts to a process of (inter)active decoding by visitors. And this required novel media strategies. As I noted in 1998, only if we go beyond the mere buying-in of ready-made media packages developed by the multimedia industry and come up with museum-specific concepts for the presentation of interactive media artworks or interactive information systems can we ensure that the visitor, rather than degenerating into a pure user, actively co-creates the specific medium of the museum.[23] We may have overstated our case a bit back then. But in any event, in its initial stages – which as with any decent reform project seems to be limited to around a decade – the media museum was an appealing place for a host of visitors to grapple with the new, and not only within the sphere of the digital.

The scope for experiments in museum practice is of course always contaminated to some extent by that 'scorn of implementation' which Swiss-German author Max Frisch ascribed to every attempt to give practical form to the conceptual.[24] So it was fortunate indeed that the experiences gained from the practice of making exhibitions and museums found expression in the curriculum of an art school, which was subject to major reforms at the time. Indeed, the scenographic impulse, with its border-crossing ambitions, may even be seen as the dynamic centrepoint around which those fields of art taught, explored experimentally and produced at the Zürcher Hochschule der Künste revolved. For the 'house of art' established in Zurich in the first decade of the new century is meant to be an open house with lofty rooms, enabling the development of that unique sense of individual artistic purpose through which virtuoso artists mature. But above all, it has generously apportioned connecting routes and points of contact where artists

foreword

come together as researchers, learners and teachers. Here they may collectively bring their particular capacities, their particular engagement, their disciplinary dynamism as well as their transdisciplinary curiosity to projects which lead to practicable visions of the future and necessarily always extend beyond the arts. From this point of view, this house of art has a good deal in common with the vision of just what a new, other scenography might offer, to which the contributions in this volume bear such striking witness.

Increasing numbers of European art schools have introduced variously labelled courses of 'new' scenography in recent years. This demonstrates the growing importance of this form of cultural mediation – which addresses both the sensory and intellectual receptors – to a society which wants and needs to face up to the consequences of the global reduction in autonomous cultural expression. But it also points to the fact that what I here call 'new scenography' has long since attained classical status. Intensive and comprehensive investigation of its methods, results and the motives of its leading lights are overdue. This publication asks the right questions and provides some important answers.

Hans Peter Schwarz

space.time.narrative

Notes

1. See: Thomas Bernhard, *Old Masters: A Comedy*, University of Chicago Press, 1992, pp 1–4. Bernhard (1931–1989) was an Austrian playwright and novelist, often criticised for his provocative texts. *Alte Meister: Komödie* was published in German in 1985 and translated into English by Ewald Osers in 1989. Its opening is situated in the Kunsthistorisches Museum (Museum of Art History), where the cynical art critic Herr Reger and the attendant, former policeman Irrsigler keep a conversation going for more than 30 years, in which Tintoretto's *White Bearded Man* and the Bordone Room where it hangs play a central role. The relationship between the two protagonists is that Irrsigler is the mouthpiece of Reger, and every sentence Reger ever spoke – like the opening quote here – has been appropriated by Irrsigler word for word.
2. Peter Greenaway (b.1942) is a British artist and film director. For his *Tulse Luper Suitcases* project, see: http://www.tulselupernetwork.com/basis.html. See also: essay 1, 'The Battery', note 6, p.67.
3. Andrea Gleiniger, 'Stil oder Code – Von den Paradigmen des architektonischen Ausdrucks im Zeitalter der Digitalisierung', in: Andrea Gleiniger and Georg Vrachliotis (eds), *Code: Narration und Operation*, 'Context Architektur: Architektonische Grundbegriffe zwischen Kunst und Technologie', vol.4, Basel–Boston, 2010; translation: Alex Skinner. Andrea Gleiniger (b.1957) is a German architectural historian, specialising in the relationship of modern architecture and new media.
4. Ibid.
5. See: Gilles Deleuze, *Difference and Repetition*, Columbia University Press, New York, 1994. For a profound analysis of the streaming film medium, see Deleuze's essays 'Cinema 1: the movement-image' and 'Cinema 2: the time-image', both published in English by the University of Minnesota Press, in 1986 and 1989. For a reflection on these essays, see also: Ronald Bogue, *Deleuze on Cinema*, Routledge, London–New York, 2003.
6. John Cage (1912–1992) was an American composer, Robert Rauschenberg (1925–2008) an American artist, Coop Himmelb(l)au an architectural design firm founded in 1968 in Vienna, Austria, and Archigram a British avant-garde group of architects, based at the Architectural Association in London in the 1960s. Stan Vanderbeek (1927–1984) was an American experimental filmmaker. Cage, Rauschenberg and Vanderbeek met at the famous Black Mountain College in Asheville, North Carolina, USA, in the 1950s, where the former was teaching and the latter two were students.
7. 'Auratic' relates to the notion of the aura. See the Introduction, note 3; see also the interview with Uwe Brückner, note 41, p.367.
8. Billy Klüver (1927–2004) was a Swedish engineer who worked on laser systems for Bell Laboratories in the 1950s and founded the now legendary E.A.T. (Experiments in Art and Technology) in 1966. E.A.T. encouraged the collaboration of artists and engineers in interdisciplinary technology-based art projects. His efforts to bridge the divide between the arts and the sciences was driven by a desire to nurture the collaborative spirit through which the scientist would increasingly engage with issues critical to society and culture. Charles (1907–1978) and Ray (1912–1988) Eames were American architects and artists, who are famous for their industrial and modernist furniture design.

foreword

9 'Hermeneutics' is the study of interpretation theory, and can be either the art of interpretation, or the theory and practice of interpretation. For 'auratic', see note 4 above.
10 For *Gesamtkunstwerk* and *Gesamtwerk*, see the interview with Ruedi Baur, note 51, p.270.
11 Anke Finger, *Das Gesamtkunstwerk der Moderne*, Vandenhoeck & Rupprecht, Göttingen, 2006, p.12; translation: Alex Skinner.
12 Dick Higgins (1938–1998) was a British composer and poet who studied composition with John Cage in New York and became part of a neo-Dadaist network of artists, composers and designers in the 1960s, known as Fluxus. Fluxus owes its interdisciplinary profile largely to the famous 'Statement on Intermedia', written by Higgins on 3 August 1966 and published in: Wolf Vostell (ed.), *Dé-coll/age*, no.6, Typos Verlag, Frankfurt am Main and Something Else Press, New York, July 1967. See also: http://www.artpool.hu/Fluxus/Higgins/intermedia2.html.
13 Guy Debord (1931–1994) was a French critic, filmmaker and leading figure of the International Situationists. The first chapter, 'Separation Perfected', of his 1967 publication *The Society of the Spectacle*, contains the fundamental assertions on which much of Debord's influence rests, and the very first thesis – that 'the whole of life of those societies in which modern conditions of production prevail presents itself as an immense accumulation of spectacles. All that was once directly lived has become mere representation' – establishes Debord's judgment. In thesis 2 and 3, he warns of a 'pseudo-world', 'an object of mere contemplation [...] where the liar has lied to himself', a condition which turns it into an 'instrument of unification' of a society in need of control. Thesis 4 offers the fundamental shift of insight, that 'the spectacle is not a collection of images, but a social relation among people, mediated by images'. See: Guy Debord, *The Society of the Spectacle*, Zone Books, New York, 2004.
14 Gottfried Hattinger, introduction to *Ars Electronica*, exhibition catalogue, Linz, 1988, n.p..
15 For the Situationists, see: Stefan Zweifel et al., *In Girum Imus Nocte Et Consumimur Igni*, JRP-Ringier Kunstverlag, Zurich, 2006.
16 The exhibition '*In der Tradition der Moderne: 100 Jahre IG Metall*' was a gift of the city of Frankfurt am Main to the metalworkers' union IG Metall on the occasion of its 100th anniversary in 1991. The exhibition was first shown in Frankfurt am Main (2 June to 23 August 1992), then travelled to Stuttgart (3 October to 15 November 1992) and ended in Berlin (19 December 1992 to 14 February 1993).
17 Jean Baudrillard (1929–2007) was a French sociologist, cultural critic and philosopher, known for his theory of the 'simulacrum', which is questioning the fundamentals of our knowledge of the world, focused on the role mass media play in our collective imagination. In Baudrillard's view, our cult(ure) of the image creates an illusion of reality, which is diametrically opposed to the true reality of our life. The museum, or rather the tendency of museumisation, is part of this illusion. See: Jean Baudrillard, *Simulacra and Simulation*, University of Michigan Press, Ann Arbor, 1996. See also: Wolfgang Zacharias (ed.), *Zeitphänomen Musealisierung: Das Verschwinden der Gegenwart und die Konstruktion der Erinnerung*, Klartext Verlag, Essen, 1990. And: Eva Sturm, *Konservierte Welt: Museum und Musealisierung*, Reimer Verlag, Berlin, 1991.
18 Johann Gottfried von Herder (1744–1803) was a German philosopher, a poet and a central figure in a unifying Germany in the age of Enlightenment. Romanticism origi-

nated in the second half of the eighteenth century in Western Europe and may partly be understood as a revolt against the scientific rationalisation of nature, which was embodied in the Industrial Revolution. Visual arts, music and literature in the Romantic Era therefore expressed a profound passion for natural history and the natural environment. '*Museumsstürmer*' could be understood as a special breed of iconoclasts, like Marcel Duchamp (1887–1968) for instance, who declared found objects (*objets trouvés*) to be pieces of 'readymade' art: Duchamp signed a urinal with the name 'R. Mutt' and labelled it *Fountain* (1917), a statement which broke through all the conventions of the classical bourgeois art museum.

19 Henri-Pierre Jeudy is a French sociologist, writer and researcher at the Centre National de la Recherche Scientifique [CNRS] in Paris. Jeudy teaches Aesthetics at the École d'Architecture in Paris and has written numerous essays on panic, fear, catastrophes, collective memory and cultural heritage. See: Henri-Pierre Jeudy: 'Der Komplex der Museophilie' ('Le complex muséophile'), in Wolfgang Zacharias (ed.), *Zeitphänomen Musealisierung: Das Verschwinden der Gegenwart und die Konstruktion der Erinnerung*, Klartext Verlag, Essen, 1990, pp 115–121.

20 See Ulrich Beck, *Risikogesellschaft: Auf dem Weg in eine andere Moderne*. Suhrkamp, Frankfurt am Main, 1986. Ulrich Beck (b.1944) is a German sociologist, well known for his 1986 essay on the *Risikogesellschaft* (risk society), which Beck defines as a systematic way of dealing with hazards and insecurities induced and introduced by modernisation itself. See: Ulrich Beck, *Risk Society: Towards a New Modernity*, Sage Publishers, London, 1992.

21 The postulate 'history on its own is contemporary' refers to the nineteenth-century German painter of history Wilhelm von Kaulbach (1805–1874) and was given new life as the title of an influential publication on historicism, which reflected the major theses of the so-called critical art history of the 1970s. 'History on its own is contemporary' became the battle cry in the agitated debates for and against Post-Modernist design and Post-Modernist architecture of the 1980s. See: Michael Brix and Monika Steinhauser (eds), *Geschichte allein ist zeitgemäss: Historismus in Deutschland*, Anabas Verlag, Lahn-Giessen, 1978.

22 Henri-Pierre Jeudy, 'Der Komplex der Museophilie', in: Wolfgang Zacharias (ed.), *Zeitphänomen Musealisierung*, Klartext, Essen, 1990, pp 115 ff.

23 Hans Peter Schwarz, 'Vom Besucher zum User', in: Harald Krämer and Hartmut John, *Zum Bedeutungswandel der Kunstmuseen*, Verlag für moderne Kunst, Nuremberg, 1998, p.101.

24 Max Frisch (1911–1991) was a Swiss architect, playwright and novelist. In 1954 he published his first novel *I'm Not Stiller*, which pivoted around the problem of identity, alienation and individual options of self-realisation, as did his 1957 tale *Homo Faber* and his 1964 novel *Wilderness of Mirrors / Gantenbein*.

introduction

The theatre and the exhibition both construct an island of the extraordinary, a situation where physical presence is essential. For that reason, both require moving to a place that has been charged with meaning for a specific occasion. This loop, away from ordinary life and back again, full of anticipation, transects a locus of discourse and constitutes the fundamental condition of narrative space. The theatre and the exhibition invite the visitor to their worlds. The Internet and television bring the world to his or her home. The distinction is a matter of who or what is moving. Both the Internet and television dwell on the periphery of the commonplace. The theatre and the exhibition derive their transformative potential from the intensity of a well-considered HERE in which two movements join, a physical and a mental one. This is what Bazon Brock was referring to when he spoke of the unity of 'course' and 'discourse': on the waves of the course, the mind focuses on the discourse.[1] Peripatetically. Herein lies the difference: the Internet and television deconstruct totality into singularities, whereas the theatre and the exhibition create a totality out of singularities. In the fabric of experience the Internet and television mark an end point, while the theatre and the exhibition establish a crossing.

    The theatre and the exhibition are poetic places in the landscape of our culture. They are the refuges for our words and objects; the forums where memory and imagination form a critical alliance and put society in its place. This alliance is grounded in language, in the interpretation that encodes the words and objects on stage, making them readable and understandable for the audience. The theatre and the exhibition bring forth unity, for as long as it lasts. During this interval, time contracts and past and present merge into a NOW, the metaphysics of which will be the subject of our present inquiry. This NOW is a place of a narrative nature. The theatre

space.time.narrative

and the exhibition are the mirror of society. Their history is tinged with tendencies of the informal, the anarchic and the discursive, although accents of the institutional, the propagandist and the mercantile have never been foreign to it. The theatre and the exhibition share a common rudimentary form which had its origins on the marketplace of old, where the convincing merchant would display his articles with just that extra bit of flair, and the orator or the comedian would get on his soapbox and find himself a temporary stage. The action of each of these 'performers' was ephemeral. But as everything revolved around the decisive attention of the audience, just as it does today, the intensity of the message became the foremost subject matter of a *mise en scène*, to be perfected in the course of time both in form and in content.

What I find interesting is what happens in that empty square, when, with minimal 'scenography', the merchant or the orator, the poet or the comedian presents his articles, thoughts, poems or jokes through words and gestures. In the topology of the square we witness the formation of a centre of gravity and a condensation of attention, which, for the time being, transforms the identity of the place. The well-geared 'performance' brings things and thoughts, poems and jokes to life in such a way that a field of intensity emerges in which the audience is seduced or persuaded. The keyword here is attention. Immersion. Amid the ephemeral, a narrative space comes into being, either as a play or as an exhibition, depending on the circumstances. Despite its rudimentary characteristics, the dynamic process of seduction and persuasion is essentially just as complex as any form of high-tech spectacle in multimedia opera production today. The only difference is that the scene of the action has moved from the *platea* of the town square to the programmed, formal locus of the theatre.[2] In both cases, however, everything revolves around the potential and the poetics of the place. Now, if the historical 'happening' of the market square is indeed the origin of both the theatre and the exhibition, then the subsequent history of their respective institutionalisations makes clear just how fundamental the chasm between thing and thought has become in the development of our culture, and how with time two specialisations or playgrounds have developed which, despite their common historical contexts, have failed to manifest most of their interrelations. The one playground became the principle domain of the auratic word, the other the domain of the auratic artefact of the museum.[3]

It is interesting to note that with the increasing demand for transparency, coherence and context the institutional demarcation has become more and more diffuse since the end of the 1960s. As the relation between thing and thought transformed, a different view of reality emerged in which context and coherence had a different, more critical emphasis. Urged on by the modernist avant-garde for whom transdisciplinarity meant an act of radical curiosity, at a time when Dada and Duchamp, Artaud and Meyerhold, Lissitzky and Kiesler were playing both grounds as a matter of course, John Cage's post-war 'chance operations', Alan Kaprow's 'happenings', Fluxus' 'post-dadaist actions', the Situationist 'interventions', Robert Wilson's 'theatre of visuals', The Living Theatre's 'rituals', The Wooster Group's 'narrative complexity', the Needcompany's 'object theatre', the Station House Opera's 'machinism' and Jan Fabre's 'harshness' have bridged the gap between text and thing, drama and object, performance and installation, the ordinary and the obscene, the trivial and the extraordinary, and in doing so have brought the stages of the theatre and the exhibition closer together. To be sure, the other side also sought rapprochement. Without the '*Dylaby*' exhibition (1962) at the Stedelijk Museum in Amsterdam, Harald Szeemann's 'When Attitudes Become Form' (1969) and Documenta V (1972) in Bern and Kassel, Jean Leering's experimental exhibitions '*Bouwen 20/40*' (1971) and '*De Straat*' (1972) in Eindhoven, Jean-François Lyotard's '*Les Immatériaux*' (1985) in the Centre Pompidou in Paris, Jan Hoet's '*Chambres d'amis*' (1986) in Ghent, François Confino's '*Cités-Cinés*' (1987) in Paris, and Peter Greenaway's 'The Physical Self' (1991) in Rotterdam – to name but a few – the stage of the exhibition wouldn't have been ready to accommodate far-reaching interpretations and the exhibition maker wouldn't have been able to appreciate the growing significance of the exhibition format within the overall cultural discourse. Still, the situation of the exhibition stage is radically different from the theatre.

While presentations with performative aspects have become established in museums, objects and installations as supports of the narrative have become accepted as parts of the hierarchy of signs besides the spoken word in the theatre. This tendency, of the decline of text as the dominant propelling force of drama in favour of a richer tapestry of dramatic signs, has been coined 'postdramatic theatre' by Hans-Thies Lehmann.[4] It refers to a type of theatre that uses a multitude of languages and signs to address an open field of associations and interpretations in a parallel and synchronous fashion. Lehmann explores the 'aesthetic logic' of this development in which the text as the main establishing agent of dramaturgical unity gives way to semantics that are open to multiple interpretations. This turning point in the practice of performance, sometimes called the 'Copernican turn' of the theatre, occurs in the practice of exhibition making as well, but in the opposite direction.[5] While in the theatre the dictate of the text is being replaced by a semantic experiment by all manner of means, the narrative space of the exhibition calls for a propelling tale to enhance the coherence and the identity of the place.

After and alongside the *exposition-spectacle*, which gratifies the commercial aims of the entertainment industry, we see how, in the imagination of designers especially, another type of exhibition makes its entry. Not because enough is enough. On the contrary, because it isn't enough. Because the spectacle fails to differentiate a subject according to content and only scratches the surface of form. Because it is so loud that it is incapable of any subtle exploration of what is other, unknown or hidden.

As economic demand cannot provide valid criteria for the maker or the medium in the end, the present book will focus on alternative dimensions of exhibition making, beyond spectacle. *space time narrative* is about the 'conceptual logic' of the 'post-spectacular' exhibition. The post-spectacular exhibition deals with the relations between things rather than with the things themselves. The fabric of these relations and associations forms a narrative potential that structures the interdependence of things from a withdrawn position – backstage – that was once the *skene*: the hidden refuge from where the dynamics of the performance were driven.

Faced with the apparent cultural isolation in which many exhibition designers were operating, exhibition architect Herman Kossmann and I decided to survey the above-mentioned defects and fuzzy outlines of the profession in a kind of roundabout way in the course of 2005.[6] The initiative paid off right away because of the overwhelming response of the professional community, which was simply: the wish to take part in the discussion. To meet this need, we decided on a long-term inquiry with an open approach. The substantive basis for the project was to be the assumption of regarding both the theatre and the exhibition as 'narrative environments'. The range of this approach allowed an analysis of the exhibition as a stage with a dramatic charge, and, conversely, an analysis of the theatre stage as a place with the potential to exhibit. These two dimensions of 'showing', of the theatre and the exhibition, of the world of words and the world of things, of the performative and the installational moments in art, were considered as two sides of the same coin.

We called the project 'Narrative Environments' to stress univocally the connecting aspects of our interpretation, the identity and the characteristics of the place, the narrative nucleus as a propellent for materialisation, and the dramaturgy of the assignment. By stressing these aspects we also made

introduction

clear that the point wasn't about design exclusively and that we intended to address the exhibition fully as a format involving a complex unity of content and form.

We were well aware that the matter had been raised before. Take the experimental expositions in the Centre Pompidou that won Jean Dethier an award in 1988. Or the Frans Hals Award for exhibition design that was established by the Frans Hals Museum, Haarlem (1988). Or the debates, the publications and the workshops initiated by the Camini Foundation in Amsterdam (1989–90). Or the *'Design Ausstellen / Ausstellungsdesign'* symposium organised by the Institut für Neue Technische Form in Darmstadt (1995). Or the World Fair in Hanover in 2000, where project manager Martin Roth introduced the term *Szenographie*. Or the Swiss exhibition *Expo.02*, where every exhibition maker was by now presenting himself as *Szenograf* and the notion of *arteplage* became the denominator for a new encompassing stage for the theatre, the exhibition, performance and installation.
 But however valuable and significant the initiatives may have been at the time, they failed to have a lasting impact for several reasons. Firstly, they remained too isolated in time and space to be truly effective. Also, the initiatives lacked sufficient theoretical basis. Moreover, the publications on the subject remained one-sided for the most part, albeit with a more up-to-date terminology, because they concentrated exclusively on matters of design and the material aspects of the exhibition. Finally, the numerous symposiums that universities and schools started devoting to the subject kept the fundamental dichotomy between the curator and the designer intact, even though the profession has come to accept the richer concept of 'scenography' in the German-speaking regions. The notions of 'scenography' and 'dramaturgy', both originating from the language of the theatre, have certainly brought about a turn in the discussion, but it remains to be seen if these neologisms (coined mainly by designers) will yield any new, more fundamental positions in the integral practice of both the curator and the scenographer.

The very first public manifestation of the 'Narrative Environments' project presented four seminars in the Museum Bellerive in Zurich in early 2006. These were organised and staged by professors and students of the Scenographical Design department of the then Hochschule für Gestaltung und Kunst (later to become the Zürcher Hochschule der Künste – Zurich University of the Arts). As a homage to the trailblazing work in the field of museum presentation of Jean Leering, director of the Van Abbemuseum in Eindhoven in the Netherlands, we named the series 'Museum in Motion',

space.time.narrative

after the publication of the same name edited by Carel Blotkamp and published in 1979, in which Leering's thought is central.[7]

The Zurich seminars had a consistent set-up of one public double presentation on Wednesday night followed by a closed colloquium with the students the next morning. Eight design studios were invited in pairs to present their views and works in the context of their profession and to exchange with the students afterwards. In the course of the seminar the following designers made their appearance: Uwe Brückner of Atelier Brückner in Stuttgart and François Confino from Lussan; Xavier Bellprat of Bellprat Associates in Winterthur and Frans Bevers of Opera Ontwerpers in Amsterdam; Ruedi Baur of Intégral in Paris and Tristan Kobler of Holzer Kobler Architekturen in Zurich; Dinah Casson and Roger Mann of CassonMann Designers in London; and Herman Kossmann and Mark de Jong of Kossmann.dejong exhibition architects in Amsterdam.[8]

The meetings in Museum Bellerive drew large audiences and pointed to the idea of forming an international network of professional designers. Locally, the western European situation of exhibition making had been mapped to some extent, but the designers themselves hadn't actually met except for the occasional pairs. So the next step had to be a true meeting, a closed-circle conference tailored to explore fully the issues that had been touched on only briefly at the seminars.

The expert meeting took place on 2 and 3 June 2006 in Amsterdam, in the new Dutch centre for design, fashion and creation – Platform21 – where the panoramic room on the top floor had been staged with projections of the works of the participants for the occasion.[9] We had 24 hours to survey the burning issues of the practice of design and to tackle the question of how we could perpetuate the discussion among professionals and how, in what format, we could effectively report on the results and the process. The initial suggestion, to publish a 'book of essentials' together, was abandoned almost straight away. The need for flexible exchange, recording and continuity pointed to a magazine that would have both the substance of a book and the versatility of a journal.[10]

As the feasibility of the undertaking appeared uncertain, by the end of 2006, I decided to develop the theoretical ambitions of the 'Narrative Environments' project in the form of an open-structured book that would explore narrative space in a varied and associative way on two stages: one 'abstract' stage which would demarcate the first intellectual ground formed by the conceptual triangle of space, time and narrative; and one superimposed 'concrete' stage demarcating the second intellectual arena formed by

introduction

the perceptual triangle of potential, process and packaging. I imagined the relation between the concrete stage and the abstract stage to be as a surfer is to a wave. The stage of the surfboard rides the surface of the wave for as long as it lasts. The surfer looks for an elegant trajectory and his course is the integral of a series of free positions. It is like that: *space time narrative* is an open search for a theory of narrative space in which the theatre and the exhibition, performance and installation, landscape and urban environment, physics and metaphysics, the arts and the theory of media are the guiding lines along which the discourse unfolds. This discourse is transdisciplinary and covers all categories related in any way to the concept, the execution or the use of narrative space.

In developing the book I used the metaphor of the stage. I imagined a stage on which my own guiding motives would figure as the 'conceptual personae' of narrative space.[11] These 'extras' have a present or past background in the arts or the sciences, in theory or practice, in the theatre or the exhibition. They are present, but passively so. I enter the stage and move my own protagonists into the ever-changing constellations of a dialogue that they would probably never have held themselves. The fabric of this exchange of thoughts forms a libretto for a theory of narrative space, solidified in two essays: 'The Battery' and 'The Envelope'. These two essays, the one about the potential of narrative space and the other about its packaging, flank a collection of six in-depth interviews with leading European scenographers, or exhibition designers, or exhibition architects, or *créateurs d'exposition*, or *Autoren-Gestalter*, or however it is that they prefer to present themselves. They are all designers with a common preference for the relationship between things as opposed to the things themselves. This section of the book is entitled 'Dark Matter'. It is dark, because in the very shadows of everyday practice a *terra incognita* of research and development is being explored. The interviews ground the essays in practice and they enabled me to test the validity of their initial hypotheses. The border region between the essays and the interviews is occupied by two picture essays – 'Parallax' and 'Afterimage' – in which the condition of the gaze and the cycle of memory and imagination are the central themes. Thus, the construction of the book is like a hut, a place for thought, where the speculative theory of a discursive scenography can take shelter.

space.time.narrative

Notes

1   See: Bazon Brock, *Lustmarsch durchs Theoriegelände: Musealisiert Euch!*, Dumont Buchverlag, Cologne, 2008.
2   See: Robert Weimann, *Shakespeare and the Popular Tradition in the Theater*, The John Hopkins University Press, Baltimore, 1978. The Online Encyclopedia Britannicadescribes *platea* as: 'In medieval theatre, the neutral acting area of a stage. In medieval staging, a number of mansions, or booths, representing specific locations, were placed around the acting area. The actors would move from mansion to mansion as the play demanded. The *platea* would assume the scenic identity of the mansion that was being used. The *platea* was also used as the acting area for places not specified by individual mansions, such as streets and open country.' (http://www.britannica.com, accessed May 2010.) Much of the play was staged on a scaffolding: usually referred to as the 'locus', like the formal stage in the theatre building of today. Sometimes the action was (and still is in experimental stagings) diverted to street level, off the stage, amidst the public. This open ground, which is governed by fundamentally different laws and dynamics, is usually referred to as '*platea*', being a construction plane of a different order.
3   For a thorough understanding of the notion of 'aura' (auratic) in relation to a work of art, see the essay of the German cultural critic Walter Benjamin, *The Work of Art in the Age of Mechanical Reproduction*, Penguin, London, 2008 (originally published in 1935 as *Das Kunstwerk im Zeitalter seiner technischen Reproduzierbarkeit*). See also the interview with Uwe Brückner, note 41, p.367.
4   See: Hans-Thies Lehmann, *Postdramatic Theatre*, Routledge, London–New York, 2006.
5   See: Patrice Pavis, *Vers une théorie de la pratique théâtrale*, Presses Universitaires du Septentrion, Villeneuve d'Ascq, 2007.
6   Herman Kossmann is an architect and partner of Kossmann.dejong, exhibition architects in Amsterdam. From 1987 to 1992 he was a member of the Board of the Camini Foundation, an organisation committed to the research of the boundaries of the exhibition medium.
7   Carel Blotkamp et al., *Museum in Motion? The Modern Art Museum at Issue*, Staatsuitgeverij, The Hague, 1979.
8   'Museum in Motion?' Seminars, Museum Bellerive, Zurich, January to February 2006.
9   'Exhibiting Now!' expert meeting, Platform21, Amsterdam, 2–3 June 2006.
10 *Topos*, proposal for a magazine dedicated to the survey of narrative environments.
11 The term 'conceptual personae' is derived from Gilles Deleuze. See: Gilles Deleuze and Félix Guattari, *What is Philosophy?*, Verso, London–New York, 1994, chapter 3: 'Conceptual personae'.

the battery

a device, consisting of one or more cells, in which chemical energy is converted into electricity

1.1   the renaissance of narrative space

'All the world's a stage', and every aspect of life, as Shakespeare foretold in *As You Like It*, now is part of an infinitely repetitive, global 'ex-hibition'.[1] In Room 1 we witness the appearance of *The Experience Economy* by Harvard professors B. Joseph Pine II and James H. Gilmore in 1999 in which they proclaim a new economic value, which – in succession to the traditional raw produce of agriculture, the end products of industry and the services of consumer-based commerce – culminates in the staged experience of our hyper reality that eagerly absorbs the maxim 'work is theatre and every business a stage' across the globe.[2] In Room 2 we find the Mosaic web browser making the World Wide Web accessible for everyone in 1993, and the virtual revolution seizing the power of information from television, and television desperately turning to an everyday reality in which everybody can become a 'star'.[3] In Room 3, on the eve of the Internet boom, the Zentrum für Kunst und Medientechnologie (ZKM) in Karlsruhe designs a laboratory where the interplay between art and high-end technology will demonstrate the supremacy of virtuality and marginalise the future of the organic body; a target that Peter Weibel will obliterate in 1998 in the 'Net_Condition' exhibition shortly after having taken over the ZKM after Heinrich Klotz's death.[4] In Room 4 the artistic production of the 'new machine age', which was to be facilitated by the immensely expensive Silicon Graphics Onyx supercomputers, is deemed unaffordable and out of line, and subsequently the more democratic low-budget, high-concept interaction of web art takes its place.⁵ In Room 5 Peter Greenaway is invited to act as guest curator at the Museum Boijmans Van Beuningen in Rotterdam in 1991 and to exhibit his own cross section of the collection in the exhibition 'The Physical Self', which prompts him to show naked individuals of flesh and blood in classic showcases amid the artefacts on display. This in turn radicalises our view on the potential of museums and opens up a semantic field that focuses on the fascination for the human body, bestowing an unusual grace to every other piece in the exhibition and transforming, at least in my perception, Joseph Beuys' maxim that every individual is an artist, by transferring its premise to the physical vehicle and declaring the body as an exhibitable work of art instead.⁶ Thus, 'The Physical Self' marks the dividing line between the problematic lack of direction of western reality on the one hand, and the frantic lack of fundament of the 'experience economy' on the other: every business may well be a stage, but not every stage produces interesting business. At the time, however, few people seemed to worry. If it hadn't been for the virtual business's proverbial sleeping dog of massive inflation, the dot-com industry wouldn't have burst like a soap bubble during the very same decade.⁷ If it hadn't been for the collapse of the Twin Towers in 2001, worldwide optimism wouldn't have been made to waver so dramatically.⁸ And, at the Exit just before the global stage exhibition closes, there is one final performance, in which treachery, intrigue and boundless ignorance produce the ultimate collective 'experience' of the worldwide credit crisis ...⁹ Fin. Bravo! But, on a small scale, the meteorology of the world obviously produces signs that are of a more integrative nature; almost as a fractal principle, as an inconspicuous counter-movement without any predictable results, like the stroke of a mosquito's wing on Madagascar that, according to chaos theory, may well cause a hurricane on Cuba.¹⁰

In other words, Hans Peter Schwarz's 1992 initiative to create a *Medienmuseum* as a contemplative cornerstone of the ZKM is still very relevant today, in my view, for the very reason that it was pointedly dedicated to the world of ideas, not the world of things.¹¹ For it tried to avoid the display of media technological rarities and the well-trodden paths of canonical progress in favour of a new-style museum which, on the dividing line between the tendencies of our time, would use a 1:1 line-up of our reality and our image of that reality, so that the myth of looking, the intensity of seeing and the quality of our gaze would be exposed. Thus, for the first time a possible theory of scenography emerged within my field of vision in which the contours of traditional museum display would be widened and understood as a narrative environment, the staging of which would be dominated by an

the battery

idea and would yield the potential of 'a myriad' of parallel stories, in a place that was charged with energy and that, like a battery, was only waiting to electrify 'a myriad' of visitors simultaneously.[12] In other words, an orientation emerged that was both Utopian and pragmatic; for the challenge may have been a dream, but its mission was very concrete, calling for a strategy that would stress the opposition between the relativism of the ambition and the intended openness of the end result on the one hand, and the complexity of the task on the other. Nothing seemed more exciting, more relevant, more radical, at the time than to have all mental and imaginative power turn into an 'ideal' concept that, with some subversive aid from outside, would explode like a cluster bomb and scatter its fragments of meaning across a whole field waiting to be minutely scrutinised in search of that one, ultimate semantic fractal with the expressive potential to transform into an exhibition. Having said that, it's important to note that even the preceding impulse, which resulted from the research conducted by the Camini Foundation in Amsterdam in 1989 into the experimental development of exhibitions as an open format, is still relevant today as an act of transdisciplinarity.[13] Altogether, both the discourse of the Camini Foundation as well as the development of the ZKM Medienmuseum provided the root concepts for the Scenographical Design course that I later set up and developed in Zurich when I was invited to do so by the Hochschule für Gestaltung und Kunst, and that made the curricular project of 'scenography' function as an interdisciplinary germ, connecting and absorbing like a parasite the idea that drama and exhibition, performance and installation would form one field of expertise and imagination, albeit a differentiated one, that would launch an all-out search for a place of identity, dedicated to an idea, and produce a new élan and a narrative environment of a pluralistic order.[14] So, in other words, the conceptual nucleus of the Scenographical Design curriculum became the basis of the Narrative Environments research project that focused on the practice of the exhibition maker and as such intended to release him from his cultural isolation, while at the same time promoting a transdisciplinary approach for formulating an open theory of scenography that would sensibly reconcile thing and thought, fact and effect, and mythos and logos.[15] So noted in the present book.

    What is scenography? This question, which, at least in western Europe, has occupied many minds for quite some time now, can no longer be answered within the framework of classical theatre, and it has become increasingly problematic because of cultural factors and traditions that vary according to language regions. In the English region, for instance, the

space.time.narrative

term 'scenography' appears to be interpreted in the context of the theatre exclusively and doesn't seem to be so flexible as to allow use in other contexts. When Pamela Howard handed over the charge of the Scenography master course at the Central Saint Martins College of Art in London to Pete Brooks in 2000, the course took a slightly different direction and to support the broadening of the master curriculum a subsidiary program on bachelor level, called Design for Narrative Environment, was added.[16] What is remarkable is that the concept of 'scenography' has vanished from the course directory of the Central Saint Martins altogether now, while in the German-speaking regions academies are en masse introducing programmes under that very heading. The movement is the same, but the terminology differs. What in German is now called *Szenografie*, is lectured in London in two postgraduate courses: MA Performance Design and Practice and MA Creative Practice for Narrative Environments. Both labels seem sufficiently flexible to incorporate the heritage of classical scenography. In the German region the notion of scenography doesn't seem to suffice and the concept of *Szenologie* has been introduced to cover the theoretical discourse of scenography.[17]

Although Pamela Howard's book *What is Scenography?* (2001) may deal with the practice of theatre exclusively, it nonetheless opens with a survey of some forty definitions of the term, given by theatre makers and designers from all over the world, some of which seem to include a broader orientation.[18] I will list a few remarkable examples. In Suk Suh from South Korea defines scenography in very general terms as 'the art of time and space'. Erik Kouwenhoven from Holland prefers the dramaturgical point of view in describing scenography as 'the suggestion of space which transforms in the head of the spectator to anything possible'. Stavros Antonopoulos' interpretation, which explains the term as 'the visual intersection of the ordinary, with the imaginative', is the one that I find most appealing. However, Howard's book was published in 2001 and in the meantime many international conferences have enriched the expertise. What has become apparent is that with respect to technique and, even more so, in relation to the dynamics and the poetry of the site, both stage and exhibition need to be considered as one unified thematic field that is relevant not only within the walls of the theatre and the museum, but increasingly so in the urban and rural spaces of city and landscape. A crucial pointer appears to be the francophone development from *muséographie* to *scénographie*, which essentially relates the world of things to the world of thoughts, and establishes, also in the theatre, a fundamental equivalence of the expressive

the battery

power of the dramatist's text and the curator's collection of objects.[19] In the German region we find another tendency apart from the encompassing approach of installation and performance scenography. During the EXPO 2000 Hanover world fair, the notion of *Scenographie* was for the first time associated with the making of exhibitions.[20] After the Swiss national EXPO.02 exhibition, all exhibition makers called themselves *Szenograf*; and after the first International Scenographers' Festival in Basel in 2006, not only exhibition makers, but also architects, graphic designers, curators and consultants – albeit to a lesser extent and with some hesitation – started to add the title of *Szenograf* to their business cards.[21] The label of scenography apparently has a certain attraction to it. Scenography is an independent trade and the term 'scenographer' has no fixed reference. But what can scenography be in a wider context? What is the basis of such a wider scope?

Traditionally, scenography is concerned with the image of the theatre stage, the way the scene of the action is set, and the optical conditions that determine the way the action can be perceived. Nowadays many theatre productions back out of the classical hierarchies and through crossover dialogues try to ground open performative productions. Crossovers between stage and exhibition, performance and installation, direction and scenography, curatorship and design, execution and authorship, necessitate a reassessment; for scenography – or whatever we want to call this artistic no-man's-land – is in a transdisciplinary sense a profession of increasing complexity. What is decisive for the description of its outlines and its tendencies is the way we look at scenography and what we expect of it. For instance, one of the hot issues in the scenography debate is whether scenographic interventions merely touch on the surface of things or rather deeply penetrate a given or an unfolding content? Depending on one's position the scenographic expertise that is required will vary.

Two analogies. One expects a carpenter to be able to drive a nail into wood with a hammer. As such, this is a rather banal and rudimentary skill relative to the overall framework of carpentry. It remains essential, though, that the carpenter can fix the nail in the right spot in the right way in order to produce a constructive integrity and a house that will not collapse. Once the latter, broader issue is embedded in the consciousness of the carpenter, then we are dealing with an expert. Basically, a surgeon is someone who cuts a living body with a knife. Strictly speaking, such a definition is true, but it isn't complete, because it could also apply to a murderer. So, what is essential for the definition is that the act of cutting is motivated by the intention to heal in the consciousness of the surgeon. Thus, there is this overriding principle that rules the aim of the act per se. The end literally justifies the means. As long as the end is fuzzy, the use of the means lacks precision.

A scenographer designs semantic spaces. Spaces that are charged with meaning, such as the ones we find on stage or in exhibitions, and more and more in rural and urban spaces as well, are usually hybrid compounds. An exhibition, for instance, is materially composed of space, light, colour, objects, text, sound, audio-visual and interactive media, in an infinite number of variants. These are the granules of scenography from which the vehicle of the content arises. Given the array of elements, any successful design of such a vehicle demands a well-coordinated transdisciplinary process. The control of this process largely depends on the expertise of the maker, of whom an equal mastery of the means is required as one expects from a decent carpenter. But is that sufficient? Not at all. It takes more to be a good scenographer, just as mere anatomical knowledge won't make a good surgeon. A scenographer is concerned with the identity of a place, which involves themes of a cultural nature, and only a meaningful interpretation of it and an adequate staging will produce the presentation that will convey new insights. The scenographer thus turns into an author whose skills lie in another area: where the syntax of the exhibition medium sustains the semantics of scenography. Just as a person who is cutting a body with a knife doesn't necessarily meet the description of a 'surgeon', thus we can only call someone who is staging a 'scenographer' if the design of the means is propelled by the intention to realise a semantic space. This particular view is one of the most topical trends in the current western European scenography debate. It promotes the image of a new type of scenographer, which in the German region is now commonly referred to as the '*Autoren-Gestalter*' (author-designer). Within the traditional framework of the exhibition trade the scenographer as author-designer principally takes a position in the middle of the axis that connects, or separates, curating and design.

It must be noted, however, that not only the profession of scenographer is transforming. The transdisciplinary format of the exhibition itself is in a state of revolution. This is the other important trend. The boundaries of the medium are under scrutiny and various experiments are already yielding a different set of expectations vis-à-vis the potential of the exhibition. This trend traces back the origins of museum display, analyses the historical development of the format and questions the traditional curator-designer paradigm. Besides the author-designer we see the emergence of another type of exhibition maker: the artist-curator. When viewed in terms of the form–content axis, we still find a direct opposition of the two, which is tragic, because while there is still no sign of a willingness to develop a shared language or theory of scenography, even the most confirmed curator will have to resort to it sooner or later. Curators meet and scratch each other's backs at curator congresses. Scenographers do exactly the same at scenographer festivals. In seclusion all preach for the converted and this *docta ignorantia* is what obstructs the perspective on new avenues.[22]

1.2   the paradox of scenography

'The world is all that is the case', and in the experience economy the business stage is where everything necessary is being staged and every aspect of mercantile strategy is being carefully planned and orchestrated in order to coerce the consumer's pattern of spending in one's own direction.[23] This is, in Wittgenstein's sense, the 'totality of facts' of – let's call it – 'mercantile scenography'. I, the other, the meeting of the two, society, the visibility of things, the authenticity of occurrences, the obscuration of facts, indeed life itself is staged from beginning to end. With a purely mercantile objective. Marketing and advertising have embraced scenography because its principles are so simple and its means are so simple to employ; because its appearance is so enticing, at least as long as the message is skin deep and the myth being conveyed doesn't reach beyond the condensed 'buy this' or 'choose that'. The problem of scenography is its very success. Mercantile scenography has no alternative but to reduce the variety of social phenomena to a one-sided message, the emptiness of which is masked by an appealing scenographical wrapping – atmospheric lighting, enchanting media, erotogenic music and the eternal beautiful women who are bred by the dynamics of idiosyncratic cycles, such as Tyra Banks' *Next Top Model* competitions.[24] There is no problem with that, as long as it isn't supposed to be all; as long as besides satisfying our material needs there is a heart-felt attempt to revive the increasingly stagnant discussion of our basic values. So, as opposed to the glamour of mercantile scenography, here we need to consider its counterpart: the versatile searchlight of 'discursive scenography'. While mercantile scenography announces and speaks with one voice, discursive scenography asks questions. While the message of mercantile scenography is a monologue, discursive scenography initiates dialogue. Discursive scenography is polyvalent, multi-faced, ambiguous, motivated by a deep-rooted cultural commitment and has a dialogical nature which

space.time.narrative

questions every statement with indigenous scepticism even as it is unfolding. The point is this very quality, this implicit awkwardness, which I would like to label as the 'obscenographic factor'. The obscenographic dimension of scenography entails just about everything that is unfitting or maladjusted, rationally impractical or vulgar; the dark matter that is usually filtered out of our concepts or the decisions we make; the irrelevant, the ugly, the sordid, the repulsive, indeed everything that can be considered obscene without any dominant sexual overtones. What is obscene is what is rejected by morality. It points at a certain non-conformism that has a meteorological nature, as it shifts with the prevailing views. In this respect, obscenography is also contrary: the dark side of scenography, its inconspicuous double, like Antonin Artaud must have envisaged it in *The Theater and its Double* – as a spectre that haunts the outskirts of the story, somewhere between thought and gesture.[25] Paradoxically, discursive scenography has to rely on obscenography for the splendour of its own essence and for making its narrative potential pervade all layers of staging. The obscenography is a critical agent, an intelligently correcting factor, as unpredictable as the weather, that either stabilises or destabilises depending on the field of action. It comes and goes, contingent as fate. Obscenography is the eternal, fundamental other; the primordial counterpart. Scenography relies on the dark to shine its light. Orientation relies on the light and dismisses whatever is irrelevant to darkness. As the ugly has the power to unmask the myth of beauty, thus beauty has the ability to mark the myth of ugliness. It is always there, that dark factor of interference on which discursive scenography depends. Obscenography is the embedded *advocatus diaboli* of scenography that guarantees the indispensable instability and the parasite dimensions of our stagings.

Each staging is ephemeral, volatile and unstable. Each drama passes by and we experience it as it passes. Each staging is based on an idea, an *inventio*. Each staged idea manifests as a fluent potential in space and time. In every scenography the idea materialises as staged narrative space. This expanding space, in which the idea unfolds, is the *manifestatio* of scenography. Now if we take *inventio* to be the narrative nucleus of a staging, then *manifestatio* must be the material condition for its effectiveness. *Inventio* has a half-life; it expires.[26] Narrative unfolds through time and essentially has a limited potential. Accordingly, each *manifestatio* has only limited effectiveness and sustainability. The scenographic gamma rays, to stick with the metaphor, are active only temporarily, during a limited interval, the length of which is directly proportional to the coherence of the means, the bandwidth of the contents and the social relevance of the themes.

Now, although a convincing scenographic work – the *manifestatio* – is always derived from a consistent idea – the *inventio* – the final realisation of it in a meaningful form in terms of means can never be perfectly unequivocal. The transformation will always be a critical process that is highly contingent, and inevitably it will manifest conceptual shifts, undesirable positions, dark matter, inaccessible domains and parasite dimensions – noise, in short. This is the obscenographic accent, the uncontrollable element, or, if you will, the parasite, that is significant because of its function in the cycle of drama: ensuring that the staging maintains the open, proactive nature that is needed for the visitor or the spectator to participate. Every scenographic piece of work, be it an exhibition or a play, an installation or a performance, will evoke a certain narrative space that is essentially unstable and that will cease to exist through time. Two things may happen: either the central idea, the *inventio*, will run out, or the cultural context, as a phenomenon in space and time, will lose its social, discursive relevance. Exhibition and theatre can only blossom once all internal and external conditions are met, once both materials and means are in delicate balance, and the staging is activated in the right cultural interval. A hell of a job. Scenography is unstable and its context is meteorological – per se. Only the most acute intuition and a versatile intellect can synchronise the work with the spirit of the times. *Kairos*.[27] Every drama exists in an interval, it unfolds in time passing and it manifests in an in-between space.

To make for a theory of narrative space I would like to experiment formally with a basic view vis-à-vis mercantile scenography by associatively presenting the frame of reference and the conceptual outlines of a discursive scenography. In doing so, I will assume the position of the obscenographer in order to question the seeming stability of the cornerstones and the anchor points of established scenography, and to destabilise its conformist, socially acceptable, respectable programme. To be sure, obscenography is a pun. Or is there more to it? The paradox of discursive scenography lies in its need for the destabilising nature of obscenography, its counterpart. For without it, it cannot coherently become apparent in the right interval. Without the hurricane, it cannot be the eye.

Scenography derives from the Greek notions of *skene* and *graphein*.[28] *Skene* can be interpreted as 'hut' or 'tent'. It suggests space and alludes to shelter. *Graphein*, on the other hand, means 'to write', but also 'to etch' or 'to engrave'. It suggests time, implying that the syntax of fleeting signs

space.time.narrative

carries the semantics of the message. So, the concept of scenography thus entails an n-dimensional space-time, charged with narrative potential, that gives shelter to the mythologies of our tale. The common goal, or the common task, that scenography and obscenography share between them, lies in this individuating narrative upgrade of space. Always. The implicit objective of discursive scenography is the sheltering of the idea, something that is taken care of by its explicit objective. What speaks in the space of scenography is the voice of the idea. That space is an enclave in a world of noise. Scenography is an intelligent filter, which by intervention allows for a more articulate message to be received.

To understand the principle of scenography we could introduce a metaphor depicted in an etching of the German mathematician Caspar Schott, who in 1657 at the court of Elector Friedrich Wilhelm was commissioned by Otto von Guericke, a scientist and the mayor of Magdeburg, to conduct and report an experiment with two hemispheres to which vacuum was applied, in order to demonstrate both the existence of the atmosphere and the effects of atmospheric pressure.[29] Many of us remember being fascinated by the intriguing story of the Magdeburg hemispheres, from classes in physics at high school. The story had the potential to become part of myth because the event and its account had an enigmatic, puzzling dimension for both laymen and professionals, for both the ignorant and the educated. The enigma lies in the drama of the historical event itself, in the staging of the scientific experiment and the scenography that aimed at rendering the invisible visible and that acquired mythological proportions by equating scenographically the visually inconspicuous compacting force of atmospheric pressure to the disruptive power of two times eight workhorses that, as the story goes, were unable to separate the two 51-centimetre copper hemispheres, which were loosely assembled by a thin greased leather ring. We imagine the scene. The scenography strongly evokes the drama and engrains the narrative potential in everyone's memory. Caspar Schott, who not only conducted the experiment but was also in charge of Otto von Guericke's marketing strategies, was well aware of the importance of a convincing depiction. The centre of the engraving obviously shows the section of the two hemispheres, which is the heart of the staging. Two teams of eight horses are rearing up and are steadying themselves, sweating. The two-part sphere is shaking frantically, but it won't come apart. Visually, the physical strength of sixteen horses is equalled to the perfection of the greased leather ring that is maintaining the underpressure in the inside void of the copper sphere. What an impressive scene: we see the convincing demonstration of a scientific idea of which both the materialisation and the aesthetics were chosen with a great sense of drama. For Guericke and Schott could just as well have selected half of the amount of horses to attain the same effect, for instance by attaching one of the hemispheres to a rock or a robust tree. But no, two teams of horses, working in opposite directions, is the better scenographic solution from a dramaturgical point of view. A physical abstraction is being demonstrated by a scene of flesh and blood and the smell of sweating horses. The performance is situated outdoors. The spectators form a circle and become part of the event. If the sphere yields, the horses will come storming apart and endanger everybody: the staging encompasses it all. The form is intense, it entails risk and it is completely convincing.

In December 2007 an international colloquium about the theory of scenography was organised in Dortmund, Germany, at the Fachhochschule (University of Applied Sciences and Arts), and its leitmotif was the allegory of the Magdeburg hemispheres.[30] The organising committee envisaged a science that would participate in the scientific discourse in just as evocative and appealing a fashion as Guericke's demonstration of the working of vacuum and the corresponding effects of atmospheric pressure. In his keynote address Ralf Bohn describes the staging of Schott and Guericke as a *spatium imaginarium*, as a mental space that is associated with an idea and that underlines the notion that speculative science knows no truths unless its abstract dimensions are reduced to sensory proportions.[31] Such a space of the imagination could by and large serve as a model of scenography if weren't for the fact that our tale of the Magdeburg hemispheres hasn't finished yet. Guericke's scientific experiment has another side to it that is crucial for our understanding of scenography and very relevant as such. The allegory of the sixteen horses is extremely graphic, obviously, in its sensual presentation of the force of pneuma, and surely we could only wish for similarly dramatic, intense staging of the dominant themes of our time.[32] However, the staging of Schott and Guericke only concerns the outer appearance of things, the eloquent conveyance of the outcome of the experiment. For scenography, though, the scientific content of the experiment is just as relevant, metaphorically significant, in referring to a fundamental condition and confronting us with the question of whether scenography is something that merely scratches the surface of things or, rather, something that is deeply concerned with the core content.

The scientist Otto van Guericke had, with the aid of the air pump he had invented, demonstrated the working of vacuum: the underpressure that

space.time.narrative

he had created in the interior of the empty spherical volume was so much smaller than the external pressure of the atmosphere, that even sixteen horses couldn't separate the two halves.[33] At least, for the time being. For how long, may we ask, did the experiment last? How long did the horses actually pull at the copper sphere? Ten seconds? A minute? Half an hour? Exactly how perfect was the air pump? And what about the mathematical accuracy of the hemispheres? Was all the air pressure directed exactly at the centre of the sphere? Was the greased leather ring completely airtight? Was the vacuum inside the sphere a perfect vacuum? We simply don't know. All we know is that there is no such thing as an absolute, permanent vacuum. In quantum physics the vacuum even appears as a dynamic medium with contingent fluctuations and so we can safely assume that the vacuum of the Magdeburg hemispheres wasn't perfect, but was rather an unstable and impermanent one, marked by a half-life.[34] Even without knowledge of quantum physics, Schott and Guericke knew this very well. They had conducted the experiment many times with varying numbers of horses and with varying success. Even the accounts from the seventeenth century report that after 'some' time the hemispheres would separate with a loud explosion. The duration of the interval is unknown today, but surely one could wait for it to happen. Now, this very fact of the vacuous sphere remaining intact under the influence of atmospheric pressure only 'for the time being' makes the Magdeburg experiment such an apt metaphor for scenography. Just as the interior of the twofold copper sphere was infused with a vacuum that for an undefined period of time would guarantee its unity, and just as the inherent geometric and material imperfections of the execution, or indeed other external contingent factors, would dissolve this unifying force again, thus the nuclear idea of each staging generates a narrative potential that is impermanent and that, like a necessary underpressure, lends coherence and effectiveness to the staged narrative for as long as it takes.

1.3   the interval of the open arts

In November 1994 the Charter of Transdisciplinarity was published to narrow the gap between science and the humanities specifically, but its stimulus also affected the domain of the (applied) arts.[35] Disciplines of design which traditionally used to operate in their own isolated areas, but which were nonetheless oriented towards integration, are now coming apart at the seams, be it out of necessity or curiosity. Both the necessity and the curiosity to look beyond the horizon of one's own existence have somehow exceeded a threshold value in the arts in western Europe and have caused a true wave of inter- and transdisciplinary interaction. The volcano of the imagination has erupted and in the solidifying lava streams new alloys, new islands and archipelagos have come into being, the cultural fertility of which still remains to be recognised and acknowledged.

Scenography is one of those new transdisciplinary areas that has its roots of expertise primarily in traditional disciplines. Its migrants necessarily search this new archipelago of the unknown for significant anchor points and new orientations. This state of heightened versatility is very interesting because the challenge of choosing a direction forces one to be alert and aware. Now that the gaze is turned towards the horizon, towards what is different, the readiness to investigate and to experiment – in other words, to abandon long-time positions – creates a climate of renewal in which we can discern a number of tendencies. One of these tendencies is that those who dwell in the interdisciplinary wasteland recognise themselves in the notion of 'relative' or 'open' art, which refers to the relationships between things and the structures of the connecting chains rather than to the things themselves. 'Relative' here is opposed to the absolute, to the notion of an 'absolute' art in which the work of art, the thing, is the result or the culmination of a more or less isolated, individual process of artistic invention and manifestation. This isolation of the process is the crucial borderline that marks the difference in the basic attitude. In absolute or 'closed' arts the thing is the dominating, public factor; the process is subsidiary and private. Relative, open arts on the other hand are characterised by a basic attitude that equally values product and process while emphasising the interaction between both realms. The process is an open one and the product is never finished – at least not when it leaves the seclusion of the studio or the workshop. The completion of the work manifests in the confrontation with the audience or the listener or the visitor, who participates in the authorship of the work *in actio*.[36] In his *Opera aperta*, Umberto Eco describes the poetics of the open work of art as an unstable field of interpretative options, as a configuration of implicit impulses that will prompt the recipient to a series of varying interpretations.[37] Because of these properties, both the completion and also the genesis of the open work of art will occur along different lines. Both process and product are open. Open like in 'open source'. Open in reference and in orientation. Open in the extent of resolution. The product, or the result, lives on external influences and organises itself in dialogue, as a dynamic entity. This process goes far beyond the horizon of immediate relevance and is open in all directions, even in the forward and backward directions of time. In *What is Philosophy?*, Gilles Deleuze and Félix Guattari introduce a 'plane of immanence', which we can easily take as an equivalent of the concept of *skene* in scenography. On the open and unstable stage we see new orientations and role models appear as 'conceptual personae' as if they were the actors in a theatre of the mind.[38] The basic condition of this plane of immanence is governed by fundamentally different dynamics, which are luminously described by Deleuze and Guattari in terms of some modern variants of sports.

A runner builds up the energy that is needed for his record on the 100 metres from scratch. Regardless of some minor external factors, such a process is self-contained and the result is the merit of an individual. When we look at a surfer, however, we see that for his ride he is completely dependent on the energy of the wave to which he adds, during a mere interval, his own energy, attuned to the characteristics of his board. The product becomes a tour de force when both energies perfectly coincide within the temporal unity of 'surfer + board'. Just as the open sports require different skills and a different kind of intelligence, the open arts require a different basic attitude and development. The dynamics of invention and manifestation that are typical of all arts become intensified and multiplied in the open arts; they rely entirely on dialogue and are deeply influenced by the degree of participation of the visitor, the spectator, the reader or the listener. It is precisely this parallax of work and working, of fact and effect, that makes the approach more complex. Still, there is more to the distinction between open and closed. Just as the surfer can only consistently unite the energies of body and wave during a limited interval, thus the open work of art will only open itself for the energy (i.e. the attention) of the audience during an interval as well. The temporary character of this confrontation is quintessential. Just as the in-between space is an essential quality of urban constellations, thus the in-between time, the interval, determines the dynamics of open art.

Such a temporality implicitly addresses the question of social relevance. Not as we know it from the past, but as a more fundamental issue; in search for a relative and relevant art which draws on the origins of western rhetorics, and which is driven by a very productive notion from the theatre: dramaturgy. Dramaturgy, or the knowledge of how things work, fundamentally requires a multiple perspective.[39] In Aristoteles' *Ars Rhetorica* the narrator, the story and the listener form one indivisible whole – like a hinge that cannot function with one part missing.[40] There is no story without a storyteller. There is no listener without a story. Without a listener there is nothing, EMPTINESS, a monologue in dead space. The law of the hinge again presents us with the central issue of transference, regardless of mode or gradation, style or composition. Still, different from before. Not in a moralistic, condescending sense, but rather instigated by the dialogical character of the open arts, like in the question: what can effectively be conveyed at what time and in what way? The open arts are like a window, a frame, a portal, a stage, a mental space that, like an inverted camera obscura, generates the snapshots of our culture.

The open arts have a meteorological nature and they manifest in temporality. They are the double helix of invention and manifestation, arising in conjunction with other cultural tendencies, transforming and transporting them, and then disappearing again. What remain are an altered outlook and a recollection. The open arts address the interaction between process and product, between storyteller and listener, between performer and audience. The centre of attention lies where the world of things and the world of thoughts overlap. Here we find the imaginative energy of our culture. Here memory and mnemotechnologies come in. Here virtuality and imagination abound: in the camera lucida of open art. Now, 'Camera Lucida', the Light Room, of course refers to Roland Barthes' text in which he describes his fascination for photography from the point of view of the spectator, i.e. after the images have left the apparatus, the camera obscura, of the photographer.[41] What is interesting in our context here, is that 'camera lucida' suggests an apparatus as well; an apparatus for the viewer, or at least a state, an exceptional condition of a mental space in which the focus, the framing and the diaphragm of perception and reflection can be regulated, so that the cycle of memory and imagination is activated. In terms of systematics such a light room perfectly corresponds to staging in the theatre or to the *mise en espace* of exhibitions. Both the theatre and the museum, or rather, both drama and exhibition offer this exceptional condition. They are the mnemomedia of our culture. Mnemomedia principally manifest as open arts. Drama and exhibition may each draw on a different expertise, but they are very similar when it comes to dynamics and format. Because of that, they tend to approach each other in certain respects. Especially where fact and effect of a production are concerned: the design of the vehicle on the one hand, and the principle of dramaturgy on the other. Also, in theatre, we notice a growing interest in the domains of the artefact and the physical dimensions of a performance, while in exhibition making it is rather the active psychological dimensions of a presentation that are gaining momentum.

But what is an exhibition? At one time it used to mean: to exhibit something. Usually this 'something' was part of a collection of artefacts that was sometimes consistent, sometimes eclectic, but always made up of objects which had been extracted from their original context – had been decontextualised. Exhibitions have gradually evolved from being a blatant display of valuable things, via academically sound recontextualising in museums, to a form of presentation that does indeed include objects but primarily concentrates on context and some central idea or narrative. It was André Malraux who provided a decisive impulse in publishing *Le Musée imaginaire*.[42] What is interesting is that such a trend will eventually bring the museum of cultural history closer to the art museum again in a roundabout way, for the latter, relying highly on the critical charge of works of art, assumed it could afford to stay away from recontextualisation and take on a different, superior status. But in the era of cultural migration and hybrid open art forms, even the art museum cannot stay behind, unless it wants to become a fossil.

Hybrid, nomadic, transcultural expressions, be they artistic or not, have changed the terrain of exhibitions and stretched the contours of the medium. In this expanding universe there lies a vacuum at the heart of aesthetics that is dying to be filled with content. For the present discussion of scenography, the theoretical work of Marshall McLuhan provides us with some interesting analyses, which attribute a dominant transformative potential to the medium completely irrespective of what it actually conveys.[43] McLuhan's adage 'the medium is the message', coined in his most widely known book *Understanding Media*, was at some point clarified by media critic Neil Postman when he reasoned that one cannot make philosophical statements by means of smoke signals, simply because the medium of smoke lacks the argumentational sophistication required for philosophical debate.[44] The medium is dominant and poses limitations to the message because of its intrinsic capacity. In the case of a hybrid super medium like the exhibition, McLuhan's maxim may well work the other way round: 'the message makes the medium'. In making an exhibition the scenographer has the complete array of different media characteristics at his disposal, and in designing the ensemble, each and every contour of the overall characteristic appears to be feasible. And here lies the actual problem. For the simple, but priceless fact of apparent feasibility of any medium-based curve of conveyance is at the same time the central point of criticism when

the battery

curators scorn the 'exposition spectacle' of the scenographer.[45] So here we have the dilemma. On the one hand: how may or should a complex super medium like an exhibition be charged with meaning in a sensible way? On the other: how may or should we produce a sophisticated translation of a complex content into a multimedia form that is expressive? If the medium has the capacity to transport any message, then we need to focus all of our attention on the structure, the meaning and the relevance of that message. McLuhan's 'law' may work very well in the case of single media, but it needs to be reversed with increasingly complex multi-dimensional and automated mediatechnological processes. This dilemma forms the axis that connects the curator and the scenographer and there is only one position on that axis that will enhance both views: right in the centre. Once an exhibition becomes essayistic in nature and reaches beyond the mere display of authentic works of art that have been conceived especially for the occasion – by which the necessary critical charge is imported, as it were – then the full bandwidth of potential authorship opens up and the notion of authorship takes on a whole new meaning for both the curator and the scenographer. Whether the exhibition is a collection of works of art or is considered to be a *Gesamtkunstwerk*, as long as the multimedia vehicle of space and time, colour and light, text and image, objects and media fails to SPEAK or fails to be original or to capture the spirit of the times, the interpretation of the 'author' will have failed.[46] What is crucial here is the consistency of concept and scenography. Authorship, which has the potential to realise this quality, thus transcends the traditional mono-disciplinary artistry. That is why the authorship of the open work of art will probably involve a team rather than a single person. It is versatile and nomadic, and it generates interpretations with philosophical, journalistic, scholarly, literary, even essayistic and evidently scenographic overtones. It is the authorship of the nomads of art.

An exhibition is a narrative space – a space with a narrative potential. This doesn't mean that the narrative will necessarily unfold completely in all its dimensions. For it to do that, one should define all of its components, and structure them in space and time. That is one of two mechanisms: the degree of definition of an exhibition that will eventually determine its reception. In the second chapter of *Understanding Media*, McLuhan points out that the degree of audience participation is inversely proportional to the degree of definition of the conveying medium.[47] The other mechanism concerns the structure of our narratives. Do they evolve in linear time? Or, rather, does the raw narrative potential generate a multitude of overlapping times and do the individual chains of association only get activated

space.time.narrative

once the visitor formally enters the exhibition and mentally participates in the cycle of recollection and imagination? If so, time will stop functioning as linear, mathematical and objective clock-time, and will become a subjective, personal time that is curved just like Albert Einstein imagined space to be curved under the influence of gravity.[48] Here the concept of space and time in Henri Bergson's metaphysics is of major importance.[49] Exhibitions with some narrative significance work like a battery, full of energy, aimed at activating the raw, undefined energy of the public in the form of inspiration and reflection in order to establish an optimal time curve (immersion). The task of scenography is all about this, and could be read as a sign of our times. Our society needs latently entrancing semantic spaces where the bigger and smaller explosions of life can occur.

Making an exhibition is a form of applied or open art. When we say 'applied', we don't mean the functionality we find in architecture or fashion for example, although these disciplines too are characterised by a multiple aim at the heart of the profession: both buildings and clothing create or maintain an identity on the one hand and offer physical shelter on the other. To do that, both the building and the clothing need to function properly and speak an aesthetic language that enhances the properties, the image or the self-image of the user. Architecture and fashion aim at making the user of the building or the clothing feel – more – comfortable. That is what McLuhan referred to when he called clothing the 'second skin', and by inference defined housing as the third, the city as the fourth and our electronic media as the fifth skin.[50] The tailor makes the man and our house is our status. Likewise, the city manifests our culture and our media personalise our signs. It is the thing that makes dreams come true and the importance of that fact can take on mythological proportions.

Yet, both an exhibition and a play or the performance of a symphony address a different area of reality and operate where the world of things and the world of ideas overlap. An exhibition opens collective memory and it activates the individual imagination. Meaningful clusters of objects generate meaningful clusters of words, and vice versa. Grains of memory. Thought particles. Imaginat-ions. The world of things, to which the exhibition in its final form belongs, is the vehicle of an extremely vulnerable world of thoughts; of an idea, an interpretation, which like everything precious is helpless and needs shelter for that reason.[51] This vehicle, the material and medial condensation of staging and design, should ultimately be understood as a form of shelter. Of course, it is a display as well; be it a *Wunderkammer*,[52] or design per se, or just a 'mounted book', a stamp collection

the battery

or simply a market place. In the scenography of a discursive exhibition, however, the shelter – as in *skene* – of an idea is the central notion.

It goes without saying that this type of functionality, that is the goal of the open art of exhibition making, is essentially a complex one. So how does this complexity affect the design? Let us look again at clothing. Once a jacket is supposed to do more than merely preserve bodily warmth and confirm a certain status – let's say that it is also required to stop bullets, to function as an on-line computer and as a mechanical interface for a mobile drum set – then what is needed is a multiple type of functionality that addresses the object not merely as a product, but rather as an organism with a corresponding type of intelligence. We see the same analogy in architecture where different types of expertise are called for depending on the complexity of the design and the intelligence of the building required. There is a certain correlation. The more functionality is required, the more intelligent the expertise that is needed; the result of which is an ongoing differentiation of the design, which no longer manifests as an object in space but also as a process in time and thus enters into another set of space–time dependencies. As such, the 'skin' of exhibitions can only fully be understood as a complex tissue, as an intelligent interface between idea and experience or an osmotic membrane between the vehicle and the audience, more or less like the 'fourth wall' in the theatre.[53] An exhibition is a collection that can be read, a space that provokes dialogue, an interval that entices the visitor, a story that unfolds along the various axes of time. It is a semantic space that has been conceived to facilitate the initial fantasy and expectation, the immediately present experience, the reflection a posteriori and the long-term recollection. Exciting stagings commence long before their actual starting point and they continue to the same extent after their actual conclusion.

Making an exhibition is always a 'relative' art. An exhibition is about the relations between things. On top of that, it is about the relation between the visitor and the web of associations that the exhibition brings out. Or: about the relation between the memories and the imagination of the visitor on the one hand, and the narrative immersive potential of the place on the other. Or, more complex: about the relation between the collective memories and associations of a cluster of visitors on the one hand, and a semantic space manifesting as a unitary design of matter and media on the other. Of course, an exhibition is a product, but at the same time it is also a process; an open art form with a whole array of alternative dimensions. It is a substantive organism; software that is initialised and activated through the participation of the visitor, with both an instant effectiveness on the spot

space.time.narrative

and a long-term, continued effect elsewhere. These dimensions of effectiveness, of relatedness between now and later, between fact and effect, between thing and thought, are the domain of dramaturgy and they form an integral part of the development of a concept. Because of this very relativity an exhibition is never finished. The vernissage on the opening day is just a cut in the overall editing, a single caesura in a process that introduces a new state of aggregation of the semantic space, after which the exhibition belongs to the visitor.

Like the theatre, exhibitions are a medium of memory: a place where the cycle of recollection and imagination both absorbs and generates all kinds of cultural impulses. Leon Battista Alberti already mentions it in his 1485 discourse on architecture, *De Re Aedificatoria*: a house is like a small city and a city(-state) is like a big house.[54] As an analogy we could say that an exhibition is a simple memory and that memory functions as an ultra-complex exhibition. Two images dawn. One is the image of classical mnemonics, in which memory is presented as a building whose various rooms contain certain significant mnemonic images called 'icons'.[55] The function of memory would be like an imaginary walk through the building during which the confrontation with the successive icons was supposed to provoke the right string of associations. The second image is one of extreme mnemonic sophistication: the *Ars Memoriae* – as it was realised in the Renaissance in the memory theatres by Giulio Camillo and Giordano Bruno in Italy, and later by Robert Fludd in England – the aim of which, regardless of material and conceptual differences, was to evoke instantaneous deeper insight on the part of the spectator by confronting him with an elaborate staging or classification of universal knowledge.[56] In fact little is known about the memory theatres. Thanks to the pioneering work of Frances A. Yates, we know that Giulio Camillo was inspired by the Teatro Olimpico of Andrea Palladio in Vicenza (1584), and that Robert Fludd systematically modelled his art of memory after the spatial organisation of the Globe Theatre of William Shakespeare and his ensemble on the bank of the Thames in London.[57] We don't have any spatial studies by Giordano Bruno, but what we do have is all the more interesting and abstract: a number of linguistic, recombinatory analyses based on a so-called 'memory wheel' (see p.372), that James Joyce is likely to have used to generate the labyrinthine semantics of *Finnegans Wake*.[58]

Why a memory theatre? Why did Camillo, Bruno or Fludd never consider a memory exhibition? Surely, the methodology of classical mnemonics, which inherently suggested an imaginary walk through the 'building

of memory', suggested as much. The answer lies in the objective. What the art of mnemonics aspired to was the capacity to serve, for instance, kings and others sovereigns by generating a deep insight into the hidden logic of the world. To do so it arranged a well-considered, meticulously orchestrated confrontation with the classified knowledge of that world. To achieve this strategy, it used a format of communication that had already proven its value and was easy to adapt in as far as its medial conventions suited the new functionality. The format, of course, was the theatre – albeit with an inverted spatial organisation in Camillo's case. Systemised fragments of knowledge were distributed along the layout of the amphitheatrical auditorium, and the stage – which was usually the scene of the action – now became the location for the Ladies and Gentlemen, in this case King François I of France, who sponsored the undertaking.[59] Such a one-man theatre made sense because it all revolved around the intensity of the gaze and the ideal perspective with which the encoded, 'exhibited' knowledge could be perceived from the stage through the window of the proscenium. Regardless of the fact that the exhibition as a format of communication was almost unknown in the Renaissance, Camillo, Bruno and Fludd could never have designed a memory exhibition because of the radical difference in dramaturgy. In order for it to work, the axis of observation was crucial, and, according to theatrical convention, it had to be static, unequivocal and governed by the laws of central perspective, i.e. the ideal viewpoint was centred at the front of the stage. Given the right lighting, the right concentration and the right duration of the event, a complete immersion in the secrets of the world would occur and the king would see the light, for which he had paid so dearly.
It never came to that, however, nor would it have along the lines of our proposed memory exhibition, simply because the format doesn't match with the intended immersion. From the visitor's point of view, exhibitions offer a multitude of positions with a multitude of perspectives. What is more, mnemonic processes are of a highly discontinuous nature and follow the path of associations, led by external stimuli and suggestions. Which is exactly what an exhibition is: an orchestrated path of associations through a landscape of things and thoughts. The visitor walks along this path and perceives it through a kaleidoscope of ever-changing perspectives during a random interval. Submersion, or immersion, is a complicated notion in this context. Memory and imagination surely form a cycle that is propelled by a narrative and its potential, but immersion goes much deeper than that. The experience of being immersed is no less than the degree of narrative or ritual density at which memory and imagination begin to oscillate and become

space.time.narrative

merged. Disney constructs moments like this; the liquid projections and the psychedelics from the 1960s remind us of it, as does voodoo trance dance.[60] But what is interesting about exhibitions is their potential to prevent mental oscillation, to keep it from spinning out of control; to have it reach the level of escape velocity, but keeping it a few inches above the ground so to speak.[61] Lifting us up a little is one of the exhibition maker's higher aims.

1.4 the blink of an eye

In *Signs of Performance*, Colin Counsell qualifies the theatrical work of Samuel Beckett as a 'theatre of absence'.[62] What exactly is absent, or not present? The answer could be one of various possibilities: development, future or perspective. Or, from the point of view of the subject: the ability to cognise development, the future or perspective – an ability which may be lacking because of perceptual inadequacy or a view that is impaired by existential fogginess. What is missing is a horizon; and if there is one, it constrains the situation as a tight corset that restricts movement. So, what is the situation? The situation is what is the matter, and in Beckett's case it is usually a dramatic demonstration of hopelessness. The hopelessness is depressing and acute, and it is the main carrier of the drama. It is like a polar bear who is caught on a floe that has gone adrift in Baffin Bay; aimlessly drifting with but one alternative: to leave the set. Aimlessness. As Clov says to Hamm in *Endgame* (1957): 'I'll leave you!'[63] Beckett's stage is pure isolation captured in an image. It is no less than bearing witness to the protagonists' permanent state of detachment. There is development, but it is out of reach. Hamm: 'What is happening?' Clov: 'Something is taking its course!' What happens happens incidentally. What is lacking is every sense of perspective. The emptiness of the here and now is so completely devastating, that the horizon seems to have blocked up the sight, as if the individual is blindfolded by despair. The glance itself is imprisoned. What remains is a blindfolded state of being in which the subject moves about with blinkers on.

When space has no visible contours, when the horizon is gone and has turned into a black hole of infiniteness itself, then time becomes the measure of things. Things turn into events, in-between space turns into in-between time that approaches its own limit and becomes eternity on a human scale. Blindness is an optical prison, and for Beckett we are all basically blind. Only occasionally does a fleeting moment of insight dawn, but it never brings ultimate liberation; some temporary relief at the most – a moment of short-lived happiness.

In the German version of Beckett's *Endgame* that I saw in the Schauspielhaus in Zurich in 2003, Clov wrote 'F=MC^2' on the black wall of their timeless interior.[64] The act wasn't Beckett's but it suited his universe very well. The scene of the action is a room from which there is no escape. Einstein's theory of relativity is the last straw and by carving its symbol E=MC^2 on the wall Clov hopes to cast a spell. However, because of sheer existential despair a slight inaccuracy creeps into the sign language. E becomes F. Graphically the difference is but one dash, but mathematically it leads to incomprehensible gibberish. The incantation doesn't work and Hamm, who is sitting but can't see, and Clov, who is seeing but can't sit, will have to rely on each other, imprisoned in the habitual patterns of their relationship. These patterns exclude any development. A situation in which there is a lack of meaningful stimuli and regenerative potential is doomed to degenerate and fall apart. Habit and routines are the 'corrosive force' that do the festering work, something Beckett referred to as the 'cancer of time'.[65] In *Waiting for Godot* (1953) Vladimir and Estragon live through the experience that life means waiting and that there is no alternative but to kill time with the hope for a better future, which may even arrive tomorrow.[66] That hope is personified by the unknown Mr Godot, who dominates the situation of waiting at the crossroads. As in *Endgame*, the timelessness of existential imprisonment is structured by a formula that is repeated like a mantra whenever tensions rise and lets off some of the steam for the time being: Estragon: 'Let's go!' Vladimir: 'We can't.' Estragon: 'Why not?' Vladimir: 'We're waiting for Godot!' Clearly, waiting for Godot is useless. In terms of hopelessness, *Endgame* and *Waiting for Godot* are related. In the latter we wait for Godot who doesn't arrive; in the former we wait for Clov's departure, but he doesn't leave. Because the act of waiting is principally without conclusion, the duration of the interval in terms of dramaturgy becomes equal to the absolute length of the play in clock time. For that reason, Beckett's plays stand apart from the type of theatre that makes for the illusion of place and time. It is what it is and doesn't refer to anything extraneous. It manifests in the here and now. For the discourse of scenography this is an important notion, because once the action on the stage has no development, the identity of the play is constructed in the spectator's head and engrained in his memory. The locus of Beckett's drama is not a safe remote one, as in the classical theatre. Precisely because of the absence of any particular development on the physical stage, the drama shifts to the inner arena of memories and imagination of the individual spectator. We, the audience, are waiting for Godot's arrival. We, the audience, are waiting for Clov to leave. Continuously. And by having focused on something beyond the horizon of time, we have blinded ourselves to the signs of immediate time and thwarted the liberation of events from the power of habit. Immediate time is imminent, however; pliable and open at the beginning and at the end, full of signs, contingent, as a potential in which 'something is taking its course' and it doesn't matter where it leads us. What does matter is whether we participate or not. With Beckett, time disappears and space turns into narrative potential.

Halfway through Act 2 of *Waiting for Godot*, Vladimir and Estragon receive an unexpected visit by Pozzo and Lucky, who were healthy the day before, but who are now blind and mute respectively. They aren't recognised at first and Estragon thinks that Godot has arrived at last. But it isn't Godot; it is Pozzo. Disappointed, Estragon mutters: 'Let's go.' Etcetera. Vladimir inquires after Pozzo's blindness: 'I'm asking you if it came all of a sudden.' Pozzo: 'I woke up one fine day as blind as Fortune. Sometimes I wonder if I'm not still asleep.' Vladimir: 'And when was that?' Pozzo: 'I don't know.' Vladimir: 'But no later than yesterday ...' Pozzo: 'Don't question me! The blind have no notion of time. The things of time are hidden from them too.'[67]

Samuel Beckett wrote two interesting pieces of prose on the *condition humaine* and the fundamental interval of existence: *Imagination Dead Imagine* (1965) and *The Lost Ones* (1966–70).[68] Both texts outline the utterly unstable, meteorological condition in which the individual (the former text) or the individual as part of society (the latter) can only realise his or her individuality in a strictly limited set of circumstances. Beckett denies the view that our world and our reality function within a hierarchic structure according to some transcendent principle. Instead, the Beckettian universe is grounded on the principle that reality is a perpetuum of coincidence, a contingent flow of events without any plan or purpose. In his essay on Proust we find: 'The individual is the seat of a constant process of decantation, decantation from the vessel containing the fluid of future time, sluggish, pale and monochrome, to the vessel containing the fluid of past time, agitated and multicoloured by the phenomena of its hours.'[69] The confrontation with this principally meaningless existence brings the individual to existential desperation, which Beckett calls 'the suffering of being'.[70] Being at the mercy of this state of affairs leaves the individual (us) no other option than to project form and meaning onto the reality that opposes him day after day. The cycle of memory and imagination, however unstable, is the only humble instrument that remains to try to shape this life as a perceptual act that induces an anticipation of what lies ahead or what is expected. The future is uncertain, grey and impotent as a reality. Only our imagination enables us to perceive the world as a colourful, meaningful experience. In Beckett's universe we don't perceive the world objectively. In order to survive we are forced to construct a completely subjective reality by a process that Colin Counsell terms 'the manufacture of meaning'.[71] In such a signifying act of looking, the quality of our view is central. In *Imagination Dead Imagine*, Beckett proposes the piercing gaze of the hunter's eye, 'the eye of prey'.[72] That is, the gaze without blinking. The look that stabs. The penetrating gaze as an ultimate instance of autonomy that serves the individual in a hopeless, dead-end world. The preying eye manifests an existence that revolves around seeing and being seen. *Esse est percipi.* How does one look when being means being seen and one only has the twinkling of an eye?[73]

Drama is governed by the passing of time and it has a limited duration. The staging manifests in an interval, in an in-between time, a fragment of time with either a fixed or a contingent beginning and end. Within those parameters the narrative or the event evolves. Scenography basically exists in an interval and nothing escapes from that osmotic time capsule, except memory and imagination. Drama consists of time fractals with a curved geometry, and the extent of the curvedness is proportional to the intensity of the experience. One may wonder what are the threshold values of scenography in terms of time? What is the smallest possible interval in which the transformative potential of dramatic action or of a dramatically charged space can evolve? And what is the largest possible one? The answer will be a statement about the bandwidth of scenography itself. The interval is a time fractal. When we compact or extrude time, all other scenographic elements and proportions will change symbiotically. On which axis of time does the staging unfold? Is it a linear axis or a curved one? What exactly is the tension of a staging or a performance? How long does a visitor take to walk through a museum? The *4'33"* piece by John Cage takes exactly four minutes and 33 seconds.[74] An average feature film about ninety minutes. Samuel Beckett's *Waiting for Godot* about two hours. *Einstein on the Beach* by Robert Wilson and Philip Glass about five hours.[75] The *Ring des Nibelungen* by Richard Wagner was meant as 'ein Bühnenfestspiel für drei Tage und einen Vorabend' ('a festive play for three days and a preliminary evening'), which took about sixteen hours.[76]

space.time.narrative

The Japanese-American photographer Hiroshi Sugimoto conducted a study of the dramaturgic 'elasticity' of the interval of the arts. Between 1975 and 2000 he photographed the auditoria of a number of cinemas and drive-in theatres while the film was being shown. The shutter time was equal to the duration of the show. Sugimoto commented on the *Theatres* project, as he called it:

> I'm a habitual self-interlocutor. Around the time I started photographing at the Natural History Museum, one evening I had a near-hallucinatory vision. The internal question-and-answer session that led up to this vision went something like this: Suppose you shoot a whole movie in a single frame? And the answer: You get a shining screen. Immediately I sprang into action, experimenting toward realizing this vision. Dressed up as a tourist, I walked into a cheap cinema in the East Village with a large-format camera. As soon as the movie started, I fixed the shutter at a wide-open aperture, and two hours later when the movie finished, I clicked the shutter closed. That evening, I developed the film, and the vision exploded behind my eyes.[77]

Not that it would have mattered to him at the time, but we may ask: which films did Sugimoto see? *Once Upon a Time in the West* by Sergio Leone? *A Clockwork Orange* by Stanley Kubrick? *Blow-Up* by Michelangelo Antonioni? *Paris, Texas* by Wim Wenders? *Dead Man* by Jim Jarmusch? Did it matter? No, because in the end all films looked identical: white see p. 383. By compressing all 172,800 frames of a two-hour film in the container of one static photographic interval, the specific dramatic articulation of the film was lost. The mere differentiated light that was the vehicle of the cinematographic content was now accumulated into an intensity from which all semantic content has vanished. When the interval or the structure of the interval doesn't match, being either too long or too static, the ephemeral content cannot take root. It will perish through overexposure, and for scenography only the medium will remain as the message. The passing of time itself is part of the DNA of the message. Drama – and indeed life in general – requires meteorological, variable conditions that form a breathing, pulsating structure of intervals of time.

In discussing the quality of the gaze one necessarily touches on depth of field and the notion of parallax.[78] On page 95 we find a sketch by René Descartes from his posthumous work *De Homine*, that illustrates the principle of triangulation as an aid for the blind.[79] The image is an interesting

the battery

one for several reasons. Triangulation is based on the parallax of two given geometrical or topographical points, often close by, that are clearly distinguished, on the basis of which a third, remote and unknown, point can be established. What is fascinating in Descartes' study is that the principle of triangulation, which relies entirely on sight, is being put to use in the context of blindness. The pictorial quality of the illustration is such that without much effort we can recognise a Vladimir or an Estragon next to the tree in *Waiting for Godot*.[80] Of course I'm interested in the aspect of parallax specifically in relation to the distance between two opinions, between situations or orientations in space or time – like the ones we encounter in the practice of scenography as existing between form and content, between curator and designer, between the intellect and intuition, between what is known and unknown, mythos and logos, play and everyday earnestness, dream and reality, between scenographer and audience. Here I interpret parallax as a mental phenomenon, as a basis for triangulation in the mental space of the imagination or as an axis of fundamental bipolarity that offers but one truly productive position for dialogue, development and transfer of knowledge: the middle. I'm not implying any form of consensus here. On the contrary, while maintaining every conceivable contrast I'm concerned with a dialectical foundation of scenography that allows a pithy integration of critically opposed values in order to create a meaningful relation between the centre and the periphery.

Scenography is essentially transdisciplinary, and transdisciplinarity has everything to do with peripheries, because when disciplines merge, a potential is generated between the various centres, which in turn transforms the peripheries. The interpenetration of disciplines produces a potential between different centres and transforms the peripheries. When a transdisciplinary potential unfolds, the profile of the expertise changes. Scenography is always about a relation between positions, between centre and edge, between a solid, firmly grounded sense of self and a curiosity-driven sense of other – oppositions that culminate in an urge to experiment. The other, which is to be discovered beyond the horizon of the familiar, always entails a fundamental shift of position along a centrifugal movement from centre to edge. This tenacious drive towards the periphery, in which stable self-references start to waver in the shrouds of the unknown, is a basic propensity of every scenographer. For the situation is basically bipolar. Every discipline that contributes to the *Gesamtwerk* of scenography has two anchor points: a fixed one in the domain of familiarity, and a floating one in the unfamiliar domain of what is 'other'. This dynamic bipolarity, which lends contrast to

space.time.narrative

the gaze and creates a shifting parallax, is a precondition for every intelligent, sensible scenography.

Descartes' study of triangulation as an aid for the blind is so appealing because it symbolises the problem of our situation. In the scenographic process of design we are partly blind simply because the world is uncontrollably complex. We rely on a sensorium that is able to focus beyond what is likely, so that the gaze reaches across the limits of the unknown. Having eyes doesn't mean that our gaze is all-inclusive. It is true that we usually see the interconnection and the nature of things where we first suspected it to be by intuition. The inclusive gaze entails noticing, in a metaphorical sense, not only the fixed constellation of the stars in any given universe, but also the fleeting, fluctuating and ephemeral nature of cloud formations.

In the complex context of scenography, much depends on the acute, dynamic and fluent orientation of the scenographer for determining if something works or fails, regardless of the closeness or remoteness of the 'other'. On page 84 we find a self-portrait with scorpion by Marina Abramovic.[81] Here, the other is a danger that has closed in on the artist and it transforms both the artist's gaze and our own. The portrait with scorpion exemplifies Abramovic's readiness to take risks and it addresses our own capacity for courage and our practical intelligence. A risky venture, no less. Scenographic processes occur in the unknown for the most part – where things are never known completely. The unknown is dominated by black holes that are inaccessible to both the intellect and the intuition. Every successful staging has to account for these black holes. Inclusive thinking, like designing, is a strategic approach, which defines scenography as a versatile process with a resultant rest mass that is essentially unknowable and impermanent: the enigma of the work. The enigma is a meteorological one. It pulsates between logos and mythos on an ever-sliding scale ranging from certainty to risk, under pressure varying from high to low, between clarity and obscuration, as Samuel Beckett aptly described in *Imagination Dead Imagine*.[82] The enigma of the world can only be penetrated by a preying gaze.

To what extent is there a separation between high and low, known and unknown, security and risk, logos and mythos? The answer was given to me at 'The Heart', an exhibition by the Wellcome Foundation in London in the summer of 2007.[83] It was an exhibition about the heart with various human and animal dissections as well as intriguing statistics about the potential of the organ. What particularly fascinated me were the data on the bandwidth of cardiac capacity of various endothermic organisms like humans and animals. Regardless of the size of the organism, the mammalian

the battery

heart beats about a billion times in a lifetime. That is its average capacity. On display was an elephant heart, which has an average frequency of 28 beats per minute. This is the engine speed that drives the seven tons of mammal across the African savannas. As a contrast, the exhibition also featured a hummingbird heart with a frequency of 1,200 beats per minute – a mini motor that propels the two-gram bird back and forth. The elephant pump contracts every two seconds. Its pulse determines the locomotion of the animal. Boom. Boom. The hummingbird pump has 20 contractions per second when the bird is in flight. Its motor hums. If you were to put your ear against the body of a flying hummingbird, you would hear a low bass tone. And man? With an average body weight of 70 kilograms and a heart frequency of 70 beats per minute at rest, man finds himself neatly in the middle of the axis between elephant and hummingbird. With a pulse of some one and a half beats per second, man travels through the urban and scenographic world of his own staging and design.

Endothermic organisms show a certain fixed correlation between body weight, heart frequency, the number of approximately one billion heartbeats and life expectancy. The formula is equal for both the elephant and the hummingbird. Given a pulse of 28 beats per minute, the elephant will live approximately 67 years. Given a frequency of 1,200 beats, the hummingbird will live less than two years. Man would live about 31 years according to the same formula, which was indeed the average life expectancy around the year AD 1000. Medical science and civilisation in general have increased the average age to 78 over the last 1000 years. According to the same formula, this augmentation means an expansion of the capacity with one and a half billion heartbeats. Now, what does man do with this increased potential? Is it civilisation that the surplus of energy has produced? Neither elephants nor hummingbirds are interested in a scenographic upgrade or a deepening of the content of their lives; they use the full capacity of their hearts to survive. Man only needs part of it and the remainder is idle capital: the margin of culture. About one and a half billion heartbeats per individual.

Assuming that heartbeats are time, we need to address the concept of time in the latitude of culture. When we simplify it in terms of formulae, the heart generates a linear series of pulses, which suggest a linear flow of time. Ever since Bergson, who distinguished between mathematical clock time and the actual time of life, we are aware of time being curved in experience as soon as an intense event occurs, very much like space losing its linear characteristics under the influence of gravitation in Einstein's view. The

space.time.narrative

pulse of someone who is in love will accelerate. In danger our heart jumps. Relaxation and massage lower the pulse rate. So, depending on the given interval, heart frequencies vary according to the gravity of drama. The latitude of culture operates on an axis of time that we cannot formulate easily. Time flows like a river. It pulsates like the heart. It consists of a double helix of ephemeral events that are fuzzy and are united in fusion. I get up after a good night's sleep. in a good mood. At breakfast I notice we're running out of coffee. In a bad mood. And on it goes. The ups and downs form a jagged curve of scraps of time, interpenetrating each other, each with its own orientation. The interval is the elementary particle of our culture: a fractal of time with a curved nature.

1.5   space, time and narrative

In 1989 the Stedelijk Museum in Amsterdam exhibited the work of the Russian artist Kasimir Malevich.[84] On page 382 we find a picture that the photographer Wim Ruigrok made of the exhibition. What makes the photograph especially interesting is that it shows an exhibition *in actio*. It is not an image of an empty room displaying the aesthetics of a museum interior, but instead it shows a guided tour pausing in the room where the *Black Square* is hanging. Kasimir Malevich painted several black rectangles, as well as red and white ones, but this one was the first square. It marked a turning point in his painting and it foreshadowed suprematism, which, like many other artistic trends of the day, would try to resist gravity, given its dynamic nature. In other words, it was an authentic statement with far-reaching effects. Which makes it even more remarkable that in the photograph only one person is looking at the painting, while the rest of the group are facing the guide with their backs turned towards the canvas. Or maybe even more so because the *Black Square* has a depth that is infinitely more profound than, let's say, a skin-deep optical lookalike in Photoshop, and requires close reading. Face to face with the *Black Square* one can easily imagine it being the condensation of the entire history of painting. A final destination that came into being by imaginatively adding each and every image, layer upon layer, and having every conceivable nuance of colour and shape add to the final culmination of solid black. As a painting, the square, which was painted with such sensitivity and nervous intensity, bears a tremendous conceptual burden. It is the quadrature of countless circles and as such it is the painterly singularity. The *Black Square* is a black hole with such a dense mass that its pictorial semantics are no longer readable. The light of the picture is no longer released by the paint. The image has become abstract. Yet Malevich's black – as Piet Mondrian's white, by the way – is an enigmatic surface that can only be compared to the surface of the sea. One can only explore this enigmatic dimension by 'reading' it very closely. In doing so, one acutely notices the extent to which it differs from a Photoshop square. The enigma of the canvas in fact requires its own frame of reference. One essential parameter is distance. Mental distance. Emotional distance. Looking distance. How remote, one may ask, are we from things? Are we close? Are we far away? What do we actually see? Scenography is primarily concerned with the orchestration of mental distance and intensity, and one cannot reflect on it without taking the quality and the orientation of the gaze into account. From afar and without the subtle light that is needed, the Malevich square and the Photoshop one enter into resemblance and the essence is lost. But when we take a close look, the digital version remains flat, regardless of the intensity of the gaze, whereas the Malevich brings us to the edge of an abyss. Within the confines of the event the optical pull of the painting makes our heads spin until we **BLACK** out. That is how the painting works when looked at closely. The *manifestatio* of the Photoshop square cannot sustain such intensity because it lacks the fundamental *inventio* of meaning. Discursive scenography relates to mercantile scenography as the *Black Square* relates to the digital one. The enigma determines the gravity of aesthetics.

    The *Black Square* is a sign of the times. It was first displayed at '0,10 [zero-ten]: The Last Futurist Exhibition', in Petrograd in 1915, the year when Albert Einstein presented his Theory of General Relativity.[85] Malevich had declared earlier that the Suprematists wanted to 'reduce everything to zero' and that the forthcoming magazine as well as the exhibition itself were called '0,10' because the movement would later 'break through the zero point'.[86] For scenography the *Black Square* is a bottom line as well, because even outside the strictly pictorial dimension of the painter in which Malevich operated, the work has a transcendent charisma comparable to the way in which James Joyce's *Finnegans Wake* transcends the strictly literary dimension. I will elaborate on this later.[87] Of course, the Futurists and Cubists with their fascination for movement and multiple perspectives had preceded the Suprematists, but Malevich's *Black Square* marked a far more radical departure in painting than Umberto Boccioni or Pablo Picasso had introduced.[88] From this point on the visual arts were, at least by the avant-garde, interpreted as essentially relative in space–time and free from any sentimental ballast and the obligation to portray visible reality. Instead, the force of the work could now serve a more fundamental purpose: symbolising the ideal unity of art and life by introducing new aesthetics for a new world. With Malevich's suprematism and later with Mondrian's neoplasticism, the ideal, driven by developments in physics, took on the proportions of a functional myth that surpassed Tommaso Marinetti's politically oriented futurism in taking care of business in the arts in order to pave the way for everyday life.[89] The aspect of immediate communication on the level of the subject was strictly necessary for both Malevich and Mondrian. Both assumed, at least in the period we are talking about, that their painting had the potential to address spectators across the boundaries of reason and analysis and touch them completely, directly and intuitively. Malevich emphatically exhibited a square that was charged with 'the feeling of non-objectivity', not an 'empty square'. It made a plea for the supremacy of pure feeling in the arts which declared the objective world a futile one and intuition the peak of significance.[90] Later he wrote: 'I felt only night within me and it was then that I conceived the new art, which I called Suprematism'. Thus the *Black Square* became the portal to an unknown wasteland that would for the time being be under tentative exploration. But the direction was clearly oriented towards the liberation of art; to dispose of old ballast and expose the true value of things, beyond any conventional virtuosity and pictorial representation.[91] We find similar lofty ambitions with Mondrian, who was concerned with the interrelation of delicately balanced, unequal but equivalent parts – the balance being the symbol of the evolutionary potential of life. Mondrian's paintings from the 1920s in particular represent such stills or momentary instances of an abstract space–time universe. Both Malevich and Mondrian were very precise about the exhibition of their work. In some cases we still have Mondrian's detailed instructions for the layout of an exhibition, which reveals a strong interest in the staging of the whole. It is hardly surprising that the *Black Square* was put in the most prominent spot of the Petrograd show. It was considered an icon from the word go.

Both suprematism and neoplasticism had a certain conceptual austerity that infused the work of Malevich and Mondrian with a critical charge that, in terms of dramaturgy, aimed at addressing, touching and enlightening the spectator. It is likely that both painters were inspired by Henri Bergson's metaphysics as he presented in his major work *L'Evolution créatrice* in 1907.[92] The work contains a comprehensive theory of life and evolution on the basis of a synthesis of Bergson's theory of time and his philosophy of the mind. Its vision or 'theory of knowledge' expounds a distinction between absolute and relative knowledge. A comparison of the methods and strategies of both brings Bergson to the conclusion that only absolute knowledge can grasp the phenomenological complexity of the world. The path of relative knowledge, which analyses phenomena on the basis of a series of remote assumptions, never transcends the level of approximation and therefore fails to grasp the essence. In his *Introduction à la métaphysique* (1903) Bergson already offers a number of striking examples of the deficiencies of the analysis of approximation.[93] According to Bergson, the space–time continuum of life as it manifests in the duration of actual time can only be known through absolute knowledge with the emphatic instrument of intuition. 'Absolute' refers to the immediacy of insight that is the prerogative of maximum proximity and complete identification. Relative knowledge, based on countless external hypotheses, could never achieve this. While the analytic approach is struggling with an inevitable residual mass that prevents the complex of hypotheses from evolving into the actual Whole, Bergson considers the path of intuition as the only way to access the origin of things and the essence of their existence, which is based on the breathing, pulsating, non-linear nature of actual time (duration or *durée*) as opposed to mathematical time (time or *temps*), which is a mere projection of it.

In his philosophy Bergson distinguishes between the time of physics, *le temps*, which in the analytical sciences is measured by clocks and as such is an expression of quantity, and the true time of life, *la durée*, which is an expression of quality; heterogeneous, flowing, ephemeral and irreversible. The main difference between the two concepts has to do with their flexibility. A given time interval BC as measured by a clock has a length that is equal to the mathematical difference of time C minus time B, while the calculation of the reverse time interval CB produces the same value. True time according to Bergson includes much more than analytical time. Not only does it include the interval BC in its duration, as a qualitative evolution of things, which gives it an irreversible direction, but also the residual value of a preceding interval AB and a prognostic value of a future interval CD. Time as in *le temps* forms a linear continuum in which events are measured against the singular dimension 't' with the instrument of a clock. Time as in *la durée* characterises the multiple, omni-dimensional experience of the lived NOW. But as a moment in time cannot be experienced as an isolated instance in the general flow of things, the experience of the fleeting NOW will necessarily expand in time, just like in music a played note will resound through the next one and, conversely, the next will come into being partly as a consequence of the preceding one. Because of this essential elasticity *la durée* forms a non-linear, dynamic universe in which events are propelled by the vital impulse of life and manifest on a timescale that, according to Bergson, shrinks and expands, contracts and dilates, which lends true time the characteristics of a wave.

In order to fathom the Bergsonian wave characteristics of time, I repeatedly listened to Beethoven's *Moonlight Sonata* by Vladimir Ashkenazy that was recorded by Decca in 1978 and released on CD in 1987.[94] Now, the *Moonlight Sonata* is very well known and anyone who has ever had any piano lessons must have practised it at some point. What I found intriguing was how a piece that was so familiar could be so enigmatic in Ashkenazy's performance? I too had to study the sonata in the past, but my endeavours were light years away from Ashkenazy's. Why? Did Ashkenazy come from outer space when he played it? The answer is: yes, he did! Apart from the fact that I hadn't come to understand the piece to such a degree that I could even start to interpret Beethoven's composition. I did play the notes, but I couldn't even compete with a self-playing piano in terms of correctness. Ashkenazy however plays the time intervals and the interrelations between the notes, and he reads the music at a level where his world merges with Beethoven's. I was concerned with the mechanics of the keyboard and the control of the hands, whereas Ashkenazy works with structure and the elasticity of time. His performance breathes time and one experiences duration as a wholeness that includes the listener. Ashkenazy is sometimes jokingly referred to as 'Broadhoven' because he stretches the notes and in doing so he transposes the notation to the curved time of experience. His performances seem to last longer than any other, and of course they are based on the *inventio* of the composed structure of the score that was produced by Beethoven's imagination, but in the execution, the *manifestatio*, Ashkenazy carefully places every note before, but usually after, the beat. By contracting and expanding, his playing acquires an enigmatic dimension that enthrals the listener and for the time being transports him to a different world. Such is the potential of a moving performance. Similarly, in the present context, scenography should always advocate the enigma of things. This potential doesn't reside in the idea on which the staging is based. The enigmatic quality, if any, of an exhibition or a play, of an installation or a performance, is due solely to the execution, which, needless to say, should be propelled by the proper sophistication and the right inventive mind.

It is one of scenography's basic questions how one can improve a

the battery

staging with the enigmatic dimension. Staging thrives on a certain measure of complexity. Seemingly insignificant elements with obscure qualities have the power to generate chains of associations that in turn cause the memory and the imagination to oscillate. The experience catches fire and the spectator or the visitor is invited to step into an unknown world that awaits further exploration. Such an effective enigma should be the purpose of every staging. It should transport us to a state of heightened intelligence and an emotional pliancy vis-à-vis the enigmatic dimensions of the staging. Why talk about enigma instead of mystery? Because to every enigma there is a solution. Mysteries cannot be solved. That is why they are mysteries. But enigmas we can solve. They have an outcome. It is this quality of solvability that makes the enigma intriguing and productive. It makes for the element of play in searching for and finding the solution. Mysteries do not belong to the world of play. In play, the dynamics of the world are reflected within a set of conventions that are accessible to everyone. A mystery, on the other hand, poses a question of unfathomable dimensions and as such one can only approach it through the path of ritual initiation. Like play, the mystery enthrals the participant, but what sets it apart is that its insolubility keeps hold of who is involved. Play sets free.[95] Part of the element of play is finding out what needs to be solved and what doesn't. Play confronts the participant with a structured chain of complementary questions. Mystery poses one great open question in space. Play has a structure; mystery does not. Play has form; mystery is amorphous. Play is staged, it is readable and it has a dramatic solution. Conversely, a given staging can be a playful enigma, but never a mystery. When the public experiences a staging as a mystery, scenography has failed. And, by implication, the scenographer.

Now, as every other profession, scenography is also dominated by mysteries. But those mysteries belong to the domain of the scenographer, to the field of design, and to his basic task to produce an interesting staging of the substance and the form of a given play or exhibition. This task is shrouded by layers that are impenetrable to the intellect and the intuition and therefore is to remain largely unknown and needs to be mysterious to some extent. They force the scenographer to eliminate and simplify out of sheer desperation or impotence as long as he lacks the necessary strategies to integrate the 'black holes' of the assignment as a potential in the process.[96] Especially in exhibitions, the dark matter of staging provides a precondition for rich nuances and for the contingence of narrative potential, like the chance element in playing dice. A game is an uncertain process with certain tendencies, which provoke progressive speculations about the outcome. Likewise, an enigmatic staging has the narrative potential to unfold in a myriad of interpretations as tendencies or dimensions or aggregations of one and the same story.

Assuming that Malevich's *Black Square* is a zero point and a plane of projection on which the art of painting of all times has been condensed, then it should be interpreted as a square that is charged instead of empty; charged with a whole universe of signs and narratives. Now, suppose we applied the same procedure to the *Moonlight Sonata*, and suppose it were possible to produce the sound of its many notes as one universal super chord, i.e. to compact the extensiveness of the composition in one single point; what would the acoustic explosion of the super chord, as a disharmonious Big Bang of the *Moonlight Sonata*, have to do with the harmonious performance of Ashkenazy? Both NOTHING and, depending on the frame of reference, EVERYTHING. Just like Malevich's square is both empty and charged, depending on the point of view. The thing is that we don't have the capacity to perceive this one-pointed compact mass of *Moonlight Sonata*. The structure is lacking, as is the interval to accommodate perception. The super chord contains the whole of the sonata in a compressed, folded-up format, and, besides Ashkenazy's time–space-related playing, there is nothing lacking. It is the timeless version of Beethoven's composition. But we only appreciate it when it unfolds in time and when it facilitates the evolution of the musical subject matter into a gripping performance by the impulse of inspiration. Here, evolution in the Bergsonian sense refers to nothing other than actual time, which, through Ashkenazy's interpretation, evolves in space as the 'becoming' of the *Moonlight Sonata.*

But what, we may ask, is the nature of time? Is there only one or do we have multiple ones? Does time have a direction? Does space dominate time or vice versa? Is time a separate dimension as such? Ever since Einstein had demonstrated in his publication of the *Theory of General Relativity* that space, time and matter were connected in a complex web of interdependencies on a macroscopic scale, and that the position of observation had a decisive influence on the phenomena perceived, the question of time and simultaneity dominated the ongoing debate between science and philosophy.[97] What Bergson objected to in Einstein's theory, was the confusion of the two types of time on the one hand, and the postulate of reversible time on the other. According to Bergson, the durative aspect of time had one direction only. On 6 April 1922, at a meeting of the Société Française de Philosophie in Paris, the two gentlemen clashed and Bergson appeared to get the worst of it after Einstein blamed him for not having understood his theory properly.[98] In a way, rationality got the better of intuition and Einstein's 'theory of relativity' would dominate Bergson's 'theory of knowledge' for a long time to come.

The debate on the nature of time is of crucial importance to scenography as well. There is not one aspect of scenography, be it dramatic or belonging to exhibition, that escapes the non-linear, relative, space–time characteristics of staging, and the orchestration of TIME in every staging determines whether the scene of the action remains an emotionally flat series of scenes or objects, or rather functions as an intelligent organism, rich with contrast, that evolves into an appealing narrative space. The dispute between physics and metaphysics about time and synchronicity could however only be reconciled in the aftermath of the discussion between Bergson and Einstein, by a series of new insights into the nature of turbulent processes. After it had been established that on the microscopic level of quantum mechanics light could be interpreted both as having the characteristics of a wave and as a stream of particles, Werner Heisenberg formulated the Uncertainty Principle, which stressed the uncertain space–time relationships of basic particles: the more accurately the location of a particle is defined, the less accurate the statements about the time of its observation become, and vice versa.[99] This fuzzy behaviour of matter on a microscopic level, which can only be expressed in terms of probability, prompted the French physicist Louis de Broglie to suggest that perhaps all matter has wave characteristics and that time may not be an independent dimension at all.[100] A third theoretical position was needed to explain the issue of the direction of time and to bridge the gap between Bergson and Einstein. The necessary impetus came from the Russian Belgian physicist Ilya Prigogine, who combined the laws of thermodynamics with the laws of general relativity and quantum mechanics, focusing on the notion of entropy as the tendency of turbulent phenomena to disintegrate and decline.[101] Prigogine suggested the possibility of entropy having, on a basic level and caused by the restraining forces of life, a creative force that produces order out of chaos, just like order turns into chaos when the cohesive energy runs out.[102] Many years later Prigogine looked back on the 1922 dispute in his lecture 'The arrow of time' and considered his work as a synthesis between science and philosophy.[103] The two major theories of the last century, relativity and quantum mechanics, had both denied the direction of time. But Prigogine demonstrated that thermodynamic processes in turbulent systems are indeed irreversible, just as the flow of our thoughts is part of an irreversible process that is contingent in its development. The causality of 'old' physics stated that all aspects

space.time.narrative

of a closed system are ruled by its initial conditions. Within that framework, science led to certainty. But once the irreversibility of time is brought into the equation, the outcome of dynamic processes is dominated by a degree of uncertainty, according to Prigogine. A turbulent system is open and unpredictable and needs to be interpreted as a complex network of bifurcations between one initial point A and an infinite number of end points B. The process then traverses every possible trajectory between A and B simultaneously, while the resultant outcome turns out to be the dominant route. In 'The arrow of time', Prigogine maintains that not only biology, but also human history is dominated by such bifurcations of choices, and that basically there is always the possibility of alternative outcomes, partly due to the pressure that is exerted on the decision-making process. Here it is interesting to note that Prigogine maintains that we perceive history on every level of observation: the Matterhorn, the Kingdom of the Netherlands, you and me; we all age in the same way. As Prigogine puts it:

> It seems that we can only understand the structures which surround us from a historical perspective, and that this historical perspective corresponds to a succession of bifurcations. So science today emphasizes the narrative element, becomes a history of nature: I would like to say, it becomes something like a novel, or a story of 1001 Nights, in which Scheherazade tells a story to interrupt and tell an even nicer story, and so on, and here we have cosmology which leads to the story of matter, then to life, and to man.[104]

According to Prigogine the ideals of classical science still had a geometrical outlook, which Einstein formulated to its ultimate degree in his theory of general relativity. Today, science becomes more and more of a narrative and the world increasingly appears to be a construct. Prigogine: 'We came to the end of certainty, but the end of certainty means the possibility of novelty' – which is also the principle of evolution as it was anticipated by Bergson in *L'Evolution créatrice* in 1907.[105]

In his book *Order Out of Chaos*, Prigogine points at the self-organisation of complex systems like the ones that had already been vividly described by the notorious Roman thinker and poet Lucretius some 2000 years before.[106] 'Sometimes,' Lucretius writes in *De Rerum Natura*, 'at uncertain times and places, the eternal, universal fall of the atoms is disturbed by a very slight deviation – the 'clinamen'. The resulting vortex gives rise to the world, to all natural things.'[107] Without much imagination we can easily consider Prigogine's thermodynamic fluctuations as instances of the Lucretian clinamen.[108] The creative counterforce of life lies especially in the minimal declinations of the usual course of things. Set against the turbulent system of scenography, Lucretius' vortex of atoms reminds us of a crowd of visitors of a contemporary exhibition. Or of Guy Debord's Situationists during a *dérive* through the urban space of a city.[109] The strolling individual who is guided by chance has all the time in the world, while the city and the exhibition provide the intimate entourage for the flow of things. The *flâneur* traverses the narrative environment of the city or the exhibition, and the resultant psycho-geographical cross-section, among thousands of other potential alternatives, assumes the dimension of a personal tale.[110]

In his 'sum-over-histories' theory the American physicist Richard Feynman described time simply as a 'direction in space', assuming that the probability of a series of events equals the sum total of all historical variants of those events.[111] In this respect, ordinary clock time is a spatial trajectory that has a higher probability than other more exotic alternatives would have manifested. For scenography this is important, because Feynman posits the integral of all conceivable time trajectories between A and B as being the most likely cross-section through space. This trajectory, however, is considered to be the resultant of a multitude of excursions and adventures that progress simultaneously, at sometimes widely differing speed rates, far beyond the habitual limits of time and space of a city or an exhibition. Thus, any chance occurrence that the *flâneur*'s clinamen might cause could easily produce a new set of situations altogether, which Bergson would interpret as embedded in the pulsating envelope of duration, but which Einstein would refuse to incorporate into his theory, for, in his view, 'God didn't play dice' and coincidence should be ruled out.[112]

For a scenography that seeks to establish itself on the triangular basis of space, time and narrative, the interdisciplinary debate about time and synchronicity, as it is and has been conducted in the sciences and philosophy, is an essential line of thought. However, in 1922 there was more going on in Paris that would have a great impact on the orientation of modern scenography. In the same year as the clash between Einstein and Bergson, the Parisian bookstore Shakespeare & Company published the first edition of James Joyce's *Ulysses* while the author was already preparing the work on his magnum opus *Finnegans Wake* – a labour in which Samuel Beckett, who some time later came to Paris to study, would assist the blind Joyce by doing research on the mnemonic art of Giordano Bruno and the *Scienza Nuova* of Giambattista Vico.[113]

space.time.narrative

After *Ulysses*, it was clear to Joyce during the 17 years of writing on 'Work in Progress', as *Finnegans Wake* was called from 1922 to 1939, that whereas *Ulysses* was the history of one day, *Finnegans Wake* had to be the history of one night. In *Finnegans Wake* Tim Finnegan, who was the main character in a vaudeville ballad, drops off a ladder on the bank of the river Liffey in Dublin and slips into a coma. The author envisaged the book as being the dream of the comatose Finn: as Umberto Eco puts it, in Finn the entire past, present and future of the history of Ireland, that is, of mankind, was to unfold in a dreamlike form. 'With *Finnegans Wake* I've put language itself to sleep,' Joyce remarked.[114]

While Kasimir Malevich's *Black Square* is a painterly singularity, *Finnegans Wake* is the literary one. The semantics of language have remained intact, but they have been recombined, and without the key to its impenetrable code it has become inaccessible. Joyce has uprooted the very nature of *spectatio*. *Finnegans Wake* cannot be read as a normal book. And maybe it doesn't need to be. It requires a completely different ritual to open its narrative secrets. A gripping story forges a narrative unity, consisting of *mythos* and *logos*, which immerses the reader in a different reality that comes into being through letters, words and sentences and is supported by semantics unfolding on the waves of language. *Finnegans Wake* doesn't function like that and demands a completely different paradigm on the part of the reader. It initiates the reader in a different kind of ritual. Joyce has alluded to some user instructions in a practical sense. Apart from his teasing remark that he only wrote the book to keep literary criticism occupied for the next three centuries, Joyce strongly recommends an alternative strategy that helps unlock the oral, acoustic aspects of the *Wake*: read it aloud at a rate of one page a day.[115] Thus, the labyrinthine voyage through nocturnal language would take us about two years to complete and to bring us back where we started, for the work is cyclic. Riverrun ...[116] The dramaturgy of the narrative ends up being smoothed out this way, but it opens up a whole new drama: the acoustic performance, which becomes even stronger once it is read in the company of others. *Finnegans Wake* turns into the libretto for a polyphonic work of performance in which the acoustic waves charge the environment with ephemeral shrouds of meaning. Just as surfing is an open kind of sport, pervious to external energy, so does the open character of *Finnegans Wake* allow the labour of the reader to finish the work. *Ulysses* could still be considered as a closed work, *Finnegans Wake* cannot. It demands intervention. Joyce's nocturnal labyrinth is pure time embedded in language. The vibration of the voice in the oral cavity is the source from

the battery

which the semantic space of the dream is born.

What is space other than an elastic envelope filled with dark matter and shrouds of ephemeral meaning? What is time other than a directed flow of sounds or signs passing through space? What is narrative space other than an unstable locus with the potential of a story? Which story? The reader's? The writer's? Is the writer the surfer riding the wave of the reader or is it the other way round? What is narrative other than two energies that are joined for the time being? Time is the source whence narrative springs. Time is the matter that language adheres to. A narrative that doesn't unfold in time is like a book that is waiting to be read: untrodden territory. Only once the reader crosses the wasteland does a trace of narrative reveal itself: the book is space, the reader is time. The book that unfolds under the eyes of the reader produces the narrative space of the story. The temporary unit 'book-reader' is essential: narrative space is always becoming.

An exhibition without visitors is like a potential that doesn't flow. A visitor without an exhibition is at a loss with his time. The temporary unit 'exhibition-visitor' is essential: the narrative is directly etched into the space of memory. Enriched by the imagination, experience keeps drawing new traces through the beds of the narrative. One cannot read the same book in the same way twice. Theatre without an audience is a potential that doesn't flow. The time interval to let the drama develop is lacking. The audience have the time. But a spectator without the drama will gaze into emptiness; which, depending on the imagination, can also be everything. The temporary unit 'drama-spectator' is essential: on the waves of the two-way current between actor and audience the drama reaches its final expression.[117] In the narrative space of the theatre or an exhibition time is not an independent dimension. Time doesn't operate in a play that isn't being witnessed, just as there is no time at work in an exhibition without visitors. Dinah Casson told me that she sometimes fantasises about what all the portraits in the National Gallery are discussing at night when we aren't there as witnesses.[118] That is an interesting thought, because it touches the heart of scenography. For, when we aren't there, there is no exhibition at all; at least, not one that is part of our reality.

I tried to imagine the situation in the Mauritshuis in The Hague, where the *Girl with a Pearl Earring* by Vermeer is: the small, but very powerful canvas from *c.*1665 that enchanted Tristan Kobler.[119] With her lifelike eyes (p.90) she gazes at the *View of Delft*, the no-less-famous canvas from the same period that is also in room 15.[120] Around the corner in room 14 hangs the *Laughing Boy* by Frans Hals, *c.*1625, and a little further on is a self-portrait

space.time.narrative

by Rembrandt from 1669.[121] All personalities captured in paint. But what these characters share amongst themselves after closing time is none of our business. At the most, their presence is a potential that triggers my imagination as soon as I find myself near them. An exhibition, then, is a condition that is activated by the impulse of my visit. It is my own relation with the three paintings that, for the time being, determines the relation between *Rembrandt*, the *Laughing Boy* and the *Girl with a Pearl Earring*. A narrative environment is an open landscape of possibilities. Encountering independent artefacts by chance and being confronted with seemingly unconnected ideas and concepts during our leisurely walk through the narrative in seminal state, is very much like Lucretius' colliding atoms.[122] The situation determines whether or not these connections will produce semantic clusters with a surplus value. And there is always this one deviation, the clinamen, which brings us new, unexpected insights.

Time has completely deserted Malevich's *Black Square*. It is a zero point. Pure space, space for the imagination. Space has deserted Joyce's *Finnegans Wake* completely. The *Wake* is a vibrating string. Pure time, time for the imagination. Both represent a threshold of invention and a crucially important landmark for scenography. Both manifest a radical universe that leaves the viewer or the reader unarmed. This overwhelming power is extremely interesting as a dynamic. You need a new orientation when faced with the *Black Square*. On the currents of *Finnegans Wake* there is no compass that will do. How much time does the *Black Square* require to be understood as a zero point? How much space does *Finnegans Wake* require to evolve into comprehensible semantics?

I once personally experienced the threshold values of scenography in the *Camera Silens* by Olaf Arndt and Rob Moonen.[123] Their 'silent room' is an exact reconstruction of the rooms with dead acoustics that were deployed at the Stammheim Prison in Stuttgart to bring terrorist members of the Red Army Faction to confession by means of sensory deprivation. This replica was part of the permanent exhibition of the Medienmuseum at the time of the opening of the ZKM in 1997 and was open to the public. Lying on an old dentist chair I had myself locked in and found, to my great horror, that I couldn't hear my own voice any more and that my hearing was exclusively turned inwards. What could be heard in the *Camera Silens* was the beating of the heart, and after a while, with sufficient sensitivity, the overtones of the blood rushing through the veins. The surrounding dead acoustics killed every resonance. My heartbeat was the centre of a capsule that corresponded with the contours of my body. With my inwardly listening ears I registered the pulse of my existence: the beating heart in my chest cavity. Each beat formed a sound with the potential of a word. Colliding sounds were carried to the periphery of space by the rushing of the blood. The periphery was the inside of my skin. There, the word clusters merged in a drumming melody and turned the membrane into a huge eardrum that had varying tensions in different places. I found myself locked in a cell, in a time capsule where the pressure increased with every heartbeat. The shreds of words that rushed through my veins in rhythmic patterns coagulated into one primordial sound that wanted to break free from the body, like a balloon that is about to burst when the pressure rises. Soon, I left the room that wasn't a room. During the stunning interval I had seen the *Black Square* while *Finnegans Wake* flowed through my veins. There was also a remote *Moonlight Sonata* played by Ashkenazy at a different speed, fitting my interval perfectly. *Camera Silens* accommodated bare time in its most immediate form, with myself as the source and with a duration that was lighter than existence itself. Weightless, I surfed on Bergson's *durée*. 'Time is invention or nothing at all,' as he put it.[124]

1.6 the dramaturgical hinge

In the room with the dead acoustics, time appeared to be mere invention. Where life is absent, we invent it instead. In the photographer's darkroom darkness reigns. The minute aperture of the diaphragm turns the image of the world upside down. In the lucid room of scenography a meteorological balance reigns. Even the smallest particle of dark matter suffices to stir the imagination. A small fraction of recognition will stir the memory. The cycle of memory and imagination is the source of the eventual story. The scenographer's tale is only the eye of the hurricane.

Every narrative environment is supported by an idea, an *inventio*. Every successful staging is an impulse – a *manifestatio* – that touches the receptive spectator, visitor or listener and multiplies the myth of the narrative into a myriad of variants. At this point I would like to emphasise the role of receptiveness in our discourse, if only because every play, exhibition or concert is completed by the participation of spectators, visitors and listeners. In 1980 a posthumous work by the French philosopher and semiologist Roland Barthes, *La Chambre claire*, presented a fascinating exposé on photography.[125] It focuses on the position of the spectator (i.e. of Barthes himself) and

space.time.narrative

interprets the immanent quality of the photograph from the perspective of the viewer. Barthes isn't concerned with photography as a technical medium, but instead with the effects of the photographic image in relation to the viewer who is touched by the expressiveness of the image. The intensity of the image and the receptiveness of the viewer are the central issues, and Barthes explores their relationship in terms of those qualities. What is interesting is that one could easily read *Camera Lucida* as a treatment about the dramaturgy of photography. As a theory of the effect of things, dramaturgy always entails three positions, as Aristotle demonstrated in the *Ars Rhetorica*. The interrelation of the three is like the function of a hinge that combines two movable elements.[126] Aristotle's treatment is about the art of rhetoric and it is evidently aimed at the dramatic unity of orator, speech and audience. In *Camera Lucida* Roland Barthes introduces the threefold functional hinge of the photographer as 'operator', the photograph as 'spectrum' and the viewer as 'spectator'. No photo without the operator. No spectrum to relate operator and spectator without the photo. And without the spectator there is just the photo, without the interval that is required to unfold its spectrum, which consequently remains lifeless and inert. The stage of viewing, which is essential to the completion of the photograph, is what Barthes calls its *spectatio*. Needless to say, this is also the very aspect that determines the completion of scenography. The model of the dramaturgical hinge of *inventio*, *manifestatio* and *spectatio* is the perfect analogy to sustain the design and the interpretation of any staging. *Inventio* is the domain of the scenographer, or the operator. The translation of the idea into a material form is the *manifestatio* that makes the spectrum of the staging. And finally the *spectatio* is the domain of the viewer, or the spectator, whose perception, whose avid gaze, stirs the narrative, the myth, and the narrative environment so that the spectrum of the play or the exhibition can materialise. Barthes distinguishes between two dimensions, two qualitative aspects of the spectrum which he illustrates in *Camera Lucida* by means of a series of photographic images. In the present context I will focus on one photograph that has a special relation with scenography. It is a photograph that the American photographer Robert Mapplethorpe took of composer Philip Glass and director-scenographer Robert Wilson on the occasion of the premiere of *Einstein on the Beach* in 1976.[127]

Barthes defines the information referred to in the last sentence as the *studium* of the photograph; as the collection of facts that together document the content of the photograph. Likewise, any play or exhibition always has a *studium*. But the *spectatio* contains more; it needs to. Barthes remarks

the battery

about the double portrait that his gaze is automatically drawn to the figure of Wilson, and he wonders why that is so. That is an interesting question. Mapplethorpe's shot on page 93 is a frontal double portrait with a square framing. Philip Glass is sitting on the left and Robert Wilson on the right. In other words, a symmetrical set-up with a neutral framing that divides the picture in two equal parts and that devotes an equal amount of space to both subjects. Still, there are noticeable differences that may attract the attention of the viewer. There are two wooden chairs on which both protagonists are seated astride. They are at equal distance from the camera but Wilson is physically bigger than Glass, so his figure is cut by the frame whereas Glass has ample space around him. This creates the illusion of Wilson being more prominent. The illusion is further enhanced by his body language and the way he looks at us. Wilson's attitude suggests far more tension than Glass' in every respect. Wilson seems about to make a gesture whereas Glass' hands are folded and at rest. Glass seems to be waiting for the photographer in a relaxed way, whereas Wilson is slightly squinting. Wilson is sitting up straight, while Glass is leaning towards him. Wilson's dark clothes also seem to contribute to the general impression, as does the background panel that appears to be a little larger on his side. All this may explain Barthes' shift of attention. But he himself didn't analyse the photograph in this way, at least not on paper. Nor did he intend to. What mattered to Barthes was the fact that Wilson in Mapplethorpe's picture apparently had that special aura, that special personality, which touches or moves the viewer. To put it in Barthes terminology: he 'wounds' the spectator. This potential is what Barthes calls the *punctum* of the photograph. The *punctum* is hard to describe. It is a contingent detail that 'stings' the viewer and in doing so it establishes the dramatic quality of the photograph, like a focal point that is mirrored and projected onto the viewer. In the case of Robert Wilson, Barthes didn't define the *punctum* any further, although rumour has it that Barthes once remarked that maybe it was Wilson's gym shoes.[128] A seemingly irrelevant detail ultimately determines where the anchor point of fascination lies. This is what makes the concepts of *studium* and *punctum* such useful tools for the modus operandi of scenography. Interestingly, the *studium* of staging, as an aspect of the spectrum, belongs to the scenographer, i.e. the operator, whereas the *punctum*, as the contingent aspect, mainly belongs to the domain of the spectator, or rather: to the personality of the viewer. What gives the *punctum* embedded in the spectrum its main thrust is the receptiveness or the openness of the spectator. The *punctum* is the unfathomable, enigmatic quality of a staging: the fascinating factor. It is the *punctum* that absorbs time in narrative space.

If the *studium* of a given staging belongs to the operator, and the *punctum* to the spectator, then the relationship between these two dimensions of the narrative environment must be able to inform us about the working of the spectrum that connects the scenographer and the audience in the space–time of an exhibition or a play. When we focus on this creative relation of *studium* and *punctum*, of operator and spectator, or between scenographer and audience, then we may ask: how exactly does one bring a narrative – the staging of a play, the arrangement of an exhibition – into the limelight, so to speak? What exactly are the dynamics of the dramaturgical hinge, which seems to be the crucial function of any narrative environment, regardless of the locus of the staged drama, be it the theatre, an exhibition or the public space of a city or landscape? There seems to be an unwritten contract between the scenographer and the audience that allots the space and the means to the former, while time is provided by the latter. Only when a staging meets with an audience, when space and time merge, stirred by the cycle of idea and interpretation, does a staging take off – when things work, that is. When they don't, the drama stays pinned to the ground.

The difference between things that work and things that do not work, between being lifted and staying on the ground, is a critical dividing line that can only be crossed by joint inspiration, depending on context and circumstances. By 'joint', which is the crucial point, I don't mean reduced to one single concrete solution that is supported by all designing parties involved. On the contrary. Convergence is a pluralistic concept that allows for deviation, variation and exotic derailments, while retaining its orientation towards a fairly clear goal. Convergence in a mental process is a matter of fuzzy logic. Mythologics. Convergence is divergent to some extent. Divergence – as Feynman and Prigogine pointed out – is a small-scale characteristic of a turbulent process that on the whole is a convergent one. This may seem paradoxical, but it is not. Antithesis and contradiction are part and parcel of the genesis of things and accordingly they are among the principle elements of the *spectatio* of drama or exhibition.

But where do things come into being? And when? And how? When we come to think of it, an exciting staging begins well before its actual starting point and it lasts accordingly after its ending. This too may seem a paradox, but likewise it is not. All depends on our gaze, which is guided by understanding. In our navigation system – the sum total of our sensory apparatus and the interpretative functions of our brain – Prigogine's principle of 'bifurcation' is included.[129] The convergence of *spectatio* is a fact of experience that is supported by progressive options and conducted along a pattern of relative variables. Left or right? Big or small? Close or remote? Short or tall? Warm or cold? Word or sign? Text or image? Listening or seeing? Seeing or believing? Light or dark? Complex or simple? Truth or lie? Thing or thought? Obscene or exalted? Fast or slow? – but also: to accelerate or to slow down? Loud or silent? – but also: louder or softer? Prose or poetry? – but also: more prosaic or more poetic? Rationality or emotion? – but also: more rational or more emotional? Structure or event? – but also: more structural or rather spectacular? These are the parameters of *manifestatio* that lends elasticity to the process of transmitting; cascades of options and expectations on which the eventual array of the scenographic sum-over-histories is based.[130] The options and expectations of the visitor or the spectator are the contingent components of scenography. Coincidence. Unreliability. Like the Uncertainty Principle in quantum mechanics, it determines the nature of scenography. Scenography is dominated by probabilities. Scenography meanders between mythos and logos, has a fuzzy nature. Scenography cannot be defined unequivocally and is bound to ask questions because it has no definite answers. This perpetually sliding scale of scenography we find in Webster's dictionary of 1913, in which 'scenography' is defined as: 'the art or act of representing a body on a perspective plane; also, a representation or description of a body, in all its dimensions, as it appears to the eye'.[131] The concept of scenography interconnects the staging of a corpus (i.e. a body or an object), the perspective of a space and the watching eye of the spectator in one dynamic system. As soon as the standpoint of the spectator or the condition of his *spectatio* changes, every proportion within the given spectrum starts to move. Conversely, when the relations on the plane of action of scenography alter, then the perspective space of the viewer is transformed. Scenography is concerned essentially with the design of these relations. Whatever moves implies space. With movement, time passes and with the passing of time a process is initiated in which a dramatic potential can unfold.

The British director Peter Brook probingly addressed the issue in his highly influential *The Empty Space* in 1968, albeit with a different objective and within a different context. Due to its analytical acumen and, what's more, its passionate style, the book is a uniquely relevant contribution to the general discourse about the theory of scenography.[132] The first chapter of *The Empty Space* opens with the sentence: 'I can take any empty space and call it a bare stage. A man walks across this empty space whilst someone else is watching him, and this is all that is needed for an act of theatre to be engaged.'[133] According to Brook, much of the theatre of the 1960s has lost its power, significance and meaning. Both his own dramatic works and the book should be understood as a means to liberate the theatre of the day of its conventions, to initiate new developments and to charge the theatre with new ritual dimensions. Over the centuries the form of the theatre hasn't developed all that much. Brook doesn't mind, because the average two hours of a performance may be short in one respect, but in terms of dramaturgy it is infinity. Shaping this relative eternity is a great art that, according to Brook, is only relevant as long as it is embedded in the social dynamics of the moment and is in accordance with the spirit of the time. The criterion is the synchronicity of the spectrum, not the form of the shell – the *skene* – giving 'mere' temporary shelter to the spectrum. Here we find the deeper meaning of 'empty': it is not about being filled or not, or being minimalist in its material, medial aspects, but rather about being emptied, evacuated as a tabula rasa; stripped of any superfluous cultural codes that prevent the space from opening itself to new significant signs and obstruct the recharging of the theatrical environment.

In the four chapters of the book, Brook explains his views on what the theatre is about. In the first chapter, 'The Deadly Theatre', he strongly opposes the mainstream commercial theatre that seems to have lost every bit of its ambition. Chapters two and three, 'The Holy Theatre' and 'The Rough Theatre', deal with two essentials of the theatre – holiness and roughness – in the context of various works of drama, and argue that only in some exceptional instances (such as Shakespeare) do the two come together. Finally, in 'The Immediate Theatre', Brook sheds some light on his own theatrical practice. For our purposes here, the concepts of roughness and holiness are of interest because they refer to diametrically opposed ambitions and trends, and as such seem to be highly applicable to the exhibition trade. The difference is huge, as the opening sentences of their corresponding chapters in Brook's book indicate. The chapter on 'The Holy Theatre' begins:

> I am calling it the Holy Theatre for short, but it could be called The Theatre of the Invisible-Made-Visible: the notion that the stage is a place where the invisible can appear has a deep hold on our thoughts. We are all aware that most of life escapes our senses: a most powerful explanation of the various arts is that they talk of patterns which we can only begin to recognize when they manifest

themselves as rhythms or shapes. We observe that the behaviour of people, of crowds, of history, obeys such recurrent patterns.[134]

For Brook, the choreographies of Merce Cunningham, but also the theatre of Samuel Beckett or Jerzy Grotowski, exemplify, each in their own particular way, the 'Holy Theatre', and he classifies their work according to the following properties: 'small means, intense work, rigorous discipline, absolute precision'.[135] Here Brook also refers to Shakespeare and Antonin Artaud (p. 86), whose manifestos of 'The Theatre of Cruelty' inspired him to conduct a series of experiments in 1964 in which he tried to shape Artaud's ideas into something concrete.[136] But Artaud, like Shakespeare, belongs to both categories; the former foresaw a kind of theatre that would be more complete and more profound, and the latter had done so three hundred years earlier.[137] Brook argues:

> We can try to capture the invisible but we must not lose touch with common sense – if our language is too special we will lose part of the spectator's belief. The model, as always, is Shakespeare. His aim continually is holy, metaphysical, yet he never makes the mistake of staying too long on the highest plane. He knew how hard it is for us to keep company with the absolute – so he continually bumps us down to earth.[138]

In continuously making for the creative interaction between the highest and the lowest planes, both Artaud, in his theory of the imagination, and Shakespeare, in the practice of his plays, are especially important to Brook, who strives for a 'theatre of ritual' in which 'rough' and 'holy' are two poles on the axis connecting the world of things with the world of ideas.

The chapter 'The Rough Theatre' explains why the conceptual relation between roughness and holiness should dominate every staging – as it does every ritual – no matter how they are balanced. The holy is the dimension of restraint and the rough represents the liberating potential. As Brook states:

> It is always the popular theatre that saves the day. Through the ages it has taken many forms, and there is only one factor that they all have in common – a roughness. Salt, sweat, noise, smell: the theatre that's not in a theatre, the theatre on carts, on wagons […] audiences standing, drinking, sitting around tables […] joining in, answering back; theatre in back rooms, upstairs rooms, barns, the one-night

stands, the torn sheet pinned up across the hall, the battered screen to conceal the quick changes – that one generic term, **theatre**, covers all this and the sparkling chandeliers too.[139]

There are some examples that Brook mentions explicitly: Vsevolod Meyerhold's political ambitions, the aspect of alienation in Bertold Brecht's plays and the explosiveness of Jean Genet's work.[140] Artaud is also among them. But the summit, 'the greatest of rough theatres', according to Brook is William Shakespeare, whose 'obscenity and truculence' should be regarded as the 'motors of revival' of the theatre of the period, as he puts it.[141] His affinity with Shakespeare, however great his fascination for Artaud, may well have to do with the radically different positions of the two men: Brook, the successful doer who directed his first play at 17, as opposed to Artaud who for various reasons found it difficult to find his way into the theatre and was doomed to express himself in texts.[142] Despite the distance in time and the difference in nationality, Brook finds it much easier to identify with Shakespeare. Their theatrical practice is very much alike. What is striking, though, is that although Shakespeare may be an example to Brook, it is Artaud who, some generations earlier in *The Theater and its Double*, fully blames Shakespeare for the theatre's catastrophic turn towards the bourgeois mentality.[143]

Like many before him and many who came after him in the theatre, Brook considered Artaud – who was seen by many as a lunatic – as an inspiring prophet; a voice in the wilderness. Brook writes:

> Railing against the sterility of the theatre before the war in France an illuminated genius, Antoine Artaud, wrote tracts describing from his imagination and intuition another theatre – a Holy Theatre in which the blazing centre speaks through those forms closest to it. A theatre working like a plague, by intoxication, by infection, by analogy, by magic; a theatre in which the play, the event itself, stands in place of a text.[144]

Here is where Brook and Artaud meet. The world of phenomena is but a 'crust' to both. Underneath we find the fuming matter, if we have the courage to look into the innermost of the volcano, that is. 'How can we tap into this energy?' Brook wonders, knowing that Artaud attempted to bypass rationality through ritual and in doing so came close to unifying the holy and the rough and addressing the invisible universe behind reality.[145] But how far should you go? What is feasible? Addressing hidden reality at the moment of a performance is a process shared between the audience and the actor, evolving in the space of the theatre, which is also shared. The theatre is a confrontation with the possibility to enter into contact. In the theatre the audience and the performer each have their own entrance to the place of the performance. The audience enters via the foyer, while the actors make their entrance from the wings. The quintessence of the theatre for Brook lies in the question of whether these two separate ways of access can, in the course of the performance, and depending on the theatrical 'temperature' of the play, transcend into one connecting axis, one functioning dramaturgical hinge, or whether they must fatefully remain 'symbols of separation'.[146]

1.7 the camera lucida of savage thought

It was also Artaud's intention to poke up the theatrical fire to full heat; let there be no doubt. Both Brook and Artaud are fascinated by the pure power of life as it is expressed in the symbols, myths and rituals of those cultures that are closer to nature than we are. This anthropological, ethnographical interest shows just how much importance is attached to the actor and the act of performing within the framework of theatrical dynamics. It is hardly surprising that Brook was very much inspired by the structural anthropology of Claude Lévi-Strauss who had published his fundamental studies *Totemism* and *The Savage Mind* in 1962, not long before *The Empty Space* appeared.[147] Both works were to become a compass for Brook in his search for a theatre of ritual. Brook's later works *Orghast* (1971) and *Mahabharata* (1985) in a way represent confrontations of diverging cultures and their symbols. We witness how the melting pot of direction re-forges them into a new set of symbols and rituals whose *raison d'être* in a conceptual sense we can trace back to Lévi-Strauss who, as a starting point for increasingly sophisticated lines of thought in *The Savage Mind*, eliminated every hierarchical distinction between our culture and the so-called primitive ones.[148] We find the same point of departure with Artaud, be it in a more intuitive way; not as theoretically based and as oriented towards appealing choreography and aesthetics. Moreover, Artaud had a different frame of reference than Brook had. When Artaud published *The Theater and its Double* in 1938, Lévi-Strauss was researching indigenous Indian cultures in the Amazon basin, a project that would be reflected in *Tristes Tropiques* only years later.[149] Of course, Lévi-Strauss may have been influenced by Artaud, but neither *Tristes Tropiques* nor *The Savage Mind* suggest as much, despite the obvious parallels in terms of cultural production, which in Artaud's case is a matter of metaphysics and in Lévi-Strauss' a matter of structural ethnographic empiricism.

Lévi-Strauss is interested in the way in which cultures produce and shape artifacts, i.e. in the aesthetics of the ritual. In *The Savage Mind*, he distinguishes between two types of institutions that are usually supposed to perform this task: one is the engineer and the other is the *bricoleur*, the handyman.[150] The tasks of the engineer and the *bricoleur* are fundamentally different, but Lévi-Strauss considers them as completely equivalent. In the chapter 'The science of the concrete', he makes the following comparison:

> The difference is [...] less absolute than it might appear. It remains a real one, however, in that the engineer is always trying to make his way out of and go beyond the constraints imposed by a particular state of civilization while the 'bricoleur' by inclination or necessity always remains within them. This is another way of saying that the engineer works by means of concepts and the 'bricoleur' by means of signs. The sets which each employs are at different distances from the poles on the axis of opposition between nature and culture.[151]

For a sound understanding of indigenous cultures it is, according to Lévi-Strauss, indispensable to structurally apply the concept of 'odd-jobbing' not only to craftsmanship, but also to the world of ideas, which in his view should be considered as an intellectual form of 'bricolage'. Lévi-Strauss considers it a central characteristic of mythological thinking and argues – very much along the lines of Artaud – that we could derive a tremendous cultural potential from it. The *bricoleur*

> derives his poetry from the fact that he does not confine himself to accomplishment and execution: he 'speaks' not only with things, as we have already seen, but also through the medium of things: giving an account of his personality and life by the choices he makes between the limited possibilities. The 'bricoleur' may not ever complete his purpose but he always puts something of himself into it.[152]

In *The Savage Mind*, Lévi-Strauss illustrates the savage thought of primitive culture by means of countless examples. They are evidence of a dazzling knowledge of plants and animal life, and within the given context of indigenous medicine they are as sophisticated as our own sciences, albeit without the same sustaining logic. Still, for Lévi-Strauss this doesn't rule out the possibility of this radically different constellation of mythologics producing brilliant and unexpected results both in the intellectual field and in the field of so-called 'naive' art. Each example demonstrates the possibility of a radically different view providing the impetus to initiate alternative ways of thinking in one's own system of thought. Just as the engineer may systemise the approach of the *bricoleur* by amplifying it with the aid of concepts, so the *bricoleur* may lend increased flexibility to the thought of the engineer by laying bare some relationships that otherwise remain hidden because of culturally conditioned blindness. The most beautiful example however is not one by Lévi-Strauss, but by Richard Feynman, who in his inaugural speech of 1974 at the Californian Institute of Technology pointed at the restrictions of savage thought in the sciences:

> In the South Seas there is a Cargo Cult of people. During the war they saw airplanes land with lots of good materials and they want the same thing to happen now. So they've arranged to make things like runways, to put fires along the sides of the runways, to make a wooden hut for a man to sit in, with two wooden pieces on his head like headphones and bars of bamboo sticking out like antennas – he's the controller – and they wait for the airplanes to land. They're doing everything right. The form is perfect. It looks exactly the way it looked before. But it doesn't work. No airplanes land. So I call these things Cargo Cult Science, because they follow all the apparent precepts and forms of scientific investigation, but they're missing something essential, because the planes don't land. Now it behooves me, of course, to tell you what they're missing. But it would be just about as difficult to explain the South Sea Islanders how they have to arrange things so that they get some wealth in their system. It is not something simple like telling them how to improve the shapes of the earphones.[153]

Here we have the engineer's view of the *bricoleur*. But both Lévi-Strauss and Artaud stress the equivalence of the *bricoleur*'s perspective. Feynman argues that the South Sea Islanders are lacking something. Now, this may be true in a strictly material sense, but that doesn't imply that in a 'mythopoetical' sense the airstrip rituals amount to naught or that they are a waste of time. What does the controller with the wooden earplugs in his little hut see? What does he hear? Or think, or perceive, or gather? We don't know.

space.time.narrative

We don't know which insights or orientations matter in the given context. We only know that we remain ignorant of their nature. We also have a hint of their cultural background, which may give access to another aspect of the truth, one that is hidden behind the appearance of things. Artaud and Brook recognised the potential of the Other for the stage. Of the two, Artaud went much further in wanting to strip bare the whole of theatre and release it from its formal, cultural conventions. As a result, the 'Theatre of Cruelty' manifestos offer a potentially new format of cultural production, which, in contours, suggests a programme for the emergence of an expanded scenography.[154]

Still, 'The Theatre of Cruelty' gave rise to a host of misunderstandings, most of which are related to the notion of 'cruelty'. Artaud is obviously aware of criticism and of the possible implications of the term 'cruelty'. As always, his reaction has an edge:

> With this mania we all have for depreciating everything, as soon as I have said 'cruelty', everybody will at once take it to mean 'blood'. But 'theatre of cruelty' means a theatre difficult and cruel for myself first of all. And, on the level of performance, it is not cruelty we can exercise upon each other by hacking at each other's bodies, carving up our personal anatomies, or, like Assyrian emperors, sending parcels of human ears, noses, or neatly detached nostrils through the mail, but the much more terrible and necessary cruelty which things can exercise against us. We are not free. And the sky can still fall on our heads. And the theatre has been created to teach us that first of all.[155]

Artaud, like Brook, is talking about the significance of the theatre, about the access to the Other, which haunts the performance and is its 'Double'. In the end, it is all about the right proximity, about audibility, about relevant signs, ritual and an encryption that will reveal the hidden truth of the performance and secure its readability. In Artaud's case, we need to take the notion of proximity quite literally. In the theatre of cruelty the actor and the audience have closed in on each other, for:

> if music affects snakes, it is not on account of the spiritual notions it offers them, but because snakes are long and coil their length upon the earth, because their bodies touch the earth at almost every point; and because the musical vibrations which are communicated to the earth affect them like a very subtle, very long massage; and I propose

to treat the spectators like the snakecharmer's subjects and conduct them by means of their organisms to an apprehension of the subtlest notions.[156]

To this effect, the theatre should be organised in a radically different way, attuned to a more comprehensive language and new ways of expression which transform our gestures, our sounds, words, fire, our cries, our light and our darkness into incantations.

While Artaud is opposing the predominance and the restrictions of language, we in our present context of discursive scenography are mainly concerned with a transformation which affects the format of conveyance that entails his vision. The first of his manifestos contains a plea for lifting the duality of the theatrical space:

> We abolish the stage and the auditorium and replace them by a single site, without partition or barrier of any kind, which will become the theater of the action. A direct communication will be re-established between the spectator and the spectacle, between the actor and the spectator, from the fact that the spectator, placed in the middle of the action, is engulfed and physically affected by it. This envelopment results, in part, from the very configuration of the room itself.[157]

The performance that Artaud has in mind in the theatre of action amounts to no less than a shock; a true spectacle 'like mines in a wall of rock which all of a sudden turns into geysers and bouquets of stone'.[158] But as all is metaphor with Artaud, literally honed for 'getting across' and intense communication, beyond rationality, it is the inevitable element of cruelty that lives in every spectacle. Intensity too has a cruel side, if only because the spectator needs to be touched. But what is striking above all, when Artaud describes the concrete means of performance, is the image of the modern *exposition-spectacle* in which the scenographer basically has the complete array of media characteristics at his or her disposal to modulate the envelope of communication into a form with the necessary *punctum*. Artaud again:

> Whereas, in the digestive theater of today, the nerves, that is to say a certain physiological sensitivity, are deliberately left aside, abandoned to the individual anarchy of the spectator, the Theater of Cruelty intends to reassert all the time-tested magical means of capturing the sensibility.

space.time.narrative

> These means, which consist of intensities of colors, lights or sounds, which utilize vibration, tremors, repetition, whether of a musical rhythm or a spoken phrase, special tones or a general diffusion of light, can obtain their full effect only by the use of dissonances. But instead of limiting these dissonances to the orbit of a single sense, we shall cause them to overlap from one sense to the other, from a color to a noise, a word to a light, a fluttering gesture to a flat tonality of sound, etc.
>
> So composed and so constructed, the spectacle will be extended, by elimination of the stage, to the entire hall of the theater and will scale the walls from the ground up on light catwalks, will physically envelop the spectator and immerse him in a constant bath of light, images, movements, and noises.[159]

Artaud's prophecy was a tempting one, and still is, but somehow it poses a problem. We cannot design a ritual. Ritual needs to evolve, ripen, deepen and crystallise over time. Our cultural production can merely help to develop the preconditions of unknown rituals to come. It is the task of scenography to explore this basic precondition. This doesn't detract from Artaud's discourse. Our time merely requires the appropriate signs. Which ritual is the relevant one, and for whom? The times have changed and have put Artaud's revolution into perspective. Cultures have merged in society, and the theatre failed to produce the necessary reconciling signs. For that reason the capacity of narrative environment should be interpreted in a new and more expanded way. It should dissociate from the confines of one single format and nestle as a differentiated critical potential in every refuge of our society.

I once saw *Mysteries* and *Paradise Now* by The Living Theatre of Julian Beck and Judith Malina in The Roundhouse in London.[160] Peter Brook must have attended these performances as well. It was only some years after the publication of *The Empty Space*, in his hometown London. The nomads of The Living Theatre had put up their camp in The Roundhouse for a week and they gave performances every day. In an Artaudian vein, the separation between the stage and the audience was regularly lifted and actors would enter the hall and invite the audience to participate in celebrating the ritual of love with the 'troupe' on stage. We cannot determine whether this was Artaud's interpretation of direct communication but The Living Theatre made one thing perfectly clear: proximity should, as an initiative, be in the hands of the spectator, just as the *punctum* should ultimately be taken as an aspect of his or her condition. Physical proximity initiated by the actor may easily be understood as an act of real cruelty, creating distance instead of what was intended. This cannot be what Artaud had in mind originally – unless he meant ritual. Ritual involves participation, but the theatre includes more. It is also about a projection that needs a certain distance between the actor and the audience in order to function; after all, some focus is indispensable. 'Proximity' then comes to signify something metaphorical; the clear projection of an image on the internal screen of the spectator. That image becomes the compass for the mind to participate. Even a giant like Robert Wilson, who experimented with about every aspect of the theatre, has never lifted the functional distinction of the 'fourth wall' between the performance and the audience because the connection between the two demands an agent, an intermediary. Only when proximity becomes an aspect of the anarchy of the spectator, does scenography accept the challenge and offer the hospitality of openness. Such receptiveness can only arise when the structure of *inventio* and the envelope of *manifestatio* are of a liberal, pluralistic nature. Then the *spectatio* of the spectator can embrace the spectrum of the performance.

Brook is a man of practice, a theatre director who realises a piece of work, or a *bricoleur*, if you will, who forges various hybrid elements of different cultures into a unity. Artaud on the other hand has, for some reason or other, struggled with the realisation of projects all his life. Circumstances forced him to lead the life of a solitary prophet, a voice in the wilderness, and take refuge in texts. Because he failed to establish his ideas in practice, Artaud involuntarily remained an 'engineer' who needed to charge his language ever more strongly in order to be heard.

Still, as a source Artaud is the purer of the two. Both the first and the second manifesto of 'The Theatre of Cruelty' have had an enormous impact on the world of performance, both before and after Peter Brook. Especially in his treatment of the concrete aspects of the theatrical space or the use of theatrical means, i.e. the vehicle of performance, Artaud is conceptually superior. Brook's approach never reaches beyond the scope of the theatre director, whereas Artaud breaks through the boundaries in order to radicalise other disciplines as well. When Artaud demands that the separation between the audience and the performer be lifted, and that every aspect of the space of the action be integrated, immediately the *exposition-spectacle* comes to mind. The freedom of Artaud's thought and his fascination for cultural confrontations as analysed by Claude Lévi-Strauss, make him a guiding light for today's expanded scenography.

space.time.narrative

At the beginning of this essay I pleaded for an alternative dimension, which I termed 'obscenography'. Considering the sign of the times, obscenography should be taken as a sublimation of Artaud's cruelty in the hands of Lévi-Strauss' intellectual *bricoleur*. And by now it should be obvious that, within the field of scenography, the obscenographer and the scenographer are related in a way that is similar to the relation between the *bricoleur* and the engineer. When Lévi-Strauss uncovers the tremendous potential that lies between the *bricoleur* and the engineer, we may do the same: expanded scenography is a transdisciplinary domain where the unity of the intuitive and the intellectual is a guiding principle. The *bricoleurs* and the engineers of the trade may seem to be in sufficient command of the *manifestatio* of scenography, but where the intellectual bricolage in Lévi-Strauss' sense is most desperately needed is in the moment of *inventio*, where the seed of every discursive scenography is sown. What the obscenography of the intellectual *bricoleur* has to offer to the field of scenography, may well be summed up by the words of Artaud. At a time when cognitive conveyance abounds, 'it is through the skin that metaphysics must be made to re-enter our minds'.[161]

the battery

Notes

1   William Shakespeare (1564–1616), *As You Like It* (1599), Act II, Scene VII, lines 139–66.
2   B. Joseph Pine II and James H. Gilmore, *The Experience Economy*, Harvard Business School Press, Boston, 1999.
3   The World Wide Web is a platform-independent computer network for the exchange of information – of a scientific nature initially – that was developed by the British software developer Tim Berners at the CERN Institute in Geneva from 1989 onwards. In 1993 a graphic interface, the Mosaic web browser, was added, which made the Internet a visual reality, accessible to the general public. Because of the huge success of the Internet, the 'traditional' medium of television became more and more oriented towards the format of reality TV.
4   The Zentrum für Kunst und Medientechnologie (ZKM) was founded by the German art historian Heinrich Klotz. It opened in October 1997 in Karlsruhe. Initially it comprised two museums and two research departments: the Museum für Neue Kunst, the Medienmuseum, the Institut für Bildmedien and the Institut für Musik & Akustik. Since 1998 the Austrian artist and scholar Peter Weibel has presided over the ZKM.
5   Silicon Graphics (SGI) Onyx was an American manufacturer of high-end graphical systems. Due to the arrival of the Internet and the tendency towards distributed computing, it lost its market position, at least in the arts. In the 1990s the SGI-Onyx super computers used to be the cutting edge in high-tech media art, whose primary aim it was to simulate interactive virtual environments that were largely dominated by the architectural conventions of actual spaces. The user could navigate through them by means of a complex interface. Often the interface would consist of a helmet with an electronic viewfinder that immersed the user in a weightless world in which the body no longer seemed to matter.
6   Peter Greenaway, 'The Physical Self', Museum Boijmans Van Beuningen, Rotterdam, from 27 October 1991 to 12 January 1992. The president of the Boijmans, Wim Crouwel, had invited Peter Greenaway to act as a guest curator and set up an exhibition about the human body. He allowed him to put together a selection from the collection to his own liking. Greenaway followed his fascination and produced an exhibition that showed strong parallels with his feature film *Prospero's Books* (1991) from the same period in which many extras appeared naked.
7   'The dot-com industry' refers to predominantly American internet companies that produced websites with the extension '.com'. In the 1990s the shares of the dot-com economy, without any realistic economic backup, were systematically overrated, as a result of which the speculative market collapsed between 10 and 15 March 2000 when investors lost their confidence, sold their shares and virtually annihilated the NASDAQ index.
8   The Al-Qaeda terrorist attacks on the Twin Towers of the World Trade Center in New York on 11 September 2001.
9   The global credit crisis that emerged on the stagnating American housing market. Mainly because of high-risk but extremely lucrative financial products, many business banks went broke and the financial markets collapsed in the course of 2008–9.
10 Chaos theory deals with the behaviour of certain dynamic systems, such as the weather, which is so unstable that the smallest fluctuations of one seemingly insignificant variable may have unpredictable results on a large scale. The so-called 'butterfly effect' is from a lecture by the mathematician and meteorologist Edward Norton Lorenz (1917–2008), held

	in 1972 in Washington D.C. for the American Association of Advanced Science, entitled: 'Predictability: Does the flap of a butterfly's wings in Brazil set off a tornado in Texas?'. Lorenz is generally considered as the father of chaos theory.
11	Hans-Peter Schwarz et al., *Das Medienmuseum: Geschichte, Theorie, Konzepte*, 1993. Concept for a new type of media museum in the Zentrum für Kunst und Medientechnologie in Karlsruhe. Published as an internal ZKM edition of 100 copies.
12	Matthias Michel et al., *Fakt & Fiktion 7.0: Wissenschaft und Welterzählung – Die narrative Ordnung der Dinge*, Edition Collegium Helveticum, vol.1; Chronos Verlag, Zurich, 2003.
13	Camini Stichting, Amsterdam, 1989; Fons Asselbergs, Jean Leering, Felix Valk, Herman Kossmann, Patrick van Mil, Lenneke Büller, Frank den Oudsten. The purpose of the research project, funded by the Ministry of Culture of the Netherlands, was to deepen and expand know-how in the field of making exhibitions. Publication: *Concept.Form.Exhibition: Museum Presentations as Narratives*, published on the occasion of the 15th general conference of the International Council of Museums (ICOM), held in The Hague in 1989.
14	The Scenographical Design course at the Hochschule für Gestaltung und Kunst (School of Art and Design) in Zurich, set up by Frank den Oudsten in 2001, became effective in 2002 and was led by Frank den Oudsten together with Christoph Allenspach and Hansuli Matter until 2006, following the four-year *Diplomstudium* format that was generally offered by art colleges in Switzerland at that time. When, for the sake of international compatibility, the bachelor–master system was subsequently introduced in Switzerland, it appeared that there was insufficient room for a broadly oriented, transdisciplinary curriculum of scenography at the Zürcher Hochschule der Künste (Zurich University of the Arts – as the Hochschule für Gestaltung und Kunst had become in 2007). As a consequence the subject of understanding narrative environments in the museum, the theatre and the urban and rural landscapes as a subject of coherent expertise was eliminated.
15	Narrative Environments: an international research project, set up by Herman Kossmann and Frank den Oudsten in 2005, aimed at liberating the exhibition trade from its cultural isolation. Seminars were held at the Museum Bellerive, Zurich, in January and February 2006. 'Exhibiting Now!' expert meeting, Platform21, Amsterdam, June 2006; 1st International Scenographers' Festival, Basel, November 2006.
16	Central Saint Martins College of Art and Design (since 2004: University of the Arts, London).
17	For some time now there has been a growing interest on the part of the exhibition trade in the dramatic action of the theatre. Conversely, the theatre has developed a keen interest in the language and the signs of exhibitions. The narrative environments of both domains have grown closer and we can easily consider them as one single field of expertise. We recognise the tendency in the education of the arts, especially at the Master level. Scenography, traditionally aimed exclusively at the theatre, has been expanded at the Central Saint Martins College of Art and Design and now includes Creative Practice for Narrative Environments. In the German region the production of theatre and exhibitions has wider context by labelling it *Szenografie* or even *Raumstrategien* ('spatial strategies') when the urban and rural landscapes are included.
18	Pamela Howard, *What is Scenography?*, Routledge, London–New York, 2002. See also The Theatre Design Website: http://sceno.org/articles/what-is-scenography/, May 2009.
19	Nina Gorgus, 'Scenographische Ausstellungen in Frankreich', *Museumskunde*, vol.2, 2002, pp 135–142. Gorgus explores the influence of French *muséographie* and *scénographie* on

the battery

exhibition making in Germany. The primary focus is on the works of Georges-Henri Rivière and Jacques Polieri. Two main issues are addressed: the *exposition-spectacle* and the exhibition without an auratic – the predicate that Walter Benjamin introduced – collection. The artist, critic and curator Franck Ancel did some extensive research on modern French scenography and set up an important exhibition about Jacques Polieri in the Bibliothèque Nationale de France in Paris. For further information on the auratic dimensions and the authenticity of museum objects: see also the interview with Uwe Brückner, pp.347–349.

20 World Fair EXPO 2000, Hanover. The term *Scenographie*, indicating the profession of making exhibitions, was first used by Dr Martin Roth, president of the thematic area of EXPO 2000: '*Scenographie ist, einfach formuliert, das Handwerk, dreidimensionale Räume so zu inszenieren, so einzurichten, dass Inhalte verstärkt durch gestalterische Mittel deutlicher und prägnanter in ihrer Wirkung und damit in der intendierten Aussage werden.*' ('Scenography, put simply, is the profession of staging 3-D spaces in such a way that content, enhanced by design, gains in terms of eloquence and impact, and therefore communicates its message more effectively.') Martin Roth et al., *Der Themenpark der EXPO 2000: Die Entdeckung einer neuen Welt*, vol.1, Vienna, 2000. Also: Martin Roth, 'Scenographie: zur Entstehung von neuen Bildwelten im Themenpark der EXPO 2000', in *Museumskunde*, vol.66, 2001, pp 25–32.

21 EXPO.02, the sixth Swiss national exhibition, was shown at different *arteplages* in Switzerland. See also: Bernadette Fülscher, *Gebaute Bilder: Künstliche Welten – Szenografie und Inszenierung an der Expo.02*, hier+jetzt, Baden, 2009. The 1st International Scenographers' Festival, organised by the Institut IN3 of the Hochschule für Gestaltung und Kunst, Basel, under the direction of Uwe Brückner, Andreas Wenger and Heinz Wagner in November 2006, was an important catalyst in the acceptance of the term 'scenography'.

22 *Docta ignorantia*: 'learned ignorance', used here as a self-chosen limitation of insight. The phrase refers to the writings of Nicolaus Cusanus (1401–1464), in which *docta ignorantia* is used to denote the concept that God's limitlessness renders it impossible for humankind to comprehend perfection.

23 Ludwig Wittgenstein (1889–1951), *Tractatus Logico-Philosophicus*, Amsterdam, 2006, proposition 1. Written by Wittgenstein during the First World War and first published in German as *Logisch-Philosophische Abhandlung*, 1921. See also: A.C. Grayling, *Wittgenstein: A Very Short Introduction*, Oxford University Press, Oxford, 2001.

24 Tyra Banks, *America's Next Top Model*: a popular reality-television programme, developed and presented by supermodel Tyra Banks; first broadcast in America in 2003 and subsequently spread over the entire world in a great number of local adaptations.

25 Antonin Artaud (1896–1948), *The Theater and its Double*, Grove Press, New York, 1958. Original title: *Le Théâtre et son double*, published in the 'Métamorphoses' series by Éditions Gallimard in Paris, 1938.

26 The half-life of a quantity whose value decreases with time is the interval required for the quantity to decay to half of its initial value. The concept originated in describing how long it takes atoms to undergo radioactive decay but also applies in a wide variety of other situations.

27 Ancient Greek knew two words for 'time': *chronos* and *kairos*. *Chronos* is to be understood as the 'time of the clock', being a fleeting phenomenon like in 'time is a river', which is measured in quantities. *Kairos*, on the other hand, is perhaps best explained through its negative equivalent 'untime' in English. Untime suggests an inappropriate instance of time.

space.time.narrative

If an event is 'untimely', then the adjective of 'untime' is adding a qualitative statement to the interval of time in which the event occurred. Reversely, *kairos* is NOW!, suggesting the right time for an event to occur and indicating the appropriateness of the moment.

28   In the classical theatre the *skene* originally formed a temporary space adjacent to the stage where costumes were put and to which the set was attached. As the setting and background to the stage gained importance, the *skene* itself became more complex and more permanent as well. Greek theatre became more frontal in character. The space in front of the *skene*, the *proskenion*, was the main area of the performance, but the *skene* itself served as a hidden part of the stage where some parts of the action would remain unseen; they could only be heard. In contemporary theatre the *skene* and the *proskenion* have evolved into one domain that contains the entire dramatic action. What remains of the original *skene* is the frame of the stage.

29   Caspar Schott (1608–1666) was a German scientist, writer and educationalist who presented his main scientific experiments in *Physica Curiosa* (Würzburg, 1662) and *Technica Curiosa* (Nuremberg, 1664). Otto von Guericke (1602–1686) was a German scientist who was the mayor of Magdeburg from 1646 to 1681.

30   '*Theatralität, Intermedialität, Erweiterter Raum*': colloquium on the theory of scenography in the Design Department of the Fachhochschule, Dortmund, 13 to 15 December 2007. As a result of the colloquium the first issue of the 'Szenografie & Szenologie' series appeared: *Inszenierung und Ereignis* by Ralf Bohn and Heiner Wilharm, transcript Verlag, Bielefeld, 2009.

31   Ralf Bohn, '*Szenologische Performativität: Optik und Ontologie beim Versteckspiel der Kinder*', Dortmund, 14 December 2007.

32   *Pneuma* is Ancient Greek for 'air', 'wind', 'breath' or 'spirit'. In metaphysics it signifies 'breath of life'. At some point in the history of thought the discussion about memory came down to the question of whether it was located in the heart or in the brain. As a medical, anatomical issue it fascinated the Greek-Roman physician Galen (131–c.216). P.J. van der Eijk recently addressed the matter in his speech for the Koninklijke Nederlandse Akademie van Wetenschappen [Royal Netherlands Academy of Arts and Sciences], '*Hersenen, lichaam en geest in het laat antieke wijsgerige en medische denken*', on 14 January 2008 in Amsterdam. See also: Charles G. Gross, *Brain, Vision, Memory: Tales in the History of Neuroscience*, Bradford Books, The MIT Press, Cambridge–London, 1998, pp 22–31. Also: Douwe Draaisma, *Metaphors of Memory: A History of Ideas about the Mind*, Cambridge University Press, Cambridge, 2000. Original title: *De Metaforenmachine: Een Geschiedenis van het Geheugen*, Historische Uitgeverij, Groningen, 1995, pp 33–40.

33   Otto von Guericke conducted his experiments with the hemispheres at several locations in Germany. Caspar Schott was the first to describe the experiment in his publication *Mechanica Hydraulico-Pneumatica* (Würzburg, 1657). For technical details see also the publication of the Deutsches Museum in Munich: *Meisterwerke aus dem Deutschen Museum*, vol.1, 2004.

34   A vacuum is literally an empty space, a place marked by the absence of the usual, former or expected contents (*Oxford English Dictionary*). Containing nothing solid, tangible or visible, a vacuum in a metaphorical sense also describes a place devoid of ideas, unintelligent or expressionless. Classical physics considered the vacuum to be a space from which air or other gas had been completely removed by a pump, like Schott and Guericke did. Quantum physics however, defines a vacuum as an instable, transient condition, which

could at first approximation be understood as the state with no particles, but which in time will not remain empty due to the so-called black body radiation of the walls of the vacuum chamber.

35 Charter of Transdisciplinarity, adopted at the First World Congress of Transdisciplinarity, Convento da Arrábida, Portugal, 2 to 6 November, 1994.

36 If, after a careful rehearsal of the interplay of all its elements – such as hand gestures, eye contact with the audience, intonation and modulation of the voice, etcetera – the actor or speaker is finally 'delivering' his or her speech, then the rhetorical dynamics of the event are set '*in actio*' for the first time. An exhibition therefore reaches its state of being *in actio* only after the staged environment of space, time and narrative has been engaged by an interacting and participating audience. In the rhetorics of scenography, *in actio* is a dramaturgical notion, indicating the final stage of a process of development and refinement, in which a work reaches its completion by setting all of its parameters into action.

37 Umberto Eco (b.1932), *Opera aperta*, Bompiani, Milan, 1962; English edition, *The Open Work*, Harvard University Press, Cambridge (MA), 1989; chapter 1: 'The poetics of the open work'. According to Eco, 'A work of art (...) is a complete and closed form in its uniqueness as a balanced organic whole, while at the same time constituting an *open* product on account of its susceptibility to countless different interpretations which do not impinge on its unadulterable specificity. Hence, every reception of a work of art is both an *interpretation* and a *performance* of it, because in every reception the work takes on a fresh perspective for itself' (p.4). See also the German edition: *Das Offene Kunstwerk*, Suhrkamp Taschenbuch Wissenschaft 222, Frankfurt am Main, 1967.

38 Gilles Deleuze and Félix Guattari, *What is Philosophy?*, Verso, London–New York, 1994. Especially relevant for the present discussion are chapter 2: 'The plane of immanence', pp 35–6, and chapter 3: 'Conceptual personae', p.71.

39 In theatre, dramaturgy is concerned with structuring a narrative into form by considering the representation and the effects of the main elements of the drama on stage. In the context of modern scenography, dramaturgy takes on the meaning of the discipline of the 'working of things'. Greek: *drama* = action + *ergon* = result. The American photographer Ralph Gibson (b.1939) at some point suggested the following definition: 'physical fact = psychic effect', which could prove very useful for scenography as well.

40 Aristotle, *The Art of Rhetoric*, translated by H.C. Lawson-Tancred, Penguin Classics, London, 1991. From chapter 1.2: 'Of those proofs that are furnished through the speech there are three kinds. Some reside in the character of the speaker, some in a certain disposition of the audience and some in the speech itself, through its demonstrating or seeming to demonstrate' (p.74). From chapter 1.3: 'For a speech is composed of three factors – the speaker, the subject and the listener – and it is to the last of these that its purpose is related' (p.80).

41 Roland Barthes, *La Chambre claire*, Éditions du Seuil, Paris, 1980; English edition, *Camera Lucida*, HarperCollins, London, 1984, chapter 44, p.107.

42 André Malraux, *Le Musée imaginaire*, Éditions Gallimard, Paris, 1965; *Museum without Walls*, Doubleday & Company, New York, 1967. See also: Geoffrey T. Harris (ed.), *André Malraux: Across Boundaries*, Rodopi, Amsterdam–Atlanta, 2000; especially the essay by Edson Rosa da Silva, pp 258–62.

43 Marshall McLuhan (1911–1980), *Understanding Media*, McGraw-Hill, New York, 1964.

44 Neil Postman (1931–2003), *Amusing Ourselves to Death*, Methuen, London, 1987, p.8.

In his essay 'Towards a semiological guerrilla warfare', Umberto Eco also wonders what McLuhan actually meant by the maxim 'the medium is the message'. Dutch translation in *De Alledaagse Onwerkelijkheid*, Uitgeverij Bert Bakker, Amsterdam, 1985, pp 158–68. Originally the essay was Eco's contribution to the 'Vision '67' congress, New York, October 1967.

45 Modern exhibitions without a sustaining collection, aimed at immersing the audience in the sensation of the narrative by means of every conceivable form of communication and media, are by nature spectacular and are called *exposition-spectacle*, not only because André Malraux in *Le Musée imaginaire* (op.cit., 1965) and Guy Debord in *La Société du spectacle* (1967) have recognised society's itch for the spectacular as a pivotal theme, but also because the development from museography to scenography within the context of the communicative medium of the exhibition took place predominantly in France. The work of François Confino, and particularly the first '*Cités-Cinés*' exhibition (initiated in La Grande Halle de la Villette, Paris, 1987), is a clear example. See also the interview with François Confino, pp.203–207.

46 A *Gesamtkunstwerk* is an ideal work of art in which drama, music and other performing arts are integrated and each is subservient to the whole (*Oxford English Dictionary*). The term is originally German and was first introduced by the German writer and philosopher Karl F.E. Trahndorff in the second volume of his essay '*Ästhetik der Lehre von der Weltanschauung und Kunst*' from 1827. The German composer Richard Wagner first used the term in his '*Zürcher Schriften zum Kunstwerk der Zukunft*' from 1849. See also the Foreword by Hans Peter Schwarz, p.xiii, and the interview with Ruedi Baur, note 51, p.270.

47 Marshall McLuhan, op.cit., chapter 2: 'Media hot and cold', pp 36–45.

48 Albert Einstein (1879–1955), *Relativiteit: speciale en algemene theorie*, Het Spectrum, Utrecht–Antwerp, 1978. The little masterpiece of popular science by the deviser himself appeared in 1956 as *Über die spezielle und die allgemeine Relativitätstheorie* by Vieweg & Sohn, Braunschweig. See also: Thomas Bührke, *E=mc²: Einführung in die Relativitätstheorie*, Deutscher Taschenbuch Verlag, Munich, 1999. Also: Bertrand Russell, *The ABC of Relativity*, George Allen & Unwin, London, 1969.

49 Henri Bergson (1859–1941), *Introduction à la métaphysique* (*Introduction to Metaphysics*) (1903), published in English as *The Creative Mind*, Greenwood Press, Westport, 1968, pp 187–99. See also: Henri Bergson, *Creative Evolution* (1907), Palgrave Macmillan, New York, 2007. Also, an important introduction to the philosophy and the metaphysics of Henri Bergson by Gilles Deleuze (1925–1995) in *Bergsonism* (originally: *Le Bergsonisme*, 1966), Zone Books, New York, 1988.

50 Marshall McLuhan, op.cit., chapters 12 and 13: pp 114–17.

51 The line '*Alles van waarde is weerloos*' ('Everything precious is helpless'), from *De zeer oude zingt* (1974) by Dutch poet and painter Lucebert (1924-1994), has become very well known.

52 Translated literally, a *Wunderkammer* (German) is a chamber or cabinet of wonders. More specifically, it is a place exhibiting the collection of a connoisseur of curiosities (*Oxford English Dictionary*). Famous English examples of a *Wunderkammer* are for instance the Pitt Rivers Museum in Oxford, and in a sense also Sir John Soane's Museum in London. The *Wunderkammer* was originally a sixteenth-century phenomenon in the European history of collecting, centred around the subjectivity and individual preference of its collector, usually a king, emperor or scientist. Regarded as such, the cabinet of curiosities was a microcosm,

a personal memory theatre or even a theatre of the world, which symbolically reflected the views of its owner. See: Elisabeth Scheicher, *Die Kunst- und Wunderkammern der Habsburger*, Brandstätter, Vienna–Munich, 1985. See also: Ken Arnold, *Cabinets for the Curious: Practicing Science in Early Modern English Museums*. Ph.D. dissertation, Princeton University, 1991.

53 The fourth wall refers to the imaginary 'wall' at the front of the stage in a traditional three-walled box set in a proscenium theatre, through which the audience sees the action in the world of the play. See for instance: Elizabeth Bell, *Theories of Performance*, Sage Publications, Thousand Oaks, 2008.

54 Leon Battista Alberti (1404–1472); Alberti's treatise on architecture, *De Re Aedificatoria*, published in 1485. is a theoretical exposé fashioned after Vitruvius' (c.80–c.15 BC) *Ten Books on Architecture*. Instead of treating it as a kind of labour, it presents architecture as an intellectual discipline with an important social relevance.

55 Mnemonics are a tool or a method for supporting the memory in the act of remembering. The 'method of loci' was especially prominent in the mnemonics of Antiquity. The anecdote of Simonides of Ceos (c.556–468 BC) perfectly illustrates its functionality. In the story a roof has collapsed during a banquet in the honour of Castor and Pollux. The victims need to be identified and, as it happens, Simonides has walked out of the hall just before the disaster and thus is the sole survivor. By mentally connecting the faces ('icons') of those present to the places at the table ('loci') where they were seated, Simonides is able to identify each of the victims. The story illustrates the principle of classical mnemonics. It is interesting to note that in Greek Antiquity Mnemosyne (the name derived from the noun denoting the ability to recall or memorise) was considered to be the mother of all nine Muses.

56 Functional mnemonics, as described in the anecdote of Simonides of Ceos and refined by Cicero (106–43 BC) in *De Oratore*, culminated in a veritable art of remembering, an *Ars Memoriae*, in the Renaissance. In Italy Giulio Camillo (1480–1544) and Giordano Bruno (1548–1600) were its main representatives; Robert Fludd (1574–1637) became the most well-known specialist in Britain.

57 Frances A. Yates, *The Art of Memory*, Pimlico, London, 1992. For the relationship between the spatial organisation of Camillo's mnemonic theatre and the architecture of Andrea Palladio (1508–1580), see pp 171–3; for the relationship between Fludd's Memory System and Shakespeare's Globe Theatre, see the analysis in chapter 16, pp 330–54. For a detailed study, see also: Frances A. Yates, *Theatre of the World*, University of Chicago Press, Chicago, 1969, pp 112–62.

58 James Joyce, *Finnegans Wake*, 1939. Joyce refers to Giordano Bruno on several occasions in the book. These include on p.163 as Nolanus: 'And I shall be misunderstord if understood to give an unconditional sinequam to the heroicised furibouts of the Nolanus theory … '; and on p.488 as Nola Bruno: 'When himupon Nola Bruno monopolises his egobruno most unwillingly seses by the mortal powers alionola equal and opposite brunoipso, id est, eternally provoking alio opposite equally as provoked as Bruno at being eternally opposed by Nola. Poor omniboose, singalow singelearum: so is he!' Bruno was born in Nola near Naples in 1548.

59 Frances A. Yates, *The Art of Memory*, op.cit., pp 135–6.

60 Walt Disney Imagineering is the master planning, creative development, design, engineering, production, project management, and research and development arm of The Walt Disney Company and its affiliates. Representing more than 150 disciplines, its talented

space.time.narrative

    corps of Imagineers is responsible for the creation of Disney resorts, theme parks and attractions, hotels, water parks, real estate developments, regional entertainment venues, cruise ships and new media technology projects; http://corporate.disney.go.com/careers/who_imagineering.html, May 2009. All given examples are about surrender and immersion, be it as a consciously constructed act of enthralling entertainment by Disney Imagineering or as a Haitian voodoo ritual in the form of a trance dance.

61   Mark Dery, *Escape Velocity: Cyberculture at the End of the Century*, Hodder & Stoughton, London, 1996. Escape velocity is the speed at which a body – a spacecraft, for instance – overcomes the gravitational pull of another body, such as the Earth.

62   Colin Counsell, 'Beckett and the avant-garde', in *Signs of Performance: An Introduction to Twentieth-Century Theatre*, Routledge, London, 1996, pp 112–42.

63   Samuel Beckett (1906–1989), *Endgame*, 1957. *Endgame* is a one-act play with four characters. It was originally written in French, entitled *Fin de partie*; as was his custom, Beckett himself translated it into English. The play was first performed in a French-language production at the Royal Court Theatre in London, opening on 3 April 1957. See also: James Knowlson, *Damned to Fame: The Life of Samuel Beckett*, Bloomsbury, London, 1996, pp 431–40.

64   Samuel Beckett, op.cit., German performance: *Endspiel* with Stefan Kurt as Clov and Sven-Erik Bechtolf as Hamm, Schauspielhaus, Zurich, November 2003.

65   Samuel Beckett, *Proust*, Grove Press, New York, 1970, p.7: 'But for every tumour a scalpel and a compress. Memory and Habit are attributes of the Time cancer.' The original English edition was published by Chatto & Windus, London, 1931.

66   Samuel Beckett; *Waiting for Godot*, 1953; *Waiting for Godot* is Beckett's translation of his own original French version, *En attendant Godot*, which was (in English) subtitled as a 'tragicomedy' in two acts. The original French text was composed between October 1948 and January 1949. The premiere was on 5 January 1953 in the Théâtre de Babylone, Paris. The production was directed by Roger Blin, who also played the role of Pozzo. See also: Knowlson, op.cit., pp 388–417. A notorious performance of *Waiting for Godot* in the US was one by the San Quentin Drama Group in 1957, which had inmates of the San Quentin State Prison in San Francisco perform the parts under the direction of Herbert Blau. For background material on American productions of the play, see: Herbert Blau, *Sails of the Herring Fleet: Essays on Beckett*, The University of Michigan Press, Ann Arbor, 2000.

67   Samuel Beckett; op.cit., Act 2.

68   Samuel Beckett, *The Complete Short Prose 1929–1989*, Grove Press, New York, 1995: *Imagination Dead Imagine* (1965), pp 182–5; *The Lost Ones* (1966–70), pp 202–23.

69   Samuel Beckett, *Proust*, op.cit., pp 4–5.

70   Ibid p.11; 'So that we are rather in the position of Tantalus, with this difference, that we allow ourselves to be tantalised. And possibly the perpetuum mobile of our disillusions is subject to more variety. The aspirations of yesterday were valid for yesterday's ego, not for to-day's.' See also Colin Counsell, op.cit., p.113.

71   Colin Counsell, op.cit., pp 112–13.

72   Samuel Beckett, op.cit., p.185 (the conclusion of the piece): 'Only murmur ah, no more, in this silence, and at the same instant for the eye of prey the infinitesimal shudder instantaneously suppressed. Leave them there, sweating and icy, there is better elsewhere. No, life ends and no, there is nothing elsewhere, and no question now of ever finding again that white speck lost in whiteness, to see if they still lie still in the stress of that storm, or in the

the battery

black dark for good, or the great whiteness unchanging, and if not what they are doing.' For 'the eye of prey' see also: Herbert Blau, op.cit., p.155.
73   *Esse est percipi*: to be is to be perceived.
74   John Cage (1912–1992), *4'33"*, 1952. Cage called *4'33"* a 'silent piece': the pianist walks to the piano and does not touch a key during the next 4 minutes and 33 seconds. A stopwatch is used to determine the exact interval of the piece. It is a piece for piano in which the coughing of the audience, the shuffling of feet, passing cars – chance environmental sounds, in short – form the acoustic material. As such, *4'33"* is aleatoric music. But it is also a performance. At the first performance, on 29 August 1952, pianist David Tudor stretched his arms three times to indicate that it is a piece in three movements – all silent.
75   Philip Glass (b.1937) and Robert Wilson (b.1941), *Einstein on the Beach*, 1976. For detailed information on Wilson's work, see: Katharina Otto-Bernstein, *Absolute Wilson: The Biography*, Prestel, Munich–Berlin–London–New York, 2006.
76   Richard Wagner (1813–1883), *Der Ring des Nibelungen: ein Bühnenfestspiel für drei Tage und einen Vorabend*, H. Fikentscher Verlag, Leipzig, 1863. Wagner's magnum opus, *Der Ring des Nibelungen* is based on the Middle High German *Nibelungenlied* and the Old Norse *Völsunga* saga. The cycle of the *Ring* is a musical theatre production consisting of four separate, related performances: *Das Rheingold*, *Die Walküre*, *Siegfried* and *Götterdämmerung*. The premiere of the *Ring* took place on 13 August 1876 in the Bayreuther Festspielhaus under conductor Hans Richter (1843–1916), and its sub-title refers to this occasion.
77   Hiroshi Sugimoto (b.1948), *Theatres*, 1975–2000. See also the book by Kerry Brougher and Pia Müller-Tamm, which accompanied the work of Hiroshi Sugimoto in Düsseldorf, Salzburg, Berlin and Lucerne (2007–9). Edition: Hatje Cantz Verlag, Ostfildern, 2007, pp 76–107.
78   The term 'parallax' is derived from the Greek *parallaxis*, meaning 'alteration', and is pointing at the apparent difference of orientation of an object which is viewed along two different lines of sight. Due to the angle of inclination between those lines – which is minimal in the case of a pair of eyes – nearby objects have a larger parallax than more distant objects. Therefore, when observed from different positions, parallax can be used to determine the distance of a remote object.
79   René Descartes (1596–1650), *Tractatus De Homine*, 1664, p.83. In 1628 Descartes settled in Holland and it was during this period that he composed a series of works that systematically dealt with the mind–body dualism. The first of these works, *De Homine* was completed about 1633, on the eve of the condemnation of Galileo. When Descartes heard of Galileo's fate at the hands of the Inquisition, he immediately suppressed his own treatise. As a result, *De Homine* was published only well after its author's death. From: http://serendip.brynmawr.edu/Mind/Descartes.html, May 2009.
80   Samuel Beckett, op.cit.. See picture essay 1: 'Parallax', pp. 96–7.
81   Marina Abramovic (b.1946), *Portrait with Scorpion (Open Eyes)*, 2005.
82   Samuel Beckett, op.cit.
83   'The Heart', The Wellcome Foundation, London, 21 June to 16 September 2007.
84   'Kasimir Malevich, 1878–1935', Stedelijk Museum, Amsterdam, 5 March to 29 May 1989. See the exhibition catalogue: *Kazimir Malevich, 1878–1935*, with Preface by W.A.L. Beeren. The touring exhibition was shown in Leningrad, Moscow and Amsterdam, 1988–9.
85   '0,10: The Last Futurist Exhibition'. The exhibition opened on 17 December 1915 at Na-

space.time.narrative

86 dezhda Dobychina's Art Bureau on the Field of Mars in Petrograd (now St Petersburg). Stedelijk Museum, op.cit., p.157. See also the essays that El Lissitzky (1890–1941) wrote on suprematism and constructivism in the 1920s in: Sophie Lissitzky-Küppers, *El Lissitzky*, Thames & Hudson, London, 1968, pp 331–58.

87 James Joyce, *Finnegans Wake*, Faber and Faber, London, 1939; here we used the bilingual English–Dutch edition by Erik Bindervoet and Robbert-Jan Henkes, Athenaeum-Polak & Van Gennep, Amsterdam, 2002. See also: Erik Bindervoet and Robbert-Jan Henkes, *Finnegancyclopedie*, Athenaeum-Polak & Van Gennep, Amsterdam, 2005.

88 Umberto Boccioni (1882–1916) was the main exponent of futurism, a politically oriented Italian art movement at the beginning of the twentieth century. The poet Filippo Tommaso Marinetti (1876–1944) wrote its manifesto in 1909. Pablo Picasso (1881–1973) and Georges Braque (1882–1963) were the main representatives of cubism, which introduced multiple perspectives in the art of painting.

89 Suprematism, the movement initiated by Kasimir Malevich, developed a visual language that was based on basic geometrical shapes, especially the line, the square and the circle, which were to be the anchor points of the supremacy of new form. See: Kasimir Malevich, *The Non-Objective World: The Manifesto of Suprematism*, 1926; English edition: Paul Theobald & Company, Chicago, 1959. Neoplasticism is the theory of painter Piet Mondrian (1872–1944), which provided a synthesis of all arts and is aimed at the complete unification of art and life. Neoplasticism also provided the theoretical base of the Dutch art movement De Stijl (1917–1931), which was initiated and led by *uomo universale* Theo van Doesburg (1883–1931). See: Ad Petersen (ed.), *De Stijl*, complete reprint, Athenaeum/Bert Bakker/Polak & Van Gennep, Amsterdam, 1968; vol.1 (1917–1920), volume 2 (1921–1932).

90 Stedelijk Museum catalogue, op.cit.; See D.V. Sarabyanov's contribution, pp 70–71. See also: Sophie Lissitzky-Küppers, op.cit., pp 337–8, 354.

91 ibid p.39.

92 Henri Bergson, op.cit. (note 49).

93 Henri Bergson, op.cit. (note 49).

94 Ludwig van Beethoven (1770–1827), *Mondscheinsonate (Moonlight Sonata)*, performed by Vladimir Ashkenazy (b.1937), 1978. Discography: *Piano Sonata No.14 in C sharp minor, op.27/2 'Moonlight'*, Decca, CD: 443 706-2.

95 Johan Huizinga, *Homo Ludens*, 1939. See: *Homo Ludens: A Study of the Play Element in Culture*, Beacon Press, Boston (MA), 1992; chapter 1, pp 1–27.

96 In astronomy, a black hole is a region of space in which the gravitational field is so powerful that nothing can escape its pull. It is called 'black' because it absorbs all the light that hits it, reflecting nothing. Its surface, called the event horizon, is therefore a one-way portal. In terms of energy, objects which are pulled into a black hole won't be able to leave such a region, unless their escape velocity is greater than the speed of light. See also: Stephen Hawking, *A Brief History of Time*, Bantam Books, London, 1998.

97 Albert Einstein, op.cit. (note 48).

98 For a detailed discussion of the debate between Einstein and Bergson that took place on 6 April 1922 at the conference of the Société Française de Philosophie, see: Jimena Canales, 'Einstein, Bergson, and the experiment that failed: intellectual cooperation at the League of Nations', *Modern Language Notes*, vol.120, 2005, pp 1168–91. Canales (Harvard University) states: 'It is commonly asserted that during the meeting Bergson lost to the young physicist (Einstein). Bergson, subsequent commentators have insisted, made an essential

mistake by not understanding the *physics* of relativity. Their confrontation exemplified the victory of *rationality* against *intuition*. It was a key moment demonstrating that intellectuals (like Bergson) were unable to keep up with revolutions in science (like Einstein's). [...] Bergson, however, never acknowledged defeat. According to him, it was Einstein and his interlocutors who did not understand *him*. He attempted to clarify his views in no less than three appendices to his famous book *Durée et simultanéité: A propos de la théorie d'Einstein* (1922), in a separate article 'Les temps fictifs et les temps réel' (1924), and in a long footnote to *La pensée et le mouvant* (1934).' According to Canales, 'the episode marks an essential change in the place of science and philosophy in history. Einstein and Bergson debated about much more than the nature of time and simultaneity. At stake in their debate was the status of philosophy *vis à vis* physics. It was about who could speak for nature and about which of these two disciplines was going to have the *final* word.' The minutes of the meeting were published in: *Bulletin de la Société française de philosophie*, vol.22, no.3, July 1922, pp 102–13. It was reprinted in Bergson, *Ecrits et paroles*, Presses Universitaires de France, Paris, 1957–9, vol.3, p.497, and in Henri Bergson, 'Discussion avec Einstein', in *Mélanges*, Presses Universitaires de France, Paris, 1972.

99   Werner Heisenberg (1901–1976), the Uncertainty Principle in quantum mechanics, 1925–7. In his 'uncertainty paper' of 1927, Heisenberg stated: 'the more precisely the position is determined, the less precisely the momentum is known in this instant, and vice versa.' As David Cassidy observes: 'This is a succinct statement of the "uncertainty relation" between the position and the momentum (mass times velocity) of a subatomic particle, such as an electron. This relation has profound implications for such fundamental notions as causality and the determination of the future behaviour of an atomic particle. Because of the scientific and philosophical implications of the seemingly harmless-sounding uncertainty relations, physicists speak of an *uncertainty principle*, which is often called more descriptively "the principle of indeterminacy".' David Cassidy/American Institute of Physics, 'Quantum mechanics 1925–1927: the Uncertainty Principle', http://www.aip.org/history/heisenberg/p08.htm, May 2009.

100   As David Cassidy explains: 'Most physicists were slow to accept 'matrix mechanics' because of its abstract nature and its unfamiliar mathematics. They gladly welcomed [Erwin] Schrödinger's [(1887–1961)] alternative wave mechanics when it appeared in early 1926, since it entailed more familiar concepts and equations, and it seemed to do away with quantum jumps and discontinuities. French physicist Louis de Broglie [(1892–1987)] had suggested that not only light but also matter might behave like a wave. Drawing on this idea, to which Einstein had lent his support, Schrödinger attributed the quantum energies of the electron orbits in the old quantum theory of the atom to the vibration frequencies of electron "matter waves" around the atom's nucleus. Just as a piano string has a fixed tone, so an electron-wave would have a fixed quantum of energy. This led to much easier calculations and more familiar visualisations of atomic events than did Heisenberg's matrix mechanics, where the energy was found in an abstruse calculation. [...] In May 1926 Schrödinger published a proof that matrix and wave mechanics gave equivalent results: mathematically they were the same theory. He also argued for the superiority of wave mechanics over matrix mechanics. This provoked an angry reaction, especially from Heisenberg, who insisted on the existence of discontinuous quantum jumps rather than a theory based on continuous waves.' Ibid.

101   Ilya Prigogine (1917–2003), proponent of irreversible thermodynamics, was a pioneering

researcher of dissipative structures, which won him the 1977 Nobel Prize in Chemistry. Traditional thermodynamics, as it was developed predominantly in the nineteenth century, exclusively provides quantitative descriptions of reversible processes. Modern statistical thermodynamics describes complex, turbulent systems consisting of vast numbers of moving particles. Prigogine was interested in the instability of such systems and the dynamic conditions that cause them to lose their balance.

102   Entropy is associated with the amount of order or disorder in thermodynamics, the branch of physical science that deals with the relation between heat and other forms of energy. In the isolated system of a body which is heated up, for instance, the second law of thermodynamics states that entropy is increased during an irreversible process, implying a particular direction for time, sometimes called an 'arrow of time'.

103   Ilya Prigogine, 'The arrow of time', inaugural lecture of the workshop on 'The Chaotic Universe' given by Prigogine, when the City of Pescara bestowed on him the honorary citizenship, Pescara, 2 February 1999.

104   Ibid. Probability, manifesting itself in the course of a process as a series of subsequent options or choices, is considered by Prigogine to be a structural quality of complex systems: 'In front of a bifurcation, you have many possibilities, many branches. The system *chooses* one branch; if you repeat the experiment it may choose another branch. In other words, the future is not given. [...] Imagine an ant nest, a source of food and two bridges. You see that after some time all ants are on one bridge. Should you repeat the experiment, they may be on the other bridge. The mechanism is again an autocatalytic mechanism because each ant encourages the other ants to be on the same bridge. This is a very simple example of a bifurcation in biology. Also, human history is full of bifurcations.'

105   Ibid.

106   Ilya Prigogine and Isabelle Stengers, *Order Out of Chaos: Man's New Dialogue with Nature*, Heinemann, Portsmouth (NH), 1984, pp 3, 141.

107   Titus Lucretius Carus (c.99–55 BC), *Of the Nature of Things*, translated by William Ellery Leonard, The Project Gutenberg eBook, no.785, Book 2: *Atomic Motions*, lines 216-225; July 2008. From: http://www.gutenberg.org/files/785/785-h/785-h.htm. See also the Latin version of the text, *De Rerum Natura*, at: http://www.koxkollum.nl/lucretius/lucretius02.htm, May 2009.

108   Clinamen is the name the Epicurian philosopher and poet Lucretius gave to a minimal indeterminacy in the motions of atoms, an unpredictable swerve 'at no fixed place or time'. See: Hanjo Berressem, 'Incerto tempore incertisque locis: the logic of the clinamen and the birth of physics' and Stephen Clucas, 'Liquid history: Serres and Lucretius', in Niran Abbas (ed.), *Mapping Michel Serres*, The University of Michigan Press, Ann Arbor, 2005.

109   Guy Debord (1931–1994). In the 1960s Debord led the Situationist International (SI) group, which influenced the Paris Uprising of 1968. Debord's book *La Société du spectacle*, published by Buchet-Chastel, Paris in 1967, is considered a major catalyst for the disturbances. Also: *The Society of the Spectacle*, Zone Books, New York, 1995. 'The Situationist International (1957–72) was a small group of international political and artistic agitators with roots in Marxism, Lettrism and the early-twentieth-century European artistic and political avant-gardes. Formed in 1957, the SI was active in Europe through the 1960s and aspired to major social and political transformations. The first issue of the journal *Internationale Situationiste* defined a Situationist as "having to do with the theory or practical activity of constructing situations. One who engages in the construction of situations. A member of

the battery

the Situationist International". The same journal defined *situationism* as "a meaningless term improperly derived from the above. There is no such thing as *situationism*, which would mean a doctrine of interpretation of existing facts. The notion of situationism is obviously devised by antisituationists." See: Stefan Zweifel et al., *In Girum Imus Nocte Et Consumimur Igni*, JRP-Ringier Kunstverlag, Zurich, 2006. This collection of essays was published on the occasion of the exhibition on the Situationist International, organised by the Centraal Museum in Utrecht (2006–7) and by the Museum Tinguely in Basel (2007) and includes an interesting Situationist glossary.

110 In his text 'Theory of the *dérive*', Guy Debord states: 'One of the basic situationist practices is the *dérive* [literally: 'drifting'], a technique of rapid passage through varied ambiances. Dérives involve playful-constructive behaviour and awareness of psychogeographical effects, and are thus quite different from the classic notions of journey or stroll. In a dérive one or more persons during a certain period drop their relations, their work and leisure activities, and all their other usual motives for movement and action, and let themselves be drawn by the attractions of the terrain and the encounters they find there. Chance is a less important factor in this activity than one might think: from a dérive point of view cities have psychogeographical contours, with constant currents, fixed points and vortexes that strongly discourage entry into or exit from certain zones. But the dérive includes both this letting-go and its necessary contradiction: the domination of psychogeographical variations by the knowledge and calculation of their possibilities.' Published in *Internationale Situationniste*, vol.2, 1958.

111 Richard Feynman (1918–1988). The path integral formulation of quantum theory for which Feynman won his Nobel Prize (1965) was developed at the California Institute of Technology (Caltech), Pasadena and is known for its accurate predictions. Feynman helped develop a functional integral formulation of quantum mechanics, in which every possible path from one state to the next is considered, the final path being a sum over all possibilities (also referred to as 'sum-over-paths' or 'sum-over-histories'). Feynman's theory was first published in *QED: Quantum Electrodynamics*, by Addison-Wesley, Reading (MA), 1962.

112 Albert Einstein in a letter to the physicist Max Born (1882–1970), 4 December 1926: 'Quantum mechanics is certainly imposing. But an inner voice tells me that it is not yet the real thing. The theory says a lot, but does not really bring us any closer to the secret of the "old one". I, at any rate, am convinced that the He [God] is not playing at dice.' See: *The Born–Einstein Letters, 1916–1955: Friendship, Politics and Physics in Uncertain Times*, Macmillan Publishers, New York, 2005, p.88.

113 James Joyce, *Ulysses*, Shakespeare & Company, Paris, 1st edition, 1000 numbered copies, February 1922. In 1922 Joyce embarked on a giant literary project entitled *Work in Progress*, which seventeen years later would appear under the title *Finnegans Wake* (which, it should be noted, was kept secret until the moment of publication), op.cit. (note 87). About the relationship between Beckett and Joyce and the work of the former on *Work in Progress*, James Knowlson cites Beckett on the basis of an interview held on 20 September 1989: 'It was at his suggestion that I wrote "Dante ... Bruno . Vico .. Joyce" – because of my Italian. I spent a lot of time reading Bruno and Vico in the magnificent library, the Bibliothèque of the École Normale. We must have had some talk about the "Eternal Return", that sort of thing. He liked the essay. But his only comment on it was that there wasn't enough about Bruno; he found Bruno rather neglected. They were new figures to me at the time. I hadn't read them. I'd worked on Dante, of course. I knew very little of them. I

knew more or less what they were about. I remember reading a biography of one of them.' Knowlson, op.cit., p.100. Beckett's text was part of a collection of essays by *intimi* of Joyce, published as *Our Exagmination Round His Factification for Incamination of Work in Progress*, Shakespeare & Company, Paris, 1929.

114   See Umberto Eco, op.cit. (note 37): *Das Offene Kunstwerk*, p.392.

115   Faced with the obstacles to be surmounted in 'understanding' Joyce's text, a handful of critics have suggested readers focus on the rhythm and sound of the language, rather than solely on 'meaning'. As early as 1929, Eugene Jolas stressed the importance of the aural and musical dimensions of the work. In his contribution to *Our Exagmination Round His Factification for Incamination of Work in Progress*, Jolas wrote: 'Those who have heard Mr. Joyce read aloud from *Work in Progress* know the immense rhythmic beauty of his technique' (op.cit. (note 113)). Hear Joyce reading from *Finnegans Wake* on Youtube: http://www.youtube.com/watch?v=JtOQi7xspRc, June 2009. Beckett stated: 'You cannot complain that this stuff is not written in English. It is not written at all. It is not to be read. It is to be looked at and listened to. His writing is not about something. It is that something itself.' *Our Exagmination Round His Factification for Incamination of Work in Progress*, p.14.

116   *Finnegans Wake* (op.cit. (note 87)) famously begins with the word 'riverrun', and is intended to be read in cyclical fashion so that the last words of the book lead back round to the first: 'A way a lone a last a loved a long the [...] riverrun, past Eve and Adam's, from swerve of shore to bend of bay, brings us by a commodius vicus of recirculation back to Howth Castle and Environs.'

117   Peter Brook, *The Empty Space*, 1st edition: MacGibbon & Kee, London, 1968. See: Penguin Books, London, 1990; chapter 4: 'The Immediate Theatre', pp 141–2.

118   Dinah Casson, in the interview with CassonMann Designers, p.xxx.

119   Johannes Vermeer (1632–1675), *Girl with a Pearl Earring*, c.1665, in the Mauritshuis, The Hague. See also the passage on this painting in the Tristan Kobler and Barbara Holzer interview, Zurich, November 2007, p.xxx.

120   Johannes Vermeer, *View of Delft*, c.1660–61.

121   Rembrandt van Rijn (1606–1669), *Self-Portrait*, 1669.

122   Lucretius, op.cit. (note 107).

123   Olaf Arndt and Rob Moonen, *Camera Silens*: researched and developed at the Akademie Schloss Solitude, Stuttgart in 1993, commissioned by the ZKM-Medienmuseum in Karlsruhe and realised as an installation with the support of various grants in 1997.

124   Henri Bergson, op.cit. (note 49), *Creative Evolution*, chapter IV: 'The cinematographical mechanism of thought', p.218. See also: Paola Marrati, *Gilles Deleuze: Cinema and Philosophy*, The John Hopkins University Press, Baltimore, 2008, pp 14–15.

125   Roland Barthes, op.cit. (note 41). Here the reference is to the English edition: *Camera Lucida*, HarperCollins, London, 1984.

126   Aristotle, op.cit. (note 40), pp 74, 80–81. See chapter 1.3 on the genres of oratory: 'The genres of rhetoric are three in number, which is the number of the types of audience. For a speech is composed of three factors – the speaker, the subject and the listener – and it is to the last of these that its purpose is related. Now the listener must be either a spectator or a judge, and, if a judge, one either of the past or of the future. The judge, then, about the future is the assembly member, the judge about the past is the juror, and the accessor of capacity is the spectator, so that there must needs be three types of rhetorical speech: *deliberative, forensic* and *display*.' The first two genres belong to the domain of the politi-

cal and judicial aspects of rhetorics, whereas scenography as we are now trying to interpret it, because of its orientation towards ethics and aesthetics seems to belong to the category of display oratory. See chapter 4, pp 104–10. In our discourse we focus on rhetorics as a *techne*, as a link that connects the various traditional genres and as a dramaturgical hinge that is operational in the theatre and exhibitions.

127 Robert Mapplethorpe (1946–1989), double portrait of Philip Glass and Robert Wilson, on the occasion of the premiere of the opera *Einstein on the Beach*, in Avignon, 1976. See Roland Barthes, op.cit., p.54.
128 Ibid p.51.
129 'Bifurcation' means the splitting of a main body into two parts. *Oxford English Dictionary*: 'Division into two forks or branches'. Ilya Prigogine, op.cit. (note 103).
130 Richard Feynman, op.cit. (note 111).
131 Definition from: http://www.websters-online-dictionary.org/sc/scenography.html, June 2009.
132 Peter Brook, op.cit. (note 117).
133 Ibid p.11.
134 Ibid p.47.
135 Merce Cunningham (1919–2009), is an American dancer and choreographer; Samuel Beckett (1906–1989) was an Irish writer, dramatist and poet; Jerzy Grotowski (1933–1999) was a Polish theatre director and innovator of experimental theatre.
136 Antonin Artaud (1896–1948) was a French playwright, poet, actor and theatre director. His first and second manifesto of 'The Theatre of Cruelty' were published in: *Le Théâtre et son double*, Éditions Gallimard, Paris, 1938. Grove Press, New York published the English edition in 1958. Artaud's radical vision inspired Peter Brook to a series of theatrical experiments in 1964. See: Peter Brook, op.cit., p.145. See also: Colin Counsell, op.cit. (note 62), pp 147–8.
137 William Shakespeare (1564–1616), English poet and playwright. See: Germaine Greer, *Shakespeare: A Very Short Introduction*, Oxford University Press, Oxford, 2002.
138 Peter Brook, op.cit., p.69.
139 Ibid p.76.
140 Vsevolod Meyerhold (1874–1940) was a Russian director, actor, producer and one of the seminal forces in modern theatre; Bertolt Brecht (1898–1956) was a politically motivated German poet, playwright, and theatre director of the Berliner Ensemble; Jean Genet (1910–1986) was a prominent and controversial French novelist, playwright, poet, essayist and political activist.
141 Peter Brook, op.cit., p.77.
142 In 1943, while still at Gresham's School in Holt (Norfolk), England, Peter Brook staged *The Tragical History of Doctor Faustus*, a play by Christopher Marlowe (1564–1593), which was based on the Faust story and first published in 1604.
143 Antonin Artaud, op.cit. (note 136), chapter 6: '*No more masterpieces*', pp 76–7.
144 Peter Brook, op.cit., pp 54–5.
145 Ibid p.58.
146 Ibid p.141.
147 Claude Lévi-Strauss, *Totemism*, Beacon Press, Boston (MA), 1963 (original: *Le Totémisme aujourd'hui*, Presses Universitaires de France, 1962); Claude Lévi-Strauss, *The Savage Mind*, University of Chicago Press, Chicago, 1966 (original: *La Pensée sauvage*, Plon, Paris, 1962).

space.time.narrative

148 Ibid pp 9–10; Peter Brook and Ted Hughes, *Orghast*, International Centre for Theatre Research, Persepolis, Iran, 1971; Peter Brook, *The Mahabharata*, Festival d'Avignon, 1985. See: Jean-Claude Carrière, *The Mahabharata: A Play*, Methuen, London, 1988.

149 Claude Lévi-Strauss, *Tristes Tropiques*, Plon, Paris, 1955. It is interesting to note what Artaud observes about totemism in the preface to *The Theater and its Double*: 'The old totemism of animals, stones, objects capable of discharging thunderbolts, costumes impregnated with bestial essences – everything, in short, that might determine, disclose, and direct the secret forces of the universe – is for us a dead thing, from which we derive nothing but static and aesthetic profit, the profit of an audience, not of an actor. Yet totemism is an actor, for it moves, and has been created in [sic] behalf of actors; all true culture relies upon the barbaric and primitive means of totemism whose savage, i.e., entirely spontaneous, life I wish to worship.' Antonin Artaud, op.cit., p.10.

150 Claude Lévi-Strauss, op.cit., p.17.

151 Ibid pp 19–20.

152 Ibid p.21.

153 Richard Feynman, 'Cargo Cult Science,' inauguration speech at the California Institute of Technology (Caltech), Pasadena, June 1974.

154 Antonin Artaud, op.cit., first manifesto of 'The Theatre of Cruelty': especially the themes of the spectacle, the *mise en scene* and the language of the stage, pp 93–5.

155 Ibid chapter 6: 'No more masterpieces', p.79.

156 Ibid chapter 6: 'No more masterpieces', p.81.

157 Ibid chapter 8: 'The stage – The auditorium', pp 96–7.

158 Ibid chapter 8: 'The spectacle', p.98.

159 Antonin Artaud, second manifesto of 'The Theatre of Cruelty': 'From the point of view of form', p.125.

160 The Living Theatre, Julian Beck, Judith Malina: *Mysteries* (1965) and *Paradise Now* (1968), seen in The Roundhouse, Chalk Farm Road, London, June 1969. See: Pierre Biner, *The Living Theatre: A History Without Myths*, Avon Books, New York, 1973. See also: Erika Billeter and Dölf Preisig, *The Living Theatre: Paradise Now*, Benteli Verlag, Bern, 1968.

161 Antonin Artaud, op.cit., p.99.

parallax

an apparent shift in the position of an object, caused by a change in the observer's position that provides a new and different line of sight

space.time.narrative

parallax

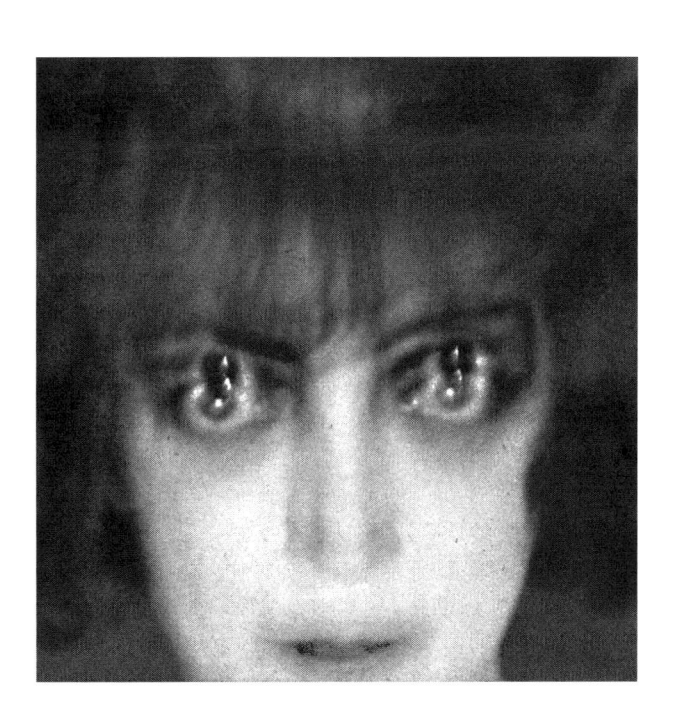

85

space.time.narrative

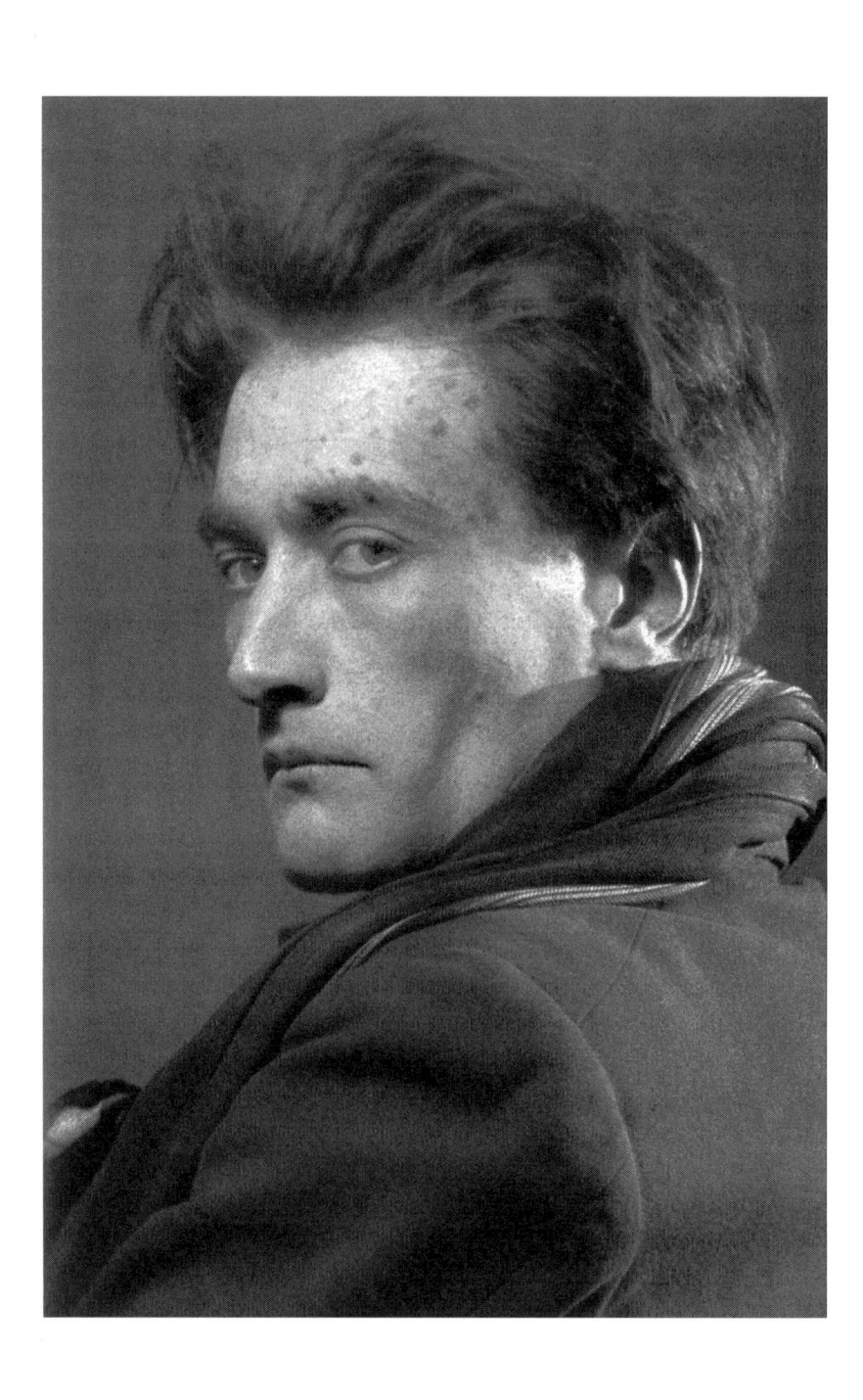

parallax

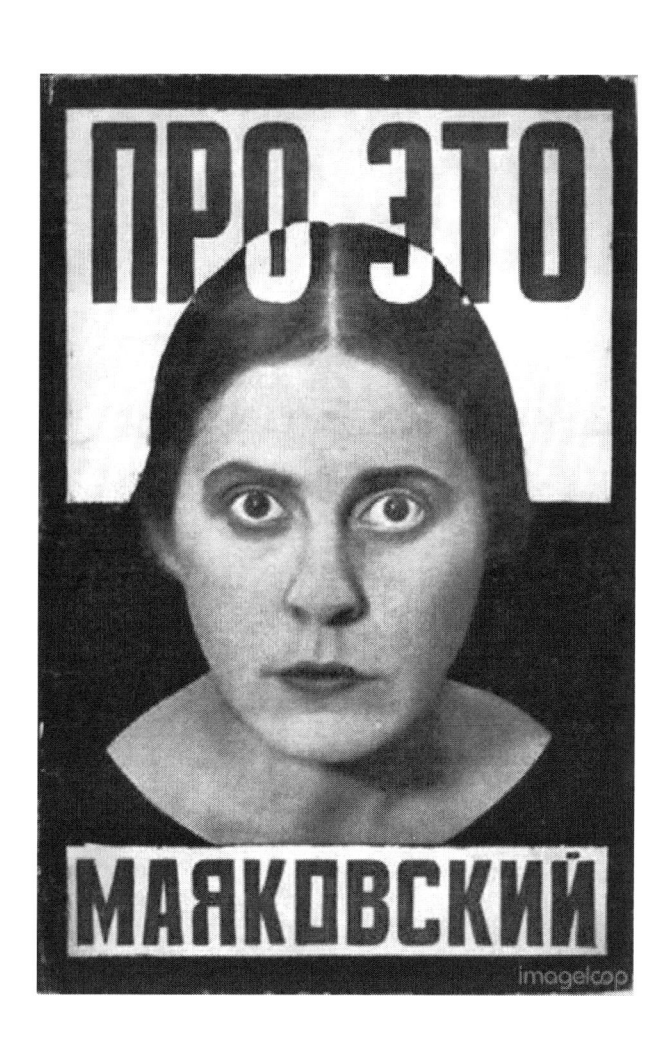

space.time.narrative

parallax

space.time.narrative

parallax

space.time.narrative

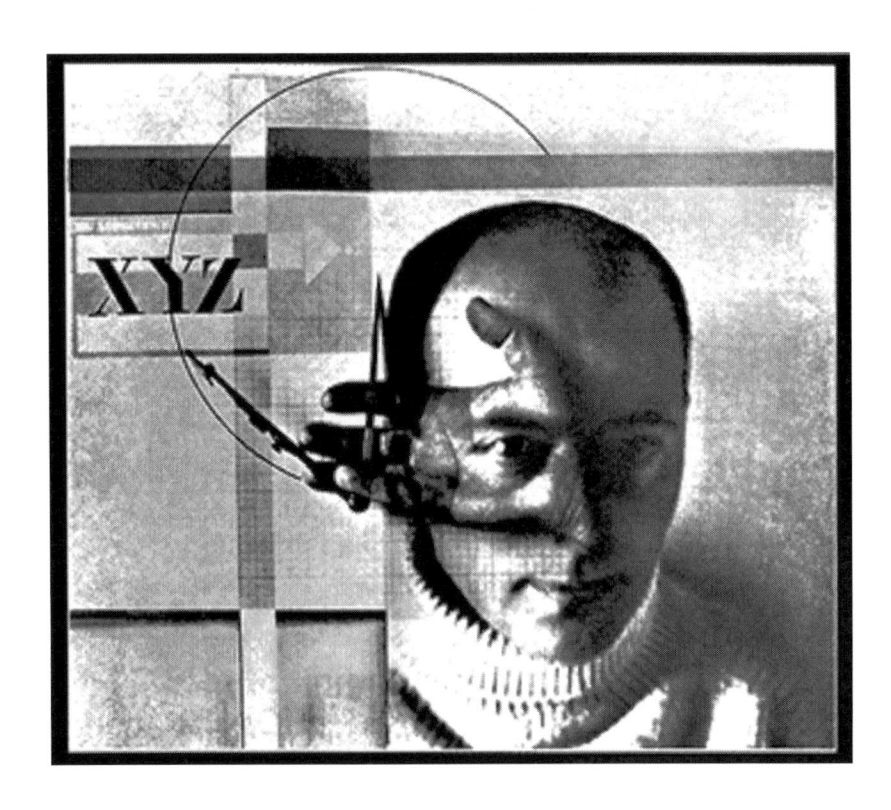

parallax

space.time.narrative

parallax

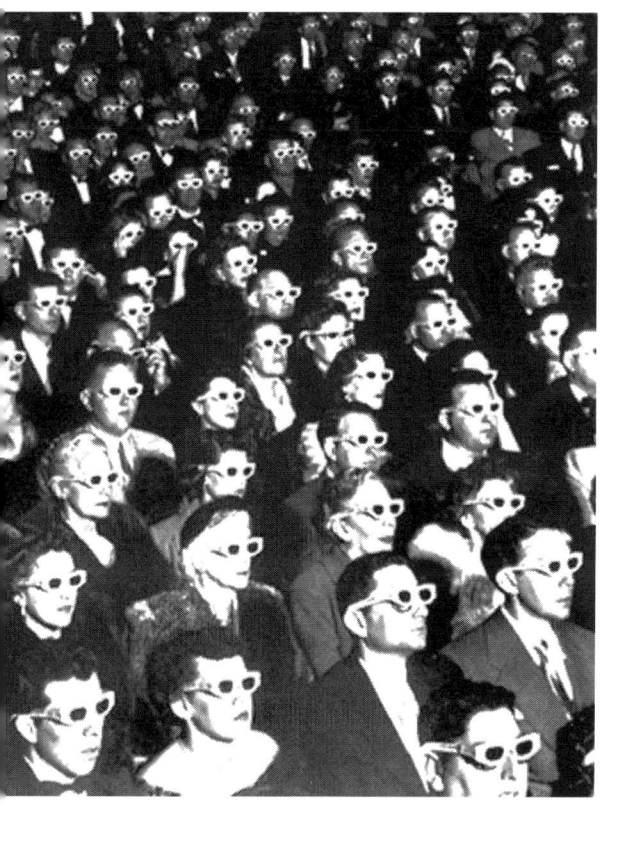

95

space.time.narrative

parallax

space.time.narrative

parallax

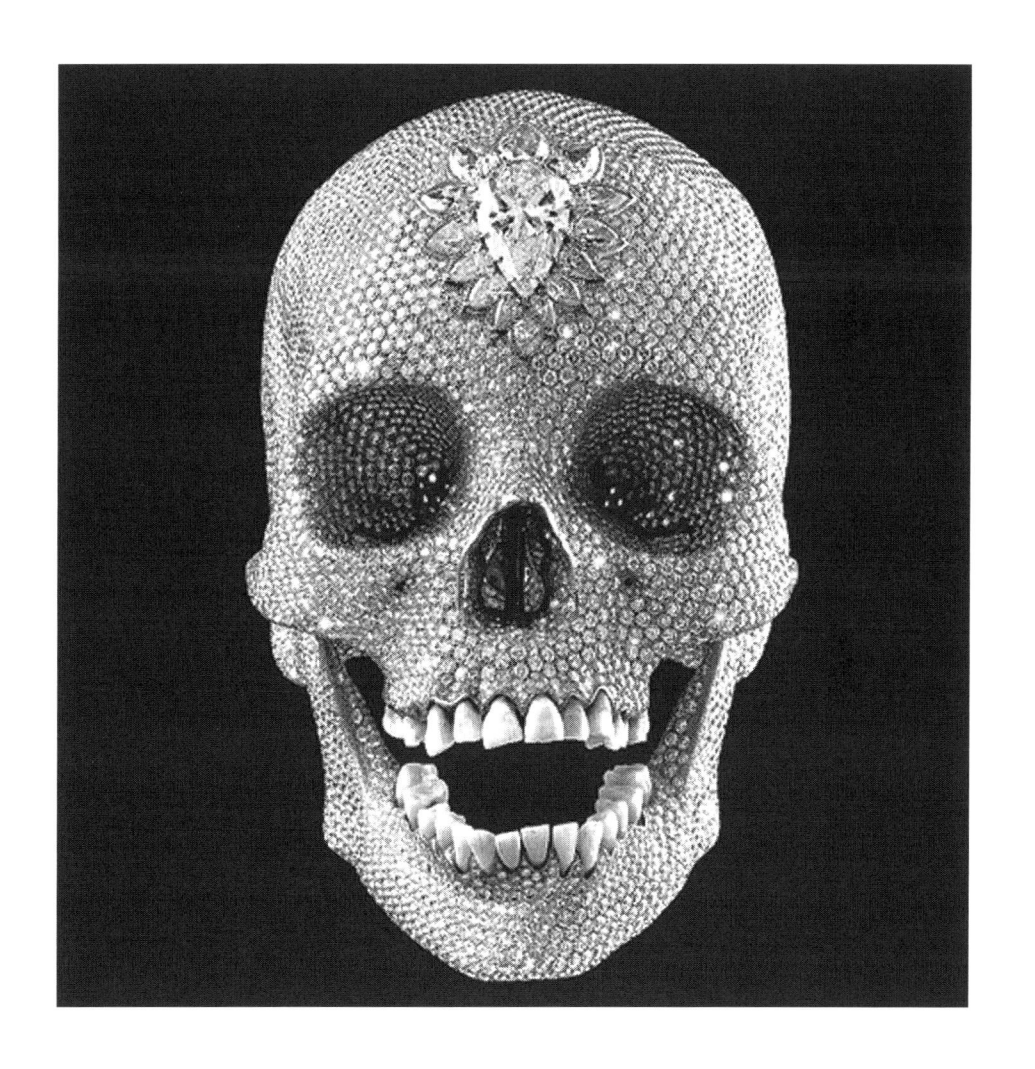

Illustrations

Ill.1 (p.84): Marina Abramovic (b.1946), *Portrait with Scorpion (open eyes)*, 2005. Courtesy of Sean Kelly Gallery, New York. The photograph is one half of a pair of twins, as Abramovic also recorded a variant with *closed eyes*. All of the work of Abramovic is about taking risks and getting as close as one can get. Here the danger is embodied in a scorpion, 'the other', which is mirrored by Abramovic's posture and haircut. Who is threatening whom? The confrontation is perfectly balanced, but both are utterly out of context. This act of alienation turns the picture into a metaphor for the courage which crossing borders basically supposes.

Ill.2 (p.85): Man Ray (1890–1976), *Marquise Casati*, 1922. © Man Ray Trust / ADAGP, Paris and DACS, London 2011. Marchesa Luisa Casati (1881–1957) was portrayed by Man Ray, but something went technically wrong, apparently. After development of the photograph, the picture displayed a triple exposure, which manifests especially in the eyes. Man Ray considered it to be a failure, but Luisa Casata thought the portrait was excellent. Its extraordinary appeal and contradictory quality lie in the fact that the freeze-frame medium of the photograph had the capacity of capturing the volatile blink of the eye. See also: http://www.marchesacasati.com/bio.html.

Ill.3 (p.86): Man Ray, *Antonin Artaud*, 1926. © ADAGP, Paris and DACS, London 2011. See essay 1, 'The Battery', para. 1.6, p. 51.

Ill.4 (p.87): Alexander Rodchenko (1891–1956), *Pro Eto. Ei i Mne*, cover for a book by Vladimir Mayakovsky, Moscow, 1923. © Rodchenko & Stepanova Archive, DACS, 2011. Vladimir Mayakovsky (1893–1930) was a Russian Futurist poet. Alexander Rodchenko was a Russian photographer and graphic designer, famous for his constructivist photomontages. He photographed and illustrated *Pro Eto* and is considered its co-author. The lady with the piercing gaze is Lilya Brik (1891–1978), Mayakovsky's muse and protagonist of the book. *Pro Eto* means *About This*: Mayakovsky's relationship with Brik. *Ei i Mne* means *To Her and To Me*; *Pro Eto* is an epic poem and an intimate statement on love.

Ill.5 (p.88): Howard Coster (1885–1959), *Portrait of W.B. Yeats*, 1 January 1930. Courtesy of Getty Images / Hulton Archive, Los Angeles. See essay 2, 'The Envelope'.

Ill.6 (p.89): The sketch of the duck-rabbit was originally employed by the American psychologist J. Jastrow (1863–1944) in his book Fact and Fable in Psychology, published in 1900, but the Austrian philosopher Ludwig Wittgenstein (1889–1951) made it famous when he used the duck-rabbit as a catalyst in his Philosophical Investigations of 1953. Wittgenstein discusses figures which can be seen and understood in different ways and uses the duck-rabbit as a simple yet ambiguous illustration that can easily be interpreted as depicting both a duck and a rabbit. When one looks at the duck-rabbit and sees a rabbit, one is not interpreting the picture as a rabbit, but rather reporting what one sees. One just sees the picture as a rabbit. But what occurs when one sees it first as a duck and then as a rabbit? The difference in perception is uncertain. However, Wittgenstein is sure that while an internal cognitive change takes place, the external world cannot stay the same.

Ill.7 (p.90): Johannes Vermeer (1632–1675), *Girl with a Pearl Earring*, c.1665. Courtesy of Royal Picture Gallery, Mauritshuis, The Hague. See the interview with Barbara Holzer

parallax

and Tristan Kobler, p.288. See also: http://www.mauritshuis.nl, and http://www.essentialvermeer.com.

Ill.8 (p.91): Marcel Duchamp (1887–1968), *L.H.O.O.Q.*, 1919. © Succession Marcel Duchamp / ADAGP, Paris and DACS, London, 2011. The work by Duchamp is a so-called readymade, assisted by the *objet trouvé* of a cheap postcard reproduction of the famous *Mona Lisa*, which was painted by Leonardo da Vinci (1452–1519) between 1503 and 1507. The title Duchamp gave to his Mona Lisa with moustache is a pun: L.H.O.O.Q. pronounced fluently as a French sentence, says: *elle a chaud au cul*, meaning: *she is hot in the ass*, and that's exactly what Duchamp meant his Mona Lisa to be.

Ill.9 (p.92): El Lissitzky (1890–1941), *The Constructor*, photomontage, 1924. © DACS, 2011. In Lissitzky's photomontage, the parallax between intuition and intellect, between hand and brain, between touch and sight, between language and mathematics forms the constructional plane for an expanded, contextualised self-portrait. Lissitzky is clearly positioning himself in the middle of the axis, which connects or divides the reason of the engineer and the sensibility of the artist. In the sense of Claude Lévi-Strauss (1908–2009), Lissitzky's photomontage is an act of intellectual *bricolage* and expresses the fundamental bond between science and art. See essay 1, 'The Battery', para. p. 59.

Ill.10 (p.93): Robert Mapplethorpe (1946–1989), *Portrait of Philip Glass and Robert Wilson*, 1976. See: Roland Barthes, *Camera Lucida: Reflections on Photography*, HarperCollins, London, 1984. See also essay 1, 'The Battery', para. 1.6, p. 51.

Ill.11 (p.94): Guy Debord (1931–1994), *Réalisation de la Philosophie*, 1963. There is a sense of irony in painting a programmatic text on a canvas, as if it were graffiti, like the phrase '*Ne Travaillez Jamais!*' ('Never Work!'), which Guy Debord had painted on the walls of the Rue de Seine in Paris, some ten years before. However, the 1963 oil painting aims at a deeper level: it acts as a manifesto and tries to bridge the gap between thinking and acting. See essay 1, 'The Battery', note 109, p. 78.

Ill.12 (p.95, left): Cover photo of Guy Debord's, *La Société du spectacle*, 1967. Debord was the leading figure of the French intellectual group who called themselves The Situationist International. His text, written in 1967, is nothing less than an accurate theoretical examination of our socio-cultural condition, describing the facts and effects of corporate globalisation which started to sweep the planet after the Second World War. His work was instrumental in sparking the student uprisings in Europe in the late 1960s. In 1988 Debord wrote his *Commentaires sur la société du spectacle*, published by Éditions Gérard Lebovici. With acuity both texts unmask the world of simulation and lies that Debord believed mankind transforms its life into. In November of 1994, at the age of 62, Debord shot himself in the heart. See: http://www.nothingness.org.

Ill.13 (p.95, right): René Descartes (1596–1650), *Triangulation for the Blind,* illustration from *Tractatus De Homine*, Amsterdam, 1664. See essay 1, 'The Battery', note 79. Somehow Cartesius' blind figure reminds me of Vladimir or Estragon cluelessly waiting at the crossroads near a dead tree in Samuel Beckett's play *Waiting for Godot*. See essay 1, 'The Battery', note 66, p. 74.

Ill.14 (pp.96+97): Richard Avedon (1923–2004), *Samuel Beckett*, 13 April 1979. Courtesy of The Richard Avedon Foundation. Richard Avedon was an American photographer, who is well known for his intensely staged portraits of artists, actors, writers and musicians, like Ezra Pound, Alberto Giacometti, Andy Warhol, Marilyn Monroe, Francis Bacon, John Cage, Pablo Picasso, Salvador Dali, Marcel Duchamp, etcetera. Courtesy of the

space.time.narrative

Richard Avedon Foundation. See: http://www.richardavedon.com. See also essay 1, 'The Battery', para 1.4, p. 30.

Ill.15 (p.98): © Frank den Oudsten (b.1949), *Blue Room*, 1973. *Blue Room* depicts a room in a deserted house, which the Dutch artist Max van der Grijn (b.1950) and I used at the time for all kinds of spatial experiments and media installations. A narrative space, in fact. If you look at it long enough, the two windows left and right remotely remind the onlooker of a mask or a face. What face? The face of a character that still needs to be defined. Defined by scenography, which is supposed to transform an empty space into a place by merely introducing character.

Ill.16 (p.99): Damien Hirst (b.1965), *For the Love of God*, 2007. Platinum, diamonds and human teeth. 6 3/4 x 5 x 7 1/2 in. (17.1 x 12.7 x 19.1 cm). Photo: Prudence Cuming Associates Ltd. Courtesy White Cube / © Damien Hirst and Science Ltd. All rights reserved, DACS 2011. In November 2008, the Rijksmuseum in Amsterdam began exhibiting a new work by the British artist Damien Hirst. The platinum cast of a skull studded with 8,601 pure diamonds transformed the city in matter of days: *For the Love of God* proved to be a real cult object. On the way to the Rijksmuseum the skull was already grinning cheekily at us mortals from large posters, and even sceptics stood in line to see the icon with their own eyes. There was a queue at the entrance. The security check involved some serious scanning. In the hall above there was another queue. Initial scepticism began to melt away, while waiting surrounded by the masterpieces of Dutch painting. Then, in a small group, I was let into a completely dark room. The eye was briefly suppressed: blind. Four spotlights came on, illuminating a cubic glass case, positioned at eye level. The diamond-studded skull reflected the light. It laughed and gleamed, blindly absorbing the gaze of the crowd. Looking through the glass case I could compare it with the heads of other visitors. Most of them were serious, some were having fun. The situation *was* funny. The blind skull appeared to be an optimistic icon, or perhaps better, a symbol with the spectacular potential of absorbing my gaze. Its radiance, I concluded, appeared to be nothing less than the accumulated, successive gazes of every visitor on the globe.

dark matter
*matter whose existence is postulated
to account for the dynamic behaviour of galaxies,
but which has not been detected*

Six interviews

in the 1930s the Swiss-American astrophysicist Fritz Zwicky (1898–1974) studied the dynamics of distant clusters of galaxies. Zwicky estimated the mass of such a remote cluster by calculating the number of galaxies and measuring their total brightness. When he compared that outcome to the estimation of the same cluster's total mass, now based on the motion of galaxies near its edge, he found a mass approximately 400 times more than was visually observable. This discrepancy has become known as 'the missing mass problem' and has not yet been solved. Apparently, the material world has a dimension which cannot be fully sensed. Dark Matter. Obviously, the dynamics of things is led by a force which cannot fully be understood. Dark Energy.

Narrative environments, whether staged or not, function a bit like that. They are like clusters of stars. There is always more than we observe and an unknown poetic potential holds the elements together, waiting to let a thousand and one tales flow. Exciting clusters of narrative, whether conciously laid out or not, are similarly characterised by 'a missing story problem'. They have an enigmatic dimension, which might be suspected, but which can only be detected in certain, hardly predictable circumstances. The condition is moody and meteorological, unstable like the weather. There is not much time: the moment is the momentum. The exhibition is a snapshot. A story is told within the blink of an eye.

Since early 2006, a changing group of western-European exhibition makers have been meeting on an irregular basis at various places, to discuss topics that keep them engaged, inspired by the narrative potential of their medium, as a point of departure for the realisation of complex semantic places with character and identity. Their expertise, however, which forms the basis for the *mise en espace* of such exhibitions, is an expertise of the belly. This applies whether the project is composed by a curator or by a scenographer, each of whom presumably works with entirely different sets of reference.

The scenographic development of an exhibition, the translation and transformation of a thesis or interpretation into an eloquent form, primarily takes place in the dark. Every design or invention knows these gloomy stages, the exhibition-practice even more so. The field lacks a language, there is no Esperanto of transdisciplinarity which might be of great help, there is no theory of scenography to fall back on. Much of it is tossing ideas around,

introduction: dark matter

guessing, groping about in the dark. In fact, most of the designers and agencies operate in cultural isolation. Their expertise therefore often bears a highly personalised signature. The six interviews which are published here are an effort to look behind the scenes, to delve into the shadows of the profession, to reflect on it from the inside out and to map personal references, positions and orientations, goals and dreams.

Damien Hirst
Marc Dion
Ilya Kabakov
CASSON MANN - SPARKING REACTION

Interview with
Herman Kossmann and Mark de Jong

Herman Kossmann (b.1958) and **Mark de Jong** (b.1960) are the founding directors of the Amsterdam-based agency Kossmann.dejong Exhibition Architects. I met Herman Kossmann as long ago as 1986, during the preparation of the exhibition '*Nieuw Nederland* 2050', on which we collaborated – he as the general director of the show and I as the designer of the introductory audiovisual installation. A few years later in 1991, in the context of another exhibition, which was also led by Herman Kossmann, I met Mark de Jong. That exhibition was '*Stadstimmeren*', held on the occasion of the 650th anniversary of the city of Rotterdam. Mark designed the section on urban planning and I produced a mixed-media environment on the city's history with the Rotterdam poet Jules Deelder as a protagonist. We have stayed in touch over the years, all fascinated by the sheer unlimited potential of the narrative environment. The interview with Herman and Mark was held on 9 and 20 March 2007, in their office, and I photographed them there in the course of our conversation.

space.time.narrative

How did you first encounter the exhibition trade?

de Jong: When I was studying constructional engineering, there was this professor who was interested in showing the results of some study projects to other students.[1] He knew that I was into graphic design so he asked me to produce the exhibition. That was very exciting. I had visited exhibitions before, of course, but they never stimulated me to take an interest in this line of work. It was pure chance, me ending up in this business after my studies. Together with my brother Pjotr I started a design company straight away and one of our first commissions was an integral design for the Union Museum: a house style, two catalogues, the overall interior design, the museum furniture and the wayfinding signs.[2] And for the first time I thought: this is an interesting combination of things, the way it produces a whole new range of possibilities.

Kossmann: In my final term at the University of Technology in Delft I lectured Constructional Engineering to some students of the interior design department of the Art College in The Hague. One major subject was draughtsmanship. So, how could I explain that floor plans, frontals and cross-sections were a two-dimensional language to grasp or represent a three-dimensional reality? One assignment was to survey a number of small pavilions nearby and translate that into a blueprint or a model, including the assembly instructions. I was fascinated by the possibility of 2-D representations of 3-D objects that could in turn be transformed into 3-D models again. It was a big hit with the students. I then collected dozens of models and blueprints from all over Holland that together with the students' projects made up a huge exhibition in the College building. A lecture gone out of control, actually.[3] Through these minor initiatives I became involved in the Nederland Nu Als Ontwerp Foundation, where I became the project manager of '*Nieuw Nederland* 2050', which was an exhibition about the future of landscape design in the Netherlands.[4] That became my first experience with large-scale interdisciplinary projects in which sociologists, architects, urban developers, landscape architects, cinematographers, copywriters, sound artists and model designers collaborated. The exhibition was to be put up in the Beurs van Berlage in Amsterdam and the challenge was how to organise this huge space.[5] Every Dutch architect and urban designer of some consequence was part of it. The project was an explosion of energy. Working at this level of professional commitment was a whole new experience for me. I entered a world that I hadn't dreamed of before.

Did you imagine at the time that this could be your profession?

Kossmann: I don't know. I was at an age at which you enjoy every bit of it. Working on the realisation of a dream collectively did however become increasingly appealing. The world of architecture is inhabited by contractors and architects who will not hesitate to play a nasty trick to get their way. In the exhibition business, on the other hand, everyone seemed to aim for the best. The content-mindedness of the profession really appealed to me. Projects such as Nederland Nu Als Ontwerp were an unbelievable inspiration to me, although I didn't exactly know where the experience would lead me. I encountered other media and areas of design that I hadn't dealt with before. Before the project I had never even heard of AV producers. Not to mention the term AV. It became an exploration of a completely new territory: the world of film and audiovisual media.[6]

de Jong: For a time, I was sort of an omnivore. I never actually designed buildings, like Herman did. I used my training as an engineer to get to know the world. I didn't go to college to become an architect. Only when I had almost finished my training did I have the feeling: when I'm done, I'll become an architect. I even considered quitting a couple of times, but I'm glad that I finished it. For a while I was part of the Waardenberg & de Jong cabaret and made a living as a graphic designer and playing in all sorts of bands.[7] After the Union Museum job I realised that making exhibitions could be something for me.

What made you work together?

Kossmann: Well, simply the fact that I had been doing a number of exhibitions, as a project manager, in which other designers worked on the design as well. Mark worked for a design company and he officially took care of the graphic aspects of it all. Meanwhile, we were in fact already running the show together. The *'Stadstimmeren'* exhibition made that very clear.[8] Later, when we officially collaborated on the *'Wederopbouw van Rotterdam'* exhibition, we took care of both the concept and the design together and that made us realise just how much working together can bring.[9] What is most significant is that the other contributes something that you yourself cannot, and vice versa. In making exhibitions that is crucial. At every stage of the project you really need to listen; truly listen. Telling a story in the shape of an exhibition is something you couldn't manage on your own. The complexity of developing a concept and finding the right metaphors, transposing it in media and form, is simply beyond the individual.

de Jong: I only contributed a minor part of the *'Stadstimmeren'* exhibition, but the *'Wederopbouw'* show became a collaboration from square one, albeit by two separate companies. Only after developing the concept of the *'Wonderbaarlijk Alfabet'* in 1998 did we decide to continue as one single company.[10] But in fact we had been working together since 1991, when we did an exhibition on Peter Loerakker. He was a mutual friend who had been extremely energetic but died very young. Doing that project already revealed some connection between the two of us.[11]

Kossmann-dejong has been around for 10 years now. Is there a professional landmark you can point at? Does the 1995 *'Wederopbouw'* exhibition stand the comparison with the Dolhuys from 2005?[12]

Kossmann: Whenever we present a project, we still show the *'Wederopbouw'* exhibition. Something intuitive happened there, that only now we are able to transmit. Nowadays, making an exhibition is a trade for us, something we quite consciously go about. But that is all based on certain discoveries we made in the early days and which we still use now. In the *'Wederopbouw'* show we apparently grounded a lot, despite the fact that it only took us a half-year to set up. It was staged as a total experience, like the *'Cités-Cinés'* exhibition, where you entered a whole new universe.[13] The *'Wederopbouw'* was also the first major exhibition, in which we were in charge and could direct things autonomously. *'Stadstimmeren'* had already hinted at a total experience, and by deciding on a great number of individual pavilions we succeeded in getting across the experience of a fair, but the exhibition somehow lacked that one unifying element. Our approach to the *'Wederopbouw'* exhibition tried to deal with this, with the question of how unity can be established. Much of what we do now is grounded there. So, if the question is: 'what has happened?', then the answer would be that we reflect on the métier with much more awareness. The other difference is working within the framework of a company. I used to work on one thing only for a whole year. I often long for that to return. Now we do ten things simultaneously. And you do get better at it. Communication! What took us a whole year to develop then, we now do in two minutes. How fast do you get to the essence of things, that's the question. After all, the process is going two steps ahead, one step back etcetera.

So, what you reap is recognising the momentum much quicker and being able to compact your actions because of that? Is that a fair representation of the ten years' harvest?

Kossmann: Every experiment we did is a valuable instrument now. But what we couldn't do then was play with those instruments.

de Jong: Experience is the reward. When you make a proposal now, you have a far more accurate picture of the consequences. Ten years ago we used to stumble into a project. It was ridiculous as far as organisation was concerned. Before the opening of a show we were slaving away with our drills all night long, which, admittedly, had a romantic feel to it. I mean, really giving a project all you've got. Nowadays it's all far more rational and businesslike. But at some point we had to admit that we couldn't keep up the all-out approach. As soon as you run more than one project at a time, you can't escape getting organised.

Kossmann: If you compare it to architecture, where you prepare a design that is executed by a building contractor, then in the exhibition trade the actual execution of the show itself is, in our perception, a crucial final stage of the designing process itself. Being present on the site to continue designing is a phase which, as an exhibition maker, you don't want to miss out on. It's extremely important that the designer of an exhibition is also the director of its final execution. It has to do with a dimension of the profession where it's not all rationality. But on the whole, we've become more efficient because of experience. We achieve more with less energy now. Certainly.

Has there been any development in the commissions since you started off? Which direction do you envisage?

de Jong: I increasingly dislike amateurism. It is the first thing to get rid of as you gain experience. People simply need to know their stuff. When you interact with different disciplines, you all have the same goal, each in their own media. As long as everybody knows where the story is heading, to what overall result, people can actually surprise you. Contributing things that you cannot offer yourself. That's the point: the art of collaborating. Interdisciplinary. You may be the director, but as long as there is no sense of the collective, all you do is control and correct without ever getting the added value.

Interdisciplinary collaboration doesn't depend on the scale of the project. But what is noticeable is that larger projects give much more space to experiment. There is the latitude, the budget and the time span available to develop. Smaller projects tend to be much more taxing. This is all part of the preconditions. I notice it more and more often: making exhibitions is a veritable trade. It's different from producing a film or writing a book. You need those professionals and the various media to appeal to all the senses, both intellectually and intuitively. The greater the ability, the better the

	team outfit, the more accurate the effect becomes. There are times when I'm so envious of the liberty that one grants Peter Greenaway when he works in a museum.[14] Because we often deal with people who don't understand what an exhibition could be like. In the old days we struggled with ourselves, but now it's the museums that commission us that we have to fight. Generally, the finest exhibitions emerge once everybody understands their own function. So that could indeed be a future perspective: having the liberty to produce, in this particular medium, the stories we imagine. We would like to have the space to become the authors of those stories. That would be an interesting direction. Right now, I think we're very submissive, too subservient.
de Jong:	But it isn't easy. We did a number of projects, like the '*Wederopbouw*' exhibition – and, to a lesser extent, the '*Interbellum*' show – where we were in charge and where we could select the team of players ourselves.[15] But sometimes we get clients who refuse to play that game and then you start spending lots of energy on matters that aren't worth it. That's a pity, but it's the price of the applied arts; you simply have to deal with clients.
Kossmann:	Still, I wouldn't mind moving in the direction I mentioned. Our narratives should gain more space and power. The Dolhuys was a success somehow because we started off with nothing. It became one of our better projects because we had the opportunity to try new things.

You have often mentioned that it's of paramount importance to become the 'managing director' of a project as soon as possible. Why is that?

Kossmann:	Well, once you acknowledge that an exhibition is a *Gesamtwerk*, a collaborative work, in which everything has to fall into place, then management becomes crucial.[16] Everything is connected, and if the funds are out of reach, then you lack the freedom necessary to balance the overall result. To fine-tune a project you have to be able to push all the buttons. Design is more than just producing beautiful draughts, come to that. It also implies being creative financially. Or being

creative in the ways you trip up your clients. For instance, we regularly work for consultancies. Now, and this I hadn't realised this until recently, these firms do nothing but consult and next they're not even interested in whether the project gets realised or not. This is reality, believe it or not. With us, however, every step is a step towards realisation. We constantly feel the pressure to achieve something and within that strategy we want to be 'bosses'.

So it's all about the conditions from which the project starts? Apparently you have the courage to make a firm stand against a client?

Kossmann: It somehow feels completely justified. You know, take it or leave it.

de Jong: We get so many offers that we are now in a position to be critical. What are the conditions? What is the latitude? What is the budget? Is everybody eager?

Kossmann: Many clients obviously have a hard time commissioning. The decision process tends to reveal a lot of schizophrenia vis-à-vis the designers as well. One finds it hard to grasp that there are designers who simply aren't afraid of other designers. Let alone the possibility that a concept or a design assignment could be developed by more than one designer through intensive discussion.

de Jong: Still, our attitude was different five years ago, I would say. In order to get a large assignment we would probably have kept a low profile. Which isn't saying we're arrogant now. But with hindsight, you're always sorry for having compromised the position to excel in exchange for getting the assignment. That's where we've become increasingly critical.

What are your main cultural points of reference in this self-made profession?

de Jong: I have never seen '*Cités-Cinés 1*', I'm sorry to say, but from what I've heard I do have a tremendously strong picture of it. So in a strange way it did become a point of reference for me. Later I did see '*Cités-Cinés 2*' in Paris, which was different from the first, but there was the resemblance of compilations of cinema in an unusual setting.[17] That Confino approach we of course later encountered in Turin in the Cinema Museum, but more toned down.[18] I suspect that Confino was seriously hampered by that particular building. In La Défense in Paris however, he had an enormous hall at his disposal. Another important reference point for me is Peter Greenaway's 'The Physical Self'.[19] That exhibition was a true collection-exhibition that made clear that one can tell exciting stories by means of collections; something that struck a note with me as an exhibition maker at the time. In a different fashion, the exhibition '*Gebed in Schoonheid*', which was put together by Henk van Os, was an important one as well.[20] It was very impressive, the fascinating lighting on those little statues, the stories that accompanied you on the way through the show.

I find it hard to name references in a wider sense. I love photography. I love music. I went to see outrageous concerts, but I'm not so sure that I actually apply those things in my work. I don't read much. I don't have a whole lot of literary reference points. The theatre doesn't really appeal to me. Imagery is very important. I have been collecting images, mainly from newspapers, for twenty years now. Images of natural catastrophes, images of personality cults, of people carrying other people's portraits. Unfortunately I haven't found the time to organise it and make it accessible yet, but still, it is an important source that I draw on quite often.

Kossmann: As I said: '*Cités-Cinés*'. When I come to think of it, I seldom visit a fine exhibition that truly inspires me. And when it does, it is usually a visual arts exhibition: Ilya Kabakov, Thomas Hirschhorn or Mark Dion, who collected objects from the Thames to produce a narrative in a cabinet in the Tate Modern.[21] Such exhibitions directly come to mind as a reference in my own work. I feel a strong affinity to that type of installation art, to the question how you can manipulate a space by means of an idea. People who find exciting solutions to that are the ones who inspire me. To me, Peter Greenaway's 'The Physical Self' is more interesting, in that respect, than what he did in Fort Asperen recently.[22] 'The Physical Self' was an eye-opener, whereas Fort Asperen is more of a repetition.

'Nightwatching' in the Rijksmuseum again was highly inspiring, not because of its form, but rather because of the notion that one single Rembrandt painting can generate a whole chain of associations.[23] Then there are the fine storytellers whom I encounter every so often; they are very inspiring as well. I'm very much impressed by people like Auke van der Woud, Geert Mak or Tijs Goldschmidt, who have such a vivid way of writing and storytelling in treating subjects like the design of the Dutch landscape, life stories or the adventures of a group of Papuans in the Vondelpark.[24] They are true storytellers. Special buildings are also a source of inspiration. Ronchamp by Le Corbusier, for example: someone imagined and realised a world there. I always found it fascinating that someone can actually do that. Most impressive.[25]

de Jong: At the 1999 Venice Biennale I saw several impressive pavilions. The Belgian one had a room full of mist.[26] As soon as you entered that room, you lost your orientation entirely. That is what I find intriguing: that something happens to you when you enter a room. I remember the Japanese pavilion had its walls covered with a grid of light bulbs that went on and off in varying patterns.[27] It's interesting how such simple interventions work on the senses and provoke extraordinary experiences. Which also makes me think of *'Chambres d'amis'* by Jan Hoet in Ghent sometime during the mid-eighties.[28] *'Chambres d'amis'* was surrounded by a collective buzz; you had to see it. You don't often have that nowadays, I feel. Being able to organise an exhibition like that all over town was something extraordinary. Having the chance to enter unknown mansions. Walking from one house to the other was part of the experience. You can sometimes really long for projects like that.

How do these references affect the substantive and aesthetic choices you make?

Kossmann: I realise we are architects and that for us the spatial aspect is the dominant one. Whenever I enter a building, I first look up to feel the building, or its potential. Walking in a cathedral I find inspiring for that very reason. So, looking precedes designing. As far as the role of cinema in exhibitions is concerned, '*Cités-Cinés*' apparently became the ultimate example, because most of what I see isn't all that interesting. As narrative, cinema offers possibilities that cannot be achieved with other media: cutting story lines, synchronising narratives. But even then the space itself remains the crucial element. When we use film, we consider the projector as a lamp and try to lay the projection over the spatial elements. Projection screens are not our business. We project the image directly into space, as a virtual wind that blows through reality.

de Jong: I've seen a lot of movies and I think it is a fantastic medium. But in our work we use it as a subsidiary. Our projections are a hybrid. It is never about that piece of cinema alone and for that reason the reference to existing cinema for us is an infelicitous one, for the story is being told out there, on the screen. So, in designing an exhibition I hardly ever fall back on movies I have seen. Of course there are instances where people commission us to present a history, such as the history of Jewry or the history of a city. At such moments cinematography is a very powerful medium that is able to bring the past to life. The spectator is drawn into the subject by the power of the medium. Thus we try to reanimate objects by the use of cinema, to make them resuscitate. But it only works when you apply the medium on a monumental scale, having the projection dominate the space. A tiny monitor with a little object beside it will not do the job.

What is the propelling motivation in your work, essentially?

Kossmann: To me, the exhibition medium gets more exciting every day. It really allows you to do things that other media cannot. There are limits of course, but I never find myself thinking: 'It's time to do some free installation.' It is about a different kind of authorship. We often start off with a theme or a collection, as a given. Our job is to supply the story with everything that the collection itself doesn't reveal or sustain. Which is one reason why we should become involved in the process of making the exhibition much earlier. I notice that the primary curatorial questions are very relevant to us. Why did they choose this particular collection? What was the purpose of juxtaposing these particular elements? Why this art-historical vision? In the Wijdeveld exhibition, for instance, we did something new.[29] By using projections, lighting and sound we created a Wijdeveld universe in which we suspended Wijdeveld's draughts. In doing that project we pushed the collection to the limits. There we conjured up an intense atmosphere with pristine light and Wijdeveld's theatrical voice cleaving through. Such projects begin to move in the right direction. In the Dolhuys we came close as well, although it was a different kind of exhibition.[30] What remains to be seen every single time, is how the various components should converge in order to create a condensed story.

Your style has become well known. The exhibitions are being honoured with awards. What makes a typical Kossmann.dejong exhibition?

Kossmann: It's true; people do speak of our exhibitions as being typically 'Kossmann.dejong' and of certain aspects corresponding. But here they tend to overlook some essentials. Of course, there are recurring ingredients, such as making the building work or the staging of the space. Or the monumentality of the story in which the spectator becomes immersed.

de Jong: What is a constant is the organisation of intensity, which can be achieved in different ways. Some of it is inherent in the subject, some of it is determined by the way you approach it as a designer.

Kossmann: We aim at an integral approach of a monumental nature. When you deploy cinema, it shouldn't appear on a miniscule monitor, but rather it should fill the space or cover the building as a projection. That is a constant and as such it is a Kossmann.dejong trademark. But apart from formal solutions we deploy cinema to charge the space with meaning.

de Jong: As a designer you never start from scratch. You're aware of the fact that some things work and those solutions become part of your stock-in-trade. But generally we are not consciously asking ourselves whether we are repeating ourselves or not. The only thing that counts is the adequacy and the intensity of the final result.

Can you tell me something about your approach? How did the Dolhuys project come about, for instance? What are the subsequent steps you take? What substantive basis or power of persuasion do you need to manage a project like that?

Kossmann: The story usually starts from square one. We tend to enter a world that is completely unfamiliar to us. In my family, for instance, I know of no one with a psychiatric history. That being unknown, the first thing you do is listen. We organise a number of brainstorming sessions that permit people to speak out and that let us explore the subject in depth without referring to design. So, what is psychiatry? What are the ambitions regarding an exhibition about psychiatry? Already after the first discussion with the Dolhuys management we noticed that three out of four people that were being discussed were not present. There was one psychiatrist and one curator who knew everything about the history of psychiatry, but no patient or representative of a patients' association was present.

What we look for in discussions like these is the full scope, the diversity and the strata of the subject matter. And here we decided fairly early on that this exhibition shouldn't be about a collection but instead about the 'normal'-versus-'abnormal' distinction. That's how it started. Next there was the building that made us think of what to do with all those separate little rooms. At the same time we realised that this very multiplicity could contribute a structure for the complex subject matter. Now, part of our methodology is working with the question of how one can achieve a succession of tension curves. In some cases the result will be a pavilion-like setup, in others a multi-layered narrative emerges. Here, the building helped to develop a vision of the exhibition as a journey through a diversity of spaces. That gave us the opportunity to make each space work individually and give each one a different psychiatric perspective. Subsequently, you deepen the matter by formulating various chapters and minor themes, and developing corresponding spatial representations. We investigated exactly how one can penetrate the world of the psychiatrist on the one hand and the world of the patient on the other. Gradually, the translation of the subject into an exhibition was crystallising. Now, if both the perspective of the psychiatrist and the perspective of the patient consist of a number of ingredients, then the question is: what mixture of media can most adequately express the richness of those narrative aspects?

de Jong: In this case things were rather complex. More complex than usual. It took us months of discussion before we put our first dot on paper.

Kossmann: Such a process immediately renders a set of rules as well. For instance, the rule of the building being the support. Or that everything should be original. Of not applying wallpaper. These are unwritten rules that together make up the language that you develop for each individual project. What happens then is that you have to rule out some things as a consequence, and that others become possible instead. At the outset, everything is possible, but after some time your options diminish. In the Dolhuys we had a rule that said that everything should be slightly damaged, slightly off track.

What is relevant, as well, is knowing who is saying what. Which authority is speaking? The psychiatrists tended to label everything, something to which the patients' representatives were very much opposed. Every word we presented had certain significance and we were acutely aware of it. This produces rules as well. They weren't simply museum signs that were put up there. Every word is carefully weighed and many have deeper levels. Such tendencies are pointers for future projects. I mean, all those indefinable curator texts you find in museums, they make you wonder: who is talking here? Why don't they have a name? Isn't it strange that in the museum trade the identity of the speaker apparently doesn't count?

With the Dolhuys, you had the opportunity to stage the project according to your own judgement for the most part, didn't you? The dilemma that I recognise nonetheless has to do with questions pertaining to collection. When you traverse the complete Dolhuys route, what goes wrong in terms of staging intensity is the last large room where the historical collection is gathered. It is so massive, in an additive rather than cumulative sense, that the potential of intensity of the individual pieces gets neutralised. It simply doesn't appear as well considered as the previous instances.

Kossmann: That was a matter of obligation. We amassed the whole collection there. I agree. That gave us a lot of trouble.

de Jong: Up to that point you encounter very few collection pieces. We just gathered the lot and presented it there.

Kossmann: And it belongs together, mind you, for it all represents one and the same theme: care.

That's all very well; the theme may be clear-cut, but the orientation is not. Did you, as a strategy, compact the collection in one room in order to gain maximum freedom in staging the other spaces?

de Jong: There is a clean break with everything that precedes it. It is the end of the route, but it wasn't a compromise. We were tied to the collection. They wanted a museum because they had the collection. You could just as well appreciate the miracle of organising so much space without any collection, with such focus on the story and the encounter of its characters.

Still, there is a huge contrast in terms of sophistication and concentration. The room of the psychiatrist invites one to take a seat at leisure, because of the clear focus of the space. It's all carefully constructed. You pass this bizarre restaurant where you have a coffee in amazement, until you finally reach the collection room. There the whole thing capsizes, because its imprint is so different. I immediately felt like, uh-oh, I'm being put

to work here. The focus that was presented to me so carefully along most of the route now no longer served to help me accurately read this other approach. The last room presupposes a completely different way of reading. Do you feel there are any parallels with the Istanbul exhibition in the Nieuwe Kerk?[31]

Kossmann: The parallel is space, I would say. In both instances the building was a given. With the 'Istanbul' exhibition it was the difficult space of the Nieuwe Kerk in Amsterdam. The first question with both projects was: how do we work with this space? What can we bring to it? At first, the 'Istanbul' show seemed to revolve around the exciting contrast of the Christian versus the Muslim worlds. Apart from a Photoshop animation, our first presentation featured just a floor plan of the church that had a Persian rug in it. As far as intensity is concerned, the big difference with the Dolhuys was that in the Nieuwe Kerk we were only in charge of the space. The collection pieces from 'Istanbul' were a constant, as were the texts. In that sense it was only half a Dolhuys. Of course, we designed the way the collection was shown; and we presented it quite handsomely. But did it contain a strong narrative? Did we actually penetrate it? The answer is: no. The same goes for the texts. In the space, however, we did manage to deliver the monumental experience through the 'close encounter' of Christianity and Islam. We added minor elements every so often, like the dervish dancers, to bring the costumes to life, but our initial ambition went far beyond that. The idea was to approach the exhibition as a city of its own; an exhibition city that would be just as dense, as crowded, and as full of life and culture as Istanbul itself. But we soon found out that such an approach would take too much time to realise. We set out to elevate the exhibition to a level beyond a mere representation of Turkey in the Ottoman Empire.[32] The relation with the present, the actual reality of Istanbul at the fringe of Europe, the frenzy of the present-day metropolis, all of that we couldn't bring to the exhibition.

de Jong: I didn't find the exhibition especially intense in that respect. It was impressive in its own way, but we didn't get to extrapo-

	late the collection and make it part of a story. The exhibition didn't get past the intricacies of a display.
Kossmann:	If only we had had more time, we would have tried to modify the choice of the collection. We did experiment with different taxonomies, but the selection of pieces was already fixed. The actual struggle came down to leaving the beautiful choir of the Nieuwe Kerk intact on the one hand, and making it work as an exhibition space on the other. The Nieuwe Kerk exhibition became a traditional collection exhibition after all, albeit with an exciting spatial layout.
de Jong:	Sound was meant to be a major aspect. I had always imagined it as a pandemonium, like a city filled with sound, with minarets calling people to prayer, and market vendors extolling the virtues of their goods. But the church wouldn't permit it, neither the building nor the organisation.
Kossmann:	We took it as far as we could.

Placing a mosque inside a church is a brilliant invention, but the realisation of the contrast is a bit half-hearted, don't you think? You look up and read the grand, monumental gesture of the space. Exciting enough. Then you look down and you read the collection in a rather straightforward traditional way. Conventional. Especially with this subject, with the European–Turkish issue and the confrontation with Islam being highly explosive, I thought that was rather a missed opportunity. All the more because the grand gesture of a mosque in a church was already there! The overall discourse could have been one in terms of clashes. The exhibition could have been a cascade of minor and major frictions – ?

Kossmann:	Absolutely. We suggested all this, but there was no room for it and nobody cared to do it. Here lay an opportunity to connect past and future if only at the level of the texts. The nice thing about Istanbul is that Christians and Muslims coexist there. Every reason to make this aspect the very heart of the exhibition. But that would have required a more thorough understanding of the subject, as well as a timely involvement in the selection of the collection.

In the Dolhuys one can experience a pitch-dark isolation cell. What is the significance of such direct sensory experiences in your concepts?

Kossmann: Sensory experience is crucial! We always try to bridge understanding and experience. What is nice about the exhibition medium is that it enables you to appeal to several senses in a parallel fashion. An exhibition allows one to walk about freely, distance oneself or close in on something. The sensory is a super theme that permeates every aspect of the exhibition, but always in relation to the intellectual aspect. That is the whole point: addressing the audience on multiple levels; which is what sets us apart from, let's say, Disney. We constantly focus on the sensory experience, but the experience occurs against the background of a wider, partly intellectual, narrative that is supported by the means of the exhibition.

It's interesting that you mention the physical freedom in the exhibition situation, which doesn't exist in the theatre, for instance. One can integrate walking and looking. Or walking and listening. You can combine sitting and looking, listening, reading, acting; there are all sorts of combinations.

Kossmann: Absolutely. The power of exhibiting essentially comes from its open nature and the multiplicity of forms with which you can address the audience.

de Jong: There is a certain charm in the fact that a spectator has the opportunity to experience things individually. In the theatre one is boxed in on all sides, really. Even if you're in the dark all the time, you're still aware of the others. Also in terms of time one is stuck in an interval that is pre-programmed. With an exhibition those aspects are fluid. The isolation room in the Dolhuys remains an individual experience, even if you're there with many people. I find it marvellous. It is a stunning demonstration of the power of sound. It is one of those moments that still sends shivers down my spine, no matter how many times I hear the fragment. It is breathtaking. It has happened a few times before with our own shows. You may have premeditated such a moment, but you never quite know if it is going to work. It is a primordial auditive experience.

It struck me as very powerful to have seen that clip where the patient is being tied to the bed immediately before. Here the staging works as a two-stage rocket.

Kossmann: We expected it would. The one is the image of coercion; the other is the sound of it. The first one is in the past; the other is in the present.

A gripping narrative is always an adventure. In your projects the adventure is always supported by a mixture of media. Are there any limits to what you can do there? I mean, you can't simulate a tsunami in an exhibition about natural disasters. Or a realistic suicide bombing in a show about terrorism, for that matter. How do you stage authentic experience?

Kossmann: That would be the primary design assignment. With an exhibition on terrorism some things are impossible, but you could just as well achieve the same goal by other means. You don't detonate a bomb for real, of course. But how does it feel to wear a bomb vest, to travel to the scene and blow other people to pieces? What are the intricacies of transposing that to an exhibition? The design assignment is exactly that transposition. That's what I mean. Lots of things are impossible with an exhibition, but you can touch a number of chords nonetheless. With the Dolhuys we often discussed it. An exhibition on psychiatry can teach you all sorts of things, but the mere fact of physically moving through the space, and being confronted with the normal and the abnormal, cannot be staged in a book.

Do you recall that when you had just received the assignment we jokingly suggested having an interactive electro shock contraption?

Kossmann: Lucky for us we didn't go through with that! From our point of view it was far more intense to stress the notion of 'being different'; to depict the notion as perceived by the patient rather than from the point of view of the psychiatrist exclusively. That was our quest. Disney would probably have introduced a machine like that as an experience, but we got rid of the idea very early on. It is too literal. And why? Who is in that chair? An average visitor! So it's fake, in short.

de Jong: Shock treatment is the first thing that comes to mind with most people. But that is not at all what it is about. It used to be one instrument to infuse lethargy with a spark of life.

Kossmann: In this particular case it was much more interesting to hear someone explain how it is to undergo shock therapy. What is the use of such a brief moment of shock for a visitor? It's useless! It is my strong conviction that already in the research phase you really have to digest the subject in order to generate the transformative power and the intensity that corresponds with the original; but through transformation.

So, that means that you don't address your audience with realism. In order to convey the impact of a tsunami, you don't have to simulate it?

Kossmann: What has to be conveyed is the authenticity and the intensity of what the victims communicate; not a report of some journalist. Suppose you make an exhibition about Borneo; you could very well put the audience in some jungle where they encounter orang-utans, but what's the point? That would be a reconstruction of reality, but it wouldn't be authentic. What is exciting is telling all about the jungle and the orang-utan. A true tale is what people take home.

So you want to dig deeper?

Kossmann: In the Science Museum in London they simulated an earthquake once. That cost an enormous amount of money. Everything allegedly collapses. And there you are, wondering: was that all? That wasn't so bad, was it? Awfully dull. It may be that people feel something similar when there is an earthquake going on, but as the context is lacking, the experience can only be a superficial simulation. Here we have hundreds of missed opportunities to make something out of the subject. For that reason we keep looking for ways to address the public both intuitively and intellectually. You want the visitor to return home with something more than mere sense perception. You want to touch something that makes people think. That is our task.

de Jong: What remains to be seen is why we care to stage intensity at all? Is that a purpose that goes without saying? For us I think that holds true. For the aim is to have people return home as different persons from the ones that came in. Something must have happened to them in the meantime. When someone leaves the exhibition completely blank, then the effort has been wasted.

In terms of intensity you not only stage immediate experience, but also the after-thought; in the slipstream, as it were?

Kossmann: Definitely! Being able to recount the experience to others is perhaps even more important than being able to recall it. When you have watched a movie with some friends, there is nothing more gratifying than sharing experiences among one another, because they are all different. That is the essence.

So each project has its own distinct horizon – such as the Dolhuys project being essentially about the question: 'What is normal?' But here I wonder, is there another reality behind the horizon? One that settles in the memory along a separate curve?

Kossmann: It's funny you mention that. Disney's designers literally state having no horizon. At Disney Studios they work on one level only, the level of experience, and they actively try to avoid the profound and the ambiguous.[33] Their sole aim is to introduce the audience to artificial worlds that can be experienced as adventures. Now, we have a similar aim, but for us these worlds are a means to end that lies beyond: make the audience go home with new insights. Otherwise we must have done something wrong.

Regarding the Wijdeveld exhibition, I would like to confront you with a quote by Rudi Nieveen in the February 2006 issue of 8Weekly**: 'The design of the exhibition is completely in keeping with Wijdeveld's cosmic, theatrical view. The blacked-out room has a centre that is a brightly lit spherical projection screen that presumably represents the illuminated mind of the visionary. On it we see projections of images, sketches and photographs accompanied by a series of deafening sound effects, which all together suggest a representation of a journey through Wijdeveld's head. Great fun, but after a few minutes I need to get out of the visual spectacle because I can't take any more of the racket and the ethereal Passion music.'[34] Was the NAi exhibition such a spectacular show?**

Kossmann: Yes, it was and it was also very much like Wijdeveld – and very much on purpose. The whole soundtrack consisted of tracks from Wijdeveld's own collection. Every bit of spoken soundtrack was taken from his own writing. And the critic is right: it is about Wijdeveld's head. We took it a long way and I feel it turned out very well. I can very well imagine that Wijdeveld would have recognised himself in it. In our perception this was what Wijdeveld was about. The dramatic deliverance with accompaniment; that is the atmosphere of Wijdeveld. So Nieveen experienced Wijdeveld, not Kossmann.dejong. Of course, we designed the whole thing, but we did so very carefully. We left no stone unturned to get close to the man.

You mean the spectacle was a functional one?

Kossmann: Yes. The spectacle was Wijdeveld too. He writes about that, you know. About architecture as spectacle. So it was all-out Wijdeveld.

de Jong: But even then, our staging was a counterpoint as well. Whereas Wijdeveld was a loudmouth with an ornate style, we produced a contemplative space. We suspended drawings as if they were hovering in a kind of vacuum. There was a tension between the bombastic on the one hand, and a serene modesty on the other. It's a pity that the quote doesn't mention that at all.

What can we learn from Disney?

Kossmann: In terms of staging intensity it is clear that Disney goes all the way to immerse the audience in a wonderful world, which already starts with the queuing. The more I think about it, the more I realise just how different our approach really is. Disney doesn't produce exhibitions, mind you. They make 3-D movies. You are in this cart and you cannot decide to retrace your steps. It's straight ahead and space passes before your eyes. With Disney everything is under control. Every section has its own script. It's a multi-sensory movie. You're moving; you feel the wind, it's 3-D. The power of an exhibition of course lies in the individual freedom of perception and movement. At an exhibition the visitor decides for himself how he spends his time, on what and in what order. Not with Disney. There everything is under control.

de Jong: But tell me, what is so bad about that? People always talk about Disney with a kind of disdain, but should we justify that?

Kossmann: The crucial difference lies in the tempo that is imposed. All sorts of things pass you by or you get carried past all sorts of things. Also, Disney is about realism, not about metaphors. A tree is a tree. As soon as something more is required than mere temporary sensation, then you have to introduce metaphors and abstractions to provoke reflection and depth. With Disney it is impossible to contemplate anything. In the Dolhuys a visit could last four minutes or four hours, and the difference between the two is huge. A Disney experience, on the other hand, has a uniform time for each and every one.

Which project produced the most coherent spatial narrative in your hands?

de Jong: I recall that the '*Wederopbouw*' exhibition had lot of that.

What really made a difference there was the fact that we had a say in the development of the building itself after we had produced the exhibition concept. Usually it's the other way round. Usually the concept of the exhibition is tuned to the building. We planned to have a time machine and that produced an extremely clear narrative form. It had a narrator who guided the audience through time and who provided continuity. In terms of narrative it was an intelligent concept throughout. Besides the grand portraits of the eras, it had a lot of detailed anecdote. It was a damn good show. We controlled both the overall structure and the minutiae.

Items magazine published an interview with you in the March/April 2006 issue and on the cover it read: 'Kossmann.dejong direct space'. Can you tell me what that is, directing space?[35]

de Jong: I like that way of putting it. But there is something lacking, because we direct so much more. We direct content. The process. We direct interaction and although space may be an important part of that whole, *Items* overemphasises the architectural, spatial aspect.

Kossmann: What I think was meant with that title, is that we handle space differently from an architect. That's how I see it. We actually try to fill space with content. In whatever way. That is the process we direct. Directing space means making it significant, charging it with significance; producing spatial narrative. Hence it is twofold: the literal designing of space, but also designing what happens in it.

Directing space doesn't exclude the architectural approach. But from the word go you two have appointed yourselves as exhibition architects. Now, the combination does produce something new, being your medium: exhibition. But what makes an exhibition? Could you define the format?

Kossmann: Exhibiting has to do with going for a walk; with the experiences that arise when one is taking a walk. Other media do not offer such a thing. At the cinema or at the theatre one sits still. It's the same with reading a book. Imagine an exciting walk through a city or a park. We can actually change the perspective and the setting of both the story and the experience of it. The setting may be static but you anticipate the visitor moving through it, and because of that we have the opportunity to offer strings of narrative bits and pieces. The pieces aren't fixed; nor is there one single medium that carries them. Besides, we have the possibility of synchronicity. Exhibitions have the potential to merge the experience of space and objects, of text, images and sounds, as well as the experience of the self and fellow visitors, with one overall image simultaneously. Most combinations of media cannot do that.

Are you suggesting a notion of the exhibition as a small-scale city?

Kossmann: One can experience an exhibition very much like one experiences a city. Imagine a walk through Rome. What you experience is the sum total of the sun shining, the people you come across, the beauty you encounter, the marvellous food you enjoy on a terrace, the synchronicity of things. There we find a correspondence with exhibitions. The experience of travelling, for me, is the image that comes closest to the essence of making exhibitions.

Mark has repeatedly defined the essence of the profession as staging intensity. When you integrate that with the image of a city, would it be fair to suggest that the exhibition is the condensation of a city? Are your exhibitions in fact small-scale cities in a controllable setting?

de Jong: Sometimes. I think that metaphor will cover a lot. In a city you have this constant shift of smells and sounds and images. You turn the corner and the situation may change instantly. In our exhibitions we look for that kind of contrast. We aim for changes of perspective and changes of mood. The comparison does carry a long way, in this respect.

Kossmann: The resemblance to an exhibition actually arises when you pause and pay attention to what draws your attention. We provide the grand gesture and the route to make a walk. People sometimes say that our exhibitions are a bit too much. We on the other hand say that it all depends on how long you intend to stay. This multitude of things has a multi-layered structure that isn't meant to be released all at once.

de Jong: You're in that street, you turn the corner and there you have this second-hand bookshop. You can pass it by, but the shop has a window that interferes with the street and, conceivably, with you as well, in a rather implicit way. But once you enter that shop, you're in a different universe where a new city arises; this time within bookshelves for instance. Now, you can snoop around for a couple of minutes and leave, or you can pick a book and stay for two hours because there again is a new universe that fascinates you. Accordingly, you can introduce shifts of attention and scale in countless ways.

Where does the city/street analogy take us? The street has doors and windows that you walk through or look through, which is the perspective of the walking visitor, but it also has its unpleasant encounters and awkward confrontations. It possibly imposes things that you don't want. The street in itself is a universe that consists of colliding worlds.

Kossmann: When I try to find a comparison with another trade, urban planning turns out to be too remote. It is excessively concerned with building blocks and creating nice spaces. Exhibitions may have more to do with the openness of a public park. Our trade has more in common with landscape design. As opposed to urban planning, landscape design is also concerned with beautiful flowers, plants, the seasons etcetera. It is about change. Such an approach is very much like ours.

That is an interesting point you mention. When people commission you to make an exhibition as a designer, does that imply designing a singular, static end result? Or

herman kossmann and mark de jong

rather a condition for what is to become a city (to stick to that metaphor) or a landscape? A living organism that mutates and develops in a certain direction?

Kossmann: No, I think we tend to design a fairly complete whole. But every time I hear a good landscape architect, designing becomes increasingly fascinating once ecology comes into play. Directing such cycles and processes, which are based on organisms that are supposed to do a certain thing at a certain moment, I find tremendously impressive. It would be fantastic if we could think and work like that in our trade.

The concept of 'ex-hibiting' refers to a form of museological presentation that implies presenting a selection from an historical collection. Nowadays we see collectionless exhibitions more and more. Even by you. What is the essence of an exhibition when there is no collection of artefacts to back it up?

Kossmann: We did collectionless exhibitions quite often and you can deal with the matter in different ways. The '*Wederopbouw*' was an example. So was the Dolhuys. And the seaport presentation at the Maritime Museum in Rotterdam.[36] These exhibitions share the story as the nuclear notion.

de Jong: Those experiences helped us develop. If we had done collection exhibitions only, we would never have arrived where we are now. Once the collection is left out, you have to change your approach. Then imagery becomes crucial. Cinema. Photography. Without the items there is no way around using images.

Kossmann: I highly value stories. Of course we did collection exhibitions. When I think of the one about children's books in the Royal Library, that's all very well, all those books, but for us it isn't enough.[37] The Royal Library has every children's book of all times from all over the world. So, there is no limit to what you can do. You need stories to present a cross-section of the collection and to structure the presentation of it. With the '*Wonderbaarlijk Alfabet*' we took the alphabet from A to Z so that we could classify every theme. Subsequently, a spatial presentation was developed where the collection itself came into play. But it didn't dominate.

de Jong: Once you've managed to make an exhibition without a collection a couple of times, you come to understand that the collection isn't always a prerequisite. That is where we stand out right now. I've got the feeling that CassonMann are sometimes envious of that: how we pull it off.[38] At times you simply have to force your way through. But you're not always in charge. A museum collects stuff and the curators want to show it in exhibitions. Period. There is no discussion. All one can do, in the margin, is say: this we'll use and that we won't. Our contribution then boils down to the overall story that holds the collection together.

When do you consider it a success? In doing an exhibition on Rembrandt's self-portraits, the magic of the collection itself is a given. You don't require much effort there. But where does the mysterious, magical, magnetic substance of a collectionless exhibition come from? You could say it is the work of the story, but then again: how does the critical charge of the narrative space come into being?

Kossmann: By a number of factors. It isn't just one story, mind you. Often it is a complex of numerous stories, which gives us the means to chop up the whole. Ultimately it is the whole we're designing, but we do it by concentrating on every single part. On elements that enable us to transport an idea, an essence. With the Dolhuys we worked with the questions: what is normal and what is abnormal? These two categories permeate every layer of the exhibition, even in terms of the spaces and the architectural decisions. The notions of 'normal' and 'abnormal' are different perspectives that enable us to introduce the story through different people, both patients and psychiatrists. That in turn produced different worlds – the one of the psychiatrists as being completely different from the patients'.

de Jong: But to get back to your question just now; you can judge a success as soon as you put the final presentation together – although we have a fairly accurate sense of quality at the designing stage now. We keep getting better at judging the final effectiveness.

But you should take the question one step further. Assuming that something worked out well, you might wonder: what exactly worked out? Take the 'Flood Warning' installation by Peter Greenaway in Fort Asperen. We all agree that a narrative space was produced there. But wasn't Fort Asperen a narrative space in itself, even without Peter Greenaway's staging? What is the difference?[39]

Kossmann: Yes, Fort Asperen is in itself a narrative space, but one that lacks the content of Greenaway's installation. Because it is a fortress, you can imagine all sorts of things happening in that space. The water, for example, that Greenaway used, had been there already. If you simply hung a sign over it saying 'FLOOD', then a number of things would happen, but not as explicitly.

The bare Fort Asperen is a narrative, essentially, and Greenaway superimposes a second narrative layer. And then there is the third layer: the web of associations that the visitor brings along. Isn't this complexity, which one also finds in a city, the secret of staging intensity?

Kossmann: It is certainly the sort of complexity that we are looking for. We develop a multi-layering and present it to the audience. However, we cannot always predict how it will work. What we do know is that it is going to function, and yes, very much like the atmosphere of a city – as it did with the '*Wederopbouw*' exhibition. There we designed three separate narrative strands and combined them in one carrier. Now you can't predict the exact result, but superimposing things like that is bound to yield something. In other words, one can direct the unpredictable.

de Jong: Yes, but Fort Asperen is a completely unique building, mind you. That is already special in itself. You feel it in everything. It is suffused with history and legend. The installation worked specifically well because Greenaway was really in touch with the mystical element and he managed to reinforce it. We try that too. At whichever place we work, be it old or new, we always try to strike those overtones. The Dolhuys worked for that very reason. The key to that success was the way we put the building to use. It would have failed had the walls been plastered white, as it said in the original restoration plans. That would have made it a vacant building. In the NAi in Rotterdam you can't rely on history, but you have to start from architectural quality.[40] In a way we negated the actual space there to do the Wijdeveld exhibition. By putting a blue lighting on every wall we created a sort of infinity that worked exceptionally well for the Wijdeveld universe that we created there. Thus we try to direct the space every time around.

Here we are discussing space and how it adopts the character of a narrative once we structure it or direct it or use it. Now, every narrative has a certain structure. A classical structure would be the tripartite structure that entails a beginning, a middle and an end, with some key scenes to mark the turning points of the narrative that prepare us for a change of perspective. What is your favourite structure?[41]

de Jong: We tend to use shifts of perspective to keep the audience alert. So, for us it is an aspect of the suspense that we organise. But we are never consciously preoccupied with narrative structure as such.

Kossmann: Well, you can't, actually. That is the main difference with a book or a movie. We don't like fixed trajectories and so we try to avoid that kind of linearity. With us, such an overall narrative trajectory tends to diversify into a variety of smaller ones almost right away. Thus a routing comes into being that has many built-in, two-way deviations where the beginning of each can at the same time be the end. In fact, there is no beginning or end. This often produces a lot of fuss with the museum people. Of course you have a sort of beginning when you enter the exhibition and an end when you exit, but we don't design any routes in between. We structure the space and design a layering. The spaces that we create do indeed resemble cities, where one can turn left or right or decide to go straight ahead, rather than Hollywood movies. Our narratives aren't linear. And deliberately so. It doesn't matter if you decide to cross the exhibition diagonally or whatever. There are many ways to traverse the presentation and we encourage people to do so. In fact we design a lot of tiny curves with spaces in between – some air – and we see to it that at the physical level things aren't jammed; that there is a pause after every experience. In a city you have the same: the house fronts are not just one massive wall. It is a great relief that every so often there is a street that allows you to take a different direction; that leads you to the next beautiful square. That is the pause I'm talking about. The experience continues without the screen ever fading out.

Like in music, where notes are played. In between the notes there is no playing, but that time interval where the duration of the preceding note anticipates the one that follows, that is essential to the acoustic experience of the musical whole. Is that what you mean by pause?

Kossmann: Yes, you could put it that way.

de Jong: It also has to do with concentration. Once intensity is required, you need concentration. Being stuck in a chair in a blacked-out cinema can certainly produce concentration, but by putting twenty objects in a showcase you make the exhibition visitor perceive just one thing. You are not going to concentrate on each and every one of those twenty objects one at a time. There is too much competition and too much distraction going on. But once you leave some space between the objects, there is room for attention for every single object. So you can reflect on concentration on different levels.

What interests me is what influences perception. Everybody is familiar with the experience of a shift in the perception of time in the cinema. You know that the film lasts for two hours, because that is what it said on the poster, but afterwards you have the impression

of having been in a different world for just one hour or, rather, for at least four hours. Depending on the narrative and on the intensity of perception, the experience of time will deviate from mechanical time. Maybe drama curves time?[42]

Kossmann: What we try to effect is the willingness to pay attention. An exhibition is a walk that either draws people's attention or not. If it does, we did well. And here of course lies the complexity of the exhibition medium. If you do not succeed in grabbing the attention of the visitor like this, the story has failed. For in an exhibition you cannot force people to pay attention to something. That is why the first glance is of crucial importance. Often, the first five minutes make clear if you are going to stay for more than an hour or not. Now, we don't stage an hour's walk. That would amount to a walking distance of three miles or so. We only do about a hundred yards. So, we have to compact those three miles in the hundred yards available. Which is quite something: a lot of pausing!

What I find intriguing, is which basic units you use. Do you think in terms of scenes?

de Jong: It all depends on the assignment. With the Dolhuys we actually constructed a walk through a cluster of building and spaces. In every room we set up a scene. You traverse the story step by step. However labyrinthine it may be, the Dolhuys has certain linearity to it in that respect. It guides you through in a linear way, doesn't it? What really mattered there was: what to present to the visitor? Should it be serene? Intense? Lively? Or peaceful, rather? That has something to do with scenography.

Kossmann: Well yes, but the word 'scene' immediately brings to mind something with a beginning and an end. We don't usually present experience in such clear-cut units, but more in a layered mode. But the Dolhuys certainly has scenes; for example the dark isolation cell where people get to witness a patient's story. That one even has a climax. It is the ultimate radio play, staged in an extraordinary environment, and as such one can very well call it a scene.

Let's look at the isolation cell. The staging you design always gets mixed with the visitor's own actions on the spot. As a visitor you enter the room. You close the door. That is a deliberate choice. Next an audio clip is played. The contrast is enormous because you enter the dark coming in from broad daylight. To some people this is a deeply moving experience. Now, let's assume I'm arriving just when another visitor is leaving the room visibly upset; what happens then is that through this encounter an unforeseen third dramatic layer arises. This complex whole, the layering of experience, the sequence of spaces, the light and dark contrast, the staging of the audio clip, the visitor's act of locking himself in; this all very much amounts to full-fledged drama, doesn't it?

Kossmann: That is very true.

When you reflect on the theatre and exhibiting – that is, on the possibilities of, say, dramatic exhibitions – what comes to mind as being the most intense exhibition that you have visited or have made yourselves over the last five years?

de Jong: Well, I found the 'Flood Warning' installation by Peter Greenaway in Fort Asperen particularly powerful. That was at an extraordinary level. It may have been a coincidence, but on my way down there, when I was driving along the Acquoy bank, it started to rain like never before. Even with the windscreen wipers at full speed you couldn't see a thing. I had to drive dead slow, otherwise I would have ended up in the ditch. This was such a tremendously beautiful intro to the Greenaway setup. But besides that chance concurrence I found the mystical quality of the space, combined with Greenaway's abundant, baroque style very intense indeed. He sometimes pushes it a bit too far to my taste. A film like *Prospero's Books* is horrible, really.[43] Often his staging remains a mere set – corny – but in Asperen, with the mouldy suitcases and the water in the rooms, it became very convincing as an installation. You entered a completely new, mystical universe. But was it an exhibition?

Does it matter? Greenaway staged a setting that presented a common Dutch problem in a condensed way that we could all relate to. Everyone who was there was wading through the water in wellies to start with. Thus a collective memory was addressed and activated by relatively simple means. And that is precisely the power of the project: the whole scenography was based on the Dutch experience of the struggle against water, and it worked. There was a unity of collection and context and that made the installation such a relevant one.

Kossmann: There were a number of installations that I also found really impressive. For instance the one that Thomas Hirschhorn did in the Bonnefantenmuseum in Maastricht.[44] Hirschhorn is able to use his papier-mâché, aluminium foil, and all that stuff to express all kinds of themes like power and powerlessness. You walk through an amazing piece of work. There is no lighting or technical stuff, but it is a very intense universe that surrounds you. There I had a feeling that I hadn't had in a long time: Wow! How does he do it? From scratch, really. In the Tate Modern I saw *The Weather Project* by Olafur Eliason.[45] You enter the gigantic, almost futuristic hall and there it is, this sun. Incredibly impressive. I also remember the 'Century Cities' very well, again in the Tate Modern.[46] The curator had selected ten cities, each in its own era: an African city in the 1950s, New York in the 1970s, Vienna in the nineteenth century etcetera. What the exhibition did was present each of these cities by combining works of art, photographs and one essential text. The exhibition didn't have any particular design. It was arranged in white, neutral rooms, but by the very combinations of things it was able to convey the essence of an entire city.

What exactly is curating?

Kossmann: Generally, in my experience, it simply means putting an exhibition together. The curator determines the ingredients as well as the style of cooking the soup. Is it going to be French style or Italian? Or plain Dutch? Knowing a lot about a subject doesn't make you a curator. A curator is someone who is able to grasp the essence of a subject and translate it into form while maintaining a contemporary feel. Someone who is able to play with a subject. So, a curator has to be both a good writer and a good storyteller. Sometimes we collaborate with the curator in doing an exhibition; sometimes we do it ourselves.

Of which exhibition do you consider yourselves to be the curators?

de Jong: The '*Interbellum*' one. With that exhibition we were actively involved both in selecting the collection pieces and in presenting them. It started out as a very high-brow, high-culture thing, with the Boijmans Museum and the Chabot Museum. Later we added collections from the Museum of Education and the Tax Museum to present as complete an image of the interwar period as possible.[47] The power of that exhibition came from the combination of very different collections on the one hand, and the monumental compilations of films from the 1930s on the other, which gave all the objects an accessible context.

Many exhibitions lack suspense, when I look at it, because the basis of the collection is too much narrowed down to the experts' vision. Exhibitions only become interesting once somebody is sent into the depot with a carte-blanche assignment. No curator is allowed that sort of free association. Everybody is taking care of his own business. And so, as soon as the material is about to be displayed in public, it is immediately burdened with a heavy substantive load. With no room for playful liberty. That's what made 'The Physical Self' such fun. Greenaway went ahead by freely associating on the basis of the various available collections.[48]

Once you have an exciting concept as a curator, you don't need much design or scenography to transform it into an exhibition that has vitality to it. Now suppose such a potent concept is lacking and all you get is some sloppy content; can you actually save the exhibition by means of scenography?

Kossmann: Maybe the design can create some veils around such insufficient substance, but it would collapse the moment one stopped to reflect on it. We talked about the effectiveness of exhibitions just now, both immediate and long-term, and with a lack of substance I expect the exhibition will fail to touch the memory. As a project it will remain mere entertainment.

How important is the audience as a factor in developing your projects?

Kossmann: It is there at the back of our minds all the time, frankly. In the end it's we who are doing the design, of course, but we never lose track of whether it will work or not. We try to look at it from the perspective of the spectator, how it will affect him and often, in the process, we actually feel like visiting the exhibition ourselves. We never consult any polls or statistics, though. We are the sole point of reference and that's what we go on.

So, you're both the director and the audience? As long as it works for you, it will for them?

Kossmann: Yes.
de Jong: (laughs)

Staging intensity is a dramaturgical notion, surely. You often mention 'first sight', which is a dramaturgical tool essentially, and you somehow seem to set great store by the perception of the audience. As such, your work is also about the quality of looking itself. How do you direct that looking?

Kossmann: First sight has several implications. Most obviously, it represents the initial visual confrontation, what is seen first, what entices the visitor to pursue the subject further. It is like being on a journey through a landscape and arriving on a hill. Down below lies a town. It has a certain attraction. On sensing its past you decide to descend.

    First sight is about the first complete impression. It is a summary, or rather, the concentrated power of the whole, as a quality. The Institute for Sound and Vision in Hilversum, for example, has failed to realise this completely. From the very first glance I lost my appetite to continue. That's what you end up with after the first confrontation: so what?[49]

de Jong: It also very much depends on the quality of the space itself. The installation has to transform the space. If we hadn't used the textiles in the 'Istanbul' exhibition in the Nieuwe Kerk, the whole exhibition would have been staged at 1 or 2 metres height. Which as such isn't altogether far-fetched, because they have exhibitions that work like that all the time. The first glance then becomes a collection of showcases filled with stuff. That isn't wrong per se, but I wouldn't call it a monumental spatial solution.

Kossmann: The first glance may very well be the last one, actually; the one you remember the exhibition by. To me, it is an image that captures the essence of the exhibition, very much like the image of a city. Take Rome, for instance; the image of Rome is a multi-layered one. It is about the history of the Romans, about Popes and Mussolini. On top of that we have hoards of men honking their horns, many, many beautiful women and long, delicious meals.

Narrative suggests a story unfolding in time. But does it need to? Wouldn't it be far more exciting to posit the narrative potential without gradual development? The narrative structure wouldn't consist of scenes, but instead the potential would become palpable as a kind of pressure that transforms our sight. All narrative layers are present simultaneously, instead of sequentially, as a juxtaposed potential. I'm touching on this because you often refer to art installations and if there is one narrative

distinction between the two formats, it must surely be this. What is your perspective on this?

de Jong: We refer to narrative often indeed, and perhaps we shouldn't. Narrative suggests telling a story from start to finish. It has a logical linear structure: a development. But that is hardly ever our concern. Our narratives consist of a multiplicity of fragments. Story fragments. That's why we seldom make linear exhibitions. From a larger supply, the spectator picks a number of fragments that together make up a story against the background of his own personal experience. At our exhibitions you could form a complete story from just two fragments. But you could just as well pick twenty as your point of departure. The story then becomes richer, or more detailed, if you will. But our exhibitions work on a self-service basis. The shelves are filled with individual stories and the spectator may decide which components are suitable to thread his narrative. But as I see it, the notion of narrative is hard to maintain. It suggests having a perfectly finished story dished out to you.

Kossmann: I agree. Exhibitions don't offer consistently linear narratives but only fragments of narrative. One doesn't need to consume each and every element to have an adequate impression of the content. Also, exhibitions are a sum total of distinct media, and we handle those distinctions with a fair deal of attention. What is feasible as a narrative in some media, simply doesn't work in others. Thus, a layering is produced that enables us to tell the same story with different means and different accents. Such an approach also makes for perspective. It produces a sandwich of layers that together make up the exhibition.

We haven't talked about language as much I had hoped. As I see it, your work shows a number of tendencies that call for such an approach nevertheless, if only because the most recent examples point towards monumental, free installation, and a great deal of depth might be gained by concentrating primarily on curatorship. We already touched on the heavy burden of collections and the freedom that results from exhibiting beyond collections.

herman kossmann and mark de jong

Whatever the premise may be, the end result should be perfectly clear. What is your reaction to the following line of thought that was originated by Ludwig Wittgenstein and further elaborated by Richard Rorty in his book *The Linguistic Turn*, **which, in short, posits language not only as an instrument to describe reality, but also as a communicative potential that creates new realities itself.[50] Would it be useful to suggest a distinction between the reactive classical exhibition of display that passively displays a given collection on the one hand, and a proactive narrative space that reveals new thoughts and avenues on the other? You seem to be on the verge of this yourselves, so is it reasonable to suggest that in five years' time you may well have stopped making exhibitions altogether? And if not, what will your exhibitions look like by then?**

Kossmann: That's a good one. I don't know about the exhibitions. What I do know is that we are in for some major changes in the meantime. We are at a point of asking ourselves whether it is actually worth doing another exhibition. We feel a great need to experiment. Not for experiment's sake, but to deepen our approach. To broaden our view and to find new ways of collaborating. We've become professionals in this line of work and we feel an urge to explore other dimensions with the same expertise.

de Jong: Up to this point our work has been determined primarily by third-party needs that were submitted to us. So far, we haven't influenced those needs beyond the point of rejecting some and accepting others. That has been our only instrument for adjusting our course. For us, traditional museums are losing much of their appeal. We have again done a number of such projects recently and got some interesting results, but the prospect is becoming increasingly less appealing. For what it's worth, Schiphol Airport recently came to us for a pitch for doing the design of Lounge 3.[51] Usually, they would select interior designers, but this time they've come to us and we may be able to come up with something new. Such an arena is far more interesting for us right now. I much prefer Schiphol to some conventional exhibition where people walk in with preconceived ideas. You know, people buy the tickets and then they have a fixed objective to visit the museum. At Schiphol, on the other hand, something completely different happens. Likewise, Johan Simons – just to make the cross-reference to the theatre – recently did a play at a railway station, exactly because other things happen than those you find on the classical theatre stage.[52] Blood is thicker than water. I think that in five years' time we will certainly do exhibitions occasionally, but we will be moving into other territories …

Kossmann: What's more, museums will have to move on too, or else they will all collapse. I can't help thinking that the old world is somehow coming apart completely. It seems like a bygone era of centuries past. Everyone feels that. Things simply must change.

de Jong: I very much doubt that they will.

Notes

1. Professor Dieter Besch at the Technische Universiteit Delft [Technical University of Delft].
2. Mark and Pjotr de Jong, design for the Vakbondsmuseum [Trade Unions Museum] in Amsterdam, 1990.
3. Herman Kossmann was teaching at the Koninklijke Academie van Beeldende Kunsten [Royal Academy of Art] in The Hague, from 1982 to 1985.
4. The NNAO (Nederland Nu Als Ontwerp) foundation was founded in 1984 to revitalise the debate on urban planning in the Netherlands. Four different political scenarios informed the research on the future situation of the country in the year 2050. This research culminated in an exhibition, which juxtaposed the visualisations of these four future scenarios.
5. The exhibition '*Nieuw Nederland 2050*' ['New Netherlands 2050'] was held in the Beurs van Berlage, Amsterdam in 1987.
6. In the exhibition audiovisual (AV) media were applied on a large scale for visualising the future.
7. Waardenberg & de Jong is a Rotterdam-based ensemble, renowned for their physical absurdist kind of theatre.
8. The exhibition '*Stadstimmeren*' [Constructing the City'], Rotterdam, 1992, was held on the occasion of the city's 650th anniversary.
9. The exhibition '*De Wederopbouw*' ['Reconstruction'], Rotterdam, 1995, conmemorised 50 years of reconstruction since the end of the Second World War, after the Nazi bombardment of the city in May 1940.
10. The exhibition '*Het Wonderbaarlijk Alfabet*' ['Amazing Alphabet'] in De Nieuwe Kerk in Amsterdam, 1994, was commissioned by the Koninklijke Bibliotheek in The Hague.
11. Peter Loerakker (1959–1991) was a Dutch architect who organised exhibitions and discussions, which made him a pivotal figure amongst the young architects of his time.
12. Kossmann.deJong, Het Dolhuys – Museum voor Psychiatrie [Museum of Psychiatry], Haarlem, 2005.
13. François Confino, '*Cités-Cinés*', La Grande Halle de la Villette, Paris, 1987.
14. Peter Greenaway (b.1942) curated various influential exhibitions, museum presentations and installations, including: 'The Physical Self' in Museum Boijmans Van Beuningen, Rotterdam, 1991–2; '100 Objects to Represent the World' at the Hofburg Imperial Palace in Vienna, 1992; 'Hell and Heaven: the Middle Ages in the North', organised by the Groninger Museum in the hamlet of Dorkwerd at the periphery of the city of Groningen, 2001; and 'Flood Warning' in Fort Asperen, Acquoy, 2006.
15. The exhibition '*Interbellum Rotterdam 1918–1940*' ['Interwar Rotterdam 1918–1940'] was presented in the abandoned storehouse 'Las Palmas' in the harbour area of Rotterdam, 2001.
16. For *Gesamtwerk*, see the interview with Ruedi Baur, note 51, p.270. See also the Foreword by Hans Peter Schwarz, p.xiii.
17. François Confino, '*Cités-Cinés 2*', La Colline, Paris–La Défense, 1995.
18. François Confino, Museo Nazionale del Cinema in the Mole Antonelliana, Turin, 2000.
19. Peter Greenaway, 'The Physical Self', Museum Boijmans Van Beuningen, Rotterdam,

space.time.narrative

        1991–2. See picture-essay 2, p. 381.
20   Henk van Os, *'Gebed in Schoonheid*' ['Prayer in Beauty'], Rijksmuseum, Amsterdam, 1994.
21   Ilya Kabakov (b.1933), Thomas Hirschhorn (b.1957). Kossmann refers here to the *Tate Thames Dig* project by Mark Dion (b.1961) in the Tate Modern, London, 1999.
22   Peter Greenaway, 'Flood Warning', Fort Asperen, Acquoy, 2006.
23   Peter Greenaway, 'Nightwatching', Rijksmuseum, Amsterdam, 2006.
24   Auke van der Woud (b.1947) is professor of the History of Architecture at the University of Groningen; Geert Mak (b.1946) is a lawyer, journalist and writer; Tijs Goldschmidt (b.1953) is a biologist, writer and a researcher at the Radboud University, Nijmegen.
25   Le Corbusier (1887–1965), chapel of Notre-Dame-du-Haut, Ronchamp, France, 1954.
26   Ann Veronica Janssens (b.1956), *Horror Vacui*, Belgian Pavilion, 48th Venice Biennale, 1999.
27   Tatsuo Miyajima (b.1957), *Mega Death*, Japanese Pavilion, 48th Venice Biennale, 1999.
28   Jan Hoet (b.1936), '*Chambres d'amis*' ['Guest Rooms'], Ghent, 1986.
29   Kossmann.deJong, 'Plan the Impossible: The World of Architect Hendrik Wijdeveld (1885–1987)', Netherlands Architecture Institute (NAi), Rotterdam, 2006.
30   See note 12 above.
31   Kossmann.dejong, 'Istanbul: The City and the Sultan', De Nieuwe Kerk, Amsterdam, 2006–7.
32   The Ottoman Empire, founded by Osman I, the ancestor of the Ottoman dynasty, lasted from 1299 to 1923 and was succeeded by the Republic of Turkey. At the height of its power in the sixteenth and seventeenth centuries, it spanned three continents, controlling much of southeastern Europe, western Asia and North Africa.
33   Herman Kossmann is referring to 'Mickey's 10 Commandments of Theme Park Design', which were compiled by Marty Sklar, creative head of Walt Disney Imagineering, for the annual meeting of the American Association of Museums in 1987. See: http://www.themedattraction.com/mickeys10commandments.htm.
34   Rudi Nieveen in *8Weekly*, February 2006.
35   *Items*, vol.2, March/April 2006.
36   Kossmann.dejong, 'MainPort Live', presentation of the port of Rotterdam, Maritiem Museum, Rotterdam, 2007.
37   Kossmann.deJong, 'Wonderland', Kunsthal, Rotterdam, 2002. The Dutch Royal Library is the Koninklijke Bibliotheek in The Hague.
38   CassonMann Designers, London.
39   Fort Asperen is a nineteenth-century fortification in the 'Nieuwe Hollandse Waterlinie' (New Dutch Waterline) near Acquoy. The building is in use now as a space for exhibitions, events and artists' installations. See: http://www.fortasperen.nl, April 2010.
40   NAi: Netherlands Architecture Institute, Rotterdam. See: http://en.nai.nl/, April 2010.
41   See: Syd Field, *Screenplay: The Foundations of Screenwriting*, Dell Publishing Company, New York, 1982.
42   See essay 1, 'The Battery,' para.1.5: 'Space, time and narrative', p.38.
43   Peter Greenaway, *Prospero's Books*, 1991.
44   Thomas Hirschhorn, *Anschool*, Bonnefantenmuseum, Maastricht, 2005.
45   Olafur Eliasson (b.1967), *The Weather Project*, Tate Modern, London, 2003–4.
46   'Century City: Art and Culture in the Modern Metropolis', Tate Modern, London, 1

February to 29 April 2001.
47 Kossmann.dejong, '*Interbellum Rotterdam 1918–1940*', Las Palmas, Rotterdam, 2001. The objects and artworks of the '*Interbellum*' exhibition were derived from various museum collections, mainly in Rotterdam: Museum Boijmans Van Beuningen, Chabot Museum, Maritiem Museum [Maritime Museum], Nationaal Onderwijsmuseum [National Museum of Education], Belasting & Douane Museum [Tax & Customs Museum] and many others.
48 'The Physical Self', op.cit. (note 19).
49 Nederlands Instituut voor Beeld en Geluid [Netherlands Institute for Sound and Vision], Hilversum. See: http://portal.beeldengeluid.nl/. Also: http://experience.beeldengeluid.nl/, April 2010.
50 In his 'very short introduction' to Wittgenstein, the British philosopher A.C. Grayling states: 'Wittgenstein's objective is *to solve the problems of philosophy* [...] by showing *how language works.*' According to Grayling, Wittgenstein's *Tractatus Logico Philosophicus* is an attempt to demonstrate how an understanding of language could solve these problems, that cannot 'be solved by empirical means – by looking through a telescope or microscope, or by conducting experiments in a laboratory', since 'they are conceptual and logical problems, requiring conceptual and logical investigation.' The recognition of the capacity of language to function as a structuring agent, informed the notion of 'the linguistic turn'. The term became popular with the anthology *The Linguistic Turn*, which Richard Rorty edited in 1967. See: A.C. Grayling, *Wittgenstein: A Very Short Introduction*, Oxford University Press, Oxford, 1996, pp 16-20. See also: Richard M. Rorty (ed.), *The Linguistic Turn: Essays in Philosophical Method*, The University of Chicago Press, Chicago, 1967. Especially noteworthy are the two additional essays 'Ten years after' and 'Twenty-five years after', which Rorty published in the 1992 edition.
51 Competition for the design of the Privium ClubLounge of Schiphol Airport, Amsterdam, 2007–8.
52 Johan Simons (b.1946), *Merlin oder Das wüste Land*, Maschinenhalle Zeche Zweckel, Gladbeck, Ruhrtriennale, 2007.

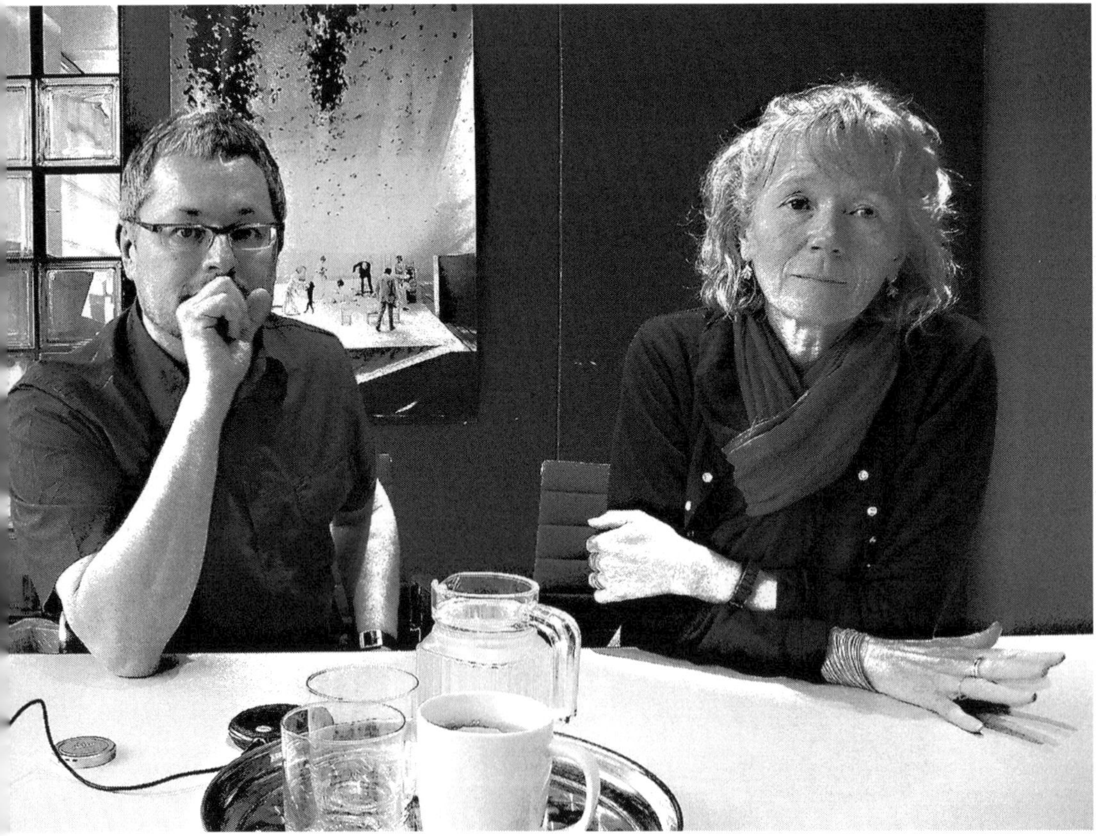

Interview with
Dinah Casson and Roger Mann

Dinah Casson (b.1947) and **Roger Mann** (b.1961) are the founding directors of the London-based agency CassonMann Designers. I met Dinah and Roger in November 2005 in their former office in Northington Street, where I invited them to take part in a series of seminars that I wanted to organise as part of the Scenographical Design course at the Hochschule für Gestaltung und Kunst in Zurich, in early 2006. I had seen impressive photographs of CassonMann projects published in the 'exhibition issue' of *Frame* magazine. Enough to be intrigued. Dinah and Roger, both genuine interior architects with a highly developed sense of detail and nicknamed by colleagues as 'the professionals', accepted the invitation and became part of the Narrative Environments research project. The interview with Dinah and Roger was held in their former office, in a tiny room packed with models, books and paperwork, on 28 and 30 March and concluded on 9 July 2007. The portrait on the opposite page was shot on the first day of our conversation.

What was the first exhibition that really touched you?

Mann: The first one I remember is the Tutankhamun exhibition, in the seventies.[1] I was 10 or something at the time. I remember queuing up for three hours. They actually had film footage of the queues in a documentary on television the other night. Somehow that is a key. I mean, queuing up for three hours to get in, when you're ten, was quite something. But also, I guess the lighting and the whole impact was something I had never really experienced before. Just the power of objects, pin-point lighting in an otherwise completely black space. That had a huge impact. The other exhibition I remember from that time, was a hologram exhibition at the Royal Academy.[2] Holograms were very new at the time and they don't seem to have moved on from then, particularly. Both of these exhibitions were kind of amazing.

Casson: I think my memories are a little bit more fragmented than that. I went to the Expo in Montreal.[3] It must have been 1967. I have a very clear memory of Technology. It was the first time I'd been in those cinemas with screens going all around you, where you have to hang on because you are flying through the Grand Canyon. It seemed pretty amazing then. Also, the monorails going through the Buckminster Fuller Dome.[4] I remember the Buckminster Fuller Dome very very clearly. I remember this whole thing, the concept of an Expo as the idea of making a temporary city. But having said that, of course, my very first big exhibition was the Festival of Britain in 1951, when I was four.[5] I remember the atmosphere of that. There is something very odd, which happens on these campuses, these Expo types of places. There is a sort of lifting of spirit, expectation and a funny mix of solidity of the pavilion-buildings and experimentation. Certainly the Expo in Montreal had a big impact on me, but it wasn't about objects. I remember a whole series of exhibitions at the Whitechapel Gallery as well.[6] They were mainly art exhibitions: Rauschenberg, Oskar Kokoschka for example. It must have been the mid-sixties. They completely hit me at the moment. Those were incredibly vivid art-experiences, but I don't remember objects or light particularly. Not the way Roger does.

dinah casson and roger mann

What exhibition made you consider becoming active in the field of exhibition-making?

Mann: Certainly the Japan exhibition at the V&A, I remember the potential role of technology as a dynamic storytelling tool, as well as the objects and all the other media.[7] It was either very early on in our endeavours in this field, or just prior to it. I didn't have much time or a great passion for objects in showcases. I enjoy them much more now, but at the time it was a gear-shift.

Casson: Somebody asked us to do an exhibition at the Boijmans Museum in Rotterdam.[8] I think that was the first time that we were actually confronted with the question of presenting objects. What can you do with them? What sense can you make of them? We had a nice time, although it was complicated. It was very hands-on: we built a lot of it ourselves.

Mann: It was the first exhibition we ever did. It was called 'British Design: New Traditions'. Malcolm Garrett did the graphics.[9] The intro was our first bit of video. We had 20 CRTs set up in a big clunky physical row with some software that cost 200 pounds.[10] Beyond that intro we ended up in a garden, which was to do with a very specific bit of Britishness. And then it moved on to a street-style installation, which was all made of mesh and graphics. Then came industrial technology, corporate identity and branding. The last thing was centred around Tom Dixon and all that designer–maker crowd.[11]

Casson: What was interesting was that we were pushed into finding ways of setting a context which didn't depend on the written word. We couldn't assume that the Dutch would understand English that well, so the installation itself had to express what normally a graphic panel would be required to say. That was the beginning of an interest in the narrative environment, if you like. It also introduced us to the idea that it was possible – and desirable – to make a landscape, within which you could place things and that this could make an enormous, silent contribution to the understanding of the objects. So, for example, the first group of objects from people like Paul Smith and Vivienne Westwood, who were working within some kind of tradition of Britishness but were rethinking and doing it with a twist, were placed in an English garden framed with a plastic hedge: this was an attempt to explain that.[12] It was a stylised landscape for these stylised objects. Similarly, each subsequent chapter of the exhibition used materials and structures to make a landscape within which these things could sit. This was one way in which the designer of the exhibition could speak, without saying anything. The industrial chapter in Rotterdam, for instance, was all on a sheet of rusted steel – of which you could say, at that moment, that it had to do with the fact that British industry was in rapid decline. We were showing the last fragments that were left, so to speak.

How did you become partners in profession?

Casson: Because of an Alitalia strike. Two people met in Rome airport, waiting for an airplane. They knew each other. One said to the other: 'Hello, how nice to see you, where are you going?' 'I'm going to London,' the other said. 'What are you going to do there?' 'I'm going, because I want to make an ice cream shop.'[13] 'Who are you going to get to make that ice cream shop for you?' 'I don't know. I have to find a shop and I have to find an architect,' said the other. 'Well, then you need to go and see Dinah! Here is her phone number.' So, when he arrived in London and rang me, he said he was going to see three or four architects. And I rang Roger and asked him if he wanted to come and help with doing this pitch against these other people, whom I didn't know. We did it and of course there were no other people. That's how it happened.

But you did the job on an entirely freelance basis? There wasn't a CassonMann office yet?

Casson: No; I had been working in the furniture industry. When I left college, I worked for Terence Conran, who was still running Habitat at that time, and my job was essentially within the manufacturing part of the company.[14] I had an interesting time working in the different factories in the organisation. Then I was freelance on my own for a while and I was doing furniture projects, mostly. And I was teaching interior designers at Kingston. Being a furniture person, I was asked by Kingston to teach interior designers about making furniture, and putting things together.[15] So, then I allowed myself to get interested in interior design, which I had resisted up to that point, because my parents were involved in all that. I had carved out another thing for myself somehow.

And you were a student of interior design at that time, Roger? Dinah was your teacher for a while?

Mann: On some projects. As a visiting tutor. A day a week or so.

Was the ice cream parlour the spark that made you decide to work together on a more regular basis?

Mann: We had a good time. It was fun!
Casson: We had fun, because we didn't really know what we were doing. We were also under a lot of pressure before it opened. We opened before we had planning permission, which in Knightsbridge was not a good idea. It was a very pretty little shop, which had the best ice cream in London, so it was popular. We were taken to court by the neighbours, because we didn't have the planning permission, so we pulled in all favours and wrote to all the big architects in London, with whom we had any sort of contact. Big guns, who wrote incredibly flattering things about this little shop. When we went to the court for this appeal, the other side said: we've got nothing to say.
Mann: They capitulated and we all went off for lunch together.

CassonMann as an office has existed for almost 20 years now?

Mann: It depends on your description of office!
Casson: For a very very long time, it was just the two of us working in a room. And our income was pathetic.

But you labelled yourself CassonMann at some point and gradually became an institution?

Mann: I don't think we labelled ourselves CassonMann very early on. But in the publicity of the ice cream shop we were referred to as CassonMann. At that time it was something of an illegal marriage. It was not formalised. There was not a partnership. There was nothing other than two individuals collaborating. The formal bit came only ten years later.

If you look at it professionally, what distance did you cover since your initial cooperation?

Casson: I think it is still the no-plan plan, really. I mean the ice cream shop was designed for some very special clients – who are still friends. We have never really enjoyed projects where the client wasn't interesting, so we try to avoid that if we can. I think we were just incredibly lucky, early on. The projects we were asked to do were all interesting and not terribly normal. They weren't necessarily in any order: one didn't lead to the other. So, from time to time we would sit down and think, if we were to market ourselves what would we say we do? We were doing all sorts of things and we thought, maybe, doing all these different things was a strength. But of course anybody looking at us was completely confused because it is not very English to do lots of things. In the design-school system in this country you are educated to be a graphic designer or a product designer, and so on. This is why the Alitalia conversation was so interesting; the fact that I wasn't an interior designer or an architect, and that I had never done a shop before, was not important. My design-head was considered as interesting and apparently that was enough.

Are you keen on that sort of challenge, which goes beyond your horizon?

Mann: That's still what we're looking for. There has been quite a nice shift in the last years. We are doing museums, hotels and other things at the moment, which we have never done before. That's great. It is still a balance to get that and to see what you can take into it. We've got a little bit more knowledge now than twenty years ago.

Would you be prepared to do another ice cream parlour?

Mann: It wouldn't become a space quite as small as the first one.

Casson: If we like the client, of course. When we finally made the decision to go into museums, it was simply because we thought that working with curators would be more rewarding than working with facility managers, because of the content.

Mann: But there was a gap. We did the 'British Design' exhibition in Rotterdam in 1989, and after that we didn't really do anything until we pitched for the basement of the Science Museum here, which was in 1993. So there was a gap of three years, before we were introduced to the museum through somebody we knew through teaching, who took up the post of Head of Design of the Science Museum. He got in all the people he liked, to look at his project. He was one of these rare people who said, I want people who haven't done this before. He was ignoring all the obvious kinds of exhibition designers that were around at the time, and deliberately went outside the box. So that was our first break, really. As a result of that, we did a small children's gallery for the Science Museum called The Garden in 1996.[16] And the most bizarre thing was to go from The Garden to the British Galleries. The weirdest thing ever, because The Garden is a very small gallery for 3- to 6-year-olds, with absolutely no objects, whereas the British Galleries, with 3,000 objects, was the biggest museum job in London that decade.[17]

Casson: It is curious how things happen. I knew the curator of the British Galleries a little bit. I rang him up and said: the project is kind of interesting, but do you think we've got a chance? He said: yes, go for it, why not? He knew our work – particularly the exhibition in Rotterdam. They didn't demand any drawing – only an essay of one thousand words. The essay got us into the last six. Then we did an interview, and at no point in the interview were we asked for any creative work on the space at all. They didn't want any of that. All we did was to produce a lot of slides of things that we liked, and we made a few, kind of curious, early, antique, photoshop illustrations of some ideas and things. But it was not specific to the V&A, really. That's how we got the job. If we'd had to the sort of pitch that you are expected to do now, I don't think we would have had a hope.

The other thing is that we had the interview on Tuesday and the Director rang up the next day. He said: we'd like you to work with David Mlinaric and his team.[18] He will do the interior design and we want you to do the interpretation, which is an unusual cut. I didn't know what that meant, but it sounded fine to me. I think what they meant was that we would be doing the discovery areas and all the interactive stuff. So, we developed an interpretative strategy (not that we would have called it that then) and, in the end, we did the galleries with David doing the five period rooms and the colours – which was a huge exercise in itself. That was a very gentle way in to the world of conservation and objects. But I don't think the full impact of what it was that we had taken on hit us until about nine months in.

You say you have more of a plan now. Is this plan related to the shift, you were talking about, from the world of the museum towards more commercial projects?

Mann: Yes. In a way it is a hard-nosed business decision about diversity. We find that these crafted, individually nested object-galleries are impossible to earn money doing. If we all want to move on in life, then we need to diversify our work. But the thing which is much more interesting is that, having immersed ourselves in narrative environments for so long, we now see the potential of our knowledge in these other markets. At about the same time these other markets are looking at museums saying, this immersive experiental stuff applies to retail, to hotels, to all sorts of things as well. We are enjoying the hotel work we are doing, because we feel we are investing an awful lot of our scenographic experience. They are contemporary hotels and they are stylish. They are not just fashionable interiors, but sort of narrative environments themselves. We are regularly assessing what stories we are telling, through all the media that we apply.

You arrived at the point where you say: these stories don't necessarily have to be told in an exhibition context – they might be told anywhere, perhaps? Like Nigel Coates having a notion of the city being a narrative environment.[19] Or like Capability Brown, who introduced the idea of the themes in landscape architecture.[20] Are these notions a point of reference for you?

Casson: Absolutely.

You are both trained as 'interior designers', but a major part of your profession lies within the field of 'exhibition design' now. What is the difference? What is, could or would be the essential difference between (interior) architecture and exhibition?

Mann: Before we did museums or exhibitions, doing interiors had far more to do with taste and style. Since we've been doing narrative stuff, our approach to interiors has changed in the sense that we now seek a justification, a rationale, for almost every decision we're making, in terms of materials and form. In almost every interior-design decision we're crafting what, even in a hotel context, could be a narrative environment, because everything is adding up to something and that something is more than just looking fashionable or whatever. Things we're doing now are much more focused than everything we did before. So, I'm not sure any longer what the difference is between interior- and exhibition design. Now, there is almost no difference in my head. Ten, fifteen years ago I would have given you a different answer.

As an exhibition maker you communicate in space, if you like. Do you consider the communicative precision, which an exhibition requires, as a burden compared to interior design for a hotel, for example?

Mann: 'A burden' implies that it is unwanted. I think after years of doing exhibitions, we know now how long it takes to do it. I still think we are passionate about doing it and intend to carry on doing it. I guess it is almost a self-imposed choice to make a hotel a narrative space, where the client wants us to be funky and make him money. We are interested in cross-fertilisation. We take some of the museum thinking and play and work with it in a different context. But that other context also allows us to explore other materials, taste, style, fashion and all the other aspects of things. It's like playing in another playground and learning some other tricks and exploring some other ideas, allowing us to take them to the other arena and start playing with them over there. So, I wouldn't say it is a burden. We are just aware of the time-consuming nature of doing exhibitions.

Casson: I think all buildings, landscapes, cityscapes, houses, are narrative environments potentially, because passing through them is a temporal experience. It is not possible to experience them in any other way. We have been going through our very very long apprenticeship on narrative spaces, where the message and the potential impact is clear. Well, it's clear in the brief, not necessarily in the exhibition, but we know what we are trying to say. I think, somehow, that these neighbouring fields of work that we have discussed have begun to realise that they also have an environment which can carry a narrative. Some of them are now interested in seeing what skills and techniques have evolved in the museum world that might be relevant.

What are your most important references, in this respect? What images do you see when you dream? What music do you hear when you close your eyes? Which book or theatre play changed your views? Which people have had an impact on your thinking and way of life?

Casson: I suppose there are a few individuals who have been important for me. I suppose my father was one of them.[21] And I think that Vico Magistretti, who was one of the people in the Alitalia departure lounge, was incredibly important for me as well.[22] He really had an extraordinarily interesting mind and we used to talk a lot. There are a few people who I brushed against, like Charles Eames, who used to come and visit us at home. I remember him as being someone with an incredibly powerful presence. I wasn't old enough to talk then, but I listened. And Ray Eames, who continued to come.[23] I met Eileen Gray for example and she looked at my portfolio.[24] These were my college heroes and although these encounters were little more than just saying hello, even those brief exchanges can be memorable and they have stayed with me.

Music is a big part of my life. Classical music, more than anything else. We probably go to a concert about once a week. Theatre has always been important. Opera is a wonderful fusion of the two. We go to movies a lot, but movies don't touch me in the same way, really. I could use opera as a metaphor for everything, I guess. Books? I usually have four books on the go, parked in different places: a mixture of novels, biographies, whatever. At the moment I'm reading a biography of Nabokov and a Nabokov novel.[25] I'm also reading a book by Anna Politkovskaya, the journalist who was shot in Russia.[26] I've got certain books that I keep going back to, like *The Art of Memory* by Frances Yates, for example.[27]

And yours, Roger?

Mann: I'm struggling. Thomas the Tank Engine is what I read most of the time.[28] I had a child rather late in life. So, the last three or four years, I've been rather focused on that. I ask myself: is that play really worth another 50 quid in baby-sitting and taxis to go and see it? Maybe not. It's quite hard. Music is a huge part of my life. Not just classical music, but also rap, jazz, everything, anything so long as it is good.

Some people are moved by a painting, for instance by a Goya they have seen at the National Portrait Gallery.[29] I wonder if I am an emotional person sometimes, because I'm not particularly moved by painting. I'm rather interested in interventions. I'm interested in land-art, in sculptural interventions. The exhibitions I enjoyed most were the ones where someone invaded a space artistically, rather than just hanging something on the wall. I'm very aware that it relates to what we do professionally, but these artists have not been burdened by anything other than it being their own personal expression within that space. It's almost about seeing the potential in what they've done, a sort of fuel that goes in. For me it's a process, in which I'm constantly looking and listening until I get to the point where I can rely on it all just being in there, and something happens. The process of designing is almost reliant on the fact that all this, whatever it is, has gone into my head. It might be books that I've read. It might be exhibitions that I've been to. I do still try to see exhibitions as much as I can. But I'm struggling to say: that exhibition or that book or that bit of music on its own was powerful enough to change me. In literature, I was very much into what was horribly called 'magic realism'. Gabriel García Márquez and Salman Rushdie and so on.[30] Their books are very gritty and naturalistic, but there is this other layer of fantasy that somehow threaded its way through what appeared to be normal life. The fascinating thing is that the South American and the Indian culture seem to take the magic bit as normal. It isn't a weird thing to them, but just another dimension of life. As far as art is concerned, I like the work of Michael Heizer, someone who went out and carved great gashes in mountainsides.[31] It's the intervention outside the gallery which I like most.

It's funny, but I've such a different background. There isn't one person in my life whom I can credit something to, really. I was floundering around in an old-fashioned grammar school. There is no history of design in my family whatsoever. The art department at school was horrendous. I didn't do art, but I always used to do the stage sets for the school plays. Mainly because I hated acting. Then very late in my time at school the art master changed and a new art master came in and we had a session together and he said, haven't you thought of going to an art school, doing design? I said what's that? He guided me through it, suggesting that interior design might be the right thing to do.

Casson: Since we last met and you asked me about painters I have realised that the artists – and this would apply to writers as well – that interest me are those who carry a veneer of the ordinary, working within a tight, proscribed form perhaps but who find a way of burrowing under our sensibilities to something way outside of that proscription: Vermeer, Velázquez, Rembrandt, Piero della Franscesco, Ingres.[32] There was recently a Velázquez exhibition in London.[33] Looking at those paintings was just so extraordinary. I saw them three times and could have gone more. Just under the surface, this painter had somehow seen something, or was able to do something, which says so much within such a little space for manouevre – in the context of something very conventional. I think that's really what is increasingly interesting to me; something which is apparently completely straightforward, but absolutely isn't straightforward at all. Why is it good? Why is a Velázquez portrait or an Ingres portrait so good? It's just that you can write fourteen novels about those faces. That interests me, because I don't know what it is, really, other than it is there.

Is it your aim or dream, perhaps, to embed such qualities into your work?

Casson: For me it is not that clear. Howard Hodgkin, the English painter, once talked about how every day is a process of desperate improvisation.[34] And that's what it feels like to me. For me there is no method in the madness. It is simply a grope in the dark. At some point in a way, once it's not like that, once it's familiar, it has lost it; you know it's boring. And if it is boring for you as a designer, it's going to be boring for the visitor as well. A long time ago, when I used to go to the Milan Furniture Fair and write about it, I realised that the things that were exciting were all things that were just sitting on the edge. Things that were sitting safely within their sphere were not of interest.

What then is the edge?

Casson: The edge is perhaps defined by the fact that everything we do is a prototype. The things we do, we've never done before, so we don't quite know if they are going to work. That's one of the edges. You could say we are pushing out the boundaries, but it is not quite like that. That might suggest that we're pushing forward. But we might have been pushing off the back. It's to do with not being quite sure: it's taking the risk. If I'm talking about edge, I'm not talking about us as a company, delivering on time and on budget and all of that. The edge may be, how many layers can we get in? The edge might be, can we just do one layer? Every circumstance is different. So I think it is quite hard to describe what edge might be. What are the edges of the moment? They are always a surprise.

Like what could happen on a stroll in the city?

Casson: Yesterday, I saw something completely wonderful. There is a church in Bloomsbury, the Hawksmoor church, and I have been past that church many times.[35] Yesterday I happened to be in the street behind it and the back of that church is completely wild. That sort of thing keeps me quiet for a day.

I guess, we need to talk about the phrase 'narrative environment', because what in fact is a narrative environment? Compared to an exhibition? An exhibition has an entrance and an exit, usually, physically both precisely defined. Are those physical boundaries of the exhibition also the boundaries of the narrative environment? Or does the narrative environment have broader boundaries, starting perhaps long before one enters the exhibition? Extending perhaps way beyond the exit of the exhibition?

Mann: In an on-line age the experience of an exhibition begins and ends not just at the doors of the exhibition. An exhibition should not just be objects in showcases and panels on walls with the rest of the internal space doing nothing to enrich the story, it is up to us to use every part of that space to heighten the experience of the story. Particularly when we start talking about narrative thinking and implementing narrative environments in other contexts, like in hotels and offices. It's interesting for us after having done exhibitions for almost over ten years. We find ourselves making decisions about what materials to use on all these other planes and surfaces, which are no longer purely driven by style and taste and aesthetics. They're also now being driven by the question: are they saying what they are supposed to say?

Casson: It's uncertain, whether the word 'narrative' suggests a linear idea or whether it's something else? In an exhibition with its sequence of little stories, there is an overarching narrative which has to do with time. It's a temporal experience, starting in one place, ending in another. What I'm getting more and more interested in is this bigger, multi-strand exchange, which is still perhaps a narrative. I keep thinking of when you walk into a cathedral, for example – because a cathedral is a narrative space, in the sense that each part of it has its meaning. And whatever liturgy you relate to or have interest in, those spaces mean something slightly different. But interestingly, in many cathedrals you can come in at any point. You don't always come in through the west door, you might come in through the east door. And you can understand all that, because the narrative, if you like, is familiar. It's a multi-strand thing. Somehow there are many many stories all happening at once, and you can hold them. This is what interests me at the moment.

Ulysses by James Joyce is the story of one day told with a multitude of perspectives, organised in various chapters with contrasting protagonists.[36] Reading Ulysses **is like entering your cathedral through many doors simultaneously, perhaps?**

Casson: But in a book you can only read one line at a time.

But being in that church at point A and remaining there for two hours because you're fascinated, that flow of time is also continuous. So, how do we want to understand this idea of the narrative environment? If we talk about exhibition in the traditional sense, it's

objects in showcases, paintings on the wall, lighting, some text, an architectural structure. But if you look at it as an experience, suddenly the flow and structure of time become extremely interesting and transform our focus on the exhibition medium.

Casson: Whatever exhibition you make, there's always a chronology in the sense that you arrive in the morning at ten o'clock and you leave two hours later at 12 o'clock. Within that time span you take a route, which could be the one the designer or the curator suggests that you take. Another way is that you set up a number of sensations and let the visitor move freely around and construct their own sort of linear narrative. In that case, both curator and designer know what the options will be. There is a point of entry and a point of exit. Between those points the visitor is always guided in a gentle way, no matter how openly the narrative is structured. But it starts to get interesting when it gets three-dimensional. For instance, in the museums about individuals like Churchill or Franklin that we have worked on recently, we are trying to paint a 3-D picture of somebody, literally like a Cubist painter, combining a multitude of perspectives into one frame. In this case you want your visitors to come in at any point and to start from there and find new ways of looking at the material – perhaps in a way you haven't anticipated. And that's when it gets exciting. And potentially chaotic of course.

I'm very much attracted by your metaphor of the cathedral. This cathedral is a sacred place, and perhaps a profane place at the same time, depending on your state of mind. But the cathedral is offering a multi-threaded narrative for everyone. Its narrative is partly unfolded, perhaps. But all the elements are there, the liturgy for the mind and icons for the eyes. So, isn't it far more exciting to focus on the composite potential of this multi-strand narrative, instead of breaking it down into singular threads of story?

Casson: It goes completely counter to everything else I think about life. What this scenario is suggesting, in a way, is that you give the visitor choice about what they do, what they see and what they learn, which direction they're going, how long they stay. You know? It's up to you to decide. Generally, I'm very anti-choice. I've had my fill of choice, I don't like it. I want editors. I want people to help me. I expect experts to help me choose things, because I think making choices is very, very tiring, if you don't know what you are doing. Why are you making these choices? What are the criteria for your decisions? But in this particular case, I think it is quite interesting.

The question is: is it choice or is it participation? No matter how detailed your exhibition will be, surely you can't control my experience entirely and you only structure my decisions to a limited extent?

Casson: You can't escape the fact that once you're in that thing, whatever you do, you're making a series of decisions: choices.

When I visited the Churchill Museum, I felt travelling through his life was like crossing the London Tube.[37] According to the various lines, I would meet Churchill in a different way. If we use this network of Tube lines as a metaphor for ways of reading a subject, then we're almost at the point of entering your cathedral – ?

Casson: There was an exhibition about national identity at the Boilerhouse in the basement of the V&A, which originally was the Design Museum.[38] That exhibition was laid out as a matrix. There were a number of portals, one for each country. And if you went through that portal, you saw a line of products which came out of that country. A motorbike, a piece of food, shoes, whatever. So, you could look at all the things which came out of Japan, for instance. But next to the country-portals, the matrix was governed by theme-portals as well. So, if you entered through the motorbike-portal, you got an overview of motorbikes from Japan to the United States. It was a very simple idea and a very interesting matrix. And actually the Dada exhibition last year at the Centre Pompidou in Paris had similar things.[39] They set up these vistas, which quite unexpectedly offered diagonal views of the exhibition landscape. Very unusual. Suddenly, you were picking up objects and ideas, which were running in other directions.

The nice thing about your cathedral, about *Ulysses* and about the matrix-exhibition is that it is all there, simultaneously. That's why the analogy of the Cubist painting, offering a multi-perspective universe, is so relevant. Perhaps the narrative environment, as we like to see it, is just the immaterial equivalent of the material display of objects and things?

Mann: We live in time and a two-hour experience is linear. If you then force that into a linear physical experience, with a start here and an end there, including a linear story, like we're going to tell you this here and that there, things get more and more controlled. It is nice that we can afford for people not to have the same experience as the person next to them. Then it becomes a matter of working with the confines of the spaces given, and with the curatorial experts – because we almost never curate our exhibitions ourselves. So there is always a sort of compromise, finding an agreed way of doing it. But we enjoy making each segment of the experience as different as the next one, so that there is freshness, big things and small things, so that there is a whole variety of experiences. The worst kind of exhibition would be like a route of which there was no breaking. Something like a boring maze, a maze where there is only one route to get through. A maze without an assignment and only a few dead ends. You can't see where you're going, you've got no sense of where you are, of what your commitment is in terms of time. I think it's important to give people the ability to gauge their own visit.

Could you describe the profile and characteristics of a typical CassonMann exhibition?

Casson: I think it's very hard for us to say. You tell us.

Well, I've seen some of your work before, and yesterday I saw some four or five other presentations in addition to that, which were all very different. My overall impression now, however, is that there is a tendency towards landscaping. Except for the 'Camouflage' exhibition in the Imperial War Museum, which was a bit disappointing to me, because unlike the British Galleries and unlike 'Digitopolis', the 'Camouflage' exhibition didn't offer this large-scale environment into which I was immersed.[40] The 'Camouflage' exhibition offered one way of reading the collection, whereas the British Galleries try to combine various ways of reading the content. I think this dimension of creating an overall environment, which is a seducing vehicle for a part of a narrative at least, seems to me to be a consistent part of your work. It's about landscaping, I would say!?

Mann: Yes! Landscape is certainly a preoccupation and one of the things we try to do. 'Camouflage' was an attempt to do an abstracted landscape that supported the narrative, but we ran into a few problems with the client in the middle of the project. One half of the client just wanted it to be simple: an art gallery space. So, it got problematic. In the end we made it as good as we could, given the circumstances. The underlying landscape concept is there but not as rigorously developed as it should have been. Do you think of the British Galleries as a landscape, Dinah?

Casson: I don't know. Perhaps, because of the scale of it. There is a vocabulary of display, which is recurring, so that there is a loose overall landscape, but I'm not sure, if it works like that there?

While preparing the interview, I was thinking of Capability Brown, and it is just a hypothesis for now, but I sense there is a correlation between Brown's thematic landscapes and the CassonMann exhibition-

scapes? This morning I visited the V&A and the sunlight was falling onto the museum building from the Cromwell Road side. And because of this light and the way it invaded the space and was reflected by those patterns of colour and form, I sensed the British Galleries very much as a landscape, as a landscape in which a narrative was embedded, as a narrative environment. But the other CassonMann characteristic for me would be the rich detail, which was also lacking in the 'Camouflage' exhibition. The carefully crafted desks in 'Who Am I?', for instance, are definitely a part of the story and a part of the pleasure of being there.[41]

Mann: Certainly in this country, a lot of exhibition designers are not also interior designers. They only do exhibitions and they come from an exhibition background. We do maintain quite a level of what we call interior design in our spaces, attention to detail. Apart from all the intensity of storytelling, we add to our burden by also wanting to make well-crafted interior design. We are enjoying the way in which that comes together. So, I think that runs through everything we do, where we can afford it, where it is allowed to be so.

I think the rich detail and the narrative landscape are consistent, because if you walk outside in a natural landscape or in a cityscape, this alternation between scales of vision, between close-up and wide-angle view occurs as well. Amongst impressive vistas you might be struck by an astonishing detail. Perhaps the preconditions for structuring perception in an exhibition may be found here? There is a nice thought about that in the work of Samuel Beckett. Beckett speaks of 'the eye of prey', which I always understood as the basic condition for capturing the right intensity and richness of things – in reality, on stage, and it might apply to exhibitions as well.[42] **Beckett's 'eye of prey' describes a layered kind of perception, in which two sorts of vision would work simultaneously. More or less like a bird of prey combines the wide-angle overview of the hunting site with the**

extreme zoom-in on the target.

Mann: That puts it in a nutshell, what we do here every day, I think. It's jumping the scales all the time.

Casson: I think we're a bit softer than Beckett. I saw *Happy Days* the other night and it is completely extraordinary.[43] It's haunting. It is tough. There is a little bit perhaps of it. We don't tend to do a lot of retrospection. You know, if you look at it too closely, it would all fall apart. That feeling. And also, if you look at it too closely, there is a chance that it would be too difficult to move on. Maybe that's why it is not easy for us to say. I think one of our weaknesses may be that things get too layered, too rich. That there is too much going on in a tiny space. I'm quite keen on deciding what is appropriate at any one point. That's easier said than done, of course. What you might think is appropriate isn't perhaps appropriate. You might think it is not appropriate to do something very rich, but actually it is really appropriate in the end. Or it comes and creates its own appropriateness.

Tell me about your design process. Your exhibitions and museum displays are complex environments, composed of space, colour, light, objects, text and time-based media. Where do you start? How do you get to grips with this mix of media? What stages of development are there in a CassonMann project?

Casson: There is always another player in all of this. The client, the curator or host, whoever that is, sometimes has already a kind of idea about how the exhibition should be. Often, one is responding to that.

Mann: Because of the creative pitch system in this country, quite often you're taking these first steps without a huge amount of information from the side of the client. You might have a brief, but there is very minimal client contact. I think, knowing how complex the space is going to finally get, we're spending quite some time getting a clear diagram which is going to underpin it all. Certainly in the Churchill Museum, we had to deal with quite a problematic space. What we actually pitched with was a logical, rational, quite simple concept for how we were going to manipulate the space. Then, the ensuing months were really to do with testing to see if that concept worked as a sort of vehicle. After having assured the client, and ourselves, that this thing was robust and could support the story, we then began to layer the layers on to this skeleton structure. I think this is true for most of the galleries we do. Before we get too far into the content, we develop a big idea, which is informed by our knowledge of the subject at the time, which obviously is not great, but hopefully sufficiently informed by enough content.

Casson: I think that is quite true. With Churchill we knew very early on that we needed a lifeline, even though the client said they didn't want a lifeline – a timeline. They had just wanted to use 'chapter-headings'. So, in a way, our push was finding a way of making that timeline engaging. That was critically important.

Mann: We knew, in that particular instance, there was an inevitable chronology to the exhibition, because it was about the man's life. We also knew that the linear experience of the rest of the Cabinet War Rooms was kind of exhausting and that we wanted this space to be much more loosely structured.[44] So we could very easily have done a guided route through the maze of columns, but we chose to set up a structure, whereby the lifeline began as a kind of device in the middle of the room that forced you to go around the room in a clockwise motion. As long as you did that, at the same time you were free to go where you wanted.

Casson: We realised, also, that one of the problems in a room like that was orientation. Because it was completely impossible to know where you actually were in this structure. So, the table became a sort of lifeline in the other sense, offering the visitor something to holding on to.

Mann: All I'm saying is that this was a diagram which wasn't described by the content. There was a chronology and we dealt with that not in the normal way. Churchill aside, I still think there is a search and a need for a certain, fairly simple, underlying structure.

dinah casson and roger mann

Could you tell me a bit about the big idea of Sellafield?[45] **You stated before that the CassonMann work looks good in pictures. I think that's true for the Sellafield pictures I saw. I wanted to go there to check that out, but it was actually too far away to squeeze a trip to the North into my schedule these days, so I have to rely on beautiful pictures once more.**

Mann: I can't guarantee that it is still there. The starting point was when British Nuclear Fuels were told by the government to get open and honest about what they do.[46] They realised that nobody would believe them, whatever they said, so they needed a kind of body who would be perceived to be honest and open to do this for them. So they approached the Science Museum, assuming people would believe what they say, and asked them to develop an exhibition on nuclear energy at Sellafield. The Science Museum's response was only on the condition that they had total editorial control. We came on board on the same basis, with the Science Museum as our client. That was the starting point. Then, with the museum, we decided to create an exhibition that would be a debate about the pros and cons of nuclear energy, about what the options were, what the future of nuclear energy could be. So, it became a forum for opinion. Lots of words – and the last thing a visitor of an exhibition wants to do is read. We then came up with the idea of an immersive space in the middle of the exhibition, in which animated text would be revealed or concealed to and from them in ways which would sufficiently intrigue people, so that they almost get tricked into reading texts. These animations became so beautiful and were so compelling to engage with, that you got drawn into reading what the text was saying, which were actually hard-hitting views on the subject. I guess we have been inspired by Barbara Kruger here.[47] Her texts are not moving in space, but she demonstrated the power of a text-based space, which we saw in an exhibition here in London, prior to the Sellafield project.

We wanted 100 per cent text, but the client wanted imagery as well. The content-team of the Science Museum

space.time.narrative

were insistent on imagery, for reasons of accessibility. Some people don't read very well. Images would help the understanding of it. I was worried the images would make it easier to ignore the text. That was the thinking. But British Nuclear Fuels never liked it. They agreed to it, but never liked it, because it was too critical. (We have subsequently learned that the exhibition has been removed.)

In your text 'The Piccadilly line' you describe your Underground brain activity on the way from your office in Holborn to the field of operation in South Kensington, where in fact three of your clients are located: the V&A Museum, the Science Museum and the Natural History Museum.[48] How different is or was your frame of mind, depending on to which museum you were going?

Casson: They are radically different clients, yes! The first thing which actually glues the three of them together, however, is that they are all national museums, which are properly funded. So, they have people, they have resources. For example in the British Galleries, at any one time there were probably sixty or seventy people in the museum, working on the British Galleries in some way or another, which is extraordinary. The situation for the Wellcome Wing of the Science Museum was not much different.[49] Those were both our first big museum projects. Then, we started a project in Newcastle for example, which is a bigger project in fact, but is entirely done by three people.[50] You realise that outside this national group, the world of museums is completely different. It has taken us a very long while to realise and to find ways of helping these regional museum to somehow deal with what it is they start. In Newcastle they said: we take everything out, we buy a dinosaur and we're going to be the best museum in the north of England. Three people, you know, who have to do everything. They have to run the entire museum and build their temporary exhibitions themselves. It's just a gap between aspiration and reality.

The British Galleries is dealing with a time span of

dinah casson and roger mann

400 years, from 1500 until 1900. In 1500 Britain was importing technology, skills, knowledge, style, art, anything to get things going and to enrich economic and cultural life. Whereas in 1900, Britain was an empire in many senses and the greatest producer of knowledge and an exporting power of technology. So I'm curious how this leading idea got embedded in the presentation? We have already compared the British Galleries to a huge narrative landscape. So, my question now is: do these two notions, the idea of Britain's transforming role and the metaphor of the landscape, blend or come together at some point in the layout of the galleries?

Casson: I think it is much more like your Capability Brown idea of that literal sort of language, like a journey through a park of some kind, where there are set pieces and if you stand at that particular point and you look in a particular direction, you would see a wonderful composition. And it all looks incredibly informal, not man-made at all. Just natural, organic. I think, when you're showing objects, your contribution as the architect, if you like, has to be very supportive. So, the touch should be light. There is no opportunity really for making big gestures. Whenever you go to a gallery of objects which has big gestures, the gesture becomes very oppressive, particularly after a bit of time. Whereas in a thematic gallery like the Science Museum, you need the big gesture, because ideas need a form to sit on. So, here is where my word 'appropriate' comes in. There is an appropriate weight of touch. I like installations where the hand of the designer is light, but just present enough for you to feel that you are being handled nicely in some way. It's just getting that weight right, which I think is very interesting. And that weight varies from project to project. The 'Camouflage' exhibition had to have quite a lot of weight, because the voices of the curators were all over the place and the objects were all over the place. To try and glue those silly hats and shoes together with this very serious business of killing people, was quite difficult. In Sellafield the subject was very difficult and the audience very resistant to hearing anything which they didn't like. Before our exhibition,

80 per cent of the people who went there thought nuclear energy was a great idea. British Nuclear Fuels employs some 30,000 people and there is nothing else to work up there in the North. So, in a way, people are forced to think it's a good idea and it is very important that they are not worried about leukemia. Our exhibition was of course saying all these things. Just for that, you have to have a very strong installation to get across something to which people are basically resistant. Finding that balance is not very easy to do.

One of the difficulties I had with the 'Camouflage' exhibition was that it was almost entirely referring to the material world, not to the mental world, whereas camouflage as such is a highly mental phenomenon as well. There was this tree: a metal tree which could cover up one soldier and function as a watch post. The watchman had to stay in that tree all day, because they could only be moved at night. What a story! A forest of metal camouflage-trees seems to me to have an almost mythological potential. So, camouflage, decoy, distortion on a mental and mythological level would have extended and deepened the exhibition in an interesting way, and perhaps could have given the presentation a Protean nature, so that the world of forms and appearances would have changed as soon as the visitor came too close?

Casson: Well, that exhibition, I mean the subject without the street stuff and so on, needed a space of minimal eight times the actual size, because the stories are just fabulous. The Imperial War Museum couldn't do it, or they refused to do it.

You wrote me once that it took the Imperial War Museum 15 years to respond to your original idea for the 'Camouflage' exhibition, which makes me curious as to what this original idea was?

Casson: It was a wonderful subject for an exhibition. It was a wonderful subject for a film. It was a wonderful subject for a book. My original idea was that we could do all three together. The film was partly because the last group of people who were doing this work were still alive. There were two things which I really liked about it. One was that the Royal College of Art was set up on the back of camouflage, because Robin Darwin, who was director after the war, was running the camouflage and all his camouflage-people went in as the first generation of professors of art.[51] They were all in camouflage. The other thing which I always liked very much about it, is this meeting of two cultures, of the artist and the soldier, who are not natural bedfellows. So, the long-haired bohemian resistant artist, forced into army gear, to work alongside and to teach these guys how to disguise themselves, is just a wonderful moment. And, as far as I know, it is one of the few times in history, apart from Leonardo of course, where the skill of the artist, of the scenographer, is suddenly on the front line.[52] The battle of El Alamein in North Africa, which turned the war, was based entirely on cardboard tanks.[53] But there are no cardboard tanks in that bloody exhibition. All of that stuff is just not there. My idea originally was to tell that story.

That's fascinating: war as a major scenographic event?

Casson: Well, the best story was about this very famous camouflage designer, who is not in the exhibition unfortunately, who taught everybody about camouflage and made some cardboard tanks himself. The general came down to inspect them and looked at these tanks and said: good god, these things are useless! You can tell a mile off that they are made of cardboard. Get rid of them! The designer then said: but the real tanks are underneath, sir. That was what El Alamein was about. These are wonderful stories.

In the exhibition, there is one astonishing piece of historic film: four guys, soldiers, are running onto the scene to set up an inflatable tank in just a couple of minutes!

Casson: Fantastic!

So far, we have put quite some emphasis on space, on form and image. I would like to shift a little bit towards time. Stories, no matter how intelligent our spaces are, imply time. Dinah talked in Basel about the linearity of a narrative.[54] The integration of these two key elements, of telling a 'story' in an 'intelligent space', would result in a narrative environment, wouldn't it?

Casson: As you know from my little piece in Basel, I was quite critical of this phrase: 'narrative environment'. It has a tendency to be a single thread. For me it is the multi-thread, it is the sort of weaving, which is interesting. Wagner's Rhinemaidens, if you like.[55] What is interesting about exhibitions is that you have no control, really. You set up these moments, but unlike a composer of music, for instance, you have no control over the tempo in which this thing is received. It's different from film, where you have a sort of passive experience. But with books and with exhibitions people can do what they want. Of course that can be very rich in itself, because the visitors always do things which you never expect. They respond in a way you never expect, which is fantastic. Incredibly important. That's a kind of wild card. But the phrase 'narrative environment' has always suggested to me, I may be wrong, a sort of single thread. I think all narratives have other threads, because what is going on in your head is in your response to what you see.

I think that the way the phrase has been used, over the last five years, has rather reduced it in a way. It is suggesting that if you set up a number of little stories within the context of one big story, that's actually it. And it is not that. It's more complicated.

I must confess that since Basel, I'm less and less convinced about this word 'narrative' being useful for what we do. I mean, yes, it's narrative in so far as visiting an exhibition is a temporal experience, like going for a walk in the woods. But an overarching narrative doesn't often come from us, as a construct. Mostly the overarching narrative is chronological, but that's kind of boring. The sort of narrative that we would more engage with is the spatial narrative, if you like, which might be connected to intelligent spaces. This has much more to do with going on a journey. With breathing. It is a little journey, which is connected to your lungs. You're looking big and then you're looking small. You're looking through and then you're looking back. Then you're turning round and round again. It is a sort of ballet of the head, that you are trying to construct. More than that, there is this word again: 'narrative'. Maybe my interpretation of this word 'narrative' is much too tight?

You would rather read 'narrative' as a dramaturgical notion? Narrative understood as a process of reception in the mind of the visitor? Like walking through the landscapes of Capability Brown? A stroll through the streets of Paris? Collecting bits and pieces of information at random? Assembling them in an overall experience which is linear and called 'narrative'? Is that it?

Casson: Yes, but perhaps this is less true for Roger than it is for me? But in museums, there is usually a top-down storyline imposed by the curator. And hitherto, we have not made exhibitions which have come from us. But my experience of narrative, if I'm reading a story in a book, or if I'm listening to somebody telling me something, if I'm watching a movie, it is not just that. It is always that, plus the other stuff, which just turns up. Isn't it?

In your presentation in Zurich in early 2006, you said: 'visitors are no empty buckets'.[56] If you think of an exhibition as a narrative environment, the entire thing is a process of participation. There is a part which is brought in by the curator and designer and there is something the visitor brings in.

Casson: I think that was a big lesson that we learned from the British Galleries. And we learned that all the people in these rooms who are looking at your architecture, if you like, are full of stuff. They bring along their past and their present, their memories and fantasies. You simply can't live in the naive notion that they are not full of stuff. So, if you can open a little gap which allows some of that to come out, the narrative environment would become much richer.

A friend of ours describes projects always like little paper boats. And you sort of craft these paper boats. Then you put them in the water and push them off. And then they start their own life. That's what exhibitions are. They interact with visitors and they provoke visitor responses, which are outside anything that you might have anticipated. So, all you're doing, in a way, is setting up a framework or a little structure, which is very fragile.

If you think of the exhibition entering a new phase at the time of its opening, because it is understood as a process of participation with the visitor, isn't there a need for a sort of control which is forcing you more in the direction of curatorship? Simply because such an exhibition would demand a degree of conception which goes beyond the task of designing a functional space with elegantly lit objects?

Mann: We're moving in that direction. We're getting more confident in contributing to the curatorial share. We are much more critical, if we think it's not good or could be better.

Casson: I think we've always been, actually.

How about an exhibition like 'Sparking Reaction' in Sellafield? Weren't you the curators there as well? Because the question is: can you communicate with the visitor, understanding the exhibition format like we just said, without being the curator?

Casson: A part of that exhibition – 'The Core', which was the name, we gave to that projected space in the middle – was absolutely our idea. There was nothing in the brief that was asking for something that did that in quite the same way. The exhibition on nuclear energy, around the periphery of that interactive element, is what the Science Museum was heavily into and that was really where they were going. But we thought we needed to do something much more immersive and theatrical to communicate it. So, we drove it. It was our thinking. But they then fed the content in as researchers. I guess we did quite a lot of editing and pushing, in terms of: we need more material. We orchestrated it.

The exhibition medium is increasingly reflected on in terms of the theatre, these days. The introduction, especially in German-speaking countries, of the notion of scenography, is one example. We have been talking about narratives and dramaturgy, about language and metaphor. To what extent is that relevant for you? How do your exhibitions relate to the theatre or to theatrical dynamics?

Casson: The main difference of course is the degree of control. In the theatre you're controlled, in the exhibition you're not, as a visitor. In the theatre you sit in the audience and the curtain goes up and the director and the actors are sort of telling you what you are going to get, when. But of course all the stuff in your head is the same. In an exhibition it is very important that you set it all off, keep things spatially apart. The studies of how people go into spaces that they're unfamiliar with are very interesting. If you watch someone walking into an exhibition for the first time, you may see that visitors are attracted by things which are faintly familiar. It can be any thing. It is a sort of process of identification and reassurance. To take on something completely new, which you have never experienced before, is very rare.

Is a CassonMann exhibition, apart from the physicalities, thought of in terms of staging?

Casson: I don't think so, actually. That rather suggests: here is a scene and there is a scene and a walk from this one to that one. It doesn't quite work with the landscape metaphor. The landscape is closer to what we do. Finding a way of setting a big scene up, within which there are things happening. It's slightly different, I guess.

In a landscape, interestingly, one could make a 'scenic' walk.

Mann: The scenic walk tends to be about a series of viewpoints.
Casson: And little surprises round the corner. I think it is more like that.
Mann: We are actively setting these moments up and we are very aware of it.
Casson: It's a fantasy. We make fantasies.

In his book *The Empty Space*, Peter Brook describes the two realms of theatre. On the one side of the theatre-space there is the audience, which enters the auditorium through the foyer. On the other side of the building the actors enter their play-world through the backstage entrance. These two realms are divided physically by the proscenium and immaterially, if you like, by the so-called 'fourth wall'. And the whole point about theatre, Brook states, is if – whether or not – these two realms get linked, during the average two hours that the performance lasts. Isn't this true for exhibitions as well?[57]

Casson: We're doing this project on Stanislavski in Moscow. So the theatre is in the front of our heads at the moment.[58] Stanislavski talks about the fourth wall in a slightly different way, because he is focusing on how you get actors to do their job. He often would rehearse with the curtain down. Then there is a moment when the curtain goes up and the fourth wall is gone, or rather changes, and as an actor you're faced with the audience instead. Suddenly it becomes an intelligent wall, if you like, because it is responding, coughing and laughing. Of course he talks about these moments of intense concentration and focused silence. That's the ambition of every performance.[59]

Brook opens his first chapter in his book with the words: 'I can take any empty space and call it a bare stage. A man walks across this empty space whilst someone else is watching him, and this is all that is needed for an act of

dinah casson and roger mann

theatre to be engaged.' Transferred to our context: what would be the bottom line in terms of exhibition?

Casson: It's one object in the middle of an empty space, or one word written on a wall. You need a mark, which might be an image, a word or an object. And you need somebody to watch it or to visit it.

Mann: Well, you can have an exhibition that no-one goes to. It's like a book before someone has bought it. It's a potential. It's about to do its job. Despite all the rehearsals, theatre only becomes itself when you finally do it in front of a live audience.

Doesn't it all come down to the heart of dramaturgy? We are talking about narratives. The story is the connecting part in the chain between narrator and listener. There is no story if there is only a storyteller. Neither so, if there is only a listener. Let alone if there is only a story. The story has to be delivered and must at the same time be received. Speaker and listener are hinged upon the narration. If one of these three elements in the chain of communication fails, there is no flow of narrative.

Mann: The whole of a theatre production before first night is done with the sole intent of communicating with the audience, and it is the same with an exhibition. All our endeavours over the years are adding up to the opening day and the rest of its life. We're not like some writer or painter who is actually doing things for himself. It's completely the opposite. We're doing it for that moment and for that life, until it stops on the day the exhibition is closed.

Casson: Assume you're in the National Gallery and it is ten o'clock at night and you walk into a room full of paintings without visitors.[60] Something happens when you walk in, you could imagine you could write a wonderful story about what these paintings are discussing when you're not there? Do they exist when you're not in? It only gets interesting when the spark is happening. I think it all depends on the way things are structured. The majority of our projects work towards this moment of the opening. Our involvement is usually over after that. But it would be very nice to try and find a way of making an installation which starts like that and evolves over time.

Will CassonMann still be making exhibitions in five years' time? What will they look like?

Mann: I hope so.

Casson: I think so, but I hope they'll be completely different. I think we're learning all the time. Certainly one of the things about us, which I always thought was actually quite a good thing, is that I still don't really know what we do and how we do it. So, when a new project comes in, I very rarely think: oh, that's easy. I tend to think: oh, how the hell do you do a thing like that. When I was working in the furniture industry, there was a brief: design a table. I thought: what is a table? Somehow all your knowledge is worth nothing, because the reality of the next task is completely new. That's terrifying. And intriguing, of course.

Mann: There is such a thing as instinct. When you ask me about what inspires me, I'm very aware that I'm feeding off everything I've ever listened to or seen. When I'm confronted with a brief, all that comes in in terms of problem solving. I can't quite analyse the process; sooner or later, the germ of the idea always seems to come. And I don't know from where it comes, half of the time.

Casson: Stanislavsky told all of his actors that they had to see and read and listen and travel all the time. You have to feed yourself and be absolutely aware of what's around you. But to answer your question, I think that we will still be making exhibitions, but whether they're exhibitions in museums or whether they're exhibitions in funny places or maybe they're exhibitions as something else, I don't know. But I think, probably, that what we've been doing the last twenty years will always be part of it.

Notes

1. 'The Treasures of Tutankhamun', British Museum, London, 1972.
2. 'Light Fantastic', Royal Academy of Arts, London, 1977. See: Anton Furst et al., *Light Fantastic*, Bergström & Boyle, London, 1977. Also: Sandy Boyle, *Light Fantastic 2: A New Exhibition of Holograms*, Bergström & Boyle, London, 1978.
3. The International and Universal Exposition, in short Expo 67, was a Category One World's Fair, held in Montreal and Quebec, Canada, from 27 April to 29 October 1967.
4. R. Buckminster Fuller (1895–1983), The Biosphere, US pavilion at the Expo, Montreal, 1967. Fuller's pavilion was a geodesic sphere, a thin shell structure based on a network of geodesics (circles) lying on the surface of a sphere. The so-called 'tensegrity' principle (tensional integrity) of continuous tension and discontinuous compression was developed by Buckminster Fuller in close collaboration with the artist Kenneth Snelson (b.1927), who had produced his innovative X-Piece, based on this principle, in 1948, after artistic explorations at the Black Mountain College in North Carolina, USA, where Fuller was lecturing.
5. The Festival of Britain was a national exhibition held in London and throughout the country, in 1951, not only as a moral impulse to the city which was in large parts destroyed in the Second World War, but also to commemorate the first World Expo ever, which had taken place in Crystal Palace in South Kensington, 100 years before.
6. The Whitechapel Gallery (founded 1901) is situated on Whitechapel High Street in East London.
7. 'Visions of Japan', Victoria & Albert Museum, London, 1991.
8. CassonMann Designers, 'British Design: New Traditions', Museum Boijmans Van Beuningen, Rotterdam, 1989.
9. Malcolm Garrett (b.1956) is a British graphic designer, who has worked for music artists such as Simple Minds, Magazine, Duran Duran and Peter Gabriel. See: http://www.malcolmgarrett.com/.
10. CRT: Cathode Ray Tube.
11. Tom Dixon (b.1959) is a Tunisian-British furniture designer, who is now Creative Director of 100% Design. Dixon also runs Design Research Studio, which specialises in interior design schemes and projects. See: http://www.tomdixon.net/. Also: www.designresearchstudio.net.
12. Paul Smith (b.1946) and Vivienne Westwood (b.1941) are renowned British fashion designers.
13. Dinah Casson and Roger Mann, Grangelato, Knightsbridge, London, 1984.
14. Habitat is a UK-based international retailer of household furnishings, founded in 1964 by the English designer, restaurateur, retailer and writer Terence Conran (b.1931).
15. Dinah Casson was teaching at Kingston Polytechnic (latterly Kingston University) from 1974 until 1993.
16. CassonMann Designers, The Garden, Science Museum, London, 1996.
17. CassonMann Designers, British Galleries, Victoria & Albert Museum, London, 2001.
18. David Mlinaric (b.1939) is an English expert in historic decoration. See: Mirabel Cecil and David Mlinaric, *Mlinaric on Decorating*, Frances Lincoln, London, 2008.
19. Nigel Coates (b.1949) is an English architect, interior designer, author, and furniture

20   designer. See: http://www.nigelcoates.com/. See also essay 2, 'The Envelope', p.415.
20   Lancelot 'Capability' Brown (1716–1783) was an English landscape architect, well known for his thematic landscape gardens.
21   The father of Dinah Casson was Sir Hugh Casson (1910–1999), architect, director of architecture of the Festival of Britain exhibition in 1951, Professor of Interior Design at the Royal College of Art in London from 1955 to 1975 and later President of the Royal Academy (1976–1984).
22   Vico Magistretti (1920–2006) was an Italian industrial designer, known principally as a furniture designer and architect.
23   Charles (1907–1978) and Ray (1912–1988) Eames were American designers, married in 1941, who made major contributions in the fields of modern architecture and furniture, as well as working in industrial design, fine art, graphic design and film.
24   Eileen Gray (1878–1976) was an Irish furniture designer who played a pioneering role in the Modern Movement in architecture.
25   Vladimir Nabokov (1899–1977) was a Russian-American writer, poet and critic of literature.
26   Anna Politkovskaya (1958–2006) was a Russian journalist, publicist and human-rights activist. She was murdered by gunshots in the elevator of her apartment on 7 October 2007.
27   Frances A. Yates, *The Art of Memory*, Pimlico, London, 2001.
28   Thomas the Tank Engine is a fictional anthropomorphic steam locomotive created by the Reverend W.V. Awdry as one of a number of characters in his Railway Series books, first published in the 1940s.
29   The National Portrait Gallery in London, founded in 1856, is as much an historical as it is an art museum, as it houses a collection of portraits of historically important and famous British people, selected on the basis of the significance of the portrayed, not that of the artist.
30   Gabriel García Márquez (b.1927) is a Colombian writer, who became well known with his novel *One Hundred Years of Solitude* (1967) and won the Nobel Prize for Literature in 1982. Salman Rushdie (b.1947) is a British-Indian novelist and essayist. His fourth novel, *The Satanic Verses* (1988), was at the centre of a controversy that led to a fatwa issued by Ayatollah Khomeini, the Supreme Leader of Iran, in February 1989.
31   Michael Heizer (b.1944) is an American artist who specialises primarily in large-scale sculptures and earth- or land art.
32   Johannes Vermeer (1632–1675) was a Dutch painter who lived in the city of Delft. Diego Rodríguez de Silva y Velázquez (1599–1660) was a Spanish painter who was the leading artist in the court of King Philip IV of Spain. Rembrandt van Rijn (1606–1669) was a Dutch painter and etcher who lived in the cities of Leiden and Amsterdam, and was renowned for his treatment of light. Piero della Francesca (c.1415–1492) was an Italian artist and mathematician of the Early Renaissance. Jean Auguste Dominique Ingres (1780–1867) was a French neoclassical painter who was renowned for his portraits, both painted and drawn.
33   'Velázquez', National Gallery, London, 18 October 2006 to 21 January 2007.
34   Sir Gordon Howard Eliot Hodgkin (b.1932), generally known as Howard Hodgkin, is a British painter and printmaker whose work is most often associated with abstraction.
35   The church referred to here is St George's Church, Bloomsbury, built between 1716

and 1731 – the last of Hawksmoor's six London churches. Confusingly perhaps it has a statue of George I on the top of the steeple – even more confusingly wearing Roman dress. Nicholas Hawksmoor (1661–1736) was one of England's few baroque architects. A pupil of Sir Christopher Wren and Sir John Vanbrugh, he worked most of his life as a surveyor and as a 'completer' of work by his masters; but he was a genius in his own right.

36 James Joyce, *Ulysses*, Everyman's Library, London, 1997.
37 CassonMann Designers, Churchill Museum, Cabinet War Rooms, London, 2005.
38 The Boilerhouse Project, first venue of the future Design Museum in the basement of the Victoria & Albert Museum in London, founded in 1981. In 1989 the Design Museum moved to its present location in Butler's Wharf on the south bank of the river Thames, London. See: http://designmuseum.org/. Dinah Casson is referring to the 1985 exhibition 'National Characteristics in Design', curated by Stephen Bayley (b.1951) and designed by Jon Wealleans (b.1946).
39 'Dada', Centre Pompidou, Paris, 5 October 2005 to 9 January 2006.
40 CassonMann Designers, 'Camouflage', Imperial War Museum, London, March 2007, and 'Digitopolis', Science Museum, London, 2000; for British Galleries, see note 17 above.
41 CassonMann Designers, 'Who Am I?', Science Museum, London, 2000.
42 Samuel Beckett, *Imagination Dead Imagine* (1965), in *The Complete Short Prose*, Grove Press, New York, 1995. For 'the eye of prey', see also essay 1, 'The Battery', para.1.4, pp 30–33.
43 See: Samuel Beckett, *Happy Days* (1961), in *Collected Shorter Plays*, Grove Press, New York, 1984. See also: *Happy Days*, film version: http://www.youtube.com/watch?v=TekdYnjIzvM.
44 The Churchill War Rooms (formerly the Churchill Museum and Cabinet War Rooms) is a museum in London and one of the five branches of the Imperial War Museum. The Cabinet War Rooms are an underground complex that was used as an operational command and control centre by the British government throughout the Second World War.
45 CassonMann Designers, 'Sparking Reaction', Sellafield, Cumbria, May 2002.
46 The Science Museum in London was commissioned by British Nuclear Fuels to develop the 'Sparking Reaction' presentation in the Sellafield Visitors' Centre.
47 Barbara Kruger (b.1945) is an American conceptual artist, known for her critical juxtapositions of imagery and text.
48 'The Piccadilly line' was the text of a lecture given by Dinah Casson at Kingston University, London, in 2002.
49 The Wellcome Wing is an extension to the Science Museum in London, which was funded by grants from the Heritage Lottery Fund and The Wellcome Trust and opened in June 2000. The Wellcome Trust was founded by Sir Henry Wellcome (1853–1936) and is a global charity dedicated to achieving extraordinary improvements in human and animal health. See also: *Frame* magazine, *The Exhibition Issue*, Amsterdam, March/April 2001, pp 64–71.
50 CassonMann Designers, Great North Museum, Newcastle upon Tyne, 2009.
51 Robin Darwin (1910–1974) was Secretary to the British Camouflage Committee during the Second World War and recommended the use of artists, designers and architects for the work. When he was appointed to take charge of the Royal College of Art in

space.time.narrative

London after the war, he appointed many of his camouflage colleagues to professorial posts. Apart from Hugh Casson, there were also Richard Guyatt, Julian Trevelyan, David Pye and Robert Goodden.

52   Leonardo da Vinci (1452–1519) was an Italian artist, engineer, inventor and writer. He is considered to be the archetypical Renaissance man, a *homo universalis*, a person with a multifaceted and well-developed talent.

53   The First and Second Battles of El Alamein, fought not far from Alexandria in Egypt, against the so-called Axis forces of Germany and Italy, in 1942, marked a major turning point in the Western Desert Campaign of the Second World War.

54   Dinah Casson at the 1st International Scenographers' Festival IN3, Basel, 24 November 2006.

55   The Rhinemaidens are the three water-nymphs who appear in Richard Wagner's (1813–1883) opera cycle *Der Ring des Nibelungen*, 1876.

56   Dinah Casson at the 'Museum in Motion' seminars in Museum Bellerive, Zurich, 15 February 2006.

57   Peter Brook, *The Empty Space*, Penguin Books, London, 1990. See also essay 1, 'The Battery', paras 1.6, 1.7, pp 51–66.

58   Constantin Sergeyevich Stanislavski (1863–1938) was a Russian actor and theatre director. For Stanislavski's method of acting, see: Colin Counsell, *Signs of Performance*, London: Routledge, 1996, chapter 1.

59   CassonMann Designers, 'Stanislavski Museolobby', Moscow, 2008.

60   The National Gallery, Trafalgar Square, London. See: http://www.nationalgallery.org.uk/.

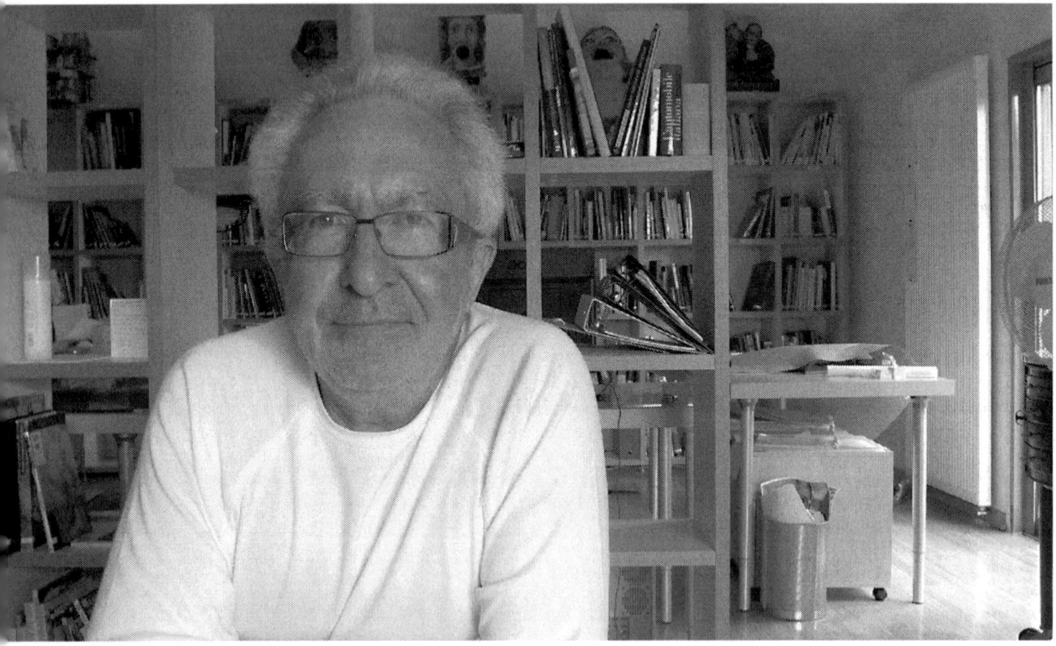

Interview with
françois confino

François Confino (b.1946) is artistic director of the Confino agency in Lussan, France. The first time I heard of him was in 1986, when the Centre Pompidou exhibition maker Jean Dethier told me about an upcoming exhibition which was expected to be a sensation. Dethier was referring to the exhibition '*Cités-Cinés*'. I visited that exhibition shortly after its opening in 1987 and it became a landmark in my experience. So, when I was in the position to initiate a research project focusing on the narrative potential of the exhibition environment, Confino had to be part of it. I didn't meet François Confino until October 2005. I had travelled to Lussan to talk and to invite him. I'll never forget his speedy style of driving to the restaurant, a few villages away, that evening. Our interview was held in two parts. Part 1 took place on the inner court of a restaurant in Turin on 10 April, part 2 on an early Saturday morning in Lussan, 2 June 2007, the day when the portrait on the opposite page was shot.

space.time.narrative

Which was the first exhibition that really touched you?

Confino: The first exhibition that touched me was the World Expo in Brussels, 1958. I found the Philips Pavilion by Le Corbusier with Iannis Xenakis and Edgar Varèse for the music most impressive.[1] It was the first time a modern expression was mixing sound, light, architecture and special effects. At that time the USSR was competing with the USA for getting the largest pavilion. I also remember that Expo very strongly too, because in the Russian Pavilion I saw the first Sputnik and in the American Pavilion I saw the first colour television. For a child of 13 who knew already that he wanted to make architecture, it was a wonderful experience. But I also have to mention my second strongest impression, which was the Swiss Expo in Lausanne, 1964.[2] After that experience I decided that architecture alone wasn't enough and from that moment on I wanted to focus on exhibition design as well. The Swiss Expo 1964 in Lausanne was a very original approach towards exhibition-making at that time, conceived by architects with a lot of imagination, which many of them seem to have lost today. There was a pavilion about consumption, for example. Imagine, it was the post-war era: 1964 was only 19 years after World War II. In Europe phenomena like supermarkets were first to be discovered. But in Lausanne some of these new concepts were directly translated into the design of the exhibition. The exhibition on consumption for instance had to be visited in a shopping cart. I loved it. I just loved it. I didn't know the word 'scenography' by then, it didn't exist. But I imagined that architecture could be so much more than what people think it is.

How did you get actually involved in the exhibition profession?

Confino: I went through all sorts of classical architectural studies together with my wife Catherine at the ETH in Zurich.[3] But we always tended to make things a little more original than our fellow students. At the end of our study we spent one year in Paris, but we didn't want to get stuck in making buildings.

françois confino

We wanted to learn about urban planning amongst other things and we got a grant from Columbia University in New York. When we arrived there, we discovered that American thinking at that time was incredibly original. You could do anything. I mean, if you wanted to propose something, even a foreign student would easily find financing. So, I founded a film festival in New York in 1973 and repeated that in 1975. I made proposals for street festivals and then Catherine and I met Haus-Rucker Inc., the utopian group which was born in Austria.[4] Haus-Rucker was making studies, for instance, of how the roofs of New York could be used. They also developed very original approaches towards exhibiting. The range stretched from happenings towards all kinds of artistic expression. There were no limits. We were the limit and all the money came from sponsoring.

How important is or was Haus-Rucker Inc. for your later work? Could you tell me about the nature of your cooperation with the group?

Confino: Before Catherine and I met with Haus-Rucker we already had a very different way of learning. For example, we had a professor whose name was John Garber. He had a big beard – you know, it was the seventies – and he came to his lectures with his dog. We could bring our son, who was two years old, and put him in the back. In Zurich a thing like that would have been impossible. Garber gave a lecture on Eskimo communities. It had nothing to do with architecture, but he made us think about society and the related human problems in a wonderful way. There was another professor, who was teaching on utopias. We had already read about Haus-Rucker Inc. and their activities in a newspaper. I said I wanted to meet them and if you want to meet somebody in the States, even someone very well known, you just call the person and say that you want to meet him. In France you will need three months to even get in touch. So, the first day we met Haus-Rucker, we had a lot of conversation and it was really love at first sight. The next day we decided to work together. Haus-Rucker was a couple, like we were: Caroll Michels and

Klaus Pinter. He was Austrian, she was American. So, there were two couples. We started imagining all kinds of studies which we wanted to launch. For instance at one point I proposed a project for Iran. My mother had studied in Geneva, together with the prime minister of the Shah of Iran: a certain Mr Hoveida, whom she knew very well.[5] So I asked my mother for a letter of recommendation, which would introduce me to him. We discovered that in the past, there had been engineers in Iran who anticipated modern technique already some 300 years ago. It was in the seventies – the time of the energy crisis – and we said, let's propose a project on how people solved their energy problems in the past. So I wrote to Mr Hoveida and two weeks later we were invited to come to Iran. I spent three weeks there. I could travel first class, which I hadn't done in my entire life so far. There was always a jeep waiting to take me wherever I wanted to go. But the problem was that Ayatollah Khomeini came to power and three months after I met him, Mr Hoveida was shot. That was the end of the project.

What was the guiding principle of Haus-Rucker Inc.? Was everything done at random?

Confino: From the beginning it was agreed upon that there was no hierarchy. The group had no president, for instance. We were the four directors. Depending on the project, we would name one of us project-director. For instance for the Iranian project, where I had all the connections, I was the director. But for the Centre Pompidou which demanded an artistic project, Klaus was the director, because he was the artist of the group. This was changing from project to project. We were brainstorming all the time and when we thought we had a good idea, we tried to push and to promote it.

You were driven by curiosity?

Confino: It was more than just curiosity. We were driven by a feeling that society needed a different view on things. But it didn't always work. Sometimes our ideas were too arty, or a little too much, or too abstract. Klaus Pinter was reasoning: if only ten people understand it, I will prefer it. And my point of view was: if 100,000 people understand it, I will prefer it. So we always had big fights. I remember we drank wine until four o'clock in the morning, fighting about the concepts, in the loft we had on Broadway. He was an artist, he didn't care. I was much more of an architect or a scenographer and I wanted the public to be happy and to have fun.

What kept you together? Political motivations?

Confino: Yes, the four of us were on the left side. At that time, I was even close to the Cuban movement. But our projects were not really political. Take our first approach for the opening exhibition of the Centre Pompidou: '*Archéologie de la ville*'.[6] When the Centre Pompidou was projected in Paris, there was a guy who had a little café exactly on the spot where building was to be erected. He refused to move. Our idea was to reinstall this café in our exhibition. People would discover this guy still remaining there and would be able to get a drink in his place. François Barré who was the director at that time, was very, very happy with this project.[7] The political dimension was how an individual may resist a project by society. If he has legal reasons and wants to fight till the end, maybe he will win. But we didn't want to make a political statement in the first place. We were looking for a different approach, for a way of solving things with fun.

Your story of '*L'Archéologie de la ville*' reminds me of way the Situationists explored and mapped the city. How important were Guy Debord and the Situationists for you?[8]

Confino: I don't know their philosophy well enough to answer that question.

You've been making exhibitions for more than 20 years now. If you look at it professionally, what distance have you covered since your first show? What did you win?

What got lost?

Confino: One of the first exhibitions I did was '*Cités-Cinés*', and it became so well known that I became Mr Cités-Cinés and everbody wanted me to repeat it worldwide.[9] We had a big discussion with François Barré, because he was involved very closely in that process. We said, do we want '*Cités-Cinés*' to be our trademark for the rest of our lives? We decided that we didn't want that. We could have made a lot of money. We were solicited from all over the world, China, Japan, everywhere. At the same time this fame was a chance, because it allowed me to do other exciting projects, like the Spanish Pavilion for the Expo in Seville, 1992.[10] People believed that what I was telling them was no bullshit. I was able to propose crazy things and they would believe it. Many architects and even friends in France wonder what I'm doing today. They don't know. For them I am still Mr Cités-Cinés. They haven't seen the other things which I have done, because my exhibitions were no longer in France. That's a kind of a handicap. I'm working worldwide. In Turin, for example, I am well known now as the man who did the Mole Antonelliana and in the near future I am probably going to be the man who did the Automobile Museum as well.[11]

But if you span a bridge from being Mr Cités-Cinés towards being Mr Mole Antonelliana, what covers that distance professionally?

Confino: Probably the most important point is that with '*Cités-Cinés*' I had no constraints. I was responsible for absolutely everything. Every square centimetre of it was ours. It was our invention. We had a roof above our heads and that was it. With the Mole Antonelliana we had a building which we had to respect. We had spaces that were very difficult: one big, tall space in the centre with only small spaces around it. And we had to deal with a collection. So, these projects were totally different in the way they had to be approached. '*Cités-Cinés*' was an exhibition of which I was the author. The Mole Antonelliana had to be turned into a museum. I wasn't in the position to say: your collection is a piece of shit and I'm not going to show it. On the contrary, it is the most wonderful collection in the world and I respected Maria Adriana Prolo, the woman who had collected it.[12] There was a given story to tell. And I liked it. So, I would say these projects are entirely different, except for the fact that they're both exhibitions on cinema.

You have been trained as an architect, but the major part of your profession lies within the field of exhibition-making. What is the difference? What is, could or would be the essential difference between architecture and scenography?

Confino: When I was an architect, I was just a good architect. Not the top. I'm not a Jean Nouvel, but generally in France I was considered as one of the good architects.[13] At some point I had the feeling of repetition, of not learning any more. I started getting bored. My associate at that time, Jean-Pierre Duval, was not bored at all.[14] He was talking about his style. But what is style? Ted Lapidus has a style. Christian Dior has a style. But it is all very superficial. Duval explained our architecture as 'movements of sliding volumes' and was talking about 'transparencies' that make things 'evanescent'. I could not speak like this, because it didn't mean anything to me. So, I started enjoying exhibition design, focusing on various subject matters. The exhibition '*Archéologie de la ville*', for instance, was a way of looking at our society from a future point in time, the year 3000. This was an effort to analyse what would remain of our civilisation in a thousand years from now. This question of framing the subject matter was much more interesting for me than the actual design of the exhibition itself. I started to enjoy the adrenaline of the first touch upon a solution. How to invent a frame through which the visitor may perceive the subject matter in a very original way? The invention of such a framework is a wonderful moment.

Does this mean that your anchor point is always in the subject matter?

Confino: Yes!

And once you found your anchor point, you need the right dose of adrenaline to let things explode in an appropriate form?

Confino: Probably.

In 2005 you published a book: Explosition**, with the subtitle '***François Confino Scénographe***'.**[15] **Could you say a few words to explain the title?**

Confino: The title is a joke. It's very simple. 'Explosition' works in French and I think in English as well. I like to characterise our work as an explosion of ideas, which we try to expose. So, it is a contraction of these two words. It's a bit simple, but we liked it.

I'm of course interested in the explosive part of it – ?

Confino: As long as a project doesn't explode, for me it is not a good project. At some point your public must be surprised. It's like walking behind somebody. If you suddenly make a bang or a lot of noise, the person jumps. I try to do that sometimes. I do not always succeed, but it's a little bit that spirit. I know so many exhibition designers who never offer any surprise. They are very very boring to me. In that respect I admire Uwe Brückner, because he also brings many surprises.[16] I think we have the same spirit.

In your book Explosition **you talk about your childhood memories and the trips you made to Algeria, Tunisia and Morocco with your parents. How important were these African trips for you?**

Confino: First of all, my father was someone who had a great sense of humour. All the time he was like second-degree joking, doing games with words etcetera. I kept that for my children and my children keep it for my grandchildren. It became the spirit of the family. My parents were travelling a lot. My mother was not working, but my father was an interpreter at the United Nations. So, we always were on a journey. Every other year the UN paid for a trip to the family's hometown. My grandfather was based in Algiers, so we got a first-class trip to Algeria. This was a wonderful experience, because we left Geneva by train, we arrived at the harbour in Marseille and a steamer would take us to Algeria in two-and-a-half days. From there we immediately left for Morocco and visited Marrakech, which was a similarly striking experience as visiting the Philips Pavilion at the World Expo in Brussels, 1958.[17] It just opened my mind and I remember these trips in North Africa as an incredible way of learning. Learning by smelling, learning by touching, learning by eating. That's the spirit of travelling.

What are your most important cultural references? What images do you see when you dream? What music do you hear when you close your eyes? Which book or theatre play changed your views? Which words echo in your head? Which people impacted your thinking and way of life?

Confino: One of the events which had a great impact was the assassination of Kennedy.[18] It is one of the most important events in the history of modern democracy. It showed that even underneath the surface of democracy, the worst things may happen. I'm sorry to say, but the second event that impacted me was 9/11 and the collapse of the Twin Towers.[19] I watched the film *JFK* by Oliver Stone recently.[20] The interesting thing is what they say about the lobby of people who are interested in making money with war. The speech in that film could exactly be the speech one would write for George W. Bush in the Halliburton case of our time.[21] The interests were exactly the same. There were people who wanted to push not only for political reasons but also for the reason of money.

If I think of cinema, all the films of Ernst Lubitsch and all the films of Billy Wilder come to my mind.[22] Why? Because Lubitsch and Wilder have this sense of humour, even in the most tragic films. And for me, humour is the most important human dimension. Even more than humanity. Even more than kindness. Even more than pity. Humour is a way of looking at things second degree. Of course there are many others, like Monty Python etcetera.[23] But Monty Python is at some points too much. Wilder is very subtle and Lubitsch is very very subtle. In theatre I went to see many of Robert Wilson's shows, which offer extraordinary moments of poetry.[24] In architecture, I like the work of Herzog & de Meuron, because they are very sober people who solve their issues in a perfect way.[25] What I don't like about Frank Gehry or Zaha Hadid for instance, is that they are repeating themselves at some point.[26] They seem to have reached the limit of their originality and their work has somehow become very boring now. The Disney hall in Los Angeles is a wonderful place, but after you have seen the Guggenheim Museum in Bilbao, you say nice, what's next?[27] And Zaha Hadid, I think, is very pretentious. In literature, I like all the books by Thomas Mann and by Stefan Zweig.[28] These are my two favourites. But I am also fond of Guy de Maupassant.[29] I can reread their texts endlessly. I tried to get interested in modern literature, but I never had the same satisfaction as from the engagement of Stefan Zweig for example.

When I think of '*Cités-Cinés*' in Paris, or the Mole Antonelliana in Turin, and now being here at your agency in Lussan, recalling our breakfast one-and-a-half years ago up there on the hill in your house, surrounded by books, masks and the automated piano from the World Expo in Hanover, I get this idea that you are living in a permanent, ever-extending exhibition. Or, thought the other way around: isn't every exhibition an extension of your living space?

Confino: Well, the exhibitions are not my home, because usually I never go back, once I have designed something and inaugurated it. It is very rare that I go back. And if I go back, it is just to show journalists or friends around. One of the reasons for that is that I avoid getting confronted with all the things that went and go wrong. Then I would like to change things, whilst everybody is happy and I'm not. But my house here and my atelier are my universe. It is my mind. So, when I see an object, I'm not thinking: is it the right object? If I have the money, I spontaneously decide to buy it. Why am I interested in that? I'm not even thinking about it. It is a spontaneous way of looking at objects. I had this period when I bought a lot of objects. But the house is quite full. My wife gets mad when I bring a new object. So, I stopped buying things. My books and my archive now have priority.

But do you agree? The place is a memory palace!

Confino: Oh yes! It represents the atmosphere of the various times.

When I visited the Mole Antonelliana for the first time, seeing that space, the light and all the things you brought together was of course a striking experience. But on my second visit, after having seen the baroque city of Turin and the Real Chiesa di San Lorenzo on the Piazza Castello, I had this sense of entering a church and I wanted to ask you: are you a religious person?[30]

Confino: At least, in my beliefs: not at all. My greatest pleasure would be to know, before I die, that there are living creatures elsewhere in the universe. Because it would destroy in terms of reasoning the monotheistic religions on earth. But there is another word for religion. For me the ethics are much more important, and the sacred. For instance the life of my granddaughter is sacred. It is not religious and that's a big difference. There are things that are sacred. I have many friends. When certain things happen, I need to talk to them and to tell them the truth about something. No lies. Telling the truth is sacred. So, I wouldn't use the word religion, but a friend of mine, Fabrizio Sabelli, is probably religious.[31] He went back to Rome, partly because of the attraction of the church and its ceremonies.

My point was, while visiting the Real Chiesa in Torino, one enters this baroque dome, a vertical space with all

these *cappelle*, which are filled with religious, catholic content. Beautiful light is pouring down from the ceiling and out of the curved niches of this baroque architecture. Then, entering the National Cinema Museum in the Mole Antonelliana, one is confronted with striking similarities. I know, originally the Mole was a religious building, but my point is that your *mise en scène* emphasises that quality and focuses implicitly on some sort of sacred truth. A long way back, I sensed that in '*Cités-Cinés*' as well. Did you ever compare the Real Chiesa and the Mole Antonelliana?

Confino: No, not really. When I first discovered the Mole Antonelliana there had already been an intervention by the architect Gritella.[32] He constructed these ramps. So, it was a building which was in between its religious origin and its transformation into something else. I was very intimidated by the space. When I saw it first, I said: this is not something for me. The building was too impressive in itself. Peter Greenaway was asked, just before me, to do the National Cinema Museum and he refused, it seems, for the same reason.[33] He came back to see what I had done. He didn't like my work and wrote: 'This is a very kitschy approach and I hate it.'

So the Mole Antonelliana, the vertical dream built by Antonelli, was a given fact. I didn't know the ramp was already there. But how about the elevator?

Confino: The elevator to the roof terrace had been installed there already in the fifties, but had been put out of operation, because it was too dangerous. It was not the invention of Gritella. But it is fun, being elevated in a church, through the dome, to the top, that's right. Your soul is flying!

Absolutely! I was waiting for the opportunity to fly high and lose my weight in this glass elevator exactly when the gods of cinema are projected onto the ceiling. I didn't succeed. I couldn't synchronise all these events. I was not in control. That would have been the ultimate moment. I thought François Confino is emphasising and reinforcing

françois confino

this vertical dream.

Confino: I intended to do so, but it was the only solution for that building as well, to be honest, and in view of the fact that the function of an originally religious building was taken over by a cinema museum. If we had left the dome unused, it would have been a huge mistake, because then we wouldn't have tried to exploit the connections between this empty building and the cinema museum. The other feature of the Mole is the main hall, which is surrounded by little chapels, the *cappelle*. In French, '*une petite chapelle*' is a group of people who think in a very restricted way. In analogy to that the Cinema Museum has a chapel of absurdity, a chapel of truth and lies, a chapel of mirrors etcetera. This was a natural solution.

These *cappelle* offer odd stories and experiences like sitting on a toilet seat whilst watching a movie. As a visitor, one has to get to grips with peculiar associations, triggering odd arrangements of thought, not much different from the religious stagings in the *cappelle* of the baroque church. And perhaps you don't agree, but in my view this choice is part of the internal logic of the Confino approach.

Confino: You have to let yourself be guided by the constraints. That's a very nice way of working. If I am in a fabulous place and the space is very small and it is a cinema museum and I like to have a big screen, I can't have that big screen. OK? In the Mole, we had to deal with a religious building. We looked in the dictionary: *cappelle*? Ah, *une petite chapelle*! This is a good idea. Let's go in that direction. Such an approach relaxes and prevents you from making your own style. If you look at my work over the last 30 years there is a style, which is non-style. If you look at the work of Frank Gehry, you see a style. It is his own style, mastered by him. My style is imposed by the environment which I am in and by the clues and traces of the content with which I am going to work.

Earlier we were talking about the stigma of being Mr

Cités-Cinés. For me, visiting the Mole Antonelliana helped me a lot in understanding and in appreciating your work. It helped me think about the truth in a Confino exhibition, about the Confino mythology, if you like. It explains a lot if you consider that to be the core of your projects. Suddenly there is some continuity revealed. But for the moment, I would like to get back to '*Cités-Cinés***'. Could you explain that title? And what was the idea behind connecting city and film?**

Confino: The first idea for '*Cités-Cinés*' came from François Barré. François Barré was the head of La Grande Halle de la Villette at that time.[34] And we had worked together at the Centre Pompidou on the inauguration exhibit before. He knew that I had a passion for cinema, and with the architectural school of Bordeaux he had discussed the possibility of organising some sort of festival about film on architecture and urban planning and things like that. I had done that in New York in 1973 and 1975, and also in Lausanne in 1979.[35]

Most of the documentary films on architecture I had seen were extremely boring. When I was lecturing at Columbia University, I invited my students to my home in the evening. I had a deal with the Museum of Modern Art in New York and they lent me 35mm copies of the greatest films like *Metropolis*, or *Things to Come*.[36] I asked the university to rent a big movie projector for me and so we made these home projections and had dinner together. That was real fun. Much more fun than looking at documentaries. So, when François Barré asked me to make this festival with documentary films, I said: no, François, this is not where the information is. There is much more information in fiction films. I said: give me two months and let me make a proposal. Two months later I came up with a project that was completely crazy, because it entirely covered La Grande Halle de la Villette and this was not what he had in mind. He had in mind a budget of 2 million French francs at that time and I had in mind a budget of 26 million French francs. Multiplied by 13. But he liked the concept so much that we immediately went to his president, who was fascinated. Everybody said: it is impossible, but let's try it. We were working at that time with Pierre-André Boutang.[37] Pierre-André Boutang was a filmmaker who was responsible for the television network Arte later on. Boutang was a nuisance, breaking down our ideas all the time. At the end we had to separate from him, because he didn't believe in it. He was a pain in the neck. He hated me later, because he saw the success. Then we started looking for money. Jacques Lang was the Minister of Culture and we went to see him.[38] He said: green light. It's a great project. Go ahead. At that time, Cinecittà in Rome was a very important place for filmmaking.[39] I visited Cinecittà. They had just made the movie *The Name of the Rose*.[40] Inspired by all that I said: let's call our project '*Cités-Cinés*'.

For many people, '*Cités-Cinés*' was an exhibition with a tremendous aftereffect. So much so that the exhibition has become an icon for exhibition makers and scenographers, even for those who haven't actually seen it.

Confino: Yes, still today. It opened doors in an incredible way.

What was the magic of '*Cités-Cinés*'?

Confino: It is very difficult to explain. The exhibition was very easy to understand. The visitor was in a world that didn't exist before. We made that, but we weren't aware of it. It offered an experience that was new for everybody. I guess that the Corbusier–Xenakis–Varèse Philips Pavilion for the 1958 World Expo in Brussels was a kind of new thing like this. I probably have this project somewhere in the back of my mind. But in '*Cités-Cinés*' everything was new. The possibility of eating in an exhibition. The possibility of sitting on roofs. The possibility of opening doors and discovering things which were hidden to the public. All these things didn't exist before. There had never been an exhibition like this before. There were probably some great experiences in the World Expos before. Also, on a small scale artists offered extraordinary experiences in installations. But at a scale of 6,000 square metres, it was new. People asked me if I considered myself to be an artist, and I always said: no, I am not an artist. I am an architect and an exhibition designer. May be I should have adopted the status of artist at that time. It would have made things a lot easier and I would have been in the position to say: well, I'm the artist who makes the biggest works of art in the world. Six thousand square metres is the minimum I want to work on. Everybody would have believed that and I would have easily found huge amounts of money to create things around the world. But I didn't choose to do that.

I saw 'Cités-Cinés' in La Grande Halle de la Villette in Paris in 1987. I was very impressed. Today, reflecting on its influence, I would say 'Cités-Cinés' materialised the idea of imaginary space, long before there was Internet. There was no virtual reality yet, so to speak – no CAVE, no AlphaWorld, no avatars.[41]

Confino: My main objective at the time was that I wanted people to enter the screen. Cinema allowed us to create what we can experience on the Internet today. But cinema is much stronger than Internet. The large screens of 'Cités-Cinés' made up the major part of the place. So, you could say, visually, the exhibition was constantly changing, because the dimensions of the screens were far more important than the fixed objects and things. With the 'Futures to Come' exhibition, which we are working on today, I want to go even further.[42] So that the people will really enter the movies.

The other aspect which contributed considerably to the impact of 'Cités-Cinés' was the fact that the visitor, the physical presence of the visitor, was an integral part of the scenography. As an active visitor you became part of the exhibition itself. Being there meant completing the exhibition. How do you regard the status of the exhibition at the time of its inauguration? Is it a finished product? Or is the process of development just tipping over and entering a new phase and developing further in a new setting? How open is this process?

Confino: You are talking about temporary exhibitions, but I apply the same methods in other places as well. The Automobile Museum in Turin will be a permanent installation. The ocean liner museum in Saint-Nazaire as well.[43] These places are adapted to changes as well. But if you take a book on architecture, for instance, and you look at the pictures, there is nobody there. The spaces are always empty. Most architects want their work to be photographed with nobody there. The day of the inauguration, for them, is the death of their building. Because they are shocked that people are going to shit in the toilets. The dirt is coming in. My work, on the contrary, becomes alive at the day of the inauguration. Before it was dead. That's exactly the opposite. But it is very difficult in advance to know if it is going to work. So far, it has almost always worked. Even in the strangest places. In my first exhibition, 'Archéologie de la ville', people were surprised, but pleasantly. I don't recall having made a place so disappointing that the next day the articles in the press were extremely bad. It has never happened to me, so I've been lucky.

In your book *Explosion*, the curator Fabrizio Sabelli refers to 'Cités-Cinés' as the founding project for a new type of exhibition, the *'exposition-spectacle'*, and he describes your profession as *'créateur d'exposition'*.[44] He characterises the Confino scenographical concept in an abstract of eight points. I would like to present them to you step by step and ask you to reflect on them. First of all, Sabelli sees: 'a principle of the arrangement of spaces, the architecture of which is inspired by a theme chosen in accordance with the message that the scenographer wishes to convey to the visitor'.[45] Could you respond to that?

Confino: Sabelli and I work a lot together and the most productive moment for us to work together is in the early stages of a project. For instance, for the Automobile Museum we started really thinking, what is interesting to say about cars? How can we conceive of spaces which tell the story of cars in the twentieth century in an appropriate way? We arrived at a number of major themes. My starting point is not: we must have ten spaces. I am saying we have to have ten themes. So, in this case we are going to have ten different spaces. It is always the subject matter which dictates the architecture.

Secondly, Sabelli suggests, Confino is seeking: 'a communication which is based on architectural structures that 'speak', that carry meaning, in the manner of early Christian, Romanesque, gothic and baroque religious buildings. These structures create an atmosphere that envelops the visitor continuously throughout his visit.'[46] Please comment on that?

Confino: When you enter an exhibition environment, you know that you are not in a normal place. The place itself is teaching you how you have to behave, at what you have to look, and in fact all the frescoes and sculptures in a church remind you that you are in a religious building. It's true that when I do an exhibition and it's going to be very immersive, all projections on the walls are part of the story, but they are telling the visitor, at the same time, that he is immersed in a sacred place with respect to the subject matter.

Sabelli's third characteristic would be: 'the implication of the visitor in the spectacle: to invest him, often despite himself, with the role of an actor; to give him a certain freedom to ascribe a meaning to the signs and spaces that are configured more as propositions aiming to invite reflection on themes than as occasions for the consumption of objects or of aesthetic forms.'[47] So, how central is the visitor in your projects?

Confino: When you are in a special place like a cathedral, even if you don't believe in God, there is still a religious feeling imposed on you, somehow. You are going to whisper. You are not going to run. But the choice of believing or not believing is still there. No different with exhibitions. When you enter a certain kind of space, for instance the space I showed you with all the eyes looking at you, probably, if we do it very well, also depending on the sound, on the degree of lighting, people will refrain from speaking loud. They will be impressed by being observed like this. They may say or think what they want, but the statement will be: spectator, I am watching you and you are becoming somebody who has an emotion, a feeling, and you are no longer behaving like you behaved in the preceding space. We are a bit naughty. We are manipulators. But it only lasts for two hours and we are not hurting people. So?

As the fourth aspect, Sabelli emphasises the narrative bandwidth from straightforward didactics to stories with a fantastic dimension: 'a stroll along a route, sometimes tortuous, the stages of which compose a story that the scenographer wishes to relate to the public; a narrative which, depending on the exhibition, takes the form of a fable, a fantastical tale or simply a story-message with a didactic essence that translates the theme of the exhibition into a scenographic form.'[48] This interests me a lot. Please tell me about your fables?

Confino: We never try to tell stories in an obvious way. Many museums do that and we don't need to do that as well. I am sorry to talk about the Automobile Museum again, but it is a good example, because 'automobile' is so much more than automobiles. It was the expression of the last century. It was the expression of individualism. It has transformed the structure of cities. But an average person who comes into an automobile museum is not ready to listen to these stories, because he came to see nice cars – and usually the visitors are macho guys who force their family to come along, and some children are happy, but the wives are not. If you change or widen the scope of the museum, so that the cars tell much more, rather than just being on a podium with good lighting, then you transform the subject and you bring people to discover the other dimensions of the car. We try to bring these added values into the exhibition.

There is for instance a car, the 40 hp Itala, which drove from Beijing to Paris in 1907 in 61 days.[49] Imagine the roads in 1907! Behind that event is a mechanic performance, but much more there is a human will to explore the world, and there is the courage to look at things in an original way, and all these stories are as necessary to present that car as just the mere facts of the nice mechanics. I had a big fight about that with the director last Wednesday. He said: this car made it because there was a new kind of motor. And I said: you are totally wrong. The motor was part of the issue of course, but there is also the fact that there were courageous people risking their lives. That's the other part of the story.

The fifth characteristic of a Confino exhibition, according to Sabelli, would be: 'a *mise en scène* **that reduces the descriptive function [of the exhibition] in favour of the extensive use of visual metaphors: poetic processes of the imagination which suggest and mask, at the same time, the concepts chosen to illustrate each thematic space'.[50] How important are metaphors in your scenography?**

Confino: If you make a museum, and if you are going to speak in that museum about Egypt or about the sea, and if you then propose a room with Egyptian statues or with photographs of the sea or the ocean, nobody is going to be surprised, because it is all first degree. And the spectator will say: oh yes! This is what I expected! One day I entered the British Museum in London and I went to the Egyptian section. There were interventions by Rebecca Horn and many other artists, and I didn't see Egyptian statues, but a very strange world of which a part was Egyptian.[51] And the other part was interpretation of what could have been Egyptian magic. And suddenly the entire presentation told me much more, because I was surprised and I wanted to see and understand more. The search for the right metaphor, in the initial phase of a project, is essential.

Sabelli's sixth point is about light: 'the use of fixed and moving images (cinema), their projection onto flat surfaces or three-dimensional structures, the whole associated with lighting effects; a way of re-creating atmospheres that are totally unreal and surprising, capable not only of stimulating the public imagination, but

also of making the messages more easily accessible'.[52] **Tell me about the syntax and semantics of your projections?**

Confino: Alors, we talked already about the use of projections, of images, fixed images, etcetera. I'm trying not to have the classic screens. Small or big, I try to avoid that. Of course sometimes we have screens, but if we have a real screen, I will bring the image down to the ground, so that the space shown in the film is at the same level as where you are. And not at a higher level where it looks like a screen. Projecting images on objects is like bringing two ideas together. For example, if you project a landscape on an Egyptian statue, the two elements are either contradictory, or harmonious and tell another message. We like to play with that a lot. But it has to be very well done, otherwise it will be very lousy.

The seventh point is about humour. Sabelli proposes: 'the inclusion of installations in the *mise en scène,* **in order to inspire in the visitor either laughter or a smile, or a critical reaction; a technique of provocation, the aim of which is to call out to the visitor and to establish with him a relationship of complicity, or sometimes even of disapproval'.**[53] **How provocative are your exhibitions?**

Confino: Well, we made the Musée Juste Pour Rire in Montreal and there we pushed the provocation and the humour very far.[54] At the entrance of the museum (it no longer exists) we had a scientist who was letting people in, and he gave a very serious speech about the 12 different types of humour. In the first room you saw these 12 forms of humour in glass showcases. In each of these glass cases there was in fact a second- or third-degree object, which was supposed to make people laugh in the genre that had been explained by the scientist. For the black humour section, the vitrine had fallen onto a little child and you would see only the two feet under the glass case. But in every exhibit we bring humour, because humour is the most wonderful characteristic of the human being. Maybe some cats have humour, if you see them smile. But the real humour is the privilege of the human being.

Sabelli's eighth point is about immersion: 'the organisation of the itinerary conceived as a sort of initiation rite during which one remains constantly immersed in the artificial landscape [of the exhibition], in order to avoid any breaking of the atmosphere'.[55] **If your exhibitions initiation rites, then what do they initiate?**

Confino: If we have two rooms and there is a corridor or a staircase in between, the corridor and the staircase has to be part of the *mise en scène*, because otherwise the visitor drops back to the state of his everyday conscience, and I want people to be totally manipulated – or at least, I want them never to walk away from the *fil rouge*.[56] For the initiation of the visitor, we usually work out the entrance. It is the point where one should forget about the world outside and where one enters an exhibition. I like, for instance, a long corridor. A corridor where the light is gradually dimming and the sound starts playing its part etcetera. In '*Cités-Cinés 2*' in La Défense, people walked through a corridor with microphones under their feet, and we transformed that sound as if they were walking on snow, because the first room where you arrived presented an Ice Age in the year 3000.[57] This is a *rite d'initiation*, because automatically you have the emotion or the feeling that you're part of an experience. It is different from entering any room in a normal museum. Likewise, the way one gets out of an exhibition is also very important.

In the Zurich seminars, in early 2006, you called yourself 'a professional liar'.[58] **In your book** *Explosion*, **there is a section called 'True lies:** *le musée mensonge*'.[59] **Please tell me all about your 'truth' and about your 'lies'. What's the importance of being a 'liar' in this profession?**

Confino: The first thing is to be aware of it, because you cannot reproduce reality. Never. So, in this case it's better to tell the public that you are maybe not lying, but imitating or faking. Whatever the right term may be. I thought lying was more provocative than faking. There is this sort of misunderstanding about the meaning of objects in a museum today. Why are they there? This doesn't necessarily count for the old objects. But for the new objects, like the new works of art by for instance Rebecca Horn or Anselm Kiefer and all these people, whom I admire very much.[60] You see their works in a museum usually, but they are already out of context. Even if the visitor admires the work of art, the relation between him or her and the work of art is never going to be the same as the relation between Anselm Kiefer and his work. I always try to include this second-degree aspect in the representation of the objects that I show, so that people know that I didn't show them as the most exceptional artefacts. I'm always trying to tell a little bit of a story about this context of the object.

Doesn't a 'lie' imply some sort of 'truth'? What sort of 'truth' may a Confino exhibition convey?

Confino: We had a big discussion on that in 1992, when we did the Pavilion of Discoveries for the World Expo in Seville.[61] That's the pavilion that got burnt completely, just before the Expo opened. We tried to get the original telescope of Galileo Galilei.[62] Unfortunately it was already reserved by the city of Genoa. In fact that was very fortunate, because it would have been burnt in the fire. Many people in the Expo said: don't worry, we are going to make a replica of that telescope. I said: no, that's impossible. If you don't show the real telescope, you have to say it and then it loses any interest. The real telescope is something with DNA on it, that you can almost touch. The DNA of Galileo on the telescope can't be replaced by an imitation. The real object can't be replaced by a copy, even if it's so well done that you can't tell it from the real thing. I don't believe in God or anything like that, but there is something in there, which is physical.

A few minutes ago I heard that the whole proposal of making this reality-television show on donating organs, in Holland, was a fake.[63] It was a joke, because they wanted people to be aware that donating living organs is a very rare thing to do and so, with that show, they proved that lying is a good way of getting to the truth. Here, at our office, we were very much shocked by that idea. But to come back to the main question: a museum is always a place of lies. I would like to insist on this, because all the objects which are found there are not in the right place. The nice thing about a museum, however, is, that it opens doors which are usually closed to the public. There is this ambiguity. And there is the question of context. The object is basically in the wrong place. So, how do you show it? Do you try to show it as if it were in the right place? In the new Automobile Museum in Turin, for instance, I do that. There is a wonderful handmade car, a Cisitalia, of which there is one copy in the Museum of Modern Art in New York and one copy in Turin. The one in New York is shown as if it were a sculpture in a white cube. Wonderful. In Turin, I show it as if it were under construction, with all the plans on the walls, together with the tools of the engineers. All these sorts of things. Who is right? The Museum of Modern Art presents the pure aesthetics of the car. The Automobile Museum emphasises the intelligence which lies behind the creation of that car. These are two points of view. I don't think that anybody is right or wrong, but nobody is telling the truth: it is, let's say, an 'interpretation'.

How important, in that respect, is the book by André Malraux – Le Musée imaginaire – for you?[64] Because Malraux emphasises the point that placing an object in a museum is an act of decontextualisation. The bigger part of the story remains out there, so there is a need for recontextualisation.

Confino: Most of the classical art museums, be it the Prado or the Louvre, don't really give additional information. When you are in front of Le Déjeuner sur l'herbe, you don't know why it was painted like this.[65] What was the story behind it? What were the notions on sexual activity at that time? All this information is not given to the public. Maybe it would be interesting to give at least some clues as to why such a picture was made in the first place. It became very famous. It is about female sex. It's very provocative. At that time it was much more provocative than it is now. Even children today are hardly shocked or surprised by it when they see it in the gallery. Then, there is the relation between the different objects in the exhibition space. The Tate Gallery in London, for instance, does that very well. They don't comment on one picture, but they group certain pictures in one room to explain a movement. Futurism, for example. Impressionism etcetera. In that case there is always a panel at the entrance of the room, explaining why this movement was born at the time, and why it died away.

You don't seem to me the type of scenographer who is that much interested in didactics. Your proposed presentation of the famous car in the Automobile Museum seems to show a magic object and a magical act of engineering in a magical *mise en scène*?

Confino: You're wrong. I am very much interested in the pedagogical message, except I don't want this message to be given to the public in the same way as in other places. I just came back from Turin and I had a big fight with the director of the museum. He said: where is the information? How do you communicate with the public? You have made nice decors, nice sets, but there is nothing else. I was really mad at him, because at the entrance of each bigger space, there will be an explanation, like in the English museums. They can be read in 30 or 40 seconds. Not more. It is printed in large typeface and hung over the heads of the people, so that more visitors can read the message at the same time. But that's it. Then the public goes out to see the cars. At discreet places, each car will have an explaining panel. Not only giving technical details, like the amount of horsepower, speed etcetera. That's not interesting. The information I give is about why this car is symbolic for its time. There are many reasons: the development of a new motor or the prestige of being seen in that car, or a car made for women, because it was easier to drive. All these little stories are also very important. In almost each of the spaces there will be sound, ambient sound and sometimes spoken commentary. There is for example a huge garage with 15 cars. We hear the mechanics discuss a new motor that has just arrived. Listening to that discussion is a way of getting immersed in that place. Then, there are projections of films. In Turin it will be a mixture of fiction and documentary films. At some point we arrive at *les années folles*, the 1920s.[66] At that time there were engineers who designed airplanes. Some of them were fascinated by cars, so they started to design cars like they designed airplanes. That is a fascinating story, which had not so much to do with elegant ladies, wanting to drive like Isadora Duncan.[67] Or with rich people, driving big cars. That was the other movement: *The Great Gatsby*.[68] In our movie we are going to show them both and at some points we are going to make interesting connections. For instance, Le Corbusier was very interested in cars and one of his good friends was Gabriel Voisin.[69] Voisin was an engineer who designed airplanes, and Le Corbusier drove a Voisin. That was one of the most innovative cars of those years. That's how the information will be on the screens, at the cars and at the entrances of the exhibition spaces. It's always a combination.

Coming back to the subject of the telescope of Galileo, the nice thing about that is that it is a vehicle for the story of truth and lie in itself, because the truth Galileo saw through his telescope was declared to be the ultimate lie at the time. But let me ask you a last question. If you had the chance to make an exhibition at free will, what sort of exhibition would you make? You once told me it would be about God! Is such still the case? Why?

Confino: Oh yes! But I guess the exhibition would get blasted the next day. So, it could only be done second, third, fourth, fifth degree. We did a competition for a museum in Lyon: Le Musée des Confluences.[70] For a long time people thought our plan was the best, but we finally lost. In our project the confrontation between human beliefs and science was central. This is what interests me a lot. If we do the Science Museum in Suzhou, I will bring back this subject matter.[71] One cannot understand science without understanding human belief first. Today, for instance, we are very critical about what we eat. But if you study the history of chemicals and eating, it is not a new story. Salt, vinegar, oil, all these things were invented a long long time ago. These sorts of subjects, I'd like to bring to the Milan World Expo on food, focusing on the religious rules related to food and why they exist.[72]

space.time.narrative

Notes

1 Philips Pavilion, Expo 58 (World's Fair), Brussels, 1958. Le Corbusier (1887–1965), born as Charles-Édouard Jeanneret-Gris, was a Swiss-French architect, designer, urbanist, writer and painter, well known for being a pioneer of what now is called Modern architecture or the International style. Le Corbusier was commissioned by Philips to conceive of a pavilion. It was Iannis Xenakis (1922–2001) however, working at the Le Corbusier office at the time, who became its senior designer. Xenakis was a Greek-French composer, music theorist and architect. As a composer Xenakis had a great influence on the development of electronic music. Most of his compositions are structured by mathematical models, by set theory and the use of various stochastic processes. Together with the French Edgar Varèse (1883–1965), Xenakis and Le Corbusier realised a genuine *Gesamtkunstwerk*, an interdisciplinary total work of art: *Le Poème Électronique*, which was set free from the usual need to display the company's industrial products and was supported in any way by the state of the art in electronics from the Philips Research Lab.

2 Expo 64 (Swiss National Exhibition), Lausanne, 1964.

3 François Confino studied architecture at the ETH Zurich from 1966 to 1970.

4 Haus-Rucker Co was a group of architects, artists and designers founded in Vienna in 1967 by Laurids (b.1941) and Manfred (b.1943) Ortner, Günter Zamp Kelp (b.1941), Klaus Pinter (b.1940), with others representing different disciplines. The group quickly became international, opening offices in Düsseldorf (1970) and New York City (1971), where the conceptual artist and writer Caroll Michels (b.1943) joined the activities as executive director. Haus-Rucker specialised in 'disposable architecture', pneumatic structures, air mattresses and life-support systems. Its projects, often featuring plastics, included Balloon for Two (1967), the external shell around the Haus Lange Museum, Krefeld (1971), and Oasis no.7 at Documenta V in Kassel (1972). Since 1972, the New York office has worked independently under the name Haus-Rucker Inc.

5 Amir Abbas Hoveida (1919–1979), Iranian political leader, prime minister of Iran (1965–77). After serving (1958–64) with the National Iranian Oil Company, he became (1964) minister of finance in the liberal government of Hassan Ali Mansur. When Mansur was killed by right-wing Muslim extremists, Hoveida was named (1965) prime minister. He continued his predecessor's policy of land redistribution and sought to maintain friendly ties with both the United States and the Soviet Union. Hoveida was re-elected in 1967 and 1971. He fell out of favour with the Shah in 1977, surrendered to the Ayatollah Khomeini in 1979, and was shot.

6 François Confino and Haus-Rucker Inc., '*Archéologie de la ville*' ['Archaeology of the Town'], Centre Pompidou, Paris, 1977.

7 François Barré (b.1939), co-founder of the Centre de Création Industrielle in 1969, former director of the Grande Halle de la Villette, president of the Centre Pompidou, 1993–6.

8 Guy Debord (1931–1994); see essay 1, 'The Battery', note 109, p.78.

9 François Confino, '*Cités-Cinés*', La Grande Halle de la Villette, Paris, 1987.

10 Spanish Pavilion, Expo '92, Seville, 1992.

11 François Confino built the Museo Nazionale del Cinema [National Museum of Cinema]

françois confino

      in the Mole Antonelliana in Turin in 2000. Since 2004 Confino has been developing the Museo dell'Automobile [Automobile Museum] in Turin, which is scheduled to open in 2010.
12   The Mole Antonelliana is a major landmark of Turin that is named after the architect who built it: Alessandro Antonelli (1798–1888). Construction began in 1863 and was completed 26 years later, after the architect's death. Originally conceived as a synagogue, the declining Jewish community donated it to the town while it was still under construction. Today it houses the National Museum of Cinema, which was founded after Maria Adriana Prolo (1908–1989) died and the town inherited her outstanding collection of pre-cinema-, cinema- and photography-related objects, posters and souvenirs. After a few local quarrels among architects, Turin Town Council awarded the Confino agency the project in November 1998, imposing record deadlines. With a touch of humour to highlight the former religious vocation of the building, Confino transformed it into a temple of cinema with its own series of chapels on a variety of themes. It is believed to be the tallest museum in the world.
13   Jean Nouvel (b.1945) is a French architect. His prize-winning design for the Institut du Monde Arabe (1981) in Paris brought him international fame.
14   Jean-Pierre Duval (b.1949) is a French architect who studied architecture and scenography at the École d'Architecture in Nancy. Duval was associated with François Confino from 1980 until 1993.
15   François Confino et al., *Explosition*, Éditions Norma, Paris, 2005.
16   Uwe R. Brückner (b.1957), architect, scenographer, founder of Atelier Brückner in Stuttgart. See the interview with Uwe Brückner, pp 319.
17   See note 1 above.
18   John F. Kennedy (1917–1963), the 35th president of the United States of America (and often referred to as JFK), was assassinated on November 22, 1963 in Dallas, Texas.
19   On 11 September 2001, two American civil airplanes, hijacked by the terrorist network Al-Qaeda, struck the two towers of the World Trade Center in New York, which made them collapse. The historical event, in which thousands of people lost their lives, initiated the American War on Terror and is generally referred to now as 9/11.
20   Oliver Stone (b.1946), *JFK*, 1991.
21   Halliburton Energy Services is a US-based multinational corporation, which became controversial because of its ties to vice-president Dick Cheney of the George W. Bush government and its alleged involvement in the Iraq War of 2003, for which the company was accused of gaining billions of dollars, in an audio recording by Al-Qaeda's founding leader Osama Bin Laden in April 2004.
22   Ernst Lubitsch (1892–1947) was a German filmmaker renowned for his humour and 'the Lubitsch touch'; Billy Wilder (1906–2002) was an Austrian-American journalist, filmmaker, screenwriter and producer. Lubitsch and Wilder both went to Hollywood and collaborated in the film *Ninotchka* (1939), starring Greta Garbo. *Ninotchka* was directed by Lubitsch on the basis of Wilder's screenplay.
23   Monty Python were a British comedy group that created the influential British television comedy show *Monty Python's Flying Circus*. Broadcast by the BBC from 1969 to 1974, the series was conceived, written and performed by Graham Chapman, John Cleese, Terry Gilliam, Eric Idle, Terry Jones and Michael Palin. Loosely structured as a sketch show but with an innovative stream-of-consciousness approach, it challenged the ac-

space.time.narrative

24   Robert Wilson (b.1941); see essay 2, 'The Envelope', para.2.1: 'A space full of time', p.391.

25   Herzog & de Meuron Architekten is a Swiss architecture firm based in Basel. Founded in 1978 by Jacques Herzog (b.1950) and Pierre de Meuron (b.1950), it is perhaps best known for the new home of the Tate Modern at Bankside in London and the Beijing National Stadium for the 2008 Olympic Games. Both Herzog and de Meuron have been visiting professors at the Harvard University Graduate School of Design since 1994 and professors at ETH Zurich since 1999.

26   Frank Gehry (b.1929) is a Canadian-American architect based in Los Angeles, one of whose best-known works is the titanium-covered Guggenheim Museum in Bilbao (1997); Zaha Hadid (b.1950) is a British-Iraqi deconstructivist architect, who was a partner of the Office for Metropolitan Architecture in Rotterdam from 1977 until 1980 when she founded her own office in London.

27   Frank Gehry, Walt Disney Concert Hall, Los Angeles (2003). The building is aesthetically comparable to the Guggenheim Museum, Bilbao (see note 26 above).

28   Thomas Mann (1875–1955) was a German novelist, short story writer, essayist and 1929 Nobel Prize laureate, known for his series of highly symbolic and ironic epic novels and novellas. Stefan Zweig (1881–1942) was an Austrian novelist, playwright, journalist and biographer.

29   Guy de Maupassant (1850–1893) was a popular French writer and is considered one of the fathers of the modern short story.

30   The Royal Church of San Lorenzo, Piazza Castello in Turin, designed by the Italian baroque architect Camillo-Guarino Guarini (1624–1683), was built in 1666–80.

31   Fabrizio Sabelli (b.1940) is a writer and a consultant, who specialises in economical anthropology. As associate professor, Sabelli was affiliated to the universities of Geneva and Neuchâtel, Switzerland, where he got involved in the development of scenographic concepts for the Musée d'Ethnographie. He contributed to the *mise en scène* of various thematic exhibitions, including the masterplan for the Expo 2000 in Hanover, Germany, which was directed by François Confino. Since then, Confino and Sabelli have collaborated on various projects, including the Los Angeles County Museum of Natural History (2003), the Museo dell'Automobile [Automobile Museum] in Turin (2003–4) and the Science Museum of Suzhou in China, which opened in 2008.

32   Gianfranco Gritella (b.1959) is an Italian architect, restorer, architectural historian and writer.

33   Peter Greenaway (b.1942) is a British artist, film- and exhibition maker.

34   See note 7 above.

35   François Confino organised film festivals in New York in 1973 and 1975, and in Lausanne in 1979.

36   *Metropolis* is a 1927 German expressionist film in the science-fiction genre directed by Fritz Lang (1896–1957). *Things to Come* is a 1936 British science-fiction film directed by William Cameron Menzies (1896–1957), on the basis of a screenplay written by H.G. Wells (1866–1946).

37   Pierre-André Boutang (1937–2008) was a French documentary filmmaker.

38   Jacques Lang (b.1939), is a French politician. Lang entered politics as a Socialist member of the French National Assembly from Paris in 1977. He is best known for having

served as Minister of Culture (1981–6) and (1988–93) and as Minister of Education (1992–3 and 2000–2002).

39 Cinecittà is a large film studio in Rome which is widely considered the hub of Italian cinema.

40 Umberto Eco (b.1932), *The Name of the Rose*, first published in Italian (*Il nome della rosa*) in 1980. *The Name of the Rose* was made into a film in 1986, directed by Jean-Jacques Annaud (b.1943) and starring Sean Connery as William of Baskerville and Christian Slater as Adso.

41 CAVE stands for Computer Assisted Virtual Environment, which is an advanced total-immersive simulation tool, initially explored by media artists, but because of the expenses mainly used in the automobile industry, in medical surgery and other scientific applications. The first CAVE was developed by the Electronic Visualization Laboratory of the University of Illinois in Chicago, and announced and demonstrated at the SIGGRAPH conference in Chicago, 1992. For AlphaWorld and avatars, see essay 2, 'The Envelope', note 88, p.453.

42 The 'Futures to Come' ('*Avenirs à venir*') project is planned to be a huge exhibition on the future, developed in close collaboration with François Schuiten (b.1956), Benoit Peeters (b.1956) and Serge Kirszbaum (b.1947). Its location has yet to be confirmed.

43 Escal'Atlantic, Saint-Nazaire, 2000. Saint-Nazaire is the town that gave birth to the *France* and to many other prestigious ocean liners. This is why the Town Council decided to open a museum to pay homage to them all. During the Second World War, Saint-Nazaire also had to shelter German submarines in an enormous bunker built by the Nazis. Indestructible and empty, it took the courage of the mayor to decide to convert the tragic remains into a cultural venue. It was here that the architect François Seigneur (b.1942) and the scenographer François Confino divided the bunker into two immense areas for each of them to work on. One was to be the outside of an ocean liner, the *Grand Large*, and the other, the inside of an ocean liner, from the engine room or the hold to the captain's gangway, not omitting the dining room, the hairdressing saloon and all the cabins.

44 Fabrizio Sabelli (b.1940). See: *Explosition*, op.cit. (note 15).

45 Ibid: '*un principe d'organisation des espaces dont l'architecture s'inspire d'un thème choisi en fonction du message que le scénographe souhaite adresser au visiteur*'; translation: Abigail Grater.

46 Ibid: '*une communication qui s'appuie sur des structures architecturales parlantes, porteuses de sens, à la manière des bâtiments religieux paléochrétiens, romans, gothiques, baroques. Ces structures créent une atmosphère qui enveloppe le visiteur tout au long de son parcours sans discontinuité*'; translation: Abigail Grater.

47 Ibid: '*l'implication du visiteur dans le spectacle; lui confier, souvent malgré lui, une rôle d'acteur; lui donner une certaine liberté d'attribuer un sens aux signes et aux espaces configurés davantage comme des propositions dont le but est de faire réfléchir à des thèmes que comme des occasions de « consommation » d'objets ou de formes esthétiques*'; translation: Abigail Grater.

48 Ibid: '*une promenade le long d'un chemin, parfois tortueux, dont les étapes composent une histoire que le scénographe souhaite raconter au public; une narration qui, selon les expositions, prend la forme d'un fable, d'un conte fantastique ou simplement d'une histoire-message à vocation didactique qui traduit en forme scénographique le*

		thème de l'exposition'; translation: Abigail Grater.
	49	Itala was an exotic car manufacturer based in Turin from 1904 to 1934. In 1907 a 7,433-cc, 35/45-hp model driven by Count Scipione Borghese won the Peking to Paris motor race by three weeks.
	50	Fabrizio Sabelli in *Explosition*, op.cit. (note 15): '*une mise en scène qui limite à l'extrême la fonction descriptive et qui fait largement usage de métaphores visuelles: des procédés de l'imagination poétiques qui suggèrent et masquent, en même temps, les concepts choisis pour illustrer chaque espace thématique*'; translation: Frank den Oudsten and Abigail Grater.
	51	Rebecca Horn (b.1944) is a German installation artist most famous for her body modifications such as *Einhorn* (Unicorn).
	52	Fabrizio Sabelli in *Explosition*, op.cit. (note 15): '*l'utilisation d'images fixes et en mouvement (cinéma), leurs projections sur des surfaces plates ou sur des structures tridimensionelles, le tout associé à des effets d'éclairage; une façon de recréer des atmosphères totalement irréelles et surprenantes, capables non seulement de stimuler l'imaginaire du public, mais aussi de lui rendre plus facile l'accès aux messages*'; translation: Abigail Grater.
	53	Ibid: '*l'inclusion dans la mise en scène d'installations afin de déclencher soit le rire ou le sourire du visiteur, soit une réaction de critique; une technique de la provocation dont le but est d'interpeller le visiteur et d'établir avec celui-ci une relation de complicité ou, parfois même, de désapprobation*'; translation: Abigail Grater.
	54	François Confino, Le Musée Juste Pour Rire (Just for Laughs Museum), Montreal, 1993.
	55	Fabrizio Sabelli in *Explosition*, op.cit. (note 15): '*l'organisation du parcours de visite conçu comme une sorte de rite d'initiation au cours duquel l'on demeure constamment immergé dans le paysage construit et cela pour éviter toute rupture d'atmosphère*'; translation: Frank den Oudsten and Abigail Grater.
	56	The *fil rouge* here is to be understood as the thread of the story laid out by the scenographer as a route through narrative space.
	57	François Confino, '*Cités-Cinés 2*', La Défense, Paris, 1995.
	58	'Museum in Motion' seminars in Museum Bellerive, Zurich, 18 January 2006.
	59	*Explosition*, op.cit. (note 15), pp 41–4.
	60	For Rebecca Horn, see note 51 above. Anselm Kiefer (b.1945) is a German painter and sculptor, whose work is characterised by the use of raw materials such as ash and straw in his paintings, and stone, lead and waste in his sculptures. Kiefer studied occasionally with the German artist Joseph Beuys (1921–1986) at the Staatliche Kunstakademie in Düsseldorf, in the early 1970s.
	61	Expo'92 in Seville was organised to celebrate the 500th anniversary of the discovery of the Americas in 1492 by Christopher Columbus. The Pavilion of Discoveries was one of the four theme pavilions proposed by Spain.
	62	Galileo Galilei (1564–1642) was an Italian physicist, mathematician, astronomer and philosopher who built a 30-power telescope, which allowed him to observe three satellites rotating around Jupiter with such scrutiny that the heliocentric cosmology, which the German astronomer Nicolaus Copernicus (1473–1543) had claimed in his *De Revolutionibus Orbium Coelesticum* (1543), could be proved.
	63	Endemol, *De Grote Donorshow* (The Big Donor Show), broadcast by BNN in the Netherlands on 1 June 2007. The show was a hoax reality television programme which

involved a supposedly terminally ill 37-year-old woman, Lisa, donating a kidney to one of three people requiring a kidney transplantation. Viewers were invited to send text messages advising her as to whom they thought she should choose as the recipient of her kidney. The show received heavy international criticism in the run-up to the broadcast, due to its controversial nature. In the end, it was revealed during the course of the screening that the terminally ill woman was in fact an actress, and that although the three candidates were real kidney patients, they were aware that Lisa was an actress, and participated because they supported BNN's aim to raise awareness of the limited number of organ donors in the Netherlands.

64 André Malraux (1901–1976), *Le Musée imaginaire*, Éditions Gallimard, Paris, 1965. Malraux was a French author, adventurer, statesman and France's first Minister of Cultural Affairs from 1959 to 1969, serving throughout the presidency of Charles de Gaulle.

65 Edouard Manet (1832–1883) was a French painter. His famous oil canvas *Le Déjeuner sur l'herbe* (1863) is currently in the Musée d'Orsay in Paris.

66 *Les années folles* in France cover the period 1920–29, from the end of the First World War until the beginning of the economic crisis.

67 Isadora Duncan (1877–1927) was an American dancer, considered by many to be the creator of modern dance. She died in a freak car accident. Duncan was fond of wearing large silk scarfs that were flowing in the wind, which looked good, especially when driving a cabriolet. This act of elegance, however, proved fatal in Nice, where her scarf, still draped around her neck, got entangled around one of the vehicle's open-spoked wheels and broke her neck.

68 *The Great Gatsby* is a novel by the American author F. Scott Fitzgerald (1896–1940). First published in 1925 as a critique of the American Dream, it is set on Long Island and in New York City during the summer of 1922.

69 For Le Corbusier, see note 1 above. Gabriel Voisin (1880–1973) was a French pioneer of aviation who created Europe's first engine-powered, heavier-than-air flying machine, and later became a major producer of military aircraft, notably the Voisin III, during the First World War, as well as designing and building exceptional automobiles bearing the name Avions Voisin during the 1920s and 1930s.

70 Competition for the Musée des Confluences, Lyon, 2006.

71 François Confino, Science Museum, Suzhou, China, 2008.

72 François Confino, 'Hollyfood', masterplan for World Expo 2015, Milan.

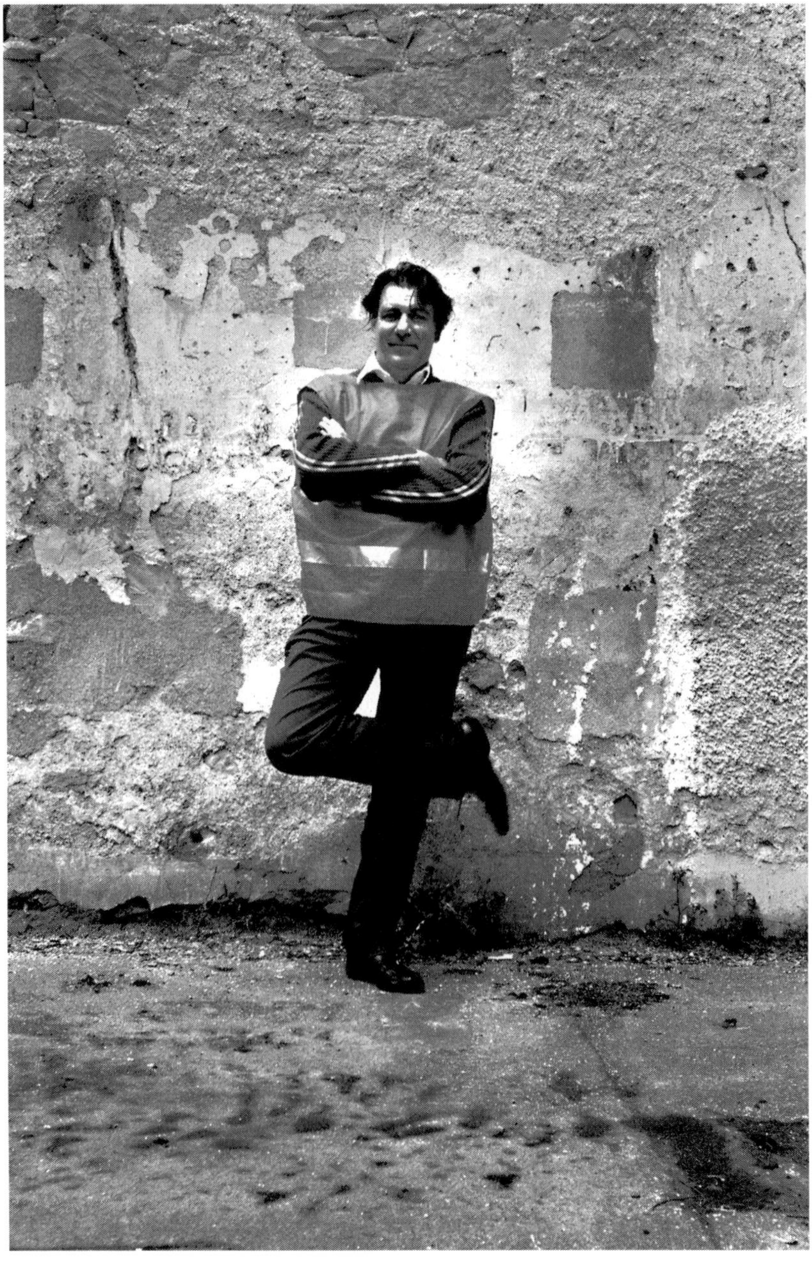

Interview with
Ruedi Baur

Ruedi Baur (b.1956) is the co-founder of the loosely arranged creative network Intégral, which operates partly undercover in different design disciplines and doesn't promote itself. This qualification pretty much resembles the *auctor intellectualis* of it all: Ruedi Baur. The various nodes of the network identify themselves with the formula: Intégral [Name]. So, there is an Intégral Ruedi Baur, originally based in Paris, now also in Zurich and in Berlin. I met Ruedi Baur in his Zurich office on a hot day in June 2004. We found a place outside in the shade, where I invited him to do a project in my Scenographical Design class. In return he invited me to do one in his System Design class in Leipzig, where he had been the dean of the Hochschule für Grafik und Buchkunst. I sensed much common ground and we've stayed in touch ever since. The following conversation was recorded in Zurich and on the Monte Verità in the southern part of Switzerland, on 13 September and 3 and 17 October 2007. Somehow we didn't manage to take photographs. The portrait on the opposite page was shot by Michael Scherrer in 2005.

What was the first exhibition that really touched and affected you?

Baur: The first exhibition I was consciously aware of and can still remember was Expo 64 in Lausanne.[1] I was young, eight years old to be exact, and my parents and I came from France to see the Expo. It's one of the first conscious experiences that helped me understand, later on, what a profound long-term impact extraordinary spatial events can have. The image within the exhibition space was less strongly influenced by media than is the case now. The real space was crucial. Experiments like those of Max Bill focused unambiguously on the relationship between exterior and interior space.[2] The information was secondary. What I particularly remember is the pavilion with the 360-degree film projection. This confrontation with a moving image that dominated the space was really fascinating, but seems utterly banal today.[3] And this constant, ritualised shifting between inside and outside: stepping out of one pavilion, finding yourself in an interior-exterior space, before sinking into the next inner interior world, was something that touched me deeply as a child, a special experience. It was my first encounter with scenography, though the term wasn't used for that kind of design back then.

Which exhibition aroused your interest in making exhibitions and for the exhibition as a multimedia communicative format? What guided your interests towards exhibitions professionally?

Baur: My route into scenography was far from direct. And I don't regard myself as a specialist in scenography. I want to make that clear right from the outset, though staging is an important element in my projects. I got into scenography via a long and circuitous route. I was fascinated by the potential of space as such as a communicative medium. Far more than by the specific format of the exhibition as such. I was interested in this idea of the conveyance of a subject matter. What can an exhibition do compared with a book or a website? For me, the problem of orientation, identification and information within a given space was crucial. How do you convey the subject matter in a spatial context through which the visitors move and in which they are embedded? This is a fascinating topic, one I'm still working on today.

When I wrote a book on new typography, at times I engaged deeply with the Constructivists.[4] I was astonished by the communicative capacity of the exhibition as medium, generally as well as in the specific installations created by El Lissitzky, László Moholy-Nagy and Herbert Bayer.[5] Their experiments were more or less the last act of the early avant-garde period, before the ideology of modernity was developed further, both functionally and pragmatically, in the 1930s. I found constructivist attempts to get to grips with space interesting. El Lissitzky's *Lenin Tribune* and 'Proun' rooms, the futurist Fortunato Depero's pavilions, Gustavs Klucis' radio tribunes, Lajos Kassák's kiosks and other similar experiments in avant-garde art sensitised me to scenography, which, interestingly enough, entered the realm of the avant-garde in the 1990s.[6] I also discovered the even more fascinating problem of the staged object in public space.

While I was training as a graphic designer with Michael Baviera, towards the end of the 1970s here in Zurich, I got to grips with contemporary art and a bridge was built for me between art and design.[7] I was very impressed by the Baviera family. Because I was interested in wayfinding, I applied for a position with Theo Ballmer in Basel.[8] Theo Ballmer had a very functionally oriented studio where I learned the basic know-how of wayfinding and was sensitised to text in architectural spaces. I went on to use this Ballmerian wayfinding in my own studio for a time, but I found it extremely boring and repetitive. I hadn't yet managed to come up with new approaches to it.

Were you simply driven into public space by your interest in the Constructivists, and perhaps your enthusiasm for the Pressa exhibition, for the orator tribunes and the cloud irons of El Lissitzky – all in fact manifestations of text in space and anything but expressions of New Objectivity – combined with your boredom with

functionalist graphic design?[9]

Baur: Absolutely. I was still very interested in architecture and at some point I was asked to create a sign-system in a public space. This is how the relationship between space and information, which I continue to regard as the core of my work, took centre stage for the first time. As a graphic designer I gradually found and adopted a new stance. That this new stance was far closer to scenography than classical wayfinding was something I became aware of only later. My boredom with functionalist graphic design, which no-one actually wants to look at, led me back to the experimental field of constructivism. For me, the confrontation with public space entailed an exciting political dimension because even the unnecessary, the beautiful or the unique fulfil important functions in relation to that which is necessary within society. I then went on to grapple with the rupture that occurred in the arts in the late 1920s and early 1930s, particularly in Germany and the Soviet Union. How does an avant-garde come to an end? Why is creative subversion transformed into functionalist boredom? Why was the Constructivists' enthusiasm for experimentation suddenly lost?[10]

How did you end up making exhibitions?

Baur: After working with Theo Ballmer in Basel, I founded a small studio here in Zurich, which began in the same way as all small studios begin.[11] In other words, we were asked to design notepaper. That really annoyed me. I made decent money, but after a year I looked for something else, because there was no scope for development there. So I went to Lyon with very little money and there I had the opportunity to work on some decent, important projects. In Lyon I got into the contemporary art scene quite quickly. I had the chance to design the catalogues for various museums. This opened up the possibility of renting a larger studio in one of the outlying districts of Lyon. I divided up the space as follows: one quarter for work, one quarter to live in and the rest was to be the exhibition space. It was there that I first began to think about the medium of the exhibition. To begin with my aim was simply to convey key aspects of design to my clients and the people around me. Put simply: how can I explain the things that get me so fired up? I believe we created a series of really important exhibitions there, which live on in people's memories. All of them with no budget. We just did it. Through dialogue with figures from the field of graphic and industrial design, like Sambonet, Enzo Mari, A.G. Fronzoni, Otl Aicher, Dieter Rams, Anton Stankowski, Peter Saville and Ross Lovegrove, I engaged intensively with the staging of creative works.[12] In small but high-quality exhibitions, alongside the objects themselves, our primary aim was to present the spirit of the designers.

A case of adding 'context to design'?[13]

Baur: Yes, exactly, even back then. But these exhibitions were not as yet major scenographic endeavours, more a kind of initiation into the relationship between graphic design, objects and spaces. Things then began to speed up for two reasons. First of all, the mayor of Villeurbanne, near Lyon, picked up on the idea, providing us with a more official platform. For three or four years we had a place at our disposal where we could create really professional and large-scale exhibitions.[14] Second, I was appointed by the École des Beaux-Arts de Lyon to head a department that was to be dedicated to urban design. The deal was that I would do 'something' with this department, which already included an artist and the scenographer Philippe Délis.[15] We had very little money and there was no proper basic course of study, as was the case in these art schools in France and as is, unfortunately, often still the case. In light of this, there were really only two possibilities for us. Either we could develop a classical course in the field of 'space', only worse than all the others because of the lack of money and capacity. Or we could take a totally new approach and develop something modest but original. Given the teaching staff's mix of professional experience, it was almost inevitable that we would go for the latter option and adopt an interdisciplinary perspective. We chose to focus on the theme of *espace-information*, our aim being to bring together the culture of space and the culture of information, graphic design and the new media. Our courses focused on those places where graphic design and architecture come into contact: exhibitions, wayfinding, reception rooms. A few years later we also began to offer a postgraduate course called 'Civic City'. This pedagogical project then gave rise to my first major exhibition, '*Mode d'Emploi*', and my collaboration with Philippe Délis in the field of scenography.[16]

[Interview question:]

So Lyon was a laboratory? Which period are we talking about here?

Baur: From 1984 to 1989, Lyon was a tremendous opportunity for me. There were lots of cultural institutes and almost unlimited possibilities. I worked at the École des Beaux-Arts a bit later on, from 1990 I think. By then I was already settled in Paris.[17]

I'd like to talk to you about the staging of text within space, as implemented, for example, in the Centre Pompidou, but also in the Kalkriese Museum in Osnabrück.[18] In your Bellerive seminar you stated that with Confino the text disappears, but with you it becomes ever more important.[19] When a graphic designer says something like that, people may quickly accept and understand it without asking themselves what exactly it might mean. When I visited the Kalkriese Museum yet another level occurred to me. This dense overlaying of texts on the glass surfaces between the display cases provoked a moment of positive hesitation in me and triggered an interval in which I really had to focus, as if I was looking through a camera and had to sharpen the image. This act of focusing requires time and prevents you from directly consuming what you see. It slows things down in other words, and I found that interesting. Can you relate to that?

Baur: I belong to a generation on the interface of two worlds. I was educated without computers but was then very quickly confronted with them. I simply had to learn how to deal with this tool. I had to invent a new logic for digital design and confront this with the old logic of analogue design. That was of course a very exciting moment, when new aesthetics and new forms of production were developed and suddenly a new form of space came into being through work done on-screen. Graphics were suddenly light, the depth came from behind, you could overlap layers, create transparencies and work spatially on two-dimensional graphics.[20] It took some time for us to become aware of this phenomenon and my generation was deeply marked by that. Just like the sterile perfection generated by this medium of the computer. The perfection of the machine is too perfect and therefore uninteresting. Throughout history, human beings have sought perfection and now attempt to compensate for the absolute perfection of the machine with artificially produced errors. A veritable paradigm shift. But that wasn't so clear at the time.

There were also interesting developments in real space. Walls became ever thinner. Spatial boundaries dematerialised and became multi-layered. The air between the transparent layers became part of this new form of wall. Graphics takes on the role of materialisation. The overlapping of two-dimensional graphic and constructive elements corresponds to the principle of the screen on a large scale.[21] This architectural development has also been a constant source of inspiration in various scenographic projects. What does multi-layered complexity mean in this medium? The opportunity to celebrate plurality? In the Centre Pompidou it's the plurality of languages that is concentrated in the form of information and which thus symbolises an openness to the world.

Is it because of this that you introduced the idea of the sandwich – two textual objects back to back with colour or light wedged between them – both in wayfinding and in the Centre Pompidou? Graphics extruding into the room?

Baur: In the Centre Pompidou we tried to develop wayfinding on the basis of a certain logic. This is the logic of the design of the information bearers, on which the graphic elements are distributed, embedded and hierarchised in space. The room itself becomes the bearer and the objects become information. Because of this it was also important to transform text into an object. With the doubling of the graphic elements and their spatial extrusion, this effect was achieved with few resources. The interspace was given a different colour and the information was illuminated like an exhibited object. This is how we staged and highlighted the gap that had been created.

This problem of multi-layered complexity is often a feature of my work. I'm interested both in the transition from the two-dimensional to the space or the object as well as the interactions that ensue. For a while, I unconsciously tried to conceal the fact that I come from a graphic design background. But now I've grappled enough with space to allow me to work autonomously on this space–graphics interface and celebrate it as a designer. In other words, I want to forget the whole problem of 2-D and 3-D and just look at the whole thing as a unity so I can really focus on the rhetoric and form of conveyance.

At the moment I'm working with the concept of '*inscription*', which links my work in the scenography of exhibitions with my work in the wayfinding field. The word comes from *scriptum*. What I'm interested in is the difference and interaction between '*inscrire dans l'espace*' and '*s'inscrire dans l'espace*', between inscribing the space and inscribing oneself into the space. Of course, the term '*inscrire*' not only has to do with text, but also with that which becomes readable through the text: the message.

An exhibition space must be readable, to a greater extent than other spaces. In this readable room, through his or her conduct, the visitor inscribes a new readability. This gives rise to a subtle relationship between the dance of the visitors and that which the space conveys. It also gives rise to interference between the intelligent visitors and our pre-planned inscription within the space. So the visitors move through a dual space: that of their own thoughts and the real space of the exhibition, where they ultimately organise the information themselves. Through a dynamic process consisting of that which the staging has inscribed, the dance of the visitors and the perception of the whole thing, both spaces are connected.

I'm deeply interested in this process of inscription, inspired by the art of writing, because *scriptum* carries the narrative within it. For me, this interpretation of scenography also emphasises the significance of text as such. Unlike some of my colleagues, I don't reject text. I don't try to replace text with other things. On the contrary, I celebrate it as a fundamental part of our culture and I try to present it – as the foundation of our post-national global culture – in a multilingual form if possible, whether in exhibitions or in public spaces.

By expressing your fascination for text in these terms, you've also immediately defined the core of your work as a scenographer. In my interpretation of the term 'scenography', the word is made up of the Greek skene **and** graphein. **You could translate** skene **both as 'hut' or 'tent' as well as 'accommodation', while** graphein **may be rendered as 'to write', as 'text' or even as 'idea'. In essence, this would make scenography a matter of accommodating an idea.**

Baur: I think that brings us to one of the origins of scenography and also of graphic design. Through inscriptions in prehistoric caves, human beings made marks in space, thus transforming space. Certain marks were permanently scratched or carved into the rock face. Others faded away over time. Yet others were sketched with a water-based medium and vanished within a few seconds. But all these marks were *inscriptions* and in each case the space was changed through human intervention. This is the core of my interests. The image, as the staged object, as well as the space as such, are elements of this inscription.

Now that you've related this temporality to the material

of the mark or the materialisation and mediality of the conveyance, I'd like to add another temporality to this aspect of time, namely that through which the mark must be read and understood and which therefore implies a cultural code with a particular half-life.

Baur: This problem is always part of the equation. Who or what leads to the disappearance of a cultural code? How do new cultural codes emerge? Are we as designers involved in this emergence and what is our role? I would claim that I as a designer have a role vis-à-vis the readers. I'm in the middle of writing about multilingualism in public spaces and I have realised that my fascination for the Italian language developed partly in those silly trains. I often found myself confronted with the sentence '*e pericoloso sporgersi*', which was printed on a little notice on the train window.[22] I found this text far more pleasant than the authoritarian messages printed next to it – '*Attention* … !' or '*Achtung* … !' So I was absolutely determined to learn this language, and I'm glad I did so.

The entire history of signs and their meaning can be divided into two levels, which overlap: the meaning of the sentence as such and the meaning of its staging. If for example 'DANGER' has been inscribed into a space in a number of languages, I understand the immediate message in my own language, but also the fact that this message is aimed at people from various cultures who are clearly all welcome in this space, and thus that I am in a cosmopolitan space. In this sense, the staging and design of the message are just as important as the message itself, and this applies both to brief warnings as well as more complex narratives.

It's interesting to turn now to how this second level of perception may influence the first. This brings us to the centre of both visual communication and scenography. The design of a message influences, for instance, the seriousness of the perception. Design is a means of lending credibility. By giving something form, you give it credibility. Even beyond a purely commercial effect, design can make things credible and this is one of its most important functions. It's interesting to observe that this second level of perception exercises an influence on the intensity of the message and on temporality. I often try to integrate these aspects holistically into the spaces I've staged, because both the quantity and intensity of that which is read as well as the rhythm of perception are all linked.

I'd like to come back to your time at the École des Beaux-Arts in Lyon.

Baur: As I mentioned, we had our studio in Lyon, which had a gallery called Projets in which we held design exhibitions. We were getting an increasing number of requests from clients in Paris. They aren't too keen on heading for the provinces to commission designers. So like many French people, at some point we had to make the move to Paris, which we were quite happy to do. At the same time, I was officially appointed to a position at the École des Beaux-Arts in Lyons.[23] So I began to make the same journey but in the opposite direction.

Teaching at the École des Beaux-Arts was an important learning experience for me. Fundamentally, I see teaching as a learning process: if I'm no longer learning anything, I can no longer teach. An educational establishment is always complex, and usually involves a great deal of administration; in contrast to a studio, the working conditions are never really optimal. In an independent studio, you can take a project in any direction you like as the fancy takes you. But in an educational establishment this direction is partly determined by the students and that's a good thing, because it's more a matter of supporting the students than leading them.

Because of the difficult conditions, we relied on interdisciplinarity and on one another as a survival strategy. None of us could achieve anything by ourselves, so we had to share our perspectives and our projects. Philippe Délis taught the culture of architecture, Sonja Dicquemare the culture of art, the poet Patrick Beurard-Valdoye was responsible for theory and I taught the culture of design.[24] These different cultures all shared a concern with specific artistic problems within the framework of a common political stance, and that's what we'd set out to achieve. So in practice three of us always had to depart from our traditional area of expertise and enter new territory, where we were all outsiders, but where we could bring in our specific disciplinary impulses. In both practical and theoretical terms, I carried out this intellectual exercise for a long time, particularly in collaboration with Philippe Délis.

The interaction between space and information was the core theme. How do you break down the classical hierarchy between space and information? How do you dissolve the division between space and information? How can the message guide spatial design and vice versa? How do you develop image and text at exactly the same time as, and through feedback with, spatial experience? What we were striving for was a multi-sensory or synaesthetic experience. Changing the hierarchy of things was key to this process. Rather than first designing the space and then the information for this space, we would sometimes begin the other way round, by designing the information, which would then influence the spatial design in a parallel process.

In this way, Philippe Délis gained experience in graphic design and gave me a deeper knowledge of 3-D design. Furthermore, we both knew exactly how the other one ticked and could work together perfectly. The idea of interdisciplinarity was crucial here. It was almost a dogma. We tried to persuade our clients that two- and three-dimensional design are equally important and must be dealt with simultaneously. This led to the development of teams in which the graphic designer had a hand in the spatial design right from the outset, and so on. One exhibition which perhaps demonstrated this approach most radically at the time was 'Machine à Communiquer'.[25] The rules which we had set ourselves were that the length of the texts and the surface area of the titles would define the dimensions of the furnishings and spaces. So a long title required a large pedestal and vice versa. The whole exhibition was conceived in such a way that the graphic design had an influence on the space and the space had an influence on the graphic design. The principle was that the information is part of the space, just as the space is part of the information.

Wasn't this conscious embrace of interdisciplinarity as a principle also the basis of Intégral? Can you talk a bit about how Intégral got off the ground?

Baur: When we set ourselves up in Paris I met up with Pippo Lionni, who had worked in my studio in Lyon for a while.[26] He had a studio with a modest staff and worked in similar areas, with a similar attitude towards design. We decided to merge our studios. We thought long and hard about how a design studio ought to work in future and sensed very early on that a strong network was the alternative to an ever-bigger studio. We were fairly critical of the mammoth bureaux like Total Design and Pentagram and felt that the potential of difference was paid too little attention in such structures.[27] So Intégral was conceived as a network. Originally, Intégral was called Intégral Concept and for us this was undoubtedly a statement that our goal was breadth of design rather than specialisation. Even more importantly, we didn't see ourselves as concerned solely with concepts but wanted to be involved in the entire design process.

But of course Intégral has a secret history. No-one knows exactly what Intégral is. I like that a lot. No-one knows who's part of the team and who isn't. There are various Intégrals in the world, but we've never made it clear who runs them. Intégral works on the basis of a belief in the culture of difference. We have great faith in the Other and therefore we even sign with the same name. But we do not interfere commercially with the Other's work. And it's not always the same people who collaborate. That's open as well. Sometimes you reach a point where the collaboration has to stop. It's like being in a marriage. In a certain sense, my 'marriage' with Philippe Délis eventually broke down. At some point it was simply over between us. He no longer accepted our dogma and we'd exchanged too much. We're still great friends, even within Intégral, but each of us goes his own way.

At the moment I'm grappling with urban issues. That brings me closer to Lipsky & Rollet Architectes, or Jean Beaudoin, an architect in Montreal.[28] This summer I did a workshop with the Vinaccia studio, our Milanese contingent, who tend to base their work on the object. Lars Müller are constantly producing publications.[29] So it's a network, and reflects the way networks tend to be. It's an option rather than a must. The network may grow, but we don't want to become too enormous. There are no commercial considerations and no grand strategies at Intégral. It's really more about wanting to collaborate and a similar view of design, and of trust and the desire to share design. That's Intégral's philosophy, and it's a strong and durable one. We are friends and partners within a network. So there are also rituals and moments of meeting, when we celebrate the exchange of ideas.

In Darmstadt in 1997 you initiated a symposium entitled 'Design Ausstellen – Ausstellungsdesign'.[30] What was the core thesis of this symposium?

Baur: I held a visiting professorship in Offenbach and the symposium was organised, in collaboration with Philipp Teufel, at the Institut für Neue Technische Form in Darmstadt. The Institut für Neue Technische Form was a very important place for design. It was important to me because I put on one of my first exhibitions there and because the prevailing atmosphere there was conducive to design as a humanistic endeavour, going far beyond commercial concerns. The head of the institute was Michael Schneider, one of the great figures in the world of design.[31] In the Institut für Neue Technische Form we debated the ethics of product design and confronted the entire Frankfurt School with the issue of design.[32] I also got to know Dieter Rams there.[33] So it was a very important place, even if the town of Darmstadt didn't see it that way.

The symposium *'Design Ausstellen – Ausstellungsdesign'* was a get-together with Philipp Teufel, who was working as a scenographer for various museums in Frankfurt at the time. We chose that particular topic because it was rooted in our own experience. We had both explored the question of what it actually means to collect and exhibit design. Both of us also had experience designing exhibitions. The central theme of the symposium was the crossover of these two fields of experience and the resulting publication was, I believe, one of the first books on scenography.

For us, the symposium was a chance to take stock of ten years of experimentation in the field of exhibition design. But it was also an occasion when we attempted to give this specialist field a name, in order to assess the design of exhibitions in a professional manner and determine the importance of this for design itself. The aim here was to flesh out design as a profession and raise clients' awareness.

You've been making exhibitions for more than 15 years now. From a professional point of view, what's changed over this period of time?

Baur: I definitely think that the nature of reception has changed greatly. Reception has developed tremendously, as have the expectations of the exhibition as format. On the one hand, there are certainly populist needs, whether artificially cultivated or real, which lead to a culture of the emotional and are often accompanied by the thinning down or even total disappearance of content. On the other hand there is an opposing tendency, a tremendous desire to get away from the hollowness of the permanent spectacle in order to endow life with new meaning and content. I also see a certain division there. There are scenographers who are prepared to stage everything, regardless of content. And there are others whose chief preoccupation is the transmission of cultural knowledge in our post-liberal society. The latter are by no means more pitiable than the former.

I like the term 'espace récréatif', which my colleagues from Quebec have introduced to describe the spectacular, purely entertaining European stagings. I think a large part of our culture at the moment is based on recreation and conveys very little apart from emotions. And that is in fact one of the origins of the exhibition. Think of the deformities and exotica that used to be displayed in the market square. That doesn't hold much appeal for me. As a scenographer, I also take a critical view of exhibitions conceived purely as a marketing strategy. I'm really only interested in designing exhibitions where there's something to convey, or at least ones that set out to convey something. In a society already overloaded with messages, that's a far from simple task.

But the same phenomenon also exists in the newspapers. There are newspapers that are becoming ever more visual, superficial and empty, and then there's a counter-movement which suddenly generates new newspapers that really tackle the subject matter head-on and devote ten pages to a particular topic. It's the latter variant that interests me and I really hope to win over new clients to this approach.

But what interests me far more these days is the question of how a city can deploy staging for the good of its citizens. How, within public spaces, do you transmit those things of urgent importance to the society? I no longer want to merely withdraw the subject matter into a 'white cube', but offer it up directly within the everyday reality of the city.[34]

Alongside the question of where scenography manifests itself is the question of what scenography actually touches on. Is scenography something that scratches the surface of things? Or does it probe deeply into the heart of the matter?

Baur: I always develop my design on the basis of the subject matter, and the more interesting the subject matter, the more inspired I am. It's no different with books. I can't imagine designing a book with no substance. For me, a book that merely conveys emotions is unthinkable. The wonderful thing about both books and exhibitions is that readers or visitors can define the degree of their absorption themselves. If the book or exhibition doesn't facilitate that, then every effect becomes superficial and every emotion deeply frustrating. But there are still plenty of perspectives and topics for the serious exhibition. I'm thinking for example of a museum of democracy where citizens can access information and debate with their fellow citizens. The citizen not only has to be able to recognise a politician's face, but also what he or she stands for. Every town hall ought to have a museum like that. My focus is absolutely on the confrontation with the subject matter, and the staging of this subject matter should facilitate greater understanding. I see it as the unambiguous task of scenography to make readable those aspects that the object leaves unreadable. This doesn't mean, to repeat, that a staging can't be poetic, emotional or experimental.

So you're calling for the recontextualisation of the object in a relevant and compelling way?

Baur: Yes, that's right, partly because the object in the museum was ripped out of its reality. The 'white cube' is anything but neutral and we should be clear about that. And I'm not at all sure whether the presentation of physical objects can be the sole aim of an exhibition these days. I love exhibitions in which the objects instead act as witnesses to a reflective context. I'm interested in the space between the objects, the relations between the artefacts, the immaterial elements such as rituals and habits, which must also be preserved. In order to understand them better, there is an urgent need to reflect on and explain our society. Here, the object is the centrepiece of the museum at most in a classical, museographic sense. The object needs a context – a lively, topical context, in fact. Its relationship with contemporary reality is crucial. The exhibition resembles a stage backed by another stage, which is real life.

You operate between disciplines. You move between information and space. You were trained as a graphic designer. You grew up in a climate in which architecture and urbanism played a crucial role. The axis of information and space is the core of your artistic activity. What do you see as the difference between architecture and the exhibition?

Baur: Architecture and the exhibition are radically different. This whole problem of the exhibition has very little to do with architecture. If you're creating an exhibition, then of course you have to get to grips with the architectural aspects. But you don't decide on the colour of the rooms before turning to the transmission of meaning. Instead you ask yourself which resources you require to transmit meaning, and then you think about how this can be reinforced through the use of space. So the focus is quite different. Sometimes there are elements within the architectural space that can't be used. So you 'remove' them. You don't illuminate them, you leave them in the dark, because they contribute nothing to the transmission of meaning. There's also a connection with theatre here. In theatre you have the scenery and the actors, and as the play develops there are moments when the relationship between the two elements is very strong, and vice versa. There are moments when the work of the actor would be impossible if the scenery didn't support the dramatic action. This interaction is highly important, and that applies to the exhibition as well.

What are your cultural references?

Baur: It may be that I draw on a greater mix of sources than others because I've always lived in two worlds. I grew up in both the Latin, Catholic culture and its Germanic, Protestant counterpart and I'm fascinated by the profound differences between these two worlds.[35] On the one hand I'm fascinated by the minimal and the functional, but as soon as these qualities hold sway, I miss the poetry and complexity. As soon as the latter dominate, I look for logic again. This alternation has come to dominate my professional culture as well.

In common with many architects of my generation, my scenography has been greatly influenced by the contrast between the designed or planned western cities on the one hand and the South Asian phenomenon of urban chaos and complexity on the other. I find this dialectic really fascinating. This contrast between individual and society, peace and commotion, everything and nothing, adding and taking away, the spontaneous and the philosopher, the useful and the non-useful, the rational and the intuitive, and so on, has always inspired me. I'm not making any judgements here, I'm just greatly interested in the tension between these spheres. As a scenographer, I work with contrasts like these. My scenography asks you to concentrate and then let your thoughts disperse again. My scenography offers moments in which you can find yourself as an individual and moments when you have to experience something through a process of exchange.

How important to you is the work of John Cage?

Baur: The works of James Joyce, Samuel Beckett, Marcel Duchamp and John Cage are very important sources of inspiration for me.[36] The works of Duchamp perhaps even more than those of Cage. The way they play earnestly with life and the world, with the absurd aspects of concepts and systems, which you also find in Borges, is an important point of reference, as is the whole Dada movement.[37] The absurd as a form of protection from the absurd. These seriously meant nonsense worlds both generate and rupture their own rigid systems in order to cultivate the exception. This is an important attitude for me.

But filmmakers such as Jean-Luc Godard or Wim Wenders also remain a great source of inspiration.[38] The shifting between image and sound in the films of the former, between what you see and what you hear, is actually just as important to me as the work of John Cage. For all of these figures, though, experimenting openly with the nature of the message is a key preoccupation. In the field of music, what interests me is the culture of interpretation. The same score, the same musical structure, constantly gives rise to new performances that reinterpret the same piece and produce an infinite number of variations. There isn't really anything like it in scenography, nor in art. You always start again at the beginning. The Chinese, on the other hand, may see their calligraphy and some of their art in that way. They paint according to styles whose origins are sometimes 500, 1,000 or 3,000 years old. They're actually interpreting a score and endowing it with new aspects. This culture of interpretation plays an important role in the transmission of meaning.

As a developer or designer, you need an interpretation in order to be able to guide the genesis of the exhibition as a process, just like the conductor, who steers the tone quality and dynamics of the musical performance.

Baur: In the Kalkriese Museum, which is dedicated to the Battle of the Teutoburg Forest against the Romans, we tried to constantly reinterpret the interpretation, and that led to the alternation of perspective in the spatial structure of the exhibition.[39] The visitor zigzags through the staging. A new perspective opens up at every turn, a new interpretation of the same phenomenon. You look at the subject matter from the perspective of the Romans, then that of the Teutons, the archaeologists, symbolic analysis, and so on. This allows the visitor to develop his or her own perspective or orientation on the basis of a more in-depth understanding of the problem. So the exhibition wasn't arranged according to the principle of good and evil. The world is more complex than that, and should be understood as such.

In the new BMW Museum in Munich, which we designed together with Uwe Brückner, I again tried to bring this factor in, in such a way that the interpretation is undergirded by a logic, so that a structure emerges that allows the public to read the connections between the individual interpretations.[40]

If the connections between the various elements don't work, neither does the exhibition as a whole. Each element may be good in itself, but the sequence of scenes may be wrong and as a result the narrative fails to develop. The great art of scenography is actually the creation of these links between the scenes. It can't just be a matter of designing pretty rooms. That's a small part of the overall task. A harmonious and readable connection between the elements, which gives the visitors the freedom to come up with their own readings, is the most crucial aspect of scenography in my opinion.

Behind a seemingly chaotic, aesthetic surface there's a meaningful structure and a language that determines the readability and makes it possible for the visitor to find his or her way around within the spatial structure of the exhibition. The visitor is fundamentally free within an exhibition. The web of spatial and temporal structures is the fascinating thing about this media format. There's no hierarchy or chronology vis-à-vis the visitors, unless you put them into a tunnel. Visitors choose their route through the space, measure out their own time and we're expected to stage the exhibition as a logical, consistent unity without ruptures, irrespective of this diversity of possible routes. This is what makes the whole thing so complex.

The staged exhibition is unique in its materiality and mediality. The system is programmed, even if time-based and unstable elements are embedded within the whole. But doesn't that mean that a thousand different visitors experience a thousand different stories?

Baur: Nonetheless, you can almost read the system of the exhibition as a score, and suddenly we're back with John Cage again.[41] There are these little moments and propositions where the visitor can still make a free choice. But moments and propositions that are bound up with other moments and propositions, which are at times even simultaneous. And despite the great number of variables, this web has to function in terms of reception. All of this also has everything to do with language.

Expressed in those terms, the exhibition as format closely resembles the city.

Baur: Absolutely. The simultaneity of the exhibition is similar to that of a city. If an exhibition achieves this simultaneity but still manages not to lose the coordination and the differences between the elements, it becomes very exciting. But a city also operates in accordance with a number of simultaneous systems. The coordination between the individual systems is an important topic these days. Even if it looks chaotic, a city is highly structured. It's no longer a matter of chaos but of complexity. The structure remains in the background but allows for constant choice. Urban freedom is generated by the complexity of the hidden structures, and not only through so-called open spaces. But the art of exhibitions hasn't got that far yet.

It's clear to me that you're fascinated by the system of the city, by the potential to intervene in this system by means of graphic design or scenography. But imagine another exhibition, one in which you have the maximum degree of freedom as author. To what extent would this exhibition, irrespective of its thematic content, be dominated by this system of the city?

Baur: It would of course be a dream come true to create an important exhibition as both author and designer with no constraints. In the early stages of the development of the French Pavilion for the World Exhibition in Shanghai we managed to do that in a certain sense, but the Republic and its representatives suddenly woke up to reality and demanded a different discourse. It was at this point that Intégral dropped out.[42] But back to the question.

It's an ongoing dream for me to reinterpret the 'Musée de l'Homme' as author, with a score that makes it possible to ask the old questions again: What is the human being? Which societies have we created? How do our bodies work? Our brains? How do we conduct ourselves, alone and in relation to others? In the most varied of contexts? To rethink and develop, without constraints, such a 'Museum of People' or 'Museum of Humanity' or 'Museum of Evolution' in collaboration with experts and curators, with or without a collection, would be wonderful and extremely attractive.

Exhibiting is not a trivial thing, it's a mirror of society. How do you see to it that this mirror isn't boring and full of poor compromises? A good exhibition transforms our view of reality.

That's also the original function of theatre! In the theatre too there's an espace récréative**. So you go to** Cats **or whatever. But there's also the kind of theatre that generates an** espace créative**. Beckett, for example.**[43]

Baur: Both spheres could form a unity. A good Molière for example obviously entailed savage social criticism, but also provided entertainment.[44] Lots of contemporary authors also entertain.

My aim is not to straightforwardly critique recreational space. It's a necessary thing. But what annoys me is that nowadays the cultural space, the *espace culturel*, is being transformed into an amusement park, out of sheer terror of content. It annoys me when colleagues promote or support this. It annoys me when they themselves talk only of the emotional effect and no longer see the difference between a shopping centre and a city museum. And of course it also annoys me if the museum acts as though it were a shopping centre. The museum as amusement park really doesn't interest me. The private company museum even less so. The transmission of meaning is usually nothing but propaganda in such places.

Sometimes I give myself assignments. The last exhibitions I authored were called '*Quotidien Visuel*' and '*Juste avant la Transformation*'.[45] The first was concerned with everyday life. The question was how to make the everyday visible. We no longer see it, and function as though there were no alternatives. The second project asked how and where society can be changed or remade, as a possibility and necessity. These were interesting experiments in terms of the visitors' participation.

You were curator, scenographer and author of these exhibitions, weren't you?

Baur: That's precisely the discussion I recently had with Philippe Délis. Both of us established that we disagree entirely with those designers who say they can't work on a given assignment without a detailed briefing. We're far more interested in an open, basic discussion that sets out the aims of the operation than a briefing. How you achieve this goal is part of our work and no-one will produce a clearer briefing than we do by questioning the question.

Every staging has something to do with authorship. Not in the sense that you don't work together with curators, but because every staging is a formal translation. However faithful such a translation may be, there is still room for interpretation. Umberto Eco brought great insights to this subject.[46] As a scenographer you have to become an author, and authorship means that you bring together the theme and curatorial knowledge, turning all this expertise into an expressive media form.

Your work revolves around two key elements: information and space. You are concerned equally with 'informative spaces' and 'spatial information'. Do you work simultaneously as a graphic designer and architect?

Baur: Yes, that's definitely how I see it. The ways I approach an exhibition and, for example, conceive of a book, are quite similar. First of all there's always a desire and certain things which have to be done, and then what you have to do (I'm missing out lots of stages) is give form to this ensemble. This form has a narrative dimension and the information contains a creative component. In theatre there's a beginning, middle and end: a linear narrative. You don't usually find this kind of linear narrative in an exhibition. In an exhibition there are often several meta-discourses which manifest themselves spatially and which can be built into points of concentrated meaning and various subdivisions in such a way as to generate a whole network of narrative linkages. In this way, the visitors are confronted with a certain degree of disorientation, which I think is productive. The visitors are allowed to lose themselves in an exhibition. They're allowed to fritter away their time. For me, that's exactly where the great potential of both a book and an exhibition lies. You could conceive of both in a linear way, like a novel. But the visitors are familiar with the hypertext structures of the Internet and expect to be able to 'channel surf'. They decide autonomously which micro-problem to concentrate on and thus when and where to invest their time.

The exhibition format as such is certainly highly discontinuous and non-linear. Yet there is an aspect which comes to the fore, for example, in Peter Brook's book *The Empty Space*, admittedly in the context of the theatre but with just as much relevance to the exhibition. Brook describes the universe of a theatrical production as a temporary totality made up of two worlds. The real world of the auditorium and the fictional world of the drama create a sandwich consisting of audience and actors, and the theatrical act manifests itself as a communicative interval, as a ritual that lasts an average of two hours. At issue here is the confrontation between these two worlds: the performed world versus the real world of the audience. Each world has its own point of entry. The audience enter the auditorium through the foyer. The actors come on stage through the wings. Initially these worlds are separate, and what is now at stake is whether or not a connection is formed between these two worlds. According to Brook, this is the great art of the theatre, because the entire system is highly complex and unstable.[47] I think he's absolutely right. As with a book, I think you can pre-programme and anticipate a great many things in an exhibition. But there's the moment when the exhibition first opens and only then do you know whether the composition really works, whether the public wants to join in. Before the opening you plan things and guess how they'll turn out but, fortunately perhaps, you're not in control of the magic that makes a work a success. You've brought together a great many different elements, you do all you can to establish this connection between the public or *récepteur* and the *diffuseur*, but it's very difficult to anticipate the actual process of an exhibition in terms of its impact.

So the exhibition is a completely open system?

Baur: Yes, partly because there's no failsafe recipe for the exhibition. An exhibition can't be expressed as a mathematical formula. And that's a good thing. There are too many parameters and too many variables, which elude the author even in more simple projects. You develop prototypes, but even then the execution inevitably entails an element of surprise, and then comes the reception by that crucial, as yet absent group, the visitors. This is why I refer to magic. There's a moment when the format itself springs into action. First you design, manipulate, control, try to structure and plan everything, and then you let go. Then the exhibition lives on autonomously. Or it may be only then that it really comes alive. The scenographer really plays no role in the concrete interaction between exhibition and visitors.

In wayfinding, for example, we know that people using the Paris métro find their bearings in different ways. There are those who remember the numbers of the lines, others who know the final stops like the back of their hands, and others again who find their way with the help of colour coding, which would be of no use to the colour-blind. So there's a variety of complementary navigation systems that function in parallel. For this reason alone you mustn't take an overly analytical approach to the problems of navigation and reception.

You have to offer a number of solutions in parallel and create complementary worlds, in such a way that the exhibition becomes error-resistant as a communicative medium. This is the art of complexity.

I'd like to return briefly to the linearity of information and the direct communicative link in light of the Peter Brook example. You spend two hours in a constructed setting, and the time you spend there is modulated: something happens, something occurs, with the intention of bringing about a connection. How then, with respect to the event structure of this interval, are we to understand the relationship between the two pillars of your work, information and space? Is there a hierarchy? Do you begin with information and then move on to space? Or does information come after space? Or are both complementary and interchangeable?

Baur: For me all these things have to be conceived in a complementary and simultaneous way. Ultimately, the question is always how I can link the two elements as strongly as possible in such a way that they become one. For me that goes for books, websites, urban interventions and of course exhibitions as well. The space is part of the information. As such, it has a magic about it, because it conveys something, even when empty, and we work with this condition. This distinction is very important. We don't insert something into space, we change it.

So you try to read the space in its ultimate state, as a charged space, a space charged with information?

Baur: For me the exhibition space is both a real space and a virtual space, both a fixed space and a fluid space, both a transitional space and certainly a loaded space as well. As I see it, an exhibition has succeeded only if you can't immediately perceive and decode it. Though I'm very much in favour of free movement through an exhibition, the visitor should perhaps be taken by the hand and constantly surprised. Not by the transmission of opinions, but by the transmission of questions. It's the contrasts and contradictions that should be cultivated rather than the assertions. I always prefer those exhibitions that offer a number of standpoints. Perhaps it's between these standpoints that the magic comes in? I'm also fascinated by doubt. I want to place doubt at the centre of the exhibition. In the first briefings the experts often tell you why they're so keen to realise the exhibition. It would be wonderful if you could retain the narrative intensity of what has been said and conveyed to us in an interesting way, for there's often not much left of it at the end.

How important to you is the cultural and political work of Guy Debord and the Situationists, who crisscrossed the city in a state of heightened consciousness with their notions of *dérive* and *psycho-géographie*?[48]

Baur: For me the Situationists are absolutely essential, and that goes way beyond their methodology. I see Guy Debord as one of the intellectuals who have explained this relationship between politics and the manufacture of consumption-related emotions. Debord explored and outlined the contours of the new society with the greatest clarity. In my view, it was Marcuse and Sartre who tended to analyse the pre-spectacle society.[49] The only one, however, who could foresee the status quo in the year 2000 was Guy Debord. It's no coincidence that our institute at the Zürcher Hochschule der Künste is called 'Design2Context'. I could also have called it 'Design2Situation'. But that was less pleasing phonetically. So the

Situationists were so important to me that I see myself as at least a kind of Situationist, or perhaps Post-Situationist.

The question of how you render our everyday life visible, and how you make the problems of our society readable through subversive viewpoints, remains a certain obsession for me. We are informed, but much remains abstract, distanced. Is that a form of protection? I like to use the term *pérégrination* to describe the methodology of *dérive*. That's a wonderful French word. *Pérégriner* means to take off and go for a walk without a clear goal. It points to a fundamental openness towards coincidence and the new. A *pérégrination* doesn't link one place with another; it links a here and now with an 'I don't know yet'. For me a good exhibition is like a *pérégrination*. It offers visitors an open situation in which they can experience the unexpected.

Your idea of *pérégrination* links up with the highly potent Situationist concept of *la dérive*, which is a psycho-geographical cross-section of the urban space. Are you trying to re-establish the ancient linkage between the cosmos of the world and the cosmos in our heads?

Baur: Yes, *pérégrination* in French also suggests the idea of the current or stream that is taking you somewhere regardless of countervailing forces. This also means that the flow of the city, the processes occurring in the urban context, may suddenly bring you into a space of history, a narrative space. This is where the strength of scenography lies. A *pérégrination* in an exhibition also suggests a narrative potential, which generates stories you didn't plan. This means that scenographers don't have to pre-programme everything and must leave certain open spaces that may change through the mere presence of the visitor. A small child unexpectedly enters and suddenly the situation changes. In this way everything can suddenly become magical and have a far greater impact than the scenographer anticipated.

The very fact that the Situationists invented psycho-geography as a cartographic instrument to visually notate their forays into the city, forces us, in analogy to dramaturgy in the theatre, to introduce a similarly powerful tool into the practice of exhibitions. The exhibition is after all a city in miniature and we're interested in better understanding the scenographic dynamics and the impact of things in this little city.

There is a dimension which is present throughout my work and which is pithily expressed in the question of how you can create systems that are not based on authoritarianism and are not perfect. Systems which don't try to anticipate everything and which are open enough to allow in coincidence and human imperfection without destroying the system itself. The culture of corporate design, for example, is quite crass in this respect. Corporate design generally tries to anticipate everything. Enormous 'manuals' define everything right from the outset. Even in school I resisted this system-based mentality. But the question of how you can create open systems adapted to evolution and the specific situation, is very interesting. How do you ensure that the system is read in an open way and may be defined over time? In my view, open systems that allow for differentiation are particularly important to the exhibition as a format.

Because we don't want to restrict the idea of the exhibition to traditional notions of museums, fairs and art galleries and wish to extend it to include performative, urban and even rural spaces, we've called our international research project 'Narrative Environments'. But what's a narrative space? The term requires definition.

If you look into the concept of narratives in depth, you may ask yourself whether there are any spaces that are not narrative. What is a non-narrative space? A space that conveys nothing? This may be where the term ceases to apply. I think every space has its narrative, regardless of how anonymous or succinct this space itself may be. So the key thing is the additional narrative which may have nothing directly to do with the space, but which is embedded in the space by the scenographer as a kind of double narrative. To look at it positively, I find it very exciting to engage with the traces left behind in the space by the narrative. Does a space in which something important has happened bear specific narrative traces? To what extent must we, or can we, stage and render tangible such a specific narrative dimension? How do you make stories tangible, narratable and readable, without killing their character? In my view, we shouldn't talk sweepingly about narrative spaces, but always specifically about the narrative potential of a space. For me, a space with narrative potential would be one that manages to tell us clearly and originally what it is, including the message that it also has to impart. How do you ensure that the staging of this message doesn't destroy the basic poetic potential of the space?

In the previous discussion you talked about *scriptum* and the inscribing of an idea in space. We also reflected briefly on Peter Brook's 'empty space' and contrasted this with a 'charged space'. Do you think that the term 'narrative environment' in itself goes some way to helping us understand the mission and potential of scenography differently, regardless of whether we are talking about an exhibition, a play or a staging within urban space?

Baur: The space that narrates what it itself is can certainly be described as narrative. But we are talking about staged spaces, spaces designed in such a way that they narrate precisely what was intended. What interests me here is whether the term 'narrative' also entails a certain contrast or alternative to advertising. Advertising strategists have of course noticed the narrative power of scenography and make use of it in their adverts. The flood of commercial stagings that are empty because there's no author behind them, no profound idea, and which are based on speech bubbles because their sole aim is to sell something, confront us with a new problem.

Would you say that the scenographer who makes use of the powerful tools of staging and deploys them to convey shallow messages is nevertheless confronted with the question of authorship?

Baur: Authorship is one thing, the other is power. What is the manipulative potential of scenography? Does the scenographer have the power to define the subject matter? How and where? These questions are paid too little attention. In Venice there was recently a scenography workshop in which we attempted to determine the difference between the masked ball as a scenographic act on the one hand, and Mussolini's fascist interventions in the city as political staging on the other.[50] The masked ball as such can't be regarded as fascist, because in principle each actor within the ball still has the potential to change the whole thing and understand it in different ways. If, on the other hand, all the actors behave in exactly the same way, if difference is lost, something quite different emerges. To polarise or differentiate are thus the key tasks of scenography. The question of orientation is crucial. The very awareness that you don't just say a sentence, but perhaps ask three questions instead, in such a way that you contrast various aspects with lots of friction, opens up a space that gives the spectator the chance to take new paths. Questioning the question is crucial to every form of the transmission of meaning, whether in graphic design or scenography.

This brings us back to the question of positioning, personal relevance and scenographic responsibility, which is embedded in the assignment. In my view, you can only deal with these questions intellectually if you see yourself as an author, regardless of whether the authorship is shared or not.

Baur: Yes, that certainly has to be specified as well. You become an author from the moment you conduct yourself responsibly in a design context. That is, from the moment you think autonomously and distance yourself from the service mentality. From the moment when you concern yourself with the content. And you become even more of an author, this is how I would use the word, when you take on the content and design on your own or in collaboration with another author. But authorship vanishes if designers uncritically carry out their assignments, despite having their own quite different insights. If they have to work against their will. If you define authorship within the client–designer relationship in this way, the definition is nothing other than a call for dialogue, for a reciprocal, horizontal process of argumentation. The designer who bears more than purely formal responsibility for the result is also an author. Responsibility is a fact and we designers must unambiguously take it on. And this responsibility can't be denied by saying 'They told me to do it!'. This is a topic of current interest. The attitude that I'm doing something because the client asked me to might have terrible results. We're familiar with this behaviour from history: 'I'm only responsible for the trains, what they carry has nothing to do with me.'

Exhibition makers call themselves scenographers these days. That's fairly new and is in fact a phenomenon found only in the German-speaking world. Now we're proposing to extend the concept of exhibition by using the term 'narrative environment'. Alongside the museum and the art gallery as classical venues for exhibitions, modern scenographers are coming to view urban space and the stage as viable settings. A conceptual unity is emerging between installation-based and performative scenography. What do you see as the benefit of this extended concept of the narrative milieu?

Baur: I'm not quite sure. In the urban space, the scenographer's contribution may make an even greater impact than in the classical exhibition space. But we have to look at these complex things in a nuanced way. The function of the narrative environment isn't just to be narrative, it is always a multi-layered overall work and the scenographer will never have all the necessary skills, even if he or she holds to the ludicrous belief in the *Gesamtkunstwerk*.[51] With regard to the problem of the city, the scenographer's skills would certainly be of great value as a means of reinforcing the narrative potential of things. But that works only if scenographers are prepared to work in a team and capable of integrating themselves into it, and if they can see themselves as co-authors of the overall narrative environment. In the case of the exhibition, I see scenographers as standing at the centre of a multidisciplinary team that brings together the broadest range of skills. Each member of the team has her or his importance. But there is a tendency to view the scenographer as the sole author, with the others having to fall into line with his or her approach. I don't think that this way of working leads to the optimal use of the various skills. So I'm in favour of a more open, creative form of teamwork designed to be horizontal in nature and underpinned by the principle of interdisciplinarity, an approach in which the suggestions put forward by one person positively influence another's project and vice versa. Everyone has to surrender a bit of ego, but the result will certainly be more interesting.

But back to the city. As with design as a whole, scenography in an urban context has to do with the elevation of certain elements. I call this 'credibilisation'. Designers give form to objects and make them credible. But there are other needs than this need to endow things with value. For me there's always this triangle of equal concepts or aspects: orientation, identification and information. Scenography structures information and on a broader level it enables orientation and identification. In the context of the classical exhibition, information is the most important thing because it is the object of the transmission of meaning. In public space, orientation and identification are much more important than the descriptive explanation. As my whole conceptual triangle revolves around the written and the narrated, around the narrative dimension of things, the term 'narrative environment' contains my three aspects on a higher level.

As I see it, the advantage of the new term 'narrative environment' compared to the old term 'exhibition' lies above all in the fact that it enhances our understanding of the media format. You might still see the exhibition, in the shape of the conventional presentation of a collection of museum objects in a room, as a spatial phenomenon. The narrative environment, on the other hand, clearly links space and time. Narrative implies reading, listening or watching. A story is unfolding and the time flies past. Right from the outset, the immaterial, soft dimension of

the content is part of this. So I'd like to talk to you about time, because narrative space implies time. What is your concept of time in this context?

Baur: Two examples. We're in the process of creating a sign system for a library.[52] We're trying to play with a dialectic between longer texts on the one hand and symbolic data that can be read as an image on the other. In the longer texts we're highlighting certain words, accentuating them through graphics, and in this way we're creating a space featuring two parallel intensities of reading or two temporalities. There are long sentences that you can grapple with for a long time which simultaneously contain short, compact, symbolic messages. This permanent simultaneity of reading rhythms might generate a poetic narrative dimension. As a second example, I'd like to tell you about how we are intervening in downtown Montreal in the Quartier des Spectacles.[53] In this area there are about thirty cultural institutions, sources of information for us, whose messages we would like to orchestrate in one of the central streets of the district. We're trying to bring together all the cultural information and to create a dramatised space out of this flood of information. We're talking here about the current information relating to the individual theatres, which is also presented on their own facades. In the narrative space of the central street, all the information accumulates and – through the multiplication of projections and data media – forms a flow of text and images that reminds us of radio, because the dramatised street functions 24 hours a day and the programme is always a little bit different, since there are no simple repetitions. The theatres in Montreal get airtime in the Quartier des Spectacles only in sync with the performances they're staging. The Quartier des Spectacles shows what is happening right now. The projected flood of information is online and in real time: the onlooker is absorbed into the endlessness of the narrative and confronted with the simultaneity of the city's times, rhythms and impulses. Time is extremely important in this project. The scenographic problem is how we orchestrate and harmonise the thirty languages of the various institutions without descending into total chaos.

In your Bellerive Seminar you talked about the possibility of speaking loudly and quietly. I found that a highly productive metaphor. You also talked about the fact that we are usually confronted with an ultra-radiant aesthetic.[54] If this narrative urban space in Montreal is supposed to carry the simultaneous presentation of thirty visual languages, what means do you have as a scenographer-cum-graphic designer to differentiate between these languages?

Baur: In the case of Montreal we opted to speak only in 'black and white'. We decided not to deploy every instrument in our toolkit, but to concentrate instead on something that is recognisable, something that may not be perfect, that doesn't allow us to do everything, something where the limited possibilities partly define the language. A language is limited by its grammar. A thing is defined by what you aren't able to do. But to whisper is something else again.

We find ourselves in a society that cultivates noise, speed and roar. This applies to the sentiment, 'I have nothing to say, but I'm going to roar about it.'

Everyone's had the kind of conversation in which you get louder and louder at certain moments. Your opponents make new arguments, but in reality you're in the midst of a lot of roaring, and you can no longer reflect much on things or hear very much. If someone capable of focusing everyone's attention on a meaningful sentence then speaks in a quiet voice, everything quietens down again and there is a sense of calm. This is also a level I deal with in scenography. How do you evaluate certain things in this respect? From this point of view the enigmatic is a far more powerful factor than the sensational. The hidden or the veiled, *le secret*, the thing you don't entirely understand, entails a certain power. So in Montreal we proposed that each institution in the Quartier des Spectacles may become visible only if there is currently something happening there. So disappearing also makes it possible to reappear. Presence cannot and should not be permanent. If a performance is being staged in a theatre for example, the corresponding information in the Quartier des

Spectacles is activated. If the play is over or the institution is not currently producing anything, the information disappears or there is none. So wiping away is just as important to this concept as switching on or appearing.

Because I find this scale extending from loud to quiet so relevant, I'd like to speak to you about micro-differences. At some point you mentioned a book whose design was based on these micro-differences and whose pictures, for instance, became one per cent smaller for every page. At first sight you can't tell the difference, but in time you experience the difference in a very real way. Would you deploy such micro-differences in your spatial scenographies as well?

Baur: In scenography you can produce contrasts but you can also create mild transitions. Indistinct transitions make it possible for the visitor to slip into a new situation without noticing. The space itself might slowly transform. It was one way and, without you being consciously aware of the transformation, after a while the space is different. The staging of transitions is a really fascinating issue. There are centres and there are transitions. You move from one centre to another but sometimes you don't notice that you're leaving a particular territory at all. When exactly does the narrative flip over and when do you find yourself in another world? You really don't know exactly where the tipping point lies. The boundaries are simply blurred and the border areas coloured in shades of grey.

My aim is not to manipulate the visitors. On the contrary, it is to make them aware of their manipulability. That is, to give them the opportunity to decide. For me, that's also a dream for the world. That we stop saying 'there are borders' and instead say 'there are centres'. With cities this works very well, whereas nations are dreadful in this respect.

If we were to assume that the world functioned on the basis of centres, then there would be less concentrated places between the centres. The centres generate a certain energy and thus a certain degree of control that hardly manifests itself in the intervening spaces. A gradual transition manifests itself in these spaces. The limits of these spaces are important. The intervening space is either a border featuring a sharp transition or an open space featuring an almost imperceptible transition. Genuine open spaces are multilayered, pluriform and weakly defined, and you always notice that interesting people dwell there, people who are trying to find space to live their own lives in this hyper-controlled society.

If you weave together two or more narrative threads in an exhibition and you resolve, as author or scenographer, to determine and lay down precisely the positioning of the centres of the narrative, is it possible that you might get it wrong? Could it be that the narrative nuclei shift when the exhibition is finally materialised?

Baur: But that can be a good thing! It's good that we don't control everything, that people can still feel disoriented. After the opening, the exhibition belongs to the visitors, who do as they wish with the setup we've constructed. This is an element that can't be anticipated even with the help of major academic studies. Shifts and open spaces emerge regardless, with the possible exception of highly authoritarian scenographies. This is precisely the difference between Mussolini and the masked ball that we discussed earlier. Where can the visitors insert themselves into the story, and in what cases does the facade of scenography reduce them to yes-women and -men?

An average visit to an exhibition lasts about two hours. The narrative structure of the exhibition may be discontinuous. Nonetheless, the accumulated experience is linear and runs like a thread through narrative space. These two hours are an important interval for the scenographer. The visitor's attention may be attracted but also lost during this focused period. How do you deal with this interval? On which temporal axes do your exhibitions turn? Immediate experience in a particular location? People's conversations about what they've seen

when they get home after the exhibition? Or perhaps also the exhibition's key metaphors and leitmotifs, which take root in the visitor's memory over the longer term?

Baur: I have to say, as a consumer of exhibitions, that I very rarely spend two hours in one. I am one of those people who, with the odd exception, tends to march quickly through the exhibition. Chance or fascination may sometimes cause me to engage more deeply, and this process may last far longer. That's the nice thing about an exhibition. Everyone can freely determine his or her own rhythm and intensity. The staging of the French Pavilion for the World Exhibition in Shanghai, which we were involved in, was meant to be adapted to a maximum visiting time of fifteen minutes. Almost a TV commercial. Dreadful.[55] But in a real exhibition, where you are still addressing individuals, there is actually a kind of expansible time, which I'm keen to cultivate. An exhibition must be understandable in ten minutes as well as a concentrated phenomenon you can experience over ten hours. But at the moment there are a great many exhibitions in which you quickly reach the maximum time for a visit. Unfortunately, these exhibitions lack the potential for deeper engagement.

In other words, the centres that you create and the transitions you allow to emerge also require this kind of differentiation. They require a certain complexity in order to express the enigmatic dimensions and depths of the theme in the first place.

Baur: But complexity not in the sense of hermetics, but in the sense of Deleuze and the capacity for a gradual, staggered entry.[56] In other words, in line with the principle: 'I'll explain it to you very simply. If you like, you can come again, then I'll explain it to you in a more complicated way. And if you're still hungry for more, I'll explain it to you in a really, really complex way. And every time you get a little more. But it's no problem if you're finished in no time.' In other words, it's not the effect that's important, but the connection. The connection structures the experience and takes root in your memory.

There are various analogies to the exhibition. The exhibition is a landscape. A city, a battery, a church. Do you have other analogies? Your comments please!

Baur: The exhibition as landscape is really exciting. There is a horizontal aspect to exhibiting; it does in fact generate a cultivated landscape. A good exhibition may also become a city. Certain exhibitions by Harald Szeemann for example, were cities, which means that you can spend a great deal of time in every house, that the exhibition doesn't babble, that you don't have to see everything, that the world of the exhibition is complex and varied, that it's alive.[57] Conceiving of the exhibition as a battery is definitely not a priority for me. I can imagine that certain exhibitions are the exact opposite of a battery. It depends on the theme. In some cases, it's vital that the exhibition is not a battery. I don't think that an exhibition provides energy in such a direct way. I have no time at all for the exhibition as church. That's precisely what annoys me about certain exhibitions. One language. One God. One vision. That's not a route I want to go down at all.

But perhaps the exhibition may also be a scattering of Polynesian islands. You move from one island to the next and each one opens up an aspect of the whole. This would make the exhibition an archipelago. That's one possible analogy. But I would almost say that the exhibition as a process without end is what interests me most. Simply to assert that the exhibition has no end and always generates new exhibitions is to expand the concept of the exhibition.

Will Ruedi Baur still be making exhibitions in five years' time? And if so, what will they look like?

Baur: I really hope I have another period of intense engagement with exhibitions. After this current break, I'd like to be able to approach the problem in a totally fresh way. With clients who want to carry out an experiment with me. I've consciously distanced myself from these enormous exhibitions, though it would have been easy to go on making a name for myself with those. But I drew back because the whole thing seemed meaningless to me. If our society is willing to face up to certain things again and sees certain things clearly again, then I think the exhibition will begin to fulfil its function again. At the moment we find ourselves in a phase of empty spectacle, and I'm not too keen on being overly involved in that. But I'll be back. I'll be back!

Notes

1. Swiss National Expo, Lausanne, 1964.
2. Max Bill (1908-1994) was a Swiss architect, artist, painter, typeface designer, industrial designer and graphic designer. He was the head architect of the sector '*Bilden und Gestalten*' ['Form and Design'] at the Swiss National Exhibition in Lausanne, 1964.
3. Baur is referring to the 20-minute 'Circlarama' film *Magic of the Rails* at the National Swiss Railways transportation exhibit in the Lausanne exhibition of 1964. The surround film was shot and produced by the Swiss filmmaker Ernst A. Heiniger, who developed and refined the so-called Circle Vision technique for the Walt Disney Company. Circle-Vision 360° is a film technique that uses nine cameras for nine huge screens arranged in a circle. The cameras are usually mounted on top of a motor vehicle for scenes through cities and highways, while films such as *The Timekeeper* (1992) use a static camera and many animated effects. The first film was *America the Beautiful* (1955 version) in the Circarama Theater, Disneyland, California (or 'Circlarama', as it was called in Europe), which would eventually become Circle-Vision Theater in 1967. See: http://www.in70mm.com/news/2004/swissorama/index.htm, April 2010; Haig Khatchadourian, 'Space and time in film', *British Journal of Aesthetics*, vol.27 (1987), pp 169–77.
4. Ruedi Baur, *La Nouvelle Typographie*, Centre national de documentation pédagogique (CNDP), Paris, 1993. Constructivist architecture was a form of modern architecture that flourished in the Soviet Union in the 1920s and early 1930s. It combined advanced technology and engineering with an avowedly Communist social purpose. Although it was divided into several competing factions, the movement produced many pioneering projects and finished buildings, before falling out of favour around 1932.
5. El Lissitzky (1890–1941) was a Russian artist, designer, photographer, typographer, polemicist and architect. László Moholy-Nagy (1895–1946) was a Jewish-Hungarian painter and photographer who was highly influenced by constructivism; a professor in the Bauhaus school, he was a strong advocate of the integration of technology and industry into the arts. Herbert Bayer (1900–1985) was an Austrian graphic designer, painter, photographer, sculptor, art director, environmental and interior designer and architect, known for being the last living member of the Bauhaus.
6. Lissitzky's *Lenin Tribune* (1924) was a constructivist project, also known *as Proun no.85*, dedicated to Lenin and designed in his own suprematist style, which Lissitzky called 'Proun': the station where one changes from painting to architecture. See: Sophie Lissitzky-Küppers, *El Lissitzky*, Thames & Hudson, London, 1968. Fortunato Depero (1892–1960) was an Italian futurist painter, writer, sculptor and graphic designer: Gustavs Klucis (1895–1938) was a pioneering Russian photographer and major member of the Constructivist avant-garde in the early twentieth century. Lajos Kassák (1887–1967) was a Hungarian poet, novelist, essayist, painter, editor and avant-garde theoretician.
7. Michael Baviera (b.1946) is a Swiss graphic designer. In 1981 Baviera co-founded the BBV-Studio (Baur-Baviera-Vetter) together with Ruedi Baur and Peter Vetter in Zurich, Lyon and Milan. Today Michael Baviera teaches corporate design at the art school in Konstanz, Germany.

8		Theo Ballmer (b.1936) is a Swiss graphic designer, who is renowned for his signage system (German: *Signaletik*) for the Paris métro. Ruedi Baur worked for the Theo Ballmer & Partner studio in Basel from 1979 to 1980.
9		Constructivism was an experimental movement in art and life which had its centre of gravity in Russia from 1917, when it was considered to be the art of the Revolution, to 1932 when the Russian Constructivists were forced to give up their inspirational ideal of developing a 'new aesthetics' for a new world and had to turn to an officially declared 'socialist realism', proclaimed by the Soviet state. Constructivism originated in Malevich's suprematism and was conceptually rooted in futurism, cubism, Dadaism, De Stijl and Bauhaus. Important constructivist artists were the painter Vladimir Tatlin (1885–1953), the sculptor-architect Naum Gabo (1890–1977) and the photographer, graphic designer and architect El Lissitzky (1890–1941) who was affiliated with Bauhaus and De Stijl. Lissitzky is well known for his own suprematist style, which he called 'Proun', and for his designs for the Lenin Tribune (1920), the Cloud Iron skyscrapers for Moscow (1923–5) and the Pressa Pavilion of the Socialist Soviet Republics, designed for the International Press Exhibition in Cologne, May to October 1928. See: Sophie Lissitzky-Küppers, *El Lissitzky*, London: Thames & Hudson, 1968.
10		Meant here, is the phase in which modernism in art and architecture was gradually taken over by an officially declared turn towards Socialist-Realism in Russia, culminating in the 1932 speech by Lazar Kaganovich (1893–1991) in which Stalin's decree 'On the Reconstruction of Literary and Art Organisations' was presented. Kaganovich was a Soviet politician and administrator and a close associate of Joseph Stalin. He is considered to be one of the Bolshevik leaders responsible for the Soviet famine of 1932–3. See: Hugh D. Hudson Jr, *Blueprints and Blood: The Stalinization of Soviet Architecture, 1917–1937*, Princeton University Press, Princeton (NJ), 1994. At the same time the Nazis in Germany were gaining power, culminating in the Hitler government in 1933.
11		Ruedi Baur founded the Plus Design studio with Swiss artist and graphic designer Sereina Bucher-Feuerstein (b.1957) in Zurich, in 1980.
12		Robert Sambonet (1924–1995) was an Italian industrial designer. Enzo Mari (b.1932) is an Italian writer, artist and product designer. A.G. Fronzoni (b.1923) is an Italian graphic and furniture designer. Otl Aicher (1922–1991) was a German graphic designer. Dieter Rams (b.1932) is a German product designer and architect. Anton Stankowski (1906–1998) was a German painter, photographer and graphic designer. Peter Saville (b.1955) is a British graphic designer and art director. Ross Lovegrove (b.1958) is a British industrial designer.
13		Ruedi Baur has led the design research institute Design2Context at the Zürcher Hochschule der Künste [Zurich University of the Arts] (ZHdK) since 2004.
14		Ruedi Baur was the founding director of the Projets gallery in Villeurbanne from 1984 to 1988.
15		École Nationale des Beaux-Arts, Lyon, 1989–94; Baur coordinated the Design Department together with Philippe Délis (b.1951), who is a French architect and scenographer.
16		The postgraduate course Civic City was organised by the École Nationale des Beaux-Arts, Lyon, 1994–6. The exhibition '*Mode d'Emploi*' was organised within the framework of the 2nd Design Biennale '*Caravelle*' and shown in the Espace Lyonnais d'Art Contemporain (ELAC) in Lyon, in 1991.

ruedi baur

17 In 1989 Ruedi Baur developed the 'Intégral' concept together with the American designer Pippo Lionni (b.1954) and founded his Paris office Intégral Ruedi Baur & Associés.
18 The Centre Pompidou's signage system was designed by the Intégral Ruedi Baur & Associés agency for the reopening of the building in 2000. Together with the Norwegian-Swiss designer Lars Müller (b.1955), Ruedi Baur developed the concept for the exhibition and pavilions of the Museum and Park Kalkriese, in Kalkriese near Osnabrück, Germany, 1998–2002.
19 'Museum in Motion' seminars, Museum Bellerive, 8 February 2006.
20 Baur compares working on a computer screen with working on paper as is used to be. For instance, on paper graphics are composed of black ink, but typeface on a screen is 'semantic light'. Layers of paper appear on top of each other, opaque, filling the space between the design and the viewer. Behind layer 1 there's nothing. The computer screen on the contrary seems to be the top layer of an infinite virtual space behind. In a paper collage there is hardly any transparency between layers, on a computer screen it's easy to construct any kind of transparency you like. For the computer there is no fundamental difference between 2-D and 3-D design, as it is in the analogue realm. Any 2-D piece of graphic design is constructed in the virtual 3-D environment of the computer. That was new at the time.
21 Here, the ambivalent 2-D–3-D phenomenon of the computer screen is copied to the analogue space of architecture: a wall becomes a space in itself.
22 In Italian, '*e pericoloso sporgersi*' means 'it's dangerous to lean out' (of the window of the train).
23 Ruedi Baur took on the position of head of the Design Department at the École Nationale des Beaux-Arts in Lyon, in 1989. See notes 13 and 14 above.
24 Sonja Dicquemare is a French architect and choreographer, who teaches Urban Representation at the École Nationale des Beaux-Arts in Lyon. Patrick Beurard-Valdoye is a French poet, who teaches both the Culture of Philosophy and Literature at the École Nationale des Beaux-Arts in Lyon.
25 Ruedi Baur and Philippe Délis, '*Machine à Communiquer*' ['Interface'], Cité des Sciences et de l'Industrie, Parc de la Villette, Paris, 1990.
26 See note 15 above. For Pippo Lionni, see: http://www.lionni.com, April 2010.
27 Total Design was a Dutch multidisciplinary design agency in Amsterdam, founded in 1963; Pentagram is a multidisciplinary design agency which originated in London in 1972 and opened offices in New York in 1978, San Francisco in 1986, Austin in 1994 and Berlin in 2002.
28 Intégral Lipsky+Rollet Architectes is a Paris based office, which was founded by Florence Lipsky (b.1960) and Pascal Rollet (b.1960); see: http://www.lipsky-rollet.com/. Intégral Jean Beaudoin is an architectural and design studio in Montreal focusing on space and identity, founded by Jean Beaudoin (b.1967); see: http://www.integral.jean-beaudoin.com/
29 Intégral Studio Vinaccia was created in 1987 in Milan by Giulio (b.1955) and Valerio (b.1955) Vinaccia. The studio works mainly with product design, packaging and corporate graphic image. See: http://www.vinaccia.it/. In addition to his work as a publisher, Lars Müller is the founder of Intégral Lars Müller, one of five studios that share an

space.time.narrative

  intellectual approach to a range of disciplines from architecture to product design. See: http://www.lars-mueller-publishers.com/en/publisher/integral, April 2010.
30 The symposium '*Design Ausstellen – Ausstellungsdesign*' ('Exhibiting Design – Design Exhibitions), Darmstadt, 1997, was organised by Ruedi Baur and Philipp Teufel. Philipp Teufel (*b.*1958) is a German graphic designer and professor of graphic design at the Exhibition Design Institute (EDI) in Düsseldorf. See: Ruedi Baur and Philipp Teufel, *Design ausstellen – Ausstellungsdesign*, Lars Müller Publishers, Baden, 1997.
31 Institut für Neue Technische Form (INTEF), Darmstadt. See: http://www.intef.de/, April 2010. Michael Schneider (*b.*1946) has been head of INTEF since 1976.
32 The Frankfurt School (*Frankfurter Schule*) was a German sociological and philosophical movement in the 1960s, in which neo-Marxist critical theory of capitalist society was central. The movement was founded by Theodor Adorno (1903–1969) and Herbert Marcuse (1898–1979), on the basis of the 1937 programmatic essay 'Traditional and critical theory' by Mark Horkheimer (1895–1973). All three sociologists-philosophers were affiliated with the Institute for Social Research in Frankfurt am Main, although Marcuse lived in the USA from 1940. See: David Held, *Introduction to Critical Theory: Horkheimer to Habermas*, University of California Press, Berkeley–Los Angeles, 1980, p.14.
33 Dieter Rams (*b.*1932) is a German industrial designer closely associated with the consumer products company Braun and the Functionalist school of industrial design.
34 See: Brian O'Doherty, *Inside the White Cube: The Ideology of the Gallery Space*, expanded edition, University of California Press, Berkeley–Los Angeles, 2000.
35 Ruedi Baur was born in Paris in 1956, went to school in Chambéry, Savoie, France, and received his professional training as a graphic designer at the Schule für Gestaltung (now Zürcher Hochschule der Künste – ZHdK) in Zurich, Switzerland from 1975 to 1979.
36 For James Joyce (1882–1941) and Samuel Beckett (1906–1989), see essay 1, 'The Battery', paras 1.4 and 1.5, pp 30–51; Marcel Duchamp (1887–1968) was a French-American artist whose work is most often associated with the Dadaist and Surrealist movements; John Cage (1912–1992) was one of the leading figures of the post-war avant-garde.
37 Jorge Luis Borges (1899–1986) was an Argentine writer, essayist and poet. In our context, Borges is of special interest for the 'sceonographical' topics he addresses in many of his stories, like the nature of time and the problem of identity. In *The Library of Babel* (1941), for instance, the theme of the labyrinth and the infinity of variation through mirroring and recombination is central. The protagonist of *Funes the Memorious* (1942) is a person who isn't capable of forgetting anything that has been experienced. In *The Secret Miracle* (1944) time freezes, and *The Aleph* (1949) is about an interface through which all of the universe can be observed, to name just a few. It is Borges' mix of fact and fiction, of the real and the fantastic, which makes him such a deep source of inspiration for a profession which almost entirely relies on the power of the imagination. Dada or Dadaism is a cultural movement that began in Zurich, Switzerland, during the First World War and peaked from 1916 to 1922. The movement involved visual arts, literature, poetry, art manifestoes, art theory, theatre and graphic design, and concentrated its anti-war politics on a rejection of the prevailing standards in art through anti-art cultural works. Its purpose was to ridicule what its participants considered to be the meaninglessness of the modern world. In addition to being anti-war, Dada was

also anti-bourgeois and anarchistic in nature. See: Hans Richer, *Dada: Art and Anti-Art*, Thames & Hudson, London, 1965. Also: Marc Dachy, *Dada: la révolte de l'art*, Éditions Gallimard/Centre Pompidou, Paris, Découvertes no.476, 2005, and: *Dada, catalogue d'exposition*, Centre Pompidou, Paris, 2005.
38 Jean-Luc Godard (b.1930) is a French and Swiss filmmaker and one of the founding members of the *Nouvelle Vague*; Wim Wenders (b.1945) is a German film director, playwright, author, photographer and producer.
39 Ruedi Baur and Lars Müller, Museum and Park Kalkriese, 1998–2002. In autumn of the year 9 AD, the Cheruscan Prince Hermann led the Teutonic tribes into a battle with the Romans under command of Publius Quintilius Varus, which he won and thus proved that the Roman legions were not unconquerable, which was a genuine act of liberation. The Battle took place in the Teutoburg Forest, near the city of Osnabrück in Germany. Hence the name, but the battle is also referred to as Varus' Battle or Hermann's Battle. The exhibition which Ruedi Baur staged and designed in the Museum and Park Kalkriese is devoted to the archeology of the historic event. See also note 18 above.
40 Atelier Brückner, BMW Museum, Munich, 2008. The visual identity and the graphic design of the new BMW Museum has been developed by Intégral Ruedi Baur Zurich.
41 Ruedi Baur is referring to the chance operations by John Cage. See: James Pritchett, *The Music of John Cage*, Cambridge University Press, Cambridge, 1993.
42 Intégral Ruedi Baur Paris was asked to design the French Pavilion for Expo 2010 in Shanghai, but withdrew from the assignment in 2009, disagreeing with what the scenography should aim at.
43 *Cats* is a musical composed by Andrew Lloyd Webber (b.1948) based on *Old Possum's Book of Practical Cats* by T. S. Eliot (1888–1965). The musical first opened in the West End in 1981 and then on Broadway in 1982. The London production ran for 21 years and the Broadway production ran for 18 years, both setting long-run records. *Cats* has been performed around the world many times and has been translated into more than 20 languages.
44 Jean-Baptiste Poquelin (1622–1673), better known by his stage name Molière, was a French playwright and actor who is considered one of the greatest masters of comedy in western literature.
45 Intégral Ruedi Baur, '*Quotidien Visuel*', 2002–8. '*Quotidien Visuel*' is a work in progress in the form of an ongoing travelling exhibition on everyday backstage life at the Intégral Ruedi Baur agencies. The exhibition has been on show in Paris, Cologne, Leipzig, Lausanne, Montreal, Shanghai and develops further month by month, project by project, and may be considered as a visual and verbal log book of the activities of Intégral Ruedi Baur. Ruedi Baur and Sébastian Thiery, '*Juste avant la Transformation*', International Design Biennale, Saint-Étienne, France, 2006.
46 See: Umberto Eco, *The Open Work (Opera Aperta)*, Harvard University Press, Cambridge (MA), 1989 (originally published in Italian in 1962).
47 Peter Brook, *The Empty Space*, Penguin Books, London, 1990.
48 For Guy Debord and the International Situationists, see essay 1, 'The Battery', notes 109, 110, pp.78–79.
49 Herbert Marcuse (1898–1979) was a German philosopher, sociologist, and political theorist, associated with the Frankfurt School of critical theory; see also note 32 above. Jean-Paul Sartre (1905–1980) was a French philosopher, political activist, playwright

	and novelist. His existentialism profoundly influenced the young generation of artists and writers in the 1950s and 1960s. Sartre was also renowned because of his long-term relationship with the French writer, philosopher and feminist Simone de Beauvoir (1908–1986). Sartre refused the Nobel Prize for Literature that was awarded him in 1964.
50	Ruedi Baur is referring to the KESHMA workshop 'Staging the City', held in Venice, 28 June to 1 July 2007. KESHMA stands for (K)nowledge (E)nvironments & (S)hared (H)ybrid (M)edia (A)ccess. KESHMA is a network, a platform and an archive in support of sharing knowledge through digital classrooms. The workshop 'Staging the City' was the tenth part of the Urban Identity & Design postgraduate course at the Design2Context Institute of the Hochschule für Gestaltung und Kunst (now Zürcher Hochschule der Künste (ZHdK)), October 2006 to July 2007.
51	The German word *Gesamtkunstwerk* refers to Wagner and reflects a kind of artwork: the total work of art, which could and has been misused for political reasons because of its high or elitist aspirations. Ruedi Baur opposes this idea and indeed calls it 'ridiculous', judging the ambition implied in the *Gesamtkunstwerk* to be a ludicrous belief. The German language differentiates between a *Gesamtwerk* = an overall work (of art) and a *Gesamtkunstwerk* for which there is no proper English translation. See also the Foreword by Hans Peter Schwarz, p.xiii.
52	Ruedi Baur is referring to the Médiathèque André Malraux in Strasbourg, built in 2008 by the architects Jean-Marc Ibos (b.1957) and Myrto Vitart (b.1955). See: http://www.ibosvitart.com
53	Intégral Ruedi Baur and Intégral Jean Beaudoin, Quartier des Spectacles, Montreal, 2007–10.
54	See note 19 above.
55	See note 42 above.
56	See: Gilles Deleuze and Félix Guattari, *A Thousand Plateaus*, The Athlone Press, London, 2004.
57	Harald Szeemann (1933–2005). Ruedi Baur is referring to Szeemann exhibitions such as Documenta V in the Neue Galerie and Museum Fridericianum in Kassel, 1972, or the Biennale d'Art Contemporain in Lyon in 1997, but also to smaller exhibitions like the '*Monte Verità – Berg der Wahrheit*', in the Kunsthaus, Zurich, 1978.

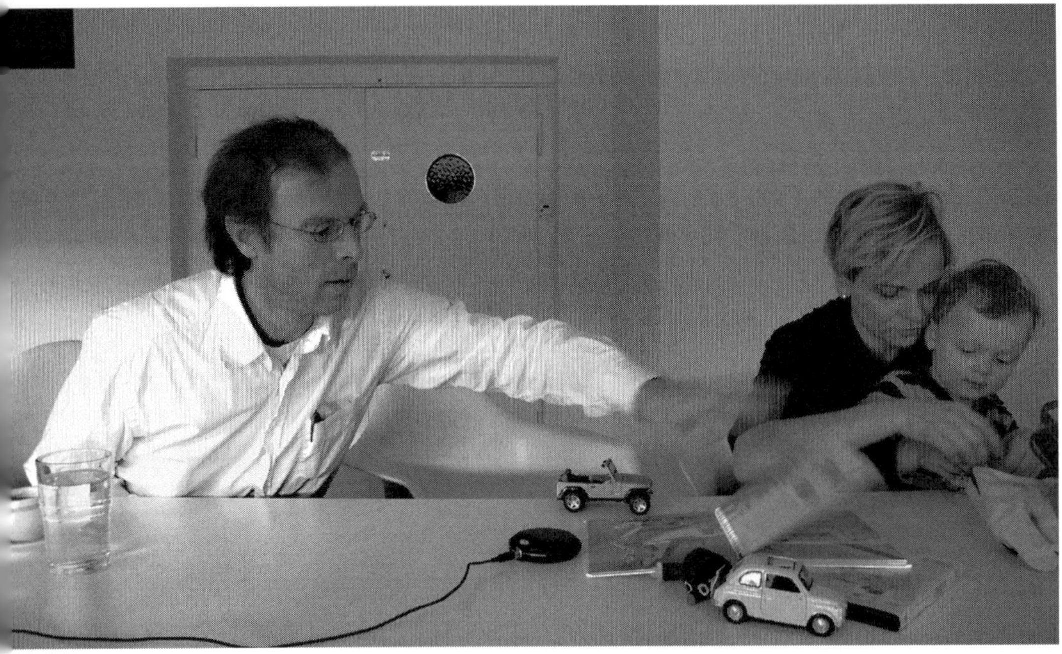

Interview with
Barbara Holzer and Tristan Kobler

Barbara Holzer (b.1966) and **Tristan Kobler** (b.1960) are the founding directors of the Zurich-based agency Holzer Kobler Architekturen. In the Zurich Landesmuseum they had staged an exhibition called '*Waffen werfen Schatten*', which had impressed me because of its intriguing scenographical arrangements of museum objects that are usually displayed in a traditional way. Somehow, something new came alive, through delicate lighting and delicate staging in space. Barbara and Tristan had convincingly turned the Landesmuseum into a narrative environment with impacting imagery, which triggered me to invite them to take part in the 'Museum in Motion' seminars. We first met in a back room of their office in the Ankerstrasse in June 2005. It was all a bit chaotic. Tristan came later and Barbara primarily had to take care of her newborn son Ian, but we managed. Our interview was held on 22 November 2007, to be continued on 19 and 20 January 2008. It was during the second of these meetings when the portrait on the opposite page was made. On a sunny Saturday morning just before we started recording again.

Barbara, what was the first exhibition that really touched and affected you?

Holzer: That's really difficult. My long-term memory just isn't that good. What I tend to remember is individual objects that influenced me. That may have something to do with the fact that I spent much of my childhood in classical museums or that back then there were no staged exhibitions. For example, I remember the *Water Lilies* by Monet, which I saw as a girl.[1] Or pictures and sculptures somewhere in one of Europe's historical cities or in one of the classical galleries. These are my memories of exhibitions. As far as themed exhibitions are concerned, first there's a huge gap in my memory and then I remember the exhibitions here in Zurich, in the Museum für Gestaltung, where I suppose Tristan and I must have met.[2] I found Tristan's exhibitions beautiful and quite refreshing. There was no logical form. In terms of the overall staging they were quite chaotic spaces, but they were very poetic because somehow they had a unique structure of their own rather than any kind of formal language.

Tristan, which exhibition do you remember most?

Kobler: In fact, I didn't actually see any of my first exhibitions. But the first one I can really remember was the *Landesausstellung* in Lausanne.[3] That was in 1964 and I was four years old. I was dragged along and chucked into a crèche, which was quite futuristic, with holes to crawl through, and I was probably spoken to in French. That was the most disastrous day for me and that's why I remember it. I wasn't taken along into the exhibition. Of course, the crèche was equipped in accordance with the latest ideas of the 1960s. It was very modern. That's why I remember that day so clearly. It was an absolute nightmare.

Later on, when I was working on EXPO.02, I refused to create a crèche because I feel that people should bring the kids along with them.[4] I also have clear memories of the art exhibitions by Jean-Christophe Ammann in the Lucerne Kunsthaus; that was also in the 1960s.[5] They were highly progressive. My parents went to see all the exhibitions but they were always appalled once they got back home. Unfortunately, they never took me with them. Gilbert & George were singing on platforms, Joseph Beuys' *Fat Corners*, Luciano Castelli, I knew all the works of all these people, but never got to see them.[6] It was during piano lessons that I got my real introduction to these things. With John Cage and his new musical notations and quadrophonic sound reproduction.[7] I had a piano teacher, a woman who lived in a commune with the most modern furniture. The opposite of my own home, in fact. Though we always played classical music, the whole culture was different. There I listened to the concert using 100 typewriters and bells by Rolf Liebermann, and to pieces by Karlheinz Stockhausen.[8] The other thing that really impressed me was the churches. Religious images have always fascinated me, all the symbolism and staging, the incense. It was only in other countries that I went to art museums, because we would go to Paris or London or wherever it might be. I saw the *Water Lilies* by Monet and the most incredible pictures while abroad. It was then that I first became involved in creating exhibitions, though without realising it.

Are the memories beginning to flow for you?

Holzer: I was generally taken along to exhibitions as a child. There you are confronted with these images that influence you. The *Water Lilies* by Monet are just one of many examples. In the case of Beuys' *Fat Corners*, as a child you think, what's that all about? I do have the feeling that a certain process of sensitisation occurred, to observation in general. But the question of what you are actually thinking about when you talk about an exhibition is an interesting one. Are you thinking about the space, as it were, about the staging within the space? Generally, what I remember is the content of what I saw. Funnily enough, in terms of scenography I can't really remember any exhibitions. I find this interesting, where and how do you begin to perceive spaces as such? The church, for example, never enters my head. I was raised as a Protestant so there were no pictures involved.

Which exhibition awakened your interest in creating exhibitions and in the exhibition as a multimedia communicative format? How did you end up in this interdisciplinary field?

Kobler: It's not something I wanted at all. I actually took a degree in architecture, which I eventually completed. I was then invited to an interview at the Museum für Gestaltung here in Zurich, for a job designing exhibitions.[9] In reality I wasn't the least bit interested in it. There were plenty of jobs around at the time and I thought, I'll go to a well-known architect and build a big box. But I also wanted to find out what an interview involved, so I went there with absolutely no intention of doing anything like that. I didn't know how these things go, and had brought nothing along with me. Then they asked me whether I had brought anything with me. And I asked them what they meant. A portfolio! Haven't got one. Then there was a second interview and I had nothing but slides. This they found amusing in some way or other and ultimately they decided they wanted me. I had no idea what I was supposed to do, but I found the mixture of creating and designing while still doing research here and there exciting. I was also interacting with quite different people, different from architects, with a very different background, and I learned a lot of other new things as a result. Actually, that prompted me to take the job. The curators were responsible for content and they needed someone to take care of the design. I was the exhibition architect or designer. The term 'scenography' didn't exist at the time.

Holzer: I did a great deal of acting throughout my school years. That was my great passion. And I wanted to become a professional actress. I was very clear about that. But this led to terrible arguments with my parents. They said they would pay for a degree in any (sensible) subject, and then I could do as I pleased. So I studied architecture and learned stage-setting during an internship in Frankfurt.[10] I actually got into the exhibition world via the theatre. I continued to work as a stage-setting assistant for a time and that's still one of the most important references for me. I haven't developed exclusively within one discipline. I don't call myself a scenographer either. It was basically classical architecture that I was involved in, making boxes large and small for the major architects and again that gave me an insight into a quite different world, one I hadn't learned about from the ETH.[11] And I think that moulded me. For me, this exclusive way of looking at things just doesn't exist. Of course, the nice thing about exhibitions or scenography is that you think about content, that you think on a smaller and faster scale, but it is always the relation between the concept and the experience of space that is the real focus of attention in my work. In this, I was influenced on the one hand by the theatre and on the other by classical architecture. And actually less so by exhibitions, which I had no connection with. It was through Tristan that I got into exhibitions. The first exhibition that we did together was the one with, and about, Daniel Libeskind.[12] That's how it all came about. I would never have said: I've decided to be an exhibition designer. That sounded like window-dresser. Which sounds quite awful, doesn't it?

Holzer Kobler Architecturen hasn't been around for very long. You used to have your own companies. How did you find each other and what is the basis of your collaboration?

Holzer: We've known each other for ages. I lived in Berlin for a long time and then I came back to Zurich with two or three people and a small architectural firm. Then, like some kind of vagabond, as it were, I dropped in on my old friend Tristan and asked, would you take us on? Could you fit us in somewhere? And that's how things got going again.[13]

Kobler: It's just that we were interrupted for a couple of years, but we had worked together before.

Why do you work so well together? Do you sing from the same hymn sheet?

Kobler: No, not at all. That's why we decided to do it – because we go about things differently and think differently. Otherwise you merely duplicate one another and that would be boring.

Holzer: I feel that conflict has exciting potential!

You're good at arguing?

Holzer: Yes!
Kobler: Not arguing, we simply have different approaches.
Holzer: Fundamentally, we approach things in quite contrary ways. There's not the slightest doubt about that. That's what makes the process so exciting, the fact that you're constantly being questioned. Which is a terrible nuisance, isn't it? When you're working away on something with three people and then along comes the other person and says it's no good at all. You continually pull one another out of the process, so to speak. You might get back on to the same track, but with one more observation in mind. And because we know each other so well, there is a basic trust. At the end of the day, you don't have to discuss every last thing. But I do think the fact that we always adopt an opposing stance is very productive. And if we switch roles, no doubt everything will change again.

An exhibition such as 'All We Need' in Luxembourg couldn't have been created by just anyone. It's a genuine Holzer Kobler exhibition. I don't know what your respective roles were in that project, but at some point you must have come to some kind of agreement.[14]

Kobler: You don't have to agree, but you do get to a certain point. Again, in Luxembourg, Barbara kept throwing a spanner into the works, but that helped develop the project further. Things happen in a certain order, of course, and at some point, invariably shortly before the opening, you know what you have to do. By then it's almost too late, but up to that point we're making constant changes. Until it feels right. But that doesn't work so well when we're dealing with complex projects.

With respect to this opposition, is it apparent that your background, Barbara, is in architecture and theatre while yours, Tristan, basically lies in museum-based curatorial and design work?

Kobler: I don't think so. Barbara takes a much more museum-oriented approach than me. This is something I've noticed with respect to presentation. People expect more of her when it comes to dealing with objects than they do of me, though I worked in a museum for nine years. It has something to do with the fact that I take a different view of the conservation-related aspects. It's not that I don't know how that side of things works. But I enjoy the different perspective that you get from discourse with the client, because it's interesting. Some clients think, he doesn't understand a thing. It's more in this way that our differences make themselves felt, but it has nothing to do with our backgrounds.

Holzer: Where we work well together is in conceptual development. We really do complement one another by bringing in different perspectives. Just as with architecture, we start with the content rather than the formal aspects of a given project. Our approach to an architectural assignment and an exhibition is in fact much the same in terms of our attitude. What we are always trying to do is write a kind of story about the subject matter. Whether I'm writing that story for an exhibition or a house, the methodology is exactly the same. It's probably on this level that the common ground exists between us. Sometimes I think Tristan is better at that than I am, but it's more a question of character. For example, Tristan is better at working with scientists. I can do that to a certain extent, but eventually I reach my limits. It simply gets too detailed for me and I lose patience. That's not the way I go about things. Then I have a hard time keeping on the ball. Tristan is much better at that. So we have our different emphases. Tristan tends to take care of the curatorial aspects for example. If we have to rework the content of an exhibition, Tristan is the main point of contact.

Kobler: There is a process of back and forth between us until we reach a settled view.

Holzer: We're going through a lot of changes at the moment. Our exhibitions are heavily influenced by Tristan's earlier work at the Museum für Gestaltung.[15] At the beginning our exhibitions were temporary. But in the last years we started designing permanent exhibitions like the Swiss National Museum.[16]

I can't say to clients, go and have a look at our exhibition. There aren't any. We are now planning four or five permanent exhibitions and that changes a few things. Our attitude is the same, but the whole structure of the assignment and the way we deal with it is something else again.

Kobler: Yes, this is something fairly new. Previously I resisted doing permanent exhibitions. Back then, I got into an exhibition culture in which people basically only wanted to create temporary exhibitions. At the Museum für Gestaltung I decided to take the same approach, and that gives you an unbelievable drive. You ask quite different questions. You have to work far more quickly and precisely. You can also bring in a much stronger statement, because it doesn't have to hold up for five or ten years. You know it'll all be gone again in two months and that creates a quite different dynamic. I really enjoyed all of that.

Barbara has talked about your strengths. What do you think her strengths are?

Kobler: I always spend a long time questioning things, projects, until they feel right. Not everyone is convinced of this approach. They think I have no idea how to proceed. But Barbara can come up with something very concrete and precise in short order, so she comes across as far more committed. I remain uncommitted for far longer. Barbara is very good at negotiating and can persuade people of things very quickly indeed. Far more quickly than me. Don't you think?

Spatially, all of your exhibitions tend to offer a well-formed overall image, a 'big picture'. This applied to '*Waffen werfen Schatten*', **while in the case of '***In Heikler Mission***'** **the space was generously structured using a huge tented roof. In 'All We Need' in Luxembourg your stagings were defamiliarised in a compelling way by the context of the abandoned steel foundry. You're of one mind on this level, I assume?**[17]

Holzer: As you say, the big picture is an important goal. We look for big, simple pictures that are impressive and easy to understand. That's a very important strategy. These pictures offer the public a way in to all those things that get complex, multifaceted and delicate later on. I'm absolutely convinced of the need for hooks of this kind. You can convey the heart of the matter to people through these pictures. We're not interested in coming up with some nice packaging. Any designer can do that. That's a piece of cake. And it's not interesting either. The aim is really to achieve this translation and find a metaphor for the content. The big pictures simplify the translation and sum up the themes, in such a way that a thesis is inserted into space.

Kobler: In order to develop a fitting thesis, you have to know a great deal about the theme, because if the picture is wrong it can also have the opposite effect. When working on the big picture, you also have to do a great deal of thinking in stories and memories. What do people actually have in their heads in our culture? What points of reference can you pick up on? That kind of question. We always develop the big picture in light of the theme, and the themes are always completely different. Ultimately, the most important thing about an exhibition is the message and we try to define or even push the message through the big pictures, in order to make it visible and clear. Why this exhibition now, in this place and at this time? Sometimes you build a construct around these questions until the exhibition's relevance becomes clear. We always attempt to come up with this construct, in other words the answer to the question of why here and now, in light of the theme and location.

A particular exhibition may be quite mediocre in one place but work very well in another, always depending in part on timing. Holding an exhibition a year earlier or later can change it completely. Not in terms of the content, but in terms of the message. Exhibitions have a contemporary dimension, like theatre. The key thing is always people's stories and typologies, which have a certain archaic quality. These are the primal stories that make sense to people in different eras and different cultures. We seek out stories of this kind because they tap the pulse of what it is to be human and

space.time.narrative

Holzer: that's the heart of the matter. Our task is to tap that pulse.

Holzer: We're not collectors and we don't work with props. The key thing is always the approach, which involves seeking out pictures of relevance today and hopefully tomorrow as well. Even pictures of the day after tomorrow. Yet in many museums I simply get a dust allergy and if we are to work there you first have to bring some fresh air into these rooms through a grand gesture. For me it's an almost physical feeling to, say, keep 20 per cent of the collection and get rid of the rest. Let's do some radical tidying up! When I say this to the clients and curators, their jaws drop, but they think, she's right. It has something to do with how you work, but I think you just have to shock people so that they wipe the slate clean and say, OK, I get it.

You reinvent the assignment so that you can realise the subject matter in a compelling way, so you can anchor it in a particular place and time. Is this radicalism not an impediment to permanent exhibitions?

Kobler: What I'm trying to do now is work out what I think a permanent exhibition is. Most exhibitions are gone in 50 or 100 years and the few that may still be there are wonderfully refreshing because they're so different. In terms of architecture as well, I always ask myself which buildings is it that people look at? And undoubtedly the buildings that the general public look at are always clear, compelling documents of a given time: the pyramids, the Taj Mahal, cathedrals and so on. Such buildings have a great deal to do with a particular historical period and are not built to be timeless, even if they're solidly built, but are always a strong expression of their time. They may be the craziest, most excessive, most useless buildings in existence. Almost all of them are idiotic and useless, completely over the top, and went bankrupt several times. In reality they're disasters, but the interesting thing is that you can attach them to a particular period and attitude. This is the common feature of all these works. This is why a permanent exhibition may also be very much bound up with a given time and we can read and categorise it as such, because it adopts a particular position or attitude.

In your search for the grand gesture, which I see as one of your strengths, you are very much representatives of an author-designer approach. In a lot of ordinary museums I suppose you simply don't get the room for manoeuvre you need for that.

Holzer: Of course with a contract the obligations are different, because there's a standard programme, for us but also for the curators. You have to learn to deal with that. Actually I would not like to say: I'll build you a cabinet which has two glass doors, and here you have a selection of suitable objects for it – help yourself. You get 100 of those and then I'll come back again in five years. That's not how I approach things. You can differentiate between the arrangements for the various showcases, by classifying the objects. You can process and articulate the differences in advance.

    In permanent exhibitions you simply can't always work with the same meticulousness or precision, the same eye for detail, as in some temporary ones. But the museum says: I expect you to develop a dramaturgical concept for every display case. But that's just not possible in a permanent exhibition. The quantity may be of interest here: the big picture conceived in terms of a hundred display cases, for example. That's where I begin to see differences.

Kobler: Yes, but not just that. What you're talking about there is also a question of choreography. In the theatre, you have two or three high points where everything becomes very condensed, then there's a lot of noise, and afterwards there are long drawn-out stretches during which everything opens up. And you can't have one beat of the drum after the next in an exhibition either. Between the drumbeats you also need less intense stretches or unexpected twists and surprises. You generally can't approach everything on the same level when it comes to design either, for straightforward financial reasons. There's certainly not a lot of money available. In other words, you 'gold-plate' two or three elements and you make everything else out of cardboard and sheet metal. But the two or three key components have to be gold-plated. In conceptual terms, even in terms of the physical construction, as well as materials. It's like the handle of a heavy door. The door has the mass and the door handle gives you the feeling.

Holzer: Perhaps this needs to be expressed in another way as well. It's not that I don't work on certain things because I don't want to work on them, because of lack of interest or time. It's more a question of reducing the strain of looking, for example through the design of the display cases, which are to some extent constant factors in the staging. The display cases are gorgeous, well installed, always aesthetically pleasing. What we do is also always aesthetically pleasing. Every spoon is well positioned, the captions are excellent and so on. But in the case of the Militärhistorisches Museum in Dresden for example, I certainly envisage the visitor being able to give his or her eyes a rest from time to time, away from the aesthetics.[18] For me, these are important contrasts. Most exhibitions, put together by whatever exhibition designers in whichever city museums, are generally quite well done. Excellent wooden models. Tables five metres long. Everything nicely arranged in rows and worked out to the last detail. Really good. Yet in reality these museums are crap. Why? Because the logic of the exhibition is too simple. A scenographer always has to make sure he is permitting other systems. In a permanent exhibition, it would be interesting if we could create receptacles in which you can work repeatedly with ruptures. Otherwise there's a great danger that the design remains merely fashionable.

Holzer: Perhaps that's the crux of what we do. There are plenty of people who can do design. So can we. But to develop a spatial staging, on the basis of a choreography, which goes beyond mere design and terms like 'nice', with regard to both thematic content and choreography, is a quite different matter.

You've been creating exhibitions for a number of years now. What direction are you moving in? What have you got better at?

Holzer: What I can say is that we look for a 'a big picture' for every exhibition, regardless of how this picture manifests itself. That doesn't always have to mean large-scale installations. The goal is to transmit the core thesis of the exhibition in a visual way. So we are always confronted with the question, what is the big picture? Why are we doing this? We've increasingly found ourselves in situations in which we are actually providing comprehensive packages: media, artwork, spaces, everything, in fact, that makes up the medium of the exhibition, sometimes including the subject matter. We are no longer asked for individual elements, such as designing a display case, while the artwork or VDU comes from elsewhere. This has more or less automatically changed our working methods in that the subject matter which we have to convey takes centre stage and we and the client work out the nature of this conveyance together. You design the level of conveyance together, as it were, a level which is always present in an exhibition. However boring this word *conveyance* may sound, you have to get across the subject matter, regardless of how you do it. As a result we actually work very closely with the experts and curators, far more closely than we used to.

Does that mean that for you the classical division between curator and designer de facto no longer exists? Is there just one point left on the axis between the two, namely the mid-point?

Kobler: The best thing would be if this division ceased to exist altogether. Naturally, there are different areas of expertise. What interests me, increasingly, is the installation as such, without the whole package of sub-tasks relating to what the various objects have to say individually. I'm concerned with the central message, because this is the core reason why you want to create the exhibition in the first place. If you can't identify this core reason, you should forget about the exhibition. It's not remotely enough to say that you're opening the drawer in order to show people something yet again. When it comes to the core statement, I want to be able to select objects with greater freedom.

Would you agree that as scenographers you have very much adopted the stance of the artist? That your work is strongly influenced by an artistic approach?

Kobler: Yes, that's right, only we don't put it like that. There is the subject matter, the statement and the execution, which can be read in multiple ways. For me, the plethora of different readings is what makes a good work of art.

Holzer: You could also put it in another way again. If I had to define our exhibitions by stating whether they are works of art or examples of design, then I would certainly go for the former, because we are not chiefly concerned with pleasing design. Our primary concern really is with the subject matter, with finding powerful images to express it and putting these into concrete form. I don't regard myself as an artist, but our exhibitions represent an artistic perspective. That is certainly true.

Could we go so far as to say that not every topic is a Holzer Kobler topic? Are there topics you don't take on, while others may be dominant or be well suited to your synthetic way of working?

Holzer: It all depends. There are lots of assignments which at first glance make you say, for God's sake, I'm not doing that! But if you manage to rethink everything from the bottom up in dialogue with the client, any topic can be turned into an exciting exhibition. That's the point. I need a key that unlocks the topic for me, that awakens my fascination and enables me to read the topic down to the fine details, because the exhibition has to do much the same thing for the visitors. I need this key because I don't create an exhibition out of a sense of duty. If you find this key, every topic is interesting because together with the experts you explore how to arrange things in new ways and get them across in a compelling fashion. It's like a game of chess. What you are creating is a system of interpretation and a new strategy that you build on top of that.

Kobler: Initially it's often difficult to find your way into a topic. Sometimes it seems hopeless. But that very fact often gives you an idea. For example, I might say to myself, I'm going to destroy this topic completely. A negative approach like this often leads to conversations in which you say, it all amounts to nothing. This fundamental scepticism, and the question of the project's relevance, gradually takes you to the heart of the matter, to what might be fascinating about this topic. You can often find your way back into the topic in this way.

Is it that you have to get really fired up about what you're doing?

Kobler: That's the main problem. If that doesn't happen, then we simply shouldn't go ahead with the exhibition. If you can't become fascinated with the topic yourself, then working on it is just a waste of time.

We've looked back and refreshed our memories about formative exhibitions. Now I'd like us to look forward and pick up the thread of a passage in our dialogue which centred on the search for a visual metaphor for the thesis of the exhibition. For you, the role of this metaphor was to help people get to grips with the structure of the content and form of the exhibition, to realise the thesis in a given space in the shape of a big picture and define how the exhibition may be read. Tristan then stated that good exhibitions are in fact always documents of a given era, which hit on something fundamental about the human condition. I'd like to pick up on that and ask you what you currently consider to be your key cultural references.

Kobler: At the moment I'm constantly fascinated by my son, all the things he learns so quickly, how he looks at things. He's two years old, a blank slate. I'm fascinated by how he approaches things. Again and again, the question arises, what is it that attracts a person? Does something have to move or does it have to be big in order to impress people?

Holzer: There are individuals and works that impress me. There are also one or two women who have been key figures for me from very early on. Frida Kahlo is an example of such a key figure, someone who managed to construct a reality of her own and also managed to live that reality.[19] There's this black-and-white photograph that I've been carrying around with me for years that shows Frida Kahlo in an enormously long skirt with a clay pigeon. These are important figures for me, like Simone de Beauvoir.[20] Women who claimed a bit of freedom so that they could be creative, produce art and take a strong political stand.

Kobler: There are a great many, but for me it's not systematically linked with individuals, but more incidental. I remember the paintings in the Mauritshuis gallery in The Hague.[21] You only need to walk through it once and you've got the stereotypical image of the Dutch in your head. They also have the painting by Johannes Vermeer there, *Girl with a Pearl Earring*.[22] The painting is 400 years old or so, but you have the feeling the woman is breathing. It's alive. That's an event. I can't get that picture out of my head. I also have a postcard of this painting, but it doesn't have the same effect. But in the gallery in the Mauritshuis, you really have to look to make sure she's not moving. That's a timeless picture that will still be incredible in another 200 years.

Holzer: Images like that represent a state of mind. In terms of my own biography the time with Daniel Libeskind was important because I was confronted with an energy and a faith that it is in fact possible to make certain things happen.[23] What are you working on? How are you investing your time? Where does this power come from? Where is it taking you? This state of mind involves saying, in the first instance, anything is possible. If you lack this faith, you simply give up after filling out the first form, don't you? For artistic work it is extremely important that at some point someone tells you: open the doors, it is possible. This is something I was presented with in a very radical way and it's something I practised. That was a major inspiration.

Kobler: It's always about works produced by a certain kind of free thinking, because this thinking is able to break with conventions and there's always an element of freedom in these works themselves. And you can feel that freedom. This is a crucial point for me. In school I was always told that you can't do anything. You hear that over a long period of time and at some point you do something and suddenly people appear saying, that's brilliant! If you create exhibitions in Switzerland when you're young, you get nothing but criticism. If you allow yourself the freedom to make certain statements, you are immediately given a dressing-down. But in New York for example, where no-one knows us, you find a totally different, positive enthusiasm; people say, that's a good idea, you must do it. And if you reply that it lies far outside your area of expertise, they say: it doesn't matter, just do it, that's how I started out. Suddenly you notice that if you have a strong idea, you will get somewhere with it. Here you tend to be held back.

You've said, we're not collectors and we don't work with props. But my understanding is that you're always on the lookout for compelling images, for expressive words. So what do you collect in your own minds?

Holzer: It's always about experiences in one way or another, experiences which impress because of a certain attitude. It has something to do with ways of seeing and also with provocation, with seeking out the limits of the tolerable, of the achievable. The desire simply to amaze and astonish is a key driving force. The idea is not to shock people. If you manage to do that in a positive way, that's fine as well. In everyday life as well there are people who impress and don't even work in an art-related context. When I was a child I had an Italian teacher who had long brown hair and thick-lensed glasses. She was a small woman and always walked through the schoolhouse in slow motion carrying a big pile of books, looking at no-one. At some point she came into the classroom, slammed the door shut, banged the books down on the table and was there. That's something I remember with complete clarity. A very normal woman really, with such radicalism in her character. My interpretation was always that for her this was the only way to endure this environment: I'm somewhere else, I arrive when I wish. I think that's pretty special.

How provocative or radical are your exhibition projects?

Holzer: The aim is still to produce a strong, expressive picture. But that doesn't mean that our solution is to offer the same answer to varying questions. The greatest shock would probably be if we were to celebrate the absence of outlandish form and merely presented a couple of small display cases. After all, the task is always to surprise, to break through certain public expectations. This is still the goal of our work. We recently spent a long time arguing over a small installation in Luxembourg.[24] Tristan had a picture. I didn't like it. We spent ages fine-tuning it. The question is always, what kind of picture is it that you're selling. Is it special enough? Are people amazed by it? Is it funny? Is it provocative? But we always try to find an abstract metaphor. We try yet again to convert whatever is amazing about a topic into a strong image. That has to be the ultimate destination. I would like to move a bit away from the work we're known for. Though that's also significant: how do you quote yourself? You did something at some point – can you do it again? Do we have to change it or come up with new solutions despite these past experiences? These are the kind of demands we make of ourselves because we are also trying to take our vocabulary further. For me, that vocabulary is not complete with what we have now. This aspiration to develop our vocabulary further also gives rise to new things.

Kobler: In theatre and in a performance you can condense things to an incredible degree. If I manage to do that in an exhibition, then that's the ideal. The exhibition is based on other devices, entails different possibilities, is not based on the individual actors, who may surprise us, offers very little drama of the kind that unfolds over time in linear fashion. The exhibition has no beginning or end like a film or a piece of music. Yet the goal is still to create such condensed moments and dramatically loaded intervals, using different devices than in the theatre. That's rather more difficult in an exhibition because you can't get a group of people simultaneously into a hyped-up state, into a general state of hysteria and then knock them for six. In an exhibition, you can achieve that kind of thing only in a differentiated way, tailored to individuals and small groups. This is why you always need a strong message, and as we don't create art installations in a gallery or museum, but impart the thematic content of exhibitions, your interlocutor, the client, has to play a role as well. So the question then becomes: is this the message they want? Is it too strong for them? Does it even mean anything to them? You can of course produce certain messages in advance, without the client noticing. But ideally you come together on these levels at the planning stage, so that you get the desired strength right.

Holzer: I have the feeling that in future, alongside the need for well-designed and well-lit display cases, museums might require you to search for these relevant messages or a certain symbolism that expresses these messages. This may not apply to every museum, but particularly to those places outside of the major cities, to cities of medium size and importance, where people are open to different approaches and willing to consider something different. You need something sensational, that has a certain outlandishness and that makes a statement, so that people talk about it and it tends to draw people in. Because that certainly doesn't happen through the objects and the collection. So the question of how exhibition design can help to communicate and can help to place things within an interesting setting, is certainly one aspect of our work. That's how it works in the field of architecture. You go for Frank Gehry or Daniel Libeskind, because they are also the best marketing tools and in fact fairly inexpensive. It's all over the media and everyone's been talking about it. I have the feeling that something like that might also take hold in the exhibition world.

Kobler: I've noticed that even in conventional museums increasingly what they're looking for is an experience. They're quite simply ready to sacrifice a great deal of good subject matter for the sake of an experience. I think that's very dangerous because mostly the experiences have nothing to do with the subject matter. So you pass through the exhibition in a little train and say, this is great! But even with Rembrandt's *Night Watch*, a Cy Twombly or an oil painting you can create experiences geared towards the subject matter, which are expressive and lead you away from the dead end of mere entertainment. I don't mean that the works are enough in themselves, though sometimes they are. But the key thing is always to achieve the right contrast between the original and the staging, so that the right questions are thrown up, ones that lead to new conclusions. It's a matter of identity or even uniqueness. The important thing is that the exhibition offers something that I can't find anywhere else. The crucial point is that I am confronted with a powerful image that I can't see at home. Places with a strong identity generate experiences.

You've said that an exhibition must offer a big picture, put forward a thesis within a given space, something that you enter into and take part in, and only then does the whole thing begin to work; something suddenly opens up and this moment of opening is the real goal of scenography. What does Disney have to teach us here?

Kobler: I think you can learn a great deal from Disney, because they turn highly controlled, well-thought-out projects into reality.[25] What Disney actually do is present us with the reality of a surreal, non-existent world, and these worlds offer us the chance to take some time out. You know that you have to return to the real world at some point. Disneyland is an alternative world. This is the interesting thing, which has nothing to do with the question of whether it is formally correct or incorrect. They simply manage to get the visitor to dive into this alternative world. Such moments have something to do with intensity. The ideal would be to achieve a similar intensity in your own work.

But don't you create alternative worlds? What I remember most about 'All We Need', for example, is two rooms. The pink room right at the top with the enormous long bed which you could lie down on to listen to stories. This room was simply a dramatic proposition, an opportunity for the visitor to be absorbed completely into the overall picture and that picture was intense, generous, inviting, poetic and unforgettable: bewitching.

I simply lay down. The other room whose identity remains clear in my mind's eye was far more intellectual in character but was also poetic. This was the room with the statistics presented through grains of rice. Abstract subject matter in the form of statistical facts were transformed – in formally coherent and consistent fashion – in a way that was instantaneous. Despite a totally different language, here too an alternative world came into being because it contained elements that allowed me to see differently.

Kobler: And that's always the work that you do as a designer. You sift something out and then you have to repackage it in a striking way, trying to leave out external influences as much as possible, so that you can really concentrate on one message or one sentiment. That's important.

Holzer: It's interesting that you pick up on those two rooms, because they really are spaces which work well because they are so straightforward, simple and reduced. The other thing is what you might call the Alice in Wonderland effect. By breaking with familiar scale – a normal bed is 2 metres by 1 metre and here suddenly 20 metres x 3 metres – you generate a quite different feeling for themes that you're used to dealing with in daily life.[26] The huge bed, which makes the visitor very small – such distortions have the ability to amaze, and awaken emotions, because anything that changes the scale takes the visitor into a bit of a wonderland. When proportions change and the messages are borne by unfamiliar means, like the statistics in rice, the way in which the exhibition is read may shift. For example, if we'd presented the statistics with normal pie charts, no-one would have looked at them.

Kober: It's the methods of alienation that you're using there. Extracting but also defamiliarising things and not trying to depict the world realistically. Perhaps this is the difference from Disney, artistically speaking? Because in the case of Disney the means of alienation can often be understood, and read, as real.

The statistics in rice introduced a compelling metaphor.

Through the rice heap, a key thesis was placed in the room in easily readable form. The big picture gave the place an identity people were sure to relate to, because rice is quite simply the basic food of the masses, and the grain of rice an atom of life, as it were. The visual language of the rice room worked on both a large and a small scale.

Kobler: Interesting. The rice installation is by Stan's Café.[27] It's not one of ours. That was the aim of the exhibition, to collaborate with lots of artists. Stan's Café aren't even artists, they're an English theatre group from Birmingham and actually what they did here was to transform a performance, which they often stage in a theatre for just two or three days, into an installation. There are actually two or three more people who constantly create new patterns out of the rice. But financially it was impossible to engage a theatre group for six months. In principle we try not to separate art and didactics, information and entertainment in our stagings. On the other hand, we want to interweave the complex of different levels in such a way that a new unity is generated.

You chose this theatre group for the exhibition in order to give form to and represent this aspect of the 'All We Need' theme in a compelling way that appeals to the senses. This surely means that you took on the role of curator and therefore began to blur the boundaries between your curatorial and scenographic approaches, and that the curatorial and scenographic perspectives merge into a new integrated standpoint.

Kobler: In 'All We Need', I think there was no dividing line between scenography and curation. There was simply a group of people who did everything, including the execution. When everything comes together like that, you can actually get around a whole number of obstacles that you're otherwise faced with, and achieve the desired intensity more easily.

You've rejected the idea of exclusivity, in other words that

you're either a curator or a scenographer, because, so it seemed to me, you feel that it is precisely in the fusion of the two roles that you can discover new potential. In 'All We Need', it makes absolutely no difference that you didn't develop the statistics in rice yourselves. You went for this expressive staging by Stan's Café. That's the key thing.

Kobler: That's right. In the end what you have is an overall picture and this overall picture has to ring true. I'm glad it worked for you. You don't need to do everything yourself. What you have to do is bring together the right constellation of people.

Holzer: That's also part of the work you have to do.
It simply happens to be the case that we often curate. We not only play the role of designer, but also that of curator and this means, for example, that it's not us who are the artists, but instead we bring in artists whenever relevant. In a great many of the exhibitions that we've also curated, we've often worked up close to the art. Or we've worked the big picture into a given topic in collaboration with artists. For us, artists are simply crucial partners in the execution itself. There may be a broad form that comes from us. But the individual chapters are often adapted in a quite different way.

You've just said, we're not artists. Why not? What's the difference?

Holzer: We're exhibition designers and we're architects. The work that an artist does is free of the constraints of a contract. Our work isn't, though we also explore a topic and create a work. There's always a difference depending on whether an artist does it or we do it. As designers, we always work within an overall context. We bring everything together and try to define it from a stylistic point of view. That's our task. And we don't bring in artists to take on the work of designing the exhibition, but to deal with specific themes. In the case of certain themes, statements have already been made by artists with such precision that we want to work with these people. Tristan and I develop a script for a work as a whole; together with a group of people, this is put into action and realised in as coherent a way as possible. Stan's Café has already been working with these statistics in rice for ten years and we made use of this potential. How would you begin to do something like that yourself? The work done by Stan's Café is a work of art. The thing is to discover these works by artists who have been working on a given theme for years. You can't just substitute design for that kind of intensity.

Your role is sometimes not much different from that of a composer who writes a violin solo, can imagine it and already hear it in his head as it were, but cannot himself play the solo on the violin and needs a suitable musician to do so. What you have here is simply two states of the same work.

Holzer: I would make a similar analogy with the role of a film director. If I take our project '*Heimatfabrik*', we were what you might call the directors.[28] We chose the artists and the artists created their works within the framework of our directorial plan for the exhibition. That was a very tough battle because we had very clear ideas about where these artists should be going. This was far from easy for the artists because they aren't used to creating art to order or operating within the framework of a big picture. Our approach, if you like, is certainly strongly influenced by art, but for me it's also shaped by theatre and film. And it's also shaped by a style. If I take Robert Wilson for example in the case of theatre, this clearly corresponds to what we do.[29] We are fascinated by the strong, translated, abstract images found in art, film and theatre. But that's a matter of both style and of an approach that draws on an artistic aspiration. We simply work on a different type of artwork.

How important is Robert Wilson to you?

Holzer: For me, the significance of Robert Wilson lies in his extreme abstraction and distortion of scale. I find that brilliant, these images: abstraction in the colours and in the light and the defamiliarisation of scale, absolute reduction. These things

	make Wilson one of the greatest figures in the world of stage direction. This very slight degree of surrealism that you also find in his work also fascinates me. This rupture, where the whole thing suddenly flips over into a dream world, using the most meagre of devices.
Kobler:	What I find interesting about Wilson is when he manages to give you the feeling that nothing further can be taken away, that everything's been reduced down to a skeleton. I think that's brilliant. His aim is to utilise whatever is needed for the message and no more. He reaches a point where nothing further can be taken away without losing the message. In other words, how do you maximise the message with the minimum of resources? That's the key question.

And Peter Greenaway?[30]

Holzer:	Yes, of course. Greenaway works in exactly the same way. These very dark films, where all you can see is the emergency exit sign, are incredibly impressive. But that's the same style.
Holzer:	It's the earlier films in particular that I found incredibly impressive. *A Zed & Two Naughts*, *The Cook, the Thief, His Wife and Her Lover*. These were films where half the audience left after the break.[31] The first half of the film was so penetrating and unbearable that a lot of people couldn't stand it. Then after the break there's a radical rupture in the film. I think that Greenaway wanted to chase people out of the cinema and then he can begin to tell a story. I found this incredibly powerful and intense; his productions are nothing less than baroque. But this richness is necessary because it allows him to tell another two or three little stories in the background, which have nothing to do with the main narrative. That fascinates me. It's actually an interweaving of several stories in which you know that the connections between the stories create purely random levels of meaning. This has stayed with me as an image and this is also what we're always trying to put into practice in our exhibitions. There's a main story, but at the same time another two or three contrasting stories, which endow the exhibition with a certain openness, so that people can also interpret it in an open way.

Holzer: But when you analyse where and when these films become almost unbearable, you notice that almost nothing happens. That's the astonishing thing. There's this emptiness and long drawn-out patches. This is another key point. The tension doesn't come from hyperactivity at all, but through the construction of emptiness, colour, light, darkness and brightness, which suggest that a great deal is happening though you don't see anything. This may also be the little stories that Tristan senses in the background. That's the potential of film. But an exhibition is something different than film, or art or theatre. With time-based media, through dramatic images and dramatic lighting, we try to bring emotionality into the exhibition. This is probably always the key thing. How do you implant moments of movement in the static form of the exhibition? In the exhibition '*Waffen werfen Schatten*', for example, there was no movement at all. Instead, the main image functioned as a state of frozen movement and this, as it were, is what made the exhibition interesting. And often this is the key question: how to liberate the collection from the sense of its having been stored away in some dusty vault, how to set it in motion imaginatively. Suggestive images of frozen movement can have a tremendous impact. The task of the big picture in an exhibition is to hook the visitors. It should throw a switch in their heads, in such a way that they ask themselves: what's this? Through this fascination, you express your readiness, so to speak, to take an interest in the information presented in the exhibition. Through the big picture and the first look connected with it, the visitor hopefully feels curious and really gets involved in the exhibition. In the case of '*In Heikler Mission*', which was about Swiss diplomacy, we also tried to liberate the reading of the exhibition from the expectations typical of visitors to historical museums. First there's duty. Then history. And then the collection. Instead, we tried to proceed through a very different type of fascination, namely that of a picture, a spatial image, which ultimately makes a meaningful statement.

So you use the big picture to grab people by the collar and set them down in another world?

Kobler: It's the story that can be told in three sentences, just as a Hitchcock film forms a compact tale that can be quickly told.[32] But as in film, the big picture merely accompanies the first impressions. You have an idea of who the murderer is and you might now be done with the film, only there's a rupture. It's not him. Maybe it's the other guy. Points of view shift and new facts unsettle our view of the thing. This unsettling is also hugely important in an exhibition in order to open visitors' minds. Initially the visitor sees this clear picture, which gets semantically fragmented, dissolved and reinterpreted through a constant change of perspective as he or she moves through the exhibition.

Holzer: The rice room in 'All We Need' worked in exactly the same way. We cannot assume any interest in the statistics per se, far from it. You're always coming across these statistics in the newspapers. They don't sink in. Somehow you know how many millions of people have died of hunger, or how many die of hunger each second. But through this staging with rice heaps, through this spatial image, you're suddenly open to these facts. You suddenly perceive these facts in a quite different way. Of course, you don't always manage to do this in such a powerful way. But that's certainly the goal.

You also work in a commercial context. Is there a difference for you between a cultural exhibition and a project such as Ebisquare?[33]

Kobler: The projects are totally different but I think our approach is much the same. The point of departure is very different. In a cultural exhibition I want to make a strong statement and intellectual work is required. I can also bring that into a commercial context, but then more as an aside, with 'infotainment' for instance. But here the aim is more to create a place where people like to be, somewhere I myself would like to be. A place with various qualities, where I can sit down and have a coffee, go shopping or simply while away the time.

Holzer: It's no easy matter teasing apart the commercial from the cultural. I no longer believe you can really do that. As far as the process of design is concerned, I see the task of creating a striking commercial space in exactly the same way as a cultural one. I approach Ebisquare in exactly the same way as the development of an exhibition. That may be putting it in slightly radical terms, but in both cases the first priority is to work out what kind of place has to be 'performed' and what statement is to be made. Not even a commercial space is free of some kind of meaningful statement. In an exhibition the task at hand tends to be didactic or cultural. But in principle the task is the same. In both cases, for the people who go there for whatever reasons, you have to create a place that functions and that has a certain uniqueness. This is the key point. If you're creating a shopping centre with 120 shops, the various elements also have to be fitted into a complex overall scheme. I see that as much the same as the assignment we were given by the Militärhistorisches Museum in Dresden, where we had to exhibit 10,000 items on military history in display cases.[34] These are different tasks, of course. But in terms of methodology, our creative approach to these tasks is really not so different.

Kobler: The goals are different, but the work is not much different.

Holzer: You have culture and commerce, which are often still separate realms here. But in America this has already been turned on its head. You have private sponsors. Every work of art is private. Every museum is privately owned and bears the name of the sponsor. And the most important, most significant spaces in American museums are rent-out spaces for the shop and catering. And this mixing up of elements, which means that cultural places also have to be commercially successful, is a trend that can no longer be halted. That's the way things are going at the moment. There are of course still the protected, luxurious public spaces where culture is to be found. But even these are increasingly compelled to include commercially successful elements, whether it's a shop, a restaurant or rent-out spaces where you can hold weddings or where the board of directors can have meetings in the historical setting of an armoury hall. And so on. And that's why I find the challenge we're faced with in our office exciting, ranging from the exhibition, through scenography for shopping centres, to high-end commercial spaces. In our office, these seemingly very different spaces and assignments flow together. For me, this also shows that these differences are becoming ever more slight and that a commercial setting can suddenly incorporate a cultural assignment and vice versa. I don't know where this movement is leading but it's certainly there.

Kobler: I think the two spheres should be far more strongly connected. Even in a museum it is the shop and cafeteria that bring in the money. I think you should have good clothes shops and bookshops in the foyers, to make some money that can be used to rent spaces for exhibitions. It's not happening here yet but I expect that in ten to 15 years the museums will be in the shopping centres. That's a great idea. There's incredible potential in that.

Holzer: If you send someone from a really old cultural milieu to the MoMA, I'm not sure whether he can distinguish whether he's in a building containing one of the most valuable art collections or in a warehouse.[35]

Kobler: The MoMA is also one of the most successful shopping centres. It has an incredibly high turnover per square metre.

Holzer: In terms of area the MoMA shop has an enormous shop front: the entire museum!

We've labelled our research project 'Narrative Environments', in part to get away from the old notions of 'exhibition' as opposed to 'stage' as opposed to 'commercial space' and so on. In other words, in order to be able to redefine and re-evaluate the boundaries. How would you sum up the concept of 'narrative space'?[36]

Kobler: Is there actually such a thing as a non-narrative space? All spaces are narrative in one way or another, no matter how boring or interesting they are. Every space tells a particular story. The way I look at it is that narrative spaces are spaces that tell stories. The dentist's waiting room is a narrative space. There are no non-narrative spaces. So in our context the key question is which stories we wish to tell in a given space.

Holzer: Is it a case of which story we're telling or which story the visitor reads? These differences between the one who creates the space and the one who experiences the space are fascinating.

Both of you mentioned Monet's *Water Lilies* **earlier as a key reference. Why were these paintings so important to you?**

Kobler: I saw the *Water Lilies* in London during my first visit to the city. I remember this big museum and these big pictures. My father painted as a hobby and we always had the Impressionists in our house in the form of books and pictures. And then suddenly you're standing in front of the originals, which are far larger and better than you'd imagined. I could sit there for hours looking into these paintings without it becoming boring, though they're actually no more than ponds with a few leaves. I found that really fascinating. It's representational painting, but it's not about the objects at all. You simply get into a dream-like state as you stand looking at these paintings.

Holzer: I was also fascinated by the size of the pictures of course, but there's something else as well. Yesterday we talked about the subject of time and for me Monet's *Water Lilies* present us with a frozen moment. These are images that suggest infinity. You lose yourself when you look at them. You can read them on an incredible number of different levels. You can read expanses into them. It's a picture that awakens a great many associations. It fascinates me that it can capture all of this through such a simple, obvious motif. The ability to translate into art the strength of nature at this particular moment in this particular place is truly impressive.

Kobler: It's also a question of the defamiliarisation in painting. A photograph of this motif on the same scale would be something quite different. The motif dissolves. It's actually no more than dabs of paint. It's not what you think it is at all. And the exciting thing about this image is precisely the fact that you see it as representational one moment and non-representational the next. The incredibly varied colours which then resolve into a blue or a green. This incredible variety. As you look at them, the images disperse into other facets that then become visible. The *Water Lilies* combine a superficial clarity with a subtle complexity and multi-layered quality. That's what I find fascinating.

When you stand eye to eye with these paintings, the situation has become completely unstable and the way you read it is transformed. That in itself is an exciting model for the development and design of narrative spaces, don't you think?

Kobler: It does work in a very similar way. When we talk about a powerful image, we don't mean reduction to an interpretation, but a powerful superordinate image, one with which a great number of influences and references are woven and which allows for multiple readings.

Holzer: I also think it's important that the *Water Lilies* are paintings in which you can lose yourself.

Tristan stated that there are no non-narrative spaces. But if every space is a narrative space, what is an exhibition?

Kobler: An exhibition is of course also a narrative space. That's unavoidable. And if it's unavoidable it has to become part of the plan. In other words, I can guide the narrative. And a lot of exhibition designers don't think that it's narrative and therefore they make no attempt to guide the narrative. This aspect is paid no attention in a lot of exhibitions. The presentation certainly tells a story, but perhaps not the intended one.

Holzer: As silly as it may sound, every exhibition has a didactic task, a thematic assignment. The exhibition should convey a message. In other words, there is a narrative. The exhibition maker has to bring along a narrative. In other narrative environments the narrative may arise in part from the circumstances and realities of a given location. The narrative of an exhibition is not present from the outset as a basic tone pervading the exhibition site. The narrative of an exhibition has to be inscribed into the space and constructed artificially by the curator and scenographer. It hasn't grown over time. I think that's the key difference. In an exhibition you create an artificial world, just as you do in the cinema or theatre.

How important is the title with respect to the narrative potential of an exhibition? Take 'In Heikler Mission' ('On a Delicate Mission'). *Heikel* **(delicate, awkward) is of course a compelling and productive term because it suggests a certain instability. To what extent was** *heikel* **a parameter in the design?**

Kobler: We thought up the title after the exhibition had been designed. Sometimes there's a working title and depending on various factors a title may be the very thing that sparks off ideas. The working title of '*In Heikler Mission*' was simply '*Diplomatie in der Schweizer Geschichte*' ('Diplomacy in Swiss History') and far more neutral. After the change of title, we could no longer make major changes to the design of the exhibition. I liked the title '*In Heikler Mission*' a great deal.

Holzer: But often the title goes hand in hand with the design, the title is defined in connection with the design. This was very much the case with '*Waffen werfen Schatten*' ('Weapons Cast Shadows'). The title developed out of the image and theme of the exhibition.

The title '*Waffen werfen Schatten*' itself largely determined the reading and facilitated understanding. The title had an immediate metaphorical potential. Brilliant!

Kobler: But even in that case there was a lot of to-ing and fro-ing. There were several possible titles. This also inspired us, and the curators noticed that the title '*Waffen werfen Schatten*' simply hits the mark, and then of course when we opted for this title it had an enormous influence on the lighting.

I remember that in the first instance you got nowhere with the topic of diplomacy, until the moment when the mural painting by Ferdinand Hodler was discovered on the ceiling of the hall of fame gallery.[37] This image could

barbara holzer and tristan kobler

be seen as an icon of Swiss history and it gave impetus to the visual concept of the exhibition.

Kobler: It wasn't due to lack of interest in diplomacy. It's just that we knew nothing about it. It meant nothing to us. For a long time, diplomacy was almost non-existent in Switzerland. It didn't spark anything off in our minds.

Holzer: The painting by Ferdinand Hodler, *Rückzug von Marignano* [*Retreat from Marignano*], hangs above the hall of fame and shows the retreat of the Swiss soldiers following their defeat in battle at Marignano in 1515, and this defeat triggered the Swiss policy of neutrality.[38] This is interesting because on the one hand the image of a battle is of course the antithesis of diplomacy, yet on the other hand it opened the way to diplomacy. This turn from battle to diplomacy was important to the staging of the exhibition.

Kobler: Hodler's painting determined the scenography. In the centre of the exhibition there was a large negotiating table under an enormous white tented roof that we'd installed in the room. From the table, all you could see high up in the room was the Hodler triptych on one side and the triptych developed by us on the other, as a reminder of the lost battle and the necessity for diplomacy. There used to be another painting by Hodler in the room as well: *The Battle of Murten*, but that was away for restoration.[39] So we showed contemporary lost battles of diplomacy there in a bespoke montage. So the scenography of these two images dictated the space completely.

I had certain difficulties with the adjective *heikel*, because it very much suggests unstable situations, yet the image of Switzerland in the world tends to be one of security. Why was this tendency towards delicacy, or instability, so hard to detect in the end product?

Kobler: Because that wasn't the intention. '*In Heikler Mission*' is a figure of speech which is even used in the newspapers here in Switzerland. We say that people are '*in heikler Mission*' if they are about to engage in diplomacy. The fact that we use this expression implies a number of things. Switzerland is far from being a superpower. Delicacy doesn't come into it for superpowers. A superpower simply says that's acceptable and that isn't. But we have to negotiate and manoeuvre. You're always in the weaker position and somehow have to try and skilfully thread your way through. Also, Switzerland never sent professionals, but always various successful businessmen, who weren't paid but who thought it interesting to negotiate with the king in Paris. Because they weren't paid, they were actually regarded as superfluous.

Holzer: You're touching on a point which is definitely *heikel*. It's always a question of narrative and history. The issue of political correctness also always plays a role in a national museum. So far, diplomacy hasn't been researched much in this country and you need a considerable amount of time before you can develop the topic to a point where the narrative can be broken down into a sequence of entirely distinct episodes. I have the feeling that we and the people at the national museum really lacked the time to take the research to a point where you can tell clear-cut stories that bring this delicate aspect home to people. There are stagings and exhibits that manage this and that function through this ambiguity. But this only works if the interpretation of the subject matter and scenographic execution are consistent in terms of concept and design. This is why in principle you can never separate things in an exhibition and say the subject matter is good but the design is bad or the other way round. It all has to be of one piece.

If everything is a narrative space, articulated or not, which makes a statement, then the question that immediately arises is, under what conditions can this statement be read? What is the readability of the space and what is the quality of the looking through which the visitor reads the room? That would be my second point with respect to 'In Heikler Mission'. Through the large white tented roof, the scenography placed enormous emphasis on the centre of the room. This was a really surprising spatial effect. What I then felt was missing, simply because the

expectation had been aroused, was the dramatic charge of the staging of the dining table in the centre. It was the right ambience for a passionate, tricky after-dinner speech. Instead there was just a mixture of whispering and chatter. Why was that?

Kobler: That was our original intention. We put forward two people from five different eras who had been important at the time. We wanted to seat these people at the table with foreign diplomats through auditory and virtual means. So the image was: people from different times, with different problems on their hands, sit together at the table and have a discussion. But we weren't allowed to do that. Ultimately, all we were able to do were things emptied of content. We weren't allowed to do what we wanted because it was impossible to assess the risks. People didn't understand that our aim was simply to bring out the potential points of friction in the conversations. So what we ended up with was literally incomprehensible. The delicate narratives were not even recorded because we already knew that we wouldn't be able to use them.

That's a shame.

Holzer: This is what I meant by the political correctness of an exhibition. You're only going to be able to address the problematic aspects of diplomacy or give voice to imaginary diplomats in a place like the national museum if you manage to carry the museum and the historians with you on the adventure. That takes a lot of time. You can't do it in two or three weeks. It really takes a long time, and that we didn't have. And most museum staff aren't trained to think like that. They can't judge what the effect will be. If we'd been able to implement our idea, then the staging, with the table in the centre, would have been far more impactful than a mere spatial gesture because it would have been powerfully undergirded by the subject matter. In the museum world you can't really take it for granted that you'll find people who are able to assess and support these processes. It actually astonishes me that we managed to carry people with us along this path at all. We had to do a test and show them what it would look like. Then they could see, aha, this doesn't enter the danger zone. So these really are processes that can't be speeded up.

Kobler: It's a shame because it's always at the precise moment when you say, it's getting dangerous, that it's actually getting interesting. Then you can be criticised and you have to lay yourself open to attack and clarify your ideas. Fiction isn't allowed in a historical museum. This is a tricky area and usually it's almost forbidden, though official histories also contain lots of fictional elements. It's at exactly this point that it becomes exciting. Once in the danger zone, the museum, curator and scenographer are open to attack and that gets the discussion going.

Because you potentially cover all the bases required to develop a radical exhibition, I guess that at some point there will be a moment when you are given carte blanche by a museum with respect to curation and scenography. I remember 'The Physical Self' in the Museum Boijmans in Rotterdam, where Peter Greenaway was given carte blanche by the director Wim Crouwel to use all the museum's collections relating to the theme of the body as his canvas when putting together his exhibition.[40] This caused internal arguments and conflicts within the museum. But Greenaway was shielded and got his way, doing some radical things with the living bodies of real people in display cases. This idea, simple in itself, radicalised the entire exhibition and lent dynamism to how people viewed the other exhibits.

Kobler: The interesting thing about this example is that if one of the Boijmans curators had made a similar suggestion, he would have got nowhere, because his colleagues simply wouldn't have given him the Botticelli or the Breughel. A project like that can really only be done by someone from outside, in this case Greenaway, who people know is creating an artwork and is a brilliant individual who doesn't have to continue to exist within this institution. Many museums are familiar with these

Holzer: internal turf wars and conflicts and sometimes you need guest curators to break through this dynamic.

Holzer: It's a fascinating example. If you bring in Greenaway, you can be sure that you're going to get a radical story. That's the expectation. The exciting thing here is that suddenly what you get is more than the usual room for objects, you get a discourse. It's then that it becomes interesting. But the discourse doesn't always have to be brought in by the so-called straightforward exhibition designers. In general, it's content-related approaches capable of breaking with conventions that need to be encouraged. Museums often work with external designers, but most productions fail to go much beyond self-satisfaction. But for concepts like 'The Physical Self' you need brilliant minds, from the museum side as well, because the stirring idea often carries within it the desire for discourse and what you need is someone who wants to take his museum or collection down that road in the first place. You can count the museums like that on the fingers of one hand.

Is it your ambition to bring discourses into a given space?

Holzer: That's part of the struggle, let me put it like that. When we present ourselves to institutions and museums, we're the people who constantly question everything, sometimes in a provocative way, sometimes in a laid-back way, and we simply do not stop. Sometimes the door is opened wide and they let you do whatever you want, and sometimes you have to adapt and make choices while trying to get a grip on the thing through a kind of creative solution. But I have the feeling over the time we've been working and in light of the feedback we get, that people are increasingly keen for us to get involved. That people are keen for us to contribute to the content and give them our opinion. This reputation is gradually beginning to take hold.

What does it actually mean to be an author-designer in this context?

Holzer: If I take another step back, then there's the classical architects' question, what would you most like to build? The ideal scenario is self-evident: no restrictions, an owner who lets you do anything you want and an architect with total freedom. Or is it? That's probably the most boring thing that could possibly happen to you. Of course it's great that you can work on the content and develop an overall concept. But I wouldn't say it's any less interesting collaborating with people who have been dealing with a particular topic all their lives and can bring in the discourse right from the outset. Of course they have to get involved in new images or a discourse that they have never carried on before. But when you encounter a team like that you notice how much know-how they have and how ignorant we actually are. We have no idea. We try to get a grip on this knowledge as though we were the first visitors. Everything's completely new. In terms of the subject matter we are simply uneducated people surrounded by educated people. In itself, the discourse which then unfolds generally has incredible potential.

Kobler: I agree. Otherwise we'd be in the wrong job and would have to become curators. But if you say you're a scenographer then you involve yourself in exactly these kinds of discourse. You need an interlocutor. That gives rise to certain points of friction and ideas that can then be put into practice. If there's no friction or interlocutor, it's much more difficult. Sometimes we work in a purely curatorial capacity. But even then we bring in experts, either as critics, or as sub-curators, so that we again have this interlocutor. It is only through discourse that you get to a point where the essence of the exhibition can be defined and realised. Through dialogues and the inevitable misunderstandings, images emerge that you would never have thought of. It can only happen through this kind of exchange.

Doesn't being a scenographer implicitly mean that the curatorial side is part of the deal?

Kobler: Yes, but you can't always say that.

Doesn't Harald Szeemann embody what we would wish to

barbara holzer and tristan kobler

understand by the term 'curator'?

Kobler: Absolutely, but Szeemann wasn't a scenographer.[41] His strength lay in the thematic field, in the subject matter, and not necessarily in the visual side of the exhibition, in terms of how it looked when completed. I don't know if he was less interested in that side of things, but it certainly wasn't his strength.

Isn't it the case that the successful exhibition maker of the future will basically be positioned at the centre of the classical axis between curator and scenographer?

Kobler: I would argue that sometimes the curatorial work is far more important than the scenographic. If the curatorial work is done right, the scenographic work is fairly simple. But you have to move between both fields to achieve quality. The most important thing, I always think, is not how the exhibition looks but what statement it's making. The curatorial work is crucial in this respect. It's either done already or gets done through a dialogue with us.

Holzer: It's rare to come across a good concept without a lot of intensive effort. It just doesn't happen that everything is ripe for execution from the word go. In most museums, you need a year or two to work on it before you reach that point. Before that there is a confusing mass of possibilities and one of the key questions is, how do you sort through and hierarchise it all?

Will Holzer Kobler still be creating exhibitions five years from now? What will they look like? What are your dreams?

Holzer: In principle I'd say yes to the first question. What I'm primarily interested in is the question of the attitude with which you approach a project and make it your own. We're constantly trying to realise a powerful, exciting concept in order to produce a powerful overall picture and a powerful message. This kind of goal stays interesting as long as the individual projects remain challenging. If the job becomes a repetition, it becomes easy. I think that's the moment when we'll stop and say, it's all over. But you keep on trying to see whether you can reinvent the wheel, which does take a great deal of effort. As long as this is the case, making exhibitions is still a creative act and I find it fascinating. My dream would simply be for certain processes to go more quickly, to get to certain points more quickly and deal with these processes more effectively. So far, every component that we've created has been unique, and you can always improve or modify how you achieve these things.

Kobler: I have stopped at certain points and didn't want to create any more exhibitions. I actually never really started but simply slipped into the field. And I never studied it either, I'm completely self-taught. Formerly, almost no-one approached exhibition design in a conscious way. Nowadays people know that there's tremendous potential in the medium of the exhibition. This consciousness has now reached every provincial museum and become a matter of course. I remember that after Mario Botta had created an exhibition, the Kunsthaus here in Zurich suddenly began referring to 'staged spaces'.[40] It was obviously the first time that the museum had become aware that you can stage spaces. I found this absolutely astonishing, because we had almost abandoned the term by then. We were already elsewhere by then, at the Museum für Gestaltung.[42]

Looking to the future, what direction do you see yourself moving in?

Kobler: If I allow myself to dream a little, all I'm really interested in is a competent interlocutor. It's sometimes quite an effort to start with the basics again. I'm on the lookout for curators or clients who are courageous, competent, and as clever as possible, people who have equally powerful images in their heads and are not afraid of them. That's when things get most interesting and you make the greatest progress.

But that's a factor beyond your control.

Kobler: True, but that's what I dream of.

barbara holzer and tristan kobler

Notes

1 Claude Monet (1840–1926), *Water Lilies*, 1906–1919. The *Water Lilies* (or *Nymphéas*) is a series of approximately 250 oil paintings which depict Monet's flower garden at Giverny, and were the main focus of Monet's artistic production during the last thirty years of his life.
2 The Museum für Gestaltung is part of the Zürcher Hochschule der Künste [Zurich University of the Arts] (ZHdK).
3 Expo 64 (Swiss National Exhibition), Lausanne, 1964.
4 Barbara Holzer and Tristan Kobler were involved in the following projects at EXPO.02, the Swiss National Exhibition of 2002: 'Theater Mondial' and 'BarRouge', both at the Arteplage in Yverdon-les-Bains; the 'sWISH' exhibition at the Arteplage in Biel; the 'Biopolis' exhibition in Neuchâtel; and the '*Heimatfabrik*' ['Homeland Factory'] in Murten.
5 Jean-Christophe Ammann (b.1939) is a Swiss art historian and curator, who assisted Harald Szeemann in the Kunsthalle Bern in 1967–8 and with the plan for Documenta V in Kassel in 1972. Ammann was head of the Kunsthaus Lucerne from 1968 to 1977.
6 Gilbert & George is a London-based duo of fine artists and sculptors comprising Gilbert Proesch (b.1943) and George Passmore (b.1942); their work has a performative touch, including *tableaux vivants* such as The Singing Sculpture (1970), created when they were students at the St Martins School of Art in London (now Central Saint Martins College of Art and Design). Joseph Beuys (1921–1986) was a German performance and installation artist, perhaps best known for his cultural-political statement in 1973, that 'EVERY HUMAN BEING IS AN ARTIST', which was first published in English in: Caroline Tisdall, *Art into Society, Society into Art*, ICA, London, 1974, p.48. He began using fat in the 1960s with the installations *Fat Corners* (1960, 1962) and a sculpture entitled *Fat Chair* (1964). Fat, the material found in animal tissue composed of glycerides of fatty acids, was an ideal material for Beuys to use to signify chaos and the potential for spiritual transcendence. Fat has the ability to exist as a physical example of two extremes: a flowing liquid when warm and a defined solid when cold. Luciano Castelli (b.1951) is a Swiss painter, who was a member of the Berlin group of painters named the 'Junge Wilden', in the 1970s and early 1980s.
7 John Cage (1912–1992) was an American composer and poet, whose experiments in instrumentation, notation and chance operations in the 1950s and later, usually performed on a 'prepared' piano by David Tudor (1926–1996), changed our understanding of music. Famous quotations of John Cage are: 'I have nothing to say / and I am saying it / and that is poetry / as I need it', published in 'Lecture of nothing' (1949), or: 'Which is more musical, a truck passing by a factory or a truck passing by a music school?', published in 'Silence' (1957). See: John Cage, *Silence: Lectures and Writings*, Wesleyan University Press, Hanover, 1996. See also essay 1, 'The Battery', note 74, p.75.
8 Rolf Liebermann (1910–1999) was a Swiss composer and opera director, who wrote the version for 156 typewriters of his symphony *Les Échanges*, for the Swiss National Exhibition in Lausanne, 1964. Karlheinz Stockhausen (1928–2007) was a German composer, who is widely known for his unconventional compositions and often spectacular musical

performances, such as his 'String Quartet with Helicopters' (1993); see the official Stockhausen website: http://www.stockhausen.org/

9   Tristan Kobler (b.1960) studied architecture at the ETH Zurich from 1981 to 1987 and was a scenographer of exhibitions at the Museum für Gestaltung in Zurich from 1987 to 1996.

10 Barbara Holzer (b.1966) studied architecture at the ETH Zurich from 1986 to 1992 and had an internship in stage design in Frankfurt am Main, Germany, in the course of her study.

11 The ETH is the Eidgenössische Technische Hochschule [Swiss Federal Institute of Technology] in Zurich, a science and technology university with an outstanding research record, which ranks the institution in the top of continental Europe. The ETH has associations with 21 Nobel Prize winners, who at the time of their awards were engaged as professors at ETH Zurich, or had studied or researched there, and who received the Nobel Prize in recognition of their singular performance. Among them is Albert Einstein (1879–1955), who received his Nobel Prize for physics in 1921. See: http://www.ethz.ch/index_EN

12 '*Radix, Matrix – Daniel Libeskind Architekturen*', Museum für Gestaltung, Zurich, 3 September to 6 November 1994.

13 Holzer Kobler Architekturen was founded as a fusion of Tristan Kobler's office (Morphing Systems) and Barbara Holzer's office (d-case), in 2004.

14 Holzer Kobler Architekturen, 'All We Need', Luxembourg, 21 April to 28 October 2007. 'All We Need' explored the world as a global market through the human efforts to dream, imagine and live a happy life. The exhibition showed, in particular through the fair trade example, alternatives in consumption and lifestyles. It provided reflections and proposals for action on the essential questions touching the future of mankind: which are our fundamental needs, and how can we satisfy them without endangering neither the survival of our planet, nor human rights? See: http://www.allweneed.lu/id_article/35, April 2010.

15 See note 9 above.

16 Holzer Kobler Architekturen, '*Galerie Sammlungen*' ['Collections Gallery'] and '*Geschichte Schweiz*' ['History of Switzerland'], Schweizerisches Landesmuseum [Swiss National Museum], Zurich, 2009.

17 Holzer Kobler Architekturen, '*Waffen Werfen Schatten*' ['Weapons Cast Shadows'] and '*In Heikler Mission*' ['On a Delicate Mission'], Schweizerisches Landesmuseum [Swiss National Museum], Zurich, 2003 and 2007. For 'All We Need', see note 14 above.

18 Holzer Kobler Architekturen, Militärhistorisches Museum, Dresden, 2010.

19 Frida Kahlo (1907–1954) was a Mexican painter. Her vibrantly coloured paintings were influenced both by the indigenous cultures of Mexico and by European styles including realism, symbolism, and surrealism. Many of her works are self-portraits that symbolically articulate her own pain, caused by a serious bus accident in 1925, which she miraculously survived.

20 Simone de Beauvoir (1908–1986) was a French writer, existentialist philosopher, feminist, Marxist, Maoist and social theorist. She is most widely remembered for her metaphysical novels, and for her 1949 treatise *The Second Sex*, an analysis of the oppression of women which had a profound influence on contemporary feminism. She is also noted for her lifelong polyamorous relationship with Jean-Paul Sartre.

barbara holzer and tristan kobler

21 Mauritshuis, The Royal Picture Gallery, The Hague. See: http://www.mauritshuis.nl/, April 2010.
22 Johannes Vermeer (1632–1675), *Girl with a Pearl Earring*, c.1665. See picture essay 1, 'Parallax', p.90.
23 Daniel Libeskind (b.1946) is an American architect and set-designer, who is widely known for his Jewish Museum in Berlin (1999), the Imperial War Museum North in Manchester (2001), and for his masterplan for the reconstruction of the World Trade Center site in Lower Manhattan, New York, with which he won the 2003 architectural competition. Barbara Holzer has been working with Libeskind, primarily in the field of museums and exhibitions, since 1994.
24 Holzer Kobler Architekturen, 'Greetings from Luxembourg', Musée d'Histoire de la Ville de Luxembourg [City History Museum], Luxembourg, 2008.
25 See: John Hench, *Designing Disney: Imagineering and the Art of the Show*, Disney Editions, New York, 2003.
26 'All We Need', op.cit. (note 14); Barbara Holzer is referring to the installation with the 20-by-3-metre pink bed in Space 9 on the top floor of the exhibition – *Dream (transcendence)* – where visitors could comfortably listen to promising tales and fantasies before literally sliding back to reality on the ground floor.
27 'All We Need', op.cit.; Tristan Kobler is referring to Space 7 of the exhibition – *UNDERSTAND* – which was staged on the basis of a work by the Birmingham-based performance group Stan's Café, who use piles of rice where each corn represents one human being. By carefully weighing out quantities they represent a host of human statistics and manage to make knowledge visible and hence tangible and comprehensible. The notably differing sizes of each pile and their respective labels make for interesting and surprising results. According to critics reviewing their work, Stan's Café, established in 1991, has become 'one of Britain's major contemporary theatre exports' with an 'international reputation'.
28 Barbara Holzer et al., '*Heimatfabrik*', EXPO.02, Murten, Switzerland, 2002.
29 Robert Wilson (b.1941). See essay 2, 'The Envelope', para.2.1: 'A space full of time', p.391.
30 For Peter Greenaway (b.1942), see essay 1, 'The Battery', note 6, p.67.
31 Peter Greenaway, *A Zed & Two Naughts*, 1985; *The Cook, the Thief, His Wife and Her Lover*, 1989.
32 Alfred Hitchcock (1899–1980) was an English filmmaker, best known for thrillers such as *Vertigo* (1958), *North by Northwest* (1959), *Psycho* (1960) and *The Birds* (1963).
33 Holzer Kobler Architekturen, Ebisquare entertainment and shopping centre, Lucerne, Switzerland. Ebisquare is still under construction at the time of going to press, and Holzer Kobler Architekturen is involved in what they call 'mall creation' and the design of the public spaces.
34 Holzer Kobler Architekturen, Militärhistorisches Museum, Dresden, 2010.
35 Museum of Modern Art (MoMA), New York.
36 Tristan Kobler and Barbara Holzer participated in the 'Narrative Environments' project right from the start. See the Introduction, p.6.
37 Ferdinand Hodler (1853–1918) was a Swiss painter. The *Ruhmeshalle* of the Schweizerisches Landesmuseum (Swiss National Museum) in Zurich houses the mural painting

space.time.narrative

  Rückzug von Marignano (*Retreat from Marignano*), which Hodler designed for a competition held in 1897.
38 Ferdinand Hodler, *Retreat from Marignano*, 1897–9.
39 Ferdinand Hodler, *The Battle at Murten*, 1917.
40 Peter Greenaway, 'The Physical Self', Museum Boijmans Van Beuningen, Rotterdam, 1991–2.
41 Harald Szeemann (1933–2005) was a Swiss art historian who curated legendary exhibitions, such as 'When Attitudes Become Form' in the Kunsthalle, Bern, in 1969; Documenta V in Kassel, in 1972; and '*Der Hang zum Gesamtkunstwerk*' in the Kunsthaus, Zurich, in 1983. Szeemann also co-hosted the Venice Biennale in 1980, where he created the '*Aperto*' exhibition for young artists. He was among the few to curate the Biennale twice, in 1999 and 2001. See also: Hans-Joachim Müller, *Harald Szeemann: Ausstellungsmacher*, Benteli Verlag, Bern, 2006.
42 Mario Botta (b.1943) is a Swiss architect. Botta designed the *exhibition* 'Friedrich Dürrenmatt: Portrait eines Universums – Das zeichnerische und malerische Werk', *Kunsthaus, Zurich*, 1994.
43 Museum für Gestaltung, Zurich.

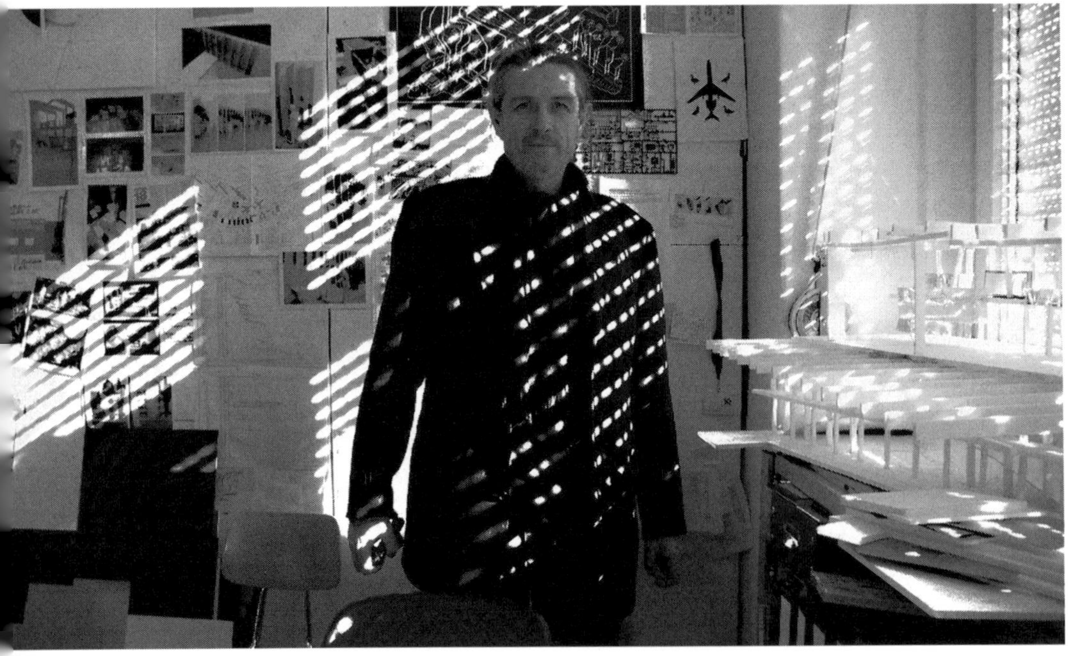

Interview with
Uwe R. Brückner

Uwe R. Brückner (b.1957) is the founder of Atelier Brückner in Stuttgart, which he runs together with his wife Shirin Brückner and colleague Eberhard Schlag. Years ago, in the late 1990s, I saw their 'Expedition Titanic' exhibition in Zurich and was struck by the well-balanced dramaturgy of it all. Later, students of mine told me about him, about his intense style of lecturing and the impressions they gained from a visit to his office. I was intrigued and we met in Stuttgart in September 2005, near the Haus der Geschichte, which he had designed. He showed me around. There was a lot to discuss. I was struck by his hospitality. Later, I sensed more of his relentless energy, which made me privately call him 'the marathon man'. Uwe Brückner just never stops. He stands up for a case and takes it to the end. Our interview therefore had to be a marathon in itself, and so it was. For three days, from 15 to 17 February 2008, we sat together in his former office in Stuttgart. There, we recorded nine hours of conversation and shot the portrait on the opposite page.

What was the first exhibition that really affected you?

Brückner: The first exhibition that deeply impressed me was the Max Ernst exhibition at the Haus der Kunst in Munich.[1] That was in my student days, between 1977 and 1985. It was his surrealism, his creative diversity and diagonal way of thinking that always impressed me; his work showed an unconditionality, a faithfulness to his own path, a sense of being en route. These things characterised his life and also his attitude towards his art, an attitude that held sway over his entire environment. There's one thing I'll never forget – I hope I get the quotation about right – and that's the poster caption: 'My only merit probably lies in the fact that I never found myself', which no doubt implies that he never stopped searching. That left a lasting impression, alongside all the influences a person could have in that post-1968 period. We were no longer the 1968 generation and the punks were yet to come. Somehow, we were always in-between – between the students' movement and the higher-education reforms towards the end of the 1970s, with 20,000 students demonstrating on the streets.

We demonstrated against Franz Josef Strauss and, within the peace movement, against the stationing of Pershing II missiles; we appreciated the aims of the Red Army Faction but were strictly against violence. It was the time of the Blues of Jimi Hendrix and Cream, the Rhythm & Blues of Creedence Clearwater Revival and Carlos Santana, the concerts of Bob Dylan, John Mayall, B.B. King and Pink Floyd, but also of Django Reinhardt, Manfred Mann's Earth Band, Klaus Doldinger's Passport, Keith Jarrett and Thelonious Monk; it was a wonderful time, you had room to move, which was perhaps the best thing of all.

That was more or less identical with my first period of study, when I did architecture at the Technical University of Munich. Alongside all the spectacular art exhibitions, concerts, parties and trips, there was also Dachau and the exhibition in, and about, the concentration camp or the demonstration of the unthinkable, the becoming tangible of rage, sorrow and shame, which left a lasting impression on me.

uwe r. brückner

What exactly did you find impressive about the Max Ernst exhibition? Was it the works of Max Ernst? Or perhaps the message of the exhibition as well?

Brückner: What I remember explicitly is the dialectic built into the exhibition – between Max Ernst, a 'degenerate' with little time for the Nazis, and the Haus der Kunst, former temple to the Nazis, in which his works were exhibited.[2] I thought that was a remarkable rupture, and there were also two different messages that were brought head to head – which turned out to be a challenge for the architecture rather than being to the disadvantage of Max Ernst. On the contrary. They didn't subordinate themselves to the architecture of the building, they tried to get as much out of the spaces as possible for the benefit of the art. But as far as staged exhibitions are concerned, the Munich Stadtmuseum was the most famous venue in Germany at the time. The director, Christoph Stölzl, put on a series of exceptional exhibitions there, on the theme, for example, of '*Das Oktoberfest – 175 Jahre bayerischer National-Rausch*', or on Karl Valentin, all of which went beyond the normal art exhibitions and took an unconventional cultural history approach that was no less spectacular and highly successful.[3]

Which exhibition aroused your interest in making exhibitions and in the exhibition as a communicative format?

Brückner: In 1989, to mark the 200th anniversary of the French Revolution, there was a public staging or performance, as we would put it today, in the Königsplatz in Munich. A gigantic Tricolour and the head of Robespierre were projected onto two enormous water screens, while at the same time a great troop of actors and bit players entered through the Propyläen.[4] They basically put on a translated performance of the French Revolution. The staging was a wonderful interplay of light and projection. The Propyläen and the nearby museums, the Glyptothek and the Staatliches Museum Ägyptischer Kunst, and thus the entire Königsplatz, were staged through the interplay of light and projection. Theatrical effects – that I could decipher as such only later on – were also deployed, such as the combination of front and back projection on the same screen or design using choreographed light. That was a performance on a massive scale, using technology that still seems amazing. I was deeply impressed by that. It wasn't an exhibition, but it was a public staging of space. For me, this event was a key experience in terms of narratives within and through space; it was neither cinema nor theatre, nor was it a proclamation to me as spectator. Rather, the space itself became the narrative medium and I was part of it, part of a complex, authentic experience – something I've often been preoccupied with since then.

[Interview question:]

How did you end up working in this interdisciplinary field? What was your first exhibition or staging in space?

Brückner: I worked as a conventional architect after completing my studies in architecture at the Technical University of Munich. First I spent three years with Sampo Widmann in Munich, who was well known for his experimental housing.[5] I built a number of houses and apartment blocks there and learnt how to turn plans into built reality. That was a very instructive experience. But then Sampo told me that I needed to do something else. It was a matter of principle for him that his staff should try something different after three years. I'm still grateful to him for that. It was at just that point that I got an offer from Stuttgart. The Lohrer studio was looking for someone who could build.[6] They had won a competition but the project was making little headway and they needed someone who could get on with the planning of this museum and sort it out. I accepted, for one year. The only question that Knut Lohrer – a friend and mentor for the last 20 years – asked me, was: 'When can you begin?' That impressed me. He had assumed that I would begin the same day. One year became two, and ultimately I stuck around in Stuttgart. ... Knut Lohrer constantly overloaded me with intellectually challenging jobs such as the conceptual planning of the Internationale Gar-

tenausstellung or IGA in Stuttgart in 1993.[7] For him, exhibition concepts were always informed by the subject matter, and we simply hadn't been taught how to work on that. We'd learned to build, to create functional designs, to make accurate, static plans in great detail, but we were unaccustomed to working on subject matter from a theoretical or conceptual standpoint. This was a tough experience for me, far more than I could cope with, and I felt pushed beyond my limits. Eventually I had to say, 'Knut, I can't do this.' But he insisted, 'Yes you can. Keep going with it and I'll help you. You can do it, just wait and see.' From Knut Lohrer I learned to develop ideas out of content I'd researched myself and at the same time I discovered that in this way you can also come up with creative arguments. Knut then involved me in more and more exhibition projects, including giving me overall responsibility for them. Two projects exercised a formative influence on me: The Schloss Trautenfels Museum of Nature and Culture in Styria, Austria, and the Archaeological Museum in Dayr az Zawr on the banks of the Euphrates in the Syrian desert.[8] 100 kilometres from the Iraqi border, about 400 kilometres from Damascus and 200 kilometres east of Palmyra, the nearest city. Everything was very basic there, in the cradle of civilisation, far from western society as I knew it. With the simplest of means, plaster, battens, wire, nails and screws, with tremendous personal effort on the part of friends and local craftsmen, and with Knut in charge, the museum was planned, fitted out and partly built by our team. This was my first direct experience of designing exhibitions and museums.
[Interview question:]

You have a dual educational history: you were trained as both architect and stage designer. How were these two disciplines incorporated, or I should say integrated, within you?

Brückner: On my fiftieth birthday, Sampo Widmann said that I had turned out exactly as he had expected me to. I replied that it's easy to say that after the event. 'Do you remember what I told you back then?' he asked. And I did in fact remember.

He had said: 'You're far too restless to sit there on a chair the whole time. You need to try out a few other things.' This was his metaphorical way of saying that I was in search of something, that I needed to try out several different things, without knowing what they would be.

And that's how it turned out. Two years later I was provoked into action by my friend Hans-Martin Scholder,[9] who was studying stage design under Jürgen Rose at the Staatliche Akademie der Bildenden Künste in Stuttgart.[10] 'You can't spend the rest of your life in an architectural bureau! You need to find something else to do, such as the stage design course. I bet you'd enjoy that.' Hans-Martin then kept on at Rose until he agreed to see me. I'll never forget that meeting. There sat the great Jürgen Rose with his mottled grey crew cut, one of Europe's most important stage designers. He smirked at me with his typically smug smile and said impassively, 'I can't see this going anywhere. You're far too old.' That was how he greeted me. Then he said: 'What do you have in mind? You'll mess up the whole caboodle!' Without knowing what that meant, more as a reflex, I said I'd like to try anyway. But my portfolio was incomplete, dull, un-artistic and boringly architectural, in other words hopeless.

Hans-Martin Scholder then coached me for the entrance exam. For six weeks, I worked day and night on my portfolio in the unoccupied house next door and was finally accepted onto the course with portfolio number 13, my favourite number. Rose said, 'Oh well, let's give it a go.'

What was driving you on? Was it Rose saying that you'd never make it? Or was there already a strong tendency towards stage design in the exhibition work you'd done at Knut Lohrer's studio?

Brückner: Both. There were in fact people from three or four different disciplines working together at Knut Lohrer's studio. So it wasn't a normal architect's studio in that sense. Knut Lohrer made as many exhibitions as he did buildings. This is why I consider him among the pioneers of modern exhibition design. He was one of the first to work with graphics in space.

It wasn't a matter of illustration, but of using graphics in order to design spaces. For him graphics was an integral component of design. Of course, the beginnings of this can be seen in the work of the Constructivists and Friedrich Kiesler in the 1920s and 1930s or François Confino from the 1960s, but here in Germany Knut Lohrer was one of the first to do it in a professional way, and I too came to feel a strong need to move beyond my purely technical and function-oriented architectural training.[11] Of course, I knew that there were other ways of expressing yourself beyond a sound training in a 'technical' field, but initially I didn't think I was up to it. I wormed my way into the Coop Himmelb(l)au in Vienna and had seen installations by Haus-Rucker Co in Kassel, visited every building by Carlo Scarpa and studied 'offbeat' role models who had done away with the norms of conventional architecture, such as Future Systems, Peter Eisenmann and Frank Gehry.[12] I also climbed up Jørn Utzon's Sydney Opera House.[13] However, I have to admit that at that point my entire generation probably hadn't gone much deeper than to question things on a visual and formal level. We didn't ask, Where does this come from? What it is capable of? Or: What can I make out of this? This only radically changed for me as a result of the stage design course. Also, there erupted within me a possibly latent, hallucinatory enthusiasm for the theatre, for the staging of spaces using texts and a fascination for the narrative environment and the dynamics involved in the transformation of spaces. Having been so sweepingly rejected by Jürgen Rose, my tenacity now really began to click in. I asked him later on whether he had done that deliberately? But no, he had been quite serious.

I'm interested in this phase at Knut Lohrer's studio, where broad thinking and a transdisciplinary approach to solving problems clearly influenced the work. I assume that your time there inspired you to expand, to adopt an approach in which design or staging is developed in light of the subject matter. Did Knut Lohrer's studio function as a point of departure for you in this way?

Brückner: Absolutely. A lot of famous designers have come from his school. H.G. Merz began his career at Knut Lohrer's studio, as did Hans-Martin Scholder.[14] A lot of people started out working with Knut before going on to found their own studios or switch over to related fields. Knut Lohrer and his free-thinking attitude, the openness with which he tackled design projects and his multidisciplinary approach were the prerequisites for my personal development. I know no-one, literally no-one, who approaches a project in such an unprejudiced way, who permits as much as Knut Lohrer. Knut questioned our complacency and challenged our indolence. He taught me how important it is to think, at least once a day: Wow, fantastic, this is a completely new world for me. He selflessly supported my application to the academy with the words, 'If you don't do it now, you never will.' Of course, the Lohrer studio was no cruise ship on which the grapes simply fell into one's mouth. It was hard graft and we usually worked round the clock. I was constantly pushed beyond my limits. But it was the best school I could imagine. On top of that, I always had the good fortune that at those moments when I felt completely lost, people turned up who believed in me and my potential – including of course my wife Shirin and my colleagues from the studio.

Atelier Brückner has been going for almost 11 years now. Qualitatively, how has it developed since its foundation?

Brückner: Atelier Brückner was originally called Atelier Uwe Brückner and from 1993 it consisted of me and one or two assistants, until my wife Shirin and then our partner Eberhard Schlag got involved. Outwardly, the studio may seem ambitious, strategic and single-minded and it may all look as if it were planned this way. But that's not how it was at all. The studio was a garage, a chaotic, spontaneous, but always demanding and enthusiastic group of artists – outside of the mainstream and always on the verge of bankruptcy. The stage design course was fantastic and it changed my world-view permanently and completely. My perspective on the same creative challenge was completely different after that. For the first time I saw the task at hand in terms of its message rather than purely in terms of function or physical conditions. My thinking became a kind of permanent questioning. I can sum this up by the question, still valid today: What can this do? By studying architecture in Munich, we became functionalists, functioning service providers that could be called up at a moment's notice, always ready to shoot from the hip with a suitable response to any problem; on the stage design course the key thing was to question what you were doing, to develop associations in the form of the overall imagery of space and to generate effects, while still leaving the recipients room for their own interpretations. Later, we transferred this artistic mode of design to the conception and design of exhibitions. That was costly and time-consuming and theatrical budgets were tiny compared to architectural ones – with Spartan fees to match.

So, stage design was perhaps economically unfeasible but made a huge contribution to getting you into a transdisciplinary field. Would you say that your architecture degree taught you architecture, but you got your independence of thought while studying stage design?

Brückner: After completing my architecture degree, I was nothing but a carpenter in academic garb. Though I wasn't dissatisfied. I didn't get out of architecture because of dissatisfaction. It was the curiosity I felt about engaging with the meaningful content of things and the need to turn the viewer's perspective upside down and the joy of 'swimming against the tide', as an artist friend of mine once put it.[15]

Stage design taught me about the overall image of space, about the dynamic staging of space. Peter Stein went out of his way to emphasise that the stage is a meaningful space in which things are charged with meaning or we charge them with meaning, and he underlined that the viewer always assumes that there is meaning to every last thing, which is why the stage as image must also have the potential of a metaphor, irrespective of didactics or morality.¹⁶ At the time I imagined that I was gaining a tiny insight into how you might deal with the fact that it is near impossible to do justice to a Shakespeare play, or to cope with the complex demands of a Wagner opera – how you might not only survive the rapids of such pieces, but skilfully navigate them.

    Stein related an anecdote about a cleaning lady who left her rag on the stage between two acts. The rag remained untouched as the actors continued with their performance, because it was an unintentional item, one, in fact, that didn't exist. The audience, however, read this cleaning rag as a focal point on the stage set, and awaited its activation. A dramaturgical diversionary manoeuvre of this kind may also be deployed consciously and productively and may enrich the imagery and narrative structure. The 'cleaning rag effect', as I now call it, means that while random events will always occur (in the creative process), the viewer will continue to assume that everything on the stage has its meaning. This principle also holds true for other creative endeavours. It was stage design that taught me this for the first time.

What prompted the establishment of Atelier Brückner?

Brückner: It was more or less a result of the Titanic exhibition.¹⁷ The idea for this exhibition came from Holger von Neuhoff and Rainer Esser, who were looking for a team to take on the project and came across the architects Götz Schulz Haas in Stuttgart, who then put me forward as exhibition maker.¹⁸ So together with a lot of other people, the 'Titanic team' was formed. The exhibition was financed by Rainer Esser, a businessman from Düsseldorf, without whose obsessiveness, commitment and management abilities the project would have been inconceivable. So I was part of the core team, but at the same time this was commissioned work. At the time I didn't have a studio large enough to cope with the project, so we put together a team of fourteen capable of realising the project in six months, from a faxed inventory from New York to the opening in Hamburg. This was an incredibly demanding task. Because of the short production time, we could only complete the project by working in shifts. For purely formal and organisational reasons, Atelier Uwe Brückner was renamed Atelier Brückner when my wife came on board in 1997.

Despite the massive success of the Titanic exhibition, it was a year before we got another assignment. Everyone involved thought the phone would be ringing off the hook after this high-publicity exhibition. But nothing happened. No-one called, no jobs, no income, just frustration and disappointment. It was Knut Lohrer who helped me and my little family out of this tight spot by letting us design the Schloss Trautenfels museum in Austria.

Since the Titanic exhibition in 1997–8, the studio has grown from a staff of 14 to one of 70, and Atelier Brückner has created many exhibitions and museums both in Germany and in other countries. If you had to sum up the key characteristics of an Atelier Brückner exhibition, what would they be?

Brückner: That's the ultimate question. Even back in the Titanic days, I modified a famous architectural maxim in order to define my philosophy. My credo was 'form follows content', an adaptation of Louis Sullivan's famous 'form follows function'.[19] This is a very important yardstick for the studio. Ideas and concepts don't drop into our laps fully formed from above, and it's not the function alone that determines the whole; rather, we always ask ourselves what we want to achieve. So in everything we do, we ask: What can this do? Why are we doing that? Why don't we drop that?

In dealing with these 'why?' questions, I generally trust in my intuition, reflexes and instincts, and of course my colleagues. Our central European culture has developed a particularly large stock of cultural instincts. Instincts that relate to aesthetics, to the capacity for judgement and acceptable, generally valid criteria of quality. There are created spaces or created things which we can agree about – a kind of collective perception which is of course heavily dependent on the particular cultural area, but which is now being highly globalised. All of us can cite at least ten examples of why something is better, more interesting, less successful or more innovative than a comparable effort. At the very least there are demands (the clients), criteria (the selection committee) and parameters (for the designers) that we can agree on. For the most part, the key thing is the Other, the exceptional, the unique, the unmistakable – what matters is a certain increase in value that we wish to produce, and must produce, through our creativity. Because of this, and because the results are always measured in terms of accessibility and the enthusiasm of the recipients, the question 'What can this do?' is an omnipresent one for us. In line with this, we ask ourselves how we can reach the visitors. In exhibitions, we allow various situations of dialogue to develop. These bring about mutual interaction, which facilitates a holistic experience. In analogy to the design process, we try to establish a dialogue between the architecture (the space) and the content (object, story), to create a relationship between exhibit and recipient so that the visitor becomes part of the overall staging of space. In exhibitions all the participants play a certain role, if you will, and for this to be able to work at all you need a certain dramaturgy, a sequence of different events or, better, a sequence of experiences in sync with an arc of tension.

    Building on my experiences in stage design, making exhibitions, architecture (not forgetting my work as a craftsman), having seen countless plays, concerts, films and museums, and not least through intensive exchange with internationally acclaimed artist colleagues, I've built up a big repertoire of reference projects. I've analysed these in an attempt to discover their underlying structures. This is the next key word. I've learnt to adapt dramaturgical structures from various disciplines for use in our design: from literature, music, opera, theatre, film, radio plays and exhibitions you can pick out dramaturgical structures, narrative structures, atmospheric structures, and physical structures, which may in turn be used as the basic structure for the development of new ideas and new concepts. An example. I have of course often been asked why, over the years, we haven't created any more exhibitions like the Titanic exhibition. I would have liked to make another exhibition of that kind, and there have been many, many attempts to do just that. Most of them have failed. Why? There are many reasons. In any event, a lot of stars have to be favourably aligned for a seed like the Titanic exhibition to thrive and bear fruit. First of all, there was a bold, enthusiastic financier. Despite the high financial risks to himself, he said: Yes, something's going to come of this. I trust these guys, I'll let them get on with it. Rainer Esser never gave us an earful with respect to the design, or even the organisation of the project. The second factor was the curators, who are extremely important. Designers can never replace the content people. In the case of the Titanic exhibition, we had acclaimed historians on the payroll. They worked constructively with our team, rather than working against us out of a sense of superior knowledge. They challenged us, animated us and of course provided content. In other words, they acted in the interests of the project as a whole. The relationship between us was harmonious rather than competitive. And quite incidentally this also gave rise to genuine friendship. Everyone tried to contribute the very best that they could to the project on the basis of their own specialism.

A museum director once described the Titanic exhibition as a *Gesamtkunstwerk*, and that's only achievable through a multidisciplinary team and an integrative approach to design.[20] But perhaps the most important, and at the time highly unusual, aspect was the conceptual approach: for this exhibition, I selected an existing dramatic structure as my model, as the likes of Peter Greenaway have also done. My model here was Akira Kurosawa's film *Rashomon*, a serial film that relates one and the same event from five different eyewitnesses – with completely different results.[21]

I'd like to return briefly to the characteristic feature of an Atelier Brückner project. I think we would agree that both an exhibition and a work for the stage consists partly of invention. This is the fuel you need if you're to have any chance of getting a project done in such a way that a certain aesthetic becomes manifest in materials and media. Can you describe the aesthetic hallmarks of

an Atelier Brückner project?

Brückner: Our exhibitions are staged exhibitions. In a lecture I once asserted that you can't *not* stage something.[22] Every exhibition is a staging to some degree, a *mise en scène* of things or events. To what extent this occurs is another matter. Let me put it from the designer's perspective: every designer who puts a grain of rice in a display case, illuminates it effectively, considers where and how the case should be located within the room and in what context it is placed, is engaged in staging. You can call yourself an architect or stage designer or product designer – none of that matters in the least. To work with time and space means to stage, and for me it's quite clear that a staging consists of a dramaturgical process that implies a Before, depicts a Now and tries to make a prediction for the After, with all of this arranged in alignment with an arc of tension through artificial means, drawn from a range of disciplines, not all of which you necessarily have to master. But you should have at least some idea about them. At some point, for instance, the electric light made its appearance and it first revolutionised the theatre rather than the exhibition. In Vienna, there were still exhibition halls without electrical lights until a few years ago. These were daylight museums, which were simply closed around 3pm during the winter because there was no longer enough light to illuminate the artefacts. Whenever technological innovations occurred there was a revolution in the theatre. With some time delay, this then spread to exhibition design. Incidentally, I feel that this happens the other way around nowadays. The impulses emanate from exhibition design and find their way to the stage only after a certain amount of resistance.

In our exhibitions we use media – graphics, light, sound, recordings and moving images – in a measured way. We don't deploy media for their own sake, but as a tool, in order to achieve a certain overall effect and staging. ATB exhibitions are staged exhibitions based on a dramaturgical structure. Hopefully they always have an identifiable signature.

The Titanic exhibition was held ten or eleven years ago and ATB has worked on a large number of varied projects since then. There have been no more projects similar to Titanic. If you consider these ten years in overview, what has ATB gained? Or perhaps even lost?

Brückner: What we've lost is undoubtedly our innocence. No-one knew us before the Titanic exhibition and very few knew us after it. There were no promotions and no public relations. We always acted as a team. People had to ask us who had made a particular exhibition. Much of what we designed was spontaneous, some of it clumsy, but all of it authentic. We thought in artistic rather than strategic terms. Marketing played no role for us. Atelier Brückner has certainly lost this naivety in the sense of the carefree attitude with which we took on the monster task of designing two huge pavilions for Expo 2000 at the same time.[23] The bigger the business, the more sumptuous the steamer became. For many years we were a small, manoeuvrable speedboat. We didn't cut through the waves, we surfed them. But now we've become a huge tanker of great length, and our course can't be corrected quickly; at the very least, we take longer to turn ourselves around. For the first five years, we were the terror of the exhibition world with our agility. In the first three years we won eight out of ten competitions. Competitions were like a drug, and we threw ourselves into them with pleasure and enthusiasm. It didn't matter which race we'd run before – we were determined to put ourselves to the test and were always out in front.

Initially, there was a phase during which we were constantly taking on new people. We started out with five people and had grown to a staff of 20 within a year. By the time of the Expo in Hanover, there were more than 25 of us. It was a peculiar high, an infectious fever that carried all of us away. No matter what we took on, it led to success. Even a massive failure, such as the plan for a permanent exhibition at the Hygiene-Museum in Dresden, became the martyr's anecdote that failure was part of the deal.[24] Every studio, by the way, goes through such phases. It's an inherent feature of young disciplines that you may rise meteorically only to crash to earth again just as rapidly, as we saw in the IT sector a few years ago. This perhaps makes it all the more amazing that we managed to keep going, though people said that ATB was just a flash in the pan. Shortly after Expo 2000 in Hanover, where the term 'scenography' was introduced in Germany for the first time, there were gloomy predictions that scenography wouldn't survive for long and that it was a mistaken approach. People said explicitly that Atelier Brückner wouldn't be around for very long. What they totally failed to grasp was that certain repressed needs on the part of both designers and curators, that had long existed, had found creative expression at Expo 2000. We had suddenly found an outlet, and the visitors felt the effects of this. As a method of design, scenography could give the invisible, the unreal and the narrative a material form and allow people to experience them. Scenography was a new way of thinking – like a new way of climbing mountains. Over the years I've always taken the same approach and have never been forced to abandon it.

Then in 1999 I moulded the ATB philosophy into a so-called *Kreativstruktur*, originally in order to create a medium of education and instruction for staff. In revised form, this *Kreativstruktur* was then integrated into the syllabus at the college in Basel. This is what we've gained.[25]

What we've lost – what have we actually lost? Perhaps the fact that we've ventured into dimensions and worked on projects so complex that sometimes we can't even count on having a specific point of contact, not even with a specific impresario, a committed curator or director with the authority to make decisions, but often merely with anonymous departments that can change their minds overnight for no reason. This has made things more complex, significantly more political and above all more strategic. In the first five years, ATB proceeded with practically no strategy in mind at all. At no point did we pursue a calculated strategy. We simply dived into a project and sounded out how we could get the best out of it for the visitors – the same even went for our budgets, which we stretched to the limit. This non-strategic approach simply doesn't work any more. We've become too big for that

– and more predictable. In shallow waters, a big steamboat like that, with a crew of around 70, simply has to navigate differently: more precisely, more long-term, more economically, more strategically. In other words, when we enter into the fray nowadays we're no longer competing against surprised competitors, but sometimes against colleagues who now take great delight in beating us. The sector has grown and the competition has become more intense. Production times have become vastly shorter, and there's almost no elbowroom left, even for orderly failure. You can't win major competitions now unless you put in a massive amount of effort and resources.

What currently determines your orientation? Who influences your thinking and way of life? Which words resonate in your mind? What images do you see when you dream?

Brückner: Since I've been leading the IN3 in Basel, together with my colleague Andreas Wenger, I've had intensive contact with a large number of internationally acclaimed artists whose work I'm impressed by.[26] Most of them are multi-talented author-designers. Rather than reeling off a list of more than a hundred names, I'll mention just one representative example: Peter Greenaway, who is a constant presence for me. I consider him one of the champions of richly imagined spatial installations – not just an outstanding filmmaker, by the way, but also an exceptionally gifted exhibition designer. If you look at his film *The Pillow Book*, it represents a two-dimensional reality, namely text, which he handles in an extraordinarily masterful way, projecting texts onto bodies or having them painted onto the messengers' bodies.[27] It's ingenious the way the written messages become readable only when the eyelids are closed – wow! This is staging turned intravenous, with the text suddenly revealed in 3-D. I think that's a wonderful metaphor, one that always stimulates me and spurs me on to see my installations, and develop them, in 3-D. So often, the words on my mind sound as if they come from Walter Benjamin's 'The work of art in the age of mechanical reproduction'[28] or like Baudrillard, sometimes like Umberto Eco, less often like Peter Sloterdijk, very often like the music of Mozart, Puccini or Wagner.[29] In more difficult situations I prefer Jimi Hendrix, Pink Floyd or Massive Attack. Apart from that, I always have a load of 'project literature' at hand.

Increasingly, my dreams are a cryptic chaos in which figures within collages of different stagings blur into each other and get up to the craziest things with one another. I used to get up at four in the morning and note these things down. Now I generally sleep in a coma-like state of exhaustion, and I spend relatively little time unravelling the web of dreams. It's a shame actually. Yes, it really is a shame, a genuine loss – it's my restlessness that's to blame.

But certain visual enclosures of space become lodged in the mind that I could spontaneously sketch, such as Bill Viola's *Fire, Water, Breath*, Robert Wilson's *Einstein on the Beach* or Achim Freyer's *Krankheit Tod*.[30] Anish Kapoor's profound spaces of colour and light or Olafur Eliasson's cloud suspension bridge come to mind because they've left a lasting impression on me, because these installations require the visitor's personal, physical presence, because their potential is best realised in real, physical spaces that you can walk through.[31] It is this staged space that fascinates me. I feel at home in 3-D. That's my métier.

You once sailed across the Atlantic. Do you have strong memories of that?

Brückner: That was one of the most important experiences I've ever had. That was a 21-day journey with two architect colleagues, who became good friends. Sampo Widmann, my first employer and mentor, had a little 36-foot Westerly Conway. It's an English model, built for long journeys rather than speed, very sturdy and reliable, and I felt good on it even in dangerous situations. We had agreed to go on a long journey together. Then one day Sampo said, 'It's time.' He wanted to sail across the Atlantic, on to the Pacific and then make our way back to European waters via Asia and Australia. It was a far-from-straightforward decision, because at the time my wife had just fallen pregnant with our first daughter. And no sooner had I agreed than there was a call from Zurich from my friend Hans-Martin Scholder, asking me if I'd like to be involved in the opera *Don Carlos* – a major production that could easily provide enough work for two stage designers.[32] That would have been my route into large-scale opera, but I opted for the Atlantic crossing instead. Those 21 days at sea were the most relaxed and harmonious that I can remember. To be directly exposed to the elements in a tiny cockleshell, to feel that sense of responsibility for your own conduct, for the ship and for your friends, to feel your own limitations and the power of nature – that was a very, very important experience. When I'm faced with situations in my current job that appear hopeless, I try to remember how I dealt with such situations while sailing the Atlantic, or on the mountain during our other expedition. Then the so-called problems seem insignificant or trivial.

The ATB logo is a fish. Can you tell me the story of the Brückner fish?

Brückner: Strictly speaking, the Brückner fish is a salmon. I got this salmon from my painter friend Thomas Deyle on my thirtieth birthday. He sent me a little postcard for my birthday with a picture of this salmon and the following brief text: 'The salmon is a traveller between worlds. It lives in both salt and fresh water and can swim against the current for several hundred miles.' And then he added the Latin '(sic!)', which means something like *so it is*, or might be translated as 'this is the way things are'. And finally 'Happy Birthday dear Uwe, don't ever change.' At some point, someone in the studio needed a full-size fish for a design and one of the assistants used the fish to create a one-metre-long blow-up. This salmon hung above the door in the old studio for years like a pair of antlers or a trophy. It was the last thing packed when we moved from our country studio into our city studio in 1997 and of course it was the first thing we unpacked. Our chief graphic designer, Birgit Kölz, thought we needed a logo. I asked: Why? Our logo is ATELIER BRÜCKNER, isn't that enough?

But she still thought that we needed a proper logo. In order to get the discussion over and done with, I said 'Use the fish then.' So the fish ended up on our notepaper, and of course now it stands for our approach as well. Not because Atelier Brückner is a streamlined team of designers, but because we prefer to swim against the tide.

So you like to travel between worlds and you'll continue to swim against the tide. Where are you headed? What are your ambitions? Which project, whether one you've already completed or one you'd like to do, comes closest to fulfilling your dreams?

Brückner: We haven't yet had the chance to create a museum *in toto*, taking in both the architecture and the exhibition. Only in the case of temporary pavilions for expos were we able to do that. The most prominent example of this was the Cycle Bowl, the pavilion for the Duales System at Expo 2000 in Hanover. In this project we created both the architecture and the exhibition. Our role was that of general planner, and that of course was a major advantage because the architecture could be developed in light of the exhibition concept. In this case, we could take our credo, 'form follows content', quite literally. It wasn't the architecture that came first, but the exhibition, in light of which a suitable building was developed. The Cycle Bowl is a kind of prototype of this. From the plan to the last screw, the entire project was generated in light of the idea of recycling and the Expo motto, 'People–Nature–Technology'. The '*Grenzen (er)leben*' pavilion at EXPO.02 in Biel in Switzerland was also moulded by the subject matter in this way. Initially, this was a really laborious, difficult project. It took a very long time to successfully convey the subject matter, which involved the staging of personal experiences of boundaries; it was a painful birth. But in the end it was a highly sophisticated, artistic project that was more than presentable. For me this was a new type of pavilion, one that allowed visitors to experience things that cannot be exhibited. Unfortunately, we weren't yet able to find clients from the classical museums who would support a concept of this kind. We often came close to doing so, and it's bound to happen one day, the 'ideal museum'. The prospects aren't bad at all. There are four or five as yet unrealised projects on ice that would have that kind of potential to link together the essence of architecture and exhibition. The Innovarium, a research project on a science centre for sustainable energy, comes very close to representing a new type of museum for the twenty-first century.[33]

Are there still unexpected niches and undiscovered paths that haven't yet been tried?

Brückner: Oh, most definitely. There is an *Ideenkonzept* [idea in outline], as I like to put it, for an underwater museum, a Museum of the Seas, that would be anchored on or in the sea floor. I'd love to do that. Another possible project would create a Museum of Silence. I'd also really like to do something relating to deceleration. Not as an empty cliché, but out of a genuine need to think about what you might be able to do with silent, contemplative things. Basically, what I'm interested in are the anti-cyclical topics, the shift of perspective, the opposite of the obvious, the room for interpretation that you get from a really good play. What interests me is what a place of enlightenment would look like in our contemporary era. Perhaps we need an Observatory of Tolerance or a House of Neutrality, Peace, Timelessness and Unconditionality – something more meditative, in other words.

Do you also view your exhibitions as islands of silence in a noisy world? As places characterised by a different focus and a different orientation? Irrespective of whether they talk loudly or softly?

Brückner: The Titanic exhibition in particular was generally quiet and subtle in its staging. The archaeology exhibition in Herne is also very unobtrusive.[34] What distinguishes most of our projects is the unusual, surprising, unexpected perspective on familiar things. We don't reinvent the wheel of course, but we do try to provide a totally different perspective and we always want to integrate the visitors into what they're experiencing. The visitors are part of the staging rather than consumers. They participate, and have no need of a teacher. Our aim is not to fill in the gaps in people's education. We prefer to impart knowledge by presenting the subject matter in an exploratory way, rather than playing the schoolmaster. Even when it comes to complex topics, we try to create a route into the material that reaches the averagely interested or even uninterested individual in such a way that he or she is happy to engage with it. '*Grenzen (er)leben*' is a good example of how you can get pleasure-oriented families, who have paid lots of money to visit the expo and are looking for light-hearted entertainment, interested in fairly unwieldy, perhaps even unpleasant topics. You don't normally go and pay 100 euros only to be confronted with everyday problems such as euthanasia, cloning, transsexualism, domestic violence and so on. Those aren't exactly the kind of topics that entice people to visit an expo. Yet people queued up in front of the pavilion for up to one and a half hours and spent far longer inside than we expected. We provided a way into these unwieldy topics by means of an ingenious, centrally placed 360-degree projection that roused the visitors' curiosity about what lay behind it through an unusual, collective experience of space. Arranged around the projection room were 28 cabinets in which visitors could listen to seven recordings in four languages. Each of them showed a short excerpt from the film, which was linked with each cabinet both spatially and in terms of content. Thus, as well as a collective experience, a highly personal, individual experience was also possible. This was the key to the decoding in which we invited the visitors to engage: the protagonists' individual fate and personal experience of boundaries created tremendous potential for identification. What we hadn't predicted and what was therefore all the more impressive was that people didn't leave this exhibition in a state of depression but alert and shaken up, and this was confirmed by our subsequent surveys. No-one complained about the presence of topics like these in an expo. On the contrary, this pavilion was rated very highly, despite the difficult complex of themes.

So would you say that if the dramaturgical structure of the scenography is right, even a serious topic like that can be tackled at an entertaining expo?

Brückner: Gio Ponti, a designer back in the 1960s, said once that the great potential of the exhibition, in contrast to theatre or cinema, was that the visitors get the chance to move around within it, to look behind things and change perspective at any moment.[35] What makes it different is that you yourself are physically present, having an authentic, individual experience that no-one else necessarily shares with you and which can be experienced only through personal presence. The kind of exhibitions I prefer demand personal involvement. Communication occurs only through direct dialogue between subject matter and recipient, in an authentic space and within a given amount of time, which can't be delegated or stored. A DVD of a visit to an exhibition makes little sense to me and can't compensate for a personal visit. This is a really important point.

In *'Grenzen (er)leben'*, we used film in such a way that the physical boundaries of the space no longer played any role. The recipients now perceived the space itself as a medium, as a spatial experience. The actual dimensions of the space were suddenly no longer important. This was a case of genuine time- and place-related perception, of authentic, personal perception, which is yours alone, of a space which was itself capable of functioning as a narrative. For the viewer, space and experience are identical. Of course, we move through a physical world, one still dominated by the force of gravity, but as soon as I involve myself in the story related there, I become part of this story – I myself am immersed in the staging as a whole. The distance between viewer and stage is abolished. I find myself on a stage, and I'm an actor rather than an observer. This is what interests me about spaces created through scenography.

An exhibition is a place imbued with an idea. As soon as you manage to create a certain balance between materiality and narration, you open up this ensemble to

participation. Visitors can engage with the exhibition on a number of levels and the scenography comes to life. As a result, you yourself as a visitor help create this authentic experience.

Brückner: Over the years, what I've worked on constantly and gradually developed is a usable structure, a simple formula that makes this experience applicable to other projects. To this end I've developed four spatial parameters that deal with precisely this phenomenon. I call the first parameter the 'physical–substantive' space. The second is the 'atmospheric–adjectival' space. The third is the 'narrative–verbal' space and the fourth the 'dramaturgical', or better, 'dramatized' space, the space which features effective choreography or which leaves behind a choreographic sequence of spaces. All of these terms have strong linguistic connotations.

For example, we generally define space through substantives that describe dimensions, materials or construction. Through substantives such as wall, floor or ceiling, I can define a space physically, while atmospheric aspects are mostly conveyed through adjectives or adverbs that describe how something is or how it seems. A narrative space is a storytelling medium expressed chiefly through verbs. In the dramatised space, the dimension of time and the ordering of content, the sequence of impressions and the choreography of all the different parameters play a key role – of the kind familiar to us from an operatic score or film script. I think these four parameters are a highly effective means of both analysing existing spaces and creating new, staged spaces. Along with content parameters and the *Kreativstruktur*, I think these spatial parameters provide the best navigation system for sophisticated design – or at least for the kind of design developed on the basis of subject matter. As a rule, sophisticated scenography provides an ideal route, featuring a choreography that makes the thematic content real to people and facilitates associative access to it – or at least creates a certain affinity to something which they may well not grasp at first sight. What you end up with is a plausible and natural connection between visitor and subject.

uwe r. brückner

If you had the opportunity to initiate and develop an exhibition right now as an author-designer, with total freedom and autonomy, what kind of exhibition would it be?

Brückner: There are two things I'd like to make an exhibition about at the moment. One is the global climate, its effects and relevance to our spaceship Earth, and the other is the world religions, their social significance and the fascination they hold for us. We've already put in a lot of work on this and were extremely close to making it happen on several occasions – in the style of the Titanic exhibition. But somehow something always came up just before we reached the finishing line, as if it were jinxed, though this topic is not only in the air, but is a burning issue. We started on this six years ago and we're still looking for coalitions, particularly partners and sponsors who'd like to get on board, so that we can at last stage this vital topic in all its breadth and depth, without restriction. One major reason why this hasn't got off the ground so far is that it's politically explosive and it's hard to find sponsors at the moment. But I'd absolutely love to do these projects – together with lots of artist colleagues, on a really broad, international basis and with globally relevant subject matter, with our masterplan as the point of departure. These are the projects I'd love to do.

The Titanic exhibition consisted of quotations, presented as layer upon layer of narrative perspectives, with authentic stories from the rescue boats. Would you take a similar approach to presenting different opinions in this new climate exhibition? Would there be the same kind of layering of perspectives as the basis for the expressiveness and potential of the exhibition?

Brückner: When you're dealing with topics involving lots of unknowns, an exhibition obviously has to provide clear explanatory models of highly complex realities. The Titanic exhibition managed to do that without becoming didactic. Generally, popular science exhibitions ask 'Why are things as they are?'

343

and 'Where do their origins lie?', but they rarely ask 'Where is this taking us?'. Though sea levels are measurably rising and that is undoubtedly due to the melting of the polar icecaps, which is in turn due to global warming, there are various scientific explanatory models. The graphics or animations illustrating the effects in Holland or the Seychelles vary only slightly, but the perspectives and behavioural potential of the different cultural areas vary enormously. You can of course simply present these things side by side without comment, but the risk is that two hundred opinions are more likely to confuse the visitors than inform them effectively. But in my view the task of those responsible for content is to develop a comprehensible matrix out of these things, to both tease out the greatest common denominator of these analyses and opinions, as well as the greatest dissent, in order to arrive at perspectives or possible solutions that are as objective as possible – and which also reach the visitors.

Why do you say it's the task of those responsible for content? It seems to me that it's also a dramaturgical task, because you somehow have to derive an expressive superstructure from this plethora of opinions.

Brückner: As you know, I like to refer to us scenographers as author-designers. But this doesn't mean that we can compose scientific reports or that we should take it upon ourselves to bend scientific reports to our will as designers. But the visual processing, the rendering understandable of these reports, in order to make a script or score out of them – that, of course, is authorship. In my opinion, good scenographers are also good storyboarders and scriptwriters. If you want to develop a score for an exhibition that describes what, when, where and why things are happening in the exhibition, then as a scenographer, beyond design skills, you need the skills of an 'author'. In the spatial reality of the exhibition, everything comes together in real-time and you can walk through it. Design is concerned, as it were, with the translation of thematic structures into three-dimensional environments, into narratives you can walk through, if you will. This is why the four spatial parameters are so significant. But you need to add the thematic, scientific substance. That's why it's a good idea to sit down with acclaimed experts at the earliest possible date.

You refer to exhibitions that function as narratives you can walk through. The Titanic exhibition included the staging of so-called 'knee plays', dramatic interludes, because the dramaturgy demanded a switching between contrasting perspectives as the narrative progressed. This too is closely bound up with how the exhibition is read.

Brückner: These knee plays were invented by Robert Wilson in order to link two scenes together, to free up time between scenes in order to make alterations and open the way for new props to make their appearance, or in order to link dramatically two scenes between which the rupture would otherwise have been so great that the narrative flow would have broken down.[36] In the Titanic exhibition, I used the principle of the knee plays to build in gaps that briefly take the visitors out of the main narrative and slow them down so that they can shift perspective or focus their attention on a new topic. The other possibility with regard to these knee plays would be to build in scenes that act as a powerful stimulus to contemplation on the part of the visitors, thus triggering a totally different train of thought purely through association. It's enough if this occurs subliminally and in the end the visitors can say that the exhibition had a varied and exciting narrative rhythm. These knee plays can make a contribution to that. Sometimes I use them offensively, sometimes defensively, sometimes not just between two spaces but even as a dialectical irritant within a space. I also use knee plays as a sluice between two spaces or topics, when the course of the exhibition changes or between two floors – a kind of transition during which visitors can take a deep breath, slow down and reorient themselves. So these are spaces and spatial structures that trigger a different perception than the spaces already seen. Finally, I also use knee plays to add rhythm to the course of the exhibition and I position them in line with an optimal arc of tension. This is why they work so well.

Does this mean that the structure of the exhibition should be open, so that an unfamiliar, different kind of noise resonates within the narrative?

Brückner: Generally speaking, curators prefer recognisable structures which are, if possible, the same for all thematic fields. This looks as follows: ten thematic fields in ten rooms; the objects placed in a modular system of display cases, a few panels with relevant texts and a monitor or projector showing background material or documentary footage. Even if the exhibits are outstandingly good, this rapidly becomes tedious. These are outmoded, additive exhibition concepts in my opinion. We, in contrast, prioritise integrative stagings which establish a relationship between exhibits, information and the overall image of space. This means that the selection of design media should be appropriate to the themes, rather than being forced into the straightjacket of a display case or media structure. So you don't put a projection or interactive terminal in every room. On the contrary, there are spaces without projections and others in which there are several. In Schloss Dyck near Düsseldorf, our task was to exhibit the diary of Prince Dyck.[37] To be honest I don't like books in exhibitions, because you only ever see two pages, while the rest of the pages are at best summarised on a panel next to it. Rather than an electronic book, we opted for an analogous solution – and, moreover, a poetic one, in my opinion. We created facsimiles of all the pages, and covered all four walls of the room with them. The pages were printed on a translucent material and lit from behind so that it was impossible to confuse them with the original. The texts float within the room in such a way that the physical dimension receded into the background and a narrative space was produced in two senses of the word. We expected people to spend ten minutes in this room at most. In fact, they spent about 40 minutes there. Why? Because in this space, reading is the experience. At no point is anyone being told, 'Either you read this now or you'll remain ignorant!' Rather, this visual enclosure contains what it promises:

the pleasure to be had here is reading. This may be akin to your 'unfamiliar noise'. And all of this without electronic media. My point is that both the so-called 'auratics' and the hard-core display-case fetishists often wrongly equate staging with the massive use of electronic media. That's wrong, at least as far as we're concerned.

Exhibits have an aura and the exhibition requires staging. What's an 'auratic' and what's a 'stager'?

Brückner: This distinction between auratics and stagers has actually come about because of a highly polemic debate that has raged over the last few years. It has been carried on by the so-called auratics on the one hand, those who put all their faith in the auratic capabilities and qualities of exhibits and dismiss everything else – especially attempts to create a staging – as unnecessary trimmings; and the so-called stagers on the other, who are nothing but window-dressers in the eyes of the auratics. The article 'Lost in decoration' kicked off this debate.[38] The origins of the auratics' approach actually lie in the nineteenth-century art museum, but these only make up around ten per cent of museums. Since then, objects have been assumed or expected to have a self-explanatory potential that they rarely live up to. Auratics more or less believe that objects possess an exclusive claim to mediation (of knowledge) and thus require no design input. We know the results. Objects end up in expensive display cases, correctly illuminated and ventilated, and labelled and provided with catalogue numbers or tags, against the most neutral background possible, appropriate to the aesthetics of the room. That's all you need. But not quite. You also need a text on the specific topic, one on the general field, then another on the exhibit itself, illustrations and visual graphics, a film or interview, in order to get across all the things the exhibit can't convey by itself. This approach to design is interchangeable, tiresome and does justice neither to the object nor the conveyance of subject matter. Unfortunately, this misconceived approach is still common in Germany, especially in the big-budget national and *Landesmuseums*.

As a reaction to this, I tried to unmask this artificial delimitation, which, by the way, is almost exclusively characteristic of the auratics, in a lecture in Vienna.[39] I contrasted the notion of the 'good auratic' and the 'wicked stager' and asserted that you 'can't *not* stage' an exhibition.[40] Every act of design within an exhibition is a *mise en scène*, and thus an act of staging. Design that is in keeping with the times means staging, because exhibiting has always involved acts of staging. You could also quote Walter Benjamin or Jean Baudrillard at this point. The latter stated that you have to arouse the aura of an object. This is exactly what the 'stagers' do. They breathe new life into the hidden, lost potential of objects, translate content-related and narrative aspects into realities that can be experienced and, not least, they get the visitors interested.[41]

It continues to be the case that the big budgets are made available for classical exhibition design and generally meagre budgets for so-called staged exhibitions. There are also mercantile motives concealed behind the ideological stance; much-sought-after benefices must be secured. In our opinion at least, it's better to invest 80 per cent of the budget in interesting staging rather than in the aestheticisation of display cases.

I very strongly believe that in object-oriented exhibitions scenography must begin by recontextualising these objects and clusters of objects. But what exactly can and should staging contribute to this? Is scenography something that scratches at the surface of things or is its task actually to delve more deeply into the heart of the subject matter?

Brückner: If we wish to avoid long-winded texts and explanatory reports, in order to achieve a comprehensible recontextualisation of objects, scenography can produce an inviting reality that does justice to the topic, one that also makes complex themes accessible to the visitors. An example of how this can work are the science-based reconstructions of Ice-Age landscapes as the background for animal skeletons from that era in the exhibition '*Leben in Extremen*'.[42] This exhibition was also concerned with our ancestors' eating habits in comparison with today. The exhibits included findings of bones and seeds. After an intensive dialogue with the experts, to ensure that we could accurately convey the essence of the messages inherent in this exhibition, we created a spatial structure of a laid table, which visualised the development of eating habits as conditioned by climate and environment.

If I manage to go beyond merely shedding light on the original meaning, use and effect of an exhibit and portraying these things in an interesting way, then I can also convey the context of supposedly uninteresting exhibits and create a relationship with the viewer. Above all, staging means activating visitors' awareness, so that they read and enjoy the exhibition with a different level of intensity.

Staging is often equated with decoration, which distorts people's view of the exhibit or, even worse – and auratics stoke these fears among curators and clients – the idea that stagers misuse their objects and exhibits as a cover-up for their own schemes. On this view, stagings are suited only to temporary exhibitions or for those featuring less valuable exhibits. That may happen, of course, but ultimately it is the choice of means and their dosage that is crucial to both your plans and their implementation. The *Well-Tempered Clavier* is well-tempered because the dosage of the composition used is in balance.[43]

The aura is bound up with authenticity. But how is authenticity achieved?

Brückner: Authenticity is something you have to look at it a nuanced way.[44] People often mistake an authentic exhibit for an original. An original is always authentic in the sense of being unique. But a non-original can also seem authentic because, being physically present at a particular time and in a particular place, it may be perceived as something truly authentic. But this doesn't mean that it has to be an original. So a replica may also touch off an authentic experience. From the point of view of impact, the aura of a replica and that of an

original may be equally effective, with the difference between original and replica being a matter of purely academic interest. But in designing an exhibition you have to distinguish between an original and a replica. We always protect the originals, but we can be far more hands-on with the replicas. Replicas don't replace the original, but they allow for direct contact with the visitors, which is impossible in the case of originals because they have to be preserved. We use simple design tools to let the visitors know whether they're looking at an original or a replica. The pleasure they experience may be equally
authentic.

Because we wish to avoid limiting the idea of the exhibition to traditional notions of museums, fairs and art galleries and instead wish to extend it to include performative, urban or even rural spaces, we've called our international research project 'Narrative Environments'. But what does this term actually mean?[45]

Brückner: As far as its German-speaking reception is concerned, a narrative environment [*Raum*] means that a spatial enclosure is capable, per se and independently, of telling stories. If space in itself is capable of having a narrative impact, if space enters into a dialogue with me as a recipient, challenges me to explore its visual boundaries more closely and more thoroughly, provides me with a kind of choreography, touches me, this would be my definition of 'narrative environment'. A narrative environment is a space which has something to say. In a narrative environment there is some kind of two-way flow going on.

For me, one of the models of a narrative environment is the *Violence* project by Barbara Kruger.[46] This is an environment that is completely covered in texts and images. I once tried something similar with the students in a one-day seminar and we came to realise that Barbara Kruger did a good deal more in her project than simply chucking a bunch of messages onto the wall. She had considered carefully, from a number of perspectives, how these messages would come across. Once again we see the impact of three-dimensionality and the anarchistic factor represented by the visitors. This is a factor that is not entirely controllable but which we as scenographers can help stage in such a way that we create a place that is more than a room with texts all over the walls.

But from a historical perspective, what exactly is an exhibition? Can you describe the character of the medium and perhaps tell us something about the message that this vehicle may convey? What is the format of the exhibition good for?

Brückner: If we go back to the Latin roots of the term, *exponere*, then to expose something means to show something, to show oneself or an object, which you believe has validity and value and potential for people other than yourself. I don't know how far back the exhibition dates as a medium for the imparting of knowledge, but some theorists believe its origins lie in the market stall. As far back as ancient Egypt, Persia or Greece, the traders no doubt had to come up with something to make their stalls more appealing, to display their wares in a more attractive way than the neighbouring traders. With the Enlightenment and the increasing importance of the bourgeoisie in the eighteenth century, the collection and presentation of curiosities in *Wunderkammer* and museums took on increasing social relevance.[47] With the beginning of the industrial revolution in the mid-nineteenth century at the latest, markets then became shows presenting the achievements of the nation state, as demonstrated among other things by the legendary exhibitions of 1851 in London, featuring Joseph Paxton's Crystal Palace, and in Paris in 1889. These spectacular events, which displayed art, exotica and even military equipment alongside all the newly developed products, are considered by many the birthplace of modern scenography.

In parallel to the increasing power and importance of the bourgeoisie in Europe, the emerging democracy movements and the beginnings of parliamentarianism, a great number of the aristocracy's private collections were opened up to the public. Once education had gained the status of sociopolitical necessity for modern states in the nineteenth century, museums, alongside literary salons and theatres, developed into the educational mainstay of the rapidly growing population. Collecting, preserving, researching and imparting knowledge were stylised as a mission; the exhibition became the point of (public) access to the Other, to the unfamiliar, to scientific discoveries.

For auratics, the *Wunderkammer* are the origin of collecting, preserving and exhibiting. But interestingly, both the auratics and the stagers put forward these curiosity cabinets in order to advance their case. The auratics do so as evidence of the aura theory, which asserts the exhibit's sole claim to representation within the exhibition, while the stagers cite the *Wunderkammer* as early examples of stagings in space.

But I think the scenographic approach goes back much further. For me, the cave paintings of Lascaux, Stonehenge, the temple complexes of the Egyptians, Greeks and Romans and – crucially – the church paintings of the Middle Ages and Renaissance, are tremendous stagings.[48] Because what we're seeing here is not only individual visual endeavours and representations, but also true environments – place, architecture, design, narrative and rituals create a space, one that is charged with meaning and staged for the viewer. This is why I prefer your original title, 'narrative environment', to the German term *'narrativer Raum'*. In German you would translate environment as *Umgebung* ['surroundings'] or *Umfeld* ['environment', 'milieu'], but also as *Ausstattung* ['decor', 'furnishings'], and this includes the surrounding spaces, the non-spaces, the intervening spaces and the meta-spaces ... I believe we can locate scenography above all within these intervening spaces.

The exhibitions of the nineteenth century as yet paid very little attention to these meaningful environments. They were largely a case of imperialist collecting and hoarding. With the triumph of didactics, after the Second World War at the latest, the focus shifted to the imparting of knowledge, to explaining and informing. Exhibitions became ever more weighed down with texts and ever more pedagogical – a kind of continuation of the school lesson in public space. In the 1980s, people were then shocked by staged exhibitions such as Hollein's exhibition on the Turks held in Vienna and 'Berlin–Berlin' by Hans Dieter Schaal.[49] In the 1990s, there was a whole number of exhibitions of a strongly scenographic flavour, such as *'7 Hügel'*, *'Traum vom Sehen'* and of course 'Expedition Titanic'.[50] All of these were spectacular, highly successful temporary exhibitions.

With the new conception of the Muséum National d'Histoire Naturelle in Paris, we had hard evidence that it's possible to successfully stage exhibit-oriented permanent exhibitions in a listed building. For me the Paris natural history museum continues to be a courageous and highly successful example of design in keeping with the times. This museum has acquired a lively character all of its own. With the spectacular 'Procession of Animals' as a compelling, central installation, it also gained an unmistakable identity. The exhibition provokes a dialogue between the institution of the museum and the visitors. Here, the exhibition becomes a medium, an intermediary and a vehicle, as you put it.[51]

At the same time, all of these events are examples of the exhibition format. The common denominator is the scenographic space, the translation of content and message into visual enclosures, the staging of objects as a scenographic reality suited to the exhibition themes, the appropriate choice of design tools and the integration of the visitors into the overall staging. The museum of the twenty-first century is not just a place of learning, but also an authentic location for both collective and individual experiences. The exhibition is a scenographic format that fascinates me. I think its staging potential is far from being exhausted. What I find particularly interesting is the freedom of artistic interpretation, the influence of modern media on our perception, but also the inherent laws of scenography. Amazingly, this has a great deal to do with rituals, which I believe exercise a great influence on scenography. These rituals appealed to, and continue to appeal to, all the senses. The ritual is not an architectural or aesthetic measure; it has always had a specific goal, it has always been a matter of achieving an overall state or condition, but it also involves a meta-level. The ritual is not a matter of rational values, but provides room for interpretation. This makes me think of magical places such as the tombs in the Valley of the Kings, the rock drawings of the Aborigines, the altar of the Incas in Machu Picchu or, far more recently, the Jantar Mantar Observatory in New Delhi.[52] There's a whole string of examples that have a very powerful ritual character in my opinion. In every case, a place was defined or a new place was created or an existing site recreated to meet the needs of the ritual, in the sense of a choreography. Rituals are always about creating a total experience. What people attempted to do with rituals was to capture and enthral the recipients, the addressees, in a total way. Alongside theatre, I see these early rituals as one of key wellsprings of scenography.

When these three dimensions – the narrative potential, the inclination to expose and the drama of the ritual – flow together, what, roughly, would you say is the potential of the exhibition format?

Brückner: As a format the exhibition is currently flourishing because it's clearly meeting a need for authentic experiences, for individual experiences. People might say that a visit to the cinema or theatre does that as well. And that's basically true. But the big difference lies in the individual freedom of action. While I'm stuck in my seat at the theatre, I can move around freely in an exhibition, choosing my own route through it. Of course, for dramaturgical reasons, well-designed exhibitions offer to guide the visitor through the exhibition or at least indicate an ideal route. This will follow a choreography of impressions that intensifies the experience but which is never limiting. So the visitors represent a remarkable anarchistic potential. They may tap into an exhibition from their own perspective. The Titanic exhibition is an example of this. The visitors had the option of leaving the meandering ideal route through the display cases at any moment and to pass through this ideal route in their own individual way starting from the central corridor, and thus to take another look at, or even pass over, specific rooms or stagings.

uwe r. brückner

Would you say that the exhibition is an open work that, in contrast to film and theatre, provokes this anarchistic factor of individual freedom through the qualities of the format itself?

Brückner: That's right. And what's hugely important is that the authentic experience of an exhibition cannot be enjoyed by proxy. You can't have an exhibition brought into your home in the form of a DVD, which is possible with film and, up to a point, with a filmed play – though the TV version can't really replace the live experience of a theatrical performance. The distance of the orchestra pit is completely absent from an exhibition. The visitors come into direct contact with the exhibits and are part of the overall staging. So to make a comparison, the visitors are on the stage rather than in the auditorium. Only as they follow the multiple trajectories of the exhibition does the succession of individual scenes, in the spatial enclosure of the scenography, open up to the visitors; to follow a particular route is to be the thumb turning the pages of the flip-book that is the exhibition. A format based on the visitors' personal interaction and participation simply cannot be transferred to another medium.

If the exhibition is an open work and the spatio-temporal contours of the narrative environment may differ from the architectural boundaries of the physical space, might that imply that the exhibition begins before it opens in a given location and continues even after the visitors have left? This idea of the exhibition goes beyond the notion of the exhibition as a product and takes its lead just as much from a process in which space and time are interlocked or interlinked. So far we've talked a lot about space, about how one may structure space, about how space can be undergirded with dramaturgical structures, but what about time? What is your concept of time?

Brückner: I like to use the term 'enclosure' to describe space because I want to get across that scenographic space cannot be defined by limitation or exclusion and that scenographic design is not a purely indoor event. Scenography is just as much an outdoor affair, on the meta-level of theory and in the virtual realm. Scenographers do not think and work solely within a limited, fixed interior space, and they shouldn't settle for the arrangement of rooms in black box or white cube. What they need to do, in a nuanced way, beyond the physical space, is look at the potential of staging in the temporal sphere. I learned to deal with time as a medium of design only after studying stage design and gaining some idea of how theatre actually works, and especially how the stage works. Everything that occurs on stage is charged with meaning, even if it's supposedly unimportant. In contrast to the architectural space, the stage area is always time-based. Not because of the length of a performance, but because a concentrated narrative is being negotiated within a succession of the most varied scenes that shift repeatedly in time and place – 24 scenes in a total of five acts in the case of Shakespeare's *Romeo and Juliet*.[53] Stage design has to be able to cope with that.

Stage areas – and I also view our exhibition spaces as such – are spaces of meaning with no time for random occurrences. Within them, we as viewers read not only the moment, but also, in its patina, the Before, and, in its transformation, that which is presumably going to happen. The character of the protagonists is reflected in the spatial reality of the stage; the fate of Romeo or Tosca is decided on the stage set – this occurs again and again anew in every performance, yet in a different way than on the thousands of previous occasions.[54] Everyone would agree that it's vital to interpret a play in order to stage the likes of Hamlet – from which a dozen quotations have entered into our language – in a manner in keeping with the times, so that a 400-year-old text still feels relevant to us.[55] Can't this also apply to an exhibition? It can, as 'That's Opera' shows, an exhibition about 200 years of Italian opera featuring valuable exhibits from the Archivio Ricordi.[56] The visitors pass through a typical backstage environment with access to six exhibition cubes, stages you can walk through, each of which displays unique objects. At the same time, these can also be seen as an important step in the process of creating an opera, from the composition of the libretto to the performance.

What this means is that as soon as you find yourself in this different context of the theatre and accept its different conventions, your perspective is transformed as well. So a narrative environment would not only be a place in which an idea is translated in a compelling way through a combination of materials and media, but also one capable, with respect to the ritual dimension of scenography, of transforming the visitors' or viewers' perspective. Again, time plays a role here and this raises the issue of the readability of the narrative potential of things and thus of the quality of the viewing eye itself.

Brückner: As the saying goes, time becomes manifest only through change, through ageing, through becoming and ceasing to exist. This implies a Before, the Now of the viewer, and also an After. In theatre and film this Before and After is of course used in a quite explicit way. Both represent a concentrate in which a whole life may be narrated in ninety minutes. We read from the costumes, the props, the protagonists' behaviour and the stage set – in parallel to the action. One example that I like to show my students is Sally Potter's *Orlando*. This film, based on a novel by Virginia Woolf, covers around four hundred years of history, during which the protagonist even switches gender, changing from a young man into a woman.[57] The narrative roams across centuries in time-lapse, centuries during which entire historical eras and political systems come and go, centuries through which Orlando's fate runs like a thread. This is staged wonderfully through the varying shapes and the multitude of forms of the hedges within the same castle grounds; in a stylistically assured way, these hedges tell us which era we are now in, from the Renaissance to the modern age, though we only ever see this set for a few seconds. This means that you can use appropriate scenography to create realities that facilitate subtle or direct access to the narrative and at the same time show the course of events from a new perspective. This brings out how important the visual enclosure of the narrative environment and its choreography are to getting the visitors onto the right track.

In theatre or film there is a clearly defined moment A when the performance begins and a moment B when everything stops. During the interval between A and B, the members of the audience all sit in the auditorium looking straight ahead in the same direction. There's no such clear interval in an exhibition. The visitors move around freely, coming, staying and going as they please. So there are thousands of non-simultaneous, asynchronous intervals in the exhibition. For this reason alone the exhibition is an open work. And this is also why I want to ask you: To what extent are ATB exhibitions defined?

Brückner: As I see it, there are only three different possibilities in exhibition making, which you can offer either individually or all together. The first is so-called forced guidance, or to put it in more politically correct terms, a defined route. Here the visitors have no choice and there is no possibility of leaving the pre-set route. Then there is the option of the ideal route, which promises the maximal experience from a dramaturgical point of view and is paced accordingly. This corresponds roughly to the dramaturgy of a play or a film with the build-up of tension. Finally, there's the democratic route, the so-called free-flow trajectory, in which the visitors can move around freely and can choose their own way through. This usually begins with a general look over the exhibition as a whole. Within a moment or two you've taken it all in and can then decide where you want to go first. As a rule, this is how art museums are organised. There is no ideal route because everything is offered up on equal terms. We have already created free-flow exhibitions, such as the '*Themenpark Umwelt*' at Expo 2000 in Hanover. In the Landesmuseum für Archäologie in Herne there is what appears at first sight to be another free-flow exhibition, which then merges into a democratic exhibition with an ideal route. The visitors can walk through the entire staged landscape of excavations, but can also find their bearings again at any time with reference to a metal walkway that marks the ideal route.[58] If you look at these three main categories, it's easy to see that you can't use exactly the same dramaturgy for each, that the trajectory has to be developed in accordance with the dramaturgy.

If you combine the integrative approach, which is an approach that includes the visitors' perspective, with the idea of authorial design, then the curatorial aspect, the curatorial factor is more or less automatically guaranteed. I assume that you take the same view, that this means there is only one – dialogical – position left on the classical axis of curator and designer, namely at the centre of this axis?

Brückner: Absolutely. The author-filmmakers of the fifties, sixties and seventies showed us the way. Wim Wenders and Alexander Kluge were not just directors but also authors.[59] We can go back even further, to Luis Buñuel or Karl Valentin, who wasn't just a satirist but also a film director and author who wrote and filmed his own pieces.[60] The surrealist Luis Buñuel, whom I revere, also occurs to me because he developed screenplays with many other artist colleagues such as Salvador Dali and Max Ernst. Initially the influence of his artist colleagues was still very obvious, particularly if you think of *Un chien andalou* with its spatial imagery, with its mad and mutant pianos and donkeys.[61] All of this, of course, bears a very strong sculptural and artistic signature, which you only get from a team of experienced colleagues – before you get anywhere near your own authorship. Well, perhaps that's not the best example, as the two of them could only stand to work together in that way once.

Peter Greenaway as a filmmaker and Robert Wilson or Achim Freyer as theatre directors would certainly be further role models for me and my notion of author-designers within scenography – because of the way in which they created a dialogue between space and narrative and dramatised these things. The way I see it, author-designers are generalists able to make brilliant use of a number of disciplines simultaneously, with the aim of creating a *Gesamtkunstwerk*.

There are author-designers and artist-curators. Is Harald Szeemann a key reference for you?[62]

Brückner: Undoubtedly. I think Szeemann achieved a great deal. A lot of people refer to him or see him as one of those figures who broke through traditional boundaries. Particularly in the case of Szeemann, the question arises as to whether he was purely a curator or was himself an artist. I think in the end he was viewed as an artist because his '*Geld und Wert*' pavilion at the EXPO.02 in Switzerland, for example, was not based solely on curation.[63] Through his selection and placing of exhibits, Szeemann was clearly doing scenography as well. Essentially, he was the nucleus of his teams of professionals, whom he needed in order to realise his complex projects. For me he was like the artistic director of an opera. The biennial festivals in Venice that he curated were also imbued with his directorial energy.[64] Szeemann was undoubtedly one of the most influential artist curators of the late twentieth century, but he was also a role model who played his cards close to his chest.

What's your view of intensive collaboration between scenographers and curators?

Brückner: For me, intensive and constructive collaboration, with a common aim, is the precondition for the success of a demanding project. Collaboration between curators and designers is the norm, but the outcome isn't necessarily positive. But there are some very exciting examples of effective, successful collaboration. We might think of '*Kosmos im Kopf*' at the Hygiene-Museum in Dresden by Via Lewandowsky, or even our Titanic exhibition.[65]

In reality, designers are keener on working with curators than the other way round. There's a rift between the two camps that has been kept alive artificially, an artificial distrust felt by curators towards designers. Generally what happens is that major personalities in the design field are quickly suspected of wanting to take over the entire project. This misunderstanding is really past its sell-by date, because there are plenty of good examples of successful cooperation.

I can definitely state that all our projects that have turned out particularly well and have continued to be successful over the years, without exception, are projects in which we worked with curators or directors on an equal footing. We didn't always have a firm foundation of trust right from the outset. In some cases this developed only during the course of the project. Sometimes the beginning of the project was laborious and it took quite a long time to find a common language. But at some point it all began to work, the Gordian knot unravelled and in the end we had a result we could all live with, live with very happily in fact.

It would certainly help a lot to have joint seminars for curators and designers at university level, because curators often have no idea what it means to give a spatial structure to the subject matter. They too suffer from an educational deficit. They have almost no lessons in three-dimensionality and there are almost no designers offering seminars or workshops in the departments or faculties to work on this area. ATB has held such workshops on several occasions, with great success. We call the first stage of getting to know one another 'deBabelising', which simply means coming up with a common language by working together on a project. The ideal thing is if a project can be developed jointly, like a game of ping pong between content and form, and both parties feel free to think in an open way and make suggestions about how to give form to, or translate, the themes in such a way that you end up with an exciting staging. Projects have become very complex and there are many different tools for realising them. This is why it's a good idea to 'think outside of the box' together.

I'd like to mention one other project in which the collaboration between curators and scenographers was an outstanding success. This is the exhibition '*Menschen–Zeiten–Räume*', the great national archaeology exhibition in the Martin-Gropius-Bau in Berlin, in which every German Land was represented and intended to exhibit its treasures, its archaeological discoveries of the last ten or twenty years.[66] The Land of Mecklenburg-Western Pomerania had submitted a Slavic boat. A Slavic boat, however, which consisted of nothing but a load of rusty nails, which, moreover, were almost too fragile to be transported. Opinion within the team of curators was divided, and in the end Mecklenburg-Western Pomerania almost withdrew from the exhibition project. The problem was ultimately resolved through a scenographic masterstroke. We took casts of all the bolts and nails. The originals were all neatly exhibited in display cases but we put the casts in forensic bags and hung them on hundreds of nylon threads at precisely the location where they were originally attached. The reference point was a negative of the ship, which had survived in the sandy riverbed. This overall spatial image of nails and bolts became a reproduction, a model, a simulation of the original Slavic boat. This staging was one of the highlights of the exhibition as a whole because, on the basis of an authorly translation, using scenographic tools, it had recontextualised something opaque, something which otherwise always remains hidden in scientific documents. Suddenly, the full-size Slavic ship was floating above the original negative on the floor. On a scale of 1:1 in other words, and everyone got it straight away without explanations of any kind. By fusing different skills in an unprejudiced way, we were able to achieve an authentic and impactful outcome that would previously have been hard to imagine.

Will Uwe Brückner still be making exhibitions in five years' time? What will they look like?

Brückner: No idea. What I'd really like in five years' time is to create only those exhibitions I can initiate myself. It is, I think, the dream of everyone in an artistic field that at some point the clients come to you and say, can you do this or that for me, but you've got a free hand. So far there hasn't been that much trust and that many unearned laurels. Though I can't complain, because I'm certainly one of the designers with the greatest possible scope to engage in autonomous design and with the greatest freedom of action. Yet, to get to the point where people come to you and say, 'I'd like a staging in this or that location, I have an adequate budget for it and I trust you to put together something quite exceptional' – that's what I'd like, that's where I'd like to be in five years' time.

space.time.narrative

Notes

1. '*Max Ernst – Die Retrospektive*', Haus der Kunst, Munich, 1979. Max Ernst (1891–1976) was a German painter, sculptor and poet. Ernst is a fellow-thinker of Marcel Duchamp (1887–1968) and considered to be one of the primary pioneers of Surrealism.
2. During the Nazi dictatorship in Germany, 'degenerate art' was the official term for modern art, which the Nazis attacked in light of their racial theories. Under the Nazi regime, all works of art and cultural movements that could not be reconciled with the Nazi view of art and ideal of beauty were considered 'degenerate art': Expressionism, Dadaism, New Objectivity, surrealism, cubism and fauvism.
3. Christoph Stölzl (b.1944) was director of the Munich Stadtmuseum from 1980, and in 1987 was appointed general manager of the Deutsches Historisches Museum in Berlin, a post he held until late 1999. He then moved to the newspaper *Die Welt*, where he was in charge of the culture pages. From April 2000 to mid-2001, Stölzl was Berlin's minister of culture. '*Das Oktoberfest – 175 Jahre bayerischer National-Rausch, 1810–1985*' ['The Octoberfeast – 175 years of Bavarian nationalist euphoria, 1810–1985'] celebrated, commented and criticised the traditional Munich *Oktoberfest* in a jubilee-exhibition on the occasion of the 850th anniversary of the city of Munich; the exhibition was held in the Stadtmuseum from 25 July to 3 November 1985. Karl Valentin (1882–1948) was a German comedian, a cabaret performer, the 'Charlie Chaplin of Germany' and a star of many silent films in the 1920s; on the centenary of his birth, the Munich Stadtmuseum organised the exhibition '*Karl Valentin: Volkssänger? Dadaist?*' ['Karl Valentin: Folk Singer? Dadaist?'], 2 July to 3 October 1982.
4. Maximilien de Robespierre (1758–1794) was a French lawyer and politician at the time of the French Revolution.
5. Sampo Widmann (b.1942) is a German architect based in Munich. See: http://www.sampowidmann.de/en/index.html
6. Knut Lohrer (b.1937) is a German architect and senior partner of Atelier Lohrer in Stuttgart, which focuses on architecture and design for museums. See: http://www.atelierlohrer.de/
7. The International Garden Exhibition (IGA) of 1993 took place in Stuttgart and was designed by a group of architects and artists led by Atelier Lohrer, who had won the competition.
8. Schloss Trautenfels is a castle built on a rock in the valley of the river Enns in Styria, Austria. It houses a 'landscape museum', which is devoted to the natural and cultural history of the region. Uwe Brückner was involved in the design of the exhibition, in 1988. Dayr az Zawr is a city in eastern Syria, capital of Dayr az Zawr Governorate, situated at the point where a bridge crosses the river Euphrates near the site of an ancient city. Dayr az Zawr houses an archaeological museum devoted to that city; it was founded in 1974 and Uwe Brückner was involved in its realisation in 1973.
9. Hans-Martin Scholder (b.1959) is now a freelance stage designer.
10. Jürgen Rose (b.1937) is a German theatre designer and director, who was a professor for Stage Design at the Staatliche Akademie der Bildenden Künste (State Academy of Art and Design) in Stuttgart from 1973 to 2000.

uwe r. brückner

11 Friedrich (or Frederick) Kiesler (1890–1965) was an Austrian-American artist, theatre designer and architect. All stages of his artistic development hold important references for the field of scenography – from his stage design for Karel Capek's piece *R.U.R.* in 1921, his *City in Space* for the Exposition Internationale des Arts Décoratifs et Industriels Modernes in Paris in 1925, his collaboration with Marcel Duchamp and the Surrealists, and his *Art of This Century Gallery* which he designed for Peggy Guggenheim in New York in 1942, to the various architectural and scenographic concepts of his 'Endless House' in the 1950s and 1960s. See: Lisa Phillips et al., *Frederick Kiesler*, Whitney Museum of American Art and W.W. Norton & Company, New York, 1989. See also: http://www.kiesler.org, the website of the Austrian Frederick and Lillian Kiesler Private Foundation.

12 Coop Himmelb(l)au is an architectural office which was founded by Wolf D. Prix, Helmut Swiczinsky and Michael Holzer in Vienna, Austria, in 1968; see: http://*www.coop-himmelblau.at/*. For Haus-Rucker Co, see the interview with François Confino, note 4, p. xxx. Carlo Scarpa (1906–1978) was an Italian architect and furniture designer. Future Systems is a London-based architectural and design practice, founded by Jan Kaplicky in 1979 while he was working at Foster Associates. Peter Eisenman (b.1932) is an American architect, whose work has been labelled 'deconstructivist'. For Frank Gehry, see the interview with François Confino, note 26, p. 220.

13 Jørn Utzon (1918–2008) was a Danish architect who worked for Alvar Aalto and studied with Frank Lloyd Wright. Utzon is most notable for designing the Sydney Opera House in Australia, for which he won the architectural competition in 1957, and which was declared a World Heritage Site on 28 June 2007, a year before Utzon's death.

14 Hans-Günter Merz (b.1947) is a German architect and museum and exhibition designer.

15 See also the remarks on p.337 of this interview.

16 Peter Stein (b.1937), director, formerly of the Schaubühne in Berlin. Statement made during the stage design class visit to Stein's staging of Anton Chekhov's (1860–1904) *The Cherry Orchard* in 1995.

17 Atelier Brückner, 'Expedition Titanic', Speicherstadt, Hamburg, May 1997 to September 1998.

18 Holger von Neuhoff (b.1965) is a German exhibition-maker who was deeply involved in the realisation of the 'Expedition Titanic' exhibition in the Hamburg Speicherstadt in 1997.

19 'It is the pervading law of all things organic and inorganic, of all things physical and metaphysical, of all things human and all things super-human, of all true manifestations of the head, of the heart, of the soul, that the life is recognizable in its expression, that form ever follows function.' Louis Sullivan in the essay 'The tall office building artistically considered', published in *Lippincott's* magazine in March 1896.

20 Response of Dr Barbara Rüschoff-Thale when asked why she invited Atelier Brückner to put forward a proposal for the LWL-Museum für Archäologie in Herne. For *Gesamtkunstwerk*, see the Foreword by Hans Peter Schwarz, p.xiii, and the interview with Ruedi Baur, note 51, p.270.

21 Akira Kurosawa (1910–1998), *Rashomon*, 1950.

22 Uwe Brückner is referring to Paul Watzlawick's axiom 'One Cannot Not Communicate', which is derived from Gregory Bateson's *Steps to an Ecology of Mind*, which was published in 1972. Paul Watzlawick (1921–2007) was an Austrian-American psychologist

space.time.narrative

and philosopher. Gregory Bateson (1904–1980) was a British anthropologist, linguist and semiotician. See: Paul Watzlawick, *Pragmatics of Human Communication*, W.W. Norton & Company, London–New York, 1967. See also: Gregory Bateson, *Steps to an Ecology of Mind: Collected Essays in Anthropology, Psychiatry, Evolution, and Epistemology*, University of Chicago Press, Chicago, 1972.

23 Cycle Bowl for the Duales System Deutschland and Themenpark Umwelt, Expo 2000, Hanover.

24 Quotation from Jürgen Rose: 'When you study stage design, failure is part of the deal.'

25 The 'creative structure' is to be understood as a scenographic navigation system, as a structure of thinking and organisation of value to conceptual work and planning.

26 IN3 is the name of the Institut für Innenarchitektur und Szenografie (Institute for Interior Architecture and Scenography) of the Fachhochschule (University of Applied Arts) Nordwest-Schweiz, in Basel, Switzerland.

27 Peter Greenaway, *The Pillow Book*, 1996.

28 Walter Benjamin, 'Das Kunstwerk im Zeitalter seiner technischen Reproduzierbarkeit', in *Gesammelte Schriften I*, vol.2 (*Werkausgabe*, vol.2), edited by Rolf Tiedermann and Hermann Schweppenhäuser, Suhrkamp, Frankfurt am Main, 1980, pp 471–508. This essay appeared in a condensed French version in 1936 and was first published in unabridged form posthumously in 1963.

29 Jean Baudrillard (1929–2007) was a French sociologist, philosopher and cultural theorist, whose work is associated with post-structuralism. Umberto Eco (b.1932) is an Italian semiotician, philosopher and novelist, best known for his novel *The Name of the Rose* (1980). Peter Sloterdijk (b.1947) is a German philosopher and rector of the University of Art and Design in Karlsruhe, Germany. Wolfgang Amadeus Mozart (1756–1791) was a highly influential Austrian composer, performer and conductor of now world-famous classical music and operas, such as *Le Nozze di Figaro* (1786), *Don Giovanni* (1787), *Così fan tutte* (1790), *The Magic Flute* (1791) and his *Requiem*, which remained unfinished because of his early death in 1791. Giacomo Puccini (1858–1924) was an Italian opera-composer, perhaps best known for his operas *Tosca* (1900) and *Madame Butterfly* (1904). Richard Wagner (1813–1883) was a German composer, conductor and theatre director, perhaps best known for his opera cycle *Der Ring des Nibelungen* (1876). See also the interview with Ruedi Baur, note 51, p.xxx on *Gesamtkunstwerk*.

30 Bill Viola (b.1951), *Fire, Water, Breath*, 1997; Robert Wilson and Philip Glass, *Einstein on the Beach*, 1976; Marguerite Duras (1914–1996), *Die Krankheit Tod*, staged by Achim Freyer (b.1934) for the Schaubühne, Berlin, 1991.

31 Anish Kapoor (b.1954) is an Indian sculptor, who lives and works in London and received the prestigious Turner Prize in 1991. Olafur Eliasson (b.1967) is a Danish-Icelandic artist, who established his studio in Berlin in 1995, and is renowned for his installation *The Weather Project* in the Turbine Hall of the Tate Modern in London, in 2003.

32 Giuseppe Verdi (1813–1901), *Don Carlos*, Opernhaus, Zurich, 1993.

33 Atelier Brückner developed the concept and the masterplan for an International Science Centre, focused on climate and ecology, in 2001. The centre was called Innovarium and planned for the city of Oberhausen, Germany, but not executed.

34 Atelier Brückner, LWL-Museum für Archäologie, Westfälisches Landesmuseum, Herne, 2003.

35 'In contrast to cinema, where the audience members are at rest and allow a series of images and events to pass over them, visitors to exhibitions move through a motionless space. Through their movement, they create a shifting array of scenes. An exhibition designer must take this fact into account: colours, forms, spatial units, ceilings of different heights, a series of different perspectives – all these elements unfold as the visitors make their way through the exhibition. But should an exhibition be designed according to these factors, it must also be borne in mind that the visitors also stop, turn and go back, in other words that the spectacle the designer offers them must be effective from different angles.' Gio Ponti (1891–1979) quoted in: Ulrich Schwarz and Philipp Teufel (eds), *Handbuch Museografie und Ausstellungsgestaltung*, avedition, Ludwigsburg, 2001, p.12).

36 See essay 2, 'The Envelope', para 2.1, 391.

37 Atelier Brückner, Zentrum für Gartenkunst und Landschaftskultur, Schloss Dyck, Jüchen, Germany, 2003.

38 Hans-Günter Merz, 'Lost in decoration', in: Anke te Heesen and Petra Lutz (eds): *Dingwelten: Das Museum als Erkenntnisort* [*Worlds of Things: The Museum as a Place of Discovery*], Cologne, etc., 2005, pp 37–43.

39 Uwe R. Brückner, 'Wirkung und Einfluss von szenographischen Gestaltungsmitteln auf die Vermittlung von Inhalten im "inszenierten Raum"', published in: Österreichischer Museumsbund (ed.), *Neues Museum: Die österreichische Museumszeitschrift*, 4/05–1/06, Linz, 2006, pp 32–40.

40 See note 22 above, referring to Watzlawick's axiom of communication.

41 In 'Das Kunstwerk im Zeitalter seiner technischen Reproduzierbarkeit' ['The work of art in the age of mechanical reproduction'] (1935) (see note 28 above), Walter Benjamin examines the effect of the mechanical reproducibility of art on its meaning. According to Baudrillard, even the body seems to lose a certain aura, an aesthetic form or quality. 'Authenticity is lost and the original no longer exists, because it bears within it its own endless reproducibility.' Quoted in Jens Holze, *Simulation des Körpers – der moderne Körperbegriff nach Jean Baudrillard*, a reader of the '*Medienbildung*' (Media Education) course at the Otto-von-Guericke Universität in Magdeburg, Germany, 2005, p.8.

42 Atelier Brückner, '*Leben in Extremen*' ['Living in Extremes'], LWL-Museum für Archäologie, Herne, 30 May 2006 to 30 May 2007.

43 *The Well-Tempered Clavier* (*Das Wohltemperierte Klavier* in the original German) is a collection of solo keyboard music composed by Johann Sebastian Bach (1685–1750).

44 See: Thomas Knieper and Marion G. Müller (eds), *Authentizität und Inszenierung von Bilderwelten*, Herbert von Halem Verlag, Cologne, 2003. Erika Fischer-Lichte and Isabel Pflug (eds), *Inszenierung von Authentizität*, Francke Verlag, Tübingen, 2007.

45 See the Introduction, p.4.

46 Barbara Kruger (b.1945) is an American artist and activist, known for her critical juxtapositions of text and image in space, such as the 1991 installation *All Violence is an Illustration of a Pathetic Stereotype*.

47 The baroque collection of art and natural history owned by August Hermann Francke in Halle, opened in 1698, is considered the oldest public museum space in Germany. The technical terms *Kunstkammer* ['chamber of art'] and *Wunderkammer* ['chamber of wonders'] gained currency through Julius von Schlosser's *Die Kunst- und Wunderkammern der Spätrenaissance*, Leipzig, 1908.

48 The Lascaux cave paintings are estimated to date from the early Magdalenian period, around 15,000 BC; for the most part they are realistic images of large animals such as buffalo, aurochs, horses and deer which existed at the time. Another popular motif is the outline of the human hand. Stonehenge is an early Stone Age edifice in England used into the Bronze Age; it consists of a burial complex surrounded by a megalithic structure made up of several concentric circles of stones. In Egypt, the temple complex at Luxor, erected during the New Kingdom (1550–1070 BC), is an example; likewise the Renaissance frescoes of the Sistine Chapel in Rome.

49 Hans Hollein (b.1934) is an Austrian architect and industrial designer who has also designed exhibitions including *'Die Türken vor Wien'* ['The Turks at the gates of Vienna'], Künstlerhaus, Vienna, 1983; he was awarded the Pritzker Prize in 1985. Hans Dieter Schaal (b.1943) is a German architect, stage designer and artist who has designed numerous influential exhibitions, such as 'Berlin–Berlin', Martin-Gropius-Bau, Berlin, 1987.

50 '*7 Hügel: Bilder und Zeichen des 21. Jahrhunderts*' ['7 Hills: Images and Symbols of the 21st Century'], Martin-Gropius-Bau, Berlin, 2000; '*Der Traum vom Sehen*' ['The Dream of Seeing'], Gasometer, Oberhausen, 1997; 'Expedition Titanic', Speicherstadt, Hamburg, May 1997 to September 1998. See also p.343.

51 The Galerie de Zoologie, built by Jules André (1819–1890), was inaugurated in the same year as the Eiffel Tower – 1889 – and with equal success. It underwent a metamorphosis in 1994 to become the Grande Galerie de l'Evolution, under the guidance of the architects Paul Chemetov (b.1928) and Borja Huidobro (b.1936), assisted by the French filmmaker and theatre director René Allio (1924–1995). Since the reopening, the Museum's zoological collections are presented from a new and dynamic angle, the evolution of life. They form a spectacular ensemble (3,000 specimens exhibited in the nave alone, 7,000 total in the Galerie), installed in a space which is 55 metres by 25 metres and 30 metres high.

52 The Valley of the Kings was a necropolis in ancient Egypt in which 63 graves have so far been discovered; it is above all the rulers of the New Kingdom (c.1552–c.1069 BC) who were laid to rest here. The Australian Aborigines possess an artistic tradition thousands of years old, which, among other things, has taken the form of rock drawings and cave paintings. Machu Picchu consists of the well-preserved ruins of an Inca city, located on a mountain peak in the Andes; probably built around 1450 by Pachacútec Yupanqui, an Inca ruler who reigned from 1438 to 1471. Jantar Mantar is an eighteenth-century observatory in New Delhi, India.

53 William Shakespeare, *Romeo and Juliet*, tragedy, 1595–7.

54 Giacomo Puccini (1858–1924), *Tosca*, opera in three acts, first performed in 1900 in Rome.

55 William Shakespeare, *Hamlet, Prince of Denmark*, tragedy, 1600–1603.

56 Atelier Brückner designed a touring exhibition called 'That's Opera – 200 Years of Italian Music', based on the collection of the Archivio Ricordi in Milan. The premiere of 'That's Opera' was in Brussels at the Royal Depot, on 14 November 2008.

57 Sally Potter (b.1949), *Orlando*, 1992. Potter's film was based on: Virginia Woolf, *Orlando*, Hogarth Press, London, 1928. German edition: *Orlando – eine Biographie*, Fischer Verlag, Frankfurt am Main, 1992.

58 Atelier Brückner, LWL-Museum für Archäologie, Westfälisches Landesmuseum, Herne, 2003. See: Landschaftsverband Westfalen-Lippe (ed.), *Das Museum – The Museum*,

Westfälisches Museum für Archäologie, Landesmuseum Herne, Landschaftsverband Westfalen-Lippe with Westfälisches Museum für Archäologie – Landesmuseum and Amt für Bodendenkmalpflege, Münster, 2004.
59 Wim Wenders (b.1945) is a German film director and playwright, best known for his movies *The State of Things* (1982), *Paris, Texas* (1984) and *Wings of Desire* (1987), which received awards at various film festivals. Alexander Kluge (b.1932) is a German author and film director.
60 Luis Buñuel (1900–1983) was a Spanish filmmaker. For Karl Valentin, see note 3 above.
61 Luis Buñuel (1900–1983) and Salvador Dali (1904–1989), *Un chien andalou*. The film was first screened in Paris, 1929.
62 Harald Szeemann (1933–2005) was a Swiss curator and art historian.
63 Harald Szeemann, '*Geld und Wert – Das letzte Tabu*' ['Money and Value – The Final Taboo'], held as a part of EXPO.02, the Swiss national exhibition of 2002.
64 Harald Szeemann curated the 48th and 49th Venice Biennales in 1999 and 2001.
65 Via Lewandowsky (b.1963), '*Kosmos im Kopf: Gehirn und Denken*' ['The Cosmos in your Head: The Brain and Thought'], Deutsches Hygiene-Museum, Dresden, 2000.
66 '*Menschen–Zeiten–Räume – Archäologie in Deutschland*' ['People–Times–Spaces: Archaeology in Germany'], Martin-Gropius-Bau, Berlin, 2002–3.

afterimage

*optical illusion that refers to a (ghost) image
continuing to appear in one's vision after
the exposure to the original image has ceased*

space.time.narrative

afterimage

space.time.narrative

afterimage

space.time.narrative

afterimage

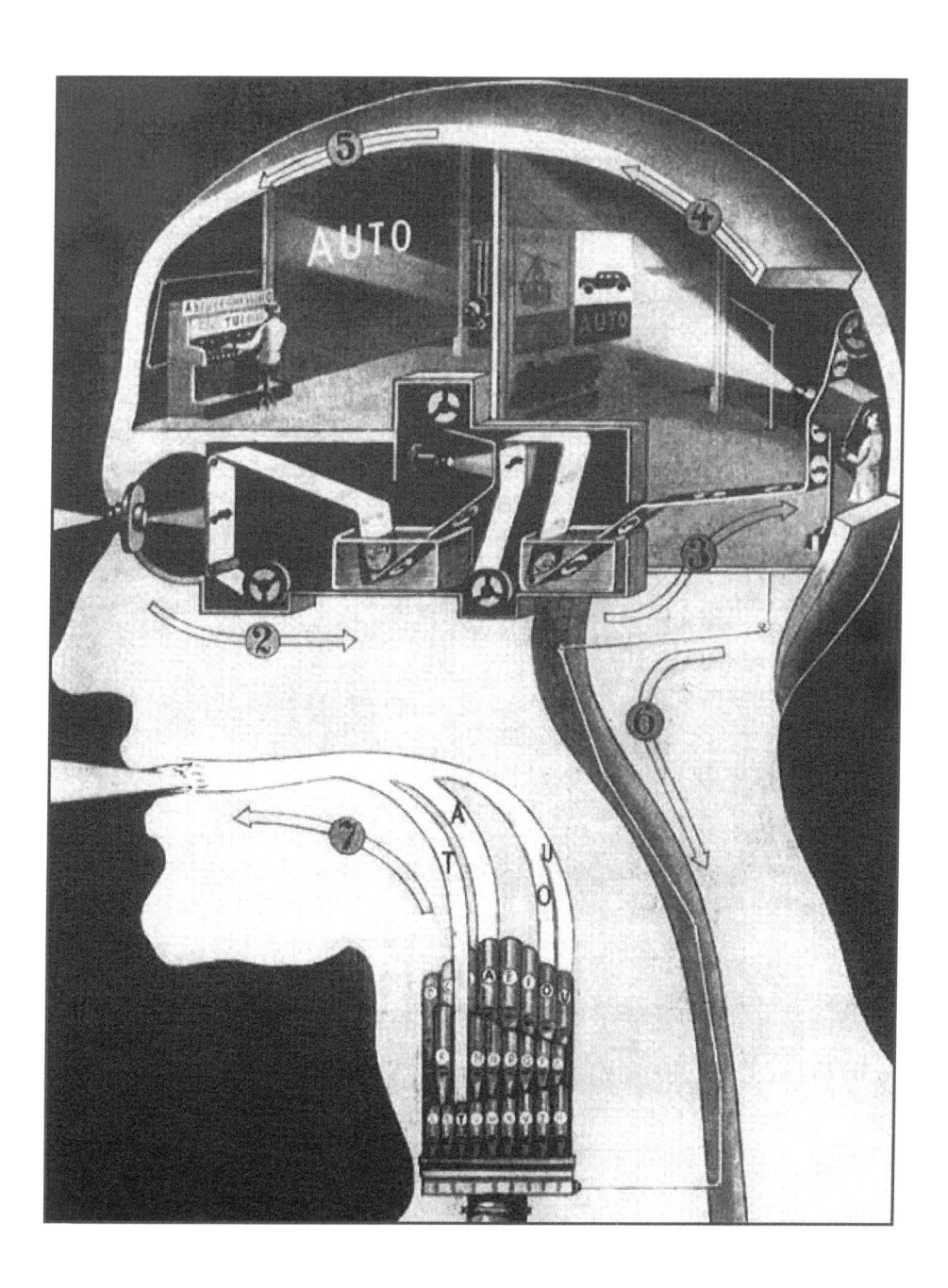

space.time.narrative

afterimage

space.time.narrative

奏崁

afterimage

space.time.narrative

afterimage

space.time.narrative

afterimage

space.time.narrative

afterimage

space.time.narrative

Illustrations

Ill.1 (p.372): Giordano Bruno (1548–1600), *Wheels of Memory*, from *De Umbris Idearum*, Paris, 1582. Until Giordano Bruno, the *Ars Memoriae* was centred around the systematical classification of the knowledge of the world and the problem of inventing the mnemotechnical algorhythms for the remembrance of its semantic structure. With his *Wheels of Memory*, Bruno radicalised this principle by reintroducing the *Ars Combinatoria* of the Spanish writer and philosopher Ramon Llull (1232–1315), but now on a more complex, encrypted and hermetic level, which supposed the knowledge of a secret code, described by Bruno in his *Clavis Magna* – a text which unfortunately got lost and leaves us with the problem of finding the key to Bruno's mystic system of five rotating concentric rings with 30 symbols each, which would allow us to decode the narrative of every single combination. See: Frances A. Yates, *The Art of Memory*, Pimlico, London, 1992. See also essay 1, 'The Battery', notes: 55–8, p.73.

Ill.2 (p.373): Ugo Mulas (1928–1973), *Lucio Fontana in action*, Milan, 1964. Courtesy the Estate of Ugo Mulas. Fontana's (1899–1968) *Concetto Spaziale* (1949) is a *cosa mentale*, an action that involves the body as well as the brain. Cutting a canvas is both an act of matter and a poetic act upon the world. The exhibition catalogue *Brasil, Lucio Fontana* makes reference to a text by Pier Luigi Tazzi, who states: 'On this side, there is language, the space taken by the subjective I; on the other side, beyond, is the unknown. The incision is the mark of passion, a passion that the rigour of reason has cooled down, but that was not completely extinguished; a nameless and limitless desire': See: Centro Cultural Banco do Brasil, *Brasil, Lucio Fontana*, Edizione Charta, Milan, 2001. See also essay 2, 'The Envelope', notes 127, 135, p. 455.

Ill.3 (p.374): Thomas Eakins (1844–1916), *Nude Broad Jumping*, 1884–5. The Library Company of Philadelphia. See: Frances P. Smyth and Mary Yakush (eds), *On the Art of Fixing a Shadow: One Hundred and Fifty Years of Photography*, National Gallery of Art and The Art Institute of Chicago, Bulfinch Press, Boston, 1989.

Ill.4 (p.375): Athanasius Kircher (1602–1680), *De Ars Magna Lucis et Umbrae* (The Great Art of Light and Shadow), Janossius, Amsterdam, 1671. Courtesy Herzog August Bibliothek, Wolfenbüttel, Germany. The spectator at point Z who entered the 'immersive environment' of Athanasius Kircher was confronted with a Wheel of Icons, a powerful media machine activated by a lever, that superimposed the heads of eight (mythological) animals onto the virtual body of the visitor, as seen in the mirror at point K, which could reflect the complex imagery, due to the sunlight entering the room through the window at point A. The optical reflections should give rise to spiritual reflections and transform the room into a genuine narrative space.

Ill.5 (p.376): © Frank den Oudsten (b.1949), *Floating Identities*, 1995–7. *Floating Identities* was developed for the Media Museum of the Zentrum für Kunst und Medientechnologie (ZKM) in Karlsruhe, Germany. The installation consists of 10 steel sculptures, each of which carries a stripped video-monitor. The sculptures are based on an ergonomical template of the human figure, which is used for drawing or modelling purposes. They are all similar, but set up in a different posture, suggesting the human body in animation. The ten figures are placed in line and form an axis in space. The ten monitors they carry are controlled by videowall technology. The main imagery, consisting of a dancer

afterimage

who jumps to reach escape velocity and float, is shot with a high-speed movie camera. Laid out as a volatile, ten-part freeze-frame on the monitors of the installation, *Floating Identities* refers to the early motion studies by British photographer Eadweard Muybridge (1830–1904).

Ill.6 (p.377): Cinematographic metaphor of the visual memory, from Fritz Kahn, *Das Leben des Menschen*, volume 4, Stuttgart, 1929. At point A in the frontal brain, a hand-driven camera shoots a scene. Its images are developed chemically at B and projected onto an internal screen at C at the back of the brain, where the sequence is watched and classified by a man, before being stored in what is called 'the visual memory centre', shaped like a film archive. See: Douwe Draaisma, *Metaphors of Memory: A History of Ideas about the Mind*, Cambridge University Press, Cambridge, 2000, p.214.

Ill.7 (p.378): Thomas Heatherwick (b.1970), *Seed Cathedral*, British Pavilion for the World Expo in Shanghai, © Frank den Oudsten, 2010. The spatial structure of the Seed Cathedral is a symbol of a seed itself, a shell with a spiny appearance. This manmade husk is composed of 60,000 transparent optical strands, each 7.5 metres long and each with a unique seed embedded at its tip, which stick into the inner chamber and guide the daylight into its interior. Thus, the visitor to the *Seed Cathedral* is encapsulated in a silent narrative space composed of 60,000 seeds from the Royal Botanical Gardens at Kew, which bring the incredible diversity and potential of life on earth within touching distance.

Ill.8 (p.379): Adolphe Mouron, alias Cassandre (1901–1968), design of Bifur typeface, 1929. Adolphe Mouron was a Ukrainian-French painter and poster-artist, born in Kharkov, who spent his childhood in Russia until the First World War. He studied art in Paris at the Académie Julian, at the Académie de la Grande Chaumière and at the Ateliers libres de Montparnasse. His paintings where greatly influenced by Cézanne. To earn his living, he worked at the printing office Hachard. By 1919, he became interested in the approach and work of the Bauhaus. In 1929 Cassandre designed Bifur, a new Art Deco advertising typeface. The term 'bifur' refers to 'bifurcation', which means division into two forks or branches, and addresses the parallax of our perception. See essay 1, 'The Battery', p. 46.

Ill.9 (p.380): © Xu Bing (b.1955), Far West logo, 2008. Xu Bing is a New York-based Chinese artist, who experiments with crossovers of the western alphabet and the Chinese character, in which meaning dissolves. See: Britta Erickson et al., *The Art of Xu Bing: Words Without Meaning, Meaning Without Words*, University of Washington Press, Seattle, 2002. See also: http://www.xubing.com.

Ill.10 (p.381): Peter Greenaway (b.1942), 'The Physical Self', Museum Boijmans Van Beuningen, Rotterdam, 1991–2. See essay 1, 'The Battery', note 6, p. 67.

Ill.11 (p.382): © Wim Ruigrok (b.1939), *Black Square with visitors*, in the Kasimir Malevich exhibition, Stedelijk Museum, Amsterdam, 1989. See essay 1, 'The Battery', p. 38.

Ill.12 (p.383): © Hiroshi Sugimoto (b.1948), *Union City Drive-In*, Union City (US), 1993. See essay 1, 'The Battery', p. 34.

Ill.13 (p.384): Fulvio Roiter (b.1926), *Einstein on the Beach*, Robert Wilson, Philip Glass, 1976. Courtesy of the Byrd Hoffman Watermill Foundation. See also essay 2, 'The Envelope', p. 402.

Ill.14 (p.385): © Thomas Struth (b.1954), *Pergamon Museum*, Berlin, 2001. Struth, who is well known for his 'museum photographs', documented here the inherent conceptual

space.time.narrative

friction, or 'parallax', of a spectacular staging of Hellenistic architectural fragments in an early-20th-century German museum building. See: Thomas Struth, Wolf-Dieter Heilmeyer and Annette Philip, *Pergamon Museum 1–6*, Schirmer/Mosel Verlag, Munich, 2004.

Ill.15 (p.386): © Associated Press / Kathy Willens, *The Mexican Suitcase*, 2008. In an article entitled 'The Capa Cache', published on 27 January 2008, the *New York Times* reported that 'thousands of negatives of photographs taken by Robert Capa during the Spanish Civil War, long thought to be lost forever, have resurfaced'. In order to escape from the Nazi invasion, Capa (1913–1954) fled Europe for America in 1939, leaving behind the contents of his Paris darkroom. He assumed that the work had been lost during the war, and when he died in 1954 on assignment in Vietnam, Capa was probably still thinking so. The so-called 'Mexican Suitcase', already rediscovered in Mexico City in 1995, was finally given in custody to the International Photography Center in New York. Its three flimsy cardboard boxes in red, green and beige contain a wealth of historic photographs, but not the evidence that could put the controversy around Capa's *Falling Soldier* to an end.

Ill.16 (p.387): Robert Capa, *The Falling Soldier*, probably near Cerro Muriano (Cordoba Front), 5 September 1936. Courtesy The International Photography Center (IPC), New York. In Capa's image, a lone anti-fascist soldier pitches backwards at the instant bullets seem to rip through him. The publication in the French magazine *VU* in 1936, and in *Life* magazine in 1937, made the photographer an international celebrity. The Falling Soldier seems to embody Capa's mantra: 'If your pictures aren't good enough, you're not close enough.' The circumstances in which Capa took the picture, however, have been the subject of an ongoing dispute ever since. Did Capa stage the scene, or is the picture really the authentic photograph, which is supposed to have changed the style of war journalism? Not even the 'Mexican Suitcase' could reveal the mystery.

the envelope

the limits within which a system can safely operate as defined by its performance boundaries; 'to push the envelope': to go beyond established limits

2.1 a space full of time

When Robert Wilson was staging Mozart's *The Magic Flute* for the Opéra Bastille in Paris in 1991, he was simultaneously working on an exhibition entitled 'Mr Bojangles' Memory ... Og, Son of Fire', which would open at the Centre Pompidou by the end of the same year.[1] Two weeks before the premiere of the opera, some six months before the opening of the exhibition, Umberto Eco asked Wilson about the rationale of the project, which would feature the legendary tap dancer Bill 'Bojangles' Robinson in a staging that involved a *mise en espace* with intricate pathways, gates and open spaces reminding us of labyrinthine urban structures.[2] Mr Bojangles' adventures were shown on video screens mapping out the staging like illuminated beacons. The videos transcended the significance of mere indicative signs, however. The animations, in which Mr Bojangles met the prehistoric character Og, enhanced the fictional nature of Wilson's exhibition stage.[3] The scaled contrasts produced an experience of a dream-like nature, which became the anchor point of the exhibition's symbolism. Mr Bojangles himself acted as the virtual memory of a narrative environment in which the spectator became involved like an actor having entered the stage to do an improvisation.

The year 1991 marked a turning point in Wilson's career, which had hitherto revolved mainly around large-scale, experimental theatre productions and, less conspicuously, around classical gallery presentations of drawings, sculptures and furniture that had been produced for these theatre productions. With 'Mr Bojangles' Memory', his exhibitions turned into ensembles that were equally complex and dramatic as his works for the theatre. It is for this reason that the staging of the Paris exhibition is of particular interest here, as comparing the two strands of artistic production in terms of design may enrich our present discourse.

The 'Robert Wilson's Vision' exhibition at the Boston Museum of Fine Arts earlier that year, a retrospective of 20 years of drawings, paintings, furniture, sculpture and video put together by curator Trevor Fairbrother, had been a turning point.[4] Despite the retrospective nature of the initial project, the exhibition evolved into a genuine Wilsonian 'environment' to which Wilson's sound artist at the time, Hans Peter Kuhn, contributed a soundscape very much like the one at the 'Mr Bojangles' exhibition six months later.[5] From a staging point of view, the Boston exhibition must surely have aroused Wilson's interest in the dramatic potential of the exhibition format and the possibilities of curatorship. The staging of works of art in the spatial environment of the exhibition became a leading principle, which he had already tested on a more modest scale in the *Room for Salomé* installation at the group exhibition *Energies* at the Stedelijk Museum in Amsterdam a year before.[6] What was new in 'Robert Wilson's Vision', and even more so in 'Mr Bojangles' Memory', was that Wilson was now in full control of every aspect of the exhibition, as if he were directing a stage production.

Robert Wilson's multi-track output could perhaps help us bridge certain philosophical, theoretical differences between the various disciplines and the laws that govern them. The field of expertise that we should primarily focus on, then, is the domain of scenography, which is often closely associated with the stage, but in my view has its bearing on this other area of cultural production as well: the exhibition. Despite formal differences, the two areas of creativity have much in common. The stage and the exhibition are the mnemonic media of our culture. But whereas the dramatic artist is being supported by an age-old tradition, the exhibition maker finds himself culturally isolated.

To bridge the gap, we unified both categories under the more general header of 'narrative environment' in essay 1: 'The Battery'. This header was required to enable us to connect the conceptual 'space–time–narrative' triangle, which dominates both disciplines, to the laws of scenography – which, we may add, also needed some stretching and transformation in order for it to apply to the more general complex of variables that make up narrative environments. Essay 1, which focuses on the narrative potential of things, could be regarded as a quest for the elastic counterpart of classical scenography, or a 'topology' of scenography, if you will, that for the sake of argument was labelled 'expanded scenography'.[7]

Expanded scenography is to classical scenography as the 'rubber sheet geometry' of topology is to classical Euclidean mathematics.[8] Whereas in the classical theatre scenography is predominantly governed by the authority of dramatic text, expanded scenography is more elusive and relative. One could interpret it as a mindset of classical orientation enriched with the subversive dimensions of obscenography, which within the cycle of dramaturgy guarantees an underlying discursive diversity.[9] Parataxis, parallax and tendencies that deviate from the leitmotif are the fertile biotope of expanded scenography. Its laws pertain to a wider area because they have a different, more comprehensive intellectual source, from which they gain a more profound and subtle radius that does not separate form and content, but merges them on an essential level instead. The scenography of narrative environment is essentially synthetic and monadic for that reason.[10] Through contrast the scenographer of narrative environment maps out conditions for an intensive odyssey along a more or less contingent series of positions and situations. Contingent, because within the narrative order that is set up by the scenographer, chance and choice are the leading principles for the nomadic spectator. This contingent succession of situations is no less than an individual cross section of an apparently infinite semantic field that is as complex as a city. Such a situationist universe requires a cubistic view on the part of the spectator who needs to edit deferring perspectives into one meaningful orientation – at least temporarily so.[11] There always remains this spectrum of oppositions, delicately balanced, but as inconstant as the weather. Narrative environments are veritable waves of imagination, spectacles, be they loud or silent, in which spectators maintain their balance for as long as it lasts. Such a fluent positioning creates, let's say, quantum mechanical uncertainties about the relation between thing and thought, work and working, time and space, tale and listener, performance and audience, dramaturg and scenographer – the polarities that dominate the dynamics of stage and exhibition. Does space accommodate narrative with time? Or, conversely, does narrative diachronically unfold as space? What else is time besides the individual experience of the spectator? What more is time than the interval in which memory and imagination open up? No time without an audience. Myriad spectators: myriad times. There is always the alternative take on things. Myriad interpretations. The spectator doesn't move through time; time moves through the spectator. Things aren't in space; space is in things. Like Alice in Wonderland who falls through the world and finds out that every relation is reversible and elastic.[12]

Back to Paris, where on 16 June 1991 Umberto Eco and Robert Wilson are having a conversation about interpretation, orientation and amnesia, about the participating visitor and the scenographical concept of 'Mr Bojangles' Memory'. The scale model, which was the starting point of the discussion, appears to have been of crucial importance for the development of the staging of the exhibition, for it not only expressed its architectural aspects, but apparently also its metaphors and its dramaturgical structure.[13]

Umberto Eco: 'It's always silly to ask an author: "What did you mean by this or that?" It also happens to me and I answer: "If I meant something more, I would have written it." It can be more silly with you because it's notorious that when you are asked something like that, you say: "Well, I did it because it is beautiful!" So I won't ask you about the meaning of your works, but rather about your feelings before and during some of them. Today I saw a maquette of the exhibition. As a first impression, I saw there a city that I can focus from different perspectives. I don't know if you are familiar with David [sic] Lynch's book *A View from the Road*, on the American city designed so as to be viewed from the highway. When I think about your work – what I loved most was *Einstein on the Beach* – I have the suspicion that you start doing something thinking of a city, of somebody who moves into a city, who can drop one thing and look at something else, who changes his own perspective, who is allowed to refuse to consider something today, in order to reconsider it tomorrow. It seems that you foresee an audience able to complete your work. I have written a book, *The Open Work*, in which the same ideas were used for literature.'[14]

Robert Wilson: 'Yes, I think it's a good analogy to compare it to a city. I'm looking out of my office window now and I see a contemporary building. Next to it is a building from the eighteenth century and over there is a building under construction. I see not only the Parisian present but also traces of its past and premonitions of its future. I look above and I see clouds changing. An airplane crosses. On the street I see a man walking and a car passing. All of these events happen simultaneously and at different speeds. The exhibition is a little bit like that, full of various spatial and temporal layers. The space is like a battery with different energies. It is a space that is full of time; I would not call it timeless, but a space for memories.'[15]

Be Eco's city analogy as it may, the Centre Pompidou exhibition made the impression of a primordial, barren landscape of black earth, gravel and lava that one could traverse via a network of levelled-up pathways. The meandering paths led one past gently rolling hills in which some forty pieces of furniture were put, some of which were flanked by works of art from the vaults of the Centre Pompidou. The most striking example was the silhouette of a Giacometti sculpture against the background of a volcano.[16] As always with Wilson, light and sound were an integral and quite impressive part of the installation, which enabled one to keep track of Mr Bojangles' adventures through video monitors, the colourful counterpoints in the poetic park of memory. But what exactly was being exhibited? As we saw, Wilson described the environment as 'a battery with different energies'. But what was the charge of this battery? And how did the accumulated energy discharge in the imagination of the audience? Eco brought up the subject of the readability of the exhibition: 'It seems that you foresee an audience able to complete your work.' Apparently Eco imagined an environment in which audience participation would complete the staging. Wilson didn't respond directly to this suggestion. But what clues did the exhibition offer in terms of accessibility?

The central pieces were the furniture sculptures that had figured in various operas. They were the carrier of the critical charge of the exhibition. Wilson designed quite a number of chairs for his operas. First we have *The Life and Times of Sigmund Freud* in 1969. Later we find *The Life and Times of Joseph Stalin*, *Letter for Queen Victoria*, *Einstein on the Beach* and numerous other productions. To Wilson a chair is always the nucleus of a more elaborate piece of work. The chair is private, the opera is public. The chair is the condensation of the content, its aesthetics the metaphor. They have names: Saddam Hussein, Sigmund Freud, Joseph Stalin, Medusa, Parsifal, Rudolf Hess, Heiner Müller, Queen Victoria, Albert Einstein, Franz Kafka, Herod, Salomé, John the Baptist, Lucinda Childs, Anton Chekhov, Piet Mondrian, King Lear, Virginia Woolf etcetera. A stage for the legendary name. Thus the chairs become the personification of protagonists of different eras.[17] Condensed into chairs they are to Wilson 'the gods of our time', each playing a part in a highly personal myth. In the Centre Pompidou their names resonated in the space of exhibition. Every chair in the landscape carried an immense history whose narrative nucleus, the idiosyncratic condensation of an era, was hurled into space by the ultra-centrifuge of Mr Bojangles' memory, on its way to a head-on collision with the receptive spectator's time. Such a fusion could produce room for a story. In that sense 'Mr Bojangles' Memory' was indeed a battery, an environment charged with countless latent stories. A space full of time.

In the discussion with Eco, Wilson referred to zap culture on television, and exactly this freedom to keep switching channels offered him a parallel with the exhibition in which every chair presented a junction of a new semantic network: 'There are an infinite number of possibilities. It is a space in which we hear and see and experience, and then we make associations.'[18] It is hard to estimate the actual capacity of this bundle of possibilities. Wilson assumed that every visitor would have sufficient knowledge of the various contemporary mythological figures and would thus make the connection necessary to have the exhibition trigger the cycle of memory and imagination. But it was this very aspect that made the Mr Bojangles exhibition a vulnerable one. For the chain of associations was provoked by the names attached to the chairs rather than by their aesthetics. So, the question came up of how the imagination of the individual visitor could relate to the wondrous landscape of Wilson's exhibition. How was one to read Mr Bojangles' memory? Critics were sceptical about Wilson's intentions and this was further reinforced by the soundtrack, which had a voice that continuously proclaimed the futility of the whole thing.[19]

Did Wilson consciously aim for alienation in 'Mr Bojangles' Memory'? Did the exhibition contain any narrative at all? Or was it Wilson's intention to 'denarratise' the narrative elements of the display, to eliminate everything temporal from the space and thus evoke, for the time being, a timeless pantheon for his collection of chairs? Did we witness a private memory landscape that was no more – and no less, to be sure – than a cubistic portrait that resembled the author? A mythological landscape, to which we could only relate as fish in deep sea to a panorama at the top of a mountain? Did the things on display actually belong to the core of the exhibition? Perhaps the visitor was rather facing the materialisation of a dream, overlooking an alternative world, very much like the walker in Caspar David Friedrich's famous painting who gazes at a virtual landscape shrouded in a sea of mist?[20]

If 'Mr Bojangles' Memory' was indeed an hermetically autobiographical universe that could only be read by means of a cross section, all possible mental trajectories that spun off the exhibition's given track in the sense of Feynman's 'sum-over-histories' would necessarily be obscure.[21] Except of course for that one completely individual, unequivocal cross section: ours.

That was the time we spent at the exhibition without any orientation, measured in hours, minutes and seconds. Tabula rasa. Memory dump. Can we encounter radically different worlds and gain new insights by doing so? The answer is: yes, we can! Which is essentially the power of scenography. In his conversation with Eco, Wilson himself hinted at the possibility of the exhibition being about loss of memory, and he mentioned that during the production of his opera *Death, Destruction & Detroit II* he had been preoccupied with the idea of designing an environment where amnesia could be experienced.[22] Eco immediately brought the city metaphor back into play and came full circle by stating that 'walking through a new city always implies a loss of memory' and, we may add, a fresh outlook.[23]

If the objective had indeed been to provoke a temporary loss of memory on the part of the spectator in order to make room for a new orientation, then alienation and disorientation were the director's main dramaturgical tools. Whether this fitted the bill remains questionable because the criticism of the inaccessibility of 'Mr Bojangles' Memory' wasn't completely unfounded. It's not that Wilson's theatrical work is any the less alienating, but with an equally alien staging, the streamlined communicative format of the theatre still has a more coherent net experience. On a structural level there are fundamental differences between Wilson's theatrical work and his exhibitions. Wilson may well maintain that his objective is not to impose his own feelings or interpretations of his work on the audience, but even if he considers his stagings to be 'open-ended situations', the scene of the action by its mere impressive visual nature will – even despite itself – still take on a narrative charge that requires guidance of our gaze and navigation. In Wilson's dramatic work this differentiation of focus is formally taken care of by organising the theatrical space, in which the frame of the proscenium serves as a window looking onto the poetic world of the performance. Its function resembles a book in which pages can be turned scene by scene, so that the theatrical action takes on a linear, sequential character.[24] At the same time the frame serves as an effective filter that determines what needs to be seen in sync with the score of the production as it progresses scene by scene, dramatic interval by dramatic interval. It is a selective instrument that enables the scenographer to choose what needs to be seen or unseen at any given moment. Thus the proscenium articulates scenography. Such a differentiation is completely lacking in exhibitions if only because the medium doesn't allow a strict formal separation between staging and audience. The intensity of the gaze in exhibitions therefore requires a whole new structural approach in which the simultaneous emergence of dramatic elements within the landscape of the narrative environment replaces the sequential one within the frame of the stage. What is frontal in the perspective alignment of the stage image is replaced by a cubistic montage of the shifting panorama of the exhibition. Exhibitions lack a fixed focus. The fabric of various narrative strands, which in the theatre appears as the semantically charged 'fourth wall' between the audience and the stage, is transformed into a fuzzy, unstable narrative outline mediating the domain of the presentation and the domain of the spectator.[25] A moving cloud, offering a fluctuating view on shreds of star-spangled sky. The proximity to the staging is a radically different one in the exhibition. As the filtering instrument of the proscenium arch is absent, the optical continuity, the narrative density and the dramatic effects are all modulated by a much more complex set of parameters in the exhibition. The visual direction that the exhibition imposes on the scenographer would roughly correspond to a filmmaker having to shoot wide-angle shots exclusively – which would seriously limit the communicative bandwidth of his medium. The dynamics of exhibition therefore spring from something other than a carefully composed rhythm of images that are carefully edited in time. A close-up in an exhibition will occur only when the visitor physically approaches the *mise en scène* or when his or her attention becomes obsessed by an element by some expectation that was triggered earlier and is subsequently met. And as expectations mount, the temperature of experience increases as well. As Mark de Jong remarked earlier, exhibitions are primarily about staging intensity.[26]

The extent of intensity in exhibitions is governed by the parameter of 'proximity' in every sense of the word. Guided attraction. Guided curiosity. Guided imagination. Exhibitions are designed in terms of attention and they are therefore topological entities.[27] To define the 'scenes' of an exhibition, dramaturgically speaking, one would speak of narrative density and mental closeness. However, such closeness can never be a univocal notion, as a neatly defined no-man's-land in between subject and object. Closeness will always be a zone with hazy contours, subject to the fuzzy logic of the complex whole.[28] An exhibition is always an aggregate of soft parameters and hard ones, very much like a town square that has one set of physical contours when the sun shines and another set when it starts to rain and everybody leaves the pavement cafés in a hurry. The scenes of a compelling exhibition are intense occurrences within an encompassing semantic field that allows for multiple points of interest and interpretations. A walk through the actual space of such a narrative landscape comes down to a series of intervals of varying orientation and intensity that one could graphically record as

the envelope

vectors of attention. Because of the erratic nature of dramatic development, such a diagram (p.400) will necessarily display a discontinuous structure, mirroring the visitor's shifting perspectives alongside the curving *parcours* of the exhibition. Each individual vector refers to a specific event or a specific situation. The resultant of all vectors taken together indicates the narrative tendency of the scenography. The sum total of all staged events, depicted as a cascade of alternatively oriented vectors in space–time, I would call the 'event structure' of narrative environment.

However, because every narrative environment is principally a dramatic hinge connecting visitor and operator, the event structure will also consist of two sets of vectors, each producing its own individual resultant orientation. We can thus interpret the event structure of an exhibition, like the event structure of a stage play, as a complex diagram depicting not only the tendency of scenography, but also, in a parallel, simultaneous fashion, the orientation of experience or the tendency of interpretation. The route through the actual space–time of the narrative landscape will always provoke a ramble through the imaginary space of memory and imagination. The extent to which the imagination will become active is dependent on the capacity of the spectator, surely, but it is also a primary function of the staging itself. A scenographically flat exhibition will produce vectors of attention that have more or less the same orientation, whereas the event structure of a presentation that is rich in contrast will produce greater dynamics. A presentation that fails to move the spectator will produce an event structure in which the two resultants by and large coincide. A stirring exhibition will provoke interesting semantic shifts and a broader array of interpretations, as an indication of which the event structure diagram will show a greater disparity between the vector of the staging and the vector of experience. See figures 1 and 2 on the following pages.

space.time.narrative

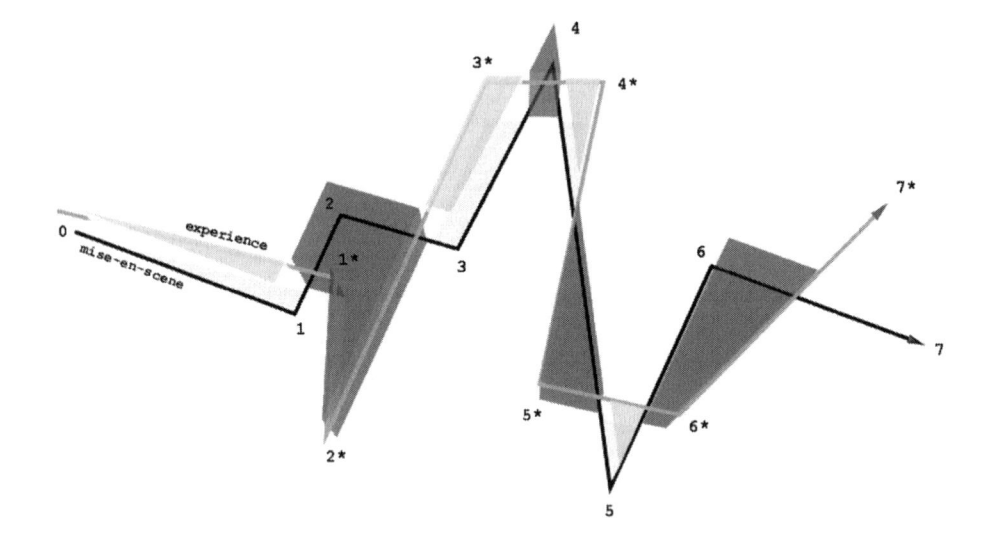

Figure 1. The scenes of a compelling exhibition are intense occurrences within an encompassing semantic field that allows for multiple points of interest and interpretations. A walk through the actual space of such a narrative landscape comes down to a series of intervals of varying orientation and intensity that one could graphically record as 'vectors of attention'. According to the twofold perspective of the 'dramaturgical hinge' which connects the scenographer and audience, every narrative space can be laid out or described in two sets of vectors: the one of the staging and the other one of the corresponding experience.

the envelope

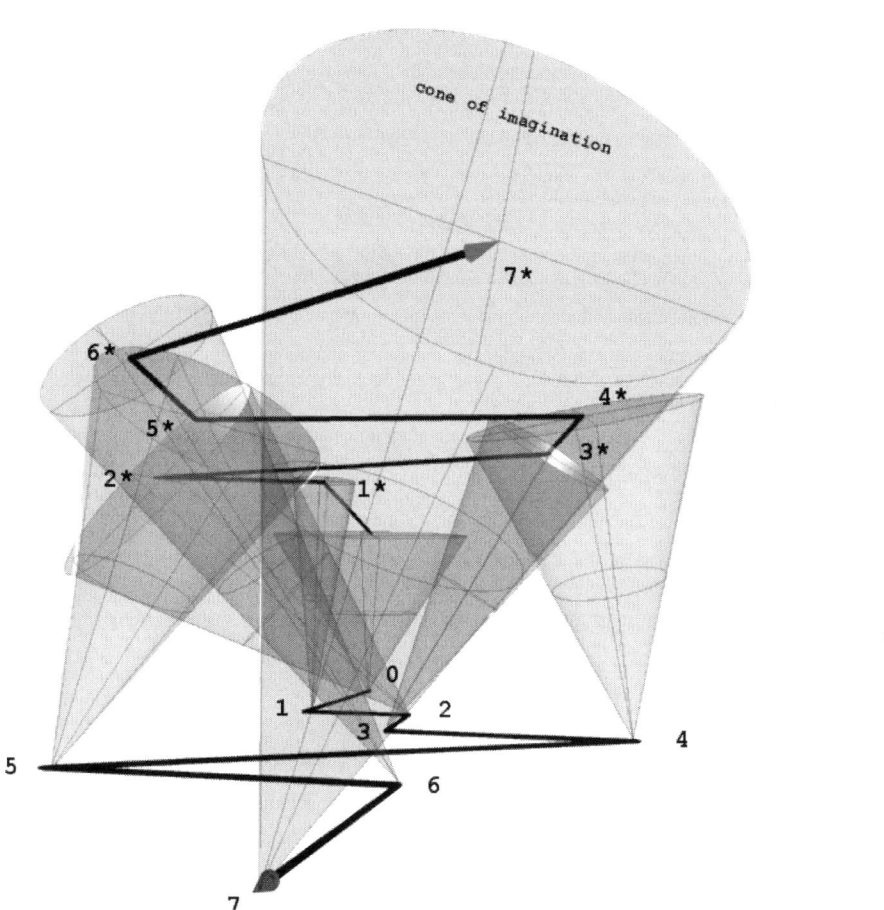

Figure 2. The 'eventstructure' of a narrative environment is based on the composed or experienced set of vectors of attention, but includes the active participation of the audience in the diagram, supposing that the individual visitor is not an 'empty bucket', but is always adding context to the staging as found. The staging activates the visitor, who in turn completes the narration. This element in the dramaturgy of the narrative environment is represented by a 'cone of imagination' in the diagram. Proportional to the imagination of the audience, the two sets of vectors are driven apart, giving way to interpretational and experiential shifts, which could be the mark of any effective narrative space.

From the point of view of the design there is still another guiding principle. Much of Robert Wilson's theatre work has an a priori 'superstructure' that articulates the total time of the play in a sequence of scenes. The aforementioned opera *Einstein on the Beach* is a good example.[29] The space in *Einstein on the Beach* was staged at three separate visual levels: A as 'still life', B as a 'portrait' and C as a 'landscape' – categories which in cinematographic terms would equal close, medium and wide shots respectively. In the course of the production, which lasted four to five hours, these three focuses alternated according to the pattern ABCABCABC. This tripartite cycle of ABC was marked or crossed at five instances by so-called 'knee plays', which Wilson invented in order to make room for some dramatic intermezzos. Suppose we label the knee plays k1–k5, the dramatic structure of *Einstein on the Beach* would be k1-AB-k2-CA-k3-BC-k4-ABC, or, in full: (kneeplay 1) Still Life, Portrait, (knee play 2) Landscape, Still Life, (knee play 3) Portrait, Landscape, (knee play 4) Still Life, Portrait, Landscape (knee play 5). Within this sequence category A (still life) would invariably establish a setting, or a staging, that is grounded in the situation in time and place; category B (portrait) would accommodate some theatrical action; and category C (landscape) would provide a choreographic accent, mainly being staged as a dance. By assigning time indications to these various structural elements, it became possible for everyone involved in the production of the opera to carry out his assignment within a concrete framework, and one had a fairly accurate estimate of the overall duration of the play. As a result, the structure of the score was fixed from the beginning for director, composer and choreographer.[30] Philip Glass explains:

> It began as a structure in time that was empty of any story or any image. It never occurred to us to begin with a story. The common ground would be how to use time. Music uses time and theatre uses time. We discovered that it was in this area that we would begin to form ideas together. We took five or six hours and we divided it into acts and scenes and time periods. Then we began to fill it in. Bob asked a lot of the performers to write their own texts, and he also wanted me to write a text. I had written the music, but I couldn't think of a text, so I began rehearsing the music with the singers and got them to sing numbers and solfège syllables: do, re, mi, fa, one, two three, four, and so on. And that became the text.[31]

the envelope

Robert Wilson remembers:

> I wanted to make a work with a theme and variations. So I picked three themes. Theme A was a train. Einstein was born in the age of the steam engine. The train was slowly crossing the stage in profile and was interrupted by a vertical line of light. The light was like an actor, like a character in the play. I scripted it in, from the beginning. Theme B would be a trial. I created a courtroom and in the centre of the courtroom would be a large bed. I thought what was really on trial was Einstein, the dreamer, the outsider. Then the bed became a prison and finally it turned into a horizontal bar of light. Theme C was a spaceship. Einstein had rung in the space age with his inventions. The splitting of the atom. Einstein, the pacifist, the splitting of the mind. The atomic explosion with grit of lights exploding. Schizophrenia. The twentieth century. I used all the possible combinations you could have with A, B and C.[32]

From a theatrical perspective the essence of *Einstein on the Beach* can be summarised by the absence of a plot and the introduction, through such mechanisms as slow motion and repetition, of a radically alternative timescale in which changes occurred at a different, more careful pace. As a result, these changes took on quite monumental proportions in the perception of the spectator. Wilson's motto came straight from the theory of general relativity itself: 'In a universe where everything goes faster, TIME itself slows down.' In the initial stages of the production design, the superstructure of the opera served as a matrix in which the scale and the resolution of the scenography – in terms of the pictorial units 'still life', 'portrait', and 'landscape' – were contrasted – in terms of clock time – with the duration and the rhythmic sequencing of the scenes. This produced a framework that enabled the composer and the director to create a production full of visual contrasts in which the metaphorical take on Einstein could be structured and shaped in an associative way. For the spectator, which in our present context is of special interest, the seemingly simplistic framework of the superstructure produced an articulation of perception by linking, on the rudimentary level of the scene, the capacity of the gaze to the intensity of attention.

Such a functional structure, as was imposed in the 'Robert Wilson's Vision' exhibition at the Boston Museum of Fine Arts by the mere architectural structure of its Gund Gallery, seemed to be lacking in 'Mr Bojangles' Memory', which was laid out in the open space of the Centre Pompidou; and we may wonder if guiding experience in exhibitions by means of what Wilson calls a 'megastructure' is feasible at all. For the structures underlying his theatrical works may be simple matrices of a Euclidean nature mathematically speaking, but the grid of the matrix will always be filled with differentiated dramatic matter of a highly Einsteinian nature. And if 'Mr Bojangles' Memory' was indeed governed by a superstructure of a Euclidean nature, then what exactly was the Einsteinian, moving element within that structure? Perhaps it was the visitor himself who on this occasion was invited to enter the empty stage of Wilson's dramatic landscape as an 'actor'? But then again, the occasional actors in this play didn't know their parts. There was a given choreography mapped out by the raised paths running through the exhibition, but the plot was lacking. That plotlessness which gave Wilson's theatrical work its extraordinary character, now deprived the exhibition stage of its deeply dramatic intensity. To be sure, 'Mr Bojangles' Memory' was intense as an environment, but merely as a large-scale image. In fact, the first glance in the exhibition space gave away too much already. On a smaller scale the staging of the exhibition fell short in terms of proximity, probably because too much communicative potential was attached to the aesthetics of Wilson's chairs.

Still, an a-priori designed superstructure, like the one we have seen time and time again in Wilson's theatrical work, could be an adequate framework for the scenography of an exhibition. Such a superstructure would very much resemble the systems of classical mnemonics in which the cycle of memory and imagination was activated by following an imaginary route through an archetypical building (the superstructure). In every room (structural element) one would, following the semantic principle of narrative (the libretto), leave (encode) or find (decode) an object with some memory value, so that the correct route through the architecture of memory would generate a coherent delivery. In the *ars memoriae*, remembering the semantic route would enable one to fish out the tale like a fisherman would bring a fish to land with the aid of hook and line.[33] Of course, in the *manifestatio* of the open arts the principle would work the other way round.[34] The stage and the exhibition offer the initial condition for an artificial external memory where the spectator is fishing for relevant associations and visions. Initially, time is still inactive, frozen, and embedded in memory particles that will only release their charge upon being associated in the flow of experience. The matrix of *Einstein on the Beach* arranges the passing of time according to the simple order of the clock. But despite its linear simplicity, this superstructure still has a complex dramaturgical dimension that manifests during the performance in terms of perception and experience.

This is crucial for the scenography of exhibitions if only because the term 'narrative' cannot be interpreted as referring to the linear thread that runs through a story, but instead it should be taken in a broader sense, for the guidance of free association in a given direction requires another type of control. This bias of free association we could term the 'inclination' of narrative space. This inclination embedded in the design requires our full attention, because in an open associative environment without proper scenographic control the course of things will lose coherence through deviation, despite the narrative framework. This conflict between the staged 'inclination' of a given narrative space on the one hand, and the randomly provoked 'deviation' of the visitor's orientation by uncontrollable factors on the other, poses the central problem of every scenographic design assignment, as it starts from the premise of the inseparable unity of form and content. All other issues are of secondary importance.

'Inclination' refers to a physical and psychological bias and it calls forth the image of a slope.[35] 'Deviation' on the other hand suggests a shift or a declination from a normal position or direction, like a compass that wanders off under the influence of a ship's magnetism.[36] It is paramount for any scenographer, theatre maker or exhibition maker to recognise this overall direction, this orientation in the spectrum of the narrative environment, as early as possible and to extract maximum clarity from it during the designing process. Even in the smallest of details. This isn't an easy task, for every narrative environment is an inclined plane that is trodden on twice: first by the operator during the *inventio* and second by the spectator during the *manifestatio*.[37] To put things in perspective: the higher the standpoint, the wider the view. But one can only fully enjoy the view when the panorama of scenography isn't shrouded in mist.

As I write this, Robert Wilson is producing Samuel Beckett's *Krapp's Last Tape* (1958) in the Teatro Mercadante in Naples.[38] Wilson is not only directing and staging the play, he is also playing Krapp, the main protagonist. It is the first time since *Hamlet: A Monologue* that he makes his appearance on the stage as an actor.[39]

In *Krapp's Last Tape* the 69-year-old Krapp looks back on his life by listening to existential comments and confessions he has spoken and recorded on tape on his birthdays in the past and has kept in private archives since.[40] In the play, Krapp is looking for one particular old recording: 'Box

3, Spool 5', which apparently contains a key moment in his life, some thirty years before, when he was at the height of his life, we are to infer.

Wilson will turn 69 in 2010. In 1980 he produced *Dialog / Curious George* together with Christopher Knowles and *Overture to the Fourth Act of Deafman Glance*.[41] Christopher Knowles suffered from a brain damage and as a result had an unusual gift for evocative language. Raymond Andrews was a deaf-mute but had a gift for pictorial expression. He was one of the protagonists in Wilson's silent opera *Deafman Glance*.[42] Wilson took both Andrews and Knowles under his wing at an early age and both had a decisive influence on his work.[43] Maybe the memories of Andrews and Knowles inspired Wilson – who is now of Krapp's age – to act in the Beckett play himself. This is mere speculation. Wilson will no doubt strictly adhere to the text. He is a professional performer and will surely pick up the part on the basis of Beckett's minute stage directions:

> *(briskly) Ah! (He bends over ledger, turns the pages, finds the entry he wants, reads.)* Box ... thrree ... Spool ... five. *(He raises his head and stares front, with relish.)* Spool! *(pause.)* Spooool! *(happy smile. Pause. He bends over table, starts peering and poking at the boxes.)* Box ... thrree ... three ... four ... two ... *(with surprise)* nine! Good God! ... seven ... ah! The little rascal! *(He takes up the box, peers at it.)* Box thrree. *(He lays it on table, opens it and peers at spools inside.)* Spool ... *(he peers at the ledger)* ... five ... *(he peers at spools)* ... five ... five ... ah! The little scoundrel! ... *(He takes out a spool, peers at it.)* Spool five.[44]

Wilson will attentively scrutinise reel 5, check the register to see if it is the right one and put it on the tape recorder with a happy smile on his face. He will rub his hands together and in the register at the bottom of the page discover a note that no longer makes any sense to him. He will read it aloud and carefully examine it to see if he can find the meaning and the significance of the 30-year-old note. He will stare in confusion and taste the words: 'Equinox, memorable equinox ... Memorable equinox? ...' Moments later he will switch on the recorder and hear his own voice, thirty years earlier: 'Thirty-nine today, sound as a ...'[45] Upon which he will accidentally knock a box off the table, swear, switch off the machine and in desperate anger sweep the entire pile of tapes and the register to the floor. For what can Krapp add to the collected reflections in the archives of his time on the day of the last recording?

the envelope

2.2 reframing scenography

In *Signs of Performance*, Colin Counsell criticises Robert Wilson's work for lacking sufficiently articulated content, as a result of which his productions are of a noncommittal nature and leave excessive room for interpretation on the part of the spectator:

> The potential for meaning his theatre offers is, as we noted, always bounded by culture; we play with the associations suggested by his images, but associations drawn from the available cultural pool. The *freedom* his work offers is therefore the freedom of the consumer, to choose whatever collection of meanings one wishes on the assumption that all are of equivalent value. Representation thus takes on the commercial logic of the marketplace, with images valued only *as* images, as spectacle.[46]

Like Guy Debord, Counsell interprets spectacle as the literal incarnation of capital, for 'prior to any *message* a work may seek to convey, spectacle first tells us what it costs.'[47] Nobody will deny the costliness of Wilson's productions, but on average they aren't more expensive than any other conventional musical theatre based on librettos and linear narrative development. In Counsell's view the audience gets too little coherent, substantive value for their money with Wilson's visual theatre. Now, it goes without saying that Wilson's work is spectacular and not primarily discursive, but to dismiss it as hollow spectacle on the basis of its costs, merely because its semiotics are ambiguously encoded, is stretching it. Counsell feels that Wilson's work is semiotically gratuitous nevertheless because it neutralises each and every intrinsic meaning of the various scenographic elements by the way they are arranged in the final production. Counsell argues: 'His theatre consists of pure expression on its own expense. It becomes the theatrical equivalent of gratuitous consumption, its expenditure of real material resources for the generation of images made more emphatic because those images are hollow.'[48]

    In terms of what is meaningful, I would certainly agree that Beckett's empty, minimalist staging has a more poignant, exact and profound quality to it, but that doesn't detract from the enormous power and cultural significance of Wilson's theatre. It is rather surprising that Counsell doesn't recognise the fact and ignores the far-reaching influence Wilson has had on stage

space.time.narrative

design in general, despite the fact that *Signs of Performance* was written some 15 years ago. This influence couldn't have occurred for formal reasons alone, or because Wilson's theatre is a theatre of meaninglessness per se.

Prior to this Counsell reflects extensively on the principle alienation and disorientation underlying most of Wilson's work:

> This lack of any apparent sense is a consistent feature of Wilson's work, for it is central to his theatrical project. Human beings, he maintains, always register the world in two ways, on two separate *screens*. The *exterior screen* is the place of conscious, public meanings, where we ascribe to objects and events the same significance as our fellows. But at the same time we each register those same images on our *interior screen*, where they are perceived subjectively, our imagination granting them meanings personal to ourselves. Both screens operate throughout our waking lives, so that we continually perceive reality in both a cultural and an individual, *acultural* way.[49]

Through the performance Wilson projects a wondrous universe of seemingly 'empty' images onto our exterior screen and with the aid of the tools of surprise and alienation he blocks and frustrates any immediate interpretation, because he sets great store by the associative potential manifesting on the interior screen of each individual. Thus Wilson's work is founded on the associative competence of the spectator who, very much in line with Eco's hypothesis, is the one who in fact completes the work.[50] Here, in the absence of any plot, we see at work one of the most basic, systematic modi operandi: physical fact = psychic effect. The consequence is obvious: dramaturgically speaking the work is adrift. Earlier, during the economically exalted ego-oriented era of the 1990s, Wilson's work had already been publicly under fire. In the catalogue of the 'Robert Wilson's Vision' exhibition, for example, Trevor Fairbrother refers to an interview with an American theatre director who was just as famous as Wilson, but more *engagé* and 15 years his minor – Peter Sellars – who points out that the excessive importance of the image in society is a threat to the theatre as a forum of discourse.[51] As Sellars wrote in 1989: 'In the age of Hollywood movies, television, and Robert Wilson, the image is a source of singular fascination. And I suspect that it is Hollywood movies, television and Robert Wilson that have rendered theatre temporarily obsolete and forced many of us who are interested in theatre to take refuge in the realm of opera and redeem our tattered selves.'[52]

In the 1980s and 1990s, Wilson's work was indeed dismissed by many as a type of drama of the past. Recently, however, as contemplation and reflection are gradually finding their way back into a multifaceted society that knows the limits of liberal capitalism by experience and is turning away from empty spectacle, Wilson's theatre and the inward gaze it provokes have become increasingly relevant and alive again. Whenever hyperrealism is in charge of daily life and the most ecstatic appearance of everyday life (as on television and the Internet) becomes the ultimate paradigm, the arts will spontaneously return to their mythological origins. Similarly, but reversed, we can see how the mythological nature of daily life in the Middle Ages is being accompanied by a distinct realism in the arts of the time.[53] In our day and age, in which conceptual thought should gradually regain their equality in keeping with the material fix of society, exuberance of form and imagination may be completely legitimate. At least, as long as it connects, deepens, promotes reflection and remains discursive. Then the stage and the exhibition may function as a counter-environment and, according to McLuhan, 'as a means of perception and adjustment' that is not only a container, but also a process with the capacity to 'change the content totally'.[54] And here, 'counter-environment' should be taken as the mental space that for the time being turns the world upside down. In *Understanding Media*, McLuhan describes a phase of transition in which the mechanical age dissolves into an electric age, and he interprets the fundamental changes that accompany the transformation as a result of the introduction of a radically different timescale on which the inertia and the clear-cut order of sequentiality are replaced by an omnipresence that occurs at the speed of light:

> After three thousand years of explosion, by means of fragmentary and mechanical technologies, the western world is imploding. During the mechanical ages we had extended our bodies in space. Today, after more than a century of electric technology, we have extended our central nervous system itself in a global embrace, abolishing both space and time as far as our planet is concerned. Rapidly, we approach the final phase of extensions of man – the technological simulation of consciousness, when the creative process of knowing will be collectively and corporately extended to the whole of human society, much as we have already extended our senses and our nerves by the various media.[55]

space.time.narrative

According to McLuhan, man acquired the ability to act in detachment by means of the technology of writing. The keyword here is 'distance', both in time and in space. Distance in thoughts and actions. In fact, action and reaction, which follows close behind, form a sequence that isn't essentially different from the fragmented production process of the assembly line. But, McLuhan states, now that electronic media have surrounded the planet and media have reduced the space–time interval between action and reaction to virtually zero by speeding up communication, distance is no longer a concept of space–time: 'We actually live mythically and integrally, as it were, but we continue to think in the old, fragmented space and time patterns of the pre-electric age.'[56]

McLuhan characterises western man and his predicament as 'the man who appears not to be involved in the action', and to illustrate the point he refers to the 'clowns' in Beckett's theatre.[57] The ultimate consequence of the dilemma is western civilisation as a collection of individuals for whom 'the medium is the message' holds true in every respect and for whom our mediatised culture has an infinitely differentiated reservoir of would-be actions in store to satisfy our existential manifestation deficiency to the subtlest of needs. Such a society has become atomised down to the level of ultimate experiential individuality, and the oscillating media are happy to give live coverage of it all. The author P.F. Thomése recently wrote an article in which he gave a poignant survey of the autistic traits of such a society:

> The real crisis is a crisis of communication. There are too many speakers, too many callers, texters, chatters, tweeters – each of them a little dictator who desperately needs to inform you of – what exactly? Their existence, for one. 'Hi, it's me.' To start with. Too many people volunteer what they are thinking, what they are doing, what they are wanting, intending, planning, what they are capable of, their good will, their ill will, showing it, exposing it, proposing it and throwing it in your face. But where are the readers, the viewers, the listeners who have to hear it, behold it and take it all in?[58]

Thomése's question is a fundamental one and it evokes a self-satisfied and consequently desperate society wallowing in its own mirror image. Narcissus. Oscillation. Ecstasy. And here Wilson's theatre comes in as a timely relevance, because it deprives spectators of their mirror and leaves them at the mercy of their own imagination. Wilson seems to be saying: go figure it out yourself. And rightly so. That is exactly the task at hand: figuring it out.

the envelope

Figuring what out? That which cannot readily be understood in relation to what is Other. Wilson's work is in its essence a call for openness and receptivity to what is other, what is unknown, unpleasant, troublesome, unfathomable – all wrapped up in an aesthetic universe of stunning beauty. With Wilson, the aesthetics are not the point, like they were at the turn of the twentieth century. Wilson's aesthetics are a means to an end, a mirror showing the unexpected. It is an optical instrument that focuses our attention on forgotten, unseen dimensions of our reality, like a prism that fractures the narcissistic attention for the egocentric in our televisionary bogus adventure by replacing the coordinates of the usual with strange signs that need to be decoded first. Deciphering and decoding thus become part of the creative task of the audience. Enigma. Scenography merely provides the algorithms as the keys to myriad interpretations of the staging. Like it is the algorithm of recited poetry that, in Paul Valéry's words, provokes 'a prolonged hesitation between sound and meaning'.[59]

If Wilson's theatre is fact the hermetic theatre of images we think it is, then it leaves the interpretation of its own critical charge to the spectator who is initially alone with his thoughts. Again we are made to think of the German romantic painter Caspar David Friedrich, whose landscapes can be understood to mirror the mind.[60] Especially in his exhibitions, Robert Wilson is a similar architect of mental landscapes in which the spectator wanders along a meandering path that leads him past serene sculptural formations when – suddenly – a visual or auditory detail addresses him and provokes a chain of personal associations, upon which the introvert individual is incorporated into the wondrous universe of the staging. Friedrich once put it like this: 'The artist should paint not only what he sees before him, but also what he sees within him. If, however, he sees nothing within him, then he should refrain from painting that which he sees before him.'[61] Wilson stages 'what he sees within him' by recollecting 'that which he saw before him'. It is all about the dream and the recollection.

Paradoxically enough, scenography depends entirely on the authenticity of this inner image and the credibility of the *inventio* that is based on it. It never depends on the aesthetics of the *manifestatio*. But what is credible? Which inner image, which type of content or message does the narrative space of the stage or the exhibition so aptly accommodate? What is worth hearing? Who is left to be listened to wholeheartedly? Or does it never get beyond seeing any more? Because seeing is believing? Because believing means having faith and faith is blind? And because blind faith is a form of ecstasy?

space.time.narrative

In early 2009 the aforementioned Museum of Fine Arts in Boston organised a conference about 'Cultural Leadership in Difficult Times' where Peter Sellars spoke about the importance of the theatre.[62] Sellars urged the necessity of a continuous, broad-based cultural discourse and argued that every mature democracy needs a place like the theatre, where contemporary issues can be discussed at a sophisticated level with the aid of the great 'poets'. Given the lack of such discourse in the hollow rhetoric of politics and parliament, Sellars recognises the theatre as the most obvious forum for dialogue, which doesn't necessarily have to be a verbal exchange, but rather a dialectical one, regardless of its actual articulation. Sellars too seems to be suggesting no less than the restoration of a mythological space, reaching far beyond the compartmentalised ecstasy of the individual in which the host of round-the-clock reality shows on television abound. The latter is scattered ecstasy, manifesting at the surface of the spectacle. What is needed is an ecstasy that unites. As such it cannot do with *mythos* alone.[63] Real profundity requires the *logos* of orientation and the *kairos* of the situation as well.[64]

The environment of dialogue accommodates the idea. It becomes a place with a personality. Shelter. When time starts to flow within the structures of the plot, an event comes into being. Action. The location and the event together produce a memorable, intelligible experience that may be mapped. Orientation. Thus scenography is more than a mere discipline of design as it focuses beyond the boundaries of staging a play. The theatre and the museum may have different conventions, but their dialectic function is a synchronous, parallel one. From a social point of view both drama and the exhibition can be interpreted as states of aggregation of one and the same cultural dynamic. The curator Hans Ulrich Obrist once described the museum as 'a site of production of knowledge, of recollection', 'a place of protest against forgetting', and 'a contact zone between past, present and future'.[65] With some minor shifts of accent these three qualifications bear upon narrative space as well. For what is a 'narrative environment' if not a contact zone where, through the discursive processing of burning issues, new insights and initiatives are generated. What is interesting is that Obrist made his remarks in an interview that focused on the psychogeography of the Situationists. Furthermore, when questioned about the very possibility of exhibiting the abstract subject matter of the Situationist International, he replied:

the envelope

> If concepts such as drift, diversion, psychogeography and dissipated strolling are to be approached in the sense of the SI, it is quite important that an oscillation be set in motion, and that we go from the museum into the city: that, for instance, walks take place. (...) It is very important that the museum works as a kind of relay, and that from there things go further.[66]

What unites the stage, the exhibition and the city under the heading of 'narrative environments' is this very concept of psychogeography. For every staging can be taken to be the creation of a particular situation that is conducive to promoting the cycle of memory and imagination – intentionally or unintentionally so. Isn't the scenographer in fact a situationist equipped with a medium and a method? In his *Introduction to a Critique of Urban Geography*, Guy Debord describes the 'psychogeographical game of the week', as it was originally published in the first edition of *Potlatch* magazine:

> In accordance with what you are seeking, choose a country, a more or less populated city, a more or less busy street. Build a house. Furnish it. Use decorations and surroundings to the best advantage. Choose the season and the time of the day. Bring together the most suitable people, with appropriate records and drinks. The lighting and conversation should obviously be suited to the occasion, as should be the weather or your memories. If there has been no error in your calculations, the result should satisfy you.[67]

The instructions to the game, which obviously criticises the mainstream technocratic approach to urban environments, can be taken as a protocol for designing narrative space, because these ten seemingly simple steps produce the same high degree of subjectivity and density that appealing drama and intriguing exhibitions are capable of producing in terms of expressive power. So we can safely conclude that the situationist urban environment equals the narrative environment of scenography in every respect, albeit with a different objective. Debord's game proposes a hierarchic orientation directed inward. The cross section of this construction of a 'situation' shows a trajectory moving from the periphery to the centre and is therefore a routine moving from a larger scale of the design to a smaller one. But can we reverse the hierarchy? For scenography of narrative space this is indispensable, because drama and exhibitions usually move the other way round, from centre to periphery. The spark of *inventio* usually sets the scenographic concept aflame at the smallest scale of the process. A given 'big idea' doesn't necessarily stem from the largest scale of the scenography. And similarly, the smallest scale of the design doesn't always represent the ultimate finesse of the narrative environment. The main environmental difference between openness and closedness is a matter of design, and in terms of shelter it becomes a matter of gradation. The essence is found in the fuzzy logic of the situation, this inseparable unity of hard and soft parameters.[68]

Now, if the geography of urban space is the domain of the engineer, then the psychogeography of narrative space is the domain of the *bricoleur*. As I have already argued, a scenographer combines the ingenuity of the one with the adventurous nature of the other.[69] The fusion of the two transforms every act of designing into a *dérive*.[70] As Debord observes:

> The sudden change of ambiance in a street within the space of a few meters; the evident division of a city into zones of distinct psychic atmospheres; the path of least resistance which is automatically followed in aimless strolls (and which has no relation to the physical contour of the ground); the appealing or repelling character of certain places – all this seems to be neglected[71]

– in the strictly logical perspective of the engineer, that is. It is the *bricoleur*, the master of nothing, who, within the given superstructure of the engineer, constructs the mythological environment of the moment by means of the irrational cross section of the *dérive*.[72] The acuteness of the intervention makes the splendour of the invention complete.

If it holds true that the situationist routine applies to the design of the stage or the exhibition, then it is language that bridges the gap between the psychogeography of urban environments and the scenography of narrative ones. Through a congenial cascade of publications, the critical experience of the urban environment was transformed into a central theme of the cultural discourse on the technological fix of western civilisation.[73]

When Guy Debord set about formulating the statements of *La Société du spectacle* in Paris, Tom Wolfe was working on his first book in New York: *The Kandy-Kolored Tangerine-Flake Streamline Baby*.[74] The first essay, 'Las Vegas (What?) Las Vegas (Can't hear you! Too noisy) Las Vegas !!!!', originally written for *Esquire* magazine, was inspired by the logic of local commerce and the way in which it manifested in the semiotics of the Strip.[75]

the envelope

Wolfe writes:

> I call Las Vegas the Versailles of America, and for specific reasons. Las Vegas happened to be created after the war, with war money, by gangsters. Gangsters happened to be the first uneducated ... but more to the point, unaristocratic, *outside* of the aristocratic tradition ... the first uneducated, prole-petty-burgher Americans to have enough money to build a monument to their style of life.[76]

Wolfe's pop prose analysis inspired Robert Venturi and Denise Scott Brown of the Yale School of Art and Architecture in 1968 to start a research project entitled 'Learning from Las Vegas', which they published under the same title and later revised in an edition with the additional title: *The Forgotten Symbolism of Architectural Form.*[77] When *Learning from Las Vegas* appeared as a book in 1972, Rem Koolhaas had just started writing his 'Retroactive manifesto for Manhattan', which would eventually appear as a book entitled *Delirious New York* in 1978.[78] It became a cult book overnight and it managed to influence just about every discipline of design by introducing fiction in architecture. In so doing, it not only changed the living perception of buildings and cities, but it also transformed the view on the architectural and related professions. Koolhaas may well have been the main catalyst for the work of Nigel Coates who in the 1980s published *NATO* magazine at the Architectural Association School in London.[79] *NATO*, short for '*Narrative Architecture Today*', created a transdisciplinary framework of design for the fictional aspects of architecture and urban development. The situationist state of mind that drove it aspired to use means of fiction in reshaping the actual urban environment. *NATO* avoided dogmas based on the ratio of invention alone. Instead it went for the proximity of intervention, for the frictions and fusions of montage, the non-conformist expression of pop culture and the intensity of authentic narrative.

The vision later appeared in Coates' libretto for *Ecstacity*, the virtual city 'that foregrounds the sensual side of all cities', in which we witness something close to an elaboration of Marshall McLuhan's 'global village' in terms of urban development.[80] But Coates isn't a ghostwriter. According to Brian Hatton, *Ecstacity* is, 'of course, a vision, and an architectural vision, but one in which plans and even buildings emerge only inter alia, among the tangles of desires and discourses that comprise the human drama inceptive to what becomes a city.'[81] Coates, the post-situationist with a route and a routine, comes quite close to the prototype of our scenographer. The principle of montage that is the blueprint of Coates' *Ecstacity* is what underlies Debord's 'game of the week', but in reverse: inside out, bottom up, from local to global. Coates' *Ecstacity*

> is about ideas, relations and blended conditions. Its premise is that, first and foremost, the city should be a place of experiences – it puts experience before the formal stylistic or functional qualities of buildings. In it, architecture – or its own broad version of it – is a vehicle for a looser and more open framework that stimulates space in each of us.[82]

Inner space: a cloud of associations appearing as the intriguing story unfolds. The city as the fluctuating totality of the complete associative potential. Not an imaginary place but a place of the imagination. Nigel Coates may well be the obscenographer of that place.

2.3   media hot and cold

'In the electric age we wear all mankind as our skin,' posited the Canadian linguist Marshall McLuhan in 1964.[83] McLuhan, who because of his poetic predictions about the potential transformations of the human nervous system rapidly became the guru of 'new media', was pointing to the fact that every technological innovation, every expansion of our physical capacity, whether it is freight traffic or information, has the intrinsic potential to radically change society. According to McLuhan, this transformative potential isn't a matter of technology as such, but rather of the environmental effects of its introduction. For example, the railways of the nineteenth century have fundamentally changed the nature of our metropolises regardless of what was being transported. Or, to use a contemporary example, the use of mobile phones has drastically changed communicative behaviour regardless of what is conveyed. In McLuhan's view it is all about the relationship between fact and effect, or, to put it in his terms, about 'figure' and 'ground'.[84] About how the introduction of new technology affects consciousness. About understanding trains and mobile phones as human artefacts within the context of their social impact.

This prompted McLuhan to posit that 'the medium is the message', as a way to provoke the insight that exclusive focusing on content was just as nonsensical as focusing on form alone. Communicating with the speed of light would reduce the planet to a 'global village', changing both the transmitter and the receiver. At once. McLuhan envisaged a world in which, as the ultimate consequence, individual consciousness would be part of a global network in which 'man becomes, as it were, the sex organs of the machine world, as is the bee of the plant world'.[85] We shouldn't take this as a logical statement, but an *ana*logical one, as is typical of McLuhan's approach, which is proportional and comparative. His analyses and prognoses were of a speculative nature, 'probes' as he called them, with a huge metaphoric potential. As such they made him more of a poet than a scholar.

The poetic ring of his line of thought, combined with the boldness of his claims, earned him a storm of criticism early on and it was only later, during the 1990s when media art was at its peak and so-called 'McLuhanism' became fashionable again, that it began to subside. New gurus, like Howard Rheingold, Nicholas Negroponte, Michael Heim – the 'philosopher of cyberspace' – and Derrick de Kerckhove, who in fact became his successor in Toronto,[86] were now expanding on his ideas in publications and conference handouts such as *The Virtual Community*, *Being Digital*, *The Metaphysics of Virtual Reality*, *Connected Intelligence* and *Doors of Perception*, in which the cyberpunk novel *Neuromancer* by William Gibson and Marvin Minsky's *Society of the Mind* were a shared point of reference.[87] 'Avatar', 'AlphaWorld' and 'artificial intelligence' were the magic words and everything seemed to indicate that soon the mind would leave the vehicle of the organic body and settle in the nanotechnological tissue of a supercomputer connected to a network of digital highways.[88] In this state of affairs, man would be reduced to a mere brain and find himself in a condition of weightlessness, floating in a universe of arithmetic imagination. I myself have increasingly come to mistrust the euphoria surrounding the digital utopia and at the height of the hype in the mid-1990s designed a counter-installation for the ZKM Medienmuseum in Karlsruhe: *Floating Identities* (p.376).[89] This was a technological *Wunderkammer* of media icons from the organic world of flesh and blood, built on ten template-like steel shapes – sculptural superstructures, as it were – which for one last time advocated the opportunities and the qualities of the burden of incarnation.[90] What in my view made the entourage of McLuhan so much more appealing – as in the New Journalism of Tom Wolfe, the semiology and the criticism of Umberto Eco, to a lesser extent the 'media ecology' of Neil Postman despite its pessimistic overtones, and the historical analyses of Bill Kuhns – was that it was based on language and critical reflection.[91]

Tom Wolfe met Marshall McLuhan for the first time in New York in the spring of 1965. The encounter produced the essay 'What if he is right?', in which Wolfe criticised McLuhan with some acute and funny analyses, but at the same time shed a clear light on McLuhan's often mistaken position:

> McLuhan is fond of quoting Daniel Boorstin's dictum, 'The celebrity is a person who is known for his wellknownness.' That pretty much describes McLuhan himself. McLuhan is one of those intellectual celebrities, like Toynbee or Einstein, who is intensely well-known as a name, and as a *savant*, while his theory remains a grand blur. Part of the difficulty is that McLuhan is presented to the world as 'the communications theorist.' His first book, *The Mechanical Bride*, was a book about communication. Since then McLuhan has barely dealt with communication at all, at least if you define communication as 'interchange of thought or opinions.' He is almost wholly concerned with the effect of the means of communication (the medium) on the central nervous system.[92]

In the column 'Towards a semiological warfare' (1976), Umberto Eco states that the medium is NOT the message. Eco finds McLuhan's analysis too undifferentiated, too generic and he poses the question: with which aspect of communication we are dealing when saying 'the medium is the message'? Eco posits:

> The communication chain assumes a Source that, through a Transmitter, emits a Signal via a Channel. At the end of the Channel the Signal, through a Receiver, is transformed into a Message for the Addressee. Since the Signal, while travelling through the Channel, can be disturbed by Noise, one must make the Message *redundant*, so that the information is transmitted clearly. But the other fundamental requirement of this chain is a Code, shared by the Source and the Addressee. A Code is an established system of probabilities, and only on the basis of the Code can we decide whether the elements of the message are intentional (desired by the Source) or the result of Noise.[93]

There is a distinct echo of the classical Shannon–Weaver model of communication theory in Eco's phraseology which McLuhan distrusts for its mechanical imagery and its reliance on a sequential interpretation of the chain of communication.[94] McLuhan points out that as communication occurs at the speed of light in the age of electricity, messages acquire an instant quality and the idea of 'transport of information' becomes obsolete. Medium and message meet and sender and receiver transform simultaneously.[95] McLuhan explains:

> All the official theories of communication [...] are theories of how you move data from point A to point B to point C with minimal distortion. That's not what I study at all. Information theory I understand and I use, but information theory is a theory of transportation, and it has nothing to do with the effects which these forms have on you. [...] My theory or concern is with what these media do to the people who use them. What did writing do to the people who invented it and used it? What do the other media of our time do to people who use them? Mine is transformation theory, how people are changed by the instruments they employ.[96]

McLuhan starts from the necessity of a radically different perception and he uses poetic language and exotic metaphors to illustrate multiple, multi-stranded cultural processes at once. So his references and his arguments are comprehensive, all-inclusive and analogy-based, because 'all words, in every language, are metaphors'.[97] To McLuhan language was primal – like 'a sense, like touch' – and the origin of any communicative chain, because 'language does for the intelligence what the wheel does for the feet and the body. It enables them to move from thing to thing with greater ease and speed and less involvement'.[98] In a television interview from about the same period, Tom Snyder of NBC Television asks McLuhan why his critics find it so hard to understand him. The answer is typically McLuhan: 'Because I use the right hemisphere [of the brain] when they're trying to use the left hemisphere. Simple.'[99]

In *Amusing Ourselves to Death*, the American media ecologist Neil Postman argues that 'all culture is a conversation or, more precisely, a corporation of conversations, conducted in a variety of symbolic modes'.[100] Postman enhances the understanding of McLuhan's metaphor by testing the communicative capacity of the 'medium' by means of a 'message', in smoke signals:

> While I do not know exactly what content was once carried in the smoke signals of American Indians, I can safely guess that it did not

include philosophical argument. Puffs of smoke are insufficiently complex to express ideas on the nature of existence, and even if they were not, a Cherokee philosopher would run short of either wood or blankets long before he reached his second axiom. You cannot use smoke to do philosophy. Its form excludes the content.[101]

In the case of a discursive scenography that manifests in the highly variegated super medium of the exhibition, this insight is a crucial one. In a practical sense it differentiates McLuhan's maxim simply by testing Eco's 'channel'. Postman writes:

> Each medium, like language itself, makes possible a unique mode of discourse by providing a new orientation for thought, for expression, for sensibility. Which, of course, is what McLuhan meant in saying the medium is the message. His aphorism, however, is in need of amendment because, as it stands, it may lead one to confuse a message with a metaphor. A message denotes a specific, concrete statement about the world. But the forms of our media, including the symbols through which they permit conversation, do not make such statements. They are rather like metaphors, working by unobtrusive but powerful implication to enforce their special definitions of reality. Whether we are experiencing the world through the lens of speech or printed word or the television camera, our media-metaphors classify the world for us, sequence it, frame it, enlarge it, reduce it, colour it, argue a case for what the world is like.[102]

Still, Postman's premise 'the medium is the metaphor' has a limited validity, adding only a subtle distinction to McLuhan's adage. If the medium is indeed the message as well as the metaphor, then medium and metaphor should coincide. This implication strikes at the heart of McLuhan's axiom. If Postman is right, then 'the medium is the message' is in itself, in its entirety, a metaphor transporting the central issue of narrative space. But a metaphor for what? For the fusion of medium and message. Against the absurdity of analysing form and content as separate, independent unities. In favour of transdisciplinarity. Against dichotomising expertise.

Apart from studying English literature, McLuhan was also involved in the theory of communication, cognitive psychology and neuroscience. But not as a scientist: his penetrating insight into the working of things made him rather a brilliant dramaturg who happened to overlook scenography, but whose work in hindsight deserves careful study nonetheless because every narrative environment is rooted in language – and McLuhan uprooted the origins of our media-technological culture by means of language itself. McLuhan is a poet. His medium is language and it is language that produces the subtlety of his insights. 'Media hot and cold', the second chapter of his renowned book *Understanding Media: The Extensions of Man*, contains a surprisingly dramaturgical accent, because it defines the effects of a given medium from the point of view of the user:

> There is a basic principle that distinguishes a hot medium like radio from a cool one like the telephone, or a hot medium like the movie from a cool one like TV. A hot medium is one that extends one single sense in 'high definition'. High definition is the state of being well filled with data. A photograph is, visually, 'high definition'. A cartoon is 'low definition', simply because very little visual information is provided. Telephone is a cool medium, or one of low definition, because the ear is given a meagre amount of information. And speech is a cool medium of low definition, because so little is given and so much has to be filled in by the listener. On the other hand, hot media do not leave so much to be filled in or completed by the audience. Hot media are, therefore, low in participation, and cool media are high in participation or completion by the audience.[103]

McLuhan speaks of the temperature of media in the same way Peter Brook, who may well have been influenced by him, would later speak of theatrical temperature.[104]

McLuhan's argument is wrapped in metaphor, as metaphors are a highly functional medium and 'all media are active metaphors in their power to translate experience into new forms'.[105] The resolution of metaphor is generally low, leaving ample room for interpretation, and consequently the suggestiveness is rich and the medium cool. Figure and configuration are brought to cold fusion in the melting pot of language.[106] Every form of poetry is eventually the meticulous result of such a fusion at room temperature. Herein lies the 'scholarship' of the poetic discipline. The ultimate example of this is beyond any doubt the poetic fusion of semantics and suggestion in *Finnegans Wake* – Joyce's nocturnal language that for McLuhan became a daily point of reference.[107] In a brilliant article on Giordano Bruno and Marshall McLuhan, media theoretician Bill Kuhns describes what connects Bruno and McLuhan and what Joyce and the *Wake* meant to him:

space.time.narrative

Across the centuries, they traded passing nods of a sort: Marshall McLuhan (1911–1980), the highly literate scourge of literacy, and Giordano Bruno the Nolan (1548–1600), rambunctious philosopher of the infinite. Thanks to James Joyce and *Finnegans Wake*, McLuhan and Bruno met, so to speak, almost every day. The *Wake* was McLuhan's vademecum. In later years he kept one copy unbound, with each page pasted onto a sleeve of 3-ring paper. The stack stood in an accessible spot just outside the door of his office. McLuhan was forever plucking fresh pages like a gambler toying with oversized cards. He liked to snap the pages into new configurations, up, down, across, and read the phrases in a kaleidoscopic collage, much as Joyce himself had written them.[108]

In 1543 the German Polish astronomer Nicolaus Copernicus a posteriori informed the world that planet Earth revolved around the sun instead of the other way round.[109] But it was Giordano Bruno, the renegade Dominican friar from Nola near Naples, who pushed the turnabout to its philosophical limits, for which he paid with his life.[110] If there were such a thing as a God, He would, in Bruno's view, descend from His throne right away, enter a heaven on earth and touch and inspire each and every building stone, each monad, with His grace.[111] In this fraction of time God no longer remained a fixed point of reference at the end of the firmament, but an all-pervading inspirational fog.

On 4 October 1957 the unmanned Russian satellite *Sputnik 1* circled the earth in 69.2 minutes.[112] The technological tour de force astonished the entire world and marked the beginning of the race for interplanetary space. However, it was Marshall McLuhan who attached some philosophical consequences to the occurrence. McLuhan writes:

> When *Sputnik* went up, it put the planet inside a man-made environment for the first time. Spaceship *Earth* has no passengers, only crew. *Sputnik* transformed the planet into Spaceship *Earth* with a program problem. Ecology became the name of the game from the moment of *Sputnik*. Nature ended. The planet became an art form inside a manned capsule, and life will never be the same on this planet again.[113]

God descended, man ascended and the Earth became a village: a mere shift of perspective. Way into the twentieth century one wasn't inclined to take the vagabond scholar Giordano Bruno seriously because it was commonly held that his views 'had not reached the point of precision at which philosophy begins'.[114] Physicists were the first to recognise Bruno's monad as a possible point of departure for a 'theory of everything'. McLuhan somehow received the same treatment. The scholarly establishment branded him Not To Be Taken Seriously. But whereas Bruno was silenced by the Inquisition and thrown into the dungeons of the Castel Sant'Angelo in Rome, McLuhan avenged himself by publishing a revised edition of *Understanding Media*. In *Laws of Media: The New Science*, McLuhan, together with his son Eric, undertook a final attempt to systematically and academically articulate his views on the dynamics of the global village.[115] Through refinement he found the consistency he was looking for and produced a methodologically uniform and critical analysis in which the interrelations of figure and ground of any given human artefact, medium or phenomenon were systematically grouped into four dimensions – a quadruple axiom which generated a heuristic and hermeneutic instrument with the obvious name of 'tetrad'.[116]

The generic approach of the tetrad was originally inspired by the work of Giambattista Vico, who elaborated on Bruno's fundamental theory of the monad and in 1725 presented his *Scienza Nuova* as the 'science of discourse'.[117] Likewise the McLuhans focused on the condition of discourse, but they laboured to replace Vico's old Cartesian 'left-brain' science with a new, more balanced, integral science that would reconcile both cerebral hemispheres and achieve a more complete understanding.

In the introduction to *The Global Village*, which appeared a year after *Laws of Media*, Marshall McLuhan and Bruce R. Powers specify their intention:

> Our research, at the Centre for Culture and Technology in Toronto, constituted an inquiry into the formal aspects of (linguistic) communication which, in the process, uncovered a tetradic structure: all media forms (a) *intensify* something in a culture, while (b) *obsolescing* something else. They also (c) *retrieve* a phase or factor long ago pushed aside and (d) undergo a modification (or *reversal*) when extended beyond the limits of their potential. The result is a four-part metaphor.[118]

The tetrad should be understood as a set of four simultaneous questions, and the consistency of its analytical trajectory **ABCD** graphically resembles a Möbius strip with four folds.[119] See figure 3 on the next page

space.time.narrative

Figure 3. The mathematical figure of the Möbius strip reflects the interwoven analytic path of argumentation, constituting the conceptual basis of McLuhan's four-part metaphor, which he called a 'tetrad'.

If it holds true, as McLuhan maintains, that every human artefact is a metaphor and that every object of design, every concept, system or technological medium speaks a language transporting ideas that can be decoded within the context of a given cultural code, then it should follow that the same objects, concepts, systems and media can be 'read' as a narrative and, moreover, that they are governed by the same dynamic dramaturgical hinge that connects the narrator and the listener, the operator and the spectator. The operator operates within the context of the spectator and vice versa. The operator's staging is the 'figure' and its 'ground' is the spectator's imagination. The spectator's interpretation is the 'figure' against the 'ground' of the operator's narrative. This is the symmetry of narrative space whose function is *analogical*. Analogy is the raw material from which the dramaturgical hinge is forged on the fire of intensity and trust. The pressure and the temperature of the tale determine the emotional value of the drama. Narrative space follows the laws of thermodynamics, as always subject to the meteorology of the moment, within the tetradic structure of the metaphor.

The Dutch author Cees Nooteboom offers us a striking comparison on the first page of his novel *Rituals*: 'Memory is like a dog that lies down where it pleases.'[120] The implication of course being that memory doesn't obey. By introducing the alien element 'dog' Nooteboom presents a metaphorical statement about the functioning of memory, as any other scientifically formulated, empirically based criterion is lacking. So here the unpredictable behaviour of a dog serves to illustrate the capricious, associative potential of memory. The metaphor conveys what cannot be said because there is no terminology, and finds analogy to suit its purpose.[121] Likewise, the phrase 'time is a river' is a clarifying statement on the nature of time. 'Time', the subject, or 'topic term', is exemplified by the transport of the 'vehicle term', 'river'. The metaphor alludes to the fact that time relates to a river like water flowing in an irreversible direction. The analogy contains four elements and this is what sets metaphor apart from parable or metonymy, the latter two consisting of only three logical constituents. Metaphors are quadruple proportional correspondences. They are tetrads of the type AB = CD. Logics are the domain of critical analysis and linear causality: A+B = C. Left brain. *Analogics* on the other hand are the domain of pattern recognition, of critical imagination. Right brain. The difference lies in the relation between the subject and its context, between figure and configuration. The two become separated in logical argument, but in the amplitude of metaphor their dual unity is preserved. The argument of logic is a closed one, whereas the structure of metaphor is an open and suggestive one. As the philosopher and linguist I.A. Richards puts it in *The Philosophy of Rhetoric*: 'When we use a metaphor we have two thoughts active together and supported by a single word, or phrase, whose meaning is a resultant of their interaction.'[122] Or, with Nooteboom in *Rituals*: self-will. My memory is to my will what Nooteboom's dog is to the place where it decides to lie down. So 'the dog that lies down where it pleases' is the vehicle term exemplifying the topic term 'memory'. Dog, place, will and memory are the four elements whose interrelations are proportional and whose interactions reinforce both the concept of memory and the concept of a dog. The metaphor simultaneously activates two associative processes, the one verbal and the other perceptual, and leaves the relation between subject and context intact. The metaphor is the go-between between analogue and semantic types of thought, and it essentially uses concrete images to clarify abstract notions.[123]

McLuhan's entire discourse is based on a concept of the metaphor reaching back to Aristotle, who formulates it in the *Poetics*:

> A metaphor is the application of a noun which properly applies to something else. The transfer may be from genus to species, from species to genus, from species to species, or by analogy. [...] By analogy I mean cases where B stands in similar relation to A as D does to C; one can mention D instead of B, and *vice versa*.[124]

The binary, proportional comparison was an especially important basis for McLuhan's tetrad. McLuhan writes: 'As we have said before, technologies, like words, are metaphors. They similarly involve the transformation of the user insofar as they establish new relationships between him and his environments. A double figure–ground relationship is brought into play with "natural man is to man-with-artefacts as is the natural environment to the man-made environment".'[125] And the complementary, 'natural man is to the natural environment as is man-with-technology to the man-made environment'. McLuhan's tetrad is a true instrument of thought, integrating as it does the functions of right and left brain hemispheres, and through the fourfold analysis of whatever medium or human artefact it completes the hermeneutic circle.[126] See figure 4 on the following page

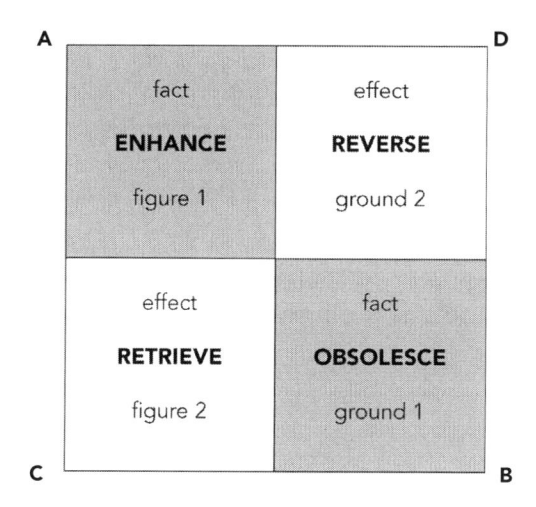

	A		D
	fact **ENHANCE** figure 1	effect **REVERSE** ground 2	
	effect **RETRIEVE** figure 2	fact **OBSOLESCE** ground 1	
	C		B

Figure 4. McLuhan's tetrad consists of a 4-step argumentation. **A**: What does the artefact or medium enhance or intensify? **B**: What does the artefact or medium obsolesce, erode or displace? **C**: What does the artefact or medium retrieve that was previously obsolesced? **D**: What does the artefact or medium reverse when pushed to its limits? **AB=CD** > physical fact = psychic effect.

From the point of view of staging a narrative environment, both on the larger scale of the score and on the smaller scale of individual scenes, the McLuhan tetrad proves a vital instrument because it provides the quadruple approach that intensifies the profundity of the design – a tool for both scenographer and dramaturg. The tetrad is a 2 x 2 matrix and we are supposed to read it twice diagonally, following the double loop of the Möbius strip: ABCD. AB represents the axis of facts. CD is the axis of effects. The intersection of AB and CD provides the critical balance between 'physical fact' and 'psychic effect': AB = CD, which we consider to be the maxim of dramaturgy. The intersection of AB and CD also represents a crossing of equations in which the 'figure' and 'ground' of facts relate proportionally to the 'figure' and 'ground' of effects. With the aid of both equations we can now test the consistency of the argument, keeping the point of view of the effects. We can do it horizontally, C:B = A:D, which means: retrieval is to obsolescence as enhancement is to reversal. But also vertically, C:A = B:D, which means: retrieval is to enhancement as obsolescence is to reversal.

To demonstrate the functionality of the tetrad I will expand on McLuhan by elaborating two examples (see figures 5 and 6) pertaining to the functionality of narrative space: theatre and exhibition.

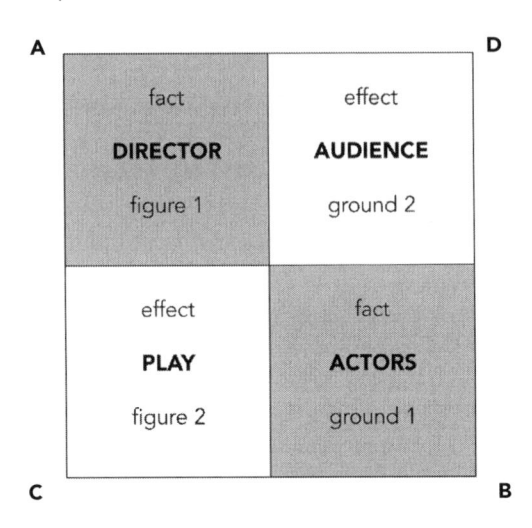

	A	D
	fact **DIRECTOR** figure 1	effect **AUDIENCE** ground 2
	effect **PLAY** figure 2	fact **ACTORS** ground 1
	C	B

Figure 5. Theatre tetrad: McLuhan's four-part metaphor applied to theatre practice. **A**: What does the theatre enhance or intensify? Cultural discourse. **B**: What does the theatre displace? The virtuality of the Internet and television. **C**: Which previously lost attainments does the theatre retrieve? The analogue space of myth. **D**: What will reverse when theatre is pushed to its limits? The logical space of causality. **AB=CD** > physical fact = psychic effect.

If the theatre tetrad applies, then it would follow that the analogue space of myth is to cultural discourse as the Internet and television are to the logical space of causality: C:A = B:D. Or, in other words: AB is always CD. So, when the cultural discourse is based on the support of a vigorous *inventio* on the part of the director and the convincing performance of the actors further renders the Internet and television obsolete at one stroke, then the stage will once more give birth to the analogue space of myth, which – for the time being – will push the logical space of causality to the background.

the envelope

```
A                               D
    ┌───────────────┬───────────────┐
    │     fact      │    effect     │
    │               │               │
    │  SCENOGRAPHY  │    VISITORS   │
    │               │               │
    │   figure 1    │   ground 2    │
    ├───────────────┼───────────────┤
    │    effect     │     fact      │
    │               │               │
    │    STAGING    │   COLLECTION  │
    │               │               │
    │   figure 2    │   ground 1    │
    └───────────────┴───────────────┘
C                               B
```

Figure 6. Exhibition tetrad: McLuhan's four-part metaphor applied to exhibition practice. **A**: What does the exhibition enhance or intensify? The poetics of cultural discourse and location. **B**: What does the exhibition displace? The attraction of the Internet and television. **C**: Which previously lost attainments does the exhibition retrieve? The analogue space of myth. **D**: What emerges when the exhibition is pushed to its limits? Noise, spectacle and mere entertainment. **AB=CD** > physical fact = psychic effect.

If the exhibition tetrad applies, then it would follow that the *analogical space of myth* is to the attraction of the internet and television as the poetics of the location is to empty spectacle and entertainment: C:B = A:D. It would also entail that the *analogical space of myth* is to the *genius loci* of cultural discourse as the attraction of media is to spectacle and entertainment. In other words: AB is always CD. When the poetry of the location is based on the support of a vigorous *inventio* on the part of the scenographer and the convincing interpretation of the curator further renders the attraction of the internet and television obsolete, then the staging will give birth to the *analogical space of myth*, which – for the time being – will push the noise and the empty spectacle to the background.

2.4 the architecture of everything

In 1949 the Argentinian-Italian artist Lucio Fontana reached the apex of his work in one single gesture, the crux of his *Concetto Spaziale*: he slit an immaculate canvas with a razor-sharp knife (p.373).[127] The act miraculously turned the medium, which according to mainstream pictorial conventions was the potential base of an image, a painting, into the message. *Avant la lettre*. Instantly, Fontana turned the mutated, mutilated base of the image into the image itself in a radical attempt to relate the art of painting to other, yet unexplored and intangible dimensions of reality. In one accurate cut, medium and message merged into one clear sign, bringing painter and painting closer together. *En taille directe*.[128] In one cut a symbol came into being that through its obscenographical immediacy incorporated the spectator in the space–time of Fontana's act, both retroactively and with prognostic clarity. Every differentiation of sign and significance, channel and information, about sender and receiver that Umberto Eco would be looking for in his criticism of Marshall McLuhan later, was now being erased from the discourse by Fontana's final cut.[129] This is the accurate cut – deep and vigorous, be it hot or cold, fast or slow, executed on a large or small scale of the work, be it within the abstract or concrete registers of our considerations – that scenography will ALWAYS and categorically have to effect. Similarly, in Luis Buñuel's film *Un chien andalou*, where the surrealist view breaks through only after the acting director himself has slit Simone Mareuil's iris with a razor.[130] Let us call it the golden section of scenography, which needs to be established time and again for every dramatic piece of work.[131] It is the quantum mechanical variant of Fibonacci's ideal proportions reflected in the uncertain universe of space, time and narrative.[132]

Robert Wilson once summarised the essence of narrative space as follows: 'Time goes to the centre of the earth and goes to the heavens. It is a vertical line. And it's crossed by space, which is a horizontal line. And this cross of SPACE and TIME is the architecture of everything.'[133] The metaphor is an appealing one, but it doesn't account for the dynamics of the discourse. What is the reality of this point of intersection? On the large scale of the design it is a prognostic one, a directive consciousness, the structure of a staging in gestation. It is abstract. However, on the small scale of the individual experience the cross of space and time is a manifest NOW: a landscape of the MOMENT. Very concrete. What is the range of that NOW in actual experience? It depends on the intensity of the situation.

the envelope

In a mechanistic NOW, time and space will coincide. But in the fluctuating reality of narrative space, Wilson's cross is never a fixed point, but always a line, a curve. However brief, be it on the stage or at an exhibition, the cross of space and time will always be a trajectory with a definite orientation, which in the abstract equals the definition of a scene. Once the participation becomes intense, the NOW is, for the time being, a timeless landscape. Without participation, the NOW will be no more than a point in time.

What I find interesting is the elasticity of this NOW. What exactly is the capacity of an audience in a narrative environment? What perceptual set of tools does a visitor bring to the occasion? What is the anticipated extent of the participation? Which cross-section of the design could conceivably make the criteria of the staging and the experience coincide?

Every environment is a narrative environment, but without the touch of scenography we are left with nothing more than semantic wasteland. Without the Las Vegas Strip the Nevada desert would still know no time.[134] Its staging – a trajectory through the sand flanked by screaming signs – opened up the space for time. For it is the elastic time of the individual visitor that completes the Strip within the framework of the spectacle.

That particular line through the sand was a final cut. But no staging is determined by one cut alone. Not even the staging of Las Vegas. There will always be this fabric of relative parameters. A complex of hypothetical intersections crossing the chaotic matter of the issue – let's call it the 'dramaturgy' – which structures both the design and the experience in a meaningful format. That is why Wilson's cross is never absolute on the small scale of the individual experience, but rather highly unstable, fluctuating and dependent on a multitude of subjective factors that will manifest at unpredictable moments. Fontana's knife being square to the pictorial space of the painting-to-be represents on one square metre what in Wilson's metaphor needs to happen in the refinement of every scene – on every conceivable temporal axis of narrative space. Earlier we coined it 'staging intensity' with the means of the scenographer, which, under the right circumstances and in a rush of immediacy, can condense into the message itself. Never without risk, to be sure: Fontana too was considered a madman with a knife.[135] But his slit exposed the essence of his *Concetto Spaziale* in one single obscenographical act.

Every narrative environment is a place with its own poetry, waiting to be discovered and made accessible. Every narrative is a multi-stranded reality, shared by narrator and listener. For that reason every staging consists of at least two equivalent, albeit unequal, *universa* in a provisional, dynamic

space.time.narrative

balance forming a vulnerable unity. The left and right brain hemispheres of scenography. Very much like Schott's and Guericke's hemispheres in the Magdeburg experiment.[136]

With every staging this relation between the centre and the peripheries needs to be established again in order to determine the consistency of the means. This applies to content. This applies to form. Form and content are inseparable and every attempt to induce the dichotomy in the multiplicity of expertise that underpins the development of narrative environments will fail because of that. Every meaningful play and every successful exhibition is the total result of an integral approach to form and content. In addition, every scenographic design is a prototype that is governed by certain laws but for which there is absolutely no manual. There is a lot of confusion about this. Even within the framework of a given template for *manifestatio* – if there is one at all – it remains a matter of one singular *inventio* that makes the work a unique event. Conversely, a hypothetical template for *inventio* doesn't preclude a wayward design, simply because of the sheer infinite array of possibilities of the *manifestatio*. Either way, there are too many variables and no recipes. There is only passion and quality, which are both individual. Ten scenographers will produce ten different solutions for a staging even if they start from the same subject matter, have the same budget and the same location for a play or an exhibition. Why? Because the human potential is elusive! What is the difference? Language; interpretation! We all know the discussions during the creative process. Too big? No, it's too small. More? No, less. Too loud! What do you mean, too loud? Too much red? Too much blue, actually. You want natural? Ham it up! Gradations! Through the design and the subjective criteria that govern it, the work will crystallise into gradations. And in gradations it will speak and address the subjective experiences of the audience. Fine-tuning these gradations is the core task of scenography.

If the architecture of 'everything' can be deducted from Wilson's cross of space and time, and furthermore if this crossing represents the NOW of the individual experience, then I can see no reason why stage design and exhibition design shouldn't allow a dramaturgical approach on the basis of a certain number of positionings towards the central issue. What does this mean? It means that the *inventio* seizes on the centre of the seminal staging, where form and content are still one, before they become separated by the specialisation of expertise. This is the moment when the work is beginning to take form and everyone involved still shares the same orientation. This orientation is necessarily grounded in actuality and its relevance is exposed by some fundamental cuts at the heart of the issue, made by Fontana's blade. As we are speaking of 'all', the incisions or intersections will as a consequence have to be all-inclusive and fit for guiding the contours of the staging. The intersections resemble the colours of the rainbow: they are lines in a spectrum. The lines do not reflect the things themselves but their interrelations. Not the thoughts but how they relate. Within the topology of the narrative environment, as we may call it, they are the parameters of the design.[137] This topology resembles the topology of music – or, to be more precise, of a symphony in a concert hall – that unites the musicians and the audience. It is a fragile whole depending entirely on passion and concentration. Stage plays and exhibitions function similarly, in fact. An orchestra *in actio* generates a polyphonic tissue in which the characteristic vibrations and timbres of the individual instruments merge into the integral 'acoustic waveform' of the orchestra.[138] Just as the waveform of an orchestra characterises the timbre and the dynamics of a given symphony, thus will the scenographic temperature and the narrative potential of a play or an exhibition express itself in a 'communicative waveform'.

It goes without saying that plays and exhibitions always present a theme or a collection or an idea within a context that is relevant both in place and time. Those are the classical elements, the granulate. Like in music, the nature of these building blocks hasn't changed all that much through time. It is the methods of building that make history. The vibration of a violin string has been the same for centuries, but the overall vibration of the orchestra, the 'envelope' of the performance, has transformed tremendously in the history of concert practice. In the course of time, orchestration has come to include dynamic parameters such as *piano* and *forte* as part of the score, whereby modulation of timbre, pitch and dynamics became tools of performance in the hands of the director, just as the dynamics of the exhibition *in actio* have become the contemporary theme in the transdisciplinary labs of scenography.

At the 1st International Scenographers' Festival IN3 in Basel, 2006, sound artist Hans Peter Kuhn mentioned in his lecture that on a scale ranging from quiet to loud, he belonged to 'the quiet ones'.[139] I found this deeply inspiring and his remark spontaneously influenced my concluding contribution to the festival programme.[140] It prompted me to suggest a '16-band parametric equalizer' for narrative space.[141] Both as a model of reflection and as an antidote to the erratic need for recipes. Without ignoring the practical fact that every scenographer benefits from intellectual tools to attune the gradations of the presentational spectrum, in exhibitions especially.

Without ignoring the spectator who would like to influence the gradations of communication itself and aspires to personalise the exhibition. Without ignoring the experts of 'ubiquitous computing' who would like to differentiate the interactivity of narrative space entirely.[142] Inspired by the fact that no two topics are ever the same, that the question of form and content is in the end an irrelevant one, because there is no content or form besides what language and interpretation make of it, I asked myself what the conceptual instruments of discursive scenography should look like. I imagined that in the course of the design of any narrative environment the entire array of relations would condense to 16 parameters defining the 'envelope' of the communication. Each parameter would represent an incision in the unknown matter of the topic and at the same time offer a structuring guideline in the fabric of its solution. They not only constitute the topological dimensions of scenography in general, but in each specific case also the constraints of the design problem.[143] Such a complex of substantive constraints poses some conditions which the variables of design will have to fulfil. The solution lies in the one combination that meets all constraints. This enables the scenographer to establish in the initial stages what the tendency of the staging is and distil a guiding principle that will reinforce the coherence and the consistency of the refinement of the design later on.

This approach stems from artificial intelligence and it resembles the parsing of natural languages.[144] Our language consists of texts and sentences: strings of words made up out of combinations of letters from the primal alphabet. Each word can only operate in a limited number of ways and the number of the ways in which a sequence of words can function simultaneously is limited by grammar. The same goes for stage and exhibition design, where the language of scenography derives its structure from the grammar of the narrative environment. Within this context we should consider the proposed 16-band equalizer as a 'thinktool', an intelligent filter with a resolution of 16 constraints for colouring the inventiveness of the designer and the effectiveness of the staging. Here I add a diagram that for the time being is somewhat sketchy. In it, the 16 parameters are divided into two groups of eight: the first group refer to material conditions, whereas the second group describe immaterial conditions.

In order to describe the functionality of the model I will now pretend that it is a type of machine, which of course it isn't really. The analogy of the filter refers to the device used by audio technicians to manipulate the bias of sound reproduction. Here we find 16 values that similarly modify the spectrum of a narrative environment into a specific curve of conveyance.

the envelope

	ordinate		parameter	bias	
01	near	far	the scale of proximity	intimacy	v
02	hot	cold	the scale of participation	temperature	v
03	fast	slow	the scale of tempo	rhythm	v
04	loud	quiet	the scale of spectacle	seduction	v
05	open	closed	the scale of structure	accessibility	v
06	image	text	the scale of communication	communication	v
07	hard	soft	the scale of character	contours	v
08	thing	thought	the scale of substance	imagination	v
09	logos	mythos	the scale of analysis	intellect	v
10	solution	invention	the scale of method	attitude	v
11	prose	poetry	the scale of language	interpretation	v
12	wake	dream	the scale of orientation	ramble	v
13	real	virtual	the scale of reality	presence	v
14	figure	ground	the scale of perception	context	v
15	truth	lie	the scale of trust	authenticity	v
16	light	dark	the scale of visibility	actuality	v

Figure 7. The 16-band parametric equalizer for narrative space is an imaginary device – a 'thinktool', in fact – which allows for a conceptual modulation of a given narrative environment, in terms of diction, dynamics and dramaturgy, based on 16 parameters which define the material and immaterial conditions of a staging. Thought of as a real device, the parametric equalizer would be a smart tool, intelligent software for both scenographer and visitor, ubiquitously embedded in the complex dimensionality of narrative space.

Filtering isn't merely a subtractive concept. On the contrary, when 'pushed to its limits', it can be positively generative in terms of selection. Like the string that is caused to vibrate and produce a tone out of thin air, an acoustic multitude of white noise can be brought to produce an equally pure tone by accurate filtering. This happens at the point where McLuhan locates the 'break boundary' of the medium.[145] This notion of a selection and filtering process, which we also find in Bergson's philosophy, is of the utmost importance to scenography and for making exhibitions especially. In terms of focus, both the theatre and the exhibition may reflect reality, but they can equally be considered as active filters articulating the multiplicity of that reality.[146] Filters, with prototypical characteristics set up by the scenographer to modulate the inclination of the theatrical and exhibited realities.

*Mo*dulation implies *de*modulation – which is what a specific curve of the parametric equalizer is intended to be: a 'modem' between the operator and the spectator.[147] A two-face instance: an interface. Both a translation from content to form, and – with inverse functionality – a translation from form to image and understanding. For, what is staging other than a transformation of a given, chosen content into a meaningful orientation grounded in actuality? Therefore the modem requires a medium. A medium with a set of characteristics imposed by the modem. The modem represents the instance of direction that modulates the materials and the means of the staging. The scenographer can be the modem, provided that he or she maintains the centre position on the sliding scale between form and content and operates the equalizer as a curator would. Alternatively, the curator could also be the modem, provided that he or she understands the procedures as a scenographer would. This is the essence: Fontana's cut isn't a dichotomy separating the scenographer and the curator, but instead it is an incision that binds them together.[148]

The intellectual model of the parametric equalizer contains 16 bands, each with its own active settings. It enables the scenographer to choose an adequate set of parameters for the modulation of his staging. This doesn't imply that when a band is switched off, its correspondent dimension will disappear from the topology altogether. At the most, that particular dimension will receive no specific attention in the design, hold a neutral position in the communicative characteristics and remain a minor agent.

The diagram of the functionality of the equalizer shows 16 'ordinates' in the first column, axes of an n-dimensional mental space whose end points have been established but remain relative. The second column presents the 16 corresponding sliding scales whose relative values depend on a given position in the ordinates column. The third column contains the 16 dimensions of the staging. These are subject to modulation depending on the variations found in the corresponding ordinates. The end result is a scenographic fabric, modulated by the equalizer, which we could label the 'bias' or the topology of the narrative environment.

We could summarise the sixteen-fold capacity of the modem as follows. **01**: On the scale of proximity, each point between 'near' and 'far' represents a statement about the intimacy of the staging. **02**: The scale of resolution, ranging from 'hot' to 'cold', in strict accordance with McLuhan, determines the extent of participation and the 'temperature' of the narrative environment. **03**: On the scale of tempo, ranging from 'fast' to 'slow', the rhythm of the narrative and the lightness of the discourse are set. **04**: Between 'loud' and 'quiet' we find the gradations of seduction, located on the scale of spectacle. **05**: The scale of structure determines the degree of accessibility, ranging from 'open' to 'closed'. **06**: The position relative to the parallel information of an 'image' and the serial information of a 'text' represents the quality of communication on the scale of communication. **07**: The quality of the periphery is a variable on the scale of character, with each element being scaled from 'hard' to 'soft' contours. **08**: The scale of substance represents a central dimension marking the domain between 'thing' and 'thought': this concerns the world of memory and imagination, the border zone where the visible coincides with the conceivable. **09**: The relation between 'mythos' and 'logos', on the scale of analysis, determines the balance between the intellect of the engineer and the intuition of the *bricoleur*. **10**: The scale of methods indicates attitude: is the objective a 'solution' or an 'invention'? **11**: Between 'prose' and 'poetry' we find the domain of interpretation set against the scale of language. **12**: On the scale of orientation we find the variable momentum between 'wake' and 'dream'. **13**: What is the relative position of the staged elements in the domain of reality: 'real' or 'virtual'? **14**: The scale of perception marks the balance between object and its surroundings, between text and context, between 'figure' and 'ground'. **15**: The eternal, ever pressing matter of 'truth' and 'lie' is set against the scale of trust; which statement is authentic? And finally, **16**: What remains in the 'dark' and what becomes 'light' by the staging on the scale of visibility? The answer is grounded in actuality. This is the anchor point that gets the experience of the audience going. It is this experience that is the target of the 'modem's' intellectual tools.

We cannot experience a punctuated 'now'. For that reason our experience of presence expands in time. Experience and drama manifest in dura-

space.time.narrative

tion. But what is subject to duration will inevitably pass. For the time being, NOW is a timeless landscape. NOW is the elastic environment temporarily encompassing the spectator for the duration of a play or an exhibition. This pliable, fluctuating NOW is no other than, in Bergson's terms, the spectator's 'mental state as it advances on the road of time'.[149] And the road of time leads us along the borders of a world that is OTHER. In the theatre the spectator reads the performance as a projection of this OTHER world on the 'fourth wall' that separates the space of the auditorium from the world of the play. This physical distance between the spectator and the world of the play brings about a liberating mental distance to everyday life within the scenographic conventions of the theatre. The fourth wall is an optical instrument. In the theatre each individual spectator perceives the stage as if through his or her own private camera obscura and witnesses the world of the play according to the laws of simple optics: upside down at first. For discursive scenography this matters, and it is an integral part of its objective. Having penetrated the darkroom of individual experience, the intelligent filter of interpretation selectively rotates the aspects and the elements of this virtual image, colours them and transforms them into a readable, meaningful imprint (registration) of the drama. This double rotation or diffraction of the spectrum of the performance, first by the prism of the fourth wall and second by the prism of interpretation, is the essence of the architecture of narrative space. However, we should modify the metaphor of optics in order to make it work for the stage and the exhibition. For, as new impressions always seek stabilisation, the spectator adds personal lenses and mental filters to the perceptual system so that the image, which is a virtual one originally, may take on a useful and coherent reality. That is the quest for a stable orientation called interpretation. It is a heuristic adventure, but it is also a function of the communicative format itself, which means that different laws apply for the theatre and the exhibition.

Expanding on the optical metaphor and assuming that within the given conventions of the theatre the mental system of the spectator does indeed function like a camera obscura, we may ask which instrument is appropriate in the case of a visitor of that other mnemonic medium: the exhibition? It would have to meet more complex requirements, for, instead of being in a fixed position and having a fixed orientation towards a stage, the visitor not only produces mental imagery, but he also needs to navigate. Thus, the question of orientation is no longer merely a mental issue; it enters the physical dimension of scenography. Designing an exhibition requires creating not only the conditions for creative imagery, but also the conditions for the emergence of a meaningful orientation. From the perspective of the spectator the 'other' world of the theatrical performance unfolds both at a distance and in a sequential progression. At an exhibition we are in that 'other' world, and as result we perceive it sequentially as well as simultaneously. There is no longer a fourth wall. Or rather: it manifests as merely fluctuating, in close reading. As the physical distance is reduced to zero, the matter of guiding the mental imagery and the navigation of the spectator is reduced to an educated guess, unless the constraints of the equalizer directly influence the reception. In that case, the mental instrument of the visitor should not only provide the intimacy of the camera obscura, but the wayfinding support of a GPS system as well.[150]

Two images. Visiting an exhibition is like a journey through a fog. The scenography determines its local density. The visitor gropes his way and enjoys a perspective as the fog momentarily lifts and the total impression reaches a sufficient degree of clarity. Alternatively, visiting an exhibition is like a ramble through a metropolis. The scenography lays out the kaleidoscope of the city and determines the local density of the sign system. The visitor is guided by conscious and subconscious connections sequentially providing the readable code needed to decipher the narrative.

The architectural footprint of a narrative environment may be a simple geometric figure, but that doesn't imply a similar simplicity of the superimposed base of the semantic space. On the contrary, the collection of planes on which the individual scenes of the narrative have been constructed is a fractal one. In the scenographical construction, each fractal plane, each 'plane of immanence' in Deleuze's terms, is a stage for discourse, a locus for concept, a space for thought, with an irregular contour and a varying angle of inclination.[151] This is the semantic patchwork of narrative space: a discontinuous discourse unfolding as a series of carvings on the walls of a prehistoric cave. Incisions indeed. Incisions revealing the enigma. Deleuze wrote: 'We will say that THE plane of immanence is, at the same time, that which must be thought and that which cannot be thought.'[152] What we see here is Robert Wilson's space–time cross being transposed to the domain of thought by Deleuze. It is this non-thought within thought which determines the constructional plane for the 'architecture of everything'.

space.time.narrative

2.5   a northwest passage

On 16 June 1903 the Norwegian explorer Roald Amundsen went aboard the cutter *Gjøa* together with a six-man crew in the harbour of Oslo – called Christiania in those days – and after having spent three winters in the Arctic region, he continued his journey on 30 August 1906, headed for the town of Nome, Alaska, via the Bering Strait.[153] The objective of the small-scale, protracted expedition was to locate the Magnetic North Pole, to explore en passant the labyrinthine, uncharted ice deserts of the archipelago north of Canada and to find a navigable route connecting the Atlantic and Pacific Oceans: the Northwest Passage.[154] The expedition, which had been carefully prepared, went off quite smoothly at first, but then disaster struck. The *Gjøa* ran aground in the James Ross Straight, near the Beaufort Islands, on 31 August, but managed to get afloat gain. The next day a fire broke out in the engine room, which was brought under control without doing too much damage. Then on 3 September a relentless north storm threw the *Gjøa* onto the rocks, which forced the crew to cut loose the deck cargo in order to save the ship and their lives. There was no indication of the Matty Island reef on any of the provisional maps made by earlier explorers, and thus the problem of the Northwest Passage was posed.[155] A matter of navigation through unknown territory with all the ups and downs: orientation based on unreliable charts, compasses rendered useless by the overpowering geomagnetics, triangulations disturbed by arctic fog, ice and shallows blocking the passage, clothing offering insufficient protection against the cold – it all made painfully clear that for this journey there was no guide whatsoever. Every aspect of the survival strategy had to be empirically discovered and acquired, including the scientific localisation of the magnetic north. Nothing was what it seemed. Everything turned out much more complicated than was expected. The Eskimos weren't the savages that were expected, but instead a people well adjusted to their circumstances, with clothing that was the perfect insulation and equipment that outmatched that of the expedition team. Furthermore, the dog sledge wouldn't glide over the snow below minus 60 degrees Celsius. The magnetic north turned out to be an unstable field of force with fluctuating contours and an unsteady, changing position instead of a point with fixed coordinates. Navigation on the basis of charts and compasses had to be discarded and replaced by the crow's nest and a lead line at the bow. The expedition could only be safeguarded by the most rudimentary means of anticipation.

the envelope

After having completed the journey through the archipelago, Amundsen again faced the ice and had to winter for the third time, now at King Point at the Yukon Coast of Canada, where another expedition lay ahead. On 24 October Admundsen set out on a 500-mile journey on skis to the nearest telegraph station in Eagle City, Alaska, to inform the world about the success of the expedition. It became a bizarre, extremely difficult journey across endless snowfields, which could never have been accomplished if it hadn't been for the hospitality of the Eskimo people. Amundsen reached Eagle City a month and a half later, but the telegraph message announcing the Northwest Passage triumph was intercepted by American newspapers. The London *Times* had originally promised a financial contribution in exchange for the exclusive right on the story, but now that it had missed out on the scoop it refused to pay the money. In Eagle City, Amundsen waited for mail for two months, in vain, and in early 1906 he returned to the *Gjøa*, famous but disappointed. It wasn't before 10 July of the same year that the ice had melted and the ship could leave King Point.[156]

By an erratic crossing through unknown territory Amundsen discovered the possibility of a northern passage between the Pacific and Atlantic Oceans. The expedition followed a route that had been mapped out, but because of unforeseen local conditions most of it turned out to be radically different. Each and every deviation from the anticipated had the potential of a crisis and required desperate measures. Only anticipation and improvisation could conquer the resistance of reality and safely complete the hazardous journey. In our present context of discursive scenography, the Amundsen expedition is a significant metaphor for both the conceptual complexity and the intricate technicalities of narrative space. But there is more to it – or, rather, beneath it. For the French philosopher of science Michel Serres, Amundsen's journey represents the relation between science and the humanities.

Serres writes: 'I'm looking for the passage that will lead us from the sciences to the humanities. Or rather – down to language or our systems of control – from us to the world. This pathway is not as easy as the classification of knowledge may lead us to think it is. In my view it is much more difficult than the notorious Northwest Passage.'[157] As such, the Northwest Passage appears to be a universal metaphor for the struggle of finding a link or a passage. In that respect each realisation of a venturesome theatre production or a meaningful exhibition will have the nature of an expedition. It always will. It will always be about that cut through the matter that will expose the potential of an urgent narrative passage. The passage is the

space.time.narrative

singular essence of discursive scenography, as opposed to the essence of propaganda, which is separation or distinction. The linking cut-through is the paradox of narrative space. On the stage it will express itself in a line of discourse unfolding in time, from scene to scene, and propelling the drama. In exhibitions it manifests as a multiple route through space, structuring the staging of the narrative and gently guiding the visitor.

The synthesising cut starts with hypothesis and forms the beginning of every linking discourse. Similarly, Bruno's monad served as a model for the link between mind and matter. Albert Einstein's inventions demonstrated the link between space and time. Henri Bergson built a bridge between physics and metaphysics. Ilya Prigogine recognised the relationship between order and chaos. Antonin Artaud argued the unity of scenography and obscenography. Lucio Fontana cut the immaculate canvas in order to link his pictorial art to imageless dimensions. Guy Debord linked the psychogeography of the city to urban design. Roland Barthes considered the photographer, the photograph and the viewer as one dramaturgical hinge. Peter Brook compacted the debate about the art of the theatre in this one question about the possibility of creating a connection between the players and the audience. Lévi-Strauss' expeditions resulted in a plea for the synthesis of the intellect of the engineer and the intuition of the *bricoleur*. Marshall McLuhan envisaged a marriage of the left and right brain hemispheres as a precondition for a more encompassing, sophisticated perception of reality. But it is never easy, nor could or should it be. As Serres explains:

> It is important to note that the passage is hardly ever successful because it is so narrow. It is never as wide as the surface of the sea where there are no reefs, like many passable straits are. The path from the humanities to the sciences and vice versa doesn't traverse an empty, homogenous space. The image of the complex archipelago, hidden under the ice for the most part, in the barren North of Canada is an accurate one. The passage is generally closed off with land or ice, or because one is lost. And when it is open, one faces a way that is unpredictable. And unique.[158]

Led by the crossover tendencies of the stage and the exhibition, I asked myself: what is scenography? I made a distinction between mercantile scenography, which primarily aims for entertainment and propaganda, and discursive scenography, which focuses on the sheltering of ideas. But how, we may ask, does an idea find shelter? Is it reasonable to suggest a sustain-

the envelope

able, protective, fostering intervention of discursive scenography when the object of protection is more volatile than Proteus himself?[159]

Ideas are tools, tools for thought. Every idea has both a unifying and a separating power. It both orientates and polarises and carves its way. It sticks where thought is receptive. It seeks form and the right moment. As such it is essentially mobile, nomadic – very much like Cees Nooteboom's memory lying down wherever it chooses. There is however one major difference between the two: the idea is an instrument of actuality, whereas memory is a tool of things past. Ideas are thought-projections onto an exterior screen; memories of events are shadows cast onto an interior screen. Memories have functions, but these functions have lost their urgency. A memory once gave guidance, the idea still does. Or, in other words, memories are like ideas having left their traces and having consumed their energy. However, a memory can be resuscitated and it is this oscillation between memory and idea that is the dynamic context of a culture. The cycle of memory and idea is the very instance that reconciles the world of things with the world of thought. This synthesis or reconciliation is the motor of what I generically would like to call a post-spectacular scenography. Where these spheres of reality overlap, we find the granulate of narrative space: memories, ideas, language, histories. In societies where spectacle reigns, a narrative space becomes a counter-environment where discourse moves upstream in a way that resembles Prigogine's order emerging from chaos. In this countermovement the idea finds shelter and we see, for the time being, the relatedness of things resurface.[160]

In 2006 the German rhetoric artist Bazon Brock organised a *Lustmarsch durchs Theoriegelände* in 11 museums in Germany, Austria and Switzerland.[161] It was a kind of action-teaching which was intended to prepare the participants for their future as citizens of Europe in an age of total globalisation (*Totalglobalisierung*). Brock interprets Europe as the future museum of the world, and he advises all citizens of the continent of the Enlightenment to 'musealise' themselves beforehand, explaining: 'To musealise oneself means to live a life worthy of interesting accounts. Not as recollections of the past, but as visions of the future.'[162]

For Bazon Brock, this way of life is all about tracking, reconstructing tracks and leaving traces. Showing the connections between seemingly singular facts, producing complexes from singularities, beyond the imaginable. 'Amaze me. Transcend my ability to anticipate. Anything short of this is mere entertainment,'[163] he urges. Brock has a lot in common with Beckett in this respect. But while for Beckett the individual is thrown upon his own re-

space.time.narrative

sources when it comes to 'the suffering of being', Brock has a motto to offer for every musealised citizen. *Exponiert euch*! Exhibit yourself! He confronts us with the image of the ancient Europe rehearsing a new part on the global stage:

> We are talking about the human potential of anticipation and empathy, the most important constructive elements of the mnemonic landscape and the mnemonic theatre. Empathy, as opposed to sympathy, isn't about a retrospective feeling of pity, but rather about a future feeling of compassion, the anticipating experience of what is yet to come and is always imminent. This ability of the imagination to look ahead before actual perception occurs is what we call anticipation.[164]

A narrative environment is about constructing a track for the idea to unfold and for the memory to conform to. That route is like Lucretius' clinamen, which is the deviant opinion, the heart of new thought, of the unimaginable.[165] And here we find the difference between the mercantile and discursive scenographies. Mercantile scenography leads us down the beaten track, through charted territory. Discursive scenography on the other hand leads us beyond familiar horizons, through virgin territory where navigation is dependent on anticipation and survival instinct. Brock's *Lustmarsch durchs Theoriegelände* aims at a synthesis of diagnostics and prognostics, of course and discourse, and in doing so it charges scenography with a substantive task. Brock suggests:

> The Greek theatre may well serve as a landscape of theory here because its spectators perform an act of *theoria* as a perception and a critical judgement of that which appears before them on the stage. And perception here means to interpret the various characters, the various dramatic instants and the linguistic and musical utterances in a meaningful relationship so that it gives rise to a comprehensible tale through the individual act of combining of the individual spectator.[166]

In Brock's 'museum of the world', every European is the author of his own mythology.

When Rem Koolhaas proposed the concept of the 'Generic City' in his book *S, M, L, XL* in 1995, he pointed out that many (European) historic city centres have a problem in common: because the vast peripheries derive their orientation from the museal identity of these distinctive centres, the

the envelope

pressure of tourism, event culture and spectacle is such that they are on the verge of collapse. So, Koolhaas suggests: down with character. What, he asks, remains once the centre is stripped: the Generic?[167] The central issue lies in the fact that the past will at some point lack the capacity to serve the ever-growing global population: we ourselves exhaust it. To meet this process of dilution head-on and avoid further pulverising of 'successful identities' into 'meaningless dust', Koolhaas proposes a city free from the 'captivity of the centre' and the 'straightjacket of identity'. For, 'as the sphere of influence expands, the area characterized by the centre becomes larger and larger, hopelessly diluting both the strength and the authority of the core; inevitably the distance between centre and circumference increases to the breaking point.'[168]

The combination of diagnostics and prognostics reminds me of a verse written by the Irish writer, poet and freedom fighter William Butler Yeats (see page 88) almost a century ago: 'things fall apart, the centre cannot hold'.[169] It is the third line of Yeats' poem *The Second Coming*, written in 1920, when Europe was recovering from the horrors of the First World War. For sceno-graphy, the line immediately preceding it is just as relevant: 'the falcon cannot hear the falconer'. The double suggestion of a broken link between the centre and the periphery offers us an inverse formulation of the task which discursive scenography is facing. However, there is one major difference: if Koolhaas is a situationist, then Yeats is a symbolist. Both analyse and interpret tendencies of everyday reality. But whereas Koolhaas is concerned with the immediacy of a given situation, Yeats refers to a higher, inspiring reality. Now, a symbolist situationism sounds rather absurd to me, but a situationist symbolism may, in the present context of discursive scenography, provide a significant propelling power to establish narrative space. What sort of chart would a *dérive* through the Generic City yield, if a group of delirious situationists should set out equipped with heightened awareness?[170] If 'the dominant sensation of The Generic City' would indeed be 'an eerie calm', then their *parcours* would have to leave behind traces as sharp as Fontana's cut.[171]

The concept of the Generic City represents the initial condition of all scenographic works. Its psychogeography resembles that of an empty stage or exhibition room: once the banal has been 'evacuated', there remains a serenity in which every sign takes on meaning and, intentionally or not, refers to something integral that is about to unfold.[172] In our interview Uwe Brückner called it the 'cleaning rag effect'.[173] Both the theatre and the exhibition are of a symbolist nature in this respect, while at the same time retain-

445

space.time.narrative

ing the situationist dimension that elegantly keeps the *mythos* within the constraints of *logos*. Now, having said that, what makes a scenographer? Simply a musealised 'European' who, equipped with an analytical sensorium and a set of prognostic tools – depending on what is required – refers to an alternative, yet unknown reality in his each and every 'uttering and outering'.[174] Such is the temporary reality of narrative space, which makes it no less majestic or compelling, to be sure. When speaking of 'the persuasive lack of urgency and insistence' in 'The Generic City', Koolhaas mentions the induction of a 'hallucination of the normal'.[175] But what matters here is that the very hallucination of the normal, which is now being celebrated in a host of reality-TV formats, is being countered by a contemplation on the extraordinary in the narrative environment of discursive scenography. Eerie calm.

Looking back on his adolescence, W.B. Yeats wrote in 1919: 'one day when I was twenty-three or twenty-four this sentence seemed to form in my head, without my willing it, much as sentences form when we are half-asleep: *hammer your thoughts into a unity*. For days I could think of nothing else, and for years I tested all I did by that sentence.'[176] Given the tremendous complexity of space–time processes in narrative environments, Yeats' leitmotif offers an important reference for the scenographer. What Yeats was looking for was an antidote at a time when human existence threatened to fall apart. For him, only an individual mythology could preserve and consolidate its integrity. Applied to our present context, Yeats implicitly argues the coherence of narrative space and its cognate concepts of nucleus, fabric, and critical charge. In a way, powerful stagings are individual mythologies indeed, operating in the border zone between truth and lies, between reality and fiction, authenticity and interpretation, transparency and mystery, memory and imagination. It is therefore beyond the question whether scenography manifests on the surface of things or not. Discursive scenography will always deeply encroach upon the relation between form and content, and it will generate a nuclear, concentrating centre of the staging. The matter will be highly explosive or the interpretation fully charged. Or both. The world is on fire. What remains is forging our thoughts into unity.

the envelope

Notes

1. Robert Wilson (b.1941), 'Mr Bojangles' Memory ... Og, Son of Fire', Centre Pompidou, Paris, 6 November 1991 to 27 January 1992.
2. A conversation between Umberto Eco and Robert Wilson, 16 June 1991. Bill 'Bojangles' Robinson (1878–1949), the dance legend from the New York Cotton Club in the 1920s. Umberto Eco (b.1932) is an Italian writer and semiotician.
3. The video animations were prepared at the IRCAM (Institut de Recherche et Coordination Acoustique/Musique) studios of the Centre Pompidou specially for the 'Mr Bojangles' Memory' exhibition. They involved blue-screen techniques that facilitated a montage with alienating scaled-down contrasts. Mr Bojangles was played by Charles 'Honi' Coles.
4. Trevor Fairbrother (b.1952), 'Robert Wilson's Vision', Museum of Fine Arts, Boston (MA), 6 February to 20 April 1991.
5. Hans Peter Kuhn (b.1952), *The Night Before The Day*, score for 'Robert Wilson's Vision', 1990. Kuhn's composition of five parts that corresponded to the spatial structure of the Boston Museum of Fine Arts exhibition: Entrance: 11'50"; Room I: 14'47"; Room II: 4'43"; Room III: 15'37"; The Space Ship: 0'20". For further details on Hans Peter Kuhn, see: Katharina Otto-Bernstein, *Absolute Wilson: The Biography*, Prestel, Munich–Berlin–London–New York, 2006.
6. *Room for Salomé*, in 'Energies', Stedelijk Museum, Amsterdam, 8 April to 29 July 1990.
7. Topology is an area of mathematics concerned with spatial properties that are preserved under continuous deformations of objects: for example, deformations that involve stretching. Because of this fundamental 'elasticity', topology is often referred to as 'rubber sheet geometry'. See: Joachim Huber, *Urbane Topologie: Architektur der randlosen Stadt*, Bauhaus University, Weimar, 2006. The concept of 'expanded scenography' was inspired by 'expanded cinema', which was introduced by media theorist Gene Youngblood in 1970. See: Gene Youngblood, *Expanded Cinema*, Clarke, Irwin & Company, Toronto–Vancouver, 1970.
8. Euclid's *Elements* is a mathematical and geometric treatise comprising 13 books that was written in Alexandria c.300 BC by the Greek mathematician Euclid.
9. For obscenography, see essay 1, 'The Battery', p.16.
10. The monad is a concept taken from Greek philosophy where it was used to denote the inseparable unity of all being. With Giordano Bruno (1548–1600) it had already taken on the meaning of a particle of reality consistent of mind and matter in equal amounts (Bruno, *De Monade Numero et Figura*, 1591). In *Monadologie* (1714), Gottfried Wilhelm von Leibnitz (1646–1716) explored the laws of this fundamental particle and tried to establish a basis for its existence by means of his infinitesimal calculus.
11. For the Situationist International, see essay 1, 'The Battery', notes 109, 110, p.78–79.
12. Lewis Carroll, *Alice in Wonderland*, Award Books Inc., New York, without date: probably 1960; Original edition: *Alice's Adventures in Wonderland*, Macmillan, London, 1865.
13. See note 2 above. The conversation between Eco and Wilson took place in the Opéra Bastille in Paris. After a first inquiry the scale model could not be located in the archives

space.time.narrative

14   of the Centre Pompidou. The premiere of this production of *The Magic Flute* was on 26 June 1991.

14   Eco mistakenly refers to David Lynch, the filmmaker. What he is in fact talking about is urban planner Kevin Lynch et al., *A View from the Road*, MIT Press, Cambridge (MA), 1964. See also: Umberto Eco, *The Open Work (Opera Aperta)*, Harvard University Press, Cambridge (MA), 1989 (originally published in Italian in 1962).

15   Conversation between Umberto Eco and Robert Wilson, published in: 'Robert Wilson Retrospective', *Performing Arts Journal*, vol.43, January 1993, pp 86–96. Published in French in *Mr Bojangles' Memory: Og, Son of Fire*, exhibition catalogue; Éditions du Centre Pompidou, Paris, 1991.

16   Alberto Giacometti (1901–1966), Swiss sculptor and painter who joined the Surrealist movement in Paris in the 1930s and became famous with the sculpture *L'Homme qui marche* (1961).

17   See: Katharina Otto-Bernstein, *Absolute Wilson: The Biography*, Prestel, Munich–Berlin–London–New York, 2006, pp 71–5. In school, Wilson supposedly maintained that he aspired to be 'the King of Spain' when he grew up – which caused considerable worries with his teacher. *The King of Spain* was to become Wilson's first theatre play, a one-acter which premiered on 30 January 1969. It had a Victorian highchair centre stage with its back faced to the audience: the throne, the symbol of power, that would become one of the scenographical centres of the action. At the end of 1969 two further acts were added to the play, which received a new title: *The Life and Times of Sigmund Freud*, staged at the Opera House of the Brooklyn Academy of Music (BAM) in New York. Wilson for the first time designed a chair specifically for the play *Freud's Hanging Chair*, the condensation of the narrative potential.

18   Wilson in the Umberto Eco interview, op.cit. (note 15), p.89.

19   Pieter Kottman, '*Het donkere doolhof van Wilson's montagekunst*', *NRC Handelsblad*, 9 December 1991: 'The visitor is shrouded in a blanket of textual and musical shreds from Wilson's theatrical productions. I can't help imagining hearing a whisper that dominates the entire pandemonium. It keeps repeating "*Das bedeutet überhaupt nichts*" and "*It doesn't mean anything at all*". This admonition compagnies the visitor on his way through a dark labyrinth where the pathway, the dimly lit objects and the monitors are his sole orientations.'

20   Caspar David Friedrich (1774–1840), *Der Wanderer über dem Nebelmeer*, 1818. Currently in Kunsthalle Hamburg.

21   See essay 1, 'The Battery', note 111, p.79.

22   Robert Wilson, *Death, Destruction & Detroit II*, 1987. In 1987, the German playwright, poet and theatre director Heiner Müller (1929–1995) wrote a letter to Robert Wilson with a Mongolian anecdote on the loss of memory, which inspired him to produce the installation *Memory/Loss* at the Venice Biennale, Italy, 13 June to 10 October 1993. See: Katharina Otto-Bernstein, op.cit. (note 17), pp 223–4.

23   The Umberto Eco interview, op.cit. (note 15), p.95.

24   Bonnie Marranca, *Performing Arts Journal*, vol.43, January 1993, p.69: 'The theatrical realm unfolds – and why not consider the proscenium as an upright book? – to present an anthology of texts and images, as it were, framing classics for contemporaries. It also recontextualizes Wilson's personal vocabulary of imagery: grid, chair, forest, cave,

25 'The fourth wall' refers to the imaginary 'wall' at the front of the stage in a proscenium theatre, through which the audience sees the action in the world of the performance. The term also applies to the boundary between any fictional setting and its audience.
26 See the interview with Herman Kossmann and Mark de Jong, p.107.
27 For 'topology', see note 7 above.
28 The basic principle of 'fuzzy logic' is that everything is a matter of degree. 'Fuzziness has a formal name in science: multivalence. The opposite of fuzziness is bivalence or two-valuedness, two ways to answer each question, true or false, 1 or 0. Fuzziness means *multi*valence. It means three or more options, instead of just two extremes. It means analog instead of binary, infinite shades of gray between black and white. It means all that the trial lawyer or judge tries to rule out when she says, "answer just yes or no".' See: Bart Kosko, *Fuzzy Thinking: The New Science of Fuzzy Logic*, HarperCollins Publishers, London, 1994, pp 18–19.
29 Robert Wilson and Philip Glass, *Einstein on the Beach*; premiere: Festival d'Avignon, 25 July 1976.
30 Megastructure of *Einstein on the Beach*, elucidated by Wilson in his lecture at the 2nd International Scenographers' Festival IN3 in Basel, 20 November 2008; the opera contained four acts, marked by five knee-plays, each with an average duration of about 40 to 50 minutes. The knee-plays had a duration of about 6 to 8 minutes. The opera as such lasted about three and a half hours. See: Katharina Otto-Bernstein, op.cit. (note 17), p.146.
31 Ibid p.148. Philip Glass states: 'We took five or six hours.' This contradicts Wilson's lecture as well as the duration of his own music as it was released bu CBS Records in 1979.
32 Ibid p.146.
33 See: Frances A. Yates, *The Art of Memory*, Pimlico, London, 2001, chapters 1 and 2.
34 As the act of scenography is basically understood here as giving 'shelter to an idea', the process of development of a scenographical work implies two major stages, which are not necessarily sequential, but rather two entwined threads of realisation: inventing a narrative potential on the one hand – *inventio* – and embedding or rather translating this potential – *manifestatio* – into materials and media in such a way that the staging may clearly speak. *Inventio* and *manifestatio* are terms derived from the five canons of the art of rhetoric: *inventio, dispositio, elocutio, memoria, actio*. However, our scenographic *inventio* and *manifestatio* both encompass all five stages, but seen from a diametrically different perspective. *Inventio* covers the entire staging from the point of view of its narrative nucleus, the idea, whereas *manifestatio* covers the entire staging in terms of its physicalities. See: Aristotle, *The Art of Rhetoric*, translated by H.C. Lawson-Tancred, Penguin Classics, London, 1991.
35 Inclination in physics or astronomy describes a certain angle between two different planes of action. In our context, inclination is a powerful notion which expresses a tendency to deviate, both in physical and in psychic respect. Inclination, therefore, is a dramaturgical parameter in the staging of narrative space.
36 Deviation is usually understood as a change of course, due to a navigational failure caused, for instance, by a malfunctioning compass. Reversely, a stroll through the city

can be full of consciously wanted positive deviations, like the Situationists advocated with their *dérive*, which promoted 'drifting' as the intense exploration of the urban environment.
37   See note 34 above.
38   Samuel Beckett (1906–1989), *Krapp's Last Tape*, 1958. Production by Robert Wilson, Teatro Mercadante, Naples, 22–24 October 2009. Wilson's version of the play had already been staged in Spoleto in June 2009.
39   Robert Wilson, *Hamlet: A Monologue*, 1995.
40   Samuel Beckett, *Krapp's Last Tape*, 1958. See: Samuel Beckett, *Collected Shorter Plays*, Grove Press, New York, 1984, pp 54–63.
41   Robert Wilson and Christopher Knowles, *Dialog / Curious George*, 1980. *Overture to the Fourth Act of Deafman Glance* was initially performed in solo by Robert Wilson, 1980. Later on, the piece was performed together with others, notably Sheryl Sutton, 1982–7.
42   Robert Wilson, *Deafman Glance*, Paris, 1970–71.
43   Lecture by Robert Wilson, 2nd International Scenographers' Festival IN3, Basel, 20 November 2008.
44   Krapp's first words after the opening sequence, *Krapp's Last Tape*, op.cit. (note 38), pp 56–7.
45   Ibid.
46   Colin Counsell, *Signs of Performance*, Routledge, London, 1996, p.206.
47   Guy Debord (1931–1994); See essay 1, 'The Battery', note 109, p.78.
48   Counsell, op.cit., p.206.
49   Ibid p.180.
50   Interview between Umberto Eco and Robert Wilson, Paris, 16 June 1991.
51   Peter Sellars, 'On opera', *Artforum*, vol.28, December 1989, pp 23–4.
52   *Robert Wilson's Vision*, exhibition catalogue, Museum of Fine Arts, Boston, 1991, p.35.
53   See: Johan Huizinga (1872–1945), *The Waning of the Middle Ages: A Study of Forms of Life, Thought, and Art in France and the Netherlands in the Dawn of the Renaissance*, Doubleday Anchor, New York, 1954.
54   Marshall McLuhan (1911–1980) and David Carson (b.1952), *The Book of Probes*, Gingko Press, Corte Madera, 2003, pp 30–31, 304–5.
55   Marshall McLuhan, *Understanding Media: The Extensions of Man*, McGraw Hill, New York, 1964, p.19. Although McLuhan's text was written in 1964, it hasn't lost any of its analytical, prognostic thrust, if only because the various forms of criticism that it provoked never seemed to have quite the same staying power and vigour as McLuhan's intense and inspired vision, which only later would become more firmly rooted in a conceptual framework.
56   Ibid p.20.
57   Ibid p.20. McLuhan surely refers to Vladimir and Estragon in Beckett's *Waiting for Godot*, 1953. The play was staged by Herbert Blau in San Quentin State Prison, San Francisco in 1957. See essay 1, 'The Battery', note 66, p.xxx.
58   P.F. Thomése (b.1958), Dutch author, *NRC-Handelsblad*, 24–25 October 2009.
59   In his text 'Repetition and stoppage: Debord in the field of cinema', Giorgio Agamben refers to Paul Valéry. See: Stefan Zweifel et al., *In Girum Imus Nocte Et Consumimur Igni*, JRP-Ringier Kunstverlag, Zurich, 2006, p.37.

the envelope

60 See note 20 above.
61 Helmut Börsch-Supan, *Caspar David Friedrich*, George Braziller, New York, 1974.
62 'Cultural Leadership in Difficult Times' conference, Museum of Fine Arts, Boston (MA), 4 February 2009.
63 In English, *logos* is the root of 'logic', suggesting logical reasoning, which was part of the semantic field of the original Greek term. *Logos* meant 'word', not in the grammatical sense, but as 'speech', 'account', 'reason', 'story', 'narrative' or even 'language'. Later *logos* received a philosophical, intellectual connotation, whereas *mythos* represented the realm of intuition, of individual, subjective feelings and experiences. Interestingly, *mythos* also refers to language and story, but now in the sense of 'plot', as defined by Aristotle in his analysis of tragedy in the *Poetics*. *Logos* and *mythos* are apparently two different but complementary modes of thinking or linguistic channels through which insight and knowledge of our world may be transported. See: Aristotle, *Poetics*, translated by Malcolm Heath, Penguin Classics, London, 1996.
64 For *logos*, see note 63 above. For *kairos*, see essay 1, 'The Battery', note 27, p.69.
65 Juri Steiner interviews Hans Ulrich Obrist in *In Girum Imus Nocte Et Consumimur Igni*, exhibition catalogue (exhibition on the Situationist International (1957–72)), Centraal Museum, Utrecht and Museum Tinguely, Basel, 2006, p.52.
66 Ibid p.51. See also essay 1, 'The Battery', notes 109, 110, pp.78–79.
67 See: 'Psychogeographical game of the week', *Potlatch*, no.1, Paris, 22 June 1954. *Potlatch* was the magazine of the International Lettrists (1952–7), a movement of writers, poets and anti-artists which could be seen as the French counterpart of the American Beat Generation. Guy Debord refers to this psychogeographical game of the week in his essay *Introduction to a Critique of Urban Geography*, which was published in *Les Lèvres nues*, vol.6, Paris, September 1955. See: http://www.nothingness.org/SI/.
68 See note 28 above.
69 See essay 1, 'The Battery', para.1.7: 'The camera lucida of savage thought', p.59.
70 See: Stefan Zweifel et al., op.cit. (note 59), p.181. In the chapter 'Situationist titles and taunts', Zweifel offers a text by Ivan Chtcheglov (1933–1998) (under 'D'), who, together with Debord, is considered the father of psychogeography. Chtcheglov: 'The dérive (in its flow, with its gestures, walking and meetings) has the same relationship to the totality as (good) psychoananalysis does to speech.'
71 Guy Debord, 'Introduction to a critique of urban geography', *Les Lèvres nues*, no.6, 1955. See also: http://library.nothingness.org/articles/SI/en/display/2, accessed: November 2009.
72 See: Guy Debord in Stefan Zweifel et al, op.cit. (note 59), p.218. Originally published in *Oeuvres*, Éditions Gallimard, Paris, 2006, p.166.
73 A 'technological fix' refers to solving a problem by using technology. See: Lisa Rosner, *The Technological Fix*, Routledge, London, 2004.
74 Tom Wolfe (b.1931) is an American writer considered to be one of the founding fathers of New Journalism who uses literary techniques similar to those of Beat Generation writers and poets. New Journalism is a style of journalism with a fictional literary touch, which was introduced by Wolfe in 1973; see: Tom Wolfe, 'The birth of the New Journalism: eyewitness report by Tom Wolfe', in *New York Magazine*, 14 February 1972. The Beat Generation was a small group of influential writers including Jack Kerouac (1922–1969), William S. Burroughs (1914–1997) and the 'beat poet' Allen Ginsberg

(1926–1997), which got together in New York in the late 1940s and moved to San Francisco in the 1950s, where it formed an important basis for the hippie counter-culture of the 1960s. Ginsberg's *Howl* (1956), Kerouac's *On The Road* (1957) and Burroughs' *Naked Lunch* (1959) are major examples of Beat poetry and writing.

75   Las Vegas, Nevada, USA, was founded in 1905 and officially appointed as a city in 1911. The desert city developed along a four-mile section of Las Vegas Boulevard, better known as 'The Strip', with its extravagant casinos and its large-scale neon lighting.

76   Tom Wolfe, *The Kandy-Kolored Tangerine-Flake Streamline Baby*, Bantam Books, New York, 1999. First Edition: Farrar, Straus & Giroux, 1965.

77   Robert Venturi (b.1925), Denise Scott Brown (b.1931) and Steven Izenour (1940–2001), *Learning from Las Vegas: The Forgotten Symbolism of Architectural Form*, The MIT Press, Cambridge (MA), 1977.

78   Rem Koolhaas (b.1944), *Delirious New York*, first edition: Oxford University Press, New York, 1978.

79   NATO (*Narrative Architecture Today*), Architectural Association, London, 1983–5.

80   Nigel Coates (b.1949), *Guide to Ecstacity*, Laurence King Publishing, London, 2003.

81   Ibid p.29.

82   Ibid p.42.

83   Marshall McLuhan, *Understanding Media*, op.cit. (note 55), p.56.

84   The concepts of 'figure' and 'ground' derive from *Gestalt* psychology and were introduced in the discourse on visual perception by the Danish art critic Edgar Rubin (1886-1951) around 1915. In 'The resonating interval', chapter 1 of *The Global Village* by Marshall McLuhan and Bruce R. Powers, the authors state that 'all cultural situations are composed of an area of attention (figure) and a very much larger area of inattention (ground). The two are in a continual state of abrasive interplay, with an outline or boundary or interval between them that serves to define both simultaneously'. See: *The Global Village: Transformations in World Life and Media in the 21st Century*, Oxford University Press, New York–Oxford, 1989, p.5.

85   Marshall McLuhan, op.cit. (note 55), p.56.

86   Howard Rheingold (b.1947) is an American writer and critic. Nicholas Negroponte (b.1943) is a Greek-American architect and computer scientist, well known for founding the Media Lab of the Massachusetts Institute of Technology (MIT). Michael Heim (b.1944) is an American writer known as 'the philosopher of cyberspace'. Derrick de Kerckhove (b.1944) is a Belgian-Canadian linguist and the director of the McLuhan Program in Culture and Technology in Toronto, Canada.

87   Howard Rheingold, *The Virtual Community*, Addison Wesley Publishing Company, Reading (MA), 1993; Nicholas Negroponte, *Being Digital*, Alfred A. Knopf, New York, 1995; Michael Heim, *The Metaphysics of Virtual Reality*, Oxford University Press, New York, 1993; Derrick de Kerckhove, *Connected Intelligence: The Arrival of the Web Society*, Kogan Page Publishers, London, 1998; William Gibson (b.1948), *Neuromancer*, The Berkley Publishing Group, New York, 1984; Marvin Minsky (b.1927), *The Society of Mind*, Simon & Schuster, New York, 1987. 'Doors of Perception' was the overarching name of a series of nine innovative design conferences with subjects as Internet, Home, Info-Eco, Speed, Play, Lightness, Flow, Infra and Food Systems. The conferences were held on an irregular basis in Amsterdam from 1993 to 2007. The authors mentioned

88 above (see note 86) participated, often as keynote speakers. See: http://www.doorsofperception.com/_conference_archive.html.
88 The term 'avatar' refers to a computer user's representation of himself/herself, whether in the form of a three-dimensional model used in computer games, a two-dimensional icon (picture) or a one-dimensional username used on Internet forums and other communities. It can also refer to the personality connected with the screen name of an Internet user. See: Bruce Damer, *Avatars!*, Peachpit Press, Berkeley (CA), 1998. By 1996 avatar space was exploding. AlphaWorld (launched 1995) is a virtual metropolis on the Internet, where millions of cyber-citizens have access to plots of virtual wasteland, which they transform into an ever-growing virtual urban environment, through their individual building activities; see: http://www.activeworlds.com/worlds/alphaworld/. Artificial intelligence (AI) is the intelligence of machines and the branch of computer science that aims to create it.
89 Frank den Oudsten, 'Floating Identities', ZKM Medienmuseum, Karlsruhe, 1995–7. See: Hans Peter Schwarz, *Media – Art – History: Media Museum ZKM*, Prestel, Munich–New York, 1997, pp 132–3. See also: http://on1.zkm.de/zkm/werke/FloatingIdentities.
90 For *Wunderkammer*, see essay 1, 'The Battery', note 52.
91 For Tom Wolfe, see note 74 above. For Umberto Eco, see note 2 above. Neil Postman (1931–2003) was an American communication scientist. William Kuhns (b.1943) is a Canadian writer and media theoretician.
92 Tom Wolfe in 'What if he is right?', *The Pump House Gang*, 11th printing, 1977, p.118. Original edition: Farrar, Straus & Giroux, New York, 1968.
93 Umberto Eco, 'Towards a semiological warfare', in *Travels in Hyperreality: Reports from the Global Village*, 1967; From: *Harvest Book*, New York, 1986, p.138.
94 For the Shannon–Weaver model of communication, see: Marshall and Eric McLuhan, *Laws of Media: The New Science*, University of Toronto Press, Toronto, 1988, pp 86–91.
95 Derrick de Kerckhove, 'Understanding McLuhan', *Canadian Forum*, vol.51, May 1981, pp 8–9, 33.
96 Marshall McLuhan, *Understanding Me*, The MIT Press, Toronto, 2005, p.230. Public lecture, 'Living at the speed of light', held at the University of South Florida, Tampa, on 25 February 1974.
97 Marshall McLuhan and David Carson, *The Book of Probes*, op.cit. (note 54), pp 239, 271.
98 Ibid p.165.
99 Marshall McLuhan, op.cit. (note 96), p.248. TV interview, *What TV Does Best*, 6 September 1976.
100 Neil Postman, *Amusing Ourselves to Death*, Methuen, London, 1987, pp 6–7.
101 Ibid p.7.
102 Ibid p.10.
103 Marshall McLuhan, *Understanding Media*, op.cit. (note 55), chapter 2: 'Media hot and cold', p.36.
104 Peter Brook, *The Empty Space*, Penguin Books, London, (1968) 1990.
105 Marshall McLuhan, *Understanding Media*, op.cit., p.64.
106 'Cold fusion' is a concept from nuclear physics referring to the – still hypothetical – fusion of atomic nuclei at room temperature.
107 James Joyce, *Finnegans Wake*, Faber & Faber, London, 1939.

space.time.narrative

108 William Kuhns, 'Reviewing the reviews: Giordano Bruno and Marshall McLuhan', *McLuhan Studies*, issue 2, Toronto, 1998; see: http://www.chass.utoronto.ca/mcluhan-studies/, accessed: November 2009.

109 Nicolaus Copernicus (1473–1543), *De Revolutionibus Orbium Coelestium*, 1543.

110 Giordano Bruno (1548–1600) was condemned to death for heresy by the Inquisition and executed at the stake on 17 February 1600 at the Campo dei Fiori in Rome.

111 See note 10 above.

112 The Sputnik programme was a series of spacecraft missions launched by the Soviet Union. The Russian word *sputnik* literally means 'co-traveller' or 'travelling companion'. *Sputnik 1* was the first manmade object launched to orbit the Earth. Its unanticipated announcement and success precipitated the Sputnik crisis in the United States and ignited the Space Race within the Cold War.

113 Marshall McLuhan, *Understanding Me*, op.cit. (note 96), p.242.

114 See: Kuhns, op.cit. (note 108). Kuhns quotes Bertrand Russell, who, as we saw earlier in the case of Bergson, doesn't think very much of the metaphysicist's intuition.

115 Marshall and Eric McLuhan, *Laws of Media*, op.cit. (note 94).

116 'Heuristic' is an adjective for experience-based techniques that help in problem solving, learning and discovery. A heuristic method is used to rapidly come to a solution that is hoped to be close to the best possible answer. A heuristic as a noun is a 'rule of thumb', an educated guess, an intuitive judgment or simply common sense. 'Hermeneutics' is the study of interpretation theory, and can be either the art of interpretation, or the theory and practice of interpretation.

117 Giambattista Vico (1668–1744), *Scienza Nuova*, 1725: the science of reasoning. See also: Samuel Beckett, 'Dante ... Bruno . Vico .. Joyce', in *Our Exagmination Round His Factification For Incamination Of Work in Progress*, Faber & Faber, London, 1929.

118 Marshall McLuhan and Bruce R. Powers, *The Global Village*, op.cit. (note 84), Preface, p.xi.

119 The Möbius strip was named after the German mathematician and astronomer August Ferdinand Möbius from Leipzig who discovered the mathematical figure in 1858.

120 Cees Nooteboom, *Rituelen*, Uitgeverij Arbeiderspers, Amsterdam, 1980, p.11.

121 Douwe Draaisma, *De Metaforenmachine*, Historische Uitgeverij, Groningen, 1995, p.20.

122 I.A. Richards (1893–1979), *The Philosophy of Rhetoric*, Oxford University Press, New York–London, 1965, p.89.

123 Douwe Draaisma, op.cit., p.24.

124 Aristotle (384–322 BC), *Poetics*, translated and introduced by Malcolm Heath, Penguin Classics, London, 1996, p.34. Aristotle's *Poetics* dates from around 335 BC and is the earliest surviving work of dramatic theory.

125 Marshall McLuhan and Bruce R. Powers, op.cit., p.8.

126 The term 'hermeneutics' refers to the theory of understanding and interpretation of linguistic and non-linguistic expressions. As a theory of interpretation, the hermeneutic tradition stretches all the way back to ancient Greek philosophy. In the course of the Middle Ages and the Renaissance, hermeneutics emerges as a crucial branch of biblical studies. Later on, it turns philosophical. Hermeneutics is no longer conceived as a methodological or didactic aid for other disciplines, but turns to the conditions of possibility for symbolic communication as such. The 'hermeneutic circle' refers to the

the envelope

idea that one's understanding of the text as a whole is established by reference to the individual parts and one's understanding of each individual part by reference to the whole. Neither the whole text nor any individual part can be understood without reference to one another, and hence it is a circle, which stresses that the meaning of a text must be found within its cultural, historical, and literary context. See: Paul Ricoeur, *The Conflicts of Interpretation: Essays in Hermeneutics*, translated by Willis Domingo et al., Northwestern University Press, Evanston, 1974; and: Gerald Bruns, *Hermeneutics: Ancient and Modern*, Yale University Press, New Haven, 1992. See also: http://plato.stanford.edu/entries/hermeneutics/

127 Lucio Fontana (1899–1968), *Concetto Spaziale*, 1949. Fontana's *Concetto Spaziale* was based on his 'White Manifesto' of 1946, in which he addressed the role of technology and science in new art forms and stated that the free development of colour and form in real space would pave the way for an art that would transcend the area of the canvas in order to become an integral part of architecture. When Fontana started to puncture (*bucare*) and to slash (*tagliare*) canvases in 1949, he had found an expressive form for this programmatic vision. See: Michel Tapie, *Fontana and the White Manifesto 1946 (Spazialismo)*, Harry Abrams, New York, 1962.

128 The phrase '*en taille directe*' is derived from the art of sculpture and indicates a technique of direct sculpting, usually in stone or wood, without any intermediate sketch, drawing or clay model. Lucio Fontana was trained as a sculptor and approached the canvases of his *Concetto Spaziale* '*en taille directe*'. He used to position himself in front of a prepared but yet untouched canvas for an hour or more, before suddenly slitting the surface with a razorblade in an explosive fashion. The act tore the canvas apart and revealed the space behind the work of art

129 Umberto Eco, op.cit. (note 93), p.453.

130 Luis Buñuel (1900–1983) and Salvador Dali (1904–1989), *Un chien andalou*, 1929.

131 The golden section is also known as the 'golden mean', 'golden ratio' and 'divine proportion'. It is a ratio or proportion defined by the number Phi (= 1.618033988749895...). It can be derived with a number of geometric constructions, each of which divides a line segment at the unique point where the ratio of the whole line (A) to the large segment (B) is the same as the ratio of the large segment (B) to the small segment (C). In other words, A is to B as B is to C. This occurs only where A is 1.618... times B and B is 1.618... times C.

132 In mathematics, the Fibonacci numbers are the numbers in the following sequence: 0, 1, 1, 2, 3, 5, 8, 13, 21, 34, 55, 89, 144, etc. By definition, the first two Fibonacci numbers are 0 and 1, and each remaining number is the sum of the previous two. The Fibonacci sequence is named after Leonardo of Pisa (c.1170–c.1250), who was known as Fibonacci (a contraction of *filius Bonaccio*).

133 NPS (Nederlandse Programma Stichting), Robert Wilson in film-interview on the occasion of the premiere of Lou Reed's *Time Rocker* opera at the Muziektheater, Amsterdam, 14 May, 1997.

134 See note 75 above.

135 Richard Flood, Chief Curator, Walker Art Center, commenting on Lucio Fontana's *Concetto Spaziale*, during the exhibition 'Art in Our Time: 1950 to the Present'. Flood: 'He slashes the surface of a painting. It's the most violent act anyone can make against a painting. It's the classic, "Oh, there's a mad man in the museum and he's got a knife."

455

I don't think there's a museum that doesn't fear that phenomena [sic]. That's what he made his art. He somehow created this incredible tension simply by doing what everyone feared, but he did it against a virgin ground.' Walker Art Center, Minneapolis, September 1999.

136 See essay 1, 'The Battery', notes 29, 33, p.70.
137 See note 7 above.
138 For '*in actio*', see essay 1, 'The Battery', note 36, p.79.
139 Hans Peter Kuhn, 1st International Scenographers' Festival IN3, Basel, 24 November 2006.
140 Frank den Oudsten, *A Scenographer's Manifesto*, closing performance with Uwe Brückner, 1st International Scenographers Festival IN3, Basel, 26 November 2006.
141 In acoustical engineering the concept of 'equalization' refers to its original function of flattening the frequency response characteristics of a system. The process of equalization is executed by channelling the stream of audio signals through a set of band pass filters, each covering an overlapping section of the audible spectrum. Such a set of in-line filters, packed as an electronic device and depending on its functionality, is called a 'graphic' or a 'parametric' equalizer. The parametric equalizer offers a more complex functionality, but beyond its original function of flattening the acoustics, both devices are capable of imposing a certain curve upon the response characteristics of a system, which affects its performance. Hence the analogy of a parametric equalizer for narrative space.
142 'Ubiquitous' means omnipresent, being everywhere simultaneously. Ubiquitous computing, therefore, offers a post-desktop model of human–computer interaction, in which the processing of information has been embedded and integrated into smart everyday furniture, architecture and activities.
143 A constraint is a limiting condition imposed upon the solution of a certain problem or the behaviour of a system. Within our context, the 16-band parametric equalizer imposes a set of 16 constraints upon the staging of a specific narrative environment, which scenography has to satisfy. Very similar for instance to constrained writing, in which a set of rules limits the syntactical options, eliminates certain letters and words or imposes certain rhythmic patterns.
144 See: Edward Tsang, *Foundations of Constraint Satisfaction*, Academic Press, London–San Diego, 1993. In linguistics, 'parsing' is the syntactic analysis of a text, in which a sentence is described grammatically and resolved into its component parts of speech.
145 See: Marshall McLuhan, *Understanding Media*, op.cit. (note 55), pp 45–51, chapter 3: 'Reversal of the overheated medium'.
146 See: Henri Bergson, *Creative Evolution*, Palgrave Macmillan, New York, 2007, pp 165–6. Bergson on unity and multiplicity: 'While, in its contact with matter, life is comparable to an impulsion or impetus, regarded in itself it is an immensity of potentiality, a mutual encroachment of thousands and thousands of tendencies which nevertheless are "thousands and thousands" only when once regarded as outside of each other, that is, when spatialized. Contact with matter is what determines this dissociation. Matter divides actually what was but potentially manifold; and, in this sense, individuation is in part the work of matter, in part the result of life's own inclination. Thus a poetic sentiment, which bursts into distinct verses, lines, and words, may be said to have already contained this multiplicity of individuated elements, and yet, in fact, it is the materiality

the envelope

of language that creates it. But through the words, lines and verses runs the simple inspiration which is the whole poem.' See also: Gilles Deleuze, *Bergsonism*, Zone Books, New York, 1988.
147 Modem: *mo*dulation-*dem*odulation: interface between sender and receiver.
148 A dichotomy is a division into two non-overlapping structures or concepts. The term comes from the Greek *dichotomia* (divided): *dich-* (form of *dícha*, in two, asunder); *tomia-* a combining form meaning cutting, incision, excision of an object.
149 Henri Bergson, op.cit. (note 146), p.1.
150 'GPS' stands for 'Global Positioning System', a structure consisting of a vast number of satellites orbiting the earth. These satellites transmit radio signals that are being received by a so-called GPS receiver down below and by means of which the receiver can then determine its own location with great accuracy.
151 Gilles Deleuze, *What is Philosophy?*, Verso, London–New York, 1994, chapter 2: 'The plane of immanence', pp 35–60.
152 Ibid p.59.
153 Roald Amundsen (1872–1928) was a Norwegian explorer who became famous for his spectacular expeditions in the Arctic regions. See: Roland Huntford, *The Amundsen Photographs*, The Atlantic Monthly Press, New York, 1987.
154 The treacherous sea route through the Canadian Arctic Archipelago, connecting the Atlantic and Pacific Oceans and called The Northwest Passage, proved to be a fatal temptation for many a sailor, before Amundsen first fully navigated it in his expedition from 1903 to 1906. See also note 153 above.
155 Although the earliest cartographical notations of the Northwest Passage stem from the mid-1500s, Amundsen based himself mainly on the expedition by the British explorer Sir John Franklin, who in 1845 sailed from London with two navy vessels. After a three-year journey he had only reached the Simpson Strait. Franklin had already lost his ships within the year in the pack ice of the Victoria Strait and in the end no-one survived the journey. Although the expedition did produce a vast quantity of maps and studies speculating on possible routes, they didn't prove very valuable to Amundsen once he arrived there, because they didn't indicate courses of navigation, but routes across frozen-over territory only accessible by dog sledge, and they didn't reach beyond the Simpson Strait.
156 For Amundsen's travel accounts see: Roland Huntford, op.cit.. See also Roald Amundsen's diaries, published in German by Detlef Brennecke, *Die Nordwestpassage: Meine Polarfahrt auf der Gjøa, 1903–1907*, Edition Erdmann, Stuttgart–Vienna, 2001.
157 Michel Serres (b.1931), *Hermes V: Die Nordwest-Passage*, Merve Verlag, Berlin, 1994, p.15. As no authorised translation of the French original could be traced, the present quote was translated by Pieter Kiewiet de Jonge. See: Michel Serres, *Hermès V: Le Passage du Nord-Ouest*, Les Éditions de Minuit, Paris, 1980.
158 Ibid p.19.
159 Proteus is an early sea-god in Greek mythology. He can foretell the future, but will change his shape to avoid having to and will answer only to someone who is capable of capturing him. See: Károly Kerényi, *The Gods of the Greeks*, Thames & Hudson, London–New York, 1951; also: Robert Graves, *The Greek Myths*, Penguin Books, London, 1992.

space.time.narrative

160   See: Marshall McLuhan, 'Canada as counter-environment', in *The Global Village*, op.cit. (note 84), p.147.

161   Bazon Brock (b.1936), *Lustmarsch durchs Theoriegelände: Musealisiert euch!*, DuMont Buchverlag, Cologne, 2008. The literal meaning of the exhibition's title is 'Enlightened Stroll through the Landscape of Theory'.

162   Ibid p.35. The quotes from Brock were translated from German by Pieter Kiewiet de Jonge.

163   Diary entry by Frank den Oudsten. Lecture by Bazon Brock at the 2nd Scenographers' Symposium: '*Identitätsausweis schafft Vertrauen – Zur Verpflichtung von jedermann, sich bis zur Kenntlichkeit zu exponieren*', Dortmund, 12 December 2009.

164   Bazon Brock, op.cit. (note 161), p.41.

165   See essay 1, 'The Battery', notes 107, 108, p.78.

166   Op.cit., p.51.

167   Rem Koolhaas, 'The Generic City', in *S, M, L, XL*, 010 Publishers, Rotterdam, 1995, p.1248.

168   Ibid.

169   W.B. Yeats (1865–1939), *The Second Coming*, 1920, line 3. See also: Stephen Coote, *W.B. Yeats: A Life*, Hodder & Stoughton, London, 1997, p.426.

170   The Situationists were notorious drinkers. See: Stefan Zweifel et al., op.cit. (note 59), p.14. The notion of 'delirium' of course also refers to Rem Koolhaas' first book *Delirious New York* (1978).

171   Rem Koolhaas, 'The Generic City', op.cit. (note 167), pp 1250–51.

172   Ibid.

173   See the interview with Uwe Brückner, p.319.

174   McLuhan uses the terms 'uttering', 'innering' and 'outering' primarily in his later work. See for example: Marshall McLuhan, *The Global Village*, op.cit. (note 84), p.4.

175   Op.cit. (note 167), p.1250.

176   Stephen Coote, op.cit. (note 169), p.xi. The introduction to Stephen Coote's Yeats biography opens with this passage.

select bibliography

Abbas, Niran et al., *Mapping Michel Serres*, The University of Michigan Press, Ann Arbor, 2005
Abbott, Edwin A., *Flatland: A Romance of Many Dimensions*, Signet Classics, New York, 1984
Abrams, Janet (ed.), *If/Then*, Netherlands Design Institute, Amsterdam, 1998
Amundsen, Roald, *Die Nordwestpassage: Meine Polarfahrt auf der Gjøa: 1903–1907*, Edition Erdmann, Stuttgart–Vienna, 2001
Aristotle, *The Art of Rhetoric*, translated by H.C. Lawson-Tancred, Penguin Classics, London, 1991
Aristotle, *Poetics*, translated by Malcolm Heath, Penguin Classics, London, 1996
Arnheim, Rudolf, *Film as Art*, Faber and Faber, London, 1969
Arnold, Ken, *Cabinets for the Curious: Practising Science in Early Modern English Museums*, PhD dissertation, Princeton University, New Jersey, 1991
Artaud, Antonin, *The Theater and its Double*, Grove Press, New York, 1958
Bachmann, Plinio et al., *All We Need*, exhibition catalogue, Holzer Kobler Architekturen & Iart Interactive (ed.), Lars Müller Publishers, Baden, 2007
Barthes, Roland, *Camera Lucida: Reflections on Photography*, HarperCollins, London, 1984
Baudrillard, Jean, *Simulacra and Simulation*, University of Michigan Press, Ann Arbor, 1996
Baur, Ruedi and Teufel, Philipp, *Design ausstellen – Ausstellungsdesign*, Hochschule für Gestaltung Offenbach and Fachhochschule Düsseldorf, Lars Müller Publishers, Baden, 1997
Baur, Ruedi et al., *Intégral Ruedi Baur*, Lars Müller Publishers, Baden, 2001
Beckett, Samuel et al., *Our Exagmination Round His Factification for Incamination of Work in Progress*, Shakespeare & Company, Paris, 1929
Beckett, Samuel, *Proust*, Grove Press, New York, 1970
Beckett, Samuel, *Collected Shorter Plays*, Grove Press, New York, 1984
Beckett, Samuel, *The Complete Short Prose 1929–1989*, Grove Press, New York, 1995
Beer, Evelyn, De Leeuw, Riet et al., *L'Exposition imaginaire*, SDU Uitgeverij, The Hague, 1989
Bell, Elizabeth, *Theories of Performance*, Sage Publications, Thousand Oaks, 2008
Belsey, Catherine, *Critical Practice*, Routledge, London, 1980

space.time.narrative

Benjamin, Walter, *Das Kunstwerk im Zeitalter seiner technischen Reproduzierbarkeit*, Suhrkamp, Frankfurt am Main, 1973
Bennett, Tony, *The Birth of the Museum*, Routledge, London, 1995
Bergson, Henri, *The Creative Mind*, Greenwood Press, Westport, 1968
Bergson, Henri, *Mémoire et vie*, Presses Universitaires de France, Paris, 1975
Bergson, Henri, *Creative Evolution*, Palgrave Macmillan, New York, 2007
Bianchi, Paolo, *Das Neue Ausstellen*, Kunstforum, vol.186, June–July 2007
Billeter, Erika, and Preisig, Dölf, *The Living Theatre: Paradise Now*, Benteli Verlag, Bern, 1968
Bindervoet, Erik, and Henkes, Robbert-Jan, *Finnegancyclopedie*, Athenaeum-Polak & Van Gennep, Amsterdam, 2005
Biner, Pierre, *The Living Theatre: A History Without Myths*, Avon Books, New York, 1973
Blau, Herbert, *Sails of the Herring Fleet: Essays on Beckett*, University of Michigan Press, Ann Arbor, 2000
Blotkamp, Carel et al., *Museum in Motion? The Modern Art Museum at Issue*, Staatsuitgeverij, The Hague, 1979
Bogue, Ronald, *Deleuze on Cinema*, Routledge, London–New York, 2003
Bohn, Ralf, Wilharm, Heiner et al., *Inszenierung und Ereignis, Beiträge zur Theorie und Praxis der Szenografie*, transcript Verlag, Bielefeld, 2009
Bohn, Ralf, *Inszenierung als Widerstand, Bildkörper und Körperbild bei Paul Klee*, transcript Verlag, Bielefeld, 2009
Born, Max, and Einstein, Albert, *The Born–Einstein Letters, 1916–1955: Friendship, Politics and Physics in Uncertain Times*, Macmillan, New York, 2005
Bredekamp, Horst, *Die Fenster der Monade*, Akademie Verlag, Berlin, 2004
Brock, Bazon, *Lustmarsch durchs Theoriegelände: Musealisiert Euch!*, DuMont Buchverlag, Cologne, 2008
Brook, Peter, *The Empty Space*, Penguin Books, London, 1990
Brougher, Kerry, and Müller-Tamm, Pia, *Hiroshi Sugimoto*, Hatje Cantz Verlag, Ostfildern, 2007
Brouwer, Joke et al., *Transurbanism*, V2-Publishing/NAi Publishers, Rotterdam, 2002
Bührke, Thomas, *E=mc^2: Einführung in die Relativitätstheorie*, Deutscher Taschenbuch Verlag, Munich, 1999
Cage, John, and Retallack, Joan, *Musicage: Cage Muses on Words, Art, Music*, Wesleyan University Press, Hanover, 1996
Cage, John, *Silence: Lectures and Writings*, Wesleyan University Press, Hanover, 1996
Campbell, Joseph, *A Skeleton Key to Finnegans Wake*, New World Library, Novato, 2005
Carlson, Marvin, *Places of Performance: The Semiotics of Theatre Architecture*, Cornell University Press, New York, 1989
Cicero, M.T., *De Oratore*, Philipp Reclam, Stuttgart, 1999
Coates, Nigel, *Guide to Ecstacity*, Laurence King Publishing, London, 2003
Confino, François et al., *Explosion: François Confino scénographe*, Éditions Norma, Paris, 2005
Coote, Stephen, *W.B. Yeats: A Life*, Hodder & Stoughton, London, 1997
Cotton, Bob, and Oliver, Richard, *Understanding Hypermedia*, Phaidon Press, London, 1993
Counsell, Colin, *Signs of Performance: An Introduction to Twentieth-Century Theatre*, Routledge, London, 1996
Debord, Guy, *The Society of the Spectacle*, Zone Books, New York, 1995

select bibliography

Deleuze, Gilles, *Bergsonism*, Zone Books, New York, 1988
Deleuze, Gilles, *Henri Bergson zur Einführung*, Junius Verlag, Hamburg, 2001
Deleuze, Gilles, *The Fold: Leibniz and the Baroque*, Continuum Press, London, 1993
Deleuze, Gilles, and Guattari, Félix, *Rhizome*, Les Éditions de Minuit, Paris, 1976
Deleuze, Gilles, and Guattari, Félix, *What is Philosophy?*, Verso, London–New York, 1994
Deleuze, Gilles, and Guattari, Félix, *A Thousand Plateaus*, The Athlone Press, London, 2004
Dernie, David, *Exhibition Design*, BIS Publishers, Amsterdam, 2006
Dery, Mark, *Escape Velocity: Cyberculture at the End of the Century*, Hodder & Stoughton, London, 1996
Dischner, Gisela, *Giordano Bruno: Denker, Dichter, Magier*, A. Francke Verlag, Tübingen, 2004
Draaisma, Douwe, *De Metaforenmachine: Een Geschiedenis van het Geheugen*, Historische Uitgeverij, Groningen, 1995
Draaisma, Douwe, *Metaphors of Memory: A History of Ideas about the Mind*, Cambridge University Press, Cambridge, 2000
Eco, Umberto, *The Open Work*, Harvard University Press, Cambridge (MA), 1989
Eco, Umberto, 'Reports from the global village', in *Travels in Hyperreality*, Harcourt, Orlando, 1986
Einstein, Albert, *Relativiteit: speciale en algemene theorie*, Het Spectrum, Utrecht–Antwerp, 1978
Eisenstein, Sergei, *Film Form: Essays in Film Theory*, Meridian, New York, 1957
Eisenstein, Sergei, *The Film Sense*, Harcourt Brace Jovanovich, New York, 1975
Eliot, T.S., *'The Waste Land' and Other Poems*, Faber and Faber, London, 1975
Ellmann, Richard, *James Joyce*, Oxford University Press, Oxford, 1983
Fairbrother, Trevor et al., *Robert Wilson's Vision*, exhibition catalogue, Museum of Fine Arts, Boston (MA), 1991
Falk, John H., and Dierking, Lynn D., *The Museum Experience*, AltaMira Press, Walnut Creek, 1992
Falk, John H., and Dierking, Lynn D., *Learning from Museums*, AltaMira Press, Walnut Creek, 2000
Field, Syd, *Screenplay: The Foundations of Screenwriting*, Dell Publishing Company, New York, 1982
Feireiss, Kristin et al., *The Art of Architecture Exhibitions*, NAi Publishers, Rotterdam, 2001
Frame magazine, *The Exhibition Issue*, vol.19, March–April 2001, Amsterdam
Fülscher, Bernadette, *Gebaute Bilder: Künstliche Welten – Szenografie und Inszenierung an der Expo.02*, hier+jetzt, Baden, 2009
Glancey, Jonathan, and Coates, Nigel, *Nigel Coates: Body Buildings and City Scapes*, Watson Guptill Publications, New York, 1999
Gleiniger, Andrea, 'Style or code: on the paradigms of the architectural expression in the age of digitalization', in *Code: Between Operation and Narration – Context Architecture*, Birkhäuser, Basel–Boston (MA), 2010
Goldberg, RoseLee, *Performance Art: From Futurism to the Present*, Thames & Hudson, London, 2001
Gorgus, Nina, 'Szenografische Ausstellungen in Frankreich', in *Museumskunde*, vol.2, Berlin, 2002, pp 135–142.

Gras, Vernon and Gras, Marguerite (eds), *Peter Greenaway: Interviews*, University Press of Missisippi, Jackson, 2000

Graves, Robert, *The Greek Myths*, Penguin Books, London, 1992

Grayling, A.C., *Wittgenstein: A Very Short Introduction*, Oxford University Press, Oxford, 2001

Greenaway, Peter, *The Physical Self*, exhibition catalogue, Museum Boijmans Van Beuningen, Rotterdam, 1991

Greer, Germaine, *Shakespeare: A Very Short Introduction*, Oxford University Press, Oxford, 2002

Harris, Geoffrey T. et al., *André Malraux: Across Boundaries*, Rodopi, Amsterdam–Atlanta, 2000

Hawking, Stephen, *A Brief History of Time*, Bantam Books, London, 1998

Hench, John, *Designing Disney: Imagineering and the Art of the Show*, Disney Editions, New York, 2003

Holl, Steven, *Parallax*, Birkhäuser, Basel–New York, 2000

Horne, Donald, *The Great Museum: The Re-presentation of History*, Pluto Press, London–Sydney, 1984

Howard, Pamela, *What is Scenography?*, Routledge, London, 2001

Huizinga, Johan, *Homo Ludens: A Study of the Play Element in Culture*, Beacon Press, Boston (MA), 1992

Huxley, Aldous, *The Doors of Perception and Heaven and Hell*, Penguin Books, Harmondsworth, 1969

Huxley, Aldous, *Brave New World*, Triad/Panther Books, London, 1977

Joyce, James, *Ulysses*, Everyman's Library, London, 1997

Joyce, James, *Finnegans Wake*, Athenaeum-Polak & Van Gennep, Amsterdam, 2002

Kaye, Nick, *Site-Specific Art: Performance, Place and Documentation*, Routledge, London–New York, 2000

Kerckhove, Derrick de, 'Understanding McLuhan', *Canadian Forum*, vol.51, Toronto, May 1981

Kerckhove, Derrick de, *Connected Intelligence: The Arrival of the Web Society*, Somerville House Publishing, Toronto, 1997

Kilger, Gerhard et al., *Szenografie in Ausstellungen und Museen*, DASA, Klartext Verlag, Essen, 2004

Knowlson, James, *Damned to Fame: The Life of Samuel Beckett*, Bloomsbury, London, 1996

Koolhaas, Rem, *Delirious New York*, first edition, Oxford University Press, New York, 1978, second edition, 010 Publishers, Rotterdam, 1994

Koolhaas, Rem, and Mau, Bruce, *S, M, L, XL*, 010 Publishers, Rotterdam, 1995

Kosko, Bart, *Fuzzy Thinking: The New Science of Fuzzy Logic*, HarperCollins Publishers, London, 1994

'Kossmann.deJong regisseren de ruimte', *Items* magazine, vol.2, March/April 2006

Kroker, Arthur, and Weinstein, Michael A., *Data Trash: The Theory of the Virtual Class*, St Martin's Press, New York, 1994

Kuhns, William, 'Reviewing the reviews: Giordano Bruno and Marshall McLuhan', *McLuhan Studies*, Issue 2, Toronto, July 1998

Lehmann, Hans-Thies, *Postdramatic Theatre*, Routledge, London–New York, 2006

Lemaire, Ton, *Claude Lévi-Strauss: Tussen Mythe en Muziek*, Ambo, Amsterdam, 2008

Leslie, Esther, *Walter Benjamin: Overpowering Conformism*, Pluto Press, London, 2000

select bibliography

Lévi-Strauss, Claude, *Tristes Tropiques*, Plon, Paris, 1955
Lévi-Strauss, Claude, *Totemism*, Beacon Press, Boston (MA), 1963
Lévi-Strauss, Claude, *The Savage Mind*, University of Chicago Press, Chicago, 1966
Lissitzky-Küppers, Sophie, *El Lissitzky*, Thames & Hudson, London, 1968
Lukas, Scott A., *Theme Park*, Reaktion Books, London, 2008
Lumley, Robert (ed.), *The Museum Time Machine: Putting Cultures On Display*, Routledge, London, 1988
Malraux, André, *Le Musée imaginaire*, Éditions Gallimard, Paris, 1965
Malraux, André, *Museum without Walls*, Doubleday & Company, New York, 1967
Marincola, Paula et al., *What Makes A Great Exhibition?*, Philadelphia Exhibitions Initiative, Philadelphia, 2006
Marrati, Paola, *Gilles Deleuze: Cinema and Philosophy*, The John Hopkins University Press, Baltimore, 2008
McLuhan, H. Marshall, *Understanding Media: The Extensions of Man*, Mentor Books, New York, 1964; critical edition, edited by Terrence Gordon, Gingko Press, Corte Madera, 2003
McLuhan, H. Marshall, and McLuhan, Eric, *Laws of Media: The New Science*, University of Toronto Press, Toronto, 1988
McLuhan, H. Marshall, and Powers, Bruce R., *The Global Village: Transformations in World Life and Media in the 21st Century*, Oxford University Press, New York–Oxford, 1989
McLuhan, H. Marshall, and Fiore, Quentin, *The Medium is the Massage*, Gingko Press Inc., Berkeley, 2001
McLuhan, H. Marshall, and Carson, David, *The Book of Probes*, Gingko Press, Corte Madera, 2003
McLuhan, H. Marshall, *Understanding Me*, The MIT Press, Toronto, 2005
Melis, Liesbeth (ed.), *Parasite Paradise: A Manifesto for Temporary Architecture and Flexible Urbanism*, NAi Publishers, Rotterdam, 2003
Minsky, Marvin, *The Society of Mind*, Simon & Schuster, New York, 1987
Moholy Nagy, László, *Vision in Motion*, Paul Theobald Press, Chicago, 1965
Müller, Hans-Joachim, *Harald Szeemann: Ausstellungsmacher*, Benteli Verlag, Bern, 2006
Mumford, Lewis, *The City in History*, Harcourt, New York, 1989
Negroponte, Nicholas, *Being Digital*, Vintage Books, New York, 1996
Noordegraaf, Julia et al., *Strategies of Display: Museum Presentation in Nineteenth- and Twentieth-Century Visual Culture*, NAi Publishers, Rotterdam, 2004
Otto-Bernstein, Katharina, *Absolute Wilson: The Biography*, Prestel, Munich–Berlin–London–New York, 2006
Oudsten, Frank den, *Concept.Form.Exhibition: Museum Presentations as Narratives*, Camini Foundation, Amsterdam, 1989
Oudsten, Frank den, 'Grenzwerte', in *Produktionsweisen: Zürcher Jahrbuch der Künste*, Zurich, 2004
Pascoe, David, *Peter Greenaway: Museums and Moving Images*, Reaktion Books, London, 1997
Pavis, Patrice, *Theatre at the Crossroads of Culture*, Routledge, London, 1992
Pavis, Patrice, *Vers une théorie de la pratique théâtrale*, Presses Universitaires du Septentrion, Villeneuve d'Ascq, 2007
Phillips, Lisa et al., *Frederick Kiesler*, Whitney Museum of American Art, W.W. Norton & Company, New York, 1989

Pine, B. Joseph II, and Gilmore, James H., *The Experience Economy*, Harvard Business School Press, Boston (MA), 1999
Postman, Neil, *Amusing Ourselves to Death*, Methuen, London, 1987
Prigogine, Ilya, and Stengers, Isabelle, *Order Out of Chaos: Man's New Dialogue with Nature*, Heinemann, Portsmouth (NH), 1984
Pritchett, James, *The Music of John Cage*, Cambridge University Press, Cambridge, 1993
Reinhardt, Uwe J. and Teufel, Philipp (eds), *New Exhibition Design 01*, avedition, Ludwigsburg, 2008
Rey, Anton et al., *Attention Artaud*, subTexte 01, Zürcher Hochschule der Künste, Zurich, 2008
Richards, I.A., *The Philosophy of Rhetoric*, Oxford University Press, New York–London, 1936
Rodtschenko, Alexander, *Alles ist Experiment!: Der Künstler-Ingenieur*, Edition Nautilus, Hamburg, 1993
Russell, Bertrand, *The ABC of Relativity*, George Allen & Unwin, London, 1969
Schade, Sigrid et al., *Curating Degree Zero*, Verlag für Moderne Kunst, Nuremberg, 1999
Schade, Sigrid et al., *Ausstellungs–Displays*, Institute of Cultural Studies in Art, Media and Design, Zurich, 2007
Schaffner, Ingrid, and Winzen, Matthias (eds), *Deep Storage: Collecting, Storing and Archiving in Art*, Prestel, Munich–New York, 1998
Schechner, Richard, *Performance Studies: An Introduction*, Routledge, London, 2002
Scheicher, Elisabeth, *Die Kunst- und Wunderkammer der Habsburger*, Brandstätter Verlag, Vienna–Munich, 1985
Schwarz, Hans-Peter, *Das Medienmuseum, Geschichte, Theorie, Konzepte*, Zentrum für Kunst und Medientechnologie, Karlsruhe, 1993
Schwarz, Hans-Peter, *Media – Art – History: Media Museum ZKM*, Prestel, Munich–New York, 1997
Sellars, Peter, 'On opera', in *Artforum*, vol.28, December 1989
Serres, Michel, *The Parasite*, The Johns Hopkins University Press, Baltimore, 1981
Serres, Michel, *Hermes: Literature, Science, Philosophy*, The Johns Hopkins University Press, Baltimore, 1982
Serres, Michel, *Hermes V: Die Nordwest-Passage*, Merve Verlag, Berlin, 1994
Sontag, Susan, *On Photography*, Penguin Books, London, 1977
Spalding, Julian, *The Poetic Museum: Reviving Historic Collections*, Prestel, London–Munich, 2002
Staniszewski, Mary Anne, *The Power of Display: A History of Exhibition Installations at the Museum of Modern Art*, The MIT Press, Cambridge (MA), 1998
Stedelijk Museum, *Kasimir Malevich, 1878–1935*, exhibition catalogue, Amsterdam, 1988
Stedelijk Museum, *Energieën*, exhibition catalogue, Amsterdam, 1990
Sturm, Eva, *Konservierte Welt: Museum und Musealisierung*, Reimer Verlag, Berlin, 1991
Szeemann, Harald, *Museum der Obsessionen*, Merve Verlag, Berlin, 1981
Szeemann, Harald, *Individuelle Mythologien*, Merve Verlag, Berlin, 1985
Szeemann, Harald, Bezzola, Tobia, and Kurzmeyer, Roman, *Harald Szeemann – with by through because towards despite*, Edition Voldemeer, Zurich, 2007
Teufel, Philipp et al., *EinszuEins: Positionen zum Ausstellen*, Modo Verlag, Freiburg, 1999
Venturi, Robert, Scott Brown, Denise, and Izenour, Steven, *Learning from Las Vegas*, revised edition, The MIT Press, Cambridge (MA), 1977

select bibliography

Weimann, Robert, *Shakespeare and the Popular Tradition in the Theater*, The Johns Hopkins University Press, Baltimore, 1978
Weitzner, Peter, *Objekttheater: Zur Dramaturgie der Bilder und Figuren*, Wilfried Nold Verlag, Frankfurt am Main, 1993
Wittgenstein, Ludwig, *Tractatus Logico-Philosophicus*, translated by W.F. Hermans, Athenaeum-Polak & Van Gennep, Amsterdam, 2006
Wolfe, Tom, 'What if he is right?', in *The Pump House Gang*, Farrar, Straus & Giroux, New York, 1968
Wolfe, Tom, *The Kandy-Kolored Tangerine-Flake Streamline Baby*, Bantam Books, New York, 1999
Woods, Alan, *Being Naked, Playing Dead: The Art of Peter Greenaway*, Manchester University Press, Manchester, 1996
Yates, Frances A., *Giordano Bruno and the Hermetic Tradition*, University of Chicago Press, Chicago, 1964
Yates, Frances A., *Theatre of the World*, University of Chicago Press, Chicago, 1969
Yates, Frances A., *The Art of Memory*, Pimlico, London, 1992
Youngblood, Gene, *Expanded Cinema*, Clarke, Irwin & Company, Toronto–Vancouver, 1970
Zacharias, Wolfgang (ed.), *Zeitphänomen Musealisierung: Das Verschwinden der Gegenwart und die Konstruktion der Erinnerung*, Klartext Verlag, Essen, 1990
Zweifel, Stefan et al., *In Girum Imus Nocte Et Consumimur Igni*, JRP-Ringier Kunstverlag, Zurich, 2006

biographical note

Frank den Oudsten is a media artist and a designer. He was a professor of scenography at the Zurich University of the Arts until 2010, but is now acting as an independent lecturer and researcher at various universities and academies of art throughout Europe. He studied applied physics and received his degree with a research project at the studio for electronic music at the Institute for Sonology in Utrecht, which meant a paradigm shift in his orientation. The field of audiovisual design became forefront, supported by courses in photography and film, of which the workshops by the experimental filmmaker Frans Zwartjes were most impressive. His professional career emcompasses both complex multimedia installations within the context of exhibitions, as performative experiments on stage. Commissioners have been the Netherlands Architecture Institute in Rotterdam, the Municipal Museum of The Hague, the Rijksmuseum Kröller Müller in Otterlo, the Centraal Museum in Utrecht, the Nederlands Fotomuseum in Rotterdam, the South Bank Centre in London, the Walker Art Center in Minneapolis, the German Museum of Architecture in Frankfurt am Main, the Centre for Art and Media in Karlsruhe, among others. In his presentations, Frank den Oudsten both uses classical analog as well as advanced digital media and mindmapping tools. His projects define the place of performance as a locus with character and identity, through the crucial unity of content and form, in which cognition and intuition are considered to be equal. In recent years the emphasis of his work has almost entirely been on discours within the context of educational projects, workshops and symposiums. His improvisations on stage however, increasingly got a performative touch. That instant, right-brain format allowed for a playful testing of his conceptual hypotheses, before they appeared in print. Reversely, text, deeply affected by the open nature of improvisation, turned into a poetic stream of speculative theory.

image credits

Man Ray – © Man Ray Trust/ADAGP, Paris and DACS, London 2011

Antonin Artaud – © ADAGP, Paris and DACS, London 2011

Alexander Rodtschenko – © Rodtschenko & Stepanova Archive, DACS 2011

Samuel Beckett – © Avedon Foundation.

El Lissitsky – © DACS 2011

For the Love of God – © Damien Hirst and Science Ltd. All rights reserved, DACS 2011

The editors and publisher gratefully acknowledge the permission granted to reproduce the copyright material in this book. Every effort has been made to trace copyright holders and to obtain their permission for the use of copyright material. The publisher apologizes for any errors or omissions in the above list and would be grateful if notified of any corrections that should be incorporated in future reprints or editions of this book.

For further copyright information see the individual image captions.

index

References to illustrations are in **bold**

Abramovic, Marina 36
    Portrait with Scorpion **84**, 100(Ill.1)
Adorno, Theodor W., 'Valéry Proust
    Museum' xvii
afterimage, definition 371
    images **372-87**
Aicher, Otl 229, 266n12
Alberti, Leon Battista, *De Re
    Aedificatoria* 28, 73n54
Ammann, Jean-Christophe 274, 313n5
Amsterdam
De Nieuwe Kerk
    Het Wonderbaarlijk Alfabet
        (1994) 110, 147n10
    'Istanbul: The City and the Sultan'
        (2006-7) 122–3, 143
    Rijksmuseum, *Gebed in Schoonheid*
        115
Amundsen, Roald 440, 441, 457n153
Archigram xii, xxn6
architecture
    of everything 432–3
    and exhibitions 241–2
Aristotle
    Ars Rhetorica 22–3, 52, 71n40
    on metaphor 426
    Poetics 425–6, 451n63

Arndt, Olaf xiv
Arndt, Olaf & Rob Moonen, *Camera
    Silens* 50–1, 80n123
Ars Electronica xiv
Ars Memoriae 28
art, and authorship 25
Artaud, Antonin 442
    Brook on 58
    portrait **86**
    The Theater and its Double 16, 58,
        59
    'Theatre of Cruelty' 57, 62–4, 81n136
        meaning 62
artefact, auratic xii
artist-curator 14
Ashkenazy, Vladimir, playing of
    Moonlight Sonata 42, 44
Associated Press/Kathy Willens, *The
    Mexican Suitcase* **386**, 390(Ill.15)
Atelier Brückner 326–7
    creative structure 334, 366n25
    exhibitions/design
        Cycle Bowl pavilion, Expo 2000,
            Hamburg 338
        'Expedition Titanic', Hamburg
            (1997-8) 328–9, 331, 333,
            339, 343–4, 345, 353, 365n17
        Innovarium Centre, Oberhausen
            (2001) 339, 366n33

'Living in Extremes', Herne (2006-07) 349, 367n42
Museum for Archaeology, Herne (2003) 339, 359, 366n34, 368n58
Schloss Dyck, Jüchen (2003) 346–7, 367n37
'That's Opera', touring exhibition 356–7, 368n56
fish logo 337–8
audiovisual media 109, 147n6
aura
   and art 8n3
   and the museum 2
auratics, exhibitions 347, 348
authenticity 349–50
author-designer, scenographer as 14, 254–6, 309–10, 344–5
authorship, and art 25
avant-garde, modernist 3
avatar 417, 453n88
Avedon, Richard, Beckett photograph **96–7**, 101(Ill.14)

Bach, J.S., *The Well-Tempered Clavier* 349, 367n43
Ballmer, Theo 227, 266n8
Barré, François 195, 196, 204, 218n7
Barthes, Roland 442
   camera lucida concept 23, 52
   La Chambre claire 51–2
   on photographic *punctum* 53
   on photographic *studium* 52
Baudelaire, Charles xiii
Baudrillard, Jean xxi17, 336, 366n29
   on the museum xvii
Baur, Ruedi 225
   on centres 260–1
   cultural references 242–3
   design process 240, 247–8

Design2Context institute 251, 266n13
École Nationale des Beaux-Arts
   appointment 229, 266n15
   'Civic City' course 230, 266n16
   teaching design 235, 236
education/training 268n35
exhibitions/designs
   BMW Museum (2008) 244–5, 269n40
   'Machine à Communiquer', Paris (1990) 236, 267n25
   Médiathèque André Malraux, signage (2008) 270n52
   'Mode d'Emploi', Lyon (1991) 230, 266n16
   Museum and Park Kalkriese (1998-2002) 244, 269n39
   see also Intégral Ruedi Baur
'*inscription*' 232–3
Intégral network 225, 237–8, 267n17
interview with 225–64
La Nouvelle Typographie 265n4
Plus Design studio 228, 266n11
portrait **224**
Projects Gallery 266n14
signage
   Centre Pompidou (Paris) 230, 231–2, 267n18
   Kalkriese Museum (Osnabrück) 230, 267n18
   Médiathèque André Malraux 270n52
on signs and meaning 234–5
symposium, 'Design Ausstellen - Ausstellungsdesign' 238–9, 268n30
Baviera, Michael 227, 265n7
Bayer, Herbert 227, 265n5
Beck, Julian & Judith Malina
Mysteries 64

Paradise Now 64
Beck, Ulrich xvii, xxiin20
Beckett, Samuel 57
   assistance to Joyce 47, 79n113
   on existence 32–3
   'eye of prey' 33, 74n72, 170–1
   portrait **96–7**
   works
      Endgame 30–1, 74n63
      Happy Days 171, 187n43
      Imagination Dead Imagine 32, 33, 36, 187n42
      Krapp's Last Tape 405–6, 450n38
      Our Exagmination 454
      The Lost Ones 32
      Waiting for Godot 31, 32, 33, 35, 74n66
Beethoven, Ludwig van, *Moonlight Sonata* 42, 44
Benjamin, Walter 336, 366n28
Bergson, Henri 37, 442
   Einstein, debate 44–5, 76n98
   metaphysics 26, 40–1
   on space-time continuum 41
   on time 41–2, 51
   on union, and multiplicity 456n146
   works
      Creative Evolution 40–1, 46, 456n146
      Introduction à la métaphysique 41
Berlin, 'People-Times-Spaces: Archaeology in Germany' (2002-3) 362, 369n66
Bernhard, Thomas, *Alte Meister: Komödie* ix, xxn1
Beurard-Valdoye, Patrick 235, 267n24
Beuys, Joseph, Fat Corners 275, 313n6
bifurcation principle, Prigogine 54–5
Bill, Max 226, 265n2
black holes 43, 76n96

Blotkamp, Carel 676
Boccioni, Umberto 39, 76n88
Bohn, Ralf 19
Borges, Jorge Luis 268n37
Botta, Mario 312, 316n42
Boutang, Pierre-André 205, 220n37
Brecht, Bertold 58, 81n140
bricoleur, and engineer 60, 61, 65, 66, 442
Brik, Lilya, portrait **87**, 100(Ill.4)
British Museum, Tutankhamun exhibition (1972) 152
Brock, Bazon 1
   Lustmarsch durchs Theoriegelände, exhibition, Cologne (2008) 443–5, 458n161
Brook, Peter 421, 442
   on Artaud 58
   Lévi-Strauss's influence on 59
   on Shakespeare 57, 58
   on theatre 56–9, 182–3
   works
      Mahabharata 59
      Orghast 59
      The Empty Space 55–6, 59, 64, 182, 248–9
Brown, 'Capability' Lancelot 159, 169, 186n20
Brückner, Uwe R. 198, 219n16, 319, 446
   design philosophy 329–31, 339–41
   on exhibitions 332
   exhibitions/designs
      Dayr az Zawr, archaeological museum 323, 364n8
      Schloss Trautenfels, landscape museum 323, 329, 364n8
   influences on 320–3
   interview with 320–63
   portrait **318**
   on space 342
   on stage design 327–8

space.time.narrative

on staging 349
on time 356, 357
see also Atelier Brückner
Bruno, Giordano 28, 47, 73n58, 421, 422, 423
Wheels of Memory **372**, 388(Ill.1)
Buckminster Fuller Dome 152, 185n4
Buñuel, Luis 359, 369n60
and Salvador Dali, *Un chien andalou* 359, 369n61, 430, 455n130
Bush, George W. 199

Cage, John xii, xxn6, 243, 245, 268n36, 275, 313n7
4'33" 33, 75n74
camera lucida concept, Barthes 23, 52
Camillo, Giulio 28
Camini Foundation, Amsterdam 11
Capa, Robert, *The Falling Soldier* **387**, 390(Ill.16)
Cargo Cult, Feynman on 61
Casati, Marchesa Luisa, portrait **85**, 100(Ill.2)
Casson, Dinah 49
on the 'edge' 163–4
influences on 160–1
portrait **150**
teaching 155
'The Piccadilly line', lecture 174, 187n48
Casson, Dinah & Roger Mann
design process 171–2, 184
diversification 158
interview 151–84
partnership formation 154
Casson, Hugh, Sir 186n21
CassonMann Designers 134, 148n38, 151, 155–6
exhibitions/designs

'British Design: New Traditions', Bojimans Museum, Rotterdam (1989) 153–4, 157, 185n8
British Galleries, V & A Museum, London (2001) 157–8, 169, 170, 174–5, 179, 185n17
'Camouflage', Imperial War Museum, London (2007) 169, 170, 175, 176–7, 187n40
Churchill Museum, London (2005) 167, 187n37
'Sparking Reaction', Sellafield, Cumbria (2002) 173–4, 175–6, 187n45
'Stanislavski Museolobby', Moscow (2008) 188n58
'The Garden', Science Museum, London (1996) 157, 185n16
'Who Am I', Science Museum, London (2000) 170, 187n41
Castelli, Luciano 275, 313n6
Cats musical 246, 269n43
CAVE 206, 221n41
Centre Pompidou (Paris) xvi, 5, 168, 187n39
signage 231–2, 267n18
centres, Baur on 260–1
Charter of Transdisciplinarity 20–1
Cinecittà, Rome 205, 221n39
Circle Vision film technique 265n3
clinamen 46–7, 78n108
clothing, functionality 27
Coates, Nigel 159, 185n19
Ecstacity 415, 416
NATO magazine 415
communication, crisis 410
computer screen, paper, comparison 267n20
computing, ubiquitous 434, 456n142
Confino, François 191, 325
architecture studies 218n3

Cités-Cinés 2 114–15, 212
exhibitions/designs
    Automobile Museum, Turin
        196, 207, 209, 214, 215–16,
        218n11, 220n31
    Cités-Cinés, Paris (1987) 111,
        117, 191, 196, 204–5, 205–6
    Expo 2015, Milan, masterplan
        217, 223n72
    'Futures to Come' 206, 221n42
    Le Musée des Confluences, Lyons
        (2006) 216, 223n70
    Le Musée Juste Pour Rire,
        Montreal (1993) 211, 222n54
    National Museum of Cinema,
        Turin (2000) 196, 202–3,
        218n11
    Pavilion of Discoveries, Expo
        1992, Seville (1992) 196
    Science Museum, Suzhou (2008)
        216, 223n71
    Spanish Pavilion, Expo 1992,
        Seville (1992) 196
Explosion 198, 207, 212
interview with 192–217
portrait **190**
projections, use of 211
on religion 201
scenographical concept 207
on style 197
Confino, François & Haus-Rucker
    Archéologie de la ville, Centre
        Pompidou, Paris (1977) 195, 197,
        207, 218n6
    cooperation 193–5
Conran, Terence 154
Constructivism 227, 228, 266n9, 325
convergence 54
Coop Himmelb(l)au 325, 365n12
Copernicus, Nicolaus 422

Coster, Howard, Portrait of W.B. Yeats
    88, 100(Ill.5)
Counsell, Colin 33
    Signs of Performance 30, 407, 408
    Wilson, criticism of 407–8
Cunningham, Merce 57, 81n135
curating, and scenography, blurring
    294–5
curator
    role 141, 311
    scenographer, collaboration 360–2

Dadaism 268n37
Dali, Salvador 359
dark matter, definition 103
Darwin, Robin 177, 187n51
de Beauvoir, Simone 269n49
    The Second Sex 288, 315n20
de Broglie, Louis 45
de Jong, Mark 107, 398
    see also Kossmann, Herman
de Kerckhove, Derrick 417, 452n86
    Connected Intelligence 452n87
de Maupassant, Guy 200, 220n29
Debord, Guy xxi n13, 47, 251, 442
    Commentaires sur la société du
        spectacle 101(Ill.12)
    Introduction to a Critique of Urban
        Geography 413
    La Société du spectacle 414
        cover 78n109, **95**, 101(Ill.12)
    Réalisation de la Philosophie **94**,
        101(Ill.11)
    'society of the spectacle' xiv, xv
    see also Situationists
Deelder, Jules 107
Deleuze, Gilles xi, 439
    and Félix Guattari, What is
        Philosophy? 22
Délis, Philippe 229, 230, 235, 236, 237,
    247, 266n15

Depero, Fortunato 227, 265n6
Descartes, René, *Tractatus De Homine*,
    triangulation 34-5, 36, 75n79, **95**,
    101(Ill.13)
Dethier, Jean 5
Deutsches Architekturmuseum (DAM)
    xv, xvi
Dicquemare, Sonja 235, 267n24
Dion, Mark 115
Disney company 30, 73n60, 124, 126,
    127
    lessons from 129, 292
Disneyland, as alternative world 292
Dixon, Tom 153, 185n11
dot.com industry 10, 67n7
drama
    and heartbeat frequencies 38
    and time 33
dramaturgy 5
Duchamp, Marcel xxin18, 243, 268n36
    L.H.O.O.Q., Mona Lisa parody **91**,
    101(Ill.8)
    portrait **98**
duck-rabbit sketch **89**, 100(Ill.6)
Duncan, Isadora 216, 223n67
Duval, Jean-Pierre 197, 219n14

Eakins, Thomas, *Nude Broad Jumping*
    374, 388(Ill.3)
Eames, Charles & Ray xii, xx n8, 161,
    186n23
Eco, Umberto 247, 336, 366n29, 391,
    394, 395, 417
    on *Finnegans Wake* 48
    on medium 418
    Opera aperta 21, 269n46, 394,
    448n14
    The Name of the Rose 205, 221n40
Eidgenössische Technische Hochschule,
    Zurich 277, 314n11
Einstein, Albert 26, 442

Bergson, debate 44–5, 76n98
    theory of relativity 31, 39, 44
Eisenmann, Peter 325, 365n12
El Alamein, battle 177, 188n53
El Lissitzky 227, 265n5
    Lenin Tribune 227, 265n6
    Proun Rooms xi, 265n6
    The Constructor **92**, 101(Ill.9)
Eliasson, Olafur, *The Weather Project*
    (2003-4) 140, 148n45, 336,
    366n31
engineer, and *bricoleur* 60, 61, 65, 66,
    442
entropy 45, 78n102
equalizer
    narrative space 434, **435**, 436–7,
    456n141, 456n143
    modem 437–8
Ernst, Max 321, 359, 364n1
    exhibition, Munich (1979) 320
Esser, Rainer 328
exhibitions xii
    and architecture 241–2
    auratics 347, 348
    Brückner on 332
    as cities 131–2, 245–6, 253
    collectionless 133–4
    and collective memory 26, 27
    commissioning 114
    event structure 399, **400–1**
    fil rouge concept 212, 222n56
    fixed focus, lack of 398
    fog metaphor 439
    future 145
    and fuzzy logic 398
    as *Gesamtkunstwerk* 25, 113
    history 351–4
    ideal routes 358–9
    and immersion experience 29
    in actio 71n36
    knee plays 345–6

as landscape 263
and 'lies' 212–14
as memorial spaces 394–5
as memory houses 28
narrative 165, 178–9
as narrative spaces 4, 25–6, 256, 303
nature of 24
as open art 26
as open systems 249–50
as *pérégrination* 252
permanent 282–3
post-spectacular 4
as process 27–8
reception 239
space direction 130–1
stagers 347, 348
success factors 134–5
tetrad concept **429**
theatre, comparison 1–2
time spent at 261–2
as topological entities 398
and topology 398, 433
transdisciplinarity 14
visitors' input 142, 181, 340, 341, 354–5, **401**, 438–9
as walks 138
see also scenography
existence, Beckett on 32–3
Expo 02 (Swiss National Exhibition) (2002) 274, 313n4
Expo 58, Brussels (1958) 192, 199, 205, 218n1
Expo 64 (Swiss National Exhibition), Lausanne 1964 218n2, 226, 313n3
Expo 67, Montreal/Quebec (1967) 152, 185n3
Expo 92, Seville
  Pavilion of Discoveries 213, 222n61
  Spanish Pavilion 196, 218n10

Expo 2000, Hanover (2000) 220n31, 333, 334, 338, 358–9
Expo 2015, Milan 217, 223n72

Fairbrother, Trevor 392, 408
Festival of Britain exhibition (1951) 152, 185n5
Feynman, Richard 79n111, 396
  on Cargo Cult 61
  on time 47
Fibonacci numbers 430, 455n132
fiction, and narrative x–xi
Finger, Anke, *Das Gesamtkunstwerk der Moderne* xiii
first sight 142–3
Fitzgerald, F.Scott, *The Great Gatsby* 216, 223n68
Fludd, Robert 28
Fontana, Lucio **373**, 442
  Concetto Spaziale 430, 431, 455n127
Frame magazine 151
François I, King of France 29
Frankfurt School 238, 268n32
Frans Hals Museum (Haarlem) 5
Freyer, Achim, *Krankheit Tod* 336, 366n30
Friedrich, Caspar David 411
  Der Wanderer über dem Nebelmeer 396, 448n20
Frisch, Max xviii, xxii n24
Fronzoni, A.G. 229, 266n12
Future Systems 325, 365n12
Futurism 40
fuzzy logic, and exhibitions 398

Galileo Galilei 213, 222n62
Garber, John 193
Garrett, Malcolm 153, 185n9
Gehry, Frank 200, 203, 220n26-7, 325
'Generic City' concept 445–6
Genet, Jean 58, 81n140

space.time.narrative

Gesamtkunstwerk xiii, 331, 360
   definition 72n46, 270n51
   exhibitions as 25, 113
   Expo 58, Brussels 218n1
   transdisciplinarity xiv
Giacometti, Alberto, *L'Homme qui marche* 395, 448n16
Gibson, William, *Neuromancer* 417, 452n87
Gilbert & George 275, 313n6
Glass, Philip 402
   see also Wilson, Robert & Philip Glass
Gleiniger, Andrea x–xi
globalisation
   challenges xv
   corporate 101(Ill.12)
   total 443
Globe Theatre (London) 28, 73n57
Godard, Jean-Luc 243, 269n38
Goldschmidt, Tijs 116, 148n24
graphein 17–18
Gray, Eileen 161, 186n24
Greenaway, Peter xii, 113, 202
   '100 Objects to Represent the World' 147n14
   A Zed & Two Naughts 297
   'Flood Warning' 135, 139–40, 147n14
   'Hell and Heaven: the Middle Ages in the North' 147n14
   'Nightwatching' 116
   Prospero's Books 67n6, 139
   The Cook, The Thief, His Wife and Her Lover 297
   'The Physical Self' 10, 67n6, 115, 141, 147n14, 308, 309, 316n40, **381**, 389(Ill.10)
   The Pillow Book 335, 366n27
   The Tulse Luper Suitcases ix–x
Gritella, Gianfranco 202, 220n32

Grotowski, Jerzy 57, 81n135
Guarini, Camillo-Guarino 220n30
Guericke, Otto von 18, 19–20

Hadid, Zaha 200, 220n26
Halliburton Energy Services 219n21
Hals, Frans, *Laughing Boy* 49
Hatton, Brian 415
Haus-Rucker Inc. 325, 365n12
   Confino, cooperation 193–5
   projects 218n4
   see also Confino, François
Hawksmoor, Nicholas 187
heartbeat frequencies 37
   and drama 38
Heatherwick, Thomas, *Seed Cathedral* **378**, 389(Ill.7)
Heim, Michael 417, 452n86
   The Metaphysics of Virtual Reality 452n87
Heisenberg, Werner, Uncertainty Principle 45, 55, 77n99
Heizer, Michael 162, 186n31
Herder, Johann Gottfried von xvii, xxi n18
hermeneutics xx n9, 454n126
Herzog & de Meuron Architects 220n25
heuristic 423, 454n116
Higgins, Dick xxi n12
   Statement on Intermedia xiv
Hilversum, Institute for Sound and Vision 143
Himmelb(l)au, Coop xii, xx n6
Hirschhorn, Thomas 115
   Anschool (2005) 140, 148n44
Hirst, Damien, *For the Love of God* **99**, 102(Ill.16)
Hitchcock, Alfred 299, 315n32
Hodgkin, Howard 163, 186n34
Hodler, Ferdinand
   Retreat from Marignano 305, 316n37

index

The Battle at Murten 305, 316n39
Hoet, Jan, *Chambres d'amis* 116, 148n28
Hollein, Hans 353, 368n49
holograms, 'Light Fantastic' exhibition (1977) 152, 185n2
Holzer, Barbara 276–7, 314n10
Holzer, Barbara & Tristan Kobler
   design process 284–7, 290–1
   influences on 287–9
   interview with 274–312
   portrait **272**
   see also Holzer Kobler Architekturen
Holzer Kobler Architekturen
   exhibitions/designs
      'All We Need', Luxembourg (2007) 278, 280, 292–3, 299, 314n14, 314n26-7
      'Collections Gallery', Swiss National Museum, Zurich (2009) 314n16
      Ebisquare shopping centre, Lucerne 299–300, 315n33
      EXPO.02, Switzerland 313n4
      'Greetings from Luxembourg' Luxembourg (2008) 290, 315n24
      'Heimatfabrik', EXPO.02, Switzerland (2002) 296, 315n28
      'History of Switzerland', Zurich (2009) 314n16
      Militärhistorisches Museum, Dresden (2010) 300, 314n18
      'On a Delicate Mission', Zurich (2007) 280, 298, 304, 305–7, 314n17
      'Radix Matrix - Daniel Libeskind Architekturen', Museum für Gestaltung, Zurich (1994) 314n12

'Weapons Cast Shadows', Zurich (2003) 273, 298, 304, 314n17
foundation 314n13
working methods 278–80
Horn, Rebecca 210, 213, 222n51
Hoveida, Amir Abbas 194, 218n5
Howard, Pamela, *What is Scenography?* 12
Huizinga, Johan 450n53

IBM pavilion, New York (1964) xii
ideas, as tools for thought 443
immanence, plane of 22, 439
Imperial War Museum, London, 'Camouflage' (2007) 169, 170, 175, 187n40
information, and space 228, 236, 248–9, 250–1
Ingres, Jean Auguste Dominique 163, 186n32
Institut für Innenarchitektur und Szenografie (Basel) 335, 366n26
Institut für Neue Technische Form (Darmstadt) 238, 268n31
Institute for Sound and Vision, Hilversum 143
Intégral Jean Beaudoin 237, 267n28
Intégral Lars Müller 238, 267n29
Intégral network 225, 237–8, 267n17
Intégral Ruedi Baur, exhibitions/designs
   'Juste avant la Transformation', Saint-Etienne (2006) 247, 269n45
   Quartier des Spectacles, Montreal (2007-10) 258, 259–60, 270n53
   'Quotidien Visuel', travelling exhibition (2002-08) 247, 269n45
Intégral Studio Vinaccia 237–8, 267n29
International Garden Exhibition, Stuttgart (1993) 322–3, 364n7
intuition, and origin of things 41

inventio, scenography 16, 17, 52, 65, 405, 411, 413–14, 432, 449n34

Janssens, Ann Veronica, *Horror Vacui* 148n26
Jantar Mantar Observatory, New Delhi 354, 368n52
Japan, 'Visions of Japan' exhibition (1991) 153, 185n7
Jastrow J. 100(Ill.6)
Jeudy, Henri-Pierre xvii–xviii, xxii n19
Die Welt als Museum xvii
Joyce, James
    Finnegans Wake 28, 39, 47, 50, 73n58, 80n115-16, 421
    cyclical nature of 48
    Eco on 48
    McLuhan, influence on 422
    Ulysses 47, 165

Kabakov, Ilya 115
Kahlo, Frida 287–8, 314n19
Kahn, Fritz, *Das Leben des Menschen* **377**, 389(Ill.6)
kairos 17, 69n27, 412
Kaplicky, Jan 365n12
Kapoor, Anish 336, 366n31
Karlsruhe Medienmuseum xv, xvi, xviii
Kassák, Lajos 227, 265n6
Kaulbach, Wilhelm von xxiin21
Kennedy, John F. 199, 219n18
KESHMA workshop, 'Staging the City', Venice (2007) 270n50
Kiefer, Anselm 213, 222n60
Kiesler, Friedrich 325, 365n11
Kircher, Athanasius, *De Ars Magna Lucis et Umbrae* **375**, 388(Ill.4)
Klotz, Heinrich 9
Klucis, Gustavs 227, 265n6
Kluge, Alexander 359, 369n59
Klüver, Billy xii, xxn8

knee plays, exhibitions 345–6
knowledge
    absolute/relative 41
    primitive, Lévi-Strauss on 60–1
Kobler, Tristan 49, 276, 313n9
    see also Holzer, Barbara & Tristan Kobler
Koolhaas, Rem
    Delirious New York 415
    'Generic City' concept 445–6
Kossmann, Herman 4, 8n6
    and Mark de Jong collaboration 110
    exhibitions
        approach 118–20, 127
        sensory experiences 124
        space direction 130–1
    interview with 107–46
    portrait **106**
    Schipol Airport, Lounge 3, design 145–6
    and Nederland Nu Als Ontwerp Foundation 108, 109, 147n4
    project manager, *Nieuw Nederland 2050*: 108
Kossmann.deJong 107
    exhibitions
        De Wederopbouw 110, 111, 113, 129–30, 133, 135, 147n9
        Het Dolhuys - Museum voor Psychiatrie 110, 119–22, 124–5, 125–6, 138–9, 147n12
        Interbellum Rotterdam 1918-1940 (2001) 141, 149n47
        'Istanbul: The City and the Sultan' 122–3, 143
        'MainPort Live' 133, 148
        'Plan the Impossible: The World of Architect Hendrik Wijdeveld (1885-1987)' 118, 128, 128–9, 148n29

Wonderbaarlijk Alfabet 133–4
'Wonderland' 148n37, 133
Kruger, Barbara 187n47
  Violence project 350–1, 367n46
Kuhn, Hans Peter 392, 433
Kuhns, William 417, 421–2, 453n91
Kurosawa, Akira, *Rashomon* 331, 365n21

Lang, Jacques 205, 220n38
Las Vegas 414–15, 431, 452n75
Lascaux cave paintings 352, 368n48
Le Corbusier 216
  chapel of Notre-Dame-du-Haut, Ronchamp 116, 148n25
  Expo 58 pavilion 192, 218n1
Leering, Jean 5
Lehmann, Hans-Thies 3
Leonardo da Vinci 177, 188n52
Lévi-Strauss, Claude 442
  influence on Brook 59
  on primitive knowledge 60–1
  The Savage Mind 59, 60
  Tristes Tropiques 59
Lewandowsky, Via, 'Cosmos in your Head', Dresden (2000) 360, 369n65
Libeskind, Daniel 277, 288, 315n23
Liebermann, Rolf, *Les Echanges* 275, 314n8
'Light Fantastic' exhibition (1977) 152, 185n2
Lionni, Pippo 237, 267n17
Lipsky & Rollet Architectes 237, 267n28
Living Theatre, The Roundhouse, London 64
Loeraker, Peter 110, 147n11
logos 412, 446, 451n63
Lohrer, Knut 322, 323, 324–5, 364n6
  studio 325–6
Lovegrove, Ross 229, 266n12
Lubitsch, Ernst 199, 219n22

Lucretius, *De Rerum Natura* 46–7
Lynch, Kevin, *A View from the Road* 394, 448n14
Lyon, exhibitions, 'Mode d'Emploi', (1991) 230, 266n16
Lyons
  École Nationale des Beaux-Arts 229, 266n15
  Le Musée des Confluences (2006) 216, 223n70

Maastricht, Bonnefantenmuseum, *Anschool* (2005) 140, 148n44
Machu Picchu 354, 368n52
McLuhan, Marshall xii, 410, 442
  as dramaturg 420–1
  on figure/ground 416, 424, 452n84
  Finnegans Wake, influence on 422
  on medium and message 24–5, 416–17, 419
  on *Sputnik* 422
  tetrad concept 423, **424**, 426, **427**
  and exhibitions **429**
  and theatre **428**
  Wolfe's criticism of 418
  works
    Global Village 423
    Laws of Media 423
    Understanding Media 24, 25, 409, 421, 450n55
Magdeburg hemispheres, scenography 18–20, 432
Magistretti, Vico 160, 186n22
Magnetic North Pole, search for 440–1
Mak, Geert 116, 148n24
Malevich, Kasimir, *Black Square* 38–9, 40, 48, 50
  history 39
  reading of 39, 44
Malraux, André, *Le Musée imaginaire* 24, 214, 223n64

Man Ray
    Antonin Artaud **86**, 100(III.3)
    Marquise Casati **85**, 100(III.2)
Manet, Edouard, *Le Déjeuner sur l'herbe* 214–15, 223n65
manifestatio, scenography 16–17, 52, 65, 405, 411, 432, 449n34
Mann, Roger
    influences on 161–2
    portrait **150**
    see also Casson, Dinah & Roger Mann
Mann, Thomas 200, 220n28
Mansur, Hassan Ali 218n5
Mapplethorpe, Robert, Glass/Wilson portrait 52-3, 81n127, **93**, 101(III.10)
Marcuse, Herbert 269n49
Mari, Enzo 229, 266n12
Marinetti, Tomasso 40
Márquez, Gabriel García 162, 186n30
Mayakovsky, Vladimir 100(III.4)
medium
    Eco on 418
    and message, McLuhan on 24–5, 416–17, 419
    and metaphor 421
    as metaphor, Postman on 420
memory
    collective, and exhibitions 26, 27
    houses, exhibitions as 28
    Nooteboom on 425, 443
    theatres 28
Merz, Hans-Günter 326, 365n14, 367n38
metaphors
    Aristotle 426
    and medium 421
    as tetrads 425
Metropolis 204, 220n36
Meyerhold, Vsevolod 58, 81n140
Michels, Caroll 193

Minsky, Marvin, *The Society of Mind* 417, 452n87
Miyajima, Tatsuo, *Mega Death* 148n27
Mlinaric, David 158, 185n18
mnemomedia 23
mnemonics 28, 73n55
    art of 29
    functional 73n56
Möbius strip 423, **424**, 454n119
Moholy-Nagy, Lásló 227, 265n5
    Room of Today xi
Molière 246, 269n44
monad 393, 442, 447n10
Mondrian, Piet 40
Monet, Claude, *Water Lilies* 274, 275, 302–3, 313n1
Monty Python comedy group 200, 219n23
Mouron, Adolphe, Bifur typeface design **379**, 389(III.8)
Mozart, W.A. 336, 366n29
Mulas, Ugo, *Lucio Fontana in action* **373**, 388(III.2)
multimedia installations xvi
Munich
    exhibitions
        'Karl Valentin' (1982) 364n3
        Max Ernst (1979) 364n1
        'The Octoberfeast' (1985) 364n3
        French Revolution, performance (1989) 321–2
Museum für Gestaltung, Zürcher Hochschule der Künste 274, 313n2
Museum of Modern Art, shops 301
'Museum in Motion' 5
Museum Studies xvi
museums
    and aura 2
    Baudrillard on xvii
    as places of memory 412

index

theatre, comparison 412
   visitors xvii
mysteries, and scenography 43
mythos 412, 446, 451n63

Nabokov, Vladimir 161, 186n25
narrative
   exhibitions 165, 178–9
   and fiction x–xi
   fragments 143–4
   and time 49, 165–6
narrative environment 50, 104, 168, 178, 393
   architectural footprint 439
   meaning 350, 412, 444
   and space/time linkage 257–8
Narrative Environments research project 5, 6, 11, 151, 253, 301
narrative space 2, 49, 134, 160
   conceptual personae 7
   definition 253
   deviation 405, 449n36
   equalizer 434, **435**, 436–7, 456n141, 456n143
      modem 437–8
   exhibitions as 4, 25–6, 256, 303
   Fort Asperen 135, 148n39
   inclination 405, 449n35
   potential 254
   and scenography 253–4
   and story telling 301–2
   structuring 136–7
   theory, search for 7, 17
   and time 258
   Wederopbouw exhibition 135
   Wilson on 430–1
National Portrait Gallery, London 161, 186n29
   'Velázquez' exhibition 163
Nederland Nu Als Ontwerp Foundation 108, 109, 147n4

Negroponte, Nicholas 417, 452n86
   Being Digital 452n87
Neoplasticism 40, 76n89
Neuhoff, Holger von 328, 365n18
'Nieuw Nederland 2050' 107–8, 147n5
Nieveen, Rudi 128, 148n34
Nooteboom, Cees
   on memory 425, 443
   Rituals 425
Northwest Passage, universal metaphor for linkage 441–2
Nouvel, Jean 197, 219n13

Obrist, Hans Ulrich 412
obscenography, and scenography 16, 17, 66, 393
open arts 20–30
   exhibitions as 26
   temporality 23
open systems 253
Osnabrück, Kalkriese Museum, signage 230, 267n18
Other, the, and the theatre 62
Ottoman Empire 148n32
Oudsten, Frank den
   Floating Identities **376**, 388(Ill.5), 417, 453n89
   with Uwe Brückner, *A Scenographer's Manifesto* 456n140

Palladio, Andrea, Teatro Olimpico 28
panorama, revival xii
paper, computer screen, comparison 267n20
parallax 75n78
   definition 83
   images **84–99**
   and triangulation 35
Paris, Natural History Museum 353, 368n51
Pentagram design agency 237, 267n27

485

Pepsi-Cola pavilion, Expo '70 (Osaka) xii
Picasso, Pablo 39
Piero della Francesca 163, 186n32
Pine, B.Joseph & James Gilmore, *The Experience Economy* 9
Pinter, Klaus 194, 195
platea 2, 8n2
Politkovskaya, Anna 161, 186n26
Ponti, Gio 341
Postman, Neil 24, 417, 453n91
   Amusing Ourselves to Death 419–20
   on medium as metaphor 420
postmodernity xi
Potter, Sally, *Orlando*, staging 357–8, 368n57
Prigogine, Ilya 45–6, 77n101, 442, 443
   bifurcation principle 54–5
   Order Out of Chaos 46
Prolo, Maria Adriana 197
Proteus 443, 457n159
proximity, actors/audience 64–5
psychogeography 252, 412, 413, 414, 442, 446, 451n70
Puccini, Giacomo 336, 366n29
punctum 53–4, 63, 64–5

Rams, Dieter 229, 238, 266n12, 268n33
Rauschenberg, Robert xii, xxn6
relativity, theory of 31, 39, 44
Rembrandt van Rijn 163, 186n32
   Night Watch 291
   Self-Portrait 50
Rheingold, Howard 417, 452n86
   The Virtual Community 452n87
Richards, I.A., *The Philosophy of Rhetoric* 425
Robespierre, Maximilien de 364n4
Rodchenko, Alexander, *Pro Eto. Ei i Mne*, book cover **87**, 100(Ill.4)
Roiter, Fulvio, *Einstein on the Beach* **384**, 389(Ill.13)

Rorty, Richard, *The Linguistic Turn* 145, 149n50
Rose, Jürgen 324, 325, 364n10
Roth, Martin 5
Rotterdam, exhibitions
   'British Design: New Traditions' (1989) 153–4, 157, 185n8
   De Wederopbouw (1995) 110, 111, 113, 129–30, 133, 135, 147n9
   Interbellum Rotterdam 1918-1940 113, 147n15
   'MainPort Live' (2007) 133, 148n36
   Stadstimmeren (1992) 110, 111, 147n8
   'Wonderland' (2002) 133, 148n37
Royal Academy of Arts, 'Light Fantastic' exhibition (1977) 152, 185n2
Ruigrok, Wim 38
   Black Square with visitors **382**, 389(Ill.11)
Rushdie, Salman 162, 186n30

Sabelli, Fabrizio 201, 207, 220n31
Sambonet, Robert 229, 266n12
Sartre, Jean-Paul 269n49
Saville, Peter 229, 266n12
Scarpa, Carlo 325, 365n12
scenographer
   as author-designer 14, 254–6, 309–10, 344–5
   curator, collaboration 360–2
   semantic spaces designer 14
Scenographers' Festival, First International (2006) 433
Scenographical Design course 11, 68n14, 151
scenography ix–x, xv, 5, 334
   architectural exhibitions xvi
   and the city 257
   courses xix
   and curating, blurring 294–5

definitions 12, 55
discursive 15–16, 17, 443, 445, 446
and enigma of things 42–3
etymology 17
expanded 393
fuzziness 55
instability 17
inventio 16, 17, 52, 65, 405, 411, 413–14, 432, 449n34
Magdeburg hemispheres 18–20, 432
manifestatio 16–17, 52, 65, 405, 411, 432, 449n34
mercantile 15, 17, 443, 444
and mysteries 43
and narrative space 253–4
and obscenography 16, 17, 66, 393
paradox 15–20
and power 254–5
scope 11–12, 12–13
spectatio 52, 65
success 15
theory 10–11, 19
and time 45, 47
transdisciplinarity 21, 35
transitions 260
and triangulation 36
and the unknown 36
and war 177
see also exhibitions
Schaal, Hans Dieter 353, 368n49
Schipol Airport, Lounge 3, design 145–6
Schneider, Michael 238
Scholder, Hans-Martin 324, 326, 337, 364n9
Schott, Caspar 18, 70n29
Schwarz, Hans Peter 10
science, as narrative 46
Science Museum, London, Wellcome Wing 174, 187n49
Sellars, Peter 408
on the theatre 412

September 11 (2001) events 199, 219n19
Serres, Michel 441, 442
Shakespeare, William 28
  Brook on 57, 58
  Hamlet 356
  Romeo and Juliet 356
signs, and meaning, Baur on 234–5
Silicon Graphics Onyx 9, 67n5
Simons, Johan, *Merlin oder Das wüste Land* 146, 149n52
Situationists 47, 78n109-110, 101(Ill.12), 185, 251, 252, 412–13
  see also Debord, Guy
skene xii, 17, 22, 56, 70n28
Sloterdijk, Peter 336, 366n29
space
  architectural xi
  Brückner on 342
  cultural 247
  direction, exhibitions 130
  exhibition, as event xii
  and information 228, 236, 248–9, 250–1
  time, and now 430–1
space-time continuum xii, xiii, xv
  Bergson on 41
Sputnik
  McLuhan on 422
  programme 454n112
stage design, Brückner on 327–8
stagers, exhibitions 347, 348
staging 431–2
  Brückner on 349
Stanislavski, Constantin S. 182, 188n58
Stankowski, Anton 229, 266n12
Stan's Café 294, 296, 315n27
Stedelijk Museum (Amsterdam) 38
Stein, Peter 327–8, 365n16
Stockhausen, Karlheinz 275, 314n8
Stölzl, Christoph 321, 364n3

Stone, Oliver, *JFK* 199
Stonehenge 368n48
Struth, Thomas, *Pergamon Museum* **385**, 390(Ill.14)
studium 52, 53, 54
Stuttgart, International Garden Exhibition (1993) 322–3, 364n7
style, Confino on 197
Sugimoto, Hiroshi
   Theatres project 34
   Union City Drive-in **383**, 389(Ill.12)
Sullivan, Louis 329
Suprematism 38, 39, 40, 76n89
Suzhou (China), Science Museum (2008) 216, 223n71
Sydney Opera House 325, 365n13
Szeeman, Harald xiii, 263, 270n57, 310–11, 316n41, 360, 369n62-4

Tate Modern
   'Century City' 140, 148n46
   Tate Thames Dig (1999) 115, 148n21
   The Weather Project (2003-4) 140, 148n45
tetrad concept 423, **424**, 426, **427**
   exhibitions **429**
   theatre **428**
tetrads, metaphors as 425
Teufel, Philipp 238, 268n30
text, decline of 3
theatre
   actors/audience, proximity 64–5
   Brook on 56–9, 182-3
   museum, comparison 412
   and the Other 62
   postdramatic 3
   Sellars on 412
   tetrad concept **428**
Thiery, Sébastian 269
Things to Come 204, 220n36
Thomèse, P.F. 410

time
   Bergson on 41–2, 51
   Brückner on 356, 357
   clock, and actual 37, 41
   and drama 33
   Feynman on 47
   irreversibility of 45–6
   and narrative 49, 165–6
   and narrative space 258
   nature of 44
   and other world 438
   and scenography 45, 47
   space, and now 430–1
   wave characteristics 41–2
topology 393, 447n7
   and exhibitions 398, 433
Total Design 237, 267n27
Trahndorff, Karl Friedrich Eusebius, *Äesthetik oder Lehre von der Weltanschauung und Kunst* xiii
transdisciplinarity xiv, xv, 3
   scenography 21, 35
triangulation
   Descartes 34–5, 36
   and parallax 35
   and scenography 36
Turin
   Automobile Museum 196, 207, 209, 214, 215–16, 218n11, 220n31
   Cinema Museum 115, 218n11
   Mole Antonelliana 196, 201, 202, 203, 204, 219n12
   Royal Church of San Lorenzo 201, 202, 202–3, 220n30
Tutankhamun exhibition, London (1972) 152

Uncertainty Principle, Heisenberg 45, 55, 77n99
Utzon, Jørn, Sydney Opera House 325, 365n13